LIABILITY AND QUALITY ISSUES IN HEALTH CARE

Fourth Edition

By

Barry R. Furrow
Professor of Law and Director, Health Law Institute
Widener University

Thomas L. Greaney
Professor of Law
Co-Director, Center for Health Law Studies
Saint Louis University

Sandra H. Johnson
Tenet Chair in Health Care Law and Ethics,
Provost, Professor of Law in Health Care Administration and
Professor of Law in Internal Medicine
Saint Louis University

Timothy Stoltzfus Jost
Robert L. Willett Family Professor of Law
Washington and Lee University School of Law

Robert L. Schwartz
Professor of Law and Professor of Pediatrics
University of New Mexico

Reprinted from Furrow, Greaney, Johnson, Jost and Schwartz's "Health Law: Cases, Materials and Problems, Fourth Edition" (West, 2001)

AMERICAN CASEBOOK SERIES®

WEST GROUP

A THOMSON COMPANY

ST. PAUL, MINN., 2001

Reprinted from Furrow, Greaney, Johnson, Jost and
Schwartz's "Health Law: Cases, Materials and Problems,
Fourth Edition" (West, 2001)

610 Opperman Drive
P.O. Box 64526
St. Paul, MN 55164–0526
1–800–328–9352

ISBN 0–314–25166–9

1st Reprint — 2003

To Donna Jo, Elena, Michael, Nicholas, Eva and Robert
B.R.F.

To Nancy, T.J., and Katie
T.L.G.

To Bob, Emily and Kathleen
S.H.J.

To Ruth, Jacob, Micah and David
T.S.J.

To Jane, Mirra and Elana
R.L.S.

This book is also dedicated to the memory of Nancy Rhoden and Jay Healey, great teachers, wonderful colleagues and warm friends.

*

Preface

Medical accidents and medical errors have emerged over the past few years as a major topic of discussion in government and health policy circles. The publication of the Institute of Medicine report **To Err is Human** has precipitated much introspection by hospitals, physicians, and regulators. It is clear that the American health care system produces too many injuries that can be avoided; there is less agreement on the best strategy for reducing those injuries. This volume allows the teacher to focus on health care quality and liability in detail, from the definitions of quality and excerpts from the new government reports on error in medicine, to the latest judicial opinions on managed care and ERISA preemption; to medical privacy and confidentiality. Sources of liability now can be found not only in the common law doctrine but in statutory regimes such as EMTALA. Liability is also channeled through the elaborate rules that have been developed by the federal courts as they interpret ERISA preemption. Discussion of liability and quality issues is an increasingly complex subject, and these materials reflect that complexity.

This softcover volume, *Liability and Quality Issues in Health Care*, is devoted exclusively to the law of health care quality control and liability. Liability has been broadly defined to include not only medical malpractice case law development, but also EMTALA, ERISA preemption, and judicial and legislative developments that address those issues. The volume is comprised of Chapters 1-6, parts of Chapters 8 and 9, and Chapter 11, from the fourth edition of our casebook *Health Law: Cases, Materials and Problems* (4th edition 2001). The previous Chapter Five, Reforming the Malpractice System, is no longer included in this edition, the result of space limitations. We have however provided it as an appendix to the teacher's manual for those who would like to explore questions of malpractice reform.

This volume is one of three softcover books aimed at the specific content of an upper level elective health law course. The other books, comprised of other portions of *Health Law*, are *The Law of Health Care Organization and Finance*, and *Bioethics: Health Care Law and Ethics.*

This book blends recent caselaw, statutory developments, and problems to maximize the flexibility of the material for teachers of health law. The notes are rich in detail and citations, allowing the teacher to spend more time on topics of particular interest. The Teachers Manual for the Health Law casebook covers the material in this book. The editorial style of this text is consistent with that of most law school casebooks. Ellipses in the text of quoted material indicate an omission of material within the quoted paragraph. Centered ellipses indicate the omission of a paragraph or more. Brackets indicate the omission of a citation, but no any substantive material.

BARRY R. FURROW
THOMAS L. GREANEY
SANDRA H. JOHNSON
TIMOTHY S. JOST
ROBERT L. SCHWARTZ

*

Acknowledgements

Annas, George J., A National Bill of Patients' Rights, 338 New England Journal of Medicine 695 (1998). Copyright 1998 George Annas. Used with permission.

Austin, C.R., Human Embryos: The Debate on Assisted Reproduction (1989). Copyright 1989, Oxford University Press. Reprinted by permission of Oxford University Press.

Battin, Margaret, A Dozen Caveats Concerning the Discussion of Euthanasia in the Netherlands, in the Least Worst Death (1994). Copyright 1994, Oxford University Press. Reprinted by permission of Oxford University Press.

Battin, Margaret, The Least Worst Death, 13 Hastings Center Report (2) 13 (April 1983). Copyright 1983, the Hastings Center. Reprinted with permission of the Hastings Center and the author.

Bernat, James, Charles Culver and Bernard Gert, Defining Death in Theory and Practice, 12 Hastings Center Report (1) 5 (February 1982). Copyright 1982, the Hastings Center. Reprinted with permission of the Hastings Center and the authors.

Callahan, Daniel, Morality and Contemporary Culture: The President's Commission and Beyond, 6 Cardozo L. Rev. 347 (1984). Copyright 1984, Cardozo Law Review. Reprinted with permission of the Cardozo Law Review.

Callahan, Daniel, Special Supplement, 19 Hastings Center Report 4 (Jan./Feb. 1989). Copyright 1989, the Hastings Center. Reprinted with permission of the Hastings Center and the author.

Capron, Alexander Morgan and Leon Kass, A Statutory Definition of the Standards for Determining Human Death: An Appraisal and a Proposal, 121 U. Pa. L. Rev. 87 (1972). Copyright 1972, the University of Pennsylvania Law Review. Reprinted with permission of the University of Pennsylvania Law Review and Fred B. Rothman & Company.

Council on Ethical and Judicial Affairs, Current Ethical Opinions 2.035: Futile Care and 9.11: Ethics Committees in Health Care Institutions, in Code of Medical Ethics: Current Opinions with Annotations (1998). Copyright 1998, American Medical Association. Reprinted with permission of American Medical Association.

Council on Ethical and Judicial Affairs, The Use of Anencephalic Neonates as Organ Donors, 273 JAMA 1614 (1995). Copyright 1995, American Medical Association. Reprinted with permission of American Medical Association.

Daniels, Norman et al., Benchmarks of Fairness for Health Care Reform: A Policy Tool for Developing Countries, 78 Bull. World Health Org. 740. Copyright 2000. The World Health Organization (2000). Reprinted with permission of The World Health Organization.

Donabedian, Avedis, The Definition of Quality and Approaches to its Assessment, 1st ed., 4-6, 7, 13, 14, 27, 79-84, 102, 119 (Health Administration Press, Ann Arbor, MI, 1980). Reprinted from Avedis Donabedian, The Definition of Quality and Approaches to its Assessment, in Explorations in Quality Assessment and Monitoring, volume 1. Copyright 1980. Reprinted with permission.

Enthoven, Alain, Health Plan: The Only Practical Solution to the Soaring Costs of Health Care 1-12 (1980). Copyright 1980 Alain Enthoven. Reprinted with permission of Alain Enthoven.

European Parliament, Directorate General Research, Working Paper: Health Care Systems in the European Union (1998). Copyright 1998, European Parliament. Reprinted with permission.

Fletcher, Joseph, Drawing Moral Lines in Fetal Therapy, 29 Clin. Obstetrics & Gynecology 595 (1986). Copyright 1986. Reprinted with permission of Lippincott, Williams and Wilks.

Fletcher, Joseph, Indicators of Humanhood, 2 Hastings Center Report (5) 1 (November 1972). Copyright 1972, the Hastings Center. Reprinted with permission of the Hastings Center.

Hacker, Jacob S., and Theodore R. Marmor, How Not to Think About "Managed Care," 32 University of Michigan Journal of Law Reform 661 (1999). Copyright University of Michigan Journal of Law Reform. Used with permission.

Hyman, David A., Regulating Managed Care: What's Wrong with a Patient Bill of Rights, 73 Southern California Law Review 221 (2000). Copyright 2000, Southern California Law Review. Reprinted with permission.

Leape, Lucian L., Error in Medicine, 272 JAMA 1851 (1994). Copyright 1994, American Medical Association. Reprinted with permission of the American Medical Association.

Morreim, E Haavi, "Redefining Quality by Reassigning Responsibility," 20 American Journal of Law and Medicine 79-104 (1994). Reprinted with permission of the American Society of Law, Medicine, and Ethics and Boston University School of Law.

National Conference of Commissioners on Uniform State Laws, Uniform Anatomical Gift Act. Copyright 1977, National Conference of Commissioners on Uniform State Laws. Reprinted with permission of National Conference of Commissioners on Uniform State Laws.

National Conference of Commissioners on Uniform State Laws, Uniform Determination of Death Act. Copyright 1980, National Conference of Commissioners on Uniform State Laws. Reprinted with permission of National Conference of Commissioners on Uniform State Laws.

National Conference of Commissioners of Uniform State Laws, Uniform Health Care Decisions Act. Copyright, National Conference of Commissioners on Uniform State Laws. Reprinted with permission of National Conference of Commissioners on Uniform State Laws.

National Conference of Commissioners on Uniform State Laws, Uniform Parentage Act. Copyright 1973, 2000, National Conference of Commissioners on Uniform State Laws. Reprinted with permission of National Conference of Commissioners on Uniform State Laws.

National Conference of Commissioners on Uniform State Laws, Uniform Probate Code. Copyright, National Conference of Commissioners on Uniform State Laws. Reprinted with permission of National Conference of Commissioners on Uniform State Laws.

Oberlander, Jonathan, Jacob Hacker, Mark Goldberg, Theodore Marmor, The Breaux Plan: Why It's Wrong Medicine for Medicare. Copyright 1999. Used by permission.

Report of the Ad Hoc Committee of the Harvard Medical School to Examine the Definition of Brain Death: A Definition of Irreversible Coma, 205 J.A.M.A. 85 (August 1968). Copyright 1968, American Medical Association. Reprinted with permission of American Medical Association.

Report of the Committee of Inquiry into Human Fertilisation and Embryology (Cmnd 9314) (1984). Copyright 1984, Her Majesty's Stationery Office. Crown copyright is reproduced with the permission of the Controller of Her Majesty's Stationery Office.

Roth, Loren, Alan Meisel and Charles Lidz, Tests of Competency to Consent to Treatment, 134 Am. J. Psychiatry 279 (1977). Copyright 1977, the American Psychiatric Association. Reprinted by permission.

Sage, William M., Physicians as Advocates, 35 Houston L. Rev. 1529 (1999).

Showalter, J. Stuart, Determining Death: The Legal and Theological Aspects of Brain-Related Criteria, 27 Catholic Lawyer 112 (1982). Copyright 1982, Catholic Lawyer. Reprinted with permission of the Catholic Lawyer.

Sinsheimer, Robert L., Whither the Genome Project?, 20 Hastings Center Report (4) 5 (July/August 1990). Copyright 1990, the Hastings Center. Reprinted with permission of the Hastings Center.

Sullivan, Mark and Stuart Youngner, Depression, Competence, and the Right to Refuse Lifesaving Medical Treatment, 151 Am. J. Psychiatry 971 (1994). Copyright 1994, the American Psychiatric Association. Reprinted by permission.

Ulrich, Lawrence P., Reproductive Rights of Genetic Disease, in J. Humber and R. Almeder, eds., Biomedical Ethics and the Law. Copyright 1986, Kluwer Academic/Plenum Publishers. Reprinted with permission of Plenum Press and the author.

Veatch, Robert, Correspondence—What it Means to be Dead, 12 Hastings Center Report (5) 45 (October 1982). Copyright 1982, the Hastings Center. Reprinted with permission of the Hastings Center and the author.

Wolf, Susan, Ethics Committees and Due Process: Nesting Rights in a Community of Caring, 50 Md. L. Rev. 798 (1991). Copyright 1991, Maryland Law Review. Reprinted with permission of the author.

Wolf, Susan, Gender, Feminism and Death: Physician Assisted Suicide and Euthanasia, in Feminism and Bioethics: Beyond Reproduction (1996). Copyright 1996, Oxford University Press. Reprinted by permission of Oxford University Press.

*

Summary of Contents

Table of Contents

*

Table of Cases

The principal cases are in bold type. Cases cited or discussed in the text are roman type. References are to pages. Cases cited in principal cases and within other quoted materials are not included.

LIABILITY AND QUALITY ISSUES IN HEALTH CARE

Fourth Edition

*

Chapter 1

DEFINING, EVALUATING AND DISTRIBUTING HEALTH CARE: AN INTRODUCTION

Part I of this chapter will consider the definition of illness and the nature of health care. Part II will examine the definition of quality and its measurement. Part III will analyze the problem of medical error, including its definition and origins and strategies for reducing its incidence. Part IV of this chapter will present issues and controversies in the distribution and supply of human organs for transplantation, using this as a paradigmatic case for an introductory analysis of values in the health care system.

I. DEFINING SICKNESS

Before examining the meaning of quality in health care, consider the meaning of health and of sickness. We all have an operational definition of health and sickness. I know when I am depressed, have a broken leg, a headache or a hangover. In these circumstances I consider myself to be in ill health because I am not functioning as well as I usually do, even though I may lack a scientific medical explanation of my malaise. But am I in poor health because my arteries are gradually becoming clogged, a process that probably began when I was a teenager? Am I sick or in poor health if I am obese, or addicted to alcohol or drugs, or if I am very old and enfeebled?

We need some definition of health in order to assess the quality of care needed to promote or restore it. A malpractice suit or medical quality audit depends on an ability to distinguish a bad from a good medical care outcome. An understanding of the nature of sickness and health is required to determine what health care society should provide the poor and how much society ought to spend on health care. Should Medicaid (a federal/state health care program for the poor) or a commercial insurer, for example, cover in vitro fertilization or abortions? Does the possibility of organ transplantation mean that replacement hearts should become the normal treatment for a condition that formerly inevitably ended in death? Should organ transplantation be available to all, without regard to the ability to pay? If the state of being old becomes a state of sickness (and particularly if that sickness must be "cured" at public expense), what will be the cost? Is this cost justified? Finally, the definition of health raises questions of autonomy, responsibility and personhood. Should health be defined by the doctor as scientist or the patient as person, or both? Is the drunkard or serial killer diseased or sinning or both or neither?

The Constitution of the World Health Organization defines health as "[A] State of complete physical, mental and social well-being and not merely the absence of disease or infirmity." When did you last feel that way? Can health ever be achieved under this definition, or is everyone always in a state of ill health? How much can physicians and hospitals contribute to health under this definition? A further provision of the WHO Constitution provides that "Governments have a responsibility for the health of their peoples which can be fulfilled only by the provision of adequate health and social measures." What are the political ramifications of these principles?

Health can be viewed in a more limited sense as the performance by each part of the body of its "natural" function. Definitions in terms of biological functioning tend to be more descriptive and less value-laden. As Englehardt writes, "The notion required for an analysis of health is not that of a good man or a good shark, but that of a good specimen of a human being or shark." H. Tristam Englehardt, "The Concepts of Health and Disease," in Concepts of Health and Disease 552 (Arthur Caplan, H. Tristam Engelhardt, and James McCartney, eds. 1981) (hereafter Concepts). Boorse compares health to the mechanical condition of a car, which can be described as good because it conforms to the designers' specifications, even though the design is flawed. Disease is then a biological malfunction, a deviation from the biological norm of natural function. C. Boorse, "On the Distinction Between Disease and Illness," in Concepts, supra at 553.

Illness can be defined as a subset of disease. Boorse writes:

> An illness must be, first, a reasonably *serious* disease with incapacitating effects that make it undesirable. A shaving cut or mild athlete's foot cannot be called an illness, nor could one call in sick on the basis of a single dental cavity, though all these conditions are diseases. Secondly, to call a disease an illness is to view its owner as deserving special treatment and diminished moral accountability * * *. Where we do not make the appropriate normative judgments or activate the social institutions, no amount of disease will lead us to use the term "ill." Even if the laboratory fruit flies fly in listless circles and expire at our feet, we do not say they succumbed to an illness, and for roughly the same reasons as we decline to give them a proper funeral.
>
> There are, then, two senses of "health". In one sense it is a theoretical notion, the opposite of "disease." In another sense it is a practical or mixed ethical notion, the opposite of "illness."

Illness is thus a socially constructed deviance. Something more than a mere biological abnormality is needed. To be ill is to have deviant characteristics for which the sick role is appropriate. The sick role, as Parsons has described it, exempts one from normal social responsibilities and removes individual responsibility. See Talcott Parsons, The Social System (1951). Our choice of words reflects this: an alcoholic is sick; a drunkard is not.

A sick person can be assisted by treatment defined by the medical model. He becomes a patient, an object of medical attention by a doctor. The doctor has the right and the ability to label someone ill, to determine whether the lump on a patient's skin is a blister, a wart or a cancer. The doctor can thus decide whether a patient is culpable or not, disabled or malingering. Illness also enjoins the physician to action to restore the patient to health.

Illness thus has many ramifications. First, it affects the individual. It relieves responsibility. The sick person need not report for work at 8:00; the posttraumatic stress syndrome or premenstrual syndrome victim may be declared not guilty for an assault. It means loss of control. The mild pain may have disproportionate effects on the individual who sees it as the harbinger of cancer or a brain tumor. The physician can restore control by providing a rational explanation for the experience of impairment. Illness costs the patient money, in lost time and in medical expenses. And someone receives that money for trying to treat that patient's illness.

Our understanding of illness also affects society. Defining a condition as an illness to be aggressively treated, rather than as a natural condition of life to be accepted and tolerated, has significant economic effects. Medical care is an object of economic choice, a good that many perceive to be different from other goods, with greater, sometimes immeasurable value. Some people are willing to pay far more for medical care than they would for other goods, or, more typically, to procure insurance that will deliver them from ever having to face the choice of paying for health care and abandoning all else. Society may also feel a special obligation to pay for the medical expenses of those who need treatment but lack resources to pay for it.

KATSKEE v. BLUE CROSS/BLUE SHIELD OF NEBRASKA

Supreme Court of Nebraska, 1994.
245 Neb. 808, 515 N.W.2d 645.

White, Justice.

This appeal arises from a summary judgment issued by the Douglas County District Court dismissing appellant Sindie Katskee's action for breach of contract. This action concerns the determination of what constitutes an illness within the meaning of a health insurance policy issued by appellee, Blue Cross/Blue Shield of Nebraska. We reverse the decision of the district court and remand the cause for further proceedings.

In January 1990, upon the recommendation of her gynecologist, Dr. Larry E. Roffman, appellant consulted with Dr. Henry T. Lynch regarding her family's history of breast and ovarian cancer, and particularly her health in relation to such a history. After examining appellant and investigating her family's medical history, Dr. Lynch diagnosed her as suffering from a genetic condition known as breast-ovarian carcinoma syndrome. Dr. Lynch then recommended that appellant have a total abdominal hysterectomy and bilateral salpingo-oophorectomy, which involves the removal of the uterus, the ovaries, and the fallopian tubes. Dr. Roffman concurred in Dr. Lynch's diagnosis and agreed that the recommended surgery was the most medically appropriate treatment available.

After considering the diagnosis and recommended treatment, appellant decided to have the surgery. In preparation for the surgery, appellant filed a claim with Blue Cross/Blue Shield. Both Drs. Lynch and Roffman wrote to Blue Cross/Blue Shield and explained the diagnosis and their basis for recommending the surgery. Initially, Blue Cross/Blue Shield sent a letter to appellant and indicated that it might pay for the surgery. Two weeks before the surgery, Dr. Roger Mason, the chief medical officer for Blue Cross/Blue Shield, wrote to appellant and stated that Blue Cross/Blue Shield would not cover the cost of the surgery. Nonetheless, appellant had the surgery in November 1990.

Appellant filed this action for breach of contract, seeking to recover $6,022.57 in costs associated with the surgery. Blue Cross/Blue Shield filed a motion for summary judgment. The district court granted the motion. It found that there was no genuine issue of material fact and that the policy did not cover appellant's surgery. Specifically, the court stated that (1) appellant did not suffer from cancer, and although her high-risk condition warranted the surgery, it was not covered by the policy; (2) appellant did not have a bodily illness or disease which was covered by the policy; and (3) under the terms of the policy, Blue Cross/Blue Shield reserved the right to determine what is medically necessary. Appellant filed a notice of appeal to the Nebraska Court of Appeals, and on our motion, we removed the case to the Nebraska Supreme Court.

Appellant contends that the district court erred in finding that no genuine issue of material fact existed and granting summary judgment in favor of appellee.

* * *

Blue Cross/Blue Shield contends that appellant's costs are not covered by the insurance policy. The policy provides coverage for services which are medically necessary. The policy defines "medically necessary" as follows: The services, procedures, drugs, supplies or Durable Medical Equipment provided by the Physician, Hospital or other health care provider, in the diagnosis or treatment of the Covered Person's Illness, Injury, or Pregnancy, which are: 1. Appropriate for the symptoms and diagnosis of the patient's Illness, Injury or Pregnancy; and 2. Provided in the most appropriate setting and at the most appropriate level of services[;] and 3. Consistent with the standards of good medical practice in the medical community of the State of Nebraska; and 4. Not provided primarily for the convenience of any of the following: a. the Covered Person; b. the Physician; c. the Covered Person's family; d. any other person or health care provider; and 5. Not considered to be unnecessarily repetitive when performed in combination with other diagnoses or treatment procedures. We shall determine whether services provided are Medically Necessary. Services will not automatically be considered Medically Necessary because they have been ordered or provided by a Physician. (Emphasis supplied.) Blue Cross/Blue Shield denied coverage because it concluded that appellant's condition does not constitute an illness, and thus the treatment she received was not medically necessary. Blue Cross/Blue Shield has not raised any other basis for its denial, and we therefore will limit our consideration to whether appellant's condition constituted an illness within the meaning of the policy.

The policy broadly defines "illness" as a "bodily disorder or disease." The policy does not provide definitions for either bodily disorder or disease.

An insurance policy is to be construed as any other contract to give effect to the parties' intentions at the time the contract was made. When the terms of the contract are clear, a court may not resort to rules of construction, and the terms are to be accorded their plain and ordinary meaning as the ordinary or reasonable person would understand them. In such a case, a court shall seek to ascertain the intention of the parties from the plain language of the policy. [ ]

Whether a policy is ambiguous is a matter of law for the court to determine. If a court finds that the policy is ambiguous, then the court may employ rules of construction and look beyond the language of the policy to ascertain the intention of the parties. A general principle of construction, which we have applied to ambiguous insurance policies, holds that an ambiguous policy will be construed in favor of the insured. However, we will not read an ambiguity into policy language which is plain and unambiguous in order to construe it against the insurer. [ ]

When interpreting the plain meaning of the terms of an insurance policy, we have stated that the " ' "natural and obvious meaning of the provisions in a policy is to be adopted in preference to a fanciful, curious, or hidden meaning." ' " [ ] We have further stated that " '[w]hile for the purpose of judicial decision dictionary definitions often are not controlling, they are at least persuasive that meanings which they do not embrace are not common.' " [ ]

Applying these principles, our interpretation of the language of the terms employed in the policy is guided by definitions found in dictionaries, and additionally by judicial opinions rendered by other courts which have considered the meaning of these terms. Webster's Third New International Dictionary, Unabridged 648 (1981), defines disease as an impairment of the normal state of the living animal or plant body or of any of its components that interrupts or modifies the performance of the vital functions, being a response to environmental factors ... to specific infective agents ... to inherent defects of the organism (as various genetic anomalies), or to combinations of these factors: Sickness, Illness. The same dictionary defines disorder as "a derangement of function: an abnormal physical or mental condition: Sickness, Ailment, Malady." Id. at 652. [ ]

These lay definitions are consistent with the general definitions provided in Dorland's Illustrated Medical Dictionary (27th ed. 1988). Dorland's defines disease as any deviation from or interruption of the normal structure or function of any part, organ, or system ... of the body that is manifested by a characteristic set of symptoms and signs and whose etiology [theory of origin or cause], pathology [origin or cause], and prognosis may be known or unknown. Id. at 481. [ ] Dorland's defines disorder as "a derangement or abnormality of function; a morbid physical or mental state." Id. at 495. [ ]

* * *

[The court looked at similar definitional disputes in other jurisdictions, noting that hemophilia, aneurysms, and chronic alcoholism had been held to be diseases or illnesses under insurance policies.]

We find that the language used in the policy at issue in the present case is not reasonably susceptible of differing interpretations and thus not ambiguous. The plain and ordinary meaning of the terms "bodily disorder" and "disease," as they are used in the policy to define illness, encompasses any abnormal condition of the body or its components of such a degree that in its natural progression would be expected to be problematic; a deviation from the healthy or normal state affecting the functions or tissues of the body; an inherent defect of the body; or a morbid physical or mental state which deviates from or interrupts the normal structure or function of any part, organ, or system of the body and which is manifested by a characteristic set of symptoms and signs.

The issue then becomes whether appellant's condition—breast-ovarian carcinoma syndrome—constitutes an illness.

Blue Cross/Blue Shield argues that appellant did not suffer from an illness because she did not have cancer. Blue Cross/Blue Shield characterizes appellant's condition only as a "predisposition to an illness (cancer)" and fails to address whether the condition itself constitutes an illness. Brief for appellee at 13. This failure is traceable to Dr. Mason's denial of appellant's claim. Despite acknowledging his inexperience and lack of knowledge about this specialized area of cancer research, Dr. Mason denied appellant's claim without consulting any medical literature or research regarding breast-ovarian carcinoma syndrome. Moreover, Dr. Mason made the decision without submitting appellant's claim for consideration to a claim review committee. The only basis for the denial was the claim filed by appellant, the letters sent by Drs. Lynch and Roffman, and the insurance policy. Despite his lack of information regarding the nature and severity of appellant's condition, Dr. Mason felt qualified to decide that appellant did not suffer from an illness.

Appellant's condition was diagnosed as breast-ovarian carcinoma syndrome. To adequately determine whether the syndrome constitutes an illness, we must first understand the nature of the syndrome.

The record on summary judgment includes the depositions of Drs. Lynch, Roffman, and Mason. In his deposition, Dr. Lynch provided a thorough discussion of this syndrome. In light of Dr. Lynch's extensive research and clinical experience in this particular area of medicine, we consider his discussion extremely helpful in our understanding of the syndrome.

According to Dr. Lynch, some forms of cancer occur on a hereditary basis. Breast and ovarian cancer are such forms of cancer which may occur on a hereditary basis. It is our understanding that the hereditary occurrence of this form of cancer is related to the genetic makeup of the woman. In this regard, the genetic deviation has conferred changes which are manifest in the individual's body and at some time become capable of being diagnosed.

At the time that he gave his deposition, Dr. Lynch explained that the state of medical research was such that detecting and diagnosing the syndrome was achieved by tracing the occurrences of hereditary cancer throughout the patient's family. Dr. Lynch stated that at the time of appellant's diagnosis, no conclusive physical test existed which would demonstrate the presence of the condition. However, Dr. Lynch stated that this area of research is progressing toward the development of a more determinative method of identifying and tracing a particular gene throughout a particular family, thus providing a physical method of diagnosing the condition.

Women diagnosed with the syndrome have at least a 50–percent chance of developing breast and/or ovarian cancer, whereas unaffected women have only a 1.4–percent risk of developing breast or ovarian cancer. In addition to the genetic deviation, the family history, and the significant risks associated with this condition, the diagnosis also may encompass symptoms of anxiety and stress, which some women experience because of their knowledge of the substantial likelihood of developing cancer.

The procedures for detecting the onset of ovarian cancer are ineffective. Generally, by the time ovarian cancer is capable of being detected, it has already developed to a very advanced stage, making treatment relatively unsuccessful. Drs. Lynch and Roffman agreed that the standard of care for treating women with breast carcinoma syndrome ordinarily involves surveillance methods. However, for women at an inordinately high risk for ovarian cancer, such as appellant, the standard of care may require radical surgery which involves the removal of the uterus, ovaries, and fallopian tubes.

Dr. Lynch explained that the surgery is labeled "prophylactic" and that the surgery is prophylactic as to the prevention of the onset of cancer. Dr. Lynch also stated that appellant's condition itself is the result of a genetic deviation from the normal, healthy state and that the recommended surgery treats that condition by eliminating or significantly reducing the presence of the condition and its likely development.

Blue Cross/Blue Shield has not proffered any evidence disputing the premise that the origin of this condition is in the genetic makeup of the individual and that in its natural development it is likely to produce devastating results. Although handicapped by his limited knowledge of the syndrome, Dr. Mason did not dispute the nature of the syndrome as explained by Dr. Lynch and supported by Dr. Roffman, nor did Dr. Mason dispute the fact that the surgery falls within the standard of care for many women afflicted with this syndrome.

In light of the plain and ordinary meaning of the terms "illness," "bodily disorder," and "disease," we find that appellant's condition constitutes an illness within the meaning of the policy. Appellant's condition is a deviation from what is considered a normal, healthy physical state or structure. The abnormality or deviation from a normal state arises, in part, from the genetic makeup of the woman. The existence of this unhealthy state results in the woman's being at substantial risk of developing cancer. The recommended surgery is intended to correct that morbid state by reducing or eliminating that risk.

Although appellant's condition was not detectable by physical evidence or a physical examination, it does not necessarily follow that appellant does not suffer from an illness. The record establishes that a woman who suffers from breast-ovarian carcinoma syndrome does have a physical state which significantly deviates from the physical state of a normal, healthy woman. Specifically, appellant suffered from a different or abnormal genetic constitution which, when combined with a particular family history of hereditary cancer, significantly increases the risk of a devastating outcome.

We are mindful that not every condition which itself constitutes a predisposition to another illness is necessarily an illness within the meaning of an insurance policy. There exists a fine distinction between such conditions, which was recognized by Chief Justice Cardozo in Silverstein v. Metropolitan Life Ins. Co., 254 N.Y. 81, 171 N.E. 914 (1930). Writing for the court, Chief Justice Cardozo explained that when a condition is such that in its probable and natural progression it may be expected to be a source of mischief, it may reasonably be described as a disease or an illness. On the other hand, he stated that if the condition is abnormal when tested by a standard of perfection, but so remote in its potential mischief that common speech would not label it a disease or infirmity, such a condition is at most a predisposing tendency. The Silverstein court found that a pea-size ulcer, which was located at the site of damage caused by a severe blow to the deceased's stomach, was not a disease or infirmity within the meaning of an exclusionary clause of an accident insurance policy because if left unattended, the ulcer would have been only as harmful as a tiny scratch.

Blue Cross/Blue Shield relies upon our decision in Fuglsang v. Blue Cross, 235 Neb. 552, 456 N.W.2d 281 (1990), and contends that we have already supplied a definition for the terms "disease," "condition," and "illness." Although we find that reliance on Fuglsang is somewhat misplaced, the opinion is relevant to our determination of the meaning of "disease," "illness," and "disorder," and whether the condition from which appellant suffered constitutes an illness.

The issue raised in Fuglsang was whether the disease from which the plaintiff suffered constituted a preexisting condition which was excluded from coverage by the terms of the policy. Blue Cross/Blue Shield relies on the following rule from Fuglsang as a definition of "disease": A disease, condition, or illness exists within the meaning of a health insurance policy excluding preexisting conditions only at such time as the disease, condition, or illness is manifest or active or when there is a distinct symptom or condition from which one learned in medicine can with reasonable accuracy diagnose the disease. [ ]

This statement concerns when an illness exists, not whether the condition itself is an illness. If the condition is not a disease or illness, it would be unnecessary to apply the above rule to determine whether the condition was a preexisting illness. In the present case, Blue Cross/Blue Shield maintains that the condition is not even an illness.

Even assuming arguendo that the rule announced in Fuglsang is a definition of "disease," "illness," and "condition," the inherent problems with the argument put forth by Blue Cross/Blue Shield undermine its reliance on that rule. Blue Cross/Blue Shield emphasizes the fact that appellant was never diagnosed with cancer and therefore, according to Blue Cross/Blue Shield, appellant did not have an illness because cancer was not active or manifest. Appellant concedes that she did not have cancer prior to her surgery. The issue is whether the condition she did have was an illness. Blue Cross/Blue Shield further argues that "[n]o disease or illness is 'manifest or active' and there is no 'distinct symptom or condition' from which Dr. Lynch or Dr. Roffman could diagnose a disease." Brief for appellee at 13. We stated above that lack of a physical test to detect the presence of an illness does not necessarily indicate that the person does not have an illness.

When the condition at issue—breast-ovarian carcinoma syndrome—is inserted into the formula provided by the Fuglsang rule, the condition would constitute an "illness" as Blue Cross/Blue Shield defines the term. The formula is whether the breast-ovarian carcinoma syndrome was manifest or active, or whether there was a distinct symptom or condition from which one learned in medicine could with reasonable accuracy diagnose the disease. The record establishes that the syndrome was manifest, at least in part, from the genetic deviation, and evident from the family medical history. The condition was such that one learned in medicine, Dr. Lynch, could with a reasonable degree of accuracy diagnose it. Blue Cross/Blue Shield does not dispute the nature of the syndrome, the method of diagnosis, or the accuracy of the diagnosis.

In the present case, the medical evidence regarding the nature of breast-ovarian carcinoma syndrome persuades us that appellant suffered from a bodily disorder or disease and, thus, suffered from an illness as defined by the insurance policy. Blue Cross/Blue Shield, therefore, is not entitled to judgment as a matter of law. Moreover, we find that appellant's condition did constitute an illness within the meaning of the policy. We reverse the decision of the district court and remand the cause for further proceedings. [ ]

Notes and Questions

1. Why did the court hold that Katskee was ill when she had no symptoms and no cancer? Can we have a variable definition of illness? For example, could Katskee be "ill" for purposes of payment for the surgery but not ill for purposes of pre-existing condition exclusions or excuse from work?

2. The syndrome in *Katskee*, if it materializes, is a medical problem for which the patient bears no responsibility. A more difficult problem area in defining "disease" involves those conditions or syndromes within the control of the individual. Consider for example alcoholism as a "disease". What difference does such a label make? What characteristics of alcohol consumption justify the label "disease"? See H. Thomas Milhorn, The Diagnosis of Alcoholism, AFP 175 (June 1988) ("... alcoholism can be defined as the continuation of drinking when it would be in the patient's best interest to stop.") See Traynor v. Turnage, 485 U.S. 535, 108 S.Ct. 1372, 99 L.Ed.2d 618 (1988) (considering alcoholism as attributable to "willful misconduct" under Veterans' Administration rules). See also Herbert Fingarette, Heavy Drinking: The Myth of Alcoholism as a Disease (1988); contra, see George Vaillant, The Natural History of Alcoholism (1983).

3. What other emerging clinical "syndromes" or diseases can you think of that raise troubling problems for the medical model of disease? How about anorexia? Obesity? "Battered wife" syndrome? What forces have led to the proliferation of these new syndromes or diseases?

Problem: The Couple's Illness

You represent Thomas and Jill Henderson, a couple embroiled in a dispute with their health insurance plan over coverage of infertility treatments. The Hendersons have been having trouble getting pregnant. Thomas has a low sperm count and motility, while Jill has irregular ovulation. They have undergone infertility treatment successfully in the past and have one child. They again sought further treatment, in order to have a second child. A simple insemination procedure failed. The health and disability group benefit plan of Thomas's employer, Clarion, paid their health benefits for this procedure.

They were then advised to try a more complex and expensive procedure, called Protocol I, which involved treating Thomas' sperm to improve its motility.

Drug therapy was prescribed for Jill to induce ovulation. Semen was then taken from Thomas, and put through an albumin gradient to improve its mobility. The semen was then reduced to a small pellet size and injected directly into the uterine cavity at the time of ovulation.

The Hendersons underwent Protocol I and submitted a bill to Clarion, which refused to pay it. Clarion cited a provision in its plan, Article VI, section 6.7, which provided:

> If a covered individual incurs outpatient expenses relating to injury or illness, those expenses charged, including but not limited to, office calls and for diagnostic services such as laboratory, x-ray, electrocardiography, therapy or injections, are covered expenses under the provisions of [the plan].

Under section 2.24 of the plan, "illness" was defined as "any sickness occurring to a covered individual which does not arise out of or in the course of employment for wage or profit." Clarion denied the Hendersons' claim on the grounds that the medical services were not performed because of any illness of Jill, as required under section 6.7. No provisions in the plan specifically excluded fertilization treatments like Protocol I.

What arguments can you make on behalf of the Hendersons that their situation is an "illness"? What arguments can you make for the insurance company that it is not?

ALAIN ENTHOVEN, PH.D., WHAT MEDICAL CARE IS AND ISN'T

In Alain Enthoven, Health Plan: The Only Practical Solution to the Soaring Costs of Health Care (1980).

[Some] Misconceptions About Medical Care

* * * In order to establish a conceptual framework that fits the realities, we must clear away seven popular misconceptions that underlie the acceptance of these inappropriate models.

1. *"The doctor should be able to know what condition the patient has, be able to answer patient's questions precisely, and prescribe the right treatment. If the doctor doesn't, that is incompetence or even malpractice."*

Of course, in many cases the diagnosis is clear-cut. But in many others there is a great deal of *uncertainty* in each step of medical care. Doctors are confronted with patients who have symptoms and syndromes, not labels with their diseases. A set of symptoms can be associated with any of several diseases. The chest pains produced by a gall bladder attack and by a heart attack can be confused by excellent doctors. Diagnostic tests are not 100 percent reliable. Consider a young woman with a painless lump in her breast. Is it cancer? There is a significant probability that a breast X-ray (mammogram), will produce a false result; that is, it will say that she does have cancer when she does not, or vice versa. There is less chance of error if a piece of the tissue is removed surgically (biopsy) and examined under a microscope by a pathologist. But even pathologists may reach different conclusions in some cases.

There are often no clear links between treatment and outcome. If a woman is found to have breast cancer, will she be better off if the whole breast and supporting tissue are removed (radical mastectomy), only the breast (simple mastectomy), or only the lump (lumpectomy)? There is considerable disagreement among doctors because there is, in fact, a great deal of uncertainty about the answer. Because of these uncertainties, there is wide variation among doctors in the tests ordered for similar cases and in the treatments prescribed. * * *

2. *"For each medical condition, there is a 'best' treatment. It is up to the doctor to know about that treatment and to use it. Anything else is unnecessary surgery, waste, fraud, or underservice."*

Of course, in many cases there is a clearly indicated treatment. But for many other medical conditions there are *several possible treatments*, each of which is legitimate and associated with different benefits, risks, and costs. Consider a few examples.

A forty-year-old laborer's chronic lower-back pain sometimes requires prolonged bed rest and potent pain medication. One doctor may recommend surgery; another, hoping to avoid the need for surgery, may recommend continued bed rest and traction followed by exercises. Whether one treatment is "better" than the other depends in part on the interpretation of the diagnostic tests (how strong the evidence is of a surgically correctable condition), but also in considerable part on the patient's values and the surgeon's judgment (how large a surgical risk the patient is willing to accept for the predicted likelihood of improvement).

As another common example with more than one treatment, consider a young woman with abnormal uterine bleeding, a nuisance but not a serious health hazard. One doctor may recommend a hysterectomy, whereas a second may advise that a dilatation and curettage be done as the first course of therapy, a third may feel that hormonal treatment is indicated, and a fourth may recommend no treatment. Any of the four might make sense, depending on the circumstances. There is no formula for calculating "the best" treatment, no clear dividing line between a "necessary" and an "unnecessary" operation.

A patient's needs, preferences, and lifestyle are important. Consider a woman who likes to ski and ride horseback and who has a partially detached retina in one eye. One ophthalmologist believes in an operation that does a minimum amount of "welding" (photocoagulation) and would minimize her loss of vision. Although that might satisfy the physician's criterion of technical excellence, it does not allow the woman to resume her athletic pursuits safely. Another ophthalmologist might propose to coagulate a complete circle around her retina. In this case the patient would lose some vision, but would have more of a guarantee that the retina will not detach again, and she could ski and ride again.

Patients suffering from severe angina pectoris (chest pain thought to be due to a lack of oxygen supply to the heart) pose another therapeutic dilemma. One doctor may recommend heart surgery; another, treatment with drugs such as nitroglycerine. For most such patients, there is no consensus among physicians today as to which is the better treatment.

What is "best" in a particular case will depend on the values and needs of the patient, the skills of the doctor, and the other resources available. The quality of the outcome depends a great deal on how the patient feels about it.

What is an annoyance for one patient may mean the inability to keep a job for another with the same condition. There is nothing wrong with the fact that doctors disagree. There is plenty of room for honest differences based on these and other factors. There are more and less costly treatments, practice patterns, and styles of medical care that produce substantially equivalent medical outcomes.

Medical care differs in important ways from repair of collision damage to your car. If you have a smashed fender, you can get three bids and make a deal to have it fixed. You can tell when it is fixed. There is one "correct treatment." Ordinarily, it should not be an open-ended task. But caring for a patient can be open-ended, especially when there is a great deal of uncertainty or when the patient has a chronic disease. Walter McClure, an analyst with InterStudy, a leading health policy research institute, put the point effectively when he wrote:

> The medical care system can legitimately absorb every dollar society will give it. If health insurance is expanded without seriously addressing the medical care system itself, cost escalation is likely to be severe and chronic. For example, why provide $50 of tests to be 95% certain of a diagnosis, if $250 of tests will provide 97% certainty. [ ]

Although there are generally accepted treatments for many diseases, and doctors can agree that there has been bad care in some cases, for many others there are no generally agreed standards of what is "the best" care. Physicians reject suggestions of what they refer to as "cookbook medicine"; recognizing the infinite variety of conditions, values, and uncertainties, they are understandably reluctant to impose such standards on one another.

The misconception that best-treatment standards exist for most cases underlies much of the belief in the feasibility of an insurance system like Medicare and the hope that regulatory schemes such as Professional Standards Review Organizations can control costs. If we understand that often there is no clear-cut best course of action in medical care, we will think in terms of alternatives, value judgments, and incentives rather than numerical standards.

3. "Medicine is an exact science. Unlike 50 or 100 years ago, there is now a firm scientific base for what the doctor does. Standard treatments are supported by scientific proof of efficacy."

In fact, medicine remains more of an art than a science. To be sure, it uses and applies scientific knowledge, and to become a physician, one must have command of a great deal of scientific information. But the application of this knowledge is a matter of judgment.

To prove beyond reasonable doubt that a medical treatment is effective often requires what is called a "randomized clinical trial (RCT)." In an RCT a large sample of patients is assigned randomly to two or more treatment groups. Each group is given one of the alternative treatments and then is evaluated by unbiased observers to see which treatment produced the better results. One of the "treatments" may be no treatment. (Of course, RCTs may not be needed in the case of "clear winners" such as penicillin, treatment of fractures, and congenital anomalies.) However, many practical difficulties stand in the way of doing a satisfactory clinical trial. As a result, RCTs are the exception, not the rule.

When medical or surgical innovations have been evaluated in this way, more often than not the innovation has been found to yield no benefit or even to be inferior to previous methods of treatment. Even when a clinical trial has established the value of a given treatment, judgment must be used in deciding whether a particular patient or set of circumstances is enough like those in the trial that the same good results can be expected in this particular case.

There are shifting opinions in medical care. Many operations have been invented and enjoyed popularity, only to be subsequently discarded when systematic testing failed to demonstrate their value. * * * Whether or not the coronary artery bypass graft operation that has recently become a billion-dollar-a-year industry will continue indefinitely at its present scale is uncertain. One good reason for not having national standards of care established by government is to avoid either imposing unsubstantiated treatments or freezing them into current practice.

Scientific and balanced analysis of the costs, risks, and benefits of different treatments is still the exception, not the rule.

4. Medical care consists of standard products that can be described precisely and measured meaningfully in standard units such as "inpatient days", "outpatient visits", or "doctor office visits".

In fact, medical care is usually anything but a standard product. Much of it is a uniquely personal interaction between two people. The elements of personal trust and confidence are an integral part of the process. Much of the process consists of reassurance and support—*caring* rather than *curing*. What doctors do ranges from the technical marvels of the heart surgeon to marriage counseling by the family doctor, each of which may fill a legitimate human need. A "doctor office visit" might last a few minutes or more than an hour. An "inpatient day" might be accompanied by the use of the most costly and complex technology or be merely a quiet day of rest, with an occasional visit by a nurse.

It is important to correct the misconception that medical care consists of standard products, because it underlies much of the thinking about costs and regulation. People will decry the rapid increase in hospital cost per day without giving recognition to the fact that the services provided during a typical hospital day now are much more complex and use much more elaborate technology than they did a decade ago. Proposals to regulate cost per day or cost per case assume that days or cases are more or less standard, so that the costs of a day in two different hospitals can be compared meaningfully. In fact, before one can make a meaningful comparison, one must specify many conditions, such as severity of illness, the length of stay, and the services provided. The belief that controls on physician fees are a feasible method of controlling the cost of physician services rests on the assumption that "doctor office visits" are more or less standard. They aren't.

Quality of medical care has many different dimensions: accessibility, convenience, style, and effectiveness. There are different systems and styles of care. This variability is desirable. It allows the medical care system to accommodate the preferences and needs of different patients and doctors. But it defies the public-utility regulators, who need standard units, such as passenger miles and kilowatt-hours.

5. *"Much of medical care is a matter of life and death or serious pain or disability."*

This view may come from watching television programs that emphasize the dramatic side of medicine. It is a foundation for the assertion that "health care is a right." As a society, we have agreed that all people should have access to life-saving care without regard to income, race, or social status.

Of course some medical care is life-saving, and its benefits are obvious and clear-cut. But most medical care is not a life-or-death matter at all. Even in the case of care for life-threatening diseases, the effectiveness of much care is measured in terms of small changes in life expectancy (for example, changes in the probability of surviving another year), as opposed to complete cures. Most medical care is a matter of "quality of life." Much of it is concerned with the relief of pain or dysfunction, with caring and reassurance.

All this is not to diminish the importance or value of medical care. But it does suggest that we are dealing with matters of darker or lighter shades of grey, conflicting values, and not clear-cut cases of life or death. Recognizing this makes it much less clear what it is that people have a "right" to or what is "necessary" as opposed to "unnecessary."

6. *"More medical care is better than less care."*

There is a tremendous amount of bias in favor of more care versus less. For example, the observation that physicians in group practices hospitalize their patients much less than do their fellow doctors in traditional solo practice is much more likely to cause suspicion that they are denying their patients necessary care than that the solo-practice doctors are providing too much care.

A.L. Cochrane, a British physician, supplied a nice example of this bias. Dr. H.G. Mather and colleagues in the National Health Service in Bristol did a randomized clinical trial comparing home and hospital treatment of uncomplicated heart attack (acute myocardial infarction) victims. They found that patients cared for in the coronary care units (CCUS) of hospitals survived in no greater proportion than did those cared for at home. Cochrane wrote:

> There is a great deal of bias, and a considerable amount of vested interest. The bias is beautifully illustrated by a story of the early days of Mather's trial. The first report after a few months of the trial showed a slightly greater death-rate in those treated in hospital than those treated at home. Someone reversed the figures and showed them to a CCU enthusiast who immediately declared that the trial was unethical and must be stopped at once. When, however, he was shown the table the correct way round he could not be persuaded to declare CCUs unethical! [ ]

In fact, more care may not be better than less care. More care may just be useless. Drs. Hill, Hampton, and Mitchell of Nottingham General Hospital recently repeated Dr. Mather's trial and got a similar result. Of 500 patients whose general practitioners called for the mobile coronary care unit (a specially equipped ambulance with a doctor), 70 percent were suspected of having a myocardial infarction. Of these, 24 percent were excluded from the trial and were hospitalized because of their medical condition or lack of suitable home environment. The rest were assigned by random method to home or hospital. The result for these patients was no discernable benefit from costly coronary care units compared with less costly home care. In many cases there may be nothing the medical care can do other than to relieve the patient's discomfort, and this relief may be accomplished as well or better at home as in a costly hospital bed.

Of course, in some cases more care will be better than less. But not in all cases. Above some minimum level that might be provided at a much lower per capita cost, more medical care may yield little, if any, discernible health benefit. This view is supported by two studies of the relationship of health resources to health indicators in different parts of the United States. One study looked at the health status of people living in different places as measured by such things as blood pressure, cholesterol concentration, abnormal electrocardiogram, and abnormal chest X-rays. The other looked at infant mortality and age-adjusted overall mortality. Each attempted to correlate these indicators with such measures of health resources as numbers and variables such as income, education, and occupation. Both found little or no significant relationship between health resources and health status.

More medical care may actually be harmful. There is such a thing as physician-caused (known as "iatrogenic") disease. People do die or are seriously injured on the operating table, and some are injured or die from the complications of anesthesia. * * *

Why Financial Incentives Make a Difference

* * *

If medical diagnoses were always clear-cut, if the best treatment were always obvious, if the element of science were large, if the timing of care were determined by medical necessity, and especially if medical care were mostly a matter of life and death, it would be easier to understand how people could believe that the institutional arrangements for providing medical care, including the financial incentives, would be irrelevant to the amounts and kinds of care provided. This kind of medicine would fit into both the casualty-insurance and public-utility models. Making it free at the time of service would not lead patients to demand more of it. Every medical treatment would be "necessary" or "unnecessary," and medical review boards could audit physician performance if unnecessary care were suspected.

Making the decision to use medical care free or almost free to consumers is bound to lead them to resolve their doubts in favor of more, and more costly, care than if they had to pay for it themselves. And think of the physicians, with their concern for the patient and a humanitarian desire to do everything possible to help alleviate suffering, professional standards that emphasize the most advanced technology, and concern over the threat of malpractice suits in a society that believes that more care is always better than less. If in addition to all that, the financing arrangements make the care free to the patient and also yield more revenue to the doctor for giving more, and more costly, care, it should not be difficult to see how fee-for-service payment contributes to ever more costly care.

Studies show that institutional settings and financial incentives do make a difference in the behavior of patients and doctors. For example, Anne Scitovsky, a leading health services researcher, did a study of visits to the doctor by Stanford University employees and their families cared for under a prepaid plan with the Palo Alto Medical Clinic. In 1966 such visits were fully paid in advance by the monthly premiums. This led to such high use of services and costs that in 1967, the plan was changed to require the families to pay one-quarter of each doctor bill. In 1968 the same people's visits to the doctor's office decreased by 25 percent. (The decline in hospital visits was by only 3 percent.) As far as Mrs. Scitovsky and other investigators could tell, the introduction of this financial disincentive was the only thing that had changed between the two years.

Incentives for the physicians can also be important; indeed, they are much more important than patient incentives from an economic point of view, because physicians make the costly decisions. George Monsma, Jr., an economist at Amherst College, highlighted this by comparing the number of operations per capita in groups of employees and their families, some of whom were cared for under group-practice prepayment plans, and some of whom were cared for under traditional insured fee-for-service plans. In the group-practice prepayment plans the surgery is free to the beneficiary, and the doctors get no more money for doing the surgery, because they are paid on the basis of a monthly per capita payment that is independent of the number of services performed. Under the traditional insured fee-for-service plans, the beneficiary pays 20 to 25 percent of the doctor bill, and the doctor gets more money for doing the operation than for not doing it.

The consumer incentive would be to have less surgery under the insured plan. But Monsma found significantly higher rates of surgery under the insured plan, thus lending support to the view that the physicians' incentives (which are in turn a function of how the physicians are organized and paid) dominate decision making on use of surgery. Numerous other comparative studies have reached similar conclusions.

To observe that financial incentives play an important role in the use of medical services is not to imply that they are the only, or even the most important, factor. Physicians are concerned primarily with curing their sick patients, regardless of the cost. That ethic has been instilled in them through years of arduous training. Many take a failure to cure a sick patient as a personal defeat. When we are sick, we want our doctors to be concerned with curing us and nothing else. Physicians and other health professionals are also motivated by a desire to achieve professional excellence and the esteem of their peers and the public. But their use of resources is inevitably shaped by financial incentives. Physicians who survive and prosper must ultimately do what brings in money and curtail those activities that lose money.

* * *

These insights also help explain why qualitative distinctions such as one finds in legal usage are not very helpful. One simply cannot divide all medical care into the categories "necessary" and "unnecessary." What is "necessary" care? Is "necessary" care limited to treatment of serious pain or life-threatening conditions? If it were, a great deal of care would not be "necessary." Even in life-and-death cases, the concept of "necessary" poorly describes many situations. Suppose that a patient with terminal cancer has 99–to–1 odds of dying within a year. Suppose that treatment costing $20,000 will reduce those odds to 97 to 1. Would that be "necessary" or "unnecessary" care? There are doubtless examples that most observers would judge to be "unnecessary." But the fact that two doctors disagree and that the doctor offering the "second opinion" says that the operation is "unnecessary" does not make it so.

Similarly, forceful assertions that "health care is a right" do not help in this large grey zone. In view of the variety of systems and styles of care and treatments, exactly what is a *right?* A *right* to *anything* health care providers can do to make you feel better? That interpretation would make "health care is a right" mean "money is no object." Our society cannot afford and will not support such a generous definition.

The concepts and language most useful for analyzing the problem of health care costs are concepts that have been developed for decision making under uncertainty and for choices of "a little more or a little less."

We need to think in terms of judgments about probabilities and in terms of the balancing of various costs, risks, and benefits. The issues are not, for example, "complete care vs. no care for a heart-attack patient." Rather, they are more of the character "seven vs. fourteen or twenty-one days in the hospital after a heart attack." What is the medical value of the extra days? How do they affect the probability that the patient will be alive a year later? What do they cost, not only in resources measured in money, but also in other terms? Are the extra benefits worth the extra costs? These are the kinds of questions we must keep asking if we want to make sense out of the problem and to get good value for the money we spend on health care. They are matters of judgment, possibly aided by calculation.

Notes and Questions

1. What are the implications of Enthoven's discussion for the regulation of health care quality? Is such regulation likely to be effective? How about the merits of a market in health care? Does Enthoven's analysis raise problems for the operation of a market in health care? What kind of problems?

2. Enthoven talks about the importance of institutional setting and financial setting. The fee-for-service mode of paying physicians has been blamed for much of the rapid inflation in health care costs over the past two decades. Physicians control up to 70% of the spending for health care, as agents for their patients. As a result, with few external controls on their ability to order health care tests and treatments, health care costs have risen much faster than the general rate of inflation of the Gross Domestic Product over the past two decades. What ideas might you propose to shift physician incentives toward a more cost-sensitive style of practice? Has managed care been successful in doing so? Are other inflationary forces at work? See Chapter 8 infra.

II. QUALITY IN HEALTH CARE

Lawyers become involved with quality of health care issues through a variety of routes. They file, or defend against, malpractice suits when a patient is injured because of a doctor's deviation from a standard of medical practice. They handle medical staff privilege cases that frequently turn on the quality of the staff doctor's performance. They represent the government in administering programs that aim to cut the cost of health care and improve its quality and providers that must adjust to these programs. Quality is a central concern in health care politics and law.

A. DEFINING THE NATURE OF QUALITY IN HEALTH CARE

AVEDIS DONABEDIAN, THE DEFINITION OF QUALITY AND APPROACHES TO ITS ASSESSMENT

(Vol. 1) (1980) 4–6.

The search for a definition of quality can usefully begin with what is perhaps the simplest complete module of care: the management by a physician, or any other primary practitioner, of a clearly definable episode of illness in a given patient. It is possible to divide this management into two domains: the technical and the interpersonal. Technical care is the application of the science and technology of medicine, and of the other health sciences, to the management of a personal health problem. Its accompaniment is the management of the social and psychological interaction between client and practitioner. The first of these has been called the science of medicine and the second its art * * *.

There may also be a third element in care which could be called its "amenities". * * * In a way, the amenities are properties of the more intimate aspects of the settings in which care is provided. But the amenities sometimes seem to be properties of the care itself * * *.

* * * At the very least, the quality of technical care consists in the application of medical science and technology in a manner that maximizes its benefits to health without correspondingly increasing its risks. The degree of quality is, therefore, the extent to which the care provided is expected to achieve the more favorable balance of risks and benefits.

What constitutes goodness in the interpersonal process is more difficult to summarize. The management of the interpersonal relationship must meet socially defined values and norms that govern the interaction of individuals in general and in particular situations. These norms are reinforced in part by the ethical dicta of health professions, and by the expectations and aspirations of individual patients. It follows that the degree of quality in the management of the interpersonal relationship is measured by the extent of conformity to these values, norms, expectations, and aspirations. * * * All these postulates lead us to a unifying concept of the quality of care as that kind of care which is expected to maximize an inclusive measure of patient welfare, after one has taken account of the balance of expected gains and losses that attend the process of care in all its parts.

Notes and Questions

1. Donabedian is a leader in the theory of health care assessment. Does his definition capture most of what you find important in thinking about quality health care?

2. The Institute of Medicine, in assessing the Medicare program, has developed its own definition:

> ... quality of care is the degree to which health services for individuals and populations increase the likelihood of desired health outcomes and are consistent with current professional knowledge.

Institute of Medicine, Medicare: A Strategy for Quality Assurance, Vol. I, 20 (K. Lohr, Ed.1990).

In order for "health services for individuals and populations to increase the likelihood of desired health outcomes," they must be used appropriately and effectively. Poor quality care can be caused by underuse, overuse, or misuse. Mark R. Chassin, R.W. Galvin, and the National Roundtable on Health Care Quality, The Urgent Need to Improve Health Care Quality, 280 JAMA 1000(1998)

Does this definition differ from Donabedian's? If so, what is the difference? Does the difference matter?

2. Unnecessary care that causes harm, by Donabedian's criteria, is poor in quality, since such care that causes harm unnecessarily is not counterbalanced by any expectation of benefit. How about care that is unnecessary yet harmless, like over-the-counter medicines that contain no therapeutic ingredients? Or medical interventions that have no proven value? Donabedian argues that such care should be judged as poor in quality.

> First, such care is not expected to yield benefits. Second, it can be argued that it causes reductions in individual and social welfare through improper use of resources. By spending time and money on medical care the patient has less to use for other things he values. Similarly, by providing excessive care to some, society has less to offer to others who may need it more. Finally, the use of redundant care, even when it is harmless, indicates carelessness, poor judgment, or ignorance on the part of the practitioner who is responsible for care. (Id. at 6–7).

Courts have generally deferred to a doctor's medical judgment as to the benefit of a particular treatment to a patient. Where the diagnostic or treatment modality is found to have no value, the physician may be negligent if a bad outcome results. In Riser v. American Medical International, Inc., 620 So.2d 372 (La.App. 5th Cir., 1993), the doctor performed a femoral arteriogram on the patient, who suffered a stroke and died. The court found that the physician had breached the standard of care by subjecting the patient to a technology which he should reasonably have known would be of "no practical benefit to the patient".

3. Effectiveness is rapidly becoming the test for a medical treatment or test. The "effectiveness initiative" in modern medicine is based on three premises: (1) many current medical practices either are ineffective or could be replaced with less expensive substitutes; (2) physicians often select more expensive treatments because of bias, fear of litigation, or financial incentives; and (3) patients would often choose different options from those recommended by their physicians if they had better information about treatment risks, benefits and costs.

Much of American medical practice does not improve health. In controlled trials, many cherished practices have been found unhelpful and even harmful. Treatments effective for one indication are frequently extended to other indications where effectiveness data do not exist. Higher quality care may cost more, raising the question of cost-effectiveness. But higher quality care may also be obtained for less money, as by cutting out ineffective services. Medicare reforms designed to contain the system's escalating costs, such as Diagnosis–Related Groups (DRGs), have been based on the assumption that the costs of caring for the elderly can be cut without affecting quality, that the corpus of health care delivery has substantial fat that can be trimmed. Empirical evidence to date supports this hypothesis. See also Volume 264, No. 15 (1990) of the Journal of the American Medical Association (J.A.M.A.)(issue devoted to a study of the prospective payment system and its effects on the quality of medical care); William L. Roper et al., Effectiveness in Health Care: An Initiative to Evaluate and Improve Medical Practice, 319 N.E.J.M. 1197 (1988); Paul M. Ellwood, Outcomes Management: A Technology of Patient Experience, 318 N.E.J.M. 1549 (1988); David M. Eddy, Variations in Physician Practice: The Role of Uncertainty, 3 Health Affairs 74 (1984); John M. Eisenberg, Doctors' Decisions and the Cost of Medical Care (1986); John E. Wennberg, Outcomes Research, Cost Containment, and the Fear of Health Care Rationing, 323 N.E.J.M. 1202 (1990).

4. What is the role of the patient and her values in the delivery of medical care? Donabedian's definition of quality combines the doctor's technical management with the patient's expectations and values, as well as cost considerations. An "absolutist" medical view, on the other hand, might define quality as a doctor's management of a patient's problems in a way that the doctor expects will best balance health benefits and risks. Donabedian characterizes this position as follows: "[i]t is the responsibility of the practitioner to recommend and carry out such care. All other factors, including monetary costs, as well as the patient's expectations and valuations, are thereby regarded as either obstacles or facilitators to the implementation of the standard of quality." (Donabedian, supra at 13).

A second view, also reflected in the judicial discussions of informed consent, is described by Donabedian as an "individualized" definition of quality:

> A long and honorable tradition of the health professions holds that the primary function of medical care is to advance the patient's welfare. If this is so, it is inevitable that the patient must share with the practitioner the responsibility for defining the objectives of care, and for placing a valuation on the benefits and risks that are expected as the results of alternative strategies of management. In fact, it can be argued that the practitioner merely provides expert information, while the task of valuation falls on the patient or on those who can, legitimately, act on his behalf. Donabedian, supra at 13–14.

How do cost considerations fit into this individualized definition of quality? If the patient has no insurance and probably cannot pay for an expensive surgical procedure, or if the patient decides to forego a treatment after making his or her own cost tradeoffs, how should the doctor respond? Must the doctor be satisfied with giving the patient less medical care than would be possible, and than would in fact help the patient?

> [I]n real life, we do not have the option of excluding monetary costs from the individualized definition of quality. Their inclusion means that the practitioner does for each patient what the patient has decided his circumstances allow. In so doing, the practitioner has discharged his responsibility to the patient, provided that he has helped the patient to discover and use every available means of paying for care. Donabedian, supra at 27.

Patients' insurance status significantly affects the procedures they receive to treat various medical problems. A study of in-hospital cardiac procedures found that patients with private health insurance, compared to patients with either Medicaid or no insurance, were 80% more likely to receive angiography, 40% more likely to receive bypass grafting, and 28% more likely to receive angioplasty. See

Mark B. Wenneker, et al., The Association of Payer with Utilization of Cardiac Procedures in Massachusetts, 264 J.A.M.A. 1255 (1990).

Even in a society with comprehensive social benefits, such as a national health insurance program, costs must be considered by the practitioner, who is still constrained by the resources available for health care. The doctor as citizen must choose whether to help the patient as much as possible, with the taxpayers absorbing the costs; or to stop short of giving the individual the maximum help.

5. The common law of battery has been applied in cases where a doctor performed a procedure on a patient against the patient's will or without his or her consent. What if the doctor's decision was correct, in the technical sense of achieving a good outcome for the patient? Consider Donabedian:

> Taken by and large, outcomes tend to be inherently valid, in the sense that there is usually no need to argue whether they are, in themselves, good or bad. For example, there is general agreement that life is preferable to death, functional integrity preferable to disability, and comfort preferable to pain. By contrast, the validity of the elements of process is fundamentally derivative, because it depends on the contribution of process to desired outcomes. But there are important exceptions. * * * [T]here are some attributes of the interpersonal process that are valid in themselves, because they represent approved or desirable behaviors in specified social situations. Attributes such as these may be valued and preserved even though they make it more difficult to achieve certain outcomes. Donabedian, supra at 102.

Should the legal system allow an individual to rank a value higher than his or her health, or than life itself?

6. A third definition of quality adds a social dimension, looking at the distribution of benefits within a population. Underuse of health care is a signification social problem in the United States, the result of lack of insurance, poor access to providers, and social attitudes by both patients and providers. As a society, we may value different segments of our population differently, based on our political choice, indifference, or social values. For example, various Federal cutbacks in maternity and child care benefits in the early 1980s disproportionately affected minorities and lower class families, reflecting political choices that seriously reduced the quality of health care received by a significant percentage of the U.S. population. Organ transplantation practices may have unduly disadvantaged African–Americans and other minorities in terms of access to organs. Access is an important measure of the quality of the American health care system.

Edward L. Hannan, The Continuing Quest for Measuring and Improving Access to Necessary Care, 284 JAMA 2374 (2000). See generally Avedis Donabedian, A Primer of Quality Assurance and Monitoring in Medical Care, 20 Toledo L.Rev. 401 (1989); A. Donabedian, The Definition of Quality and Approaches to Its Assessment (1980); A. Donabedian, The Criteria and Standards of Quality (1982); A. Donabedian, The Methods and Findings of Quality Assessment and Monitoring: An Illustrated Analysis (1985).

B. ASSESSING QUALITY

Thus far we have attempted to give some content to a definition of "quality" in health care. The next step is to examine how to evaluate quality. We need to take the definition of quality, and particularize it to describe acceptable medical procedures, and institutional structures and processes.

The elements of such an evaluation have again been provided by Donabedian, whose trichotomy is generally accepted as a starting point for thinking about the evaluation of health care.

AVEDIS DONABEDIAN, THE DEFINITION OF QUALITY AND APPROACHES TO ITS ASSESSMENT

Vol. 1 (1980) 79–84.

[T]he primary object of study is a set of activities that go on within and between practitioners and patients. This set of activities I have called the "process" of care. A judgment concerning the quality of that process may be made either by direct observation or by review of recorded information * * *. But, while "process" is the primary *object* of assessment, the *basis* for the judgment of quality is what is known about the relationship between the characteristics of the medical care process and their consequences to the health and welfare of individuals and of society, in accordance with the value placed upon health and welfare by the individual and by society.

With regard to technical management, the relationship between the characteristics of the process of care and its consequences is determined, in the abstract, by the state of medical science and technology at any given time. More specifically, this relationship is revealed in the work of the leading exponents of that science and technology; through their published research, their teachings, and their own practice these leaders define, explicitly or implicitly, the technical norms of good care.

Another set of norms governs the management of the interpersonal process. These norms arise from the values and the ethical principles and rules that govern the relationships among people, in general, and between health professionals and clients, in particular. * * *

It follows, therefore, that the quality of the "process" of care is defined, in the first place, as normative behavior. * * *

* * *

I have argued, so far, that the most direct route to an assessment of the quality of care is an examination of that care. But there are * * * two other, less direct approaches to assessment: one of these is the assessment of "structure", and the other the assessment of "outcome."

By "structure" I mean the relatively stable characteristics of the providers of care, of the tools and resources they have at their disposal, and of the physical and organizational settings in which they work. The concept of structure includes the human, physical, and financial resources that are needed to provide medical care. The term embraces the number, distribution, and qualifications of professional personnel, and so, too, the number, size, equipment, and geographic disposition of hospitals and other facilities. [Donabedian goes on to include within structure the organization of financing and delivery, how doctors practice and how they are paid, staff organization, and how medical work is reviewed in institutions] * * * The basic characteristics of structure are that it is relatively stable, that it functions to produce care or is a feature of the "environment" of care, and that it influences the kind of care that is provided.

* * * Structure, therefore, is relevant to quality in that it increases or decreases the probability of good performances. * * * But as a means for assessing the quality of care, structure is a rather blunt instrument; it can only indicate general tendencies.

* * *

I believe that good structure, that is, a sufficiency of resources and proper system design, is probably the most important means of protecting and promoting the quality of care. * * * As a source of accurate current information about quality, the assessment of structure is of a good deal less importance than the assessment of process or outcome.

* * *

The study of "outcomes" is the other of the indirect approaches that I have said could be used to assess the quality of care. [Outcome is] * * * a change in a patient's current and future health status that can be attributed to antecedent health care. * * * I shall include improvements of social and psychological function in addition to the more usual emphasis on the physical and physiological aspects of performance. By still another extension I shall add patient attitudes (including satisfaction), health-related knowledge acquired by the patient, and health-related behavioral change.

* * *

* * * [T]here are three major approaches to quality assessment: "structure," "process," and "outcome." This three-fold approach is possible because there is a fundamental functional relationship among the three elements, which can be shown schematically as follows:

Structure → Process → Outcome

This means that structural characteristics of the settings in which care takes place have a propensity to influence the process of care so that its quality is diminished or enhanced. Similarly, changes in the process of care, including variations in its quality, will influence the effect of care on health status, broadly defined.

Notes and Questions

1. Quality assurance strategies depend on evaluation tools that apply the definition of quality to a health care professional or institution. Structure evaluation is the easiest to do. Personnel, equipment, and buildings can be counted or described; internal regulations and staff organization measured against specific criteria; and budgets critiqued. Structure evaluation is the least useful, however, since the connection between structural components and quality of care is not necessarily direct.

2. Process evaluation of health care has several advantages over structural evaluations. It allows doctors to specify criteria and standards of good care or to establish a range of acceptable practice before all the research evidence is in; it assures documentation in the medical record for preventive and informative purposes; and it permits attribution of responsibility for discrete clinical decisions.

The process perspective has three major drawbacks, however. First, "[t]he major drawback * * * is the weakness of the scientific basis for much of accepted practice. The use of prevalent norms as a basis for judging quality may, therefore, encourage dogmatism and help perpetuate error." Donabedian, supra at 119. Second, the emphasis on the need for technical interventions may lead to high cost care. Third, the interpersonal process is slighted, since process evaluation focuses on the technical proficiency of the doctor.

How should process review take place within a medical practice? Within a hospital? Should surgeons or internists assess each other's work? What if an errant colleague is spotted?

3. Outcome evaluation has substantial advantages over both process and structure measures. It provides a flexible approach that focuses on what works and on integrated care that includes consideration of the patient's own contribution. The goal of all health care is, after all, the best possible outcome for the patient.

Outcome measures also have their problems, however: the duration, timing, or extent of outcomes of optimal care are often hard to specify; it is often hard to credit a good outcome to a specific medical intervention; and the outcome is often known too late to affect practice. See Katherine L. Kahn, et al., Measuring Quality of Care With Explicit Process Criteria Before and After Implementation of the DRG–Based Prospective Payment System, 264 N.Eng.J.Med. 1969 (1990).

Are outcome measures useful for comparing hospitals? Consider the Department of Health and Human Services' release of mortality figures for various medical procedures at hospitals around the country. Hospitals had widely differing mortality and morbidity rates and success rates for different procedures. This seems to be a pure outcome indicator, a kind of Consumer Reports rating of hospitals to be used comparatively for purposes of consumer information. Is release of such statistics desirable? Does it benefit the health care consumer? Does the consumer care? A recent study concluded that provider quality of care can be accurately measured and compared. Short term mortality rates following a heart attack are excellent indicators of quality of care, varying dramatically across hospitals. See Mark McClellan and Douglas Staiger, The Quality of Health Care Providers, NBER Working Paper (August 1999).

It appears that even before such explicit data became available, the relative quality of hospitals played a part in the choices made by admitting physicians and their patients. It is likely that the admitting physicians were aware of hospital differences, and chose selectively for their patients. The proliferation of specific comparative data might accelerate these tendencies to stratify hospitals by their mortality and morbidity records. Harold Luft et al., Does Quality Influence Choice of Hospital? 263 J.A.M.A. 2899 (1990); Donald M. Berwick and David L. Wald, Hospital Leaders' Opinions of the HCFA Mortality Data, 263 J.A.M.A. 247 (1990).

The Joint Commission on the Accreditation of Healthcare Organizations has moved to outcome review for the nation's accredited hospitals. Under this plan, the JCAHO gathers clinical information in order to predict outcomes and provide an ongoing survey of the clinical activities in the hospitals which it accredits. The goal is to develop clinical indicators, using outcomes data produced by hospitals, to spot potential quality control problems. See Outcomes in Action: the JCAHO's Clinical Indicators, Hospital 34 (Oct. 5, 1990).

A concept of outcomes management has been articulated for the health care industry, as a reaction to the increasing volume of outcomes data that is currently being produced. It has been defined by Ellwood as based on a "permanent national medical data base that uses a common set of definitions for measuring quality of life to enable patients, payers, and providers to make informed health choices ..." Paul Ellwood, Shattuck Lecture—Outcomes Management: A Technology of Patient Experience, 318 N.Eng.J.Med. 1549, 1555 (1988). Ellwood writes that outcomes management:

> ... consists of a common patient-understood language of health outcomes; a national data base containing information and analysis on clinical, financial, and health outcomes that estimates as best we can the relation between medical interventions and health outcomes, as well as the relation between health outcomes and money; and an opportunity for each decision-maker to have access to the analyses that are relevant to the choices they must make. Id. at 1551.

Outcomes management systems are being developed to track the effects of medical care on patients over time, measuring patient clinical condition, functional status, and satisfaction with care. See generally David J. Brailer and Lorence H. Kim, From Nicety to Necessity: Outcome Measures Come of Age, Health Systems Review 20 (Sept./Oct. 1996).

Such approaches are currently primitive, given deficiencies in studies and information gathering. One of the risks of such systems is that deceptively objective measures can be easily misapplied. In assessing hospital based care, particularly mortality, the severity of the patient's illness at admission needs to be considerably refined before many such outcome comparisons can be trusted. Jesse Green, et al., The Importance of Severity of Illness in Assessing Hospital Mortality, 263 J.A.M.A. 241 (1990). Patient satisfaction, as measured through a survey, is a central part of the outcome assessment.

4. A study by the Office of Technology Assessment proposed a variety of indicators of good or bad quality health care. Some of these quality-of-care indicators include:

a. hospital mortality rates;

b. adverse events that affect patients, such as nosocomial infections in hospitals;

c. formal disciplinary actions taken by state medical boards against physicians;

d. malpractice awards;

e. process evaluation of physicians' performance in treating a particular condition, such as hypertension screening and management;

f. physician specialization;

g. patient self-assessment of their own care;

h. scope of hospital services, evaluated by external guidelines like those of the JCAHO.

See Office of Technology Assessment, The Quality of Medical Care: Information for Consumers (1988).

Which of these indicators are structure measures? Which are process or outcome based? These indicators could be used in a variety of ways, but one common proposal is to give health care consumers information about comparative performance of providers using several of these measures. This market approach would then allow the consumers to select higher quality providers. Are individual patients likely to be good consumers? How can individuals be helped to process the kind of quantitative comparative information that can be produced? Might the other consumers of health care, such as insurers and employers, be better able to use such information than individual patients? How?

See Timothy S. Jost, The Necessary and Proper Role of Regulation to Assure the Quality of Health Care, 25 Houston L.Rev. 525 (1988); Walter McClure, Buying Right: How to Do It, 2 Bus. & Health 41 (1985); General Accounting Office, Medicare: Improved Patient Outcome Analyses Could Enhance Quality Assessment (1988). For a discussion of the legal and regulatory issues, see Maxwell Mehlman, Assuring the Quality of Medical Care: The Impact of Outcome Measurement and Practice Standards, 18 Law, Medicine & Health Care 368 (1990); Barry R. Furrow, The Changing Role of the Law in Promoting Quality in Health Care: From Sanctioning Outlaws to Managing Outcomes, 26 Houston L.Rev. 147 (1989).

C. IMPROVING QUALITY

The health care industry is rapidly reorganizing in response to market forces. The prevalence of the sole practitioner mode that dominated medical practice until the last two decades continues to decline as group practices and physicians employed by health care institutions or managed care organizations or allied with hospitals in integrated delivery systems become ever more common. The large health care corporation is coming to dominate the delivery of health care services. Both institutions that provide health care, such as hospitals or nursing homes, and entities that pay for health care, including insurers or self-insured employers, have become much more interested in overseeing the work of the professionals who practice within them or whose care they purchase. The emergence of managed care organizations that both pay for and provide care, moreover, gives lay managers even greater control over medical practice.

A revolution in information processing has accompanied the reorganization of the health care industry. Advances in information processing technology have enhanced the ability of the health care industry to collect, process, and analyze data. These advances allow the analysis of the outcomes of health care processes. Data describing large numbers of patients can be studied to determine the efficacy of alternative diagnostic and treatment modalities. This information can be used to construct practice guidelines, which can in some cases be reduced to algorithms used to enable computer review of the quality of the practices of individual practitioners or institutions. Outcome data can also be used to support pattern analysis, comparing the outcome of the care provided by individual practitioners or institutions with average or optimal practice as revealed by outcome analysis.

These new developments in information technology and industry structure have allowed the development of methods of comparing practitioners and institutions, increasingly enabling consumers to evaluate their physicians, hospitals, and managed care organizations. Several attempts have been made in recent years to enable consumers to comparatively evaluate quality in health care markets. From 1986 until 1992 the federal Health Care Financing Administration published annual data comparing the mortality experience of hospitals for certain procedures. Several states, most notably Pennsylvania, New York, and California, have begun to assemble and release comparative outcome data, permitting prospective patients to compare the performance of various health care institutions and professionals. Other information initiatives have also been proposed, such as the Joint Commission's new disclosure policy, which includes hospital report cards.

Second, information processing technology and industry reorganization enables lay managers to monitor physicians. The use of algorithms or profiles allow computes and lay managers to assess physician quality. This has led to new industry-originated practices of continuous quality improvement (CQI) or total quality management (TQM). The application of these principles is described in the following excerpt.

TIMOTHY S. JOST, OVERSIGHT OF THE QUALITY OF MEDICAL CARE: REGULATION, MANAGEMENT, OR THE MARKET?

37 Ariz. L. Rev. 825, 837 (1995).

The continuous quality improvement or total quality management movement is based on quality improvement strategies developed in the industrial setting. The ideas of Deming, Juran, Shewhart and others had a significant impact on Japanese, and then American industrial production. Within the past few years these ideas have begun to be applied widely in health care as well. Lay managers (sometimes in conjunction with physicians) are using their new-found power within reorganized health care institutions and their new and greatly enhanced access to and ability to manipulate data to improve the quality of medical care delivered in institutional settings.

The quality improvement philosophy is based on several principles:

1) Quality is defined in terms of meeting the needs of "customers," defined broadly to include not only patients but also others who consume the services of the institution, including physicians themselves. This orientation is immediately appealing to managers, who are increasingly oriented toward regarding patients as consumers. While this definition short-circuits debates over the true nature of quality, as quality is viewed as what consumers want, it is inherently problematic. If patients as consumers cannot recognize or assess the quality of medical care, as the law has assumed since Dent, how can they define quality?

2) Energy is better directed toward improving the system through which care is delivered than toward looking for "bad apples." Most quality deficiencies are caused by faulty systems, not by incompetents working within those systems. One can accomplish more, therefore, by raising the mean of the performance curve than by chopping off the tail. This emphasis on improving the average performance rather than punishing the bad actor is perhaps the clearest distinction between quality improvement and traditional quality assurance, which has tended to be preoccupied with looking for "bad apples." This orientation gives quality improvement a more positive tone than quality assurance, thus making it more palatable to hospital employees and medical staff. It also results in a heavy emphasis on process and on systems.

3) Data are very important for driving and shaping systems improvement. Outcomes data are particularly useful for identifying areas where improvement is possible or necessary. Not only must systems be monitored continuously, but improvements in systems must also be monitored to assure that they are in fact effective. Much of the arcanity of the quality improve-

ment movement (Ishikawa diagrams, Pareto diagrams, histograms, etc.) results from attempts to organize, make sense out of, and devise rational responses to patterns revealed by data.

4) Management and staff must be involved at all levels in the process of improvement. This is a particular focus of total quality management. The culture of the organization must be molded to emphasize quality.

5) Quality improvement is never finished. This is the primary insight of continuous quality improvement. There is always room for further progress. This should be reassuring, however, and not lead to discouragement.

This newfound confidence in the market and in internal management has been accompanied by a decline in confidence in external public regulation. The cost of health care quality regulation programs has long been recognized, and criticism of the high cost of regulation has become increasingly shrill. The whole range of federal and state regulatory programs, including the PRO program, CLIA, nursing home regulation, and even professional licensure have been criticized for their direct costs and for the costs they impose on the industry. Increasingly, the benefits of traditional forms of regulation that focus on competence and error have been questioned. The continuous quality improvement/total quality management program poses a serious challenge to traditional regulatory programs that focus on "bad apples." The view of TQM is that such programs depress morale, discourage innovation, and do little to improve the care provided in the vast majority of instances.

Notes and Questions

1. This approach to improving the processes of health care delivery is modelled after Japanese management practices, adopting managerial principles to improve quality:

(1) active visible support from clinical and managerial leadership for the continuous improvement of quality;

(2) focus on processes as the objects of improvement;

(3) elimination of unnecessary variation; and

(4) revised strategies for personnel management.

This ethic of continuous improvement, termed in the parlance of the industry either Continuous Quality Improvement (CQI) or Total Quality Management (TQM), assumes that processes are complex and frequently characterized by unnecessary rework and waste, whose reduction might both improve quality and reduce cost. It combines outcome measures with process technology and emphasis on personnel management, treating staff as resources central to quality improvement. The methodology was developed for use by industrial organizations by W. Edwards Deming, in Quality, Productivity, and Competitive Position (1982) and Joseph M. Juran, Managerial Breakthrough (1964). The techniques have been widely applied in health care as well as American industry. See, e.g., Donald M. Berwick et al., Curing Health Care: New Strategies for Quality Improvement (1991); Ellen J. Gaucher & Richard J. Coffey, Total Quality in Healthcare: From Theory to Practice (1993). Its application in health care was suggested by Donald Berwick, Continuous Improvement as an Ideal in Health Care, 320 N.Eng.J.Med. 53 (1989).

2. A 1994 survey found that more than two thirds of the hospitals surveyed were adopting a TQM/CQI program. Linda Oberman, Quality Quandary: Little Clinical Impact Yet, Am. Med. News, Apr. 25, 1994, at 3. Physicians typically resist such TQM/CQI programs and the high level of administrative intervention they often appear to threaten. Can you see any reason why physicians might object to the application of these management strategies to their professional services?

III. THE PROBLEM OF MEDICAL ERROR

How prevalent is medical error? How often does such error injure patients? How should a regulatory regime handle medical error that does not result in injury? If we discover that a substantial number of patients are injured by medical error, what should the legal system do about it? Even if we conclude that errors are infrequent, how do we "raise the average" of medical practice?

Medical error is a major source of iatrogenesis—disease or illness induced by medical treatment or diagnosis. Such iatrogenesis has also been characterized as medical misadventure, and we will use the two terms interchangeably. As you read through the chapter, critically evaluate the perspectives presented with an eye toward developing your own position on the problem of medical error and how to handle it through the legal system.

A. MEDICAL IATROGENESIS: DEFINITIONS AND EXTENT

Injury caused by doctors and health care institutions, or iatrogenesis, is the inverse of quality medicine. It is thus helpful to refine our understanding of injury, medical error, and medical fault, as part of our inquiry into the meaning of quality in health care. The literature on iatrogenesis is surprisingly sparse, considering the importance of the subject.

Consider a spectrum of sources of patient injury.

a. *Willful or reckless acts.* Both lawyers and doctors generally view intentional deviation from professional norms of good practice, without good cause, as culpable error. Many quality control mechanisms now in place, such as licensing and medical board disciplinary actions, seem to be aimed at these "bad apples."

b. *Negligent acts.* A negligence standard measures a physician's actions against accepted norms of practice. A doctor may fall short, injuring a patient for a number of reasons:

1. Inattentiveness on a particular occasion, even though the doctor is otherwise skillful and well trained;

2. A systematic failure of training resulting from failure to keep up with the field of practice or to be properly educated generally. In Darling v. Charleston Community Memorial Hospital, 33 Ill.2d 326, 211 N.E.2d 253 (1965), the defendant doctor had not read the latest texts on setting bone fractures;

3. A personal incapacity of the doctor to deal with this particular disease or patient, because of his or her own impairment, or inability to carry out the procedure with technical proficiency.

We feel no unfairness in generally holding doctors accountable for wilful misconduct, or for negligence based on inattentiveness, failures of education, or personal incapacity. They have failed to live up to the level of competence that their professional membership indicates they should have achieved.

Two categories of patient injury are usually viewed as based on nonculpable conduct, since it is argued that the doctor could not have done any better.

a. *Error due to patient variation.* The argument has been made that doctors cannot be held responsible for some errors because their knowledge of particular patients is necessarily limited. Each patient is unique, more than just the sum total of physical and chemical mechanisms. Each patient is a product of his or her own history. Perfect knowledge is thus impossible. If a bad result occurs, therefore, the fault lies not with any scientific ignorance but, rather, with an unavoidable "ignorance of the contingencies of the environmental context." Samuel Gorovitz and Alasdair MacIntyre, Toward a Theory of Medical Fallibility, 1 J.Med.Phil. 51 (1976). Given the uncertain results of therapeutic intervention on a given patient, regardless of the state of general knowledge about interventions of that type, every therapeutic intervention is an experiment that risks hurting the patient.

b. *Injuries of ignorance.* Much of medical treatment is still primitive: the etiologies and optimal treatments for many illnesses are not known; many treatment techniques, such as cancer chemotherapy, create substantial side-effects. Iatrogenic effects often result from the infant nature of the medical specialty. Use of the word "error" is arguably inappropriate, since the concept of error implies that an alternative error-free treatment exists.

The argument of medical ignorance has some justification. Can we in fairness ask a doctor to do more than medical science and his or her specialty have said is possible? But what if a whole profession has lagged behind, failing to discover the benefits of a desirable new practice or the risks of a generally accepted older practice? We might like more research, more efforts to bring specialty consensus on diagnosis and treatment, more systematic efforts at analysis of cost-effective medicine. Iatrogenesis due to ignorance and patient variation is, therefore, reducible with further research. Medicine is not static.

Is a concept of error also important to us as lawyers? Do lawyers have a similar set of problems with the iatrogenic effects of legal practice? Think of the harm that lawyers can do, and how it compares to the harm that doctors can do. Are the two professions comparable? Or is the doctor burdened with a heavier responsibility, and correspondingly heavier costs of error?

In Healing the Wounds: A Physician Looks at His Work (1986), Dr. David Hilfiker explores the stresses experienced by a doctor. He chronicles the stresses in the practice of medicine—the drains on a physician's time and energy, fears of making a wrong decision, lack of time to integrate experiences, and difficulties in keeping up with rapidly changing medical specialties. A busy physician—buffeted by the pressures of uncertainties in decisionmaking, the need to keep up, and the demands of a schedule—makes mistakes. As Hilfiker writes,

> it is not only in the emergency room, the operating room, the intensive care unit, or the delivery room that a doctor can blunder into tragedy. Errors are always possible, even in the midst of the humdrum routine of

daily care. * * * A doctor has to confront the possibility of a mistake with every patient visit. Id. at 82.

The well trained physician may simply be inattentive on a particular occasion; he may have failed to keep up with new developments; he may have problems dealing with a particular patient for personal reasons. Some of these causes of error can be addressed by particular correctives—an eased schedule, an expanded collegial support setting, the transfer of a patient to another doctor. How should the law respond to these exigencies in medical malpractice litigation? In disciplinary actions?

As you become familiar with the health care enterprise, and the role of physicians and other professionals within that enterprise, think about the range of regulatory tools that might be valuable in improving the quality of health care. Consider how hospitals monitor physician errors and iatrogenesis. Although the physicians are often the active agent in causing patient harm, the hospital provides an indispensable workplace for their activities. Can a health care institution also be "impaired", i.e., suffering from a systemic problem that impairs its functioning?

The law has historically focused on physician "error". Until recently, malpractice cases were brought against the treating physician and not his institution because of a variety of legal rules that shielded the hospital. State licensing boards brought disciplinary actions against the individual errant doctor. Staff privilege cases involved the individual doctor's qualifications. The narrow focus on individual error facilitated a clear definition of "bad medicine." Bad medicine was what bad doctors did, "bad apples," doctors whose incompetence was obvious and offensive.

Consider the traditional malpractice suit for a moment. Suppose that a doctor followed generally accepted, "customary," community practice in the use of a drug to control heart problems (See Chapter 4 infra), yet his patient died. In most jurisdictions, the doctor would not be liable, since he or she conformed to an accepted community practice. Now suppose that we introduce an outcome measure into our assessment. Can you design a liability rule that would take an outcome approach? Would it be desirable to apply this rule to most of medical practice?

This focus on individual responsibility and error has been the starting point for quality assessment, even though it misses many causes of poor quality health care. Such a concept of error provides a necessary starting point, but bad outcomes at the individual physician level typically occur too infrequently to identify poor or good physicians. The larger problem of quality in medical care must also address systemic failures, poor administrative design for review of health care, inadequacies in training of physicians, and the nature of practice incentives.

B. THE EXTENT OF MEDICAL MISADVENTURES

Medical errors that cause iatrogenic harms to patients also impose costs on society, including the cost of correcting the bad result (when it can be corrected) and the loss to society of that patient's productivity. How extensive are such medical mishaps?

PATIENTS, DOCTORS, AND LAWYERS: MEDICAL INJURY, MALPRACTICE LITIGATION, AND PATIENT COMPENSATION IN NEW YORK

The Report of the Harvard Medical Practice Study to the State of New York (1990).

[The Harvard Medical Practice Study in New York looked at the incidence of injuries resulting from medical interventions, "adverse events," beginning with a sample of more than 31,000 New York hospital records drawn from the study year 1984. The review was conducted by medical record administrators and nurses in the screening phase, and by board certified physicians for the physician-review phase.]

* * *

We analyzed 30,121 (96%) of the 31,429 records selected for the study sample. After preliminary screening, physicians reviewed 7,743 records, from which a total of 1,133 adverse events were identified that occurred as a result of medical management in the hospital or required hospitalization for treatment. Of this group, 280 were judged to result from negligent care. Weighting these figures according to the sample plan, we estimated the incidence of adverse events for hospitalizations in New York in 1984 to be 3.7%, or a total of 98,609. Of these, 27.6%, 27,179 cases, or 1.0% of all hospital discharges, were due to negligence.

Physician confidence in the judgments of causation of adverse events spanned a broad range, but only 1.3% of all discharges were in the close-call range (defined as a confidence in causation of just under or just over 50–50). An even smaller fraction, 0.7% of discharges were close-call negligent adverse events, but they constituted a larger proportion of total negligent adverse events.

The majority of adverse events (57%) resulted in minimal and transient disability, but 14% of patients died at least in part as a result of their adverse event, and in another 9% the resultant disability lasted longer than 6 months. Based on these figures, we estimated that about 2,500 cases of permanent total disability resulted from medical injury in New York hospitals in 1984. Further, we found evidence that medical injury contributed at least in part to the deaths of more than 13,000 patients in that year. Many of the deaths occurred in patients who had greatly shortened life expectancies from their underlying diseases, however. Negligent adverse events resulted, overall, in greater disability than did non-negligent events and were associated with 51% of all deaths from medical injury.

Risk factors

The risk of sustaining an adverse event increased with age. When rates were standardized for DRG level, persons over 65 years had twice the chance of sustaining an adverse event of those in the 16–44 years group. Newborns had half the adverse event rate of the 16–44 years group. The percent of adverse events resulting from negligence was increased in elderly patients. We found no gender differences in adverse event or negligence rates. Although the rates were higher in the self-pay group than in the insured categories, the differences were not significant. Blacks had higher rates of adverse events and adverse events resulting from negligence, but these differences overall were not significant. However, higher rates of adverse events and negligent events were found in hospitals that served a higher proportion of minority patients. At hospitals that cared for a mix of white and minority patients, blacks and whites had nearly identical rates.

Adverse event rates varied 10–fold between individual hospitals, when standardized for age and DRG level. Although standardized adverse event and negligence rates for small hospitals (fewer than 8,000 discharges/year) were less than for larger hospitals, these differences were not significant. Hospital ownership (private, non-profit, or government) also was not associated with significantly different rates of adverse events. The fraction of adverse events due to negligence in government hospitals was 50% higher than in non-profit institutions, however, and three times that in proprietary hospitals. These differences were significant. The standardized rate of adverse events in upstate, non–MSA hospitals was one-third that of upstate metropolitan hospitals and less than one-fourth that in New York City. These differences were highly significant. The percent of adverse events due to negligence was not significantly different across regions. Non-teaching hospitals had half the adverse event rates of university or affiliated teaching hospitals, but university teaching hospitals had rates of negligence that were less than half those of the non-teaching or affiliated hospitals.

The nature of adverse events

Nearly half (47%) of all adverse events occurred in patients undergoing surgery, but the percent caused by negligence was lower than for non-surgical adverse events (17% vs 37%). Adverse events resulting from errors in diagnosis and in non-invasive treatment were judged to be due to negligence in over three-fourths of patients. Falls were considered due to negligence in 45% of instances.

The high rate of adverse events in patients over 65 years occurred in three categories: non-technical postoperative complications, complications of non-invasive therapy, and falls. A larger proportion of adverse events in younger patients was due to surgical failures. The operating room was the site of management for the highest fraction of adverse events, but relatively few of these were negligent. On the other hand, most (70%) adverse events in the emergency room resulted from negligence.

The most common type of error resulting in an adverse event was that involved in performing a procedure, but diagnostic errors and prevention errors were more likely to be judged negligent, and to result in serious disability.

The more severe the degree of negligence the greater the likelihood of resultant serious disability (moderate impairment with recovery taking more than six months, permanent disability, or death).

2. Litigation data

We estimated that the incidence of malpractice claims filed by patients for the study year was between 2,967 and 3,888. Using these figures, together with the projected statewide number of injuries from medical negligence during the same period, we estimated that eight times as many patients suffered an injury from negligence as filed a malpractice claim in New York State. About 16 times as many patients suffered an injury from negligence as received compensation from the tort liability system.

These aggregate estimates understate the true size of the gap between the frequency of malpractice claims and the incidence of adverse events caused by negligence. When we identified the malpractice claims actually filed by patients in our sample and reviewed the judgments of our physician reviewers, we found that many cases in litigation were brought by patients in whose records we found no evidence of negligence or even of adverse events. Because the legal system has not yet resolved many of these cases, we do not have the information that would permit an assessment of the success of the tort litigation system in screening out claims with no negligence.

* * *

Notes and Questions

1. The Harvard Study was designed to produce empirical data to better inform the debate about reform of the tort system, including no-fault reforms. Do the findings of the study, as to level of patient injury attributable to medical error, surprise you?

A second recent study, the Utah–Colorado Medical Practice Study (UCMPS), found that adverse events connected to surgery accounted for about half (44.9%) of adverse events across both states, with only 16.9% of the surgical adverse events involving negligence. Drug related adverse events comprised the second most prevalent group. The authors concluded that the UCMPS produced results similar to the earlier New York Harvard Study. That is three to four percent of hospitalizations give rise to adverse events. "Together, the two studies provide overwhelming evidence that the burden of iatrogenic injury is large, enduring, and an innate feature of hospital care in the United States." David M. Studdert, Troyen A. Brennan, and Eric J. Thomas, Beyond Dead Reckoning: Measures of Medical Injury Burden, Malpractice Litigation, and Alternative Compensation Models from Utah and Colorado, 33 Ind. L. Rev. 1643, 1662 (2000).

A study based upon insurance company closed malpractice claims files for anesthesia-related patient injuries concluded that payment was made in more than 80% of the claims filed by patients judged to have received substandard anesthetic care. The claims were reviewed by expert anesthesiologists and divided into inappropriate and appropriate care. The authors found that a patient was much more likely to be paid if the care received was substandard. These favorable odds for payment cut across all severities of injury. The authors also concluded that when a patient files suit for anesthesia-related injury, and the care was judged to be appropriate by peers, payment was made to the patient in 42% of the cases. The authors concluded that "... the tort-based system of patient compensation for injury clearly favors payment to the injured patient, but inequities exist for both patient and physician." See Frederick W. Cheney et al., Standard of Care and Anesthesia Liability, 261 J.A.M.A. 1599 (1989).

Do these conclusions support the existing tort system's value as a quality control system in detecting and deterring error? Or do they support the need for reform? For an exploration of the role of the tort system in insuring against inadvertent negligence or accidents not caused by a professional failure, see Mark F. Grady, Why Are People Negligent? Technology, Nondurable Precautions, and the Medical Malpractice Explosion, 82 Nw.Univ.L.Rev. 293 (1988).

2. As you read Chapter 4, try to sort out the various tort doctrines and rules of admissibility to see whether they protect or ferret out medical error. Do liability doctrines adequately attack medical errors? Do the defenses available to doctors adequately protect non-errant doctors?

3. Other studies have also concluded that the hospital setting exposes patients to significant risks of iatrogenic illness. One study found that more than 36% of the patients admitted to a hospital developed iatrogenic illnesses, either a major or minor complication. Nine percent had major complications, and 2% of all patients died for reasons related to the iatrogenic illness. Exposure to drugs was an important factor in patient complications. Knight Steel et al., Iatrogenic Illness on a General Medical Service at a University Hospital, 304 N.Eng.J.Med. 638, 641 (1981). See David C. Classen et al., Adverse Drug Events in Hospitalized Patients: Excess Length of Stay, Extra Costs, and Attributable Mortality, 277 J.A.M.A. 301 (1997) (adverse drug events associated with significantly prolonged lengths of stay, increased economic costs, and an almost 2–fold increased risk of death); David W. Bates et al., The Costs of Adverse Drug Events in Hospitalized Patients, 277 J.A.M.A. 307 (1997) (found that an adverse drug event was associated with about $2,600 of additional costs to the hospital, and for preventable ADEs the figure was almost twice as high); Timothy S. Lesar, Laurie Briceland, and Daniel S. Stein, Factors Related to Errors in Medication Prescribing, 277 J.A.M.A. 312 (1997) (risks of adverse drug events can be reduced by improving focus of organization, technological, and risk management educational and training efforts).

4. Surgery is also risky. One study concluded that patients experiencing care on a surgical ward experienced about a 1% incidence or mishap rate. Diagnostic errors, and delay in performing a procedure, were major contributors to the mishaps. More than half the medical errors surveyed were errors of commission, including unnecessary or contraindicated surgery, defective execution of an indicated operation, and performance of an improper surgical procedure. The authors of the study concluded that "* * * in 31 instances, or 90 per cent of the errors of therapeutic commission, the mistakes were those of unnecessary, contraindicated, or technically defective surgical activity." Nathan P. Couch et al., The High Cost of Low–Frequency Events, 304 N.Eng.J.Med. 634, 635 (1981).

5. These medical mishaps are expensive. The hospital based study found that costs attributable to error were 1.3% of the hospital's patient-service billings for the year. The research confirmed an earlier study, which had concluded that medical misadventure contributed significantly to the costs of health care. Christopher J. Zook and Francis D. Moore, High Cost Users of Medical Care, 302 N.Eng.J.Med. 996 (1980).

Doing What Counts for Patient Safety: Federal Actions to Reduce Medical Errors and Their Impact

Report of the Quality Interagency Coordination Task Force (QuIC) To the President February 2000

Understanding Medical Errors

Growing Concerns About Medical Errors

The IOM's release of *To Err is Human* brought medical errors and patient safety the attention it has long needed but never had. The information presented in the report is not new. Indeed, many studies, some as early as the 1960s, showed that patients were frequently injured by the same medical care that was intended to help them [ ]. While evidence of medical error has existed for some time, the report succeeded in capturing the public's attention by revealing the magnitude of this pervasive problem and presenting it in a uniquely compelling fashion. The IOM estimates that medical errors cause between 44,000 and 98,000 deaths annually in the United States. Using the more conservative figure, medical errors rank as the eighth leading cause of death, killing more Americans than motor vehicle accidents, breast cancer, or AIDS. In addition to this extraordinary human toll, medical errors result in annual costs of $17 to $29 billion in the United States [ ]. Additionally, fear of becoming a victim of medical error may lead patients to delay obtaining potentially beneficial medical care, which may allow their illnesses to worsen.

Experiencing harm as a result of receiving health care is a growing concern for the American public. Front-page articles in newspapers, television exposes, and cover stories in magazine have provided the stark details of the latest and most dramatic examples of medical errors. Until recently, the perception of medical errors among health care providers and the public has been shaped by these anecdotes, and remedies have focused on fixing blame on individual providers, including health plans, hospitals, doctors, pharmacists, nurses, and other caregivers. That approach, however, has proven ineffective in addressing patient safety, as documented by the ongoing problems noted in the IOM report. The IOM's recommended alternative approaches and other ways in which the Federal agencies can work to reduce medical errors are described in this report.

Definitions and Context

The lack of standardized nomenclature and a universal taxonomy for medical errors complicates the development of a response to the issues outlined in the IOM report. A number of definitions have been applied to medical errors and patient safety. In *To Err is Human*, the IOM adopted the following definition:

> An error is defined as the failure of a planned action to be completed as intended or the use of a wrong plan to achieve an aim.

In an effort to thoroughly consider all of the relevant issues related to medical errors, the QuIC expanded on the IOM definition, as follows:

> *An error is defined as the failure of a planned action to be completed as intended or the use of a wrong plan to achieve an aim. Errors can include problems in practice, products, procedures, and systems.*

The explicit acknowledgment of the broad scope of errors reflected in this definition respects the responsibilities and capabilities of the Government agencies and departments contributing to this report. The term "patient safety" as used here applies to initiatives designed to prevent adverse outcomes from medical errors. The enhancement of patient safety encompasses three complementary activities: preventing errors, making errors visible, and mitigating the effects of errors.

It is critical to recognize that not all bad outcomes for patients are due to medical errors. Patients may not be cured of their disease or disability despite the fact that they are provided the very best of care. Additionally, not all adverse events that are the result of medical care are, in fact, errors. An adverse event is defined broadly as an injury that was caused by medical management and that resulted in measurable disability [ ]. Some adverse events, termed "unpreventable adverse events," result from a complication that cannot be prevented given the current state of knowledge. Many drugs, even when used appropriately, have a chance of side effects, such as nausea from an antibiotic. The occurrence of nausea would be an adverse event, but it would not be considered a medical error to have given the antibiotic if the patient had an infection that was expected to respond to the chosen antibiotic. Medical errors are adverse events that are preventable with our current state of medical knowledge. Figure 1 shows this set of possible outcomes of medical care.

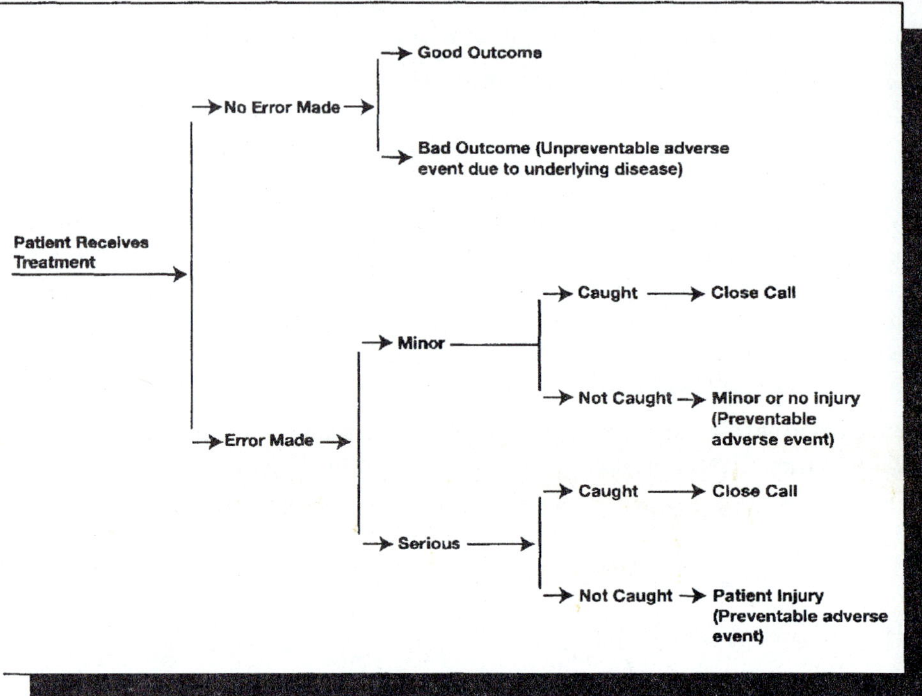

In this report, the consideration of errors is broadened beyond preventable adverse events that lead to actual patient harm to include "near misses," sometimes know as "close calls." A "near miss" is an event or situation that could have resulted in an accident, injury, or illness, but did not, either by chance or through timely intervention. Experience in other industries, including aviation, manufacturing, and nuclear energy, demonstrates that there is as much to learn from close calls as there is from incidents leading to actual harm.

It is also important to situate medical errors within the broader context of problems in health care quality. These can be classified under three categories: overuse (the service is unlikely to have net benefit), underuse (a potentially beneficial service is withheld), and misuse (a service is inappropriately used)[ ]. The majority of medical errors fall into the category of misuse, but some problems with overuse (e.g., when an unnecessary therapy is prescribed, leading to harm) or underuse (e.g., when an error in diagnosis leads to the failure to apply timely treatment) blur these distinctions. These are related quality problems and may be addressed, in part, by using some of the same approaches. In some cases, however, distinct approaches may be required. That is why the IOM has chosen to deal with the issue of errors separately in its report and plans to issue future reports on underuse and overuse quality problems. Our report will also focus exclusively on errors. Nevertheless, the QuIC participants recognize that the improvements made in patient safety will lay the foundation for, and may encourage, other quality improvements.

A Framework for Thinking About Errors

There are many possible ways to categorize medical errors, but no universally accepted taxonomy. Classifications have included:

Type of health care service provided (e.g., classification of medication errors by the National Coordinating Council for Medication Error Reporting and Prevention).

Severity of the resulting injury (e.g., sentinel events, defined as "any unexpected occurrence involving death or serious physical or psychological injury" by the Joint Commission on Accreditation of Healthcare Organizations [JCAHO]).

Legal definition (e.g., errors resulting from negligence [Institute of Medicine, 1999]).

Type of setting (e.g., outpatient clinic, intensive care unit), and

Type of individual involved (e.g., physician, nurse, patient).

Implicit in the current variety of classifications is the understanding that different types of medical errors are likely to require different solutions and preventive measures. A single approach to error reduction will fail because it does not account for important differences in types of errors. For example, for the Food and Drug Administration (FDA), product risk category may be a crucial dimension for shaping regulatory policy, but a health care provider may see this dimension as a minor consideration in shaping its error-control methods.

An "ideal" classification of errors would need to be well suited to the purpose to which it is being applied, but there is no single classification system that could be successfully applied to the full set of IOM recommendations being addressed by the QuIC. A framework for reporting may include considerations of the level of reporting (Federal versus State versus organizational), the reasons for which the reporting is being done (learning versus accountability), or the level of injury (near-miss versus minor versus severe). A framework for developing a research agenda may require more focus on the populations involved, available data, and research tools that can be applied to the problem. The experience with the Aviation Safety Reporting System (ASRS), which relies on narrative reporting without a formal framework, demonstrates that rigorous classification may not be necessary at all for some purposes.

C. REMEDYING QUALITY PROBLEMS OF HEALTH CARE SERVICES

1. *Origins of Clinical Standards of Practice*

The standard of care applied in a tort suit or a hospital peer review process does not normally derive from an external authority such as a government standard. In the medical profession, as in other professions, standards develop in a complicated way involving the interaction of leaders of the profession, professional journals and meetings, and networks of colleagues. Neither the Food and Drug Administration, the National Institutes of Health, the Department of Health and Human Services, nor state licensing boards have had much to do with shaping medical practice. Most clinical policies derive from a flow of reports in the literature, at meetings, and in peer discussions. Over a period of time, hundreds of separate comments come together to form a clinical policy. If this becomes generally accepted, we can call it "standard practice." See generally David Eddy, Clinical Policies and the Quality of Clinical Practice, 307 N.Eng.J.Med. 343 (1982).

This decentralized process of policy setting has some advantages, as Eddy notes: the individual doctor benefits from collective wisdom; unwarranted bursts of enthusiasm are dampened; the policies are tested by the best minds (through statistical and other tools); and flexibility, allowing adaptation to local skills and values, is promoted. Such a policy making process also has drawbacks: oversimplification may ignore side-effects, costs and risks; over-broad conclusions may be drawn from a few observations; examples may be chosen that tend to support the expected result; incentives may favor overuse rather than underuse; an advocacy system may arise in which proponents push and counterarguments may be ignored; the policy consensus may be based upon little more than repetition by the largest or loudest voices; and the inertia inherent in the status quo may dominate.

The diffusion of new medical technologies of diagnosis and treatment poses special problems for the individual physician. Most doctors will note new ideas as they show up in the literature. But they may not be appropriately skeptical. In spite of insufficient evidence of efficacy, doctors in various specialties have been quick to adopt new technologies such as respirator therapy, gastric freezing of ulcers, and other now-discredited techniques. Other tools, such as the CT scan and magnetic resonance imaging, have proliferated rapidly before the evidence on their efficacy was in. The adoption of what has been termed "slam-bang" technologies often precedes careful evaluation.

Even if a cautious and conscientious doctor is skeptical, the data and opinions available are often inadequate to allow evaluation of research findings. The studies may have defects; they may fail, for example, to explain how to translate limited clinical research into practice or may inadequately evaluate controversy over earlier studies. Or the doctor may not be aware of the unique nature of clinical trials.

The phenomenon of medical practice variation highlights the role of uncertainty in the setting of medical standards. Wennberg, whose studies in this area are often cited, looked at states and at regions within states for variation in surgical and other practices:

> [I]n Maine by the time women reach seventy years of age in one hospital market the likelihood they have undergone a hysterectomy is 20 percent while in another market it is 70 percent. In Iowa, the chances that male residents who reach age eighty-five have undergone prostatectomy range from a low of 15 percent to a high of more than 60 percent in different hospital markets. In Vermont the probability that resident children will undergo a tonsillectomy has ranged from a low of 8 percent in one hospital market to a high of nearly 70 percent in another.

John E. Wennberg, Dealing with Medical Practice Variations: A Proposal for Action, 3 Health Affairs 6, 9 (1984); John E. Wennberg et al., Professional Uncertainty and the Problem of Supplier–Induced Demand , 16 Soc. Sci. Med. 811, 812–17 (1982) (reviewing variations in surgical practices). See also Mark

R. Chassin et al., Variations in the Use of Medical and Surgical Services by the Medicare Population, 314 New Eng. J. Med. 285, 287 (1986); David M. Eddy, Clinical Decision Making: From Theory to Practice (pts. 1–4), 263 JAMA 287, 441, 877, 1265 (1990).

Physician variation in treatment approaches is greatest with aging-related conditions, where the outcomes of conservative treatment are unknown. By contrast, the procedures least subject to variation are those "for which there is a professional consensus on the preferred place or style of treatment." Wennberg, supra. A study of a range of medical and surgical services used by Medicare beneficiaries during 1981 confirm Wennberg's findings. The study documented large variations "linked directly to the degree of medical consensus concerning the indications for use." Mark R. Chassin et al., Variations in the Use of Medical and Surgical Services by the Medicare Population, 314 N.Eng.J.Med. 285, 288 (1986).

The appropriateness of much medical treatment has been questioned. Wide variation has been noted in the use of laboratory tests, prescription drugs, X-rays, return appointments, and telephone consultations among similarly trained doctors in a wide variety of practice settings. Research on appropriateness indicates that from one quarter to one third of medical services may be of no value to patients. Robert Brook and Kathleen Lohr, Will We Need to Ration Effective Medical Care?, Issues in Science and Technology 68 (Fall 1986). The extent of inappropriate hospital use is also significant. One study concluded that 21% of pediatric hospital use is medically inappropriate. Kathi J. Kemper, Medically Inappropriate Hospital Use in a Pediatric Population, 318 N.Eng.J.Med. 1033 (1988). Other studies have found that between 20% and 40% of hospital ancillary services are unnecessary. Robert A. Hughes, The Ancillary Services Review Program in Massachusetts: Experience of the 1982 Pilot Project, 252 N.Eng.J.Med. 1727 (1984). Carotid enterectomies, procedures that remove clots in arteries leading to the brain, were judged as appropriate in only 35% of the cases surveyed. Mark R. Chassin, et al., How Coronary Angiography Is Used, J.A.M.A. 2543 (1988).

In another study, the researchers looked at implantation of permanent cardiac pacemakers in a large population. They found that 44% of the implants were definitely indicated, 36% possibly indicated, and 20% were not indicated. Seventy-three percent of the hospitals had an incidence of 10% or more unwarranted implantations, regardless of type of hospital. Lee Goldman, et al., Costs and Effectiveness of Routine Therapy with Long–Term Beta–Adrenergic Antagonists After Acute Myocardial Infarction, 319 N.Eng.J.Med. 152 (1988). One study found a seventeen-fold variation in lab use among internists dealing with clinical patients. Steven A. Schroeder et al., Use of Laboratory Tests and Pharmaceutical Variation Among Physicians and Effect of Cost Audit on Subsequent Use, 225 J.A.M.A. 969 (1973).

The attitudes of individual doctors influence the range of variation where consensus is lacking; Wennberg has termed this the "practice style factor." This style can exert its influence in the absence of scientific information on outcomes; in other cases it may be unrelated to controversies.

Physicians in some hospital markets practice medicine in ways that have extremely adverse implications for the cost of care, motivated perhaps by reasons of their own or their patients' convenience, or because of individ-

> ualist interpretations of the requirements for defensive medicine. Whatever the reason, it certainly is not because of adherence to medical standards based on clinical outcome criteria or even on statistical norms based on average performance.

Wennberg, supra at 7. See also John E. Wennberg, The Paradox of Appropriate Care, 258 J.A.M.A. 2568 (1987). See generally John Eisenberg, Doctors' Decisions and the Cost of Medical Care (1986).

Doctors make mistakes, and some of these errors injure patients. The frequency of medical misadventures in the nation's hospitals and clinical settings is substantial. Much health care is of unproven value, but consumes consumer and governmental resources. The American health care system is therefore not of optimal quality, and could stand improvement. We have a definition of quality, we have criteria and standards for its evaluation. How do we translate the criteria into a strategy to modify behavior and performance to improve the quality of care delivered?

Several approaches to quality improvement can be pursued. We can rely on the traditional forces of professional ethics and socialization. We can expand the role of the marketplace, using dissemination of quality information to consumers and buyers of health, on the theory that prudent buyers will reject lower quality providers. We can improve the current modes of self-regulation of the medical profession and the industry, which include accreditation, medical staff privileges, and medical licensing actions. The process by which a patient sues for malpractice can be improved. And the government, as a primary source of financing for much health care in the United States, can intervene, setting standards and demanding better processes and outcomes. We will examine each of these methods of quality improvement in later sections and chapters.

The combined problems of variation in medical practice and lack of evidence of efficacy of many treatment approaches have launched a movement toward practice parameters. Specialty societies and now the Medicare program have moved to study practices, to articulate consensus on acceptable practice, and to disseminate information on the consensus. The development of practice parameters or protocols has intensified in recent years, as the medical profession attempts to sift through the available research knowledge and reduce variation in medical practice. A new agency within the Public Health Service, the Agency for Health Care Policy and Research, was created to further such research efforts. 42 U.S.C.A., Title ix, section 901. Promotion of quality work is done within this Agency by the Office of the Forum for Quality and Effectiveness in Health Care. 42 U.S.C.A. 201, § 911.

Measuring appropriateness and developing parameters has its problems: it is easier to study overuse than underuse because of difficulties in defining relevant populations; the scientific evidence is always incomplete, requiring reliance on expert judgment; and parameters are slow and expensive to develop in many areas of medical practice. Robert Brook, Practice Guidelines and Practicing Medicine: Are They Compatible? 262 J.A.M.A. 3027 (1989).

Given the patterns of variation in medical practice, and the unscientific way in which various medical treatments diffuse into common use, is it likely that newly developed practice parameters will be adopted by physicians in practice? One study evaluated the effect of distributing practice guidelines generated under the auspices of a national specialty association—the 1986 Canadian guidelines advocating a lower rate of cesarean sections. The dissemination of guidelines had little effect on actual physician practice. Physician awareness of them was high, and the attitudes of obstetricians were positive toward the recommendations. One third of the obstetricians and hospitals reported changing their practices because of the guidelines.

> * * * [T]his high level of awareness, the apparently positive attitudes, and the reported changes in practice coexisted with a demonstrated poor knowledge of the actual recommendations and very little actual change in practices. These results agree with the findings in other evaluations in this area.

See Jonathan Lomas et al., Do Practice Guidelines Guide Practice? The Effect of a Consensus Statement on the Practice of Physicians, 321 N.Eng.J.Med. 1306 (1989). The authors speculated that many forces besides research evidence affect physician decisions, including financial incentives favoring one approach over another, patient pressure, and fears of malpractice. "In the absence of any accompanying strategies to overcome these other influences, the dissemination of research evidence in the form of practice guidelines issues by a national body is unlikely to have much effect on inappropriate practices that are sustained by powerful nonscientific forces." Id. at 1310.

2. *Strategies for Reducing Medical Error*

LUCIAN L. LEAPE, ERROR IN MEDICINE

272 JAMA 1851 (1994).

* * *

Why Is the Error Rate in the Practice of Medicine So High?

Physicians, nurses, and pharmacists are trained to be careful and to function at a high level of proficiency. Indeed, they probably are among the most careful professionals in our society. It is curious, therefore, that high error rates have not stimulated more concern and efforts at error prevention. One reason may be a lack of awareness of the severity of the problem. Hospital-acquired injuries are not reported in the newspapers like jumbo-jet crashes, for the simple reason that they occur one at a time in 5000 different locations across the country. Although error rates are substantial, serious injuries due to errors are not part of the everyday experience of physicians or nurses, but are perceived as isolated and unusual events—"outliers." Second, most errors do no harm. Either they are intercepted or the patient's defenses prevent injury. (Few children die from a single misdiagnosed or mistreated urinary infection, for example.)

But the most important reason physicians and nurses have not developed more effective methods of error prevention is that they have a great deal of difficulty in dealing with human error when it does occur. The reasons are to be found in the culture of medical practice.

Physicians are socialized in medical school and residency to strive for error-free practice. There is a powerful emphasis on perfection, both in diagnosis and treatment. In everyday hospital practice, the message is equally clear: mistakes are unacceptable. Physicians are expected to function without error, an expectation that physicians translate into the need to be infallible. One result is that physicians, not unlike test pilots, come to view an error as a failure of character—you weren't careful enough, you didn't try hard enough. This kind of thinking lies behind a common reaction by physicians: 'How can there be an error without negligence?'

Cultivating a norm of high standards is, of course, highly desirable. It is the counterpart of another fundamental goal of medical education: developing the physician's sense of responsibility for the patient. If you are responsible for everything that happens to the patient, it follows that you are responsible for any errors that occur. While the logic may be sound, the conclusion is absurd, because physicians do not have the power to control all aspects of patient care. Nonetheless, the sense of duty to perform faultlessly is strongly internalized.

Role models in medical education reinforce the concept of infallibility. The young physician's teachers are largely specialists, experts in their fields, and authorities. Authorities are not supposed to err. It has been suggested that this need to be infallible creates a strong pressure to intellectual dishonesty, to cover up mistakes rather than to admit them. The organization of medical practice, particularly in the hospital, perpetuates these norms. Errors are rarely admitted or discussed among physicians in private practice. Physicians typically feel, not without reason, that admission of error will lead to censure or increased surveillance or, worse, that their colleagues will regard them as incompetent or careless. Far better to conceal a mistake or, if that is impossible, to try to shift the blame to another, even the patient.

Yet physicians are emotionally devastated by serious mistakes that harm or kill patients. Almost every physician who cares for patients has had that experience, usually more than once. The emotional impact is often profound, typically a mixture of fear, guilt, anger, embarrassment, and humiliation. However, as Christensen et al. note, physicians are typically isolated by their emotional responses; seldom is there a process to evaluate the circumstances of a mistake and to provide support and emotional healing for the fallible physician. Wu et al. found that only half of house officers discussed their most significant mistakes with attending physicians.

Thus, although the individual may learn from a mistake and change practice patterns accordingly, the adjustment often takes place in a vacuum. Lessons learned are shared privately, if at all, and external objective evaluation of what went wrong often does not occur. As Hilfiker points out, "We see the horror of our own mistakes, yet we are given no permission to deal with their enormous emotional impact.... The medical profession simply has no place for its mistakes."

Finally, the realities of the malpractice threat provide strong incentives against disclosure or investigation of mistakes. Even a minor error can place the physician's entire career in jeopardy if it results in a serious bad outcome. It is hardly surprising that a physician might hesitate to reveal an error to either the patient or hospital authorities or to expose a colleague to similar devastation for a single mistake.

The paradox is that although the standard of medical practice is perfection—error-free patient care—all physicians recognize that mistakes are inevitable. Most would like to examine their mistakes and learn from them. From an emotional standpoint, they need the support and understanding of their colleagues and patients when they make mistakes. Yet, they are denied both insight and support by misguided concepts of infallibility and by fear: fear of embarrassment by colleagues, fear of patient reaction, and fear of litigation. Although the notion of infallibility fails the reality test, the fears are well grounded.

The Medical Approach to Error Prevention

Efforts at error prevention in medicine have characteristically followed what might be called the perfectibility model: if physicians and nurses could be properly trained and motivated, then they would make no mistakes. The methods used to achieve this goal are training and punishment. Training is directed toward teaching people to do the right thing. In nursing, rigid adherence to protocols is emphasized. In medicine, the emphasis is less on rules and more on knowledge.

Punishment is through social opprobrium or peer disapproval. The professional cultures of medicine and nursing typically use blame to encourage proper performance. Errors are regarded as someone's fault, caused by a lack of sufficient attention or, worse, lack of caring enough to make sure you are correct. Punishment for egregious (negligent) errors is primarily (and capriciously) meted out through the malpractice tort litigation system.

Students of error and human performance reject this formulation. While the proximal error leading to an accident is, in fact, usually a 'human error,' the causes of that error are often well beyond the individual's control. All humans err frequently. Systems that rely on error-free performance are doomed to fail.

The medical approach to error prevention is also reactive. Errors are usually discovered only when there is an incident—an untoward effect or injury to the patient. Corrective measures are then directed toward preventing a recurrence of a similar error, often by attempting to prevent that individual from making a repeat error. Seldom are underlying causes explored.

For example, if a nurse gives a medication to the wrong patient, a typical response would be exhortation or training in double-checking the identity of both patient and drug before administration. Although it might be noted that the nurse was distracted because of an unusually large case load, it is unlikely that serious attention would be given to evaluating overall work assignments or to determining if large caseloads have contributed to other kinds of errors.

It is even less likely that questions would be raised about the wisdom of a system for dispensing medications in which safety is contingent on inspection by an individual at the end point of use. Reliance on inspection as a mechanism of quality control was discredited long ago in industry. A simple procedure, such as the use of bar coding like that used at supermarket checkout counters, would probably be more effective in this situation. More imaginative solutions could easily be found—if it were recognized that both systems and individuals contribute to the problem.

It seems clear, and it is the thesis of this article, that if physicians, nurses, pharmacists, and administrators are to succeed in reducing errors in hospital care, they will need to fundamentally change the way they think about errors and why they occur. Fortunately, a great deal has been learned about error prevention in other disciplines, information that is relevant to the hospital practice of medicine.

* * *

* * *

Prevention of Accidents

The multiplicity of mechanisms and causes of errors (internal and external, individual and systemic) dictates that there cannot be a simple or universal means of reducing errors. Creating a safe process, whether it be flying an airplane, running a hospital, or performing cardiac surgery, requires attention to methods of error reduction at each stage of system development: design, construction, maintenance, allocation of resources, training, and development of operational procedures. This type of attention to error reduction requires responsible individuals at each stage to think through the consequences of their decisions and to reason back from discovered deficiencies to redesign and reorganize the process. Systemic changes are most likely to be successful because they reduce the likelihood of a variety of types of errors at the end-user stage.

The primary objective of system design for safety is to make it difficult for individuals to err. But it is also important to recognize that errors will inevitably occur and plan for their recovery. Ideally, the system will automatically correct errors when they occur. If that is impossible, mechanisms should be in place to at least detect errors in time for corrective action. Therefore, in addition to designing the work environment to minimize psychological precursors, designers should provide feedback through instruments that provide monitoring functions and build in buffers and redundancy. Buffers are design features that automatically correct for human or mechanical errors. Redundancy is duplication (sometimes triplication or quadruplication) of critical mechanisms and instruments, so that a failure does not result in loss of the function.

Another important system design feature is designing tasks to minimize errors. Norman has recommended a set of principles that have general applicability. Tasks should be simplified to minimize the load on the weakest aspects of cognition: short-term memory, planning, and problem solving. The power of constraints should be exploited. One way to do this is with "forcing functions," which make it impossible to act without meeting a precondition (such as the inability to release the parking gear of a car unless the brake pedal is depressed). Standardization of procedures, displays, and layouts reduces error by reinforcing the pattern recognition that humans do well. Finally, where possible, operations should be easily reversible or difficult to perform when they are not reversible.

Training must include, in addition to the usual emphasis on application of knowledge and following procedures, a consideration of safety issues. These issues include understanding the rationale for procedures as well as how errors can occur at various stages, their possible consequences, and instruction in methods for avoidance of errors. Finally, it must be acknowledged that injuries can result from behavioral problems that may be seen in impaired physicians or incompetent physicians despite well-designed systems; methods for identifying and correcting egregious behaviors are also needed.

The Aviation Model

The practice of hospital medicine has been compared, usually unfavorably, to the aviation industry, also a highly complicated and risky enterprise but one that seems far safer. Indeed, there seem to be many similarities. As Allnutt observed,

> Both pilots and doctors are carefully selected, highly trained professionals who are usually determined to maintain high standards, both externally and internally imposed, whilst performing difficult tasks in life-threatening environments. Both use high technology equipment and function as key members of a team of specialists . . . both exercise high level cognitive skills in a most complex domain about which much is known, but where much remains to be discovered.

While the comparison is apt, there are also important differences between aviation and medicine, not the least of which is a substantial measure of uncertainty due to the number and variety of disease states, as well as the unpredictability of the human organism. Nonetheless, there is much physicians and nurses could learn from aviation.

Aviation—airline travel, at least—is indeed generally safe: more than 10 million takeoffs and landings each year with an average of fewer than four crashes a year. But, it was not always so. The first powered flight was in 1903, the first fatality in 1908, and the first midair collision in 1910. By 1910, there were 2000 pilots in the world and 32 had already died. The US Air Mail Service was founded in 1918. As a result of efforts to meet delivery schedules in all kinds of weather, 31 of the first 40 Air Mail Service pilots were killed. This appalling toll led to unionization of the pilots and their insistence that local field controllers could not order pilots to fly against their judgment unless the field controllers went up for a flight around the field themselves. In 1922, there were no Air Mail Service fatalities. Since that time, a complex system of aircraft design, instrumentation, training, regulation, and air traffic control has developed that is highly effective at preventing fatalities.

There are strong incentives for making flying safe. Pilots, of course, are highly motivated. Unlike physicians, their lives are on the line as well as those of their passengers. But, airlines and airplane manufacturers also have strong incentives to provide safe flight. Business decreases after a large crash, and if a certain model of aircraft crashes repeatedly, the manufacturer will be discredited. The lawsuits that inevitably follow a crash can harm both reputation and profitability.

Designing for safety has led to a number of unique characteristics of aviation that could, with suitable modification, prove useful in improving hospital safety.

First, in terms of system design, aircraft designers assume that errors and failures are inevitable and design systems to "absorb" them, building in multiple buffers, automation, and redundancy. * * *

Second, procedures are standardized to the maximum extent possible. Specific protocols must be followed for trip planning, operations, and maintenance. Pilots go through a checklist before each takeoff. Required maintenance is specified in detail and must be performed on a regular (by flight hours) basis.

Third, the training, examination, and certification process is highly developed and rigidly, as well as frequently, enforced. Airline pilots take proficiency examinations every 6 months. Much of the content of examinations is directly concerned with procedures to enhance safety.

Pilots function well within this rigorously controlled system, although not flawlessly. For example, one study of cockpit crews observed that human errors or instrument malfunctions occurred on the average of one every 4 minutes during an overseas flight. Each event was promptly recognized and corrected with no untoward effects. Pilots also willingly submit to an external authority, the air traffic controller, when within the constrained air and ground space at a busy airport.

Finally, safety in aviation has been institutionalized. Two independent agencies have government-mandated responsibilities: the Federal Aviation Administration (FAA) regulates all aspects of flying and prescribes safety procedures, and the National Transportation Safety Board investigates every accident. The adherence of airlines and pilots to required safety standards is closely monitored. The FAA recognized long ago that pilots seldom reported an error if it led to disciplinary action. Accordingly, in 1975 the FAA established a confidential reporting system for safety infractions, the Air Safety Reporting System (ASRS). If pilots, controllers, or others promptly report a dangerous situation, such as a near-miss midair collision, they will not be penalized. This program dramatically increased reporting, so that unsafe conditions at airports, communication problems, and traffic control inadequacies are now promptly communicated. Analysis of these reports and subsequent investigations appear as a regular feature in several pilots' magazines. The ASRS receives more than 5000 notifications each year.

The Medical Model

By contrast, accident prevention has not been a primary focus of the practice of hospital medicine. It is not that errors are ignored. Mortality and morbidity conferences, incident reports, risk management activities, and quality assurance committees abound. But, as noted previously, these activities focus on incidents and individuals. When errors are examined, a problem-solving approach is usually used: the cause of the error is identified and corrected. Root causes, the underlying systems failures, are rarely sought. System designers do not assume that errors and failures are inevitable and design systems to prevent or absorb them. There are, of course, exceptions. Implementation of unit dosing, for example, markedly reduced medication dosing errors by eliminating the need for the nurse to measure out each dose. Monitoring in intensive care units is sophisticated and extensive (although perhaps not sufficiently redundant). Nonetheless, the basic health care system approach is to rely on individuals not to make errors rather than to assume they will.

Second, standardization and task design vary widely. In the operating room, it has been refined to a high art. In patient care units, much more could be done, particularly to minimize reliance on short-term memory, one of the weakest aspects of cognition. On-time and correct delivery of medications, for example, is often contingent on a busy nurse remembering to do so, a nurse who is responsible for four or five patients at once and is repeatedly interrupted, a classic set up for a "loss-of-activation" error.

On the other hand, education and training in medicine and nursing far exceed that in aviation, both in breadth of content and in duration, and few professions compare with medicine in terms of the extent of continuing education. Although certification is essentially universal, including the recent introduction of periodic recertification, the idea of periodically testing performance has never been accepted. Thus, we place great emphasis on education and training, but shy away from demonstrating that it makes a difference.

Finally, unlike aviation, safety in medicine has never been institutionalized, in the sense of being a major focus of hospital medical activities. Investigation of accidents is often superficial, unless a malpractice action is likely; noninjurious error (a "near miss") is rarely examined at all. Incident reports are frequently perceived as punitive instruments. As a result, they are often not filed, and when they are, they almost invariably focus on the individual's misconduct.

One medical model is an exception and has proved quite successful in reducing accidents due to errors: anesthesia. Perhaps in part because the effects of serious anesthetic errors are potentially so dramatic—death or brain damage—and perhaps in part because the errors are frequently transparently clear and knowable to all, anesthesiologists have greatly emphasized safety. The success of these efforts has been dramatic. Whereas mortality from anesthesia was one in 10,000 to 20,000 just a decade or so ago, it is now estimated at less than one in 200,000. Anesthesiologists have led the medical profession in recognizing system factors as causes of errors, in designing fail-safe systems, and in training to avoid errors.

Systems Changes to Reduce Hospital Injuries

Can the lessons from cognitive psychology and human factors research that have been successful in accident prevention in aviation and other industries be applied to the practice of hospital medicine? There is every reason to think they could be. Hospitals, physicians, nurses, and pharmacists who wish to reduce errors could start by considering how cognition and error mechanisms apply to the practice of hospital medicine. Specifically, they can examine their care delivery systems in terms of the systems' ability to discover, prevent, and absorb errors and for the presence of psychological precursors.

Discovery of Errors

The first step in error prevention is to define the problem. Efficient, routine identification of errors needs to be part of hospital practice, as does routine investigation of all errors that cause injuries. The emphasis is on "routine." Only when errors are accepted as an inevitable, although manageable, part of everyday practice will it be possible for hospital personnel to shift from a punitive to a creative frame of mind that seeks out and identifies the underlying system failures.

Data collecting and investigatory activities are expensive, but so are the consequences of errors. Evidence from industry indicates that the savings from reduction of errors and accidents more than make up for the costs of data collection and investigation. (While these calculations apply to 'rework' and other operational inefficiencies resulting from errors, additional savings from reduced patient care costs and liability costs for hospitals and physicians could also be substantial.)

Prevention of Errors

Many health care delivery systems could be redesigned to significantly reduce the likelihood of error. Some obvious mechanisms that can be used are as follows:

Reduced Reliance on Memory.—Work should be designed to minimize the requirements for human functions that are known to be particularly fallible, such as short-term memory and vigilance (prolonged attention). Clearly, the components of work must be well delineated and understood before system redesign. Checklists, protocols, and computerized decision aids could be used more widely. For example, physicians should not have to rely on their memories to retrieve a laboratory test result, and nurses should not have to remember the time a medication dose is due. These are tasks that computers do much more reliably than humans.

Improved Information Access.—Creative ways need to be developed for making information more readily available: displaying it where it is needed, when it is needed, and in a form that permits easy access. Computerization of the medical record, for example, would greatly facilitate bedside display of patient information, including tests and medications.

Error Proofing.—Where possible, critical tasks should be structured so that errors cannot be made. The use of "forcing functions" is helpful. For example, if a computerized system is used for medication orders, it can be designed so that a physician cannot enter an order for a lethal overdose of a drug or prescribe a medication to which a patient is known to be allergic.

Standardization.—One of the most effective means of reducing error is standardizing processes wherever possible. The advantages, in efficiency as well as in error reduction, of standardizing drug doses and times of administration are obvious. Is it really acceptable to ask nurses to follow six different "K-scales" (directions for how much potassium to give according to patient serum potassium levels) solely to satisfy different physician prescribing patterns? Other candidates for standardization include information displays, methods for common practices (such as surgical dressings), and the geographic location of equipment and supplies in a patient care unit. There is something bizarre, and really quite inexcusable, about "code" situations in hospitals where house staff and other personnel responding to a cardiac arrest waste precious seconds searching for resuscitation equipment simply because it is kept in a different location on each patient care unit.

Training.—Instruction of physicians, nurses, and pharmacists in procedures or problem solving should include greater emphasis on possible errors and how to prevent them. (Well-written surgical atlases do this.) For example, many interns need more rigorous instruction and supervision than is currently provided when they are learning new procedures. Young physicians need to be taught that safe practice is as important as effective practice. Both physicians and nurses need to learn to think of errors primarily as symptoms of systems failures.

Absorption of Errors

Because it is impossible to prevent all error, buffers should be built into each system so that errors are absorbed before they can cause harm to patients. At minimum, systems should be designed so that errors can be identified in time to be intercepted. The drug delivery systems in most hospitals do this to some degree already. Nurses and pharmacists often identify errors in physician drug orders and prevent improper administration to the patient. As hospitals move to computerized records and ordering systems, more of these types of interceptions can be incorporated into the computer programs. Critical systems (such as life-support equipment and monitors) should be provided in duplicate in those situations in which a mechanical failure could lead to patient injury.

Psychological Precursors

Finally, explicit attention should be given to work schedules, division of responsibilities, task descriptions, and other details of working arrangements where improper managerial decisions can produce psychological precursors such as time pressures and fatigue that create an unsafe environment. While the influence of the stresses of everyday life on human behavior cannot be eliminated, stresses caused by a faulty work environment can be. Elimination of fear and the creation of a supportive working environment are other potent means of preventing errors.

Institutionalization of Safety

Although the idea of a national hospital safety board that would investigate every accident is neither practical nor necessary, at the hospital level such activities should occur. Existing hospital risk management activities could be broadened to include all potentially injurious errors and deepened to seek out underlying system failures. Providing immunity, as in the FAA ASRS system, might be a good first step. At the national level, the Joint Commission on Accreditation of Healthcare Organizations should be involved in discussions regarding the institutionalization of safety. Other specialty societies might well follow the lead of the anesthesiologists in developing safety standards and require their instruction to be part of residency training.

Implementing Systems Changes

Many of the principles described herein fit well within the teachings of total quality management. One of the basic tenets of total quality management, statistical quality control, requires data regarding variation in processes. In a generic sense, errors are but variations in processes. Total quality management also requires a culture in which errors and deviations are regarded not as human failures, but as opportunities to improve the system, "gems," as they are sometimes called. Finally, total quality management calls for grassroots participation to identify and develop system modifications to eliminate the underlying failures.

Like total quality management, systems changes to reduce errors require commitment of the organization's leadership. None of the aforementioned changes will be effective or, for that matter, even possible without support at the highest levels (hospital executives and departmental chiefs) for making safety a major goal of medical practice.

But it is apparent that the most fundamental change that will be needed if hospitals are to make meaningful progress in error reduction is a cultural one. Physicians and nurses need to accept the notion that error is an inevitable accompaniment of the human condition, even among conscientious professionals with high standards. Errors must be accepted as evidence of systems flaws not character flaws. Until and unless that happens, it is unlikely that any substantial progress will be made in reducing medical errors.

TO ERR IS HUMAN: BUILDING A SAFER HEALTH SYSTEM

Committee on Quality of Health Care In America
Institute of Medicine, 1999.
www.nap.edu/readingroom

Executive Summary

The knowledgeable health reporter for the Boston Globe, Betsy Lehman, died from an overdose during chemotherapy. Willie King had the wrong leg amputated. Ben Kolb was eight years old when he died during "minor" surgery due to a drug mix-up.

These horrific cases that make the headlines are just the tip of the iceberg. Two large studies, one conducted in Colorado and Utah and the other in New York, found that adverse events occurred in 2.9 and 3.7 percent of hospitalizations, respectively. In Colorado and Utah hospitals, 8.8 percent of adverse events led to death, as compared with 13.6 percent in New York hospitals. In both of these studies, over half of these adverse events resulted from medical errors and could have been prevented.

When extrapolated to the over 33.6 million admissions to U.S. hospitals in 1997, the results of the study in Colorado and Utah imply that at least 44,000 Americans die each year as a result of medical errors. The results of the New York Study suggest the number may be as high as 98,000. Even when using the lower estimate, deaths due to medical errors exceed the number attributable to the 8th leading cause of death. More people die in a given year as result of medical errors than from motor vehicle accidents (43,458), breast cancer (42,297), or AIDS (16,516).

Total national costs (lost income, lost household production, disability and health care costs) of preventable adverse events (medical errors resulting in injury) are estimated to be between $17 billion and $29 billion, of which health care costs represent over one half.

In terms of lives lost, patient safety is as important an issue as worker safety. Every year, over 6,000 Americans die from workplace injuries. Medication errors alone, occurring either in or out of the hospital, are estimated to account for over 7,000 deaths annually.

Medication-related errors occur frequently in hospitals and although not all result in actual harm, those that do, are costly. One recent study conducted at two prestigious teaching hospitals, found that about two out of every 100 admissions experienced a preventable adverse drug event, resulting in average increased hospital costs of $4,700 per admission or about $2.8 million annually for a 700 bed teach hospital. If these findings are generalizable, the increased hospital costs alone of preventable adverse drug events affecting inpatients are about $2 billion for the nation as a whole.

These figures offer only a very modest estimate of the magnitude of the problem since hospital patients represent only a small proportion of the total population at risk, and direct hospital costs are only a fraction of total costs. More care and increasingly complex care is provided in ambulatory settings. Outpatient surgical centers, physical offices and clinics serve thousands of patients daily. Home care requires patients and their families to use complicated equipment and perform follow-up care. Retail pharmacies play a major role in filling prescriptions for patients and educating them about their use. Other institutional settings, such as nursing homes, provide a broad array of services to vulnerable populations. Although many of the available studies have focus on the hospital setting, medical errors present a problem in any setting, not just hospitals.

Errors are also costly in terms of opportunity costs. Dollars spent on having to repeat diagnostic tests or counteract adverse drug events are dollars unavailable for other purposes. Purchasers and patients pay for errors when insurance costs and copayments are inflated by services that would not have been necessary had proper care been provided. It is impossible for the nation to achieve the greatest value possible from the hundreds of millions of dollars pent on medical care if the care contains errors.

But not all the costs can be directly measured. Errors are also costly in terms of loss of trust in the system by patients and diminished satisfaction by both patients and health professionals. Patients who experienced a longer hospital stay or disability as a result of errors pay with physical and psychological discomfort. Health care professionals pay with loss of morale and frustration at not being able to provide the best care possible. Employers and society, in general, pay in terms of lost worker productivity, reduced school attendance by children, and lower levels of population health status.

Yet silence surrounds this issue. For the most part, consumers believe they are protected. Media coverage has been limited to reporting of anecdotal cases. Licensure and accreditation confer, in the eyes of the public, a "Good Housekeeping Seal of Approval." Yet, licensing and accreditation processes have focused only limited attention on the issue, and even these minimal efforts have confronted some resistance from health care organizations and providers. Providers are perceive the medical liability systems as a serious impediment to systematic efforts to uncover and learn from errors.

The decentralized and fragmented nature of the health care delivery system (some would say "nonsystem") also contributes to unsafe conditions for patients, and serves as an impediment to efforts to improve safety. Even within hospitals and large medical groups, there are rigidly-defined areas of specialization and influence. For example, when patients see multiple providers in different settings, none of whom have access to complete information, it is easier for something to go wrong than when care is better coordinated. At the same time, the provision of care to patients by a collection of loosely affiliated organizations and providers makes it difficult to implement improved clinical information systems capable of providing timely access to complete patient information. Unsafe care is one of the prices we pay for not having organized systems of care with clear lines of accountability.

Lastly, the context in which health care is purchased further exacerbates these problems. Group purchasers have made few demands for improvements in safety. Most third party payment systems provide little incentive for a health care organization to improve safety, not do they recognize and reward safety or quality.

The goal of this report is to break this cycle of inaction. The status quo is not acceptable and cannot be tolerated any longer. Despite the cost pressures, liability constraints, resistance to change and other seemingly insurmountable barriers, it is simply not acceptable for patients to be harmed by the same health care system that is supposed to offer healing and comfort. "First do not harm" is an often quoted term from Hippocrates. Everyone working in health care is familiar with the term. At a very minimum, the health system needs to offer that assurance and security to the public.

A comprehensive approach to improving patient safety is needed. This approach cannot focus on a single solution since there is no "magic bullet" that will solve this problem, and indeed, no single recommendation in this report should be considered as *the* answer. Rather, large, complex problems require thoughtful, multifaceted responses, The combined goal of the recommendations is for the external environment to create sufficient pressure to make errors costly to health care organizations and providers, so they are compelled to take action to improve safety. At the same time, there is a need to enhance knowledge and tools to improve safety and break down legal and cultural barriers that impede safety improvement. Given current knowledge about the magnitude of the problem, the committee believes it would be irresponsible to expect anything less than a 50 percent reduction in errors over five years.

In this report, safety is defined as freedom from accidental injury. This definition recognizes that this is the primary safety goal from the patient's perspective. Error is defined as the failure of a planned action to be completed as intended or the use of a wrong plan to achieve an aim. According to noted expert James Reason, errors depend on two kinds of failures: either the correct action does not proceed as intended (an error of execution) or the original intended action is not correct, (an error of planning). Errors can happen in all stages in the process of care, from diagnosis, to treatment, to preventive care.

Not all errors result in harm. Errors that do result in injury are sometimes called preventable adverse events. An adverse event is an injury resulting from a medical intervention, or in other words, it is not due to the underlying condition of the patient. While all adverse events result from medical management, not all are preventable (i.e., not all are attributable to errors). For example, if a patient has surgery and dies from pneumonia he or she got postoperatively, it is an adverse event. If analysis of the case reveals that the patient got pneumonia because of poor hand washing or instrument cleaning techniques by staff, the adverse event was preventable (attributable to an error of execution). But the analysis may conclude that no error occurred and the patient would be presumed to have had a difficult surgery and recovery (not a preventable adverse event).

Much can be learned from the analysis of errors. All adverse events resulting in serious injury or death should be evaluated to assess whether improvements in the delivery system can be made to reduce the likelihood of similar events occurring in the future. Errors that do not result in harm also represent an important opportunity to identify system improvements having the potential to prevent adverse events.

Preventing errors means designing the health care system at all levels to make it safer. Building safety into processes of care is a more effective way to reduce errors than blaming individuals (some experts, such as Deming, believe improving processes is the *only* way to improve quality). The focus must shift from blaming individuals for past errors to a focus on preventing future errors by designing safety into the system. This does not mean that individuals can be careless. People must still be vigilant and held responsible for their actions. But when an error occurs, blaming an individual does little to make the system safer and prevent someone else from committing the same error.

Health care is a decade or more behind other high-risk industries in its attention to ensuring basic safety. Aviation has focused extensively on building safe systems and has been doing so since World War II. Between 1990 and 1994, the U.S. airline fatality rate was less than one-third the rate experienced in mid century. In 1998, there were no deaths in the United States in commercial aviation. In health care, preventable injuries from care have been estimated to affect between three to four percent of hospital patients. Although health care may never achieve aviation's impressive record, there is clearly room for improvement.

To err is human, but errors can be prevented. Safety is a critical first step in improving quality of care. The Harvard Medical Practice Study, a seminal research study on this issue, was published almost ten years ago; other studies have corroborated its findings. Yet few tangible actions to improve patient safety can be found. Must we wait another decade to be safe in our health system?

Recommendations

The IOM Quality of Health Care in America Committee was formed in June 1998 to develop a strategy that will result in a threshold improvement in quality over the next ten years. This report addresses issues related to patient safety, a subset of overall quality-related concerns, and lays out a national agenda for reducing errors in health care and improving patient safety. Although it is a national agenda, many activities are aimed at prompting responses at the state and local levels and within health care organizations and professional groups.

The committee believes that although there is still much to learn about the types of errors committed in health care and why they occur, enough is known today to recognize that a serious concern exists for patients. Whether a person is sick or just trying to stay healthy, they should not have to worry about being harmed by the health system itself. This report is a call to action to make health care safer for patients.

The committee believes that a major force for improving patient safety is the intrinsic motivation of health care providers, shaped by professional ethics, norms and expectations. But the interaction between factors in the external environment and factors inside health care organizations can also prompt the changes needed to improve patient safety. Factors in the external environment include availability of knowledge and tools to improve safety, strong and visible professional leadership, legislative and regulatory initiatives, and actions of purchasers and consumers to demand safety improvements. Factors inside health care organizations include strong leadership for safety, an organizational culture that encourages recognition and learning from errors, and an effective patient safety program.

* * *

The recommendations contained in this report lay out a four-tiered approach:

• establishing a national focus to create leadership, research, tools and protocols to enhance the knowledge based about safety;

• identifying and learning from errors through the immediate and strong mandatory reporting efforts, as well as the encouragement of voluntary efforts, both with the aim of making sure the system continues to be made safer for patients;

• raising standards and expectations for improvements in safety through the actions of oversight organizations, group purchasers, and professional groups; and

• creating safety systems inside health care organizations through the implementation of safe practices at the delivery level. This level is the ultimate target of all the recommendations.

Leadership and Knowledge

Other industries that have been successful in improving safety, such as aviation and occupational health, have had the support of a designated agency that sets and communicates priorities, monitors progress in achieving goals, directs resources toward areas of need, and brings visibility to important issues. Although various agencies and organizations in health care may contribute to certain of these activities, there is no focal point for raising and sustaining attention to patient safety. Without it, health care is unlikely to match the safety improvements achieved in other industries.

* * *

RECOMMENDATION 4.1 Congress should create a Center for Patient Safety within the Agency for Health Care Policy and Research. This center should

• set the national goals for patient safety, track progress in meeting these goals, and issue an annual report to the President and Congress on patient safety; and

• develop knowledge and understanding of errors in health care by developing a research agenda, funding Centers of Excellence, evaluating methods for identifying and preventing errors, and funding dissemination and communication activities to improve patient safety.

IDENTIFYING AND LEARNING FROM ERRORS

Another critical component of a comprehensive strategy to improve patient safety is to create an environment that encourages organizations to identify errors, evaluate causes and take appropriate actions to improve performance in the future. External reporting systems represent one mechanism to enhance our understanding of errors and the underlying factors that contribute to them.

Reporting systems can be designed to meet two purposes. They can be designed as part of a public system for holding health care organizations accountable for performance. In this instance, reporting is often mandatory, usually focuses on specific cases that involve serious harm or death, may result in fines or penalties relative to the specific case, and information about the event may become known to the public. Such systems ensure a response to specific reports of serious injury, hold organizations and providers accountable for maintaining safety, respond to the public's right to know, and provide incentives to health care organizations to implement internal safety systems that reduce the likelihood of such events occurring. Currently, at least twenty states have mandatory adverse event reporting systems.

Voluntary, confidential reporting systems can also be part of an overall program for improving patient safety and can be designed to complement the mandatory reporting systems previously described. Voluntary reporting systems, which generally focus on a much broader set of errors and strive to detect system weaknesses before the occurrence of serious harm, can provide rich information to health care organizations in support of their quality improvement efforts.

For either purpose, the goal of reporting systems is to analyze the information they gather and identify ways to prevent future errors from occurring. The goal is *not* data collection. Collecting reports and not doing anything with the information serves no useful purpose. Adequate resources and other support must be provided for analysis and response to critical issues.

RECOMMENDATION 5.1 A nationwide mandatory reporting system should be established that provides for the collection of standardized information by state governments about adverse events that result in death or serious harm. Reporting should initially be required of hospitals and eventually be required of other institutional and ambulatory care delivery settings. Congress should

• designate the forum for Health Care Quality Measurement and Reporting as the entity responsible for promulgating and maintaining a core set of reporting standards to be used by states, including a nomenclature and taxonomy for reporting:

• require all health care organizations to report standardized information on a defined list of adverse events;

• provide funds and technical expertise for state governments to establish or adapt their current error reporting systems to collect the standardized information, analyze it and conduct follow-up action as needed with health care organizations. Should a state choose not to implement the mandatory reporting system, the Department of Health and Human Services should be designated as the responsible entity; and

• designate the Center for Patient Safety to:

(1) convene states to share information and expertise, and to evaluate alternative approaches taken for implementing reporting programs, identify best practices for implementation, and assess the impact of state programs; and

(2) receive and analyze aggregate reports from States to identify persistent safety issues that require more intensive analysis and/or a broader-based response (e.g., designing prototype systems or requesting a response by agencies, manufacturers or others).

RECOMMENDATION 5.2 The development of voluntary reporting efforts should be encouraged. The Center for Patient Safety should

• describe and disseminate information on external voluntary reporting programs to encourage greater participation in them and track the development of new reporting systems as they form;

• convene sponsors and users of external reporting systems to evaluate what works and what does not work well in the programs, and ways to make them more effective;

• periodically assess whether additional efforts are needed to address taps in information to improve patient safety and to encourage health care organizations to participate in voluntary reporting programs; and

• fund and evaluate pilot projects for reporting systems, both within individual health care organizations and collaborative efforts among health care organizations.

The committee believes there is a role both for mandatory, public reporting systems and voluntary, confidential reporting systems. However, because of their distinct purposes, such systems should be operated and maintained separately. A nationwide mandatory reporting system should be established by building upon the current patchwork of state systems and by standardizing the types of adverse events and information to be reported. The newly established Forum for Health Care Quality Measurement and Reporting, a public/private partnership, should be charged with the establishment of such standards. Voluntary reporting systems should also be promoted and the participation of health care organizations in them should be encouraged by accrediting bodies.

RECOMMENDATION 6.1 Congress should pass legislation to extend peer review protections to data related to patient safety and quality improvement that are collected and analyzed by health care organizations for internal use or shared with others solely for purposes of improving safety and quality.

The committee believes that information about the most serious adverse events which result in harm to patients and which are subsequently found to result from errors should not be protected from public disclosure. However, the committee also recognizes that for events not falling under this category, fears about the legal discover ability of information may undercut motivations to detect and analyze errors to improve safety. Unless such data are assured protection, information about errors will continue to be hidden and errors will be repeated. A more conducive environment is needed to encourage health care professionals and organizations to identify, analyze, and report errors without threat of litigation and without compromising patients' legal rights.

SETTING PERFORMANCE STANDARDS AND EXPECTATIONS FOR SAFETY

Setting and enforcing explicit standards for safety through regulatory and related mechanisms, such as licensing, certification, and accreditation, can define minimum performance levels for health care organizations and professionals. Additionally, the process of developing and adopting standards helps to form expectations for safety among providers and consumers. However, standards and expectations are not only set through regulations. The actions of purchasers and consumers affect the behaviors of health care organizations, and the values and norms set by health professions influence standards of practice, training and education for providers. Standards for patient safety can be applied to health care professionals, the organizations in which they work, and the tools (drugs and devices) they use to care for patients.

RECOMMENDATION 7.1 Performance standards and expectations for health care organizations should focus greater attention on patient safety.

- **Regulators and accreditors should require health care organizations to implement meaningful patient safety programs with defined executive responsibility.**
- **Public private purchasers should provide incentives to health care organizations to demonstrate continuous improvement in patient safety.**

Health care organizations are currently subject to compliance with licensing and accreditation standards. Although both devote some attention to issues related to patient safety, there is opportunity to strengthen such efforts. Regulators and accreditors have a role in encouraging and supporting actions in health care organizations by holding them accountable for ensuring a safe environment for patients. After a reasonable period of time for health care organizations to develop patient safety programs, regulators and accreditors should require them as a minimum standard.

Purchaser and consumer demands also exert influence on health care organizations. Public and private purchasers should consider safety issues in their contracting decisions and reinforce the importance of patient safety by providing relevant information to their employees or beneficiaries. Purchasers should also communicate concerns about patient safety to accrediting bodies to support stronger oversight for patient safety.

RECOMMENDATION 7.2 Performance standards and expectations for health professionals should focus greater attention on patient safety.

- **Health professional licensing bodies should**

  (1) implement periodic re-examinations and re-licensing of doctors, nurses, and other key providers, based on both competence and knowledge of safety practices, and

  (2) work with certifying and credentialing organizations to develop more effective methods to identify unsafe providers and take action.

- **Professional societies should make a visible commitment to patient safety by establishing a permanent committee dedicated to safety improvement. This committee should**

  (1) develop a curriculum on patient safety and encourage its adoption into training and certification requirements;

  (2) disseminate information on patient safety to members through special sessions at annual conferences, journal articles and editorials, newsletters, publications and websites on a regular basis;

  (3) recognize patient safety considerations in practice guidelines and in standards related to the introduction and diffusion of new technologies, therapies and drugs;

  (4) work with the Center for Patient Safety to develop community-based, collaborative initiatives for error reporting and analysis and implementation of patient safety improvements; and

  (5) collaborate with other professional societies and disciplines in a national summit on the professional's role in patient safety.

Although unsafe practitioners are believed to be few in number, the rapid identification of such practitioners and corrective action are important to a comprehensive safety program. Responsibilities for documenting continuing skills are dispersed among licensing boards, specialty boards and professional groups, and health care organizations with little communication or coordination. In their ongoing assessments, existing licensing, certification and accreditation processes for health professionals should place greater attention on safety and performance skills.

Additionally, professional societies and groups should become active leaders in encouraging and demanding improvements inpatient safety. Setting standards, convening and communicating with members about safety, incorporating attention to patient safety into training programs and collaborating across disciplines are all mechanisms that will contribute to creating a culture of safety.

RECOMMENDATION 7.3 The Food and Drug Administration (FDA) should increase attention to the safe use of drugs in both pre-and post-marketing processes through the following actions:

- **develop and enforce standards for the design of drug packaging and labeling that will maximize safety I use;**
- **require pharmaceutical companies to test (using FDA-approved methods) proposed drug names to identify and remedy potential sound-alike and look-alike confusion with existing drug names; and**
- **work with physicians, pharmacists, consumers, and others to establish appropriate responses to problems identified through post-marketing surveillance, especially for concerns that are perceived to require immediate response to protect the safety of patients.**

The FDA's role is to regulate manufacturers for the safety and effectiveness of their drugs and devices. However, even approved products can present safety problems in practice. For example, different drugs with similar sounding names can create confusion for both patients and providers. Attention to the safety of products in actual use should be increased during approval processes and in post-marketing monitoring systems. The FDA should also work with drug manufacturers, distributors, pharmacy benefit managers, health plans and other organizations to assist clinicians in identifying and preventing problems in the use of drugs.

Implementing Safety Systems in Health Care Organizations

Experience in other high-risk industries has provided well-understood illustrations that can be used to improve health care safety. However, health care management and professionals have rarely provided specific, clear, high-level, organization-wide incentives to apply what has been learned in other industries about ways to prevent error and reduce harm within their own organizations. Chief Executive Officers and Boards of Trustees should be held accountable for making a serious, visible and on-going commitment to creating safe systems of care.

RECOMMENDATION 8.1 Health care organizations and the professionals affiliated with them should make continually improved patient safety a declared and serious aim by establishing patient safety programs with defined executive responsibility. Patient safety programs should

- **provide strong, clear and visible attention to safety;**
- **implement non-punitive systems for reporting and analyzing errors within their organizations;**
- **incorporate well-understood safety principles, such as, standardizing and simplifying equipment, supplies and processes; and**
- **establish interdisciplinary team training programs for providers that incorporate proven methods of team training, such as simulation.**

Health care organizations must develop a culture of safety such that an organization's care processes and workforce are focused on improving the reliability and safety of care for patients. Safety should be an explicit organizational goal that is demonstrated by the strong direction and involvement of governance, management and clinical leadership. In addition, a meaningful patient safety program should include defined program objectives, personnel, and budget and should be monitored by regular progress reports to governance.

RECOMMENDATION 8.2 Health care organizations should implement proven medication safety practices.

A number of practices have been shown to reduce errors in the medication process. Several professional and collaborative organizations interested in patient safety have developed and published recommendations for safe medication practices, especially for hospitals. Although some of these recommendations have been implemented, none have been universally adopted and some are not yet implemented in a majority of hospitals. Safe medication practices should be implemented in all hospitals and health care organizations in which they are appropriate.

* * *

Notes and Questions

1. What are the implications of a focus on system errors? Does the physician as virtuous disappear from the model of the health care system as we move toward a model of organizations that deliver care, rather than physicians that treat patients? Are we better off acknowledging the inevitability of the changes that Leape, Jost, and Enthoven describe? See Barry R. Furrow, Incentivizing Medical Practice: What (If Anything) Happens to Professionalism? 1 Widener Law Symp. J. 1, 9–10 (1996); contra, see David M. Frankford, Managing Medical Clinician's Work Through the Use of Financial Incentives, 29 Wake Forest L. Rev. 71, 96 (1994) An excellent discussion of current issues of health care quality improvement can be found in Volume 76 of The Milbank Quarterly (No.4 1998), entitled Improving the Quality of Health Care. See also Larry I. Palmer, Patient Safety, Risk Reduction, and the Law, 36 Houston L.Rev. 1609(1999).

2. If we focus on system errors and system excellence, what happens to the traditional tort suit that starts with physician error? If errors are preventable by attention to the overall organization, then physicians should no longer be viewed as at "fault" when a patient is injured. What about medical licensing? The merits of discipline for physician errors should be reconsidered, if most errors are due to failures of an organization to provide resources, support, or other structures. What about differential pay for physicians in different practice areas? As health care is integrated and outcomes used to evaluate the overall benefits to a population of patients, why should we pay differentials that reflect the older model of the physician as craftsperson or artist? Perhaps this new model suggests a salary approach to compensation, with bonuses at best for compliance with institutional norms.

3. The issue of mandatory versus voluntary reporting has loomed large for health care providers, afraid that disclosure of an error will come to plaintiff lawyers' attention. Recommendation 5.1 of the Institute of Medicine report calls for mandatory reporting by hospitals and other institutions of

adverse events that lead to death or serious bodily harm .. Critics worry that this may drive honest disclosure even further underground, deterring providers from revealing errors. The only study to date of error reporting systems found that there was little difference between systems that provided confidentiality and those that did not. Underreporting occurred in both systems at about the same levels. See National Academy for State Health Policy, Medical Errors and Adverse Events: A Report of a 50–State Survey. *www.nashp.org.*

3. As described previously, total quality management and continuous quality improvement are important methods for fostering quality in health care institutions. Other more traditional methods of quality control include the quality assurance systems that exist within hospitals and other health care institutions. Most hospitals employ two distinct but closely related systems to oversee the quality of care: risk management and quality assurance. The goals of an effective risk management program are to eliminate the causes of loss experienced by the hospital and its patients, employees, and visitors; lessen the operational and financial effects of unavoidable losses; and cover inevitable losses at the lowest cost. As such, risk management is concerned not only with the quality of patient care delivered by a hospital but also with the safety and security of the hospital's employees, visitors, and property. The risk manager also administers claims against the hospital if injuries occur and oversees the hospital's insurance programs, determining which risks the hospital ought to insure against and which it ought to retain through self-insurance or high deductibles. Finally, the risk manager must be concerned with public and patient relations, as dissatisfied patients are more likely to sue for medical errors.

4. The most important tool of the risk manager is the incident report. Hospitals require incident reports on occurrences not consistent with routine patient care or hospital operation that have resulted or could have resulted in hospital liability or patient dissatisfaction. Examples include sudden deaths, falls, drug errors or reactions, injuries due to faulty equipment, threats of legal action, and unexplained requests from attorneys for medical records. The filing of incident reports (usually prepared by nurses) is the responsibility of department heads or supervisors. Incident reports are directed to the hospital risk manager, who investigates them as necessary. The risk manager also informs appropriate administrative and medical staff about the incident. By compiling data from incident reports, the risk manager can identify problem areas within the hospital and thus help prevent errors and injuries. Incident reports also assist in claims management, permitting the hospital to avoid costly lawsuits by quickly coming to terms with injured patients where liability seems clear and facilitating early coordination with an attorney to plan a defense where litigation seems unavoidable. Some malpractice insurance contracts include reservation of rights clauses, which permit the insurer to refuse to pay claims based on unreported incidents, underscoring the importance of incident reports.

5. Hospital quality assurance programs are directly concerned with assessing and improving patient care. Quality assurance focuses more narrowly on patient care than does risk management. It is broader than risk management, however, in that it considers a wide range of quality concerns, not just discrete mishaps. Incident reports play a major role in quality assurance, as they permit the hospital to identify serious quality deficiencies. The most significant tools of hospital quality assurance, however, are the hospital committees that oversee the quality of various hospital functions. These committees carry out functions mandated by JCAHO accreditation standards, and are in some states required by state law or

regulation. See West's Ann.Cal.Admin.Code tit. 22, § 70703(e); N.Y.—McKinney's Pub.Health Law § 2805–j. Common hospital committees include a tissue committee, which oversees the quality and necessity of surgery; an infections committee, which evaluates patients' infections and oversees the disposal of infectious material and the use of antibiotics; a pharmacy and therapeutics committee, which monitors the use and handling of drugs; a medical records committee, which assures the quality and completeness of medical records; a utilization review committee, which assures that patients are not admitted inappropriately or hospitalized too long; and medical audit committees, which review the quality of care provided in the hospital as a whole or in certain departments. Some hospitals also have an overall quality control committee, which coordinates quality assurance efforts throughout the hospital. Two other very important committees are the executive and credentials committees. The former serves as the cabinet of the medical staff, and in this capacity oversees all efforts of the medical staff to ensure quality. The credentials committee passes on applications for medical staff appointments and reappointments, and establishes and reviews physician clinical privileges; i.e., it determines which doctors can practice in the hospital and what procedures they may perform. As such, it has a vital role in assuring the quality of care provided by the hospital.

Some committees, such as the credentials or executive committee, are medical staff committees; i.e., they are composed of and answerable to physicians who practice in the hospital. Others, such as the quality assurance or infections control committees, are likely to be hospital committees, answerable to the hospital administration and including other professionals besides physicians. In many hospitals, committees play an active role in assuring the quality of care; in others, they exist primarily to meet accreditation requirements and do little.

6. Risk management is outcome oriented—it operates primarily by reacting to bad outcomes. Quality assurance is more process oriented. Some quality assurance activities involve concurrent review of the care process, such as the proctoring of doctors with probationary staff privileges. Quality assurance may also include retrospective review of care, another form of process review. Risk management is a managerial function, while quality assurance is predominantly a clinical function.

7. The new JCAHO Sentinel Event Policy has adopted the view of medical errors of the Institute of Medicine report, To Err is Human. It defines a sentinel event as "an unexpected occurrence involving death or severe physical or psychological injury, or the risk thereof", including unanticipated death or major loss of functioning unrelated to the patient's condition; patient suicide; wrong-side surgery; infant abduction/discharge to the wrong family; rape; and hemolytic transfusion reactions. JCAHO, "Sentinel Event Policy and Procedures", online at *www.jcaho.org* (15 January, 2001).

Problem: ManageCare

You are the advisor to the Chief Executive Officer of U.S. ManageCare, a large managed care organization that is expanding through the country. The CEO, a physician, wants to set the standard for other organizations by providing the highest level of quality care for ManageCare subscribers at the lowest cost in the marketplace. He wants you to create a model for care that will reduce errors that occur in ManageCare affiliated hospitals, physician practices, and specialty care groups. What questions will you ask? What additional information do you need? What methods or devices might you use to improve care at all levels? Consider how a reporting system could be designed, the merits of voluntary versus mandatory reporting of adverse events, and how such a reporting system can be enforced. Examine the JCAHO Sentinel Events Policy for ideas that might be applicable to managed care.

Chapter 2

QUALITY CONTROL REGULATION: LICENSING OF HEALTH CARE PROFESSIONALS

State law controls licensure of health care professionals under the state's police power. Licensing statutes govern entry into the licensed professions and disciplinary actions against licensed health care professionals. Licensure also regulates the scope of health care services that licensed professionals may provide and prohibits unlicensed persons from providing services reserved for the licensed professions.

These statutes are implemented by boards that operate as state agencies but which are generally dominated by members of the licensed profession. Licensure in the U.S. is often described as a system of professional self-regulation, even though the boards act as state agencies; usually include lay members; are governed by procedures and standards set in the state's licensing statute and administrative procedures act; and are subject to judicial review in both their adjudicatory and rulemaking decisions.

Professional participation in licensure may further the public interest by bringing expertise to the evaluation of professionals' competency and behavior. Professional domination of licensure has been strongly criticized, however, as serving the interests of the professions at the expense of their competitors; of organizations that seek to curtail medical control of health care decisions; and of the public.

Although this debate is an old one, it has been reenergized by changes in the health care system, including the advent of managed care and its control over physician practices; the momentum of a strong movement for alternative or complementary medicine; the institutionalization of non-physician licensed health care professions; and fundamental changes in medical practice itself, including, for example, the movement to increase access to controlled substances for pain relief and the emergence of cybermedicine, especially in relation to prescribing practices.

In each of these, the traditional forms of regulation of medical practice play a significant role, at times engaging in combat against these changes but always at least molding their structure and their relationship to medical practice. For recent analyses of the debate over professional control of licensure and the role of the market as opposed to restrictive licensure, see

Carl F. Ameringer, State Medical Boards and the Politics of Public Protection (Johns Hopkins University Press 1999); Ezekiel Emmanuel and Linda Emmanuel, Preserving Community in Health Care, 22 J. of Health Policy, Politics and Law 147 (1997); Frances H. Miller, Medical Discipline in the Twenty–First Century; Are Purchasers the Answer? 60 L. and Contemp. Probs. 31 (1997); Timothy S. Jost, Oversight of the Quality of Medical Care: Regulation, Management or the Market, 37 Ariz. L. Rev. 825 (1995); and E. Clarke Ross, Regulating Managed Care: Interest Group Competition for Control and Behavioral Health Care, 24 J. of Health Politics, Policy and Law 599 (1999). For a historical perspective, see Paul Stark, The Social Transformation of American Medicine (1982); and for the classic study of medical licensure and discipline, see Robert C. Derbyshire, Medical Licensure and Discipline in the United States (1969).

I. DISCIPLINE

IN RE WILLIAMS

Supreme Court of Ohio, 1991.
60 Ohio St.3d 85, 573 N.E.2d 638.

Syllabus by the Court

* * *

... Between 1983 and 1986, Dr. Williams prescribed Biphetamine or Obetrol for fifty patients as part of a weight control treatment regimen. [Both drugs are controlled substances.]

On November 17, 1986, appellant, the Ohio State Medical Board ("board"), promulgated Ohio Adm.Code 4731–11–03(B), which prohibited the use of [drugs such as Biphetamine and Obetrol] for purposes of weight control. Dr. Williams ceased prescribing Biphetamine and Obetrol for weight control upon becoming aware of the rule.

By letter dated March 12, 1987, the board charged Dr. Williams with violating R.C. 4731.22(B)* by prescribing these stimulants without "reasonable care," and thereby failing to conform to minimal standards of medical practice. The crux of the board's charge was that Dr. Williams had departed from accepted standards of care by using these drugs as a long-term, rather than a short-term, treatment.

A hearing was held before a board examiner. The parties stipulated to the accuracy of the medical records of the patients in question, which detailed the use of Biphetamine and Obetrol for periods ranging from nearly seven months to several years. The board also introduced into evidence the Physician's Desk Reference entries for Biphetamine and Obetrol, which recommend that these

* R.C. 4731.22(B) provides in pertinent part:

"The board, pursuant to an adjudicatory hearing ... shall, to the extent permitted by law, ... [discipline] the holder of a certificate [to practice medicine] for one or more of the following reasons:

...

"(2) Failure to use reasonable care, discrimination in the administration of drugs, or failure to employ acceptable scientific methods in the selection of drugs or other modalities for treatment of disease;

"(3) Selling, prescribing, giving away, or administering drugs for other than legal and legitimate therapeutic purposes ...

...

"(6) A departure from, or the failure to conform to, minimal standards of care ... [.]"

drugs be used for only "a few weeks" in the treatment of obesity. The board presented no testimony or other evidence of the applicable standard of care.

Dr. Williams presented expert testimony from Dr. John P. Morgan, the director of the pharmacology program at the City University of New York Medical School, and Dr. Eljorn Don Nelson, an associate professor of clinical pharmacology at the University of Cincinnati College of Medicine. These experts stated that there are two schools of thought in the medical community concerning the use of stimulants for weight control. The so-called "majority" view holds that stimulants should only be used for short periods, if at all, in weight control programs. The "minority" view holds that the long-term use of stimulants is proper in the context of a supervised physician-patient relationship. Both experts testified that, though they themselves supported the "majority" view, Dr. Williams's application of the "minority" protocol was not substandard medical practice.

The hearing examiner found that Dr. Williams's practices violated R.C. 4731.22(B). The examiner recommended subjecting Dr. Williams to a three-year monitored probation period. The board modified the penalty, imposing a one-year suspension of Dr. Williams's license followed by a five-year probationary period, during which he would be unable to prescribe or dispense controlled substances.

Dr. Williams appealed to the Court of Common Pleas of Franklin County pursuant to R.C. 119.12. The court found that the board's order was "... not supported by reliable, probative and substantial evidence and ... [was] not in accordance with law." The court of appeals affirmed.

HERBERT R. BROWN, JUSTICE.

In an appeal from an administrative agency, a reviewing court is bound to uphold the agency's order if it is "... supported by reliable, probative, and substantial evidence and is in accordance with law...." [ ]. In the instant case, we must determine if the common pleas court erred by finding that the board's order was not supported by sufficient evidence. For the reasons, which follow, we conclude that it did not and affirm the judgment of the court below.

In its arguments to this court, the board contends that Arlen v. Ohio State Medical Bd. (1980), 61 Ohio St.2d 168, 15 O.O.3d 190, 399 N.E.2d 1251, is dispositive. In *Arlen*, the physician was disciplined because he had written prescriptions for controlled substances to a person who the physician knew was redistributing the drugs to others, a practice prohibited by R.C. 3719.06(A). The physician appealed on the ground that the board failed to present expert testimony that such prescribing practices fell below a reasonable standard of care.

We held that the board is not required in every case to present expert testimony on the acceptable standard of medical practice before it can find that a physician's conduct falls below this standard. We noted that the usual purpose of expert testimony is to assist the trier of facts in understanding "issues that require scientific or specialized knowledge or experience beyond the scope of common occurrences...." [ ] The board was then made up of ten (now twelve) persons, eight of whom are licensed physicians. [ ] Thus, a majority of board members are themselves experts in the medical field who already possess the specialized knowledge needed to determine the acceptable standard of general medical practice.

While the board need not, in every case, present expert testimony to support a charge against an accused physician, the charge must be supported by some reliable, probative and substantial evidence. It is here that the case against Dr. Williams fails, as it is very different from *Arlen*.

Arlen involved a physician who dispensed controlled substances in a manner that not only fell below the acceptable standard of medical practice, but also violated the applicable statute governing prescription and dispensing of these drugs. In contrast, Dr. Williams dispensed controlled substances in what was, at the time, a legally permitted manner, albeit one which was disfavored by many in the medical community. The only evidence in the record on this issue was the testimony of Dr. Williams's expert witnesses that his use of controlled substances in weight control programs did not fall below the acceptable standard of medical practice. While the board has broad discretion to resolve evidentiary conflicts [ ] and determine the weight to be given expert testimony [ ], it cannot convert its own disagreement with an expert's opinion into affirmative evidence of a contrary proposition where the issue is one on which medical experts are divided and there is no statute or rule governing the situation.

It should be noted, however, that where the General Assembly has prohibited a particular medical practice by statute, or where the board has done so through its rulemaking authority, the existence of a body of expert opinion supporting that practice would not excuse a violation. Thus, if Dr. Williams had continued to prescribe Biphetamine or Obetrol for weight control after the promulgation of Ohio Adm.Code 4731–11–03(B), this would be a violation of R.C. 4731.22(B)(3), and the existence of the "minority" view supporting the use of these substances for weight control would provide him no defense. Under those facts, *Arlen* would be dispositive. Here, however, there is insufficient evidence, expert or otherwise, to support the charges against Dr. Williams. Were the board's decision to be affirmed on the facts in this record, it would mean that a doctor would have no access to meaningful review of the board's decision. The board, though a majority of its members have special knowledge, is not entitled to exercise such unbridled discretion.

MOYER, C.J., and SWEENEY, HOLMES and DOUGLAS, JJ., concur.

WRIGHT, JUSTICE, dissenting.

The message we send to the medical community's regulators with today's decision is one, I daresay, we would never countenance for their counterparts in the legal community. We are telling those charged with policing the medical profession that their expertise as to what constitutes the acceptable standard of medical practice is not enough to overcome the assertion that challenged conduct does not violate a state statute....

HOOVER v. THE AGENCY FOR HEALTH CARE ADMINISTRATION

District Court of Appeal of Florida, 1996.
676 So.2d 1380.

JORGENSON, JUDGE.

Dr. Katherine Anne Hoover, a board-certified physician in internal medicine, appeals a final order of the Board of Medicine penalizing her and restricting her license to practice medicine in the State of Florida. We reverse because the board has once again engaged in the uniformly rejected practice of overzealously supplanting a hearing officer's valid findings of fact regarding a doctor's prescription practices with its own opinion in a case founded on a woefully inadequate quantum of evidence.

In March 1994, the Department of Business and Professional Regulation (predecessor in these proceedings to the Agency for Health Care Administration) filed an administrative complaint alleging that Dr. Hoover (1) inappropriately and excessively prescribed various ... controlled substances to seven of her patients and (2) provided care of those patients that fell below that level of care, skill, and treatment which is recognized by a reasonably prudent similar physician as being acceptable under similar conditions and circumstances; in violation of sections 458.331(1)(q) and (t), Florida Statutes, respectively. All seven of the patients had been treated by Dr. Hoover for intractable pain arising from various non-cancerous diseases or ailments.

Dr. Hoover disputed the allegations of the administrative complaint and requested a formal hearing....

The agency presented the testimony of two physicians as experts. Neither had examined any of the patients or their medical records. The sole basis for the opinions of the agency physicians was computer printouts from pharmacies in Key West where the doctor's patients had filled their prescriptions. These printouts indicated only the quantity of each drug filled for each patient, occasionally referring to a simplified diagnosis. Both of these physicians practiced internal medicine and neither specialized in the care of chronic pain. In fact, both doctors testified that they did not treat but referred their chronic pain patients to pain management clinics. The hearing officer found that this was a common practice among physicians—perhaps to avoid prosecutions like this case.* Both doctors "candidly testified that without being provided with copies of the medical records for those patients they could not evaluate Respondent's diagnoses of what alternative modalities were attempted or what testing was done to support the use of the medication chosen by Respondent to treat those patients." Despite this paucity of evidence, lack of familiarity, and seeming lack of expertise, the agency's physicians testified at the hearing that the doctor had prescribed excessive, perhaps lethal amounts of narcotics, and had practiced below the standard of care.

Dr. Hoover testified in great detail concerning the condition of each of the patients, her diagnoses and courses of treatment, alternatives attempted, the patients' need for medication, the uniformly improved function of the patients with the amount of medication prescribed, and her frequency of writing prescriptions to allow her close monitoring of the patients. She presented corroborating physician testimony regarding the appropriateness of the particular medications and the amounts prescribed and her office-setting response to the patients' requests for relief from intractable pain.

* Referral to a pain management clinic was not an option for Dr. Hoover's indigent Key West resident patients.

Following post-hearing submissions, the hearing officer issued her recommended order finding that the agency had failed to meet its burden of proof on all charges. The hearing officer concluded, for instance, "Petitioner failed to provide its experts with adequate information to show the necessary similar conditions and circumstances upon which they could render opinions that showed clearly and convincingly that Respondent failed to meet the standard of care required of her in her treatment of the patients in question."

The agency filed exceptions to the recommended findings of fact and conclusions of law as to five of the seven patients. The board of medicine accepted all the agency's exceptions, amended the findings of fact in accordance with the agency's suggestions, and found the doctor in violation of sections 458.331(1)(q) and (t), Florida Statutes. The board imposed the penalty recommended by the agency: a reprimand, a $4,000 administrative fine, continuing medical education on prescribing abusable drugs, and two years probation. This appeal follows.

For each of the five patients, the hearing officer found the prescribing practices of Doctor Hoover to be appropriate. This was based upon (1) the doctor's testimony regarding the specific care given, (2) the corroborating testimony of her physician witness, and (3) the fact that the doctor's prescriptions did not exceed the federal guidelines for treatment of intractable pain in cancer patients, though none of the five patients were diagnosed as suffering from cancer.

The board rejected these findings as not based on competent substantial evidence. As particular reasons, the board adopted the arguments of the agency's exceptions to the recommended order that (1) the hearing officer's findings were erroneously based on irrelevant federal guidelines, and (2) the agency's physicians had testified that the doctor's prescription pattern was below the standard of care and outside the practice of medicine. . . .

First, the board mischaracterizes the hearing officer's reference to the federal guidelines. The board reasoned in its final order that "[t]he record reflects that the federal guidelines relied upon by the Hearing Officer for this finding were designed for cancer patients and [the five patients at issue were] not being treated for cancer." It is true, as the hearing officer noted,

> Respondent presented expert evidence that there is a set of guidelines which have been issued for the use of Schedule II controlled substances to treat intractable pain and that although those guidelines were established to guide physicians in treating cancer patients, those are the only guidelines available at this time. Utilizing those guidelines, because they exist, the amount of medication prescribed by Respondent to the patients in question was not excessive or inappropriate.

In so finding, however, the hearing officer did not, as the board suggests, rely solely upon the federal guidelines in its ruling that the doctor's prescribing practices were not excessive. Rather, the federal guidelines merely buttressed fact findings that were independently supported by the hearing officer's determination of the persuasiveness and credibility of the physician witnesses on each side. For example, though he admitted he had not even reviewed the federal guidelines, one of the agency physicians asserted that the amounts prescribed constituted a "tremendous number of pills" and that the doses involved would be lethal. That Dr. Hoover's prescriptions fell within the guidelines for chronic-pained cancer patients may properly be considered to refute this assertion. Such a use of the federal guidelines was relevant and reasonable.

Second, Dr. Hoover testified in great detail concerning her treatment of each patient, the patient's progress under the medication she prescribed, and that the treatment was within the standard of care and practice of medicine. The hearing officer, as arbiter of credibility, was entitled to believe what the doctor and her physician expert opined. [ ] The agency's witnesses' ultimate conclusions do not strip the hearing officer's reliance upon Dr. Hoover of its competence and substantiality. The hearing officer was entitled to give Dr. Hoover's testimony greater weight than that of the agency's witnesses, who did not examine these patients or regularly engage in the treatment of intractable pain.

[T]he hearing officer explicitly recognized that the 1994 [Florida] intractable pain law was not in effect at the time of Dr. Hoover's alleged infractions but cited it for a permissible purpose—to rebut any claim that there is a strong public policy mandate in favor of the board's draconian policy of policing pain prescription practice. [ ] . . .

Reversed.

Notes and Questions

1. As you see in the dissent in *Williams*, the rationale for physicians' dominance of the membership of state medical boards is the notion of peer review. This concept holds that practitioners of the regulated profession are in the best position to judge the practices of their peers. What, then, is at the heart of this dispute over expert testimony in *Williams*? On what basis did the Florida court reject the testimony of the agency's experts in *Hoover*?

2. Both *Williams* and *Hoover* involve disputes within the medical profession concerning appropriate medical treatment, during a transition in professional standards. The Ohio State Medical Board promulgated an administrative rule, cited in *Williams*, requiring that physicians meet the "majority" standard of practice regarding the prescription of controlled substances. Should licensure boards establish standards of practice or practice guidelines that prefer one approach over another; or should they simply recognize the full range of medical practices, including minority views? Would your answer depend on whether the board was acting in a rulemaking or in an adjudicatory role? How should the boards respond in the absence of well-accepted standards of care or a well-established mainstream of practice, as in the *Hoover* case? See the *Guess* case, *infra*, for a discussion of the scope of judicial review of medical board rules and regulations.

3. The court in *Hoover* implies that disciplinary actions by a state medical board against individual physicians have an effect on other physicians' practices. Beyond penalizing the "bad apple," this is the broader intended impact of professional disciplinary actions. In the case of treatment for pain, however, the medical boards were more influenced by the "war against drugs" than they were by neglected pain. Furthermore, significant new research indicated that the traditional medical practice in the use of opioids for pain needed to be changed, as these drugs are safer than has been assumed. The change in practice that this research stimulated caused some problems in the disciplinary system, as evidenced in *Hoover*. The negative impact of medical board practices relating to the prescrip-

tion of controlled substances for pain management received considerable attention as a result. See for example, Symposium on Legal and Institutional Constraints on Effective Pain Relief, 24 Journal of Law, Medicine & Ethics (1997) and Symposium on Legal and Regulatory Issues in Pain Management, 26 Journal of Law, Medicine & Ethics (1998). The Federation of State Medical Boards developed a model policy that emphasized improvements in patient functioning and pain relief and practice management techniques (including record keeping and physical examination) over standards based merely on the quantity and chronicity of the prescriptions. See, Model Guidelines for the Use of Controlled Substances for the Treatment of Pain (1998), available at *www.fsmb.org* (visited December 27, 2000). Some states have enacted legislation generally referred to as "intractable pain treatment acts." The Florida statute referenced in *Hoover*, which is an early version of such statutes, provides:

> Notwithstanding any other provision of law, a physician may prescribe or administer any controlled substance to a person for the treatment of intractable pain, provided the physician does so in accordance with that level of care, skill, and treatment recognized by a reasonably prudent physician under similar conditions and circumstances.

Would this statute provide adequate protection to physicians such as Dr. Hoover? Should it be more specific? Is it appropriate for legislatures to enact statutes concerning permissible medical practices, or should they leave that to the licensure boards?

4. The number of disciplinary actions against physicians has increased. In the 1960s, 0.06% of doctors were disciplined, primarily for offenses involving abuse of drugs or inappropriate prescribing; and by 1981, the number disciplined had grown to 0.14% of licensed physicians. Robert C. Derbyshire, How Effective is Medical Self–Regulation? 7 Law & Human Behavior 193 (1983). The Federation's Data Bank lists approximately 4,000 disciplinary actions yearly through the 1990s. See *www.fsmb.org*. A study of California disciplinary actions published in 1998 found that 0.24% of California physicians were disciplined in 1997, with negligence and incompetence constituting about one-third of those actions. The next largest numbers related to abuse of alcohol or drugs (14%), inappropriate prescribing practices (11%), and inappropriate contact with patients (10%). The penalties levied included license revocation (21%), licensed suspension (13%), stayed suspension of license (45%), and reprimand (21%). James Morrison and Peter Wickersham, Physicians Disciplined by the State Medical Boards, 279 JAMA 1889 (1998). An accompanying commentary notes the number of physicians who were disciplined and states that "even 1% is still far too many." The Role of the Medical Profession in Physician Discipline, 279 JAMA 1914 (1998). Is 0.24% too many or too few? How would you measure whether the number of disciplinary actions in your state was too many, too few or just right? If the boards must set priorities due to limited resources, what should those priorities be? Should they focus on the more easily proven cases? Should they respond first to consumer complaints? For a general discussion see, Timothy S. Jost, et al., Consumers, Complaints, and Professional Discipline: A Look at Medical Licensure Boards, 3 Health Matrix 309 (1993).

5. In assessing incompetency, how should the board treat suits for malpractice? Settlements? Judgments? One study has concluded that the filing of a malpractice claim against a physician, even if no payment was made on the claim, was predictive of future malpractice claims. Randall R. Bovbjerg and Kenneth R. Petronis, The Relationship Between Physicians' Malpractice Claims History and

Later Claims: Does the Past Predict the Future? 272 JAMA 1421 (1994). What implication does this have for disciplinary boards, if any? See, Mich. C.L.A. § 333.16231, requiring the medical board to investigate physicians who have experienced "3 or more malpractice settlements, awards, or judgments ... in a period of 5 consecutive years or 1 or more malpractice settlements, awards, or judgments ... totaling more than $200,000.00 in a period of 5 consecutive years."

6. Most states have established programs to provide rehabilitative, non-punitive interventions for impaired nurses, doctors and other health professionals. The rehabilitative approach to impairment naturally emerges from the recent emphasis on chemical dependency as an illness rather than a failure in character, especially in professionals. It also responds to perceived concerns that a punitive disciplinary approach pushes impaired health care providers undercover, risking greater injury to the public. It is hoped that the availability of a program of non-punitive rehabilitation encourages a higher rate of reporting and self-reporting of impaired physicians. See e.g., C. Morrow, Doctors Helping Doctors, 14 Hastings Center Report 32 (1984). A focus on rehabilitation rather than punishment may be meeting more resistance in nurse discipline. H. Lippman and S. Nagle, Addicted Nurses: Tolerated, Tormented or Treated?, 55 RN 36 (1992).

Some studies of physician treatment programs indicate relapse rates of 10% to 20%. M. F. Fleming, Physician Impairment: Options for Intervention, 50 American Family Physician 41 (July 1994); B. Schneidman, Editorial: The Philosophy of Rehabilitation for Impaired Physicians, 82 Federation Bulletin 125 (1995). Other studies indicate relapse rates ranging from 30% to 57%, though the severity and duration of relapse may vary. K. L. Sprinkle, Physician Alcoholism: A Survey of the Literature, 81 Federation Bulletin 113 (1994).

Should voluntary enrollment in an impaired professional program be confidential, or should the program be required to notify the board? Can rehabilitation be coerced? Should boards allow impaired professionals to choose a rehabilitative program with discipline stayed and then expunged upon successful completion? Should physicians who are abusing alcohol or drugs or who are participating in a state-sanctioned rehabilitation program be required to inform their patients? Would this protect the public? See Barry R. Furrow, Doctors' Dirty Little Secrets: The Dark Side of Medical Privacy, 37 Washburn L.J. 283 (1998), arguing that informed consent is inadequate protection in such a case.

7. "Impairment" is a term of art in professional licensure; but it is also a central term in the federal Americans with Disabilities Act, which prohibits discrimination against persons who have a physical or mental impairment or a record of such impairment or are viewed as having such an impairment. 42 U.S.C.A. § 12101 et seq. (1990). Title II of the ADA applies to the licensing functions of the professional licensure boards of the States. 28 C.F.R. § 35.130(b)(6) (1991). See, for example, Alexander v. Margolis, 921 F.Supp. 482 (W.D.Mich.1995); *aff'd* 98 F.3d 1341 (6th Cir.1996).

8. The number of disciplinary actions for sexual misconduct has increased rapidly, nearly tripling between 1990 and 1995. Estimates of the incidence of physician sexual activity with patients vary, ranging between 5% to 10% of practicing physicians, although these estimates are viewed by some as understated. Council on Ethical and Judicial Affairs, Sexual Misconduct in the Practice of Medicine, 266 JAMA 2741 (1991); N. Gartrell, et al., Physician-patient Sexual Contact: Prevalence and Problems, 157 Western Journal of Medicine 139 (1992). The House of Delegates of the AMA formally adopted an Opinion of the Association's Council on Ethical and Judicial Affairs holding that "sexual contact or

romantic relationship concurrent with the physician-patient relationship is unethical." Opinions of the Council on Ethical and Judicial Affairs § 8.14 (1992). State statutes provide for disciplinary action against doctors for sexual misconduct with patients. In some states, such actions are brought under general provisions prohibiting "unprofessional conduct." In a few states, there are specific statutory prohibitions but their scope varies widely. For example, some states proscribe "exercising influence" over a patient for the purpose of engaging in sexual activity. See e.g., Mo.Ann.Stat. § 334.100(2)(4)(i). See also, Levin v. Idaho State Bd. of Medicine, 133 Idaho 413, 987 P.2d 1028 (Idaho 1999). For a review of the case law on disciplinary sanctions against doctors and a comparison with norms for lawyers, see Sandra H. Johnson, Judicial Review for Disciplinary Actions for Sexual Misconduct in the Practice of Medicine, 270 JAMA 1596 (1993). For an analysis of the incidence of actions and the level of sanctions against physicians, see Christine E. Dehlendorf and Sidney M. Wolfe, Physicians Disciplined for Sex–Related Offenses, 279 JAMA 1883 (1998).

9. One area of new and controversial disciplinary activity involves the state medical board's jurisdiction over the practice of utilization review. The first issue is whether utilization review is the practice of medicine so that managed care organizations must hire only licensed physicians to provide that service. See, Managed Care Industry "Under Siege" Over Utilization Review Licensure, External HMO Review Panels, BNA Health Law Reporter (May 7, 1998). See generally, the section on scope of practice regulation, *infra*. The second issue is whether a physician utilization reviewer can be disciplined for charges of incompetency or professional misconduct in the conduct of utilization review. See, State Bd. of Reg. for Healing Arts v. Fallon, 41 S.W.3d 474, 2001 WL 348980 (Mo.2001). One of the legal issues involved in this particular dispute is whether the state has authority under federal ERISA law to regulate utilization reviewers through licensure statutes. See Chapter 9.

10. Congress established the National Practitioner Data Bank in part to create an effective system for preventing doctors with disciplinary history in one state from moving to another and practicing until detected, if ever. 42 U.S.C.A. §§ 11101–11152. State disciplinary and licensure boards are required to report certain disciplinary actions against physicians. Hospitals and other entities engaging in peer review processes are required to report adverse actions as well. Licensure boards have access to the Data Bank to check on licensees, and hospitals must check the Data Bank for physicians applying for staff privileges and periodically for physicians who hold staff privileges. The general public is not allowed access to the information in the Data Bank though there have been several proposals for allowing increased access. The federal General Accounting Office has issued a report that is quite critical of the accuracy of the information contained in the Data Bank, including the information that is reported by state medical boards. National Practitioner Data Bank: Major Improvements Are Needed to Enhance Data Bank's Reliability. (GAO–01–130, Nov. 30, 2000).

Note: State Medical Boards, Licensing and Online Prescribing

In the previous material on disciplinary actions by state medical boards, you noted the problems that the state medical boards and the disciplinary system experience when there is a change in medical treatment. Medical boards must also react when there is a change in the method of delivery.

Currently, medical boards (and the federal government and professional associations such as the American Medical Association and scholars and lawyers) are struggling with the issues raised by telemedicine generally and Internet prescribing in particular. The term telemedicine encompasses a wide range of activities—including online physician consultations with specialists, review of imaging by offsite radiologists, and continuing contact with a physician's patients through e-mail—many of which do not raise unique legal issues. Online prescribing, however, captures many of the controversial attributes of telemedicine that have generated volumes examining the application of tort theory, the jurisdiction of dozens of regulatory bodies, and the scope of contract and intellectual property issues. See generally, Symposium on Electronic Medical Information: Privacy, Liability and Quality Issues, 25 Am. J. of L. & M. 191 (1999); Christopher Guttman–McCabe, Telemedicine's Imperiled Future? Funding, Reimbursement, Licensing and Privacy Hurdles, 14 Contemporary Health Law and Policy 161 (1997). For a discussion of the broader reaches of telemedicine, see Nicolas P. Terry, Cyber–Malpractice: Legal Exposure for Cybermedicine, 25 Am. J. of L. and Med. 327 (1999).

Internet pharmacy services vary in their operation. For example, patients may purchase prescription medications from an online "drug store" that operates just like a "real" pharmacy in that the entity holds a pharmacy license and requires an offsite doctor's prescription before shipping medication. Although these virtual drug stores raise some legal issues, it is a second kind of online drug purchase that raises more difficult issues for medical licensure and the state medical boards. These latter entities offer one-stop shopping for an individual seeking a prescription. The "patient" typically fills out an online medical questionnaire, which is reviewed by a physician associated with the Internet site. That physician then issues a prescription, and the drug is shipped directly to the patient. There is no other contact between the physician and the patient, and the patient does not know who the doctor is or what training the doctor has. Sites that provide prescriptions for medications for conditions that might be considered by some to be too embarrassing to see a doctor in person and for which prescription drugs have been heavily advertised seem to be the most popular. Online pharmacies also offer prices that are generally lower than other pharmacies as well as the convenience of home delivery. Chester Chuang (Note), Is There a Doctor in the House? Using Failure-to-Warn Liability to Enhance the Safety of Online Prescribing, 75 N.Y.U.L.Rev. 1452 (2000), detailing the scope of Internet pharmacy services and providing an overview of legal issues.

Naturally, these sites have raised issues of quality and access to health care. Personal knowledge of the patient and physical examination have been the traditional hallmarks of quality prescribing, and some argue that patients may be injured by taking inappropriate prescription medications when there has been no physical contact with the physician and when there is no follow-up. Others argue that telemedicine generally will improve access to care by removing the perceived stigma of certain conditions that may lead individuals to forego medical treatment entirely; by lowering cost; and by reaching geographic areas that are underserved by specialists. See, for example, Talley L. Kaleko (Comment), A Bold Step: What Florida Should Do Concerning the Health of Its Rural Communities, Licensure, and Telemedicine, 27 Fla.St.U.L.Rev. 767 (2000).

Telemedicine and online prescribing are oblivious to state boundaries. Medical licensure, however, is controlled by each state individually, and physicians, with few exceptions, must hold a license in each state in which they practice, although they are granted this license "by endorsement" if they hold a current license in another state. Even endorsement, however, involves a time-consuming application process. Should medical licensure remain the province of the states, in this one context, or should there be national licensure? Assuming that the individual states retain control of medical licensure, how should they regulate online prescribing?

Some states have already enacted legislation to govern the licensure of physicians practicing telemedicine. The Federation of State Medical Boards developed a model act in 1996 to govern the issue of electronically mediated medical practices. A Model Act to Regulate the Practice of Medicine Across State Lines (1996). This act requires licensure in the state in which the patient resides but provides for a special limited license to facilitate telemedicine. The model act has been criticized both as too liberal and as too restrictive of the practice of telemedicine.

The state of Indiana, for example, permits physicians outside of Indiana to provide consultation services to Indiana physicians but otherwise requires an Indiana medical license for any physician who is "providing diagnostic or treatment services to a person in Indiana when [those services] are transmitted through electronic communications; and are on a regular, routine and non-episodic basis ..." Ind. Code Ann. § 25–22.5–1–1.1(a)(4). Most states that have amended their licensure statutes have followed a similar form although some states do not include the exception for consultation.

Why would a state not rely on the licensure of another state? If the only contact between patient and doctor is via the Internet, has the doctor gone to the patient or has the patient come to the doctor? Will the Indiana statute encourage or impede the development of telemedicine? Should online consulting with another physician be treated differently than direct physician-to-patient online prescribing? If your state requires that a doctor using electronic communications to diagnose or treat patients residing in your state have a license issued by your state, what disciplinary standards should the medical board use to govern the practice? Should your board discipline physicians who prescribe medication without examining the patient? Rather than taking a case-by-case adjudicatory approach, should your board instead promulgate regulations for online prescribing?

For an analysis of the FSMB model act and current state legislation, see Center for Telemedicine Law, Telemedicine and Interstate Licensure: Findings and Recommendations of the CTL Licensure Task Force 73 N.D.L.Rev.109 (1997); Alison M. Sulentic, Crossing Borders: The Licensure of Interstate Telemedicine Practitioners, 25 J. Legis. 1 (1998).

II. ALTERNATIVE AND COMPLEMENTARY MEDICINE

IN RE GUESS

Supreme Court of North Carolina, 1990.
327 N.C. 46, 393 S.E.2d 833.

MITCHELL, JUSTICE.

* * *

The facts of this case are essentially uncontested. The record evidence tends to show that Dr. George Albert Guess is a licensed physician practicing family medicine in Asheville. In his practice, Guess regularly administers homeopathic medical treatments to his patients. Homeopathy has been defined as:

> A system of therapy developed by Samuel Hahnermann on the theory that large doses of a certain drug given to a healthy person will produce certain conditions which, when occurring spontaneously as symptoms of a disease, are relieved by the same drug in small doses. This [is] . . . a sort of "fighting fire with fire" therapy.

Stedman's Medical Dictionary 654 (24th ed. 1982); *see* Schmidt's Attorneys' Dictionary of Medicine H–110 (1962). Homeopathy thus differs from what is referred to as the conventional or allopathic system of medical treatment. Allopathy "employ[s] remedies which affect the body in a way *opposite* from the effect of the disease treated." Schmidt's Attorneys' Dictionary of Medicine A–147 (emphasis added); *see* Stedman's Medical Dictionary 44.

On 25 June 1985, the Board charged Dr. Guess with unprofessional conduct, pursuant to N.C.G.S. § 90–14(a)(6), specifically based upon his practice of homeopathy. In a subsequent Bill of Particulars, the Board alleged that in his practice of medicine, Guess utilized "so-called 'homeopathic medicines' prepared from substances including, but not limited to, moss, the night shade plant and various other animal, vegetable and mineral substances." . . .

Following notice, a hearing was held by the Board on the charge against Dr. Guess. The hearing evidence chiefly consisted of testimony by a number of physicians. Several physicians licensed to practice in North Carolina testified that homeopathy was not an acceptable and prevailing system of medical practice in North Carolina. In fact, there was evidence indicating that Guess is the only homeopath openly practicing in the State. Guess presented evidence that homeopathy is a recognized system of practice in at least three other states and many foreign countries. There was no evidence that Guess' homeopathic treatment had ever harmed a patient, and there was anecdotal evidence that Guess' homeopathic remedies had provided relief to several patients who were apparently unable to obtain relief through allopathic medicine.

Following its hearing, the Board revoked Dr. Guess' license to practice medicine in North Carolina, based upon findings and conclusions that Guess' practice of homeopathy "departs from and does not conform to the standards of acceptable and prevailing medical practice in this State," thus constituting unprofessional conduct as defined and prohibited by N.C.G.S. § 90–14(a)(6). The Board, however, stayed the revocation of Guess' license for so long as he refrained from practicing homeopathy.

Guess appealed the Board's decision. . . . After review, the Superior Court entered an order on 20 May 1987, which reversed and vacated the Board's decision. The Superior Court found and concluded that Guess' substantial rights had been violated because the Board's findings, conclusions and decision were "not supported by competent, material and substantial evidence and [were] arbitrary and capricious."

. . . [T]he Court of Appeals rejected the Superior Court's reasoning to the effect that the Board's findings, conclusions and decision were not supported by competent evidence. *In re Guess,* 95 N.C.App. 435, 437, 382 S.E.2d 459, 461 (1989). The Court of Appeals, nonetheless, affirmed the Superior Court's order reversing the Board's decision,

> Because the Board neither charged nor found that Dr. Guess' departures from approved and prevailing medical practice either endangered or harmed his patients or the public, and in our opinion the revocation of a physician's license to practice his profession in this state must be based upon conduct that is detrimental to the public; it cannot be based upon conduct that is merely different from that of other practitioners.

Id. at 437, 382 S.E.2d at 461. We granted the Board's Petition for Discretionary Review, and now reverse the Court of Appeals.

I.

The statute central to the resolution of this case provides in relevant part: [The Board shall have the power to deny, annul, suspend or revoke a license where the licensee has engaged in:]

> (6) Unprofessional conduct, including, but not limited to, *any departure* from, or the failure to conform to, the *standards of acceptable and prevailing medical practice,* or the ethics of the medical profession, *irrespective of whether or not a patient is injured thereby.*

N.C.G.S. § 90–14 (1985) (emphasis added). The Court of Appeals concluded that in exercising the police power, the legislature may properly act only to protect the public from harm. [ ] Therefore, the Court of Appeals reasoned that, in order to be a valid exercise of the police power, the statute must be construed as giving the Board authority to prohibit or punish the action of a physician only when it can be shown that *the particular action in question* poses a danger of harm to the patient or the public. Specifically, the Court of Appeals held that:

> Before a physician's license to practice his profession in this state can be lawfully revoked under G.S. 90–14(a)(6) for practices contrary to acceptable and prevailing medical practice that *it must also appear that the deviation complained of posed some threat of harm to either the physician's patients or the public.* [ ]

Our analysis begins with a basic constitutional principle: the General Assembly, in exercising the state's police power, may legislate to protect the public health, safety and general welfare. [ ]

Turning to the subject of this case, regulation of the medical profession is plainly related to the legitimate public purpose of protecting the public health and safety. [ ] State regulation of the medical profession has long been recognized as a legitimate exercise of the police power. As the Supreme Court of the United States has pointed out:

* * *

> Few professions require more careful preparation by one who seeks to enter it than that of medicine. It has to deal with all those subtle and mysterious influences upon which health and life depend. . . . The physician must be able to detect readily the presence of disease, and prescribe appropriate remedies for its removal. Everyone may have occasion to consult him, but comparatively few can judge of the qualifications of learning and skill, which he possesses. Reliance must be placed upon the assurance given by his license, issued by an authority competent to judge

> in that respect, that he possesses the requisite qualifications. . . . The same reasons which control in imposing conditions, upon compliance with which the physician is allowed to practice in the first instance, may call for further conditions as new modes of treating disease are discovered, or a more thorough acquaintance is obtained of the remedial properties of vegetable and mineral substances, or a more accurate knowledge is acquired of the human system and of the agencies by which it is affected.

Dent v. West Virginia, 129 U.S. 114, 122–23, 9 S.Ct. 231, 233, 32 L.Ed. 623, 626 (1889).

. . . We conclude that the legislature, in enacting N.C.G.S. § 90–14(a)(6), reasonably believed that a general risk of endangering the public is *inherent* in *any* practices which fail to conform to the standards of "acceptable and prevailing" medical practice in North Carolina. We further conclude that the legislative intent was to prohibit any practice departing from acceptable and prevailing medical standards without regard to whether the particular practice itself could be shown to endanger the public. Our conclusion is buttressed by the plain language of N.C.G.S. § 90–14(a)(6), which allows the Board to act against *any* departure from acceptable medical practice "irrespective of whether or not a patient is injured thereby." By authorizing the Board to prevent or punish *any* medical practice departing from acceptable and prevailing standards, irrespective of whether a patient is injured thereby, the statute works as a regulation which "tend[s] to secure" the public generally "against the consequences of ignorance and incapacity as well as of deception and fraud," even though it may not immediately have that direct effect in a particular case.

* * *

II.

* * *

Dr. Guess strenuously argues that many countries and at least three states recognize the legitimacy of homeopathy. While some physicians may value the homeopathic system of practice, it seems that others consider homeopathy an outmoded and ineffective system of practice. This conflict, however interesting, simply is irrelevant here in light of the uncontroverted evidence and the Board's findings and conclusion that homeopathy is not currently an "acceptable and prevailing" system of medical practice in North Carolina.

While questions as to the efficacy of homeopathy and whether its practice should be allowed in North Carolina may be open to valid debate among members of the medical profession, the courts are not the proper forums for that debate. The legislature may one day choose to recognize the homeopathic system of treatment, or homeopathy may evolve by proper experimentation and research to the point of being recognized by the medical profession as an acceptable and prevailing form of medical practice in our state; such choices, however, are not for the courts to make.

We stress that we do not intend for our opinion in this case to retard the ongoing research and development of the healing arts in any way. The Board argues, and we agree within our admittedly limited scope of medical knowledge, that preventing the practice of homeopathy will not restrict the development and acceptance of new and beneficial medical practices. Instead, the development and acceptance of such new practices simply must be achieved by "acceptable and prevailing" methods of medical research, experimentation, testing, and approval by the appropriate regulatory or professional bodies.

* * *

Reversed and Remanded.

FRYE, JUSTICE, dissenting.

* * *

... All of the evidence tended to show that Dr. Guess is a highly qualified practicing physician who uses homeopathic medicines as a last resort when allopathic medicines are not successful. He takes 150 credits of continuing medical education approved by the American Medical Association every three years and from fifty to eighty hours of homeopathic continuing medical education each year. The homeopathic medications prescribed by him are listed in the Homeopathic Pharmacopoeia of the United States and are regulated by the United States Federal Food, Drug and Cosmetic Act. The homeopathic approach is often preferred, in Dr. Guess' words, "primarily because of its well documented safety." This is not a case of a quack beguiling the public with snake oil and drums, but a dedicated physician seeking to find new ways to relieve human suffering. The legislature could hardly have intended this practice to be considered "unprofessional conduct" so as to revoke a physician's license in the absence of some evidence of harm or potential harm to the patients or to the public. Nothing in the record before the Board or this Court justifies so broad a sweep in order to secure the public "against the consequences of ignorance and incapacity as well as of deception and fraud." [ ]

* * *

... I do not believe that the General Assembly would require a physician to undergo a possibly lengthy wait for legislative action while it is attending to other matters before allowing him to make non-dangerous, beneficial treatments available to members of the public who knowingly consent. Where there is no showing of danger, I do not believe specific legislative approval is a prerequisite to a physician engaging in a practice, which is by all indications helpful when used wisely.

* * *

Notes and Questions

1. In *Williams*, the court set aside disciplinary sanction where the doctor's practice, though generally rejected, was accepted by a minority of practicing physicians. In *Guess*, the defendant produced evidence that homeopathy is a recognized system of practice in some states, but this did not cause the court to overturn disciplinary sanctions. Can you explain the different results in *Williams* and in *Guess*?

2. After the *Guess* decision, the North Carolina legislature amended the grounds for discipline to limit the section under which Guess was penalized:

> The Board shall not revoke the license of or deny a license to a person solely because of that person's practice of a therapy that is experimental, nontraditional, or that departs from acceptable and prevailing medical practices unless, by competent evidence, the Board can establish that the treatment has a safety risk greater than the prevailing treatment or that the treatment is generally not effective.

How does this amendment alter what is ordinarily required of a professional licensure board in justifying its decisions in specific cases? Does a board usually have to justify its rulemaking with empirical evidence? Does safety risk include an assessment of effectiveness? Many alternative approaches to health care are not founded on empirical scientifically-based research on effectiveness and safety. Under this amendment, does the board have to commission such research if it wants to exclude the practice?

3. The interest in alternative and complementary medicine and nonconforming practices, whether new and innovative or traditional but no longer mainstream, has increased dramatically. See e.g., David M. Eisenberg, Unconventional Medicine in the United States, 328 N.E.J.M. 246 (1993); A.L. Berrey and K.R. White, Search for the New Medicine, 100 American Journal of Nursing 45 (2000). The National Institutes of Health has established an Office of Alternative Medicine to evaluate nonconforming practices using the empirical methodology applied to allopathic medicine. This has been a controversial effort. See e.g., Clinical Practice Guidelines in Complementary and Alternative Medicine: An Analysis of Opportunities and Obstacles, 6 Archives of Family Medicine 149 (1997). For a review of legal and policy issues, see Michael H. Cohen, Complementary and Alternative Medicine: Legal Boundaries and Regulatory Perspectives (1998), suggesting that occupational licensure for practitioners of alternative and complementary medicine would encourage such practices while providing oversight for quality; Julie Stone and Joan Matthews, Complementary Medicine and the Law (1996), arguing that while some alternative or complementary practices have a technological base and are subject to the same type of verification as allopathic medicine, other practices are not amenable to such testing and, therefore, conventional quality-control regulation would be inadequate. See also, Kathleen M. Boozang, Western Medicine Opens the Door to Alternative Medicine, 24 Am.J.Law & Med. 185 (1998).

Some states allow only licensed M.D.s to provide complementary or alternative interventions such as homeopathy or acupuncture. Is this a satisfactory resolution of the interests at stake? Aside from licensure, what other barriers exist in access to nonconventional therapies?

III. UNLICENSED PROVIDERS

The state medical board generally has the primary responsibility for enforcing the prohibition against the unauthorized practice of medicine by unlicensed providers. This prohibition is enforced by criminal sanctions against the unlicensed practitioner and license revocation against any physician who aids and abets the unlicensed practitioner. The state medical practice acts define the practice of medicine quite broadly and indeterminately and prohibit anyone but licensed physicians and other licensed health care professionals, practicing within the bounds of their own licensure, from practicing medicine. For example, the Indiana statute prohibits an unlicensed person from engaging in:

> the diagnosis, treatment, correction or prevention of any disease, ailment, defect, injury, infirmity, deformity, pain or other condition of human beings, or the suggestion, recommendation or prescription or administration of any form of treatment, without limitation, or the performing of any kind of surgical operation upon a human being, including tattooing . . ., or the penetration of the skin or body orifice by any means, for the intended palliation, relief, cure or prevention of any physical, mental or functional ailment or defect of any person.

Would this prohibition extend to services offered by a health club, including fitness assessment and advice on nutrition and exercise designed to respond to specific areas needing improvement? Would it extend to the recommendation of over-the-counter medications for particular aches, pains or illnesses by a cashier at a pharmacy? What is the impact of a very broadly drawn statutory definition of the practice of medicine on patient choice? On access? On cost? On competition? On quality? On the authority of the agency itself to control services provided by non-physicians? For a case interpreting this statute, see Stetina v. State ex rel. Medical Licensing Board of Indiana, 513 N.E.2d 1234 (Ind.App.1987).

STATE BOARD OF NURSING AND STATE BOARD OF HEALING ARTS v. RUEBKE

Supreme Court of Kansas, 1996.
259 Kan. 599, 913 P.2d 142.

Larson, Justice:

The State Board of Healing Arts (Healing Arts) and the State Board of Nursing (Nursing) appeal the trial court's denial of a temporary injunction by which the Boards had sought to stop E. Michelle Ruebke, a practicing lay midwife, from continuing her alleged practice of medicine and nursing.

* * *

Factual Background

* * *

The hearing on the temporary injunction revealed that Ruebke acts as a lay midwife comprehensively assisting pregnant women with prenatal care, delivery, and post-partum care. She is president of the Kansas Midwives Association and follows its promulgated standards, which include a risk screening assessment based upon family medical history; establishing prenatal care plans, including monthly visitations; examinations and assistance in birth; and post-partum care. She works with supervising physicians who are made aware of her mode of practice and who are available for consultation and perform many of the medical tests incident to pregnancy.

* * *

Dr. Debra L. Messamore, an obstetrician/gynecologist, testified she had reviewed the Kansas Midwives Association standards of care and opined those standards were similar to the assessments incident to her practice as an OB/GYN. Dr. Messamore concluded that in her judgment the prenatal assessments made by Ruebke were obstetrical diagnoses.

Dr. Messamore testified that the prescriptions Ruebke has women obtain from their physicians are used in obstetrics to produce uterine contractions. She further testified the Kansas Midwives Association standard of care relating to post-delivery conditions of the mother and baby involved obstetrical judgments. She reviewed the birth records of [one] birth and testified that obstetrical or medical judgments were reflected. [She admitted] that many procedures at issue could be performed by a nurse rather than a physician.... She also stated her opinion that so defined obstetrics as a branch of medicine or surgery.

Ginger Breedlove, a Kansas certified advanced registered nurse practitioner and nurse-midwife, testified on behalf of Nursing. She reviewed the records [of two births] and testified nursing functions were involved. She admitted she could not tell from the records who had engaged in certain practices and that taking notes, giving enemas, and administering oxygen is often done by people who are not nurses, although education, experience, and minimum competency are required.

... The court held that provisions of both acts were unconstitutionally vague, Ruebke's midwifery practices did not and were not intended to come within the healing arts act or the nursing act, and her activities fell within exceptions to the two acts even if the acts did apply and were constitutional.

The factual findings, highly summarized, were that Ruebke had not been shown to hold herself out as anything other than a lay midwife; has routinely used and consulted with supervising physicians; was not shown to administer any prescription drugs; was not shown to do any suturing or episiotomies, make cervical or vaginal lacerations, or diagnose blood type; and had engaged only in activities routinely and properly done by people who are not physicians.

Regulatory History of Midwifery

One of the specific statutory provisions we deal with, K.S.A. 65–2802(a), defines the healing arts as follows:

> The healing arts include any system, treatment, operation, diagnosis, prescription, or practice for the ascertainment, cure, relief, palliation, adjustment, or correction of any human disease, ailment, deformity, or injury, and includes specifically but not by way of limitation the practice of medicine and surgery; the practice of osteopathic medicine and surgery; and the practice of chiropractic.

K.S.A. 65–2869 specifically provides that for the purpose of the healing arts act, the following persons shall be deemed to be engaged in the practice of medicine and surgery:

> (a) Persons who publicly profess to be physicians or surgeons, or publicly profess to assume the duties incident to the practice of medicine or surgery or any of their branches.
>
> (b) Persons who prescribe, recommend or furnish medicine or drugs, or perform any surgical operation of whatever nature by the use of any surgical instrument, procedure, equipment or mechanical device for the diagnosis, cure or relief of any wounds, fractures, bodily injury, infirmity,

disease, physical or mental illness or psychological disorder, of human beings.

* * *

In describing the history of lay midwifery, a law review comment, Choice in Childbirth: Parents, Lay Midwives, and Statutory Regulation, 30 St. Louis U.L.J. 985, 989–90 (1986), recounts that midwifery belonged to women from Biblical times through the Middle Ages. However, subsequent to the Middle Ages, women healers were often barred from universities and precluded from obtaining medical training or degrees. With the rise of barber-surgeon guilds, women were banned from using surgical instruments.

When midwives immigrated to America, they occupied positions of great prestige. Some communities licensed midwives and others did not. This continued until the end of the 19th century. In the 19th and 20th centuries, medical practice became more standardized. Economically and socially well-placed doctors pressed for more restrictive licensing laws and for penalties against those who violated them. The law review comment suggests that licensure was a market control device; midwives were depriving new obstetricians of the opportunity for training, and elimination of midwifery would allow the science of obstetrics to grow into a mature medical specialty.

There is a notable absence of anything in the history of Kansas healing arts regulation illustrating any attempt to specifically target midwives. In 1870, the Kansas Legislature adopted its first restriction on the practice of medicine . . .

[T]here can be little doubt that in 1870 Kansas, particularly in rural areas, there were not enough educated physicians available to deliver all of the children born in the state. In fact, until 1910 approximately 50 percent of births in this country were midwife assisted. [ ]

* * *

Although obstetricians held themselves out as a medical specialty in the United States as early as 1868, midwives were not seen as engaged in the practice of obstetrics, nor was obstetrics universally viewed as being a branch of medicine. In 1901, North Carolina recognized obstetricians as engaged in the practice of medicine but women midwives, as a separate discipline, were exempted from the licensure act. [ ] . . .

Although many states in the early 1900's passed laws relating to midwifery, Kansas has never expressly addressed the legality of the practice. In 1915 [ ] this court implied that a woman with considerable midwife experience was qualified to testify as an expert witness in a malpractice case against an osteopath for allegedly negligently delivering the plaintiff's child.

* * *

The 1978 Kansas Legislature created a new classification of nurses, Advanced Registered Nurse Practitioner (ARNP). [ ] One classification of ARNP is certified nurse midwives. Although the regulations permitting the practice of certified nurse midwives might be argued to show additional legislative intent to prohibit the practice of lay midwives, this argument has been rejected elsewhere. [ ]

In 1978, Kansas Attorney General opinion No. 78–164 suggested that the practice of midwifery is a violation of the healing arts act.... Although potentially persuasive, such an opinion is not binding on us.

Most probably in response to the 1978 Attorney General opinion, a 1978 legislative interim committee undertook a study of a proposal to recognize and regulate the practice of lay midwifery. However, the committee reached no conclusion.

* * *

A 1986 review of the laws of every state found that lay midwifery was specifically statutorily permitted, subject to licensing or regulation, in 25 jurisdictions. Twelve states, including Kansas, had no legislation governing or prohibiting lay midwifery directly or by direct implication. Several states recognized both lay and nurse midwives. Some issued new licensing only for nurse midwives, while others regulated and recognized both, often as separate professions, subject to separate standards and restrictions. [ ]

* * *

In April 1993, the Board of Healing Arts released Policy Statement No. 93–02, in which the Board stated it reaffirmed its previous position of August 18, 1984, that

> [m]idwifery is the practice of medicine and surgery and any practice thereof by individuals not regulated by the Kansas State Board of Nursing or under the supervision of or by order of or referral from a licensed medical or osteopathic doctor constitutes the unlicensed practice of medicine and surgery.

* * *

This historical background brings us to the question of whether the healing arts act is unconstitutionally vague. ...

Scope of Review

* * *

[A] statute "is vague and violates due process if it prohibits conduct in terms so vague that a person of common intelligence cannot understand what conduct is prohibited, and it fails to adequately guard against arbitrary and discriminatory enforcement." [ ] A statute which requires specific intent is more likely to withstand a vagueness challenge than one, like that here, which imposes strict liability. [ ]

* * *

We have held that the interpretation of a statute given by an administrative agency within its area of expertise is entitled to deference, although final construction of a statute always rests with courts. [ ] ...

We do, of course, attempt wherever possible to construe a statute as constitutional [ ]....

* * *

The definition of healing arts uses terms that have an ordinary, definite, and ascertainable meaning. The trial court's conclusion that "disease, ailment, deformity or injury" are not commonly used words with settled meanings cannot be justified.

* * *

. . . Although we hold the act not to be unconstitutionally vague, we also hold the definitional provisions do not cover midwifery. In their ordinary usage the terms in K.S.A. 65–2802(a) used to define healing arts clearly and unequivocally focus exclusively on pathologies (i.e., diseases) and abnormal human conditions (i.e., ailments, deformities, or injuries). Pregnancy and childbirth are neither pathologies nor abnormalities.

* * *

Healing Arts argues that the "practice of medicine" includes the practice of obstetrics. It reasons, in turn, that obstetrics includes the practices traditionally performed by midwives. From this, it concludes midwifery is the practice of medicine.

However, equating midwifery with obstetrics, and thus with the practice of medicine, ignores the historical reality, discussed above, that midwives and obstetricians coexisted for many years quite separately. From the time of our statehood, the relationship between obstetricians and midwives changed from that of harmonious coexistence, cooperation, and collaboration, to open market competition and hostility. [ ]

* * *

To even the most casual observer of the history of assistance to childbirth, it is clear that over the course of this century the medical profession has extended its reach so deeply into the area of birthing as to almost completely occupy the field. The introduction of medical advances to the childbirth process drew women to physicians to assist during the birth of their children. Yet, this widespread preference for physicians as birth attendants hardly mandates the conclusion that only physicians may assist with births.

. . . The fact that a person with medical training provides services in competition with someone with no medical degree does not transform the latter's practices into the practice of medicine.

* * *

Although we hold the practice of midwifery is not itself the practice of the healing arts under our statutory scheme, our conclusions should not be interpreted to mean that a midwife may engage in any activity whatsoever with regard to a pregnant woman merely by virtue of her pregnancy. . . .

. . . However, we need not decide the precise boundaries of what a midwife may do without engaging in the practice of the healing arts because, in the case before us, Ruebke was found to have worked under the supervision of physicians who were familiar with her practices and authorized her actions. Any of Ruebke's actions that were established at trial, which might otherwise have been the practice of the healing arts, were exempt from the healing arts act because she had worked under the supervision of such physicians.

K.S.A. 65–2872 exempts certain activities from the licensure requirements of the healing arts act. In relevant part it provides:

The practice of the healing arts shall not be construed to include the following persons:

(g) Persons whose professional services are performed under the supervision or by order of or referral from a practitioner who is licensed under this act.

* * *

In light of the uncontested factual findings of the trial court, which were supported by competent evidence in the record, we agree with the trial court that the exception to the healing arts act recognized by K.S.A. 65–2872(g) applies to any of Ruebke's midwifery activities which might otherwise be considered the practice of the healing arts under K.S.A. 65–2802(a) and K.S.A. 65–2869.

* * *

As we have held, the legislature has never specifically acted with the intent to restrict or regulate the traditional practice of lay midwifery. Nevertheless, Nursing argues such birth assistants must be licensed nurses before they may render aid to pregnant women. In oral argument, Nursing conceded much of its argument would be muted were we to hold, as we do above, that the practice of midwifery is not the practice of the healing arts and thus not part of a medical regimen.

* * *

The practice of nursing is defined [in the Kansas nurse practice act] by reference to the practitioner's substantial specialized knowledge in areas of the biological, physical, and behavioral sciences and educational preparation within the field of the healing arts. Ruebke claims no specialized scientific knowledge, but rather readily admits she has no formal education beyond high school. Her assistance is valued not because it is the application of a firm and rarified grasp of scientific theory, but because, like generations of midwives before, she has practical experience assisting in childbirth.

Moreover, "nursing" deals with "persons who are experiencing changes in the normal health processes." As these words are commonly understood, pregnancy and childbirth do not constitute changes in the normal health process, but the continuation of it.

. . . As we have held, the practice of lay midwifery has, throughout the history of the regulation of nursing, been separate and distinct from the practice of the healing arts, to which nursing is so closely joined. While we have no doubt of the legislature's power to place lay midwifery under the authority of the State Board of Nursing, the legislature has not done so.

We find no legislative intent manifested in the language of the nursing act clearly illustrating the purpose of including the historically separate practice of midwifery within the practice of nursing. [ ] Assistance in childbirth rendered by one whose practical experience with birthing provides comfort to the mother is not nursing under the nursing act, such that licensure is required.

Affirmed in part and reversed in part.

Notes and Questions

1. Courts have adopted many approaches to analyzing whether services provided in assistance at childbirth constitute the unauthorized practice of medicine. Some have examined individual actions that may be performed during childbirth. For example, in Leigh v. Board of Registration in Nursing, 395 Mass. 670, 481 N.E.2d 1347 (Mass. 1985), the court distinguished "ordinary assistance in the normal cases of childbirth" from that in which a lay midwife used "obstetrical instruments" and "printed prescriptions or formulas," and concluded that the former does not constitute the practice of medicine while the latter does. In People v. Jihan, 127 Ill.2d 379, 130 Ill.Dec. 422, 537 N.E.2d 751 (Ill. 1989), the court distinguished "assisting" at birth from "delivering" the child. Does dividing childbirth assistance into discrete activities reflect health and safety concerns?

2. In Hunter v. State, 110 Md.App. 144, 676 A.2d 968 (1996), the court concluded that the legislative history of provisions for certification of nurse midwives (similar to the Kansas provisions cited in *Ruebke*) required the conclusion that the statute permitted only registered nurses certified by the board as nurse midwives to provide midwifery services. In Leggett v. Tennessee Board of Nursing, 612 S.W.2d 476 (Tenn.App.1980), the court considered a case in which a nurse violating the nursing board's prohibition against assistance at home births by nurse midwives claimed to be acting as a lay midwife instead. The court concluded that the exemption for lay midwifery in the medical practice act allowed the nurse to claim that she was acting as a lay midwife rather than as a nurse midwife. See also, Marion OB/GYN v. State Med. Bd., 137 Ohio App.3d 522, 739 N.E.2d 15 (Ohio App. 2000), in which the court held that delivering infants was beyond the scope of practice allowed a physician assistant (who, though not a nurse, apparently had been certified by the American College of Nurse Midwives) although state law allowed licensed nurses to practice midwifery.

3. Should the Kansas Supreme Court have analyzed research on the quality and safety of services provided by nurse midwives as compared to direct-entry or lay midwives? The Kansas provision on certified nurse midwives describes substantial educational requirements for the provision of nurse midwife services. The court concludes, however, that formal education is unnecessary and that practical experience can be valued as highly. Given the opportunity to amend its statute, should the legislature provide for minimal educational requirements for persons assisting in childbirth? Should that education adopt an obstetrical model or a midwifery model for childbirth? Should it require certification as a nurse midwife? See Colo. § 12–37–101, as amended in 1996 for regulation of lay-midwives. See, Michael H. Cohen, A Fixed Star in Health Care Reform: The Emerging Paradigm of Holistic Healing, 27 Ariz. St. L.J. 79 (1995).

4. Part of the issue often arising in the legal status of lay midwives is access to home births. See Leggett v. Tennessee Board of Nursing, 612 S.W.2d 476 (Tenn.App.1980); Leigh v. Board. of Registration in Nursing, 395 Mass. 670, 481 N.E.2d 1347 (Mass. 1985). See also, Lori B. Andrews, The Shadow Health Care System: Regulation of Alternative Health Care Providers, 32 Hous. L. Rev. 1273 (1996). One researcher has observed:

> Home births evoke strong emotions among health professionals, and attitudes are rarely based on research data. Proponents argue that home deliveries for women who are at low risk of complications during pregnancy and delivery have perinatal outcomes as good as or better than hospital births. Opponents,

> including the American College of Obstetrics and Gynecology, argue that unexpected complications may arise during any labor, making hospital delivery a safer option for all women. Studies have compared the safety of home and hospital births in Missouri, Tennessee, North Carolina, Kentucky, and Washington State. Neonatal morbidity and mortality did not differ between planned home deliveries and hospital births when care included continuous risk assessment and a qualified birth attendant. However, studies of home births have had methodological problems, which have weakened their findings.... [T]he safety of home birth is not likely to be established by a randomized controlled trial because most women would probably refuse to be randomly allocated a birth place and a large sample size would be required to detect adverse outcomes. Jeanne Raisler, Evidence from US Suggests That Trials Will Not Alter Obstetric Behavior, 312 British Medical Journal 754 (1996).

Some states have enacted statutes concerning the legality and regulation of home births. See e.g., Alaska § 08.65.140; Mont. Code Annot. § 37–27–311 (both providing for mandatory informed consent). Given this state of evidence, how should the state medical or nursing boards assess whether home births should be regulated or prohibited?

5. Should disclosure and consent of the patient be taken into account in prosecutions for the unauthorized practice of medicine? Consider the following "release" which the lay midwife in *People v. Jihan*, cited above, provided to her clients:

> We initiated the relationship with [Jihan] and asked her to be present at the birth of our child as a midwife. We are fully aware that she is not a doctor or a nurse, and has no medical or nursing training, and agree that she is not representing that she can or will perform any tasks, which require such training. We understand that her experiences are limited to having given birth three times herself and having attended a few other births as a lay midwife or as an assistant to a doctor. We further realize that [Jihan] does not have a license as a midwife, and that Illinois does not license midwives. We understand that [Jihan] does not hold herself out to the public as a midwife, but is only agreeing to attend our birth because she feels she could be of help to us.

6. Claims of a constitutional right to choice of provider of health care services consistently fail even when made in the context of the woman's right to privacy in reproductive decision making, the lack of empirical evidence of better outcomes with commonly used obstetrical technology, and the substantial history of conflict between medical and other approaches to childbirth. See, for example, Lange–Kessler v. Department of Educ., 109 F.3d 137 (2d Cir.1997); Hunter v. State, 110 Md.App. 144, 676 A.2d 968 (1996). See also Chris Hafner–Eaton and Laurie K. Pearce, Birth Choices, the Law, and Medicine: Balancing Individual Freedoms and Protection of the Public's Health, 19 J. Health Pol. Pol'y & L. 813 (1994) (including review of state laws on direct-entry midwifery); David M. Smolin, The Jurisprudence of Privacy in a Splintered Supreme Court, 75 Marq. L. Rev. 975 (1992), with a substantial section on choices in childbirth; Lisa C. Ikemoto, The Code of Perfect Pregnancy: At the Intersection of The Ideology of Motherhood, the Practice of Defaulting to Science, and the Interventionist Mindset of Law, 53 Ohio State L. Rev. 1205 (1992).

7. Prosecution for the unauthorized practice of medicine or nursing does not require proof that the defendant actually knew that he or she was violating the

statute. That is why the *Ruebke* court refers to the statute as a strict liability statute. *Ruebke* is in the overwhelming majority in refusing to declare the medical practice act void for vagueness. See, e.g., Weyandt v. State, 35 S.W.3d 144 (Tex.App.2000); State v. Saunders, 542 N.W.2d 67 (Minn.App.1996). But see, Miller v. Medical Assoc. of Georgia, 262 Ga. 605, 423 S.E.2d 664 (Ga. 1992).

8. The court in *Ruebke* ultimately decides that where the actions of the lay midwife fell within the practice of medicine there was no violation of the statute because her actions would then fall within the statutory exception for delegated medical services performed under the supervision of a licensed physician. But see, People v. Bickham, 250 Ill.App.3d 141, 190 Ill.Dec. 217, 621 N.E.2d 86 (Ill.App. 1993), rejecting the argument by an unlicensed person who performed pelvic examinations under the direction of a physician that this activity was not the authorized practice of medicine since the exams could be conducted by physician assistants and nurses. See also, People v. Stults, 291 Ill.App.3d 71, 225 Ill.Dec. 353, 683 N.E.2d 521 (Ill.App.1997), examining practice of medical assistant as unlicensed practice of nursing. As you read the next section of materials, consider what issues the Kansas court's reliance on the authority to delegate might raise.

IV. SCOPE OF PRACTICE REGULATION

Licensed nonphysician health care providers cannot legally practice medicine, but practices that fall within their own licensure (for example, as a nurse or a physician assistant) are not considered the practice of medicine. So, for example, a nurse who is providing services authorized under the nurse practice act would not be practicing medicine while an unlicensed practitioner providing the same services could be guilty of the unauthorized practice of medicine or nursing. If a nurse engages in practices that exceed the services authorized in the nurse practice act, however, that nurse could be guilty of violating the prohibition against the unauthorized practice of medicine. In this way, the medical and nonphysician licensure statutes establish the legal framework for the roles and functions of health care professionals.

Regulation of the authorized scope of practice of the various licensed health care professions faces two inherent difficulties. First, scope of practice regulation focuses on boundary-setting between the professions and attempts to separate medicine from nursing from other health care disciplines. Second, to the extent that scope of practice regulation has depended on the identification of discrete activities that "belong" to each profession, it has applied a notion that reflects neither the overlapping competencies of health care professionals nor the nature of treatment for illness or injury.

At least two studies have advocated an integrated or multidisciplinary approach to primary care in which it would be recognized that different professions perform the same rather than different functions and activities. Linda O. Prager, Licensing Proposals Seek to Overhaul Current System, 38 Am. Med. News 9 (October 2, 1995), reviewing reports by the Pew Health Professions Commission and the Institute of Medicine. See also, Linda H. Aiken and William M. Sage, Staffing National Health Care Reform: A Role for Advanced Practice Nurses, 26 Akron L. Rev. 187 (1992).

How would you change state licensure statutes or licensing board practices to achieve more integrated care and cost-containment while assuring quality of care? How should consumer preferences be accommodated?

SERMCHIEF v. GONZALES

Supreme Court of Missouri, 1983.
660 S.W.2d 683.

WELLIVER, JUDGE.

This is a petition for a declaratory judgment and injunction brought by two nurses and five physicians* employed by the East Missouri Action Agency (Agency) wherein the plaintiff-appellants ask the Court to declare that the practices of the Agency nurses are authorized under the nursing law of this state, § 335.016.8, RSMo 1978 and that such practices do not constitute the unauthorized practice of medicine under Chapter 334 relating to the Missouri State Board of Registration For the Healing Arts (Board). ... The holding below was against appellants who make direct appeal to this Court alleging that the validity of the statutes is involved. Mo. Const. art. V, § 3. ...

I

The facts are simple and for the most part undisputed. The Agency is a federally tax exempt Missouri not-for-profit corporation that maintains offices in Cape Girardeau (main office), Flat River, Ironton, and Fredericktown. The Agency provides medical services to the general public in fields of family planning, obstetrics and gynecology. The services are provided to an area that includes the counties of Bollinger, Cape Girardeau, Perry, St. Francis, Ste. Genevieve, Madison, Iron and Washington. Some thirty-five hundred persons utilized these services during the year prior to trial. The Agency is funded from federal grants, Medicaid reimbursements and patient fees. The programs are directed toward the lower income segment of the population. Similar programs exist both statewide and nationwide.

Appellant nurses Solari and Burgess are duly licensed professional nurses in Missouri pursuant to the provisions of Chapter 335 and are employed by the Agency. Both nurses have had post-graduate special training in the field of obstetrics and gynecology. Appellant physicians are also employees of the Agency and duly licensed to practice medicine (the healing arts) pursuant to Chapter 334. Respondents are the members and the executive secretary of the Missouri State Board of Registration for the Healing Arts (Board) and as such are charged with the enforcement, implementation, and administration of Chapter 334.

The services routinely provided by the nurses and complained of by the Board included, among others, the taking of history; breast and pelvic examinations; laboratory testing of Papanicolaou (PAP) smears, gonorrhea cultures, and blood serology; the providing of and giving of information about oral contraceptives, condoms, and intrauterine devices (IUD); the dispensing of certain designated medications; and counseling services and community education. If the nurses determined the possibility of a condition designated in the standing orders or protocols that would contraindicate the use of contraceptives until further examination and evaluation, they would refer the patients to one of the Agency physicians. No act by either nurse is alleged to

* The physicians are joined for the reason that they are charged with aiding and abetting the unauthorized practice of medicine by the nurses.

have caused injury or damage to any person. All acts by the nurses were done pursuant to written standing orders and protocols signed by appellant physicians. The standing orders and protocols were directed to specifically named nurses and were not identical for all nurses.

The Board threatened to order the appellant nurses and physicians to show cause why the nurses should not be found guilty of the unauthorized practice of medicine and the physicians guilty of aiding and abetting such unauthorized practice. Appellants sought Court relief in this proceeding.

... [T]he trial court described in its memorandum opinion as the ultimate issues for determination:

> A. Does the conduct of plaintiff nurses Solari and Burgess constitute "Professional Nursing" as that term is defined in § 335.016.8, RSMo?
>
> B. If the Court finds and concludes that any act or acts of plaintiff nurses Solari and Burgess does not or do not constitute(s) "professional nursing" and, constitutes the unauthorized practice of medicine under § 334.010, RSMo the Court must then determine if § 334.010, RSMo is unconstitutionally vague and uncertain on its face and, thus, is in violation of the specificity requirements of the Fifth and Fourteenth Amendments to the United States Constitution and of Article 1, § 10 of the Missouri Constitution.

* * *

In our opinion the trial court correctly defined the issues of the case, both of which we deem to be matters of law to be determined by the Court.

* * *

III

The statutes involved are:

> It shall be unlawful for any person not now a registered physician within the meaning of the law to practice medicine or surgery in any of its departments, or to profess to cure and attempt to treat the sick and others afflicted with bodily or mental infirmities, or engage in the practice of midwifery in this state, except as herein provided.

Section 334.010.

> This Chapter does not apply ... *to nurses licensed and lawfully practicing their profession within the provisions of chapter 335, RSMo;* ...

Section 334.155, RSMo Supp.1982 (emphasis added).

> Definitions.—As used in sections 335.011 to 335.096, unless the context clearly requires otherwise, the following words and terms shall have the meanings indicated:

* * *

(8) "Professional nursing" is the performance for compensation of any act which requires substantial specialized education, judgment and skill based

on knowledge and application of principles derived from the biological, physical, social and nursing sciences, including, but not limited to:

(a) Responsibility for the teaching of health care and the prevention of illness to the patient and his family; or

(b) Assessment, nursing diagnosis, nursing care, and counsel of persons who are ill, injured or experiencing alterations in normal health processes; or

(c) The administration of medications and treatments as prescribed by a person licensed in this state to prescribe such medications and treatments; or

(d) The coordination and assistance in the delivery of a plan of health care with all members of the health team; or

(e) The teaching and supervision of other persons in the performance of any of the foregoing.

Section 335.016.8(a)–(e).

At the time of enactment of the Nursing Practice Act of 1975, the following statutes were repealed:

2. A person practices professional nursing who for compensation or personal profit performs, *under the supervision and direction of a practitioner authorized to sign birth and death certificates,* any professional services requiring the application of principles of the biological, physical or social sciences and nursing skills in the care of the sick, in the prevention of disease or in the conservation of health.

Section 335.010.2, RSMo 1969 (emphasis added).

Nothing contained in this chapter shall be construed as conferring any authority on any person to practice medicine or osteopathy or to undertake the treatment or cure of disease.

Section 335.190, RSMo 1969.

The parties on both sides request that in construing these statutes we define and draw that thin and elusive line that separates the practice of medicine and the practice of professional nursing in modern day delivery of health services. A response to this invitation, in our opinion, would result in an avalanche of both medical and nursing malpractice suits alleging infringement of that line and would hinder rather than help with the delivery of health services to the general public. Our consideration will be limited to the narrow question of whether the acts of these nurses were permissible under § 335.016.8 or were prohibited by Chapter 334.

* * *

The legislature substantially revised the law affecting the nursing profession with enactment of the Nursing Practice Act of 1975.* Perhaps the most

* The impetus for the legislation was the ongoing expansion of nursing responsibilities. Several national commissions investigated the causes of and the implications of this phenomenon during the early 1970's. One committee concluded: "Professional nursing * * * is in a period of rapid and progressive change in response to the growth of biomedical knowledge, changes in patterns of demand for health services, and the evolution of professional relationships among nurses, physicians and other health professions." Secretary's Committee to

significant feature of the Act was the redefinition of the term "professional nursing," which appears in § 335.016.8. Even a facile reading of that section reveals a manifest legislative desire to expand the scope of authorized nursing practices. Every witness at trial testified that the new definition of professional nursing is a broader definition than that in the former statute. A comparison with the prior definition vividly demonstrates this fact. Most apparent is the elimination of the requirement that a physician directly supervise nursing functions. Equally significant is the legislature's formulation of an open-ended definition of professional nursing. The earlier statute limited nursing practice to "services ... in the care of the sick, in the prevention of disease or in the conservation of health." § 335.010.2, RSMo 1969. The 1975 Act not only describes a much broader spectrum of nursing functions, it qualifies this description with the phrase "including, but not limited to." We believe this phrase evidences an intent to avoid statutory constraints on the evolution of new functions for nurses delivering [sic] health services. Under § 335.016.8, a nurse may be permitted to assume responsibilities heretofore not considered to be within the field of professional nursing so long as those responsibilities are consistent with her or his "specialized education, judgment and skill based on knowledge and application of principles derived from the biological, physical, social and nursing sciences." § 335.016.8.

The acts of the nurses herein clearly fall within this legislative standard. All acts were performed pursuant to standing orders and protocols approved by physicians. Physician prepared standing orders and protocols for nurses and other paramedical personnel were so well established and accepted at the time of the adoption of the statute that the legislature could not have been unaware of the use of such practices. We see nothing in the statute purporting to limit or restrict their continued use.

Respondents made no challenge of the nurses' level of training or the degree of their skill. They challenge only the legal right of the nurses to undertake these acts. We believe the acts of the nurses are precisely the types of acts the legislature contemplated when it granted nurses the right to make assessments and nursing diagnoses. There can be no question that a nurse undertakes only a nursing diagnosis, as opposed to a medical diagnosis, when she or he finds or fails to find symptoms described by physicians in standing orders and protocols for the purpose of administering courses of treatment prescribed by the physician in such orders and protocols.

The Court believes that it is significant that while at least forty states have modernized and expanded their nursing practice laws during the past fifteen years neither counsel nor the Court have discovered any case challenging nurses' authority to act as the nurses herein acted.

Study Extended Roles for Nurses, Dep't. of Health, Education and Welfare, Pub. No. (HSM) 73–2037, "Extending the Scope of Nursing Practice: A Report of the Secretary's Committee to Study Extended Roles for Nurses" 8 (1971). *See also* National Comm'n for the Study of Nursing and Nursing Education, An Abstract for Action (1970); National Comm'n for the Study of Nursing and Nursing Education, From Abstract Into Action (1973). The broadening of nursing roles necessitated altering existing nursing practice laws to reflect the changes in a nurse's professional duties. At the time the Missouri legislature acted, thirty states had amended their laws regulating the nursing profession. *See* Comment, "Interpreting Missouri's Nursing Practice Act," 26 St. Louis U.L.J. 931, 931 n. 1 (1982). Forty states currently have broadened nursing practice statutes similar to § 335.016.8.

The broadening of the field of practice of the nursing profession authorized by the legislature and here recognized by the Court carries with it the profession's responsibility for continuing high educational standards and the individual nurse's responsibility to conduct herself or himself in a professional manner. The hallmark of the professional is knowing the limits of one's professional knowledge. The nurse, either upon reaching the limit of her or his knowledge or upon reaching the limits prescribed for the nurse by the physician's standing orders and protocols, should refer the patient to the physician. There is no evidence that the assessments and diagnoses made by the nurses in this case exceeded such limits.

* * *

Having found that the nurses' acts were authorized by § 335.016.8, it follows that such acts do not constitute the unlawful practice of medicine for the reason that § 334.155 makes the provisions of Chapter 334 inapplicable "to nurses licensed and lawfully practicing their profession within the provisions of Chapter 335 RSMo."

This cause is reversed and remanded with instructions to enter judgment consistent with this opinion.

Notes and Questions

1. The nurse practice act in *Sermchief* contains an open-ended definition of the practice of nursing. Who has the authority to define the authorized practice of nursing under this type of definition? Why did plaintiffs file their action against the Board of Healing Arts (the board of medicine)? If the board of nursing had issued regulations embracing the plaintiffs' practice within the authorized practice of nursing, under what standard would the court review such regulations if challenged? Would the regulation of the board of nursing prevent the board of medicine from proceeding against the nurses? See e.g., Oklahoma Bd. of Med. Licensure & Supervision v. Oklahoma Bd. of Examiners in Optometry, 893 P.2d 498 (Okla.1995), allowing medical board to challenge regulations of optometry board; Washington State Nurses Ass'n v. Board of Medical Examiners, 93 Wash.2d 117, 605 P.2d 1269 (1980), challenging medical board rules expanding practice for physician assistants; Ohio Nurses Association, Inc. v. State Board of Nursing, 44 Ohio St.3d 73, 540 N.E.2d 1354 (Ohio 1989), concerning board of nursing rules expanding practice for licensed practical nurses.

2. Why did the *Sermchief* plaintiffs seek a declaratory judgment action if they had not been charged with violating the statute? See also, Group Health Plan, Inc. v. State Bd. of Registration for the Healing Arts, 787 S.W.2d 745 (Mo.App.1990), discussing the appropriateness of a declaratory judgment action in similar circumstances. See also, Lori B. Andrews, The Shadow Health Care System: Regulation of Alternative Health Care Providers, 32 Hous. L. Rev. 1273 (1996), on this point and for a comprehensive analysis of the legal issues relating to nonphysician providers.

3. The authority to prescribe medication has been a major issue in debates over the appropriate scope of practice of nurses and physician assistants. See e.g., Mary Beck, Improving America's Health Care: Authorizing Independent Prescriptive Privileges for Advanced Practice Nurses, 29 U.S.F.L. Rev. 951 (1995); Phyllis Coleman and Ronald A. Shellow, Extending Physician's Standard of Care to Non–Physician Prescribers: The Rx for Protecting Patients, 35 Idaho L. Rev. 37 (1998).

4. Physician assistants and nurses have assumed different professional identities. Physician assistants are educated in a medical model of care and view themselves as practicing medicine through physician delegation of tasks and under the supervision of physicians. In nursing, nurse practitioners or advanced practice nurses (including nurse midwives, nurse anesthetists and specialist nurse practitioners) view themselves as operating from a nursing model of health care and acting as independent practitioners who collaborate with physicians. The relationship described in *Sermchief* illustrates a collaborative practice. Currently, organized medicine asserts that both physician assistants and nurse practitioners must be supervised by physicians, a position accepted by the American Academy of Physician Assistants, but rejected by the American Nurses Association.

What is at issue in the controversy over whether the nurse practitioner is required to practice under a doctor's supervision or in collaboration with a doctor or even more independently? Will it have an impact on the location of the nurse's practice? On control of the practice? On nurses' ability to charge insurers directly for services provided?

Some advanced practice nursing statutes provide that the nurse practitioner practice under the supervision of a physician. See e.g., Cal. Bus & Prof Code § 2746.5 (certificate authorizes nurse-midwife to practice nurse-midwifery "under the supervision of a licensed physician and surgeon who has current practice or training in obstetrics"); Cal. Bus & Prof Code § 2836.1(d) (requiring physician supervision for the furnishing of drugs or devices by nurse practitioner). Others recognize advanced practice nursing in collaboration with licensed physicians. See e.g., Mo. V.A.M.S. § 334.104 (authorizing collaborative practice arrangements in the form of written agreements, protocols or standing orders, but describing the prescriptive authority of the nurse practitioner as delegated). Some describe the advanced nursing practice without reference to the participation of a supervisory or collaborative physician. See e.g., Md. Health Occup. § 8–601 (recognizing nurse midwives).

5. Some state nursing practice statutes specifically recognize advanced practice nurses or nurse practitioners. Which is preferable: explicit statutory recognition of advanced practice nurses or an open-ended nursing practice act as in *Sermchief*? The nurse practitioner statutes typically require that the nurse have completed more advanced education and training than is required for licensure as a registered nurse. In the absence of statutory requirements, how might the legal standard for adequate education and skills be established?

6. Physician assistants first practiced under delegation exceptions traditionally included in medical practice acts. Delegation exceptions in medical practice acts tend to be quite broad as you saw in *Ruebke*. See Jacobs v. United States, 436 A.2d 1286 (D.C.App.1981). *Jacobs* involved the appropriate degree of supervision required for the practice of a physician assistant under the D.C. medical practice act and specifically the use of pre-signed prescription pads by the PA. The D.C. statute exempted "the accepted use of qualified paramedical personnel" from the prohibition against unauthorized medical practice. When is delegation appropriate and when is supervision adequate in the absence of more specific statutory requirements? Two experts testified in *Jacobs* on the issue of the pre-signed prescriptions. One testified that use of pre-signed prescriptions was not an accepted use and that the doctor must be present in the same building while the PA treated patients and must approve any prescription in advance or at least review the prescription and the record within 24 hours. Another expert testified that the use of pre-signed pads was a common practice and that there was no

standard governing the appropriate time for review, though accepted practice required review of PA prescriptions within 48 to 72 hours. Are accepted use and common practice the same thing? Does uncertainty as to questions of appropriate delegation and supervision encourage or discourage the use of physician assistants? Would more specific requirements hinder or foster the growth of the scope of practice of PAs?

7. The states vary in the standards and methods they use to assure that delegation to physician assistants is appropriate and supervision is adequate. Some states take an individualized approach and require the physician assistant or supervising physician to submit particular details about the specific position for review by an agency. See e.g., Md. Health Occup. § 15–302 (requiring submission of specific "job description" for approval by the board). Some limit the number of physician assistants a doctor may supervise. See e.g., Ohio Rev. Code § 4730.21. Other states simply define "supervision," with great variations. See e.g., Mo. V.A.M.S. § 334.735(10), defining supervision as "control exercised over a physician assistant working within the same office facility of the supervising physician except a physician assistant may make follow-up patient examinations in hospitals, nursing homes and correctional facilities, each such examination being reviewed, approved and signed by the supervising physician." Some provide for specific requirements for prescriptive authority. See e.g., Cal. Bus. & Prof. Code § 3502.1 (governing "transmittal" of prescriptions).

8. Should medical boards bear the burden of proving that the practice of the nonphysician-licensed provider presents a greater risk of harm than does the practice of the licensed medical doctor? Should reductions in the cost of health care be considered as well? See Barbara J. Safriet, Health Care Dollars and Regulatory Sense: The Role of Advanced Practice Nursing, 9 Yale J. on Reg. 417 (1992), for reviews of the literature on comparative quality. See also, Jerry Cromwell, Barriers to Achieving a Cost–Effective Workforce Mix: Lessons from Anesthesiology, 24 J. Health Politics, Policy and Law 1331 (1999).

Problem: Physicians, Physician Assistants, and Nurses

Drs. Allison Jones and Emily Johnson have a practice in Jerrold, which is located in south St. Louis County. Both Drs. Jones and Johnson are board-certified internists with a rather broad family practice. They would like to expand their practice to Jackson County, a primarily rural area about seventy miles south of Jerrold. They are especially interested in Tesson, a town of approximately 6,000 that is centrally located among the four or five small towns in the area. They are interested in Tesson because it has a small community hospital and is located close to the interstate highway. They also believe the town is underserved by physicians. There is no pediatrician in Tesson, although there is one thirty miles away. The town has one internist. It has no obstetricians, although Joan Mayo, a certified nurse midwife, has an office in a small town about eighteen miles distant from Tesson.

Ms. Mayo has been providing childbirth, family planning and other women's health services. She has an agreement with an obstetrician in Jerrold through which protocols and standing orders for her practice were established and are maintained. She can consult with this OB by phone at any time, and they make it a practice to meet once a month to discuss Ms. Mayo's patients. Ms. Mayo refers patients who require special services to this OB or to the internist in Tesson. Ms. Mayo has clinical privileges for childbirth services at the community hospital, though her patients must be admitted by the internist. She also has assisted at a few home births, though it is not her custom to do so.

Drs. Jones and Johnson would like to open an office in Tesson and employ a physician assistant and a pediatric nurse practitioner to staff the office full-time. Either Dr. Jones or Dr. Johnson would have office hours at that office once a week. They are also interested in establishing an affiliation with Ms. Mayo because they see room for growth in that area. They hope to serve the needs of Tesson by establishing active obstetrical and pediatric practices.

They have a physician assistant in their office in Jerrold. The PA is not certified, but they have been impressed with her handling of the "routine" patients that come to the office with minor injuries such as cuts and sprains and illnesses such as chicken pox and strep throat. In most cases, the assistant examines the patient, decides on a course of treatment and prescribes medication using pre-signed prescription slips. In more difficult cases, the physician assistant asks for advice from one of the physicians. There is high patient satisfaction with her work. The doctors would like her to provide services in their Tesson office as well.

For their Tesson office, they would like to find a physician assistant with extensive experience in trauma so that the assistant could care for the high incidence of farming and hunting injuries expected in that area. This PA, then, would complement the doctors' own skills as the doctors have had little experience with such injuries.

Drs. Jones and Johnson have come to you for advice concerning their plans. They have many questions, but their first concerns the Board of Healing Arts, which supervises the licensing and discipline of physicians in Allstate, and whether their plans are consistent with the laws regulating practice in Allstate.

Please specify how they might comply with the law while maintaining a "low cost" practice. If for some reason the Board decides to take action against them, what is the likelihood of the physicians' success in challenging the Board's action?

If you were counsel to Ms. Mayo, would you advise her to affiliate with Drs. Jones and Johnson? What advantages and disadvantages might such an affiliation bring? Is her current practice authorized within the Allstate statutes?

In solving this problem, assume that your jurisdiction's: 1) relevant caselaw is identical to *Sermchief* and *Ruebke*; 2) medical practice act includes a delegation exception identical to the Kansas statute quoted in *Ruebke*; 3) has a nurse practice act that provides for a definition of nursing identical to the Missouri statute reproduced in *Sermchief*; and 4) has only the following additional statutory provision:

Allstate Stat. § 2746.5.

> As used in this chapter, the practice of nurse-midwifery constitutes the furthering or undertaking by any certified person, under the supervision of a licensed physician and surgeon who has current practice or training in obstetrics, to assist a woman in childbirth so long as progress meets criteria accepted as normal. All complications shall be referred to a physician immediately. The practice of nurse-midwifery does not include the assisting of childbirth by any artificial, forcible, or mechanical means, nor the performance of any version. As used in this article, "supervision" shall not be construed to require the physical presence of the supervising physician. A nurse-midwife is not authorized to practice medicine and surgery by the provisions of this chapter.

Chapter 3

QUALITY CONTROL REGULATION OF HEALTH CARE INSTITUTIONS

I. INTRODUCTION

Although hospitals, nursing homes and other health care facilities do not themselves practice medicine, the quality of the institution itself can have a very significant impact on the quality of care. The range of institutional quality issues is very broad. It extends from building design, maintenance and sanitation, fiscal and managerial soundness, through the selection, training and monitoring of the individuals directly providing care.

A major challenge for quality control regulation in health care is the vast and now rapidly changing structure of health care organizations. To illustrate the range of health care institutions regulated in a typical state, consider the Illinois Public Health and Safety Code, which includes specific regulatory requirements for the following institutional health care providers, as defined by the statute:

> Hospitals: any institution ... devoted primarily to the maintenance and operation of facilities for the diagnosis and treatment or care of ... persons admitted for overnight stay or longer in order to obtain medical ... care of illness, disease, injury, infirmity, or deformity.
>
> Long-term care facility: a private home, institution ... or any other place, ... which provides ... personal care, sheltered care or nursing for 3 or more persons ... not includ[ing] ... a hospital.
>
> Home health agency: a public agency or private organization that provides skilled nursing services [in a patient's home] and at least one other home health service.
>
> Hospice: a coordinated program of home and inpatient care providing ... palliative and supportive medical, health and other services to terminally ill patients and their families.
>
> Ambulatory surgical treatment center: any institution [or place located within an institution, subject to some restrictions] ... devoted primarily to the maintenance and operation of facilities for the performance of surgical procedures.

What health care organizations are missing from this list? Are there freestanding emergicenters, assisted living centers, rehabilitation institutes, birthing centers, mobile mammogram services, infusion centers, chemical dependency care units, sub-acute facilities or other health care facilities in your area? Are these organizations covered by the Illinois statute? Does a home care agency that provides bathing and other personal services but not nursing or other skilled therapy fit within the statutory definition? What is the reach of the statutory definition of "nursing home"? Does it cover a retirement center that provides apartments, dining facilities, supportive household services, transportation, and space for doctors and nurses to see patients? Would such an institution have to meet the statutory standards for nursing homes? If a "hospital" provides services in a person's home after discharge, is it required to get a license as a "home health agency"?

A state agency may regulate only under its statutory authority; and if there is no legislative authorization for the regulation of a specific institution, the state may not reach that entity. Consider the following case.

MAUCERI v. CHASSIN

Supreme Court, Albany County, New York, 1993.
156 Misc.2d 802, 594 N.Y.S.2d 605.

* * *

Since 1979, the plaintiff has operated a business out of her home providing patients and their families with the names of home health aides. It is up to the patient or the family to contact the home health aide and work out the specific pay scale, hours, and duties. The plaintiff receives compensation directly from the patient or the patient's family at a flat rate of 80 cents per hour for each hour the home health aide works for the client. Plaintiff does not conduct any investigation as to the qualifications of the aides, nor does she create a care plan for the patient, or maintain medical records. During 1990, the Department of Health received a complaint that the plaintiff was referring home health aides without being licensed as a home care services agency. Plaintiff took the position that the services that she rendered were not encompassed by the statutory definition of home care services agency. The defendants disagree.

* * *

If the plaintiff, and other small businesses such as hers, are forced to comply with all of the requirements of article 36 of the Public Health Law, and the regulations thereunder, the cost of home health aides to the general public will undoubtedly increase. That is because the overhead expense of the recordkeeping and supervisory duties the plaintiff and others performing similar functions will be required to perform must be passed along in the price she charges. In a time of rising health care costs, that hardly seems a worthy goal of State government. Moreover, to those adherents of free enterprise still operating within this State it is no doubt abhorrent that a patient or his or her family cannot hire an agent to assist in employing a home health aide without that agent being subject to the requirement of having a license from the Department of Health. Be that as it may, the construction given to a statute by the agency charged with implementing it should be upheld if not irrational [ ]. Subdivision 2 of section 3602 of the Public Health Law provides as follows:

"2. 'Home care services agency' means an organization primarily engaged in arranging and/or providing directly or through contract arrangement one or more of the following: Nursing services, home health aide services, and other therapeutic and related services which may include, but shall not be limited to, physical, speech and occupational therapy, nutritional services, medical social services, personal care services, homemaker services, and housekeeper or chore services, which may be of a preventive, therapeutic, rehabilitative, health guidance, and/or supportive nature to persons at home".

Clearly, the plaintiff's business is an organization engaged in arranging for home health aide services. The fact that the plaintiff does not provide or supervise those services does not mean that she is not arranging for them when she provides her clients with a list of home health aides. Since the defendants' interpretation of the statute is not irrational, it will be upheld. That being the case, plaintiff will be enjoined from operating her home health care referral service until such time she has been licensed under article 36....

Notes and Questions

1. If a family simply hired a person to provide home care services, would that person require a license as a "home care agency?" Had plaintiff made any warranties about her own services?

2. What might explain the absence of legislation regulating a particular health care organization or service? Noticeably absent from the list of facilities requiring a license are doctors' offices. Why is that? Why would Illinois define home health agency as it does rather than more broadly? See Steven J. Snyder, Providing Services to Assisted Living Facility Residents Through Home Health Agencies: Meeting the Need in Changing Times, 8 J. Affordable Housing & Community Dev. L. (Winter 1999).

II. REGULATORY SYSTEMS

The materials in this chapter focus primarily on long-term care providers. Long-term care is a critically important and growing portion of our nation's health care sector. Nursing homes are subject to a high degree of public quality control regulation by both federal and state governments, especially as compared to hospitals, home health agencies and other health care organizations. The enforcement of nursing home standards over the past three decades has created an informative case study of the challenges of public quality control regulation.

A. DIFFERENCES AMONG INSTITUTIONS

Nursing homes, home health agencies and hospitals are transforming themselves in response to significant changes in payment systems for health care, to increased competitive pressures and to forces marshaled toward integrating health care providers into seamless systems. Futurists have attempted to predict what the nursing home and the hospital will look like in the next century. See, e.g., Margaret M. Byrne and Carol M. Ashton, Incentives for Vertical Integration in Healthcare: The Effect of Reimbursement Systems, 44 J. Healthcare Management 34 (1999); Jeffrey B. Barber et al.,

Evolution of an Integrated Health System: A Life Cycle Framework, 43 J. Healthcare Management 359 (1998); and Robert E. Toomey, Integrated Healthcare Systems Governance: Prevention of Illness and Care for the Sick and Injured, 25 Health Care Management Review 59 (2000). One thing is clear: some traditional notions of what each entity does have already blurred. For example, nursing homes are treating increasingly sicker patients with increased medical as opposed to custodial or supportive needs; hospitals are dedicating portions of their facilities to longer term, lower intensity care; and home health agencies are responding to individuals who are receiving intense and highly sophisticated medical care in their homes as well as to those who need basic support in functions of daily life. Still, there are significant differences among these institutions.

Part of what makes nursing homes unique in the health care system is their responsibility for the complete and total environment of their residents over a very long time. Their involvement with the daily life of residents almost always includes assistance in bathing and often includes assistance in dressing, continence and eating. Nursing homes provide increasingly intensive health care treatment as well, though nurses, rather than physicians, direct day-to-day patient care. Of course, the term "nursing home" in the U.S. also raises the spectre of widely publicized scandals of poor care and abuse. Although the number of facilities involved in these instances is very small, the public and legislative perception of the industry is affected by this image.

Unlike hospital patients, nursing home residents are chronically rather than acutely ill. The majority of residents of a nursing home typically have resided in the facility for eighteen months, but the average length of stay for persons entering nursing homes is only a few months. Only 11 in 1000 persons 65–74 years of age reside in nursing homes compared to 46 out of 1000 persons 75–84 and 192 out of 1000 persons 85 years of age or older. E. Kramarow et al., Health and Aging Chartbook. Health, United States, 1999 (1999). Nursing home residents typically bear multiple serious, chronic and intractable medical conditions. With the increasing utilization of home care, the average nursing home patient is much sicker than the typical nursing home resident of the 1980s. Joseph L. Bianculli, Developments in Long–Term Care and Assisted Living, 700 PLI/Comm 307 (1994).

The characteristics of the nursing home population have limited their ability to bring suit for harms suffered as a result of poor care or abuse. Causation may be difficult to prove. Physical injuries in very frail elderly persons may be caused either by ordinary touching or by poor care or abuse. Mental impairment makes many nursing home residents poor witnesses. Limited remaining life spans and disabilities minimize legally recognizable damages. They do not suffer lost wages and costs of medical care for injuries for the majority of patients will be covered by Medicaid or Medicare. See Terri D. Keville et al., Developments in Long–Term Care Law and Litigation, 20 Whittier L. Rev. 325 (Winter 1998). There are indications that litigation against nursing homes has increased. Marshall B. Kapp, Malpractice Liability in Long–Term Care: A Changing Environment, 24 Creighton L. Rev. 1235 (1991); David F. Bragg, Dealing with Nursing Home Neglect: The Need for Private Litigation, 39 S. Tex. L. Rev. 1 (December 1997); and J. Thomas Rhodes III & Juliette Castillo, Proving Damages in Nursing Home Cases, 36 Trial 41 (August 2000). For a nursing home case with punitive damages awarded, see First Healthcare Corporation v. Hamilton, 740 So.2d 1189 (Fla.Dist.Ct.App.1999).

While hospitals developed in the United States as charitable institutions often under the direction of religious organizations, nursing homes developed originally as "mom-and-pop" enterprises, in which individuals boarded elderly persons in private homes. After the advent of Medicare and Medicaid, nursing homes attracted substantial activity from investors and were viewed primarily as real estate investments. Most nursing homes are for-profit, while most hospitals are not-for-profit. National for-profit chains own a significant segment of the nursing home industry.

Nursing homes have only recently developed quality assurance or continuous quality improvement systems, which have been long established internally in hospitals. Physicians are still largely absent from these facilities, and professional nurses act primarily as administrators rather than direct care providers. Further, while hospitals have long participated in a substantial private accreditation program of the Joint Commission on Accreditation of Healthcare Organizations, nursing homes do not have an equivalent influential, substantial private accreditation system (although JCAHO and others do offer accreditation for nursing homes).

The demand for nursing home spaces exceeds the supply, especially once source of payment and level of care required are considered. See Margaret M. Flint, Nursing Homes, 75 PLI/NY 721 (June 2000). Proximity to family is a common concern due to the length of stay. The choice of nursing home is still most commonly made during the hospitalization of the elderly person with the natural stress of such a decision within the short timeframe before discharge. The future resident, who is the actual consumer of services, is not usually the person who selects the home. Further, the ability of a resident to leave one facility for another is limited by the physical and mental frailty of many residents.

Over 46.3% of nursing home care in the U.S. was paid for by the Medicaid program in 1998, while about 11.9% was paid for by Medicare. HCFA, Nursing Home Care Expenditures Aggregate and Per Capita Amounts and Percent Distribution, By Source of Funds (visited Nov. 10, 2000) http://www.hcfa.glv/stats/nhe-oact/tables/t7.htm. As you will see in later chapters, Medicaid is the need-based federal-state program for health care for certain groups of poor people. Medicaid is viewed as a welfare program, while Medicare, which is not need-based but which is supported in part by general tax revenue, is generally viewed as an insurance program.

Long-term health care increasingly includes health care provided in the home. Home health care has been one of the fastest growing segments of the health care system. The total amount of expenditures on home health care has grown from around $2 billion per year in 1987 to over $18 billion per year in 1996. Brian E. Davis, The Home Health Care Crisis: Medicare's Fastest Growing Program Legalizes Spiraling Costs, 6 Elder L.J. 215 (1998). However, this spending has decreased dramatically over the past few years. See, e.g., J.P. Bender, 20 South Florida Business Journal 1 (May 26, 2000). This decline has been attributed to changes in Medicare reimbursement rates mandated by Congress in the Balanced Budget Act of 1997.

As much as nursing homes bear a negative image, home health care enjoys a positive image of "home and hearth." Yet, home health care can include high tech medical procedures that were formerly performed only in hospitals as well as basic personal care services. Home health care patients may be rehabilitation patients who are recovering from stroke or other injury, or disabled patients living at home. They may be receiving temporary follow-up care after hospital discharge, infused chemotherapy, long-term medical treatment, or palliative care in the case of terminal illness.

Home environments can be conducive to more independence and better recovery, but they can also be inadequate to the task of care. In fact, there is little known about the quality of home health services because home health by definition takes place in private home settings with providers caring for patients in many different locations, usually one patient at a time.

Home care is often "orchestrated" care, involving providers from several different agencies with the individual providers working variably as independent contractors, subcontractors or employees. The director of care formally may be the patient's physician, but in reality may be a case manager for the insurer. Home health care relies upon care provided by professionals, by paraprofessionals and by family members, with family members frequently performing functions that ordinarily are performed by licensed health care professionals.

Litigation against home health agencies for injuries to patients is relatively uncommon due to several problems including issues relating to the cause of injuries when care has been provided by both professional providers and family members; to multiple providers from a variety of agencies; and to the legal structure of the professional-agency relationship. Private accreditation reached few home health agencies in the 1980s, but has begun to extend its reach.

Notes and Questions

1. Governmental quality control regulation is only one source of quality control in health care. What role does private litigation play? The market? Internal quality assurance or quality improvement mechanisms? Professional ethics and licensure? What are some other public and private quality control mechanisms? The debate over whether government "command and control" regulation or the market is most effective in improving the quality of health care institutions has raged for decades. See, for example, William M. Sage, Regulating Through Information Disclosure Laws and American Health Care, 99 Col.L.Rev. 1701 (1999); Troyen A. Brennan and Donald M. Berwick, New Rules: Regulation, Markets and the Quality of American Health Care (1996).

2. How might the differences among hospitals, nursing homes and home health care affect the relative strength of these quality control instruments? As you read the following materials, consider what demands these institutional differences might make on a specific governmental quality control program. How will standards differ among institutions? Will the focus be the same for nursing home regulation as for hospital regulation, for example? How might the survey or inspection process differ? How would you go about inspecting home health agencies, for example? Would the tenor of the regulatory effort differ among these organizations?

3. See, for a comparison among nursing homes, hospitals and home health care: Rosalie A. Kane, et al., Perspectives on Home Care Quality, 16 Health Care Fin. Rev. 69 (1994); Bruce C. Vladeck and Nancy A. Miller, The Medicare Home Health Initiative, 16 Health Care Financing Review 7 (1994); Robert Morris, The Evolution of the Nursing Home as Intermediary Institution, 19 Generations 57 (1995); Sandra H. Johnson, Quality–Control Regulation of Home Health Care, 26 Hous.L.Rev. 901 (1989). See also John Braithwaite, The Nursing Home Industry, 18 Crime & Justice 11 (1993), for a comparison of nursing home regulation in the U.S. and Australia. See also, Randall Wainoris, Changes in Medicare Resulting from the Balanced Budget Act of 1997 and Their Affect on Home Health Care, 13–WTR NAELA Q 16 (Winter 2000).

B. LICENSURE AND MEDICARE/MEDICAID

In the 1970s, state nursing home licensure laws underwent significant reforms as to standards and sanctions. State licensure programs were central to the public quality control effort through the 1980s. Every state also licenses hospitals, but that system has been less enforcement-oriented and has received less budget support than the nursing home licensure system. In many states, hospital licensure relies extensively on the standards of the Joint Commission on Accreditation of Healthcare Organizations (JCAHO), which is discussed later in this chapter. Most states license some home health agencies, though the licensure system for home health agencies typically is the least developed and receives the least financial support, but this may be changing.

While the states have authority to regulate health care facilities under their police power, the federal government's authority arises primarily from its financing authority—its role as purchaser of health care for Medicare and Medicaid. Only providers who wish to receive payment for services to Medicare or Medicaid beneficiaries must meet federal standards in order to enter into a provider agreement with those programs. The federal government has used its authority to impose requirements that reach beyond Medicare and Medicaid beneficiaries, however. For example, hospitals receiving payment for treatment of Medicare beneficiaries must meet federal requirements in the provision of emergency care services to any person—beneficiary or not—who presents at the facility's emergency department. (See Chapter 11.)

Quality in nursing facilities is regulated at two different levels—state and federal. In order for a nursing home to operate, it must be licensed by the state. A second line of quality assurance comes from the federal government. Certification must be obtained before a nursing facility is allowed to participate and receive federal money from the Medicare and Medicaid programs.

For nursing facilities, Medicare/Medicaid certification is optional while state licensure is mandatory. If a nursing facility cannot or chooses not to participate in Medicare/Medicaid, it will only be subject to state licensure requirements. Realistically, however, most nursing homes cannot survive without Medicare and Medicaid payments. Therefore, most nursing facilities must meet both state licensure and federal Medicare/Medicaid standards.

Until the late 1980s, the federal government largely deferred quality control regulation of nursing homes to the state licensure systems. With federal nursing home reform in 1987 (the Omnibus Budget Reconciliation Act of 1987), however, the federal government undertook a very significant role in that arena. It is still struggling with the appropriate standards and enforcement system for home health care, however; and it still largely defers to private accreditation by JCAHO for Medicare and Medicaid certification of hospitals. See Senator Charles Grassley, The Resurrection of Nursing Home Reform: A Historical Account of the Recent Revival of the Quality of Care Standards for Long–Term Care Facilities Established in the Omnibus Reconciliation Act of 1987, 7 Elder L.J. 267 (1999).

C. THE REGULATORY PROCESS

The regulatory process—whether licensure or Medicare/Medicaid certification—can be divided usefully into three functions: standard setting; survey and inspection; and sanctions.

1. Standard Setting

IN RE THE ESTATE OF MICHAEL PATRICK SMITH v. HECKLER

United States Court of Appeals, Tenth Circuit, 1984.
747 F.2d 583.

McKay, Circuit Judge:

Plaintiffs, seeking relief under 42 U.S.C.A. § 1983, brought this class action on behalf of Medicaid recipients residing in nursing homes in Colorado. They alleged that the Secretary of Health and Human Services (Secretary) has a statutory duty under Title XIX of the Social Security Act, 42 U.S.C.A. §§ 1396–1396n (1982), commonly known as the Medicaid Act, to develop and implement a system of nursing home review and enforcement designed to ensure that Medicaid recipients residing in Medicaid-certified nursing homes actually receive the optimal medical and psychosocial care that they are entitled to under the Act. The plaintiffs contended that the enforcement system developed by the Secretary is "facility-oriented," not "patient-oriented" and thereby fails to meet the statutory mandate. The district court found that although a patient care or "patient-oriented" management system is feasible, the Secretary does not have a duty to introduce and require the use of such a system. *In re Estate of Smith v. O'Halloran,* 557 F.Supp. 289, 295 (D.Colo.1983).

The primary issue on appeal is whether the trial court erred in finding that the Secretary does not have a statutory duty to develop and implement a system of nursing home review and enforcement, which focuses on and ensures high quality patient care....

Background

The factual background of this complex lawsuit is fully discussed in the district court's opinion. *In re Estate of Smith v. O'Halloran,* 557 F.Supp. 289 (D.Colo.1983). Briefly, plaintiffs instituted the lawsuit in an effort to improve the deplorable conditions at many nursing homes. They presented evidence of the lack of adequate medical care and of the widespread knowledge that care is inadequate. Indeed, the district court concluded that care and life in some nursing homes is so bad that the homes "could be characterized as orphanages for the aged." *Id.* at 293.

* * *

The Medicaid Act

An understanding of the Medicaid Act (the Act) is essential to understand plaintiffs' contentions. The purpose of the Act is to enable the federal government to assist states in providing medical assistance to "aged, blind or disabled individuals, whose income and resources are insufficient to meet the costs of necessary medical services, and ... rehabilitation and other services to help such ... individuals to attain or retain capabilities for independence or self care." 42 U.S.C.A. § 1396 (1982). To receive funding, a state must submit to the Secretary and have approved by the Secretary, a plan for medical assistance, which meets the requirements of 42 U.S.C.A. § 1396a(a).

... A state seeking plan approval must establish or designate a single state agency to administer or supervise administration of the state plan, 42 U.S.C.A. § 1396a(a)(5), and must provide reports and information as the Secretary may require. *Id.* § 1396a(a)(6). Further, the state agency is responsible for establishing and maintaining health standards for institutions where the recipients of the medical assistance under the plan receive care or services. *Id.* § 1396a(a)(9)(A). The plan must include descriptions of the standards and methods the state will use to assure that medical or remedial care services provided to the recipients "are of high quality." *Id.* § 1396a(a)(22)(D).

The state plan must also provide "for a regular program of medical review ... of each patient's need for skilled nursing facility care ... , a written plan of care, and, where applicable, a plan of rehabilitation prior to admission to a skilled nursing facility...." *Id.* § 1396a(a)(26)(A). Further, the plan must provide for periodic inspections by medical review teams of:

> (i) the care being provided in such nursing facilities ... to persons receiving assistance under the State plan; (ii) with respect to each of the patients receiving such care, the adequacy of the services available in particular nursing facilities ... to meet the current health needs and promote the maximum physical well-being of patients receiving care in such facilities ...; (iii) the necessity and desirability of continued placement of such patients in such nursing facilities ...; and (iv) the feasibility of meeting their health care needs through alternative institutional or noninstitutional services. *Id.* § 1396a(a)(26)(B).

The state plan must provide that any skilled nursing facility receiving payment comply with 42 U.S.C.A. § 1395x(j), which defines "skilled nursing facility" and sets out standards for approval under a state plan. *Id.* § 1396a(a)(28). The key requirement for purposes of this lawsuit is that a skilled nursing facility must meet "such other conditions relating to the health and safety of individuals who are furnished services in such institution or relating to the physical facilities thereof as the Secretary may find necessary.... " *Id.* § 1395x(j)(15).

The state plan must provide for the appropriate state agency to establish a plan, consistent with regulations prescribed by the Secretary, for professional health personnel to review the appropriateness and quality of care and services furnished to Medicaid recipients. *Id.* § 1396a(a)(33)(A). The appropriate state agency must determine on an ongoing basis whether participating institutions meet the requirements for continued participation in the Medicaid program. *Id.* § 1396a(a)(33)(B). While the state has the initial responsibility for determining whether institutions are meeting the conditions of participation, section 1396a(a)(33)(B) gives the Secretary the authority to "look behind" the state's determination of facility compliance, and make an independent and binding determination of whether institutions meet the requirements for participation in the state Medicaid plan. Thus, the state is responsible for conducting the review of facilities to determine whether they comply with the state plan. In conducting the review, however, the states must use federal standards, forms, methods, and procedures. 42 C.F.R. § 431.610(f)(1) (1983). . . .

IMPLEMENTING REGULATIONS

Congress gave the Secretary a general mandate to promulgate rules and regulations necessary to the efficient administration of the functions with which the Secretary is charged by the Act. 42 U.S.C.A. § 1302 (1982). Pursuant to this mandate the Secretary has promulgated standards for the care to be provided by skilled nursing facilities and intermediate care facilities. See 42 C.F.R. § 442.200–.516 (1983). . . .

The Secretary has established a procedure for determining whether state plans comply with the standards set out in the regulations. This enforcement mechanism is known as the "survey/certification" inspection system. Under this system, the states conduct reviews of nursing homes pursuant to 42 U.S.C.A. § 1396a(a)(33). The Secretary then determines, on the basis of the survey results, whether the nursing home surveyed is eligible for certification and, thus, eligible for Medicaid funds. The states must use federal standards, forms, methods, and procedures in conducting the survey. 42 C.F.R. § 431.610(f)(1). At issue in this case is the form SSA–1569, [ ], which the Secretary requires the states to use to show that the nursing homes participating in Medicaid under an approved state plan meet the conditions of participation contained in the Act and the regulations. Plaintiffs contend that the form is "facility-oriented," in that it focuses on the theoretical capability of the facility to provide high quality care, rather than "patient-oriented," which would focus on the care actually provided. The district court found, with abundant support in the record, that the "facility-oriented" characterization is appropriate and that the Secretary has repeatedly admitted that the form is "facility-oriented." [ ]

THE PLAINTIFFS' CLAIMS

* * *

The plaintiffs do not challenge the substantive medical standards, or "conditions of participation," which have been adopted by the Secretary and which states must satisfy to have their plans approved. See 42 C.F.R. § 405.1101–.1137. Rather, plaintiffs challenge the enforcement mechanism the Secretary has established. The plaintiffs contend that the federal forms, form SSA–1569 in particular, which states are required to use, evaluate only the physical facilities and theoretical capability to render quality care. The surveys assess the care provided almost totally on the basis of the records, documentation, and written policies of the facility being reviewed. [ ] Further, out of the 541 questions contained in the Secretary's form SSA–1569 which must be answered by state survey and certification inspection teams, only 30 are "even marginally related to patient care or might require any patient observation. ..." [ ] Plaintiffs contend that the enforcement mechanism's focus on the facility, rather than on the care actually provided in the facility, results only in "paper compliance" with the substantive standards of the Act. Thus, plaintiffs contend, the Secretary has violated her statutory duty to assure that federal Medicaid monies are paid only to facilities, which meet the substantive standards of the Act—facilities which actually provide high quality medical, rehabilitative, and psychosocial care to resident Medicaid recipients.

The District Court's Holding

After hearing the evidence, the district court found the type of patient care management system advocated by plaintiffs clearly feasible and characterized the current enforcement system as "facility-oriented." [ ] However, the court concluded that the failure to implement and require the use of a "patient-oriented" system is not a violation of the Secretary's statutory duty. [ ] The essence of the district court's holding was that the State of Colorado, not the federal government, is responsible for developing and enforcing standards which would assure high quality care in nursing homes and, thus, the State of Colorado, not the federal government, should have been the defendant in this case. [ ]

* * *

The Secretary's Duty

After carefully reviewing the statutory scheme of the Medicaid Act, the legislative history, and the district court's opinion, we conclude that the district court improperly defined the Secretary's duty under the statute. The federal government has more than a passive role in handing out money to the states. The district court erred in finding that the burden of enforcing the substantive provisions of the Medicaid Act is on the states. The Secretary of Health and Human Services has a duty to establish a system to adequately inform herself as to whether the facilities receiving federal money are satisfying the requirements of the Act, including providing high quality patient care. This duty to be adequately informed is not only a duty to be informed at the time a facility is originally certified, but is a duty of continued supervision.

Nothing in the Medicaid Act indicates that Congress intended the physical facilities to be the end product. Rather, the purpose of the Act is to provide medical assistance and rehabilitative services. 42 U.S.C.A. § 1396. The Act repeatedly focuses on the care to be provided, with facilities being only part of that care. For example, the Act provides that health standards are to be developed and maintained, *id.* § 1396a(a)(9)(A), and that states must inform the Secretary what methods they will use to assure high quality care. *Id.* § 1396a(a)(22). In addition to the "adequacy of the services available," the periodic inspections must address "the care being provided" in nursing facilities. *Id.* § 1396a(a)(26)(B). State plans must provide review of the "appropriateness and quality of care and services furnished," *id.* § 1396a(a)(33)(A), and do so on an ongoing basis. *Id.* § 1396a(a)(33)(B).

While the district court correctly noted that it is the state, which develops specific standards and actually conducts the inspection, there is nothing in the Act to indicate that the state function relieves the Secretary of all responsibility to ensure that the purposes of the Act are being accomplished. The Secretary, not the states, determines which facilities are eligible for federal funds. [ ] While participation in the program is voluntary, states who choose to participate must comply with federal statutory requirements. [ ] The inspections may be conducted by the states, but the Secretary approves or disapproves the state's plan for review. Further, the inspections must be made with federal forms, procedures, and methods.

It would be anomalous to hold that the Secretary has a duty to determine whether a state plan meets the standards of the Act while holding that the Secretary can certify facilities without informing herself as to whether the facilities actually perform the functions required by the state plan. The Secretary has a duty to ensure more than paper compliance. The federal responsibility is particularly evident in the "look behind" provision. 42 U.S.C.A. § 1396a(a)(33)(B) (1982). We do not read the Secretary's "look behind" authority as being "nothing more than permitted authority . . .," 557 F.Supp. 296, as the district court found. Rather, we find that the purpose of that section is to assure that compliance is not merely facial, but substantive.

* * *

By enacting section 1302 Congress gave the Secretary authority to promulgate regulations to achieve the functions with which she is charged. The "look-behind" provision and its legislative history clearly show that Congress intended the Secretary to be responsible for assuring that federal Medicaid money is given only to those institutions that actually comply with Medicaid requirements. The Act's requirements include providing high quality medical care and rehabilitative services. In fact, the quality of the care provided to the aged is the focus of the Act. Being charged with this function, we must conclude that a failure to promulgate regulations that allow the Secretary to remain informed, on a continuing basis, as to whether facilities receiving federal money are meeting the requirements of the Act, is an abdication of the Secretary's duty. While the Medicaid Act is admittedly very complex and the Secretary has "exceptionally broad authority to prescribe standards for applying certain sections of the Act," *Schweiker v. Gray Panthers,* 453 U.S. 34, 43 (1981), the Secretary's authority cannot be interpreted so as to hold that that authority is merely permissive authority. The Secretary must insure that states comply with the congressional mandate to provide high quality medical care and rehabilitative services.

. . . Having determined that the purpose and the focus of the Act is to provide high quality medical care, we conclude that by promulgating a facility-oriented enforcement system the Secretary has failed to follow that focus and such failure is arbitrary and capricious. [ ]

Reversed and Remanded.

Notes and Questions

1. What explains the opposition of the federal government to patient-oriented standards in the *Smith* litigation? Should an administrative agency, as a matter of policy, simply resist all judicial mandates in standard setting? Would nursing homes oppose the implementation of a patient-oriented system?

2. Did the plaintiffs in *Smith* contest the standards as enacted in the statute? As promulgated in regulations? Would a challenge to the statute itself

likely be successful? On what basis would plaintiffs be able to challenge the regulations? Why would the survey forms themselves be of interest to attorneys representing facilities or residents?

3. In 1986, the Secretary issued final regulations to implement a new survey system as ordered by the court in *Smith.* The Secretary refused to include the survey instrument itself in the regulations, however: "[T]he new forms and instructions are not set forth in these regulations, and any future changes will be implemented through general instructions, without further changes in these regulations. This allows flexibility to revise and improve the survey process as experience is gained." 51 Fed.Reg. 21,550 (6/13/86). What else does this allow the agency to do? The federal district court rejected the final rules because they did not include the survey instruments or instructions and held the Secretary in contempt of court. Smith v. Bowen, 675 F.Supp. 586 (D.Colo.1987). What was the judge's concern here?

4. In 1987, Congress enacted comprehensive federal nursing home reform legislation as part of the Omnibus Budget Reconciliation Act (OBRA). The legislation adopted most of the recommendations of a Congressionally commissioned study of nursing homes conducted by the Institute of Medicine (IOM) of the National Academy of Sciences. See, Improving the Quality of Care in Nursing Homes (National Academy of Sciences Press 1986). OBRA 1987 represented a comprehensive change in standards, surveillance methods and enforcement. The new standards, survey process and sanctions adopted in OBRA 1987 were the result of a "partnership" among representatives of state government, the federal government, providers and consumers and shifted the emphasis toward resident-focused outcome standards that promote the quality of life of each resident and that required an individualized plan of care. Bruce C. Vladeck, The Past, Present, and Future of Nursing Home Quality, 275 JAMA 425 (Feb. 14, 1996).

5. Research indicates that standards incorporated in OBRA '87 may have had an effect on several practices although these changes may be coincidental with other factors as well. For example, the use of physical restraints has declined by 50%; inappropriate use of antipsychotic drugs has declined at least 25%; the incidence of dehydration has been reduced by 50%; the use of indwelling catheters by nearly 30%; and hospitalizations by 25%. Bruce C. Vladeck, The Past, Present and Future of Nursing Home Quality, 275 JAMA 425 (Feb. 14, 1996), reviewing the literature. But see, Catherine Hawes et al., The OBRA–87 Nursing Home Regulations and Implementation of the Resident Assessment Instrument: Effects on Process Quality, 45 J. Am. Geriatrics Soc'y 977 (1997), discussing the difficulty of proving that changes in practices and outcomes were caused by the new regulations. Marshall Kapp, in an article that is quite skeptical about research indicating that the standards of OBRA 1987 have had a significant positive effect, observes:

> In terms of OBRA 87's impact on the general quality of care and quality of life within [nursing facilities], the overall verdict to date has been largely, although not unanimously, positive. Not surprisingly, past and current HCFA Administrators have given the law (and, not coincidentally, themselves) a glowing endorsement, by pointing to such post-OBRA quality indicators as reduction in resident dehydration, decreased utilization of indwelling urinary catheters, lowering of the hospitalization rate, and an increase in the number of hearing impaired residents who now have hearing aids. Interviews with nursing home employees, regulators, advocates, and representatives of professional associations have yielded favorable perceptions regarding the law's

impact. Marshall B. Kapp, Quality of Care and Quality of Life in Nursing Facilities: What's Regulation Got To Do With It? 31 McGeorge L. Rev. 707 (2000).

Kapp notes, however, that government studies of the quality of nursing home care observe persistent problems in the quality of care and the effectiveness of the regulatory system. See e.g., General Accounting Office, Nursing Homes: Additional Steps Needed to Strengthen Enforcement of Federal Quality Standards, GAO/HEHS–99–46 (1999); General Accounting Office, California Nursing Homes: Care Problems Persist Despite Federal and State Oversight, GAO/HEHS–98–202 (1998).

6. Some advocates argue that OBRA 1987 is now outdated, "designed for an industry that no longer exists," and argue that "improvements in staff quality and the experience nursing homes have acquired in recent years have transformed today's regulations into barriers to genuine quality and efficiency." Michael J. Stoil, AAHSA Climbs on the Deregulatory Bandwagon, 44 Nursing Homes 7 (1995), quoting the president of AAHSA, the organization of not-for-profit nursing homes. How could regulations intended to improve quality become a barrier to quality? If the OBRA standards are outdated, will change require Congressional action or would HCFA be able to make needed changes?

7. The court's opinion in *Smith* describes the allocation of authority in the federal-state Medicaid quality control program. Exactly which functions are allocated to the state and which to the federal government? If Congress were to reconsider the role of the federal government in Medicaid regulation of nursing homes, should it continue the involvement of both the state and the federal governments? Should it consider requiring merely that nursing facilities receiving Medicaid or Medicare dollars be licensed by the state?

8. HCFA has initiated another round of major changes in its regulatory process overall, and particularly for nursing facilities and home health care. Barbara J. Gagel, Health Care Quality Improvement Program: A New Approach, 16 Health Care Fin. Rev. 15 (1995). One aspect is a shift in emphasis from identifying poor care providers toward the promotion of improved health status for all beneficiaries. HCFA is also emphasizing direct information to consumers to allow consumers to discriminate between the better and the poorer providers. HCFA has joined the general movement in health care toward an emphasis on outcomes rather than structure and process standards. (Review the material on measuring quality in Chapter 1.) HCFA bases this shift toward outcome standards in part on changes in the health care industry itself, including the movement toward scientifically-based practice guidelines and quality indicators, data systems technology improvements, and the adoption of quality improvement methods by the institutions themselves. Reviewing the comparative information on hospitals, nursing homes and home health provided in the beginning of this chapter, do you foresee any differences among these three providers that might determine the success of this shift in policy? For example, an emphasis on outcomes is not without its problems in nursing facilities as compared to hospitals. See Robert L. Kane, Improving the Quality of Long–Term Care, 273 JAMA 1376 (May 3, 1995). As to outcomes standards for home care, see Rosalie A. Kane, et al., Perspectives on Home Care Quality, 16 Health Care Fin. Rev. 69 (1994). What is unique to home health care that might affect reliance on outcomes as a measure of quality? As to application of quality improvement approaches to home care, see Eleanor D. Kinney, Joy A. Freedman, Cynthia A. Loveland Cook, Quality Improvement in

Community-Based Long-Term Care: Theory and Reality, 20 Am.J.L. & Med. 59 (1994).

9. What legal issues might outcome standards raise? Does an emphasis on outcome standards mean that a negative outcome must be identified in each individual case? Or that standards would be validated by research indicating that they have a direct impact on quality? Is it ever reasonable to assume that a particular process or structure standard has an effect on quality without empirical proof? If the statute specifies certain structural or process standards (e.g., requiring that a nursing home be administered by a licensed nursing home administrator, or requiring minimum staffing ratios or staff training), could a facility contest enforcement of those standards for lack of empirical evidence of an impact on quality? In Beverly California Corporation v. Shalala, 78 F.3d 403 (8th Cir.1996), the administrative law judge reviewing termination of the facility's Medicaid certification determined that termination was inappropriate because HCFA had not proved that any resident had suffered actual harm as a result of the deficiencies. The Appeals Council overturned the ALJ's decision and affirmed the Secretary's sanction stating that "deficiencies which substantially limit a facility's capacity to render adequate care or which adversely affect the health and safety of residents constitute noncompliance.... [A] strong potential for adverse effect on resident health and safety will constitute noncompliance as will an actual adverse effect or 'actual harm'." The District Court and the Eighth Circuit affirmed the Appeals Council decision.

10. OBRA '87 adopted new standards concerning the use of physical and chemical restraints which aimed at reducing their use. This represented not only a regulatory change but a fundamental change in the foundation of a customary practice. Prior to the mid 1980s, physically restraining a nursing home patient was viewed as protective of the patient in that it prevented falls. It was also believed that a nursing home would be liable for injuries due to falls if it did not restrain patients. Research in the field changed that view. See, for example, Julie A. Braun and Elizabeth A. Capezuti, The Legal and Medical Aspects of Physical Restraints and Bed Siderails and Their Relationship to Falls and Fall-Related Injuries in Nursing Homes, 4 DePaul J. of Health Care Law 1 (2000); Sandra H. Johnson, The Fear of Liability and the Use of Restraints in Nursing Homes, 18 Law, Med. & Health Care 263, 264 (1990).

Problem: Residents' Rights

Assume that you are the attorney for Pine Acres Nursing Home, located in an older section of the city. The administrator has approached you regarding problems with certain patients. One patient, Francis Scott, aged 88, has been a resident of the facility for a few months. Scott's mental and physical condition has been deteriorating slowly for several years and much more rapidly in the past six months. His family placed him in the nursing home because they wanted him to be safe. They were concerned because he had often left his apartment and become totally lost on the way back. Mr. Scott's family always promptly pays the monthly fee. Scott is angry about the placement, tends to be rude and insists on walking through the hallways and around the fenced-in grounds of the facility on his own. He has always been an early riser and likes to take his shower at the crack of dawn. He refuses to be assisted in showering by a nurses' aide. In addition, his friends from the neighborhood like to visit. They like to play pinochle when they come, and they usually bring a six-pack.

Another patient, Emma Kaitz, has fallen twice, apparently while trying to get out of bed. The staff is very concerned that she will be hurt. The physician who is medical director of the facility will write an order for restraints "as needed" for any resident upon the request of the director of nursing. Mrs. Kaitz's daughter is willing to try whatever the doctor advises. The staff have begun using "soft restraints" (cloth straps on her wrists) tied to the bedrails, but Mrs. Kaitz becomes agitated and cries. She says she feels like a dog when they tie her up. Other times they just use the bedrails alone. When she becomes agitated, she is given a sedative to help her relax, but it also tends to make her appear confused. To avoid the agitation as much as possible during the day, they have been able to position her wheelchair so that she can't get out by herself. She stops trying after a while and becomes so relaxed she nods off.

The administrator wants to know what he can do. What would you advise this administrator? Can he restrict the visiting hours for Mr. Scott? Can he require Scott to be assisted in the shower? Can Mr. Scott be transferred or discharged? Is the facility dealing with Mrs. Kaitz well? How should an inspector treat Mr. Scott's and Mrs. Kaitz's complaints? What does your nursing home client expect of you here? What role should you play in regard to quality of care standards?

The text that follows includes excerpts from the Residents' Rights section of the Medicaid statute; the regulation on the use of physical restraints; and the interpretive guidelines on physical restraints provided to surveyors for the inspection of Medicaid facilities. Find out where you can find the interpretive guidelines on other provisions of the Medicaid nursing home statutes.

42 U.S.C.A. § 1396r

(b)(1) QUALITY OF LIFE.—

(A) IN GENERAL.—A nursing facility must care for its residents in such a manner and in such an environment as will promote maintenance or enhancement of the quality of life of each resident.

* * *

(c) REQUIREMENTS RELATING TO RESIDENTS' RIGHTS—

(1) GENERAL RIGHTS.—

(A) SPECIFIED RIGHTS.—A nursing facility must protect and promote the rights of each resident, including each of the following rights:

(i) FREE CHOICE.—The right to choose a personal attending physician, to be fully informed in advance about care and treatment, to be fully informed in advance of any changes in care or treatment that may affect the resident's well-being, and (except with respect to a resident adjudged incompetent) to participate in planning care and treatment or changes in care and treatment.

(ii) FREE FROM RESTRAINTS.—The right to be free from physical or mental abuse, corporal punishment, involuntary seclusion, and any physical or chemical restraints imposed for purposes of discipline or convenience and not required to treat the resident's medical symptoms. Restraints may only be imposed—

(I) to ensure the physical safety of the resident or other residents, and

(II) only upon the written order of a physician that specifies the duration and circumstances under which the restraints are to be used (except in emergency circumstances specified by the Secretary until such an order could reasonably be obtained).

(iii) PRIVACY.—The right to privacy with regard to accommodations, medical treatment, written and telephonic communications, visits, and meetings of family and of resident groups. [Does not require private rooms.]

(v) ACCOMMODATION OF NEEDS.—The right—

(I) to reside and receive services with reasonable accommodations of individual needs and preferences, except where the health or safety of the individual or other residents would be endangered, and

(II) to receive notice before the room or roommate of the resident in the facility is changed.

(viii) PARTICIPATION IN OTHER ACTIVITIES.—The right of the resident to participate in social, religious, and community activities that do not interfere with the rights of other residents in the facility.

* * *

(D) USE OF PSYCHOPHARMACOLOGIC DRUGS.

Psychopharmacologic drugs may be administered only on the orders of a physician and only as part of a plan (included in the written plan of care . . .) designed to eliminate or modify the symptoms for which the drugs are prescribed and only if, at least annually an independent, external consultant reviews the appropriateness of the drug plan of each resident receiving such drugs.

(2) TRANSFER AND DISCHARGE RIGHTS.—

(A) IN GENERAL.—A nursing facility must permit each resident to remain in the facility and must not transfer or discharge the resident from the facility unless—

(i) the transfer or discharge is necessary to meet the resident's welfare and the resident's welfare cannot be met in the facility;

(ii) the transfer or discharge is appropriate because the resident's health has improved sufficiently so the resident no longer needs the services provided by the facility;

(iii) the safety of individuals in the facility is endangered;

(iv) the health of individuals in the facility would otherwise be endangered;

(v) the resident has failed, after reasonable and appropriate notice, to pay . . . for a stay at the facility; or

(vi) the facility ceases to operate.

* * *

(B) PRE–TRANSFER AND PRE–DISCHARGE NOTICE.—

(i) IN GENERAL.—Before effecting a transfer or discharge of a resident, a nursing facility must—

(I) notify the resident (and, if known, an immediate family member of the resident or legal representative) of the transfer or discharge and the reasons therefor,

(II) record the reasons in the resident's clinical record * * * and

(III) include in the notice the items described in clause (iii). [concerning appeal of transfer]

(ii) TIMING OF NOTICE.—The notice under clause (i)(I) must be made at least 30 days in advance of the resident's transfer or discharge except—

(I) in a case described in clause (iii) or (iv) of subparagraph (A);

(II) in a case described in clause (ii) of subparagraph (A), where the resident's health improves sufficiently to allow a more immediate transfer or discharge;

(III) in a case described in clause (i) of subparagraph (A), where a more immediate transfer or discharge is necessitated by the resident's urgent medical needs; or

(IV) in a case where a resident has not resided in the facility for 30 days.

In the case of such exceptions, notice must be given as many days before the date of the transfer or discharge as is practicable. [The statute also requires the state to establish a hearing process for transfers and discharges contested by the resident or surrogate.]

(3) ACCESS AND VISITATION RIGHTS.—A nursing facility must—

(A) permit immediate access to any resident by any representative of the Secretary, by any representative of the State, by an ombudsman . . ., or by the resident's individual physician;

(B) permit immediate access to a resident, subject to the resident's right to deny or withdraw consent at any time, by immediate family or other relatives of the resident;

(C) permit immediate access to a resident, subject to reasonable restrictions and the resident's right to deny or withdraw consent at any time, by others who are visiting with the consent of the resident;

(D) permit reasonable access to a resident by any entity or individual that provides health, social, legal, or other services to the resident, subject to the resident's right to deny or withdraw consent at any time; and

(E) permit representatives of the State ombudsman . . ., with the permission of the resident (or the resident's legal representative) and consistent with State law, to examine a resident's clinical records.

(4) EQUAL ACCESS TO QUALITY CARE.—

A skilled nursing facility must establish and maintain identical policies and practices regarding transfer, discharge and the provision of services . . . for all individuals regardless of source of payment.

42 C.F.R. § 483.13

Restraints. The resident has the right to be free from any physical or chemical restraints imposed for purposes of discipline or convenience, and not required to treat the resident's medical symptoms.

HCFA "GUIDANCE TO SURVEYORS" June 1995

Guidelines: § 483.13(a)

"Physical restraints" are defined as any manual method or physical or mechanical device, material, or equipment attached or adjacent to the resident's body that the individual cannot remove easily which restricts freedom of movement or normal access to one's body.

Restraint use may constitute an accident hazard and professional standards of practice have eliminated the need for physical restraints except under limited medical circumstances. Therefore, medical symptoms that would warrant the use of restraints should be reflected in the comprehensive assessment and care planning. It is further expected that for those residents whose care plans indicate the need for restraints that the facility engage in a systematic and gradual process toward reducing restraints. . . .

The resident's right to participate in care planning and the right to refuse treatment [ ] include the right to accept or refuse restraints.

For the resident to make an informed choice about the use of restraints, the facility should explain to the resident the negative outcomes of restraint use. Potential negative outcomes include incontinence, decreased range of motion, and decreased ability to ambulate, symptoms of withdrawal or depression, or reduced social contact.

In the case of a resident who is incapable of making a decision, the surrogate or representative may exercise this right based on the same information that would have been provided to the resident. [ ] However, the surrogate or representative cannot give permission to use restraints for the sake of discipline or staff convenience or when the restraint is not necessary to treat the resident's medical symptoms. That is, the facility may not use restraints in violation of the regulation solely because a surrogate or representative has approved or requested them.

"Physical restraints" include, but are not limited to, leg restraints, arm restraints, hand mitts, soft ties or vests, lap cushions and lap trays the resident cannot remove. Also included as restraints are facility practices that meet the definition of a restraint, such as: using bed rails to keep a resident from voluntarily getting out of bed as opposed to enhancing mobility while in bed; tucking in a sheet so tightly that a bed bound resident cannot move; using wheel chair safety bars to prevent a resident from rising out of a chair; placing a resident in a chair that prevents rising; and placing a resident who uses a wheelchair so close to a wall that the wall prevents the resident from rising.

Bed rails may be used to restrain residents or to assist in mobility and transfer of residents. The use of bed rails as restraints is prohibited unless they are necessary to treat a resident's medical symptoms. Bed rails used as restraints add risk to the resident. They potentially increase the risk of more significant injury from a fall from a bed with raised bed rails than from a fall from a bed without bed rails. They also potentially increase the likelihood that the resident will spend more time in bed and fall when attempting to transfer from bed.

2. *Survey and Inspection*

SOUTHERN HEALTH FACILITIES, INC. v. SOMANI

Court of Appeals of Ohio, 1995.
1995 WL 765161.

DESHLER, J.

The ... complaint alleged that plaintiff, Southern Health Facilities, Inc., dba Greenbriar Convalescent Center ("Greenbriar"), is an Ohio proprietary corporation licensed and authorized to operate a one-hundred fifty-one bed nursing home under the provisions of R.C. Chapter 3721, and that Greenbriar is also certified to participate in Medicare and Medicaid programs. It was averred that defendant ODH is the agency of the state designated as the "State Survey Agency" as that term is used in federal law, and that ODH is a party to an agreement with the Ohio Department of Human Services authorizing ODH to conduct inspections of Medicare and Medicaid certified skilled nursing facilities in Ohio. [Defendants filed a motion to dismiss for failure to state a claim which the trial court granted.]

* * *

The thrust of plaintiffs' complaint is that the manner in which defendants conduct certification compliance surveys is violative of federal and state law. Specifically, plaintiffs assert that defendants failed to conduct a survey in accordance with the State Operations Manual, in violation of R.C. 5111.39(C), R.C. 3721.022, and in accordance with Section 1396r, Title 42, U.S.C.A. It is averred that, while federal standards require that defendants conduct an exit conference at the conclusion of a survey, and the State Operations Manual requires that an exit conference include an opportunity to provide the surveyors with relevant additional information to assist in determining whether a deficiency occurred, defendants failed to communicate the nature of the surveyors' impressions and concerns and did not permit Greenbriar to question or provide additional documentation. The complaint alleged that the failure to follow mandated procedures resulted in defendants inappropriately citing Greenbriar for deficiencies....

The complaint further included allegations that defendants made incorrect survey determinations at the Greenbriar facility, refused to remove these improper statements regarding the care and services provided by Greenbriar, and issued public notices falsely stating that Greenbriar delivered sub-standard care. It was averred that such improper determinations are routinely made at other facilities throughout the state. The complaint also alleged that defendants have failed to properly train and assist the persons performing the surveys, that the surveys are required to be, but are not, uniformly and consistently applied between providers and from one survey to the next, and that the care delivered to residents in facilities such as Greenbriar is not assessed in a systematic manner by defendants.

* * *

Plaintiffs contend that the trial court failed to apply the proper standard in ruling on the motion to dismiss. Specifically, plaintiffs assert that the complaint sets forth sufficient facts describing in detail the deficiencies of the survey conducted at Greenbriar and that the court failed to presume the truth of the facts alleged.

We agree with plaintiffs' contention that, accepting the allegations in the complaint as true, as we must in considering a motion to dismiss, the trial court erred in granting the motion to dismiss. Upon review, we conclude that plaintiffs' complaint sufficiently alleges cognizable procedural and substantive due process claims as well as violations of state and federal provisions.

* * *

We note that the issue whether a provider is entitled to a pre-termination evidentiary hearing has been the subject of litigation in federal courts. It appears that the majority of courts which have addressed the issue have found that such a hearing is not required. [ ] Regardless of whether such an evidentiary hearing would be required, plaintiffs' complaint alleges that other procedural safeguards which are required by law were not complied with by defendants. As noted above, the complaint alleges that, contrary to federal regulations and state law, defendants failed to communicate the nature of the surveyors' impressions during the exit interview and did not permit Greenbriar to question or provide additional documentation. Presumably, compliance with mandated procedural safeguards would obviate the need for an evidentiary hearing; however, the complaint alleges that these procedures were not followed. Assuming the truth of the allegations, the complaint sufficiently sets forth a procedural due process claim.

* * *

... We note that the trial court, in addressing the factual allegations regarding the survey, concluded that the allegations merely constituted disagreements with the survey's findings. The issue, however, is whether it appears from the complaint that there can be no set of facts which would entitle plaintiffs to the relief requested. While we make no comment regarding the probable success of plaintiffs' action beyond this stage, we conclude that the allegations are sufficient to withstand dismissal....

* * *

Notes and Questions

1. Plaintiff's claim in *Southern Health Facilities* survived a motion to dismiss. What will plaintiff have to prove to succeed on the merits? How far should the courts go in testing the accuracy of the finding of a violation? Is a decision to cite a facility for a violation of standards entitled to deference? See, EPI Corporation v. Chater, 91 F.3d 143 (6th Cir.1996) and Beverly California Corporation v. Shalala, 78 F.3d 403 (8th Cir.1996), rejecting similar claims on the merits. In *EPI*, the Sixth Circuit found that the survey team had substantially complied with survey procedures; that some of the steps identified by plaintiff were optional; and that the plaintiff facility did not suffer substantial prejudice to its interests by the surveyors' failure to complete a particular form in advance of the exit conference. In *Beverly*, the Eighth Circuit also found that the surveyors

had substantially complied with the procedures described in the regulations and rejected plaintiff's claim.

2. In *Beverly,* Beverly argued that the Secretary had exceeded her statutory look-behind authority in conducting a federal survey of the facility without having first articulated some reason for believing that the state survey had been inadequate. (Refer back to *Smith v. Heckler*. What is the look-behind authority?) In this case, the court found that the federal survey team

> observed numerous regulatory violations including the following: restraints left on residents without release for periods exceeding two hours; vest restraints applied improperly creating a risk of strangulation; frail residents lifted and ambulated in a manner that posed a substantial threat of injury; failure to observe basic hygiene conventions creating a serious risk of infection; dirty and unlabeled personal items and equipment scattered throughout the facility; physical therapy administered by an unqualified employee; inadequate physical therapy regimens; and discontinuation or delay of physical therapy without physician consultation.

The court held that the Secretary had not exceeded her authority in conducting a federal inspection. The facility was one of a sample of facilities selected to test the state survey process.

3. Why might the results of a federal inspection differ from one conducted by state surveyors? What role should the courts play in the question of surveyor discretion or inconsistency? Should the survey standards be more rigid? States vary widely as to the average number of deficiencies per facility, ranging from a high of 19.48 in Nevada to a low of 2.34 in Colorado. Richard L. Butler, Jenean M. Erickson, and Vincent Mor, Avoid Survey Surprises by Being Prepared, 8 Brown University Long–Term Care Quality Letter 1 (Mar. 25, 1996). The authors of the article note that even the most frequently cited violations nationally (which are violations of requirements of comprehensive assessment, development of comprehensive care plans, and sanitary storage, preparation and distribution of food) are "rarely named in states with very low deficiency rates" and conclude that OBRA "has not been successful in 'leveling' differences between states in terms of the likelihood of receiving a deficiency." Does this range reflect varying quality of facilities or of inspection processes?

4. An evaluation of the new survey process revealed that surveyors have difficulty with the emphasis on outcomes and with the patient-focused and outcome-oriented survey techniques. In particular, researchers reported that the surveyors hesitated to cite the facility for outcome difficulties because they may be uncomfortable with the sophisticated level of assessment required for a citation on an outcome standard and may instead opt to cite the facility for less serious but more easily documented violations. For a description of this research, see Michael J. Stoil, Surveyors Stymied by Survey Criteria, Researchers Find, 43 Nursing Homes 58 (1994). See Kathy J. Vaca et al., Review of Nursing Home Regulation, 7 MedSurg Nursing 165 (June 1998). What might steer surveyors toward "documentable" citations and away from problems on which there might be more room for disagreement? A study of surveyor practices by the General Accounting Office, conducted in response to industry concerns about overly aggressive surveyors, found that surveyors were not being overzealous in their efforts. Nursing Home Oversight: Industry Examples Do Not Demonstrate That Regulatory Actions Were Reasonable, GAO/HEHS–99–154R (1999).

5. What relationship should the surveyor establish with the facility? Is the surveyor a consultant or advisor? Should the surveyor offer suggestions for

improvement? Should the surveyor commend the facility on noted improvements or other indicators of quality identified during the inspection? How might expectations concerning this relationship have affected the dispute over the exit conference described in *Southern Health Facilities*? See Facility and Surveyors: Cooperation, Not Confrontation, 9 The Brown University Long–Term Care Quality Advisor 1 (1997). For a critique of the enforcement-oriented survey process, see John Braithwaite, The Nursing Home Industry, 18 Crime & Justice 11 (1993); Mary Kathleen Robbins, Nursing Home Reform: Objective Regulation or Subjective Decisions?, 11 Thomas Cooley L. Rev. 185 (1994).

3. Sanctions

VENCOR NURSING CENTERS v. SHALALA

United States District Court, District of Columbia, 1999.
63 F.Supp.2d 1.

URBINA, DISTRICT JUDGE.

This matter comes before the court on an application by the plaintiff Vencor Nursing Centers, L.P. ("Vencor") for an order temporarily restraining the defendant, Secretary of the United States Department of Health and Human Services Donna E. Shalala ("HHS") from terminating one of Vencor's California facilities from the Medicare and Medicaid programs, and seeking other declaratory and injunctive relief . . .

Vencor owns and operates Village Square Nursing and Rehabilitation Center, a 120–bed skilled nursing facility in San Marcos, San Diego County, California ("Village Square"). During the relevant period, Village Square had between 92 and 104 residents, including about fifty Medicare and Medicaid beneficiaries . . . The California Department of Human Services ("the survey agency" or "SA") is the state agency that inspected Village Square on behalf of HHS. From November 1998 through May 1999, HHS authorized the SA to carry out three on-site surveys of Village Square. The SA conducted the first survey on November 25, 1998 and issued a Statement of Deficiencies on November 28, 1998. Village Square filed a Plan of Correction (POC) on December 18, 1998 and notified the SA that it had regained substantial compliance as of January 9, 1999. The SA conducted a follow-up survey on April 1, 1999 and issued a Statement of Deficiencies, and Village Square submitted a POC. On May 12, 1999, HCFA notified Village Square that it concurred with the SA's findings and terminated Village Square effective May 29, 1999 for failure to maintain substantial compliance for six months. In response to Village Square's representation that it was in substantial compliance, the SA conducted a third survey on May 28, 1999 and issued a Statement of Deficiencies on June 8, 1999. HCFA exercised its discretion to continue payments until June 28, 1999, thirty days from the effective date of termination. Village Square relocated 18 Medicare and Medicaid residents by July 2, 1999 and it planned to relocate the others by July 5, 1999.

* * *

A preliminary injunction may be granted only when the movant demonstrates:

(1) a substantial likelihood of success on the merits; (2) that irreparable harm will result in the absence of the relief requested; (3) that no other party will be harmed if the motion is granted; and (4) that the public interest supports granting the requested relief.

The gravemen of Vencor's dispute with HHS is its contention that a nursing home may be terminated from Medicare and Medicaid participation only where conditions at the facility place residents' health or safety in "immediate jeopardy." Therefore, Vencor argues, by terminating Village Square in the absence of a finding of "immediate jeopardy" HHS violated the Medicare Act, the Medicaid Act and the Due Process Clause. Conversely, HHS relies on 42 C.F.R. §§ 488.412 and 488.456, which provide that HHS may terminate a facility which is not in "substantial compliance," even if there is no immediate jeopardy.

In deciding whether this court is likely to adopt Vencor's interpretation of the remedy provisions, the court accords substantial deference to HHS's regulations. [ ] Broad deference is particularly warranted where the regulation "concerns a complex and highly technical regulatory program", like Medicare, "in which the identification and classification of relevant criteria necessarily require significant expertise and entail the exercise of judgment grounded in policy concerns." [ ].

The Medicare and Medicaid acts authorize HHS to impose a variety of remedies and/or sanctions against noncompliant nursing homes. Prior to 1987 the only available remedies were outright termination or a blanket ban on reimbursement for care of newly admitted residents. [ ]. While the Medicare Act formerly permitted termination without a finding of "immediate jeopardy," 42 U.S.C. § 1395cc(f), that provision is no longer in force. In 1987 Congress enacted the Federal Nursing Home Reform Act, which added a greater variety of remedies to the Medicare and Medicaid Acts. These new remedies include, inter alia, civil money penalties, imposition of independent temporary managers and orders to adopt plans of correction (POC's). The 1987 legislation establishes categories of non-compliance and provides a number of possible remedies for HHS to choose from based on the severity of the alleged noncompliance.

* * *

... There are two provisions in the Medicare Act which tend to support HHS's position. First, Congress explicitly states, "Nothing in this subparagraph shall be construed as restricting the remedies available to HHS to remedy a skilled nursing facility's deficiencies." 42 U.S.C. § 1395i–3(h)(2)(B). Second, the Act authorizes HHS to terminate the Medicare agreement of any provider which "fails to comply substantially with the provisions of the agreement, with the provisions of this subchapter and regulations thereunder...." 42 U.S.C. § 1395cc(b)(2). As the compliance provisions are "provisions of this subchapter" and § 1395cc(b)(2) does not require a finding of immediate jeopardy prior to termination, the court could infer that HHS is entitled to terminate without immediate jeopardy.

Several courts which have addressed the issue have held that HHS does not have the authority to order termination in the absence of immediate jeopardy ...

. . . In enacting the enforcement provisions to the Medicare and Medicaid Acts, Congress expressly wished to expand the panoply of remedies available to HHS. [ ]. Committee reports noted with concern the "yo-yo" phenomenon in which noncomplying facilities temporarily correct their deficiencies before an on-site survey and then quickly lapse into noncompliance until the next review. [ ]. Presumably, the new version of the statute ameliorates this problem by giving HHS a set of intermediate sanctions to choose from rather than the extreme choices of termination or no sanction. There is no indication in the legislative history that Congress wished to limit HHS's ability to terminate a persistently noncompliant facility. [ ]. In fact, the recurring theme emerging from the legislative history is that the new provisions would grant HHS remedial powers in addition to those already available. [ ].

Against this backdrop, the court could well conclude that the statute should be read as a guidepost for HHS rather than a limitation on its power. The immediate-jeopardy provision mandates that HHS must terminate or appoint temporary management when a facility's deficiencies are found to put residents' health or safety in immediate jeopardy. By contrast, the non-jeopardy provision affords HHS discretion, allowing (but not requiring) HHS to impose intermediate sanctions on facilities whose deficiencies do not immediately jeopardize health or safety. In light of the foregoing, Vencor has not shown that this court is likely to hold that HHS lacked authority to terminate Village Square absent a finding of immediate jeopardy.

Notes and Questions

1. Was termination the correct remedy in this situation? Would a less severe intermediate sanction have been more appropriate? What happens to the approximately 50 non-Medicare and non-Medicaid residents remaining in the facility? Will their care be compromised? Will the nursing facility survive without the income from Medicare and Medicaid residents?

2. If a facility is cited for but then corrects a deficiency, should it still be penalized for that violation? What arguments would support an emphasis on correction rather than punishment? What would argue against? One study concludes that the nursing home regulatory system relies extensively on correction and voluntary compliance rather than punishment even though the emphasis in OBRA was to use penalties as a deterrent. The study points out that correction may be cheaper to the facility than contesting the citation (except where there are seriously and automatically increased penalties for repeat violations), especially where agencies lack the capacity to effectively follow up on promised corrections. In addition, the study reports that nursing home chains sometimes simply shift staff from one institution to another and back again to temporarily respond to cited deficiencies in individual facilities within the chain. Still, the director of the study concludes that the emphasis on surveillance in the U.S. system has led to more regimentation and inflexibility in U.S. nursing homes than in other countries with different systems, implying that quality of care and quality of life suffer. John Braithwaite, The Nursing Home Industry, 18 Crime & Justice 11 (1993). See also, Richard L. Peck, Does Europe Have the Answers?, 49 Nursing Homes 54 (June 2000).

3. Recent reform proposals have examined the idea of federal criminal sanctions as a way of enforcing quality. See, e.g., Angela S. Quin, Imposing Federal Criminal Liability on Nursing Homes: A Way of Deterring Inadequate

Health Care and Improving the Quality of Care Delivered?, 43 St. Louis U.L.J. 653 (Spring 1999). Additionally, *qui tam* provisions have also been used to litigate quality issues. See, e.g., John T. Boese, When Angry Patients Become Angry Prosecutors: Medical Necessity Determinations, Quality of Care and the Qui Tam Law, 43 St. Louis U.L.J. 53 (Spring 1999) and Kathleen A. Peterson, First Nursing Homes, Next Managed Care?: Limiting Liability in Quality of Care Cases Under the False Claims Act, 26 Am.J.L. & Med. 69 (2000).

Problem: Restful Manor

Restful Manor is a skilled nursing facility licensed by the state and operating in its largest city. It has 117 residents, all of whom are elderly. Only twenty percent of the residents are ambulatory. Until eighteen months ago, the home had a good record of compliance with state nursing home standards. The facility has begun to have problems with compliance, although it still consistently has corrected violations or has submitted an acceptable plan of correction. The facility has also experienced some financial difficulties recently.

The most recent inspection of the facility took place four months ago. At that time, the facility was out of compliance with several standards relating to quality of meals, cleanliness of the kitchen and maintenance of patients' medical records. The facility also had some staffing problems. Other problems included the lack of a qualified dietitian and a high, though borderline acceptable, rate of errors in the administration of medications by the nurses. As a result of this inspection report, the facility was required to submit a written plan of correction in which it agreed to remedy the violations. The next on-site inspection was scheduled to take place within six to eight weeks to check on progress in correcting the violations.

Prior to that inspection, however, an investigative news team from a local television station visited the facility with a hidden camera. The news team posed as potential out-of-town buyers interested in the facility. The visit revealed several patients who were soiled and unattended and several others who were restrained in wheelchairs. A recorded conversation with the Director of Nursing indicated that there was one nurses' aide for every ten patients, which the D.O.N. thought was probably "not enough to do a good job for some of these patients." When asked about these incidents, the owner attributed these "temporary" problems to financial constraints and to his inability to hire a good administrator who was willing to work within a reasonable budget.

The news team showed portions of the videotape on the nightly news. Three days later it followed up with a report that one of the ambulatory, mentally-impaired patients at the facility had wandered out of the building. A passerby had found the patient walking aimlessly along the main thoroughfare near the facility and called the police.

The state agency felt pressured to respond. It conducted an unannounced inspection two days after the latest news report. The surveyor conducting this inspection cited the facility for violations of several regulations including the following:

1. Each resident should receive adequate skin care that supports his or her health and well-being and avoids decubitus ulcers (bed sores). (The surveyor found that the facility was not turning or positioning bed-bound patients in the manner that is advised for avoidance of ulcers. The facility also lacked supportive supplies, such as certain kinds of pads, ordinarily used to reduce the incidence of ulcers. At the time of the inspection, however, only two patients had minor incipient pressure sores. The surveyor believes, but could

not confirm, that another patient had been transferred to the hospital eight months ago for serious bedsores.)

2. The facility must assure that a resident who did not present mental or psychosocial adjustment difficulties at admission does not display patterns of decreased social interaction or increased withdrawal, angry or depressive behaviors, unless the residents' clinical condition demonstrates that such a pattern was unavoidable. (The surveyor identifies several residents who report boredom, lethargy, loss of appetite and feelings of uselessness and who complain of a lack of interesting things to do. Their medical records do not indicate any clinical diagnosis that would explain their psychosocial states.)

3. The facility shall provide a nursing staff that is appropriately trained and adequate in number to care for the residents of the facility. (The surveyor wrote in his report that the facility provided one nurses' aide for every ten patients and that this was "inadequate in light of the dependency of the residents.")

4. The facility shall employ a certified dietitian. (The surveyor noted that "the facility currently does not employ a certified dietitian, but in the exit conference the owner reported that he has been trying to hire one for the last three months.")

5. The nurses of the facility shall administer ordered medications safely and adequately. An error rate in excess of 5% in the administration of medication is unacceptable and shall constitute a violation of this standard. (The surveyor reported an error rate of 5% in one sample medications pass and an error rate of 4.9% in another.)

Even though the facility is currently in violation of several standards, families of Restful Manor's patients have rallied to the facility's support. They believe the care is good despite the problems cited. The Department disagrees. Assume that the following (an edited version of the federal regulations) is your state statute.

488.404. Factors to be considered in selecting remedies

(b) Determining seriousness of deficiencies. To determine the seriousness of the deficiency, the State must consider at least the following factors:

(1) Whether a facility's deficiencies constitute—

(i) No actual harm with a potential for minimal harm; (ii) No actual harm with a potential for more than minimal harm, but not immediate jeopardy; (iii) Actual harm that is not immediate jeopardy; or (iv) Immediate jeopardy to resident health or safety.

(2) Whether the deficiencies—

(i) Are isolated; (ii) Constitute a pattern; or (iii) Are widespread.

(c) ... Following the initial assessment, the State may consider other factors, which may include, but are not limited to the following:

(1) The relationship of the one deficiency to other deficiencies resulting in noncompliance.

(2) The facility's prior history of noncompliance in general and specifically with reference to the cited deficiencies.

488.406. Available remedies

(a) General. In addition to the remedy of termination of the provider agreement, the following remedies are available:

(1) Temporary management.

(2) Civil money penalties.

(3) State monitoring.

(4) Transfer of residents.

(5) Closure of the facility and transfer of residents.

(6) Directed plan of correction.

(7) Directed in-service training.

488.408. Selection of remedies

(a) Categories of remedies. In this section, the remedies specified in § 488.406 (a) are grouped into categories and applied to deficiencies according to how serious the noncompliance is.

(c) (1) Category 1 remedies include the following:

(i) Directed plan of correction.

(ii) State monitoring.

(iii) Directed in-service training.

(2) The State must apply one or more of the remedies in Category 1 when there—

(i) Are isolated deficiencies that constitute no actual harm with a potential for more than minimal harm but not immediate jeopardy; or (ii) Is a pattern of deficiencies that constitutes no actual harm with a potential for more than minimal harm but not immediate jeopardy.

(3) Except when the facility is in substantial compliance, HCFA or the State may apply one or more of the remedies in Category 1 to any deficiency.

(d) (1) Category 2 remedies include the following

(iii) Civil money penalties of $50–$3,000 per day.

(iv) Civil money penalty of $1,000–$10,000 per instance of noncompliance.

(2) The State must apply one or more of the remedies in Category 2 when there are—

(i) Widespread deficiencies that constitute no actual harm with a potential for more than minimal harm but not immediate jeopardy; or (ii) One or more deficiencies that constitute actual harm that is not immediate jeopardy.

(3) The State may apply one or more of the remedies in Category 2 to any deficiency except when—

(i) The facility is in substantial compliance; or (ii) the State imposes a civil money penalty for a deficiency that constitutes immediate jeopardy, the penalty must be in the upper range of penalty amounts, as specified in § 488.438(a).

(e) (1) Category 3 remedies include the following:

(i) Temporary management.

(ii) Immediate licensure revocation.

(iii) Civil money penalty of $1,000–$10,000 per instance of noncompliance.

(2) When there are one or more deficiencies that constitute immediate jeopardy to resident health or safety—

(i) The State must do one or both of the following;

(A) Impose temporary management; or

(B) Revoke the facility license;

(ii) The State may impose a civil money penalty of $3,050–$10,000 per day or $1,000–$10,000 per instance of noncompliance, in addition to imposing the remedies specified in paragraph (e) (2) (i) of this section.

(3) When there are widespread deficiencies that constitute actual harm that is not immediate jeopardy, the State may impose temporary management, in addition to Category 2 remedies.

(f) Plan of correction.

(1) Except as specified in paragraph (f) (2) of this section, each facility that has a deficiency with regard to a requirement for long term care facilities must submit a plan of correction for approval by the State, regardless of—

(i) Which remedies are imposed; or (ii) The seriousness of the deficiencies.

(2) When there are only isolated deficiencies that HCFA or the State determines constitute no actual harm with a potential for minimal harm, the facility need not submit a plan of correction.

488.410. Action when there is immediate jeopardy

(a) If there is immediate jeopardy to resident health or safety, the State must either revocate the facility license within 23 calendar days of the last date of the survey or appoint a temporary manager to remove the immediate jeopardy . . .

(b) The State may also impose other remedies, as appropriate.

(d) The State must provide for the safe and orderly transfer of residents when the facility is terminated.

(e) If the immediate jeopardy is also substandard quality of care, the State survey agency must notify attending physicians and the State board responsible for licensing the facility administrator of the finding of substandard quality of care.

488.412. Action when there is no immediate jeopardy

(a) If a facility's deficiencies do not pose immediate jeopardy to residents' health or safety, and the facility is not in substantial compliance, the State may revoke the facility's license agreement or may allow the facility to continue to participate for no longer than 6 months from the last day of the survey if—

(1) The State survey agency finds that it is more appropriate to impose alternative remedies than to terminate the facility's provider agreement;

(2) The facility has submitted an approved plan and timetable for corrective action.

488.415. Temporary management

(a) Temporary management means the temporary appointment by the State of a substitute facility manager or administrator with authority to hire, terminate or reassign staff, obligate facility funds, alter facility procedures, and manage the facility to correct deficiencies identified in the facility's operation.

(e) Duration of temporary management. Temporary management ends when the facility ceases operation or meets standards.

The Department of Health expects litigation as a result of any enforcement action it takes in this case. It has come to the office of the state's Attorney General for advice. The Director of the Department wants to be aggressive in this case in part because the poor condition of the facility has become public knowledge. She believes that the agency's effectiveness has been challenged and that the facility is seriously deficient and heading for more problems.

Several students should serve as the assistant A.G. who has been assigned to this case. Please advise the Department on the course of action they should follow in this instance.

Other students should serve in the role of attorneys representing the facility. Please identify any defenses available to the facility, your strategy and the course the dispute is likely to take.

Having worked through these provisions, what recommendations for change would you make to this state's legislature, both as to enforcement mechanisms and as to the standards?

III. PRIVATE ACCREDITATION OF HEALTH CARE FACILITIES

Private accreditation is a nongovernmental, voluntary activity typically conducted by not-for-profit associations. The Joint Commission on Accreditation of Healthcare Organizations (JCAHO), which offers accreditation programs for hospitals, nursing homes, home health, and other facilities, and the National Committee on Quality Assurance (NCQA), which accredits health maintenance organizations, are two of the leading organizations in the accreditation of health care entities.

Accrediting associations set standards for and engage in some form of surveillance of entities seeking to gain or maintain accreditation. As a voluntary process, accreditation may be viewed as providing the accredited health care entity merely with a seal of approval—a method for communicating in shorthand that it meets standards established by an external organization.

This definitional view of accreditation certainly captures the theory of health care accreditation as a private communicative device. But in practice in the U.S., there is a much closer marriage between some private accreditation programs and government regulation of health care facilities. This is especially true of the hospital accreditation program of the JCAHO. JCAHO's hospital accreditation program is the largest of the JCAHO accreditation programs and is perhaps the most influential of all private health care accreditation programs in the U.S. Virtually all U.S. hospitals with more than 25 beds are JCAHO-accredited.

A number of important economic and professional opportunities are restricted to JCAHO-accredited hospitals. For example, payers for health care services may allow payments only to JCAHO-accredited institutions. In addition, both state and federal governments have to a great extent relied on JCAHO accreditation in their hospital licensure and Medicare/Medicaid certification programs. Most states have incorporated JCAHO accreditation standards, some explicitly, into their hospital licensure standards. Some have accepted JCAHO accreditation in lieu of a state license. See e.g., Tex. Health & Safety Code § 222.024. Under the Medicare statute, JCAHO-accredited hospitals are "deemed" to have met requirements for Medicare certification. 42 U.S.C. §§ 1395x(e), 1395bb. Although the Secretary retains a look-behind authority, JCAHO substitutes for the routine surveillance process.

Originally, the acceptance of JCAHO accreditation by the Medicare program was designed to entice an adequate number of hospitals to participate in the then-new Medicare program. That original rationale has dissipated as hospitals have become much more dependent on Medicare payments. The federal government's reliance on private accreditation as a substitute for routine government surveillance has expanded considerably beyond the original hospital setting, however, and now extends to clinical laboratories and home health care.

In 1981 the Reagan administration proposed extending deemed status to nursing homes accredited by the JCAHO. This proposal was opposed vigorously by consumer advocates and was withdrawn. Should nursing homes be treated differently, and arguably more restrictively, than hospitals on the question of deemed status? What might explain this extensive reliance on private organizations for public regulation? Some would argue that private accreditation more effectively encourages voluntary compliance and avoids some of the "prosecutorial" environment of a government-conducted inspection program. Furthermore, and perhaps more importantly, deemed status allows the government to shift the cost of the inspection process as accredited facilities pay the accrediting organization for the costs of the accreditation program, including the site visit.

How does the private accreditation process compare to public regulation? Private accreditation programs traditionally have engaged in practices that encourage voluntary subscription to the accreditation program. For example, accreditation programs often perform only announced site visits and keep negative evaluations confidential, at least until the accreditation itself is reduced or not renewed. Standards established by accreditation programs, which are often dominated by professionals in the industry rather than consumer groups, may differ from those set by a process that arguably fosters broader public participation. With JCAHO, in particular, governance and policymaking is dominated by physician organization members (e.g., the American Medical Association, the American College of Physicians, the American College of Surgeons) and the American Hospital Association.

For a history of the JCAHO and a broad review of legal issues related to private accreditation, see Timothy S. Jost, The Joint Commission on Accreditation of Hospitals: Private Regulation of Health Care and the Public Interest, 24 B.C.L.Rev.835 (1983). For a discussion of the relation between private accreditation and public regulation, see Jody Freeman, The Private Role in Public Governance, 75 N.Y.U.L.Rev. 543 (2000); Symposium on Private Accreditation in the Regulatory State, 57 Law and Contemp. Prob.1 (1994).

Review the final rule reproduced below. How does the regulation alter the ordinary private accreditation process? Has the Department adequately preserved its interests and authority while granting deemed status to home health agencies accredited by JCAHO?

DEPARTMENT OF HEALTH AND HUMAN SERVICES

58 Fed.Reg. 35007 (June 30, 1993).

As a result of this notice, HHAs [home health agencies] accredited by JCAHO are deemed to meet the requirements for participation in the Medicare program and, therefore, may participate in the Medicaid program as a provider of home health services. . . .

* * *

[W]e would remove recognition of JCAHO accreditation if either of the following circumstances occur:

— JCAHO revises its standards so that the revised standards fail to provide reasonable assurance that JCAHO-accredited HHAs meet the Medicare conditions of participation. Conversely, we revise the Medicare HHA conditions of participation to such a degree that JCAHO's standards or accreditation policies would no longer provide reasonable assurance that JCAHO-accredited HHAs meet the conditions of participation; or

— Our validation or complaint surveys reveal widespread, systematic, or unresolvable problems with the JCAHO accreditation process, thereby providing evidence that there is not reasonable assurance that JCAHO-accredited HHAs meet the Medicare conditions of participation.

* * *

The proposed notice also made our recognition of JCAHO's accreditation program contingent on JCAHO's continued agreement to:

— Release JCAHO survey reports to us routinely and to the public upon request. If the reports reveal deficiencies which we believe warrant action by us, we may survey the HHAs identified as having deficiencies, withdraw recognition of the accreditation program if appropriate, and apply any other appropriate corrective measures or sanctions. The information to be released includes the accreditation findings, supporting documentation, the official accreditation survey reports of JCAHO surveyors, and other related information.

— Report to either the Office of Inspector General (OIG) (for Medicare) or to the State agency responsible for investigating fraud and abuse (for Medicaid), or to both, complaints received from persons working in the accredited HHA or any substantial complaints from others, anonymous or identified, concerning potential fraud and abuse violations, and any other indication of a Medicare or Medicaid program abuse encountered by JCAHO during a JCAHO inspection.

— Make JCAHO surveyors available to serve as witnesses if adverse action is taken by HCFA after JCAHO accreditation has been withdrawn.

Finally, we proposed to make our approval of JCAHO's accreditation program contingent on the following revisions to JCAHO's survey and accreditation process (JCAHO had already agreed to make these changes):

— Implementation of an annual, unannounced survey of those HHAs requesting JCAHO accreditation for Medicare deeming purposes.

— Adoption of the standardized functional assessment instrument used by HCFA and State agency surveyors and training of the JCAHO surveyors in its use.

— Adoption of a case-mix, stratified random sampling process and sample sizes of clinical records for review and home visits comparable to HCFA's.

— Maintenance of a timeframe and process for following up deficiencies found during an HHA survey comparable to HCFA's.

* * *

As appropriate ... we will perform announced and unannounced validation and complaint surveys of HHAs to assure that JCAHO-accredited HHAs that participate in Medicare meet the Medicare conditions of participation. As established in the proposed notice of February 3, 1992, we may withdraw recognition of JCAHO accreditation of HHAs at any time if we determine that JCAHO accreditation does not continue to provide reasonable assurance that Medicare conditions of participation are met.

In 1999, the Office of Inspector General of the Department of Health and Human Services issued a report critical of both the JCAHO surveys and the oversight provided by HCFA in relation to hospitals. External Review of Hospital Quality: A Call for Greater Accountability (OEI–01–97–00050). See also, External Quality Review of Psychiatric Hospitals (OEI–01–99–00160).

In its report on hospitals, the OIG concluded that JCAHO provided a significant tool for quality control but that its surveys are "unlikely to detect substandard patterns of care or individual practitioners with questionable skills" because the visits are fast-paced, highly structured and still tend to be consultative. The OIG noted that the states do not survey unaccredited hospitals in a timely fashion, reporting that about 50% of unaccredited hospitals had not been surveyed within the three-year period expected. The OIG also noted that HCFA failed to check on JCAHO surveys adequately. In summary, the OIG concluded that the hospital certification system was more "collegial" than "regulatory" and recommended a greater emphasis on the regulatory nature of the surveys.

JCAHO made some changes subsequent to the OIG report. For example, it issued a plan for conducting unannounced surveys, eliminating its practice of providing 24–hour notice, and for resurveying institutions anywhere between nine and thirty months after a full survey. At the same time, JCAHO surveyed its accredited institutions to see how it might make its processes more acceptable to the providers, indicating that the organization is intent on reducing the costs of the survey process perhaps by reducing the on-site visit to one day and developing more reliance on self-assessment and continuous quality improvement. Hospitals Face Random Unannounced Visits Under Amended JCAHO Survey Policy, BNA Health Law Reporter August 19, 1999; Hospital Survey Process Under Review as Joint Commission Solicits Opinions, BNA Health Law Reporter, June 22, 2000.

In 2000, HCFA extended approval of JCAHO accreditation for Medicare certification of home health agencies. In its notice of reapproval, HCFA lists several changes JCAHO made in its procedures and standards in response to HCFA concerns. 65 Fed.Reg. 8722–01 (Feb. 22, 2000).

Chapter 4

LIABILITY OF HEALTH CARE PROFESSIONALS

This chapter will examine the framework for a malpractice suit against health care professionals and the doctrinal and evidentiary dimensions of such litigation. As you read the chapter, think about the cases and materials on three levels. First, how is the plaintiff's case proved and how does the defendant counter it? Second, how does tort doctrine respond to different categories of medical error? And third, how does malpractice litigation affect medical practice and the quality of medical care?

I. THE STANDARD OF CARE

A. ESTABLISHING THE STANDARD OF CARE

HALL v. HILBUN

Supreme Court of Mississippi, 1985.
466 So.2d 856.

ROBERTSON, JUSTICE, for the Court:

I.

This matter is before the Court on Petition for Rehearing presenting primarily the question whether we should, as a necessary incident to a just adjudication of the case at bar, refine and elaborate upon our law regarding (a) the standard of care applicable to physicians in medical malpractice cases and (b) the matter of how expert witnesses may be qualified in such litigation.

* * *

When this matter was before the Court on direct appeal, we determined that the judgment below in favor of the surgeon, Dr. Glyn R. Hilbun, rendered following the granting of a motion for a directed verdict, had been correctly entered. * * *

For the reasons set forth below, we now regard that our original decision was incorrect. * * *

II.

Terry O. Hall was admitted to the Singing River Hospital in Jackson County, Mississippi, in the early morning hours of May 18, 1978, complaining of abdominal discomfort. Because he was of the opinion his patient had a surgical problem, Dr. R.D. Ward, her physician, requested Dr. Glyn R. Hilbun, a general surgeon, to enter the case for consultation. Examination suggested that the discomfort and illness were probably caused by an obstruction of the small bowel. Dr. Hilbun recommended an exploratory laparotomy [sic]. Consent being given, Dr. Hilbun performed the surgery about noon on May 20, 1978, with apparent success.

Following surgery Mrs. Hall was moved to a recovery room at 1:35 p.m., where Dr. Hilbun remained in attendance with her until about 2:50 p.m. At that time Mrs. Hall was alert and communicating with him. All vital signs were stable. Mrs. Hall was then moved to a private room where she expired some 14 hours later.

On May 19, 1980, Glenn Hall commenced this wrongful death action by the filing of his complaint * * *.

* * *

At trial Glenn Hall, plaintiff below and appellant here, described the fact of the surgery. He then testified that he remained with his wife in her hospital room from the time of her arrival from the recovery room at approximately 3:00 p.m. on May 20, 1978, until she ultimately expired at approximately 5:00 a.m. on the morning of May 21. Hall stated that his wife complained of pain at about 9:00 p.m. and was given morphine for relief, after which she fell asleep. Thereafter, Hall observed that his wife had difficulty in breathing which he reported to the nurses. He inquired if something was wrong and was told his wife was all right and that such breathing was not unusual following surgery. The labored breathing then subsided for an hour or more. Later, Mrs. Hall awakened and again complained of pain in her abdomen and requested a sedative, which was administered following which she fell asleep. Mrs. Hall experienced further difficulty in breathing, and her husband reported this, too. Again, a nurse told Hall that such was normal, that patients sometimes make a lot of noise after surgery.

After the nurse left the following occurred, according to Hall.

> [A]t this time I followed her [the nurse] into the hall and walked in the hall a minute. Then I walked back into the room, and walked back out in the hall. Then I walked into the room again and I walked over to my wife and put my hand on her arm because she had stopped making that noise. Then I bent over and flipped the light on and got closer to her where I could see her, and it looked like she was having a real hard problem breathing and she was turning pale or a bluish color. And I went to screaming.

Dr. Hilbun was called and came to the hospital immediately only to find his patient had expired. The cause of the death of Terry O. Hall was subsequently determined to be adult respiratory distress syndrome (cardio-respiratory failure).

Dr. Hilbun was called as an adverse witness and gave testimony largely in accord with that above. * * *.

Dr. Hilbun stated the surgery was performed on a Saturday. Following the patient's removal to her room, he "went home and was on call that weekend for anything that might come up." Dr. Hilbun made no follow-up contacts with his patient, nor did he make any inquiry that evening regarding Mrs. Hall's post-operative progress. Moreover, he was *not* contacted by the nursing staff or others concerning Mrs. Hall's condition during the afternoon or evening of May 20 following surgery, or the early morning hours of May 21, although the exhibits introduced at trial disclose fluctuations in the vital signs late in the evening of May 20 and more so, in the early morning hours of May 21. Dr. Hilbun's next contact with his patient came when he was called by Glenn Hall about 4:55 or 5:00 that morning. By then it was too late.

* * *

The autopsy performed upon Mrs. Hall's body revealed the cause of death and, additionally, disclosed that a laparotomy [sic] sponge had been left in the patient's abdominal cavity. The evidence, however, without contradiction establishes that the sponge did not contribute to Mrs. Hall's death. Although the sponge may ultimately have caused illness, this possibility was foreclosed by the patient's untimely death.

Plaintiff's theory of the case centered around the post-operative care provided by Dr. Hilbun. Two areas of fault suggested were Dr. Hilbun's failure to make inquiry regarding his patient's post-operative course prior to his retiring on the night of May 20 and his alleged failure to give appropriate post-operative instructions to the hospital nursing staff.

When questioned at trial, Dr. Hilbun first stated that he had practiced for 16 years in the Singing River Hospital and was familiar with the routine of making surgical notes, i.e., a history of the surgery. He explained that the post-operative orders were noted on the record out of courtesy by Dr. Judy Fabian, the anesthesiologist on the case. He stated such orders were customarily approved by his signature or he would add or subtract from the record to reflect the exact situation.

[Dr. Hilbun testified as to the post-operative orders noted in the medical records as of May 20, 1978. Mrs. Hall had a nasogastric tube, an i.v., a catheter; she was receiving medications for pain, nausea, and infections.] His testimony continued:

> Q. Now after this surgery, while Mrs. Hall was in the recovery room did I understand you to say earlier that you checked on her there?
>
> A. When I got through operating on Mrs. Hall, with this major surgical procedure in an emergency situation—and I always do—I went to the recovery room with Mrs. Hall, stayed in the recovery room with Mrs. Hall, listened to her chest, took her vital signs, stayed there with her and discharged her to the floor. The only time I left the recovery room was to go into the waiting room and tell Mr. Hall. Mrs. Hall waked up, I talked to her, she said she was cold. She was completely alert.

* * *

Q. Now, you went to the recovery room to see her because you were still her physician following her post-surgery?

A. I was one of her physicians. I operated on her, and I go to the recovery room with everybody.

Q. Okay. You were the surgeon and you were concerned about the surgical procedures and how she was doing post-operatively, or either you are not concerned with your patients, how they do post-operatively?

A. As I said, I go to the recovery room with every one of my patients.

Q. Then you are still the doctor?

A. I was one of her physicians.

Q. Okay. And you customarily follow your patients following the surgery to see how they are doing as a result of the surgery, because you are the surgeon. Is that correct?

A. Yes.

* * *

Q. How long do you follow a patient like Terry Hall?

A. Until she leaves the hospital.

Q. Okay. So ever how long she is in the hospital, you are going to continue to see her?

A. As long as my services are needed.

Insofar as the record reflects, Dr. Hilbun gave the nursing staff no instructions regarding the post-operative monitoring and care of Mrs. Hall beyond those [summarized above]. Dr. Hilbun had no contact with Mrs. Hall after 3:00 p.m. on May 20. Fourteen hours later she was dead.

The plaintiff called Dr. S.O. Hoerr, a retired surgeon of Cleveland, Ohio, as an expert witness. The record reflects that Dr. Hoerr is a *cum laude* graduate of the Harvard Medical School, enjoys the respect of his peers, and has had many years of surgical practice. Through him the plaintiff sought to establish that there is a national standard of surgical practice and surgical care of patients in the United States to which all surgeons, including Dr. Hilbun, are obligated to adhere. Dr. Hoerr conceded that he did not know for a fact the standard of professional skill, including surgical skills and post-operative care, practiced by general surgeons in Pascagoula, Mississippi, but that he did know what the standard should have been.

* * * [T]he trial court ruled that Dr. Hoerr was not qualified to give an opinion as to whether Dr. Hilbun's post-operative regimen departed from the obligatory standard of care. * * *.

* * *

Parts of Dr. Hoerr's testimony excluded under the trial judge's ruling follow:

> A. My opinion is that she [Mrs. Hall] did not receive the type of care that she should have received from the general surgical specialist and that he [Dr. Hilbun] was negligent in not following this patient; contacting, checking on the condition of his patient sometime in the evening of

May 20th. *It is important in the post-operative care of patients to remember that very serious complications can follow abdominal operations, in particular in the first few hours after a surgical procedure.* And this can be inward bleeding; it can be an explosive development in an infection; or *it can be the development of a serious pulmonary complication, as it was in this patient. As a result of her condition, it is my opinion that he lost the opportunity to diagnose a condition, which in all probability could have been diagnosed at the time by an experienced general surgeon, one with expertise in thoracic surgery. And then appropriate treatment could have been undertaken to abort the complications and save her life.*

There are different ways that a surgeon can keep track of his patient—"follow her" as the expression goes—besides a bedside visit, which is the best way and which need not be very long at all, in which the vital signs are checked over. The surgeon gets a general impression of what's going on. He can delegate this responsibility to a competent physician, who need not be a surgeon but could be a knowledgeable family practitioner. He could call in and ask to speak to the registered nurse in charge of the patient and determine through her what the vital signs are, and if she is an experienced Registered Nurse what her evaluation of the patient is. *From my review of the record, none of these things took place, and there is no effort as far as I can see that Dr. Hilbun made any effort to find out what was going on with this patient during that period of time.* I might say or add an additional belief that I felt that the nursing responsibility which should have been exercised was not exercised, particularly at the 4:00 a.m. level when the pulse rate was recorded at 140 per minute without any effort as far as I can see to have any physician see the patient or to get in touch with the operating surgeon and so on.

There is an additional thing that Dr. Hilbun could have done if he felt that the nursing services might be spotty—sometimes good, sometimes bad. This is commonly done in Columbus, Ohio, in Ashtabula, Pascagoula, etcetera. *He could put limits on the degree in which the vital signs can vary, expressing the order that he should be called if they exceeded that.* Examples would be: Call me if the pulse rate goes over 110; call me if the temperature exceeds 101; call me if the blood pressure drops below 100. There is a simple way of spelling out for the nursing services what the limits of discretion belong to them and the point at which the doctor should be called.

* * *

Dr. Hilbun did not place any orders on the chart for the nurses to call him in the event of a change in the vital signs of Mrs. Hall. He normally made afternoon rounds between 4:00 and 5:00 p.m. but didn't recall whether he went by to see her before going home. Dr. Hilbun was on call at the hospital that weekend for anything which might come up. Subsequent to the operation and previous to Mrs. Hall's death, he was called about one other person on the same ward, one door down, twice during the night. He made no inquiry concerning Mrs. Hall, nor did he see or communicate with her.

Dr. Donald Dohn, of expertise unquestioned by plaintiff and with years of practical experience, gave testimony for the defendant. He had practiced on the staff at the Cleveland Clinic Foundation in Cleveland, Ohio, beginning in 1958. Fortuitously, he had moved to Pascagoula, Mississippi, about one month before the trial. Dr. Dohn stated he had practiced in the Singing River Hospital for a short time and there was a great difference in the standard of care in medical procedures in Cleveland, Ohio, and those in Pascagoula, Mississippi. Although he had practiced three weeks in Pascagoula, he was still in the process of acquainting himself with the local conditions. He explained the differences as follows:

> Well, there are personnel differences. There are equipment differences. There are diagnostic differences. There are differences in staff responsibility and so on. For example, at the Cleveland Clinic on our service we had ten residents that we were training. They worked with us as our right hands. Here we have no staff. So it is up to us to do the things that our residents would have done there. There we had a team of five or six nurses and other personnel in the operating room to help us. Here we have nurses in the operating room, but there is no assigned team. You get the luck of the draw that day. I am finding out these things myself. Up there it is a big center; a thousand beds, and it is a regional center. We have tremendous advantages with technical systems, various types of x-ray equipment that is [sic] sophisticated. Also in terms of the intensive care unit, we had a Neurosurgical Intensive Care with people who were specially trained as a team to work there. From my standpoint personally, I seldom had to do much paperwork there as compared to what I have to do now. I have to dictate everything and take all my notes. So, as you can see, there is a difference.

Finally, he again stated the standard of care in Ohio and the standard of care in the Singing River Hospital are very different, although it is obvious to the careful reader of Dr. Dohn's testimony that in so doing he had reference to the differences in equipment, personnel and resources and not differences in the standards of skill, medical knowledge and general medical competence a physician could be expected to bring to bear upon the treatment of a patient.

At the conclusion of the plaintiff's case, defendant moved for a directed verdict on the obvious grounds that, the testimony of Drs. Hoerr and Sachs having been excluded, the Plaintiff had failed to present a legally sufficient quantum of evidence to establish a prima facie case. The Circuit Court granted the motion. * * *

III.

A. General Considerations

Medical malpractice is legal fault by a physician or surgeon. It arises from the failure of a physician to provide the quality of care required by law. When a physician undertakes to treat a patient, he takes on an obligation enforceable at law to use minimally sound medical judgment and render minimally competent care in the course of the services he provides. A physician does not guarantee recovery. If a patient sustains injury because of the physician's failure to perform the duty he has assumed under our law, the physician may be liable in damages. A competent physician is not liable *per se* for a mere error of judgment, mistaken diagnosis or the occurrence of an undesirable result.

The twin principles undergirding our stewardship of the law regulating professional liability of physicians have always been reason and fairness. For years in medical malpractice litigation we regarded as reasonable and fair what came to be known as the "locality rule" (but which has always consisted of at least two separate rules, one a rule of substantive law, the other a rule of evidence).

* * *

C. The Physician's Duty of Care: A primary rule of substantive law

1. The Backdrop

* * *

2. The Inevitable Ascendency of National Standards

* * *

We would have to put our heads in the sand to ignore the "nationalization" of medical education and training. Medical school admission standards are similar across the country. Curricula are substantially the same. Internship and residency programs for those entering medical specialties have substantially common components. Nationally uniform standards are enforced in the case of certification of specialists. Differences and changes in these areas occur temporally, not geographically.

Physicians are far more mobile than they once were. They frequently attend medical school in one state, do a residency in another, establish a practice in a third and after a period of time relocate to a fourth. All the while, they have ready access to professional and scientific journals and seminars for continuing medical education from across the country. Common sense and experience inform us that the laws of medicine do not vary from state to state in anything like the manner our public law does.

Medicine is a science, though its practice be an art (as distinguished from a business). Regarding the basic matter of the learning, skill and competence a physician may bring to bear in the treatment of a given patient, state lines are largely irrelevant. That a patient's temperature is 105 degrees means the same in New York as in Mississippi. Bones break and heal in Washington the same as in Florida, in Minnesota the same as in Texas. * * *

* * *

3. The Competence–Based National Standard of Care: Herein of the Limited Role of Local Custom

All of the above informs our understanding and articulation of the competence-based duty of care. Each physician may with reason and fairness be expected to possess or have reasonable access to such medical knowledge as is commonly possessed or reasonably available to minimally competent physicians in the same specialty or general field of practice throughout the United States, to have a realistic understanding of the limitations on his or her knowledge or competence, and, in general, to exercise minimally adequate medical judgment. Beyond that, each physician has a duty to have a practical working knowledge of the facilities, equipment, resources (including personnel in health related fields and their general level of knowledge and competence), and options (including what specialized services or facilities may be available in larger communities, e.g., Memphis, Birmingham, Jackson, New Orleans, etc.) reasonably available to him or her as well as the practical limitations on same.

In the care and treatment of each patient, each physician has a non-delegable duty to render professional services consistent with that objectively ascertained minimally acceptable level of competence he may be expected to apply given the qualifications and level of expertise he holds himself out as possessing and given the circumstances of the particular case. The professional services contemplated within this duty concern the entire caring process, including but not limited to examination, history, testing, diagnosis, course of treatment, medication, surgery, follow-up, after-care and the like.

* * *

Mention should be made in this context of the role of good medical judgment which, because medicine is not an exact science, must be brought to bear in diagnostic and treatment decisions daily. Some physicians are more reluctant to recommend radical surgery than are other equally competent physicians. There exist legitimate differences of opinion regarding medications to be employed in particular contexts. "Waiting periods" and their duration are the subject of bona fide medical controversy. What diagnostic tests should be performed is a matter of particularly heated debate in this era of ever-escalating health care costs. We must be vigilant that liability never be imposed upon a physician for the mere exercise of a bona fide medical judgment which turns out, with the benefit of 20–20 hindsight (a) to have been mistaken, and (b) to be contrary to what a qualified medical expert witness in the exercise of his good medical judgment would have done. We repeat: a physician may incur civil liability only when the quality of care he renders (including his judgment calls) falls below minimally acceptable levels.

Different medical judgments are made by physicians whose offices are across the street from one another. Comparable differences in medical judgment or opinion exist among physicians geographically separated by much greater distances, and in this sense local custom does and must continue to play a role within our law, albeit a limited one.

We recognize that customs vary within given medical communities and from one medical community to another. Conformity with established medical custom practiced by minimally competent physicians in a given area, while evidence of performance of the duty of care, may never be conclusive of such compliance. [ ] The content of the duty of care must be objectively determined by reference to the availability of medical and practical knowledge which would be brought to bear in the treatment of like or similar patients under like or similar circumstances by minimally competent physicians in the same field, given the facilities, resources and options available. The content of the duty of care may be informed by local medical custom but never subsumed by it.

* * *

4. The Resources–Based Caveat to the National Standard of Care

The duty of care, as it thus emerges from considerations of reason and fairness, when applied to the facts of the world of medical science and practice, takes two forms: (a) a duty to render a quality of care consonant with the level of medical and practical knowledge the physician may reasonably be expected to possess and the medical judgment he may be expected to exercise, and (b) a duty based upon the adept use of such medical facilities, services, equipment and options as are reasonably available. With respect to this second form of the duty, we regard that there remains a core of validity to the premises of the old locality rule.

* * *

A physician practicing in Noxubee County, for example, may hardly be faulted for failure to perform a CAT scan when the necessary facilities and equipment are not reasonably available. In contradistinction, objectively reasonable expectations regarding the physician's knowledge, skill, capacity for sound medical judgment and general competence are, consistent with his field of practice and the facts and circumstances in which the patient may be found, *the same everywhere.*

* * *

As a result of its resources-based component, the physician's non-delegable duty of care is this: given the circumstances of each patient, each physician has a duty to use his or her knowledge and therewith treat through maximum reasonable medical recovery, each patient, with such reasonable diligence, skill, competence, and prudence as are practiced by minimally competent physicians in the same specialty or general field of practice throughout the United States, who have available to them the same general facilities, services, equipment and options.

* * *

As we deal with general principles, gray areas necessarily exist. One involves the case where needed specialized facilities and equipment are not available locally but are reasonably accessible in major medical centers—New Orleans, Jackson, Memphis. Here as elsewhere the local physician is held to minimally acceptable standards. In determining whether the physician's actions comport with his duty of care, consideration must always be given to the time factor—is the physician confronted with what reasonably appears to be a medical emergency, or does it appear likely that the patient may be transferred to an appropriate medical center without substantial risk to the health or life of the patient? Consideration must also be given to the economic factors—are the proposed transferee facilities sufficiently superior to justify the trouble and expense of transfer? Further discussion of these factors should await proper cases.

D. Who May Qualify As Expert Medical Witness In Malpractice Case: A rule of evidence

As a general rule, if scientific, technical or other specialized knowledge will assist the trier of fact to understand the evidence or to determine a fact in issue, a witness qualified as an expert by knowledge, skill, experience, training or education (or a combination thereof), coupled with independence and lack of bias, may testify thereto in the form of an opinion or otherwise. Medical malpractice cases generally require expert witnesses to assist the trier of fact to understand the evidence. [ ]

Generally, where the expert lives or where he or she practices his or her profession has no relevance *per se* with respect to whether a person may be qualified and accepted by the court as an expert witness. There is no reason on principle why these factors should have *per se* relevance in medical malpractice cases.

* * *

In view of the refinements in the physician's duty of care * * * we hold that a qualified medical expert witness may without more express an opinion regarding the meaning and import of the duty of care * * *, given the peculiar circumstances of the case. Based on the information reasonably available to the physician, i.e., symptoms, history, test results, results of the doctor's own physical examination, x-rays, vital signs, etc., a qualified medical expert may express an opinion regarding the conclusions (possible diagnoses or areas for further examination and testing) minimally knowledgeable and competent physicians in the same specialty or general field of practice would draw, or actions (not tied to the availability of specialized facilities or equipment not generally available) they would take.

Before the witness may go further, he must be familiarized with the facilities, resources, services and options available. This may be done in any number of ways. The witness may prior to trial have visited the facilities, etc. He may have sat in the courtroom and listened as other witnesses described the facilities. He may have known and over the years interacted with physicians in the area. There are no doubt many other ways in which this could be done, but, significantly, we should allow the witness to be made familiar with the facilities (and customs) of the medical community in question via a properly predicated and phrased hypothetical question.

Once he has become informed of the facilities, etc. available to the defendant physician, the qualified medical expert witness may express an opinion what the care duty of the defendant physician was and whether the acts or omissions of the defendant physician were in compliance with, or fell substantially short of compliance with, that duty.

* * *

V. Disposition Of The Case At Bar

[The court reversed and remanded for a new trial, on the grounds that the testimony of Drs. Hoerr and Sachs was improperly excluded, and with their testimony, the plaintiff might have survived the defense motion for a directed verdict.]

Notes and Questions

1. How did the court in *Hall v. Hilbun* view the customary practice of the defendant's medical specialty? Why did it adopt this position? How much of a burden is it for a defendant to rebut the plaintiff's evidence on customary practice?

2. The standards by which the delivery of professional medical services is judged are not normally established by either judge or jury. The medical profession itself sets the standards of practice and the courts enforce these standards in

tort suits. Defendants trying to prove a standard of care normally present expert testimony describing the actual pattern of medical practice, without any reference to the effectiveness of that practice. Most jurisdictions give professional medical standards conclusive weight, so that the trier of fact is not allowed to reject the practice as improper. See, e.g., Holt v. Godsil, 447 So.2d 191 (Ala.1984).

3. Why should conformity to customary practice be a conclusive shield for a health care professional? In tort litigation not involving professionals, courts are willing to reject customary practice if they find the practice dangerous or out of date. See Joseph King, In Search of a Standard of Care for the Medical Profession—the "Accepted Practice" Formula, 28 Vand.L.Rev. 1213, 1236 (1975). Critics such as King worry that standard practice may at times be little more than a routine into which physicians have drifted by default.

The customary or accepted practice standard follows the general tort rule that physicians are measured against the standard of their profession, not merely the standard of a reasonable and prudent person. Medical practices are always evolving as new developments and scientific studies alter the customary practice. Such evolution in medical practices often creates tensions for the physician who believes that the customary practice is dangerous but the new standard has not yet been generally accepted. Courts have however been unwilling generally to allow a plaintiff to present evidence to attack a customary practice that the defendant physician complied with, except under rare circumstances.

In Burton v. Brooklyn Doctors Hospital, 88 A.D.2d 217, 452 N.Y.S.2d 875 (1982), the plaintiff was exposed while in the hospital as a newborn to a prolonged liberal application of oxygen. He developed retrolental fibroplasia (RFL) as a result. At the time of his birth, a "significant segment of the medical community continued to believe that the liberal administration of oxygen to prematures was important in preventing death or brain damage. Yet, a respected body of medical opinion believed that oxygen contributed to RLF." He was part of a study at the hospital examining various level of oxygen and the effects of its withdrawal or curtailment; the study found in 1954 that prolonged liberal use led to the development of RLF, and cutting off oxygen to premature infants after 48 hours decreased the incidence of RLF without increasing the risk of either death or brain damage.

> * * * [T]he jury's finding of malpractice should not be disturbed. The issue was submitted to the jury under a proper charge. "If a physician fails to employ his expertise or best judgment, and that omission causes injury, he should not automatically be freed from liability because in fact he adhered to acceptable practice."

See also Toth v. Community Hospital at Glen Cove, 22 N.Y.2d 255, 292 N.Y.S.2d 440, 239 N.E.2d 368 (1968), where the defendant doctor had ordered a reduction in the flow of oxygen to the plaintiff, and the nursing staff had failed to carry out the order.

> * * * evidence that the defendant followed customary practice is not the sole test of professional malpractice. If a physician fails to employ his expertise or best judgment, and that omission causes injury, he should not automatically be freed from liability because in fact he adhered to acceptable practice. There is no policy reason why a physician, who knows or believes there are unnecessary dangers in the community practice, should not be required to take whatever precautionary measures he deems appropriate.

4. Judicial deference to customary practice may be weakening. The Wisconsin Supreme Court observed that:

> * * * [S]hould customary medical practice fail to keep pace with developments and advances in medical science, adherence to custom might constitute a failure to exercise ordinary care.
>
> * * *
>
> We agree with the parties and the Medical Society that while evidence of the usual and customary conduct of others under similar circumstances is ordinarily relevant and admissible as an indication of what is reasonably prudent, customary conduct is not dispositive and cannot overcome the requirement that physicians exercise ordinary care.

Nowatske v. Osterloh, 198 Wis.2d 419, 543 N.W.2d 265, 272 (1996).

5. Courts expect the standard of care to be compliance with available technology at the time the diagnosis or treatment was offered to the patient. See, e.g., Klisch v. Meritcare Medical Group, Inc., 134 F.3d 1356 (C.A. 8th Cir. 1998), where the patient sued for negligent performance of surgery. The Court of Appeals held that: (1) a jury instruction that the jury should consider the state of medical technology at time of allegedly negligent surgery was appropriate; (2) under Minnesota law, the jury in a medical malpractice action should weigh information available to physicians at the time of treatment and without benefit of hindsight.

6. Could a plaintiff use the studies cited in Chapter 1 to support a position that the efficacy of a standard practice is not proven? How would a court react to such studies?

1. The Locality Rule

Hall provides an excellent discussion of the locality rule. Most courts have moved from the locality rule to a similar locality or a national standard, in part due to worries about a "conspiracy of silence" that unfairly limits the pool of available experts. Doctors do not like to testify against one another. As the court noted in Mulder v. Parke Davis & Co., 288 Minn. 332, 181 N.W.2d 882 (1970), "All too frequently, and perhaps understandably, practicing physicians are reluctant to testify against one another. Unfortunately, the medical profession has been slow to fashion machinery for making impartial and objective assessments of the performance of their fellow practitioners."

For a first hand account of physician reluctance, by an M.D.–J.D., see Robinson, Why the Conspiracy of Silence Won't Die, Medical Economics 180 (Feb. 20, 1984).

Rural communities face substantial difficulties in getting doctors: salaries are lower, availability of peers is limited, health insurance for doctor and patient may be harder to get. The locality rule has been viewed as a subsidy for rural areas, an additional incentive to attract doctors to areas that they don't otherwise find attractive. Absent the added protection of the locality rule, it is argued, rural areas will suffer even more from little or no medical care. Henry C. Karlson and Roger D. Erwin, Medical Malpractice: Informed Consent to the Locality Rule, 12 Ind.L.Rev. 653, 664–657 (1979). Most courts have proved hostile to this position, since medical practice has become national in scope and rural residents deserve the same level of care as urban residents. See Shilkret v. Annapolis Emergency Hospital Ass'n., 276 Md. 187, 349 A.2d 245 (1975). In any event, rural residents do not sue for malpractice at anywhere near the level of urban residents. Danzon concluded that urbanization was the "single most powerful predictor" of the frequency and severity of claims. Patricia Danzon, Medical Malpractice 82–83 (1985). See also Patricia Danzon, The Frequency and Severity of Medical Malpractice Claims: New Evidence, 49 Law & Contemp.Probs. 57, 69 (1986). Rural practitioners are simply not likely to get sued, perhaps because of more personal relationships with their patients or the attitudes of rural residents generally toward litigation.

The debate over the locality rule has been largely won by the national standard test, as *Hall* evidences. But many courts, like *Hall,* also allow evidence describing the practice limitations under which the defendant labors. *Hall* 's "resource component" allows the trier of fact to consider the facilities, staff and other equipment available to the practitioner in the institution, following the general rule that courts should take into account the locality, proximity of specialists and special facilities for diagnosis and treatment. Blair v. Eblen, 461 S.W.2d 370 (Ky.1970); Restatement (Second) of Torts, sec. 299A, Comment g. ("Allowance must be made also for the type of community in which the actor carries on his practice. A country doctor cannot be expected to have the equipment, facilities, experience, knowledge or opportunity to obtain it, afforded him by a large city.")

A national standard of practice may not exist for many procedures, and the "highest and best" practice may not be the safest or most effective in the long run. Substantial regional variations exist in the use of many procedures, with no apparent differences in outcome (life expectancy, morbidity, days missed from work). Different practice styles exist in different regions, and even within states, based on local concepts of good practice. What do these findings suggest? Does the evidence on variation in medical practice among regions support the locality rule? Might it be better to allow the locality rule in a tort suit as a way of supporting local practices against a monolithic national practice under some circumstances?

Note: Telemedicine and Rural Practices

Access by physicians to computer databases makes information on advances in medical knowledge instantly available whether the doctor is rural or urban. MEDLINE, the largest, has over five million references and articles from 4,000 journals. The level of skill required to access such a database has steadily decreased, with more user friendly command structures and access through commercial services such as MEDLARS and MEDIS. A physician with a phone, a modem and a personal computer can pay a monthly subscription fee and then call up information 24 hours a day. In fact such databases are now freely accessible to a consumer with a computer through such online services such as America Online, and Medline is now accessible on the World Wide Web, with free software available online to access it.

The possibilities of telemedicine go far beyond access to large medical databases. A physician in a rural area could get the assistance of a large medical center in diagnosing a patient's problems; such a physician might also be able to track a patient at home to monitor vital signs and symptoms. As Bradham et al. write,

Through telemedicine, patients and doctors in rural or economically depressed areas might immediately access specialized services that their communities lack, thereby increasing convenience, diagnostic ability, and the overall quality of local medical care. Further, telemedicine technologies might allow hospitals to release patients sooner by permitting clinicians to monitor patient progress remotely, which in turn would reduce costly hospital stays.

What exactly is "telemedicine"? Kuszler sums it up as follows:

Telemedicine's "simple, but serviceable" definition is the use of telecommunication to diagnose and treat a patient. Telemedicine encompasses a panoply of technologies and communication modalities that allow health care providers to connect with, examine, counsel and advise patients about treatment options. These include teleradiology and other teleimaging diagnostics, telesurgery and robotics, video and Internet/e-mail conferencing, transmission of electrocardiographic and other physiological data by telephone, telecommunications, or Internet lines and "telehealth" education via the Internet and cable television. Although many of these examples rely on relatively recent communications technologies, telemedicine escaped the bounds of the simple telephone call at least thirty years ago and has already acquired an impressive history.

* * *

Telemedicine is no longer limited to transmission of hazy images and telemetry data from the remote, isolated Alaskan village or orbiting spacecraft. Highly sophisticated communication and computer systems provide high-resolution images, "crunch" complex data, have analytic, even artificial intelligence, capacity, and allow access to real-time, delayed and stored information.

Telemedicine is becoming an integral part of health care delivery in diverse settings. It is breaking down boundaries between different types of health care providers, revolutionizing rural health care delivery, improving and facilitating care for underserved and difficult to manage populations and enhancing discourse between patients and providers. There is also a growing telehealth movement.

Patricia C. Kuszler, Telemedicine and Integrated Health Care Delivery: Compounding Malpractice Liability, 25 Am. J.L. & Med. 297, 299–300 (1999).

What will this do the standard of care? Kuszler writes:

Telemedicine will provide physicians in all geographic areas with the opportunity to obtain consultations from specialists, have diagnostic tests and data reviewed at state-of-the-art tertiary care centers and have the patient "examined" by another provider for a second opinion.Telemedicine potentially can conquer distance in an instant. Differences between services available to providers and patients in different geographic areas should further evaporate, resulting in greater pervasiveness of a single standard of care. Id at 316.

Ease of access to medical databases necessarily raises the standard of knowledge required of the average physician. No court has yet required an individual physician to have access to a database or to telemedicine links, but a requirement of such access seems inevitable as sophistication about the Internet and databases grows. Don't computerized databases reinforce a national standard of care against which to judge medical practice? Not only will such access continue to diminish the importance of the locality rule or its manifestations, but it may also limit the "respectable minority" rule and other judgment rules by narrowing the range of variation in medical opinion as to what is acceptable. A physician relying on a contraindicated drug, an outdated surgical technique, or an inappropriate description of risk factors in getting a patient's informed consent may be attacked by the plaintiff using the results of a computer search. See Warrick v. Giron, 290 N.W.2d 166 (Minn.1980) (the defendants introduced a computerized search they had conducted, revealing no evidence that the surgical and anesthesiological techniques utilized by the defendants were improper.) See generally Patricia C. Kuszler, Telemedicine and Integrated Health Care Delivery: Compounding Medical Liability, 25 Am.J.L. & Med. 297(1999); Jerry V. Glowniak and Marilyn K. Bushway, Computer Networks as a Medical Resource: Accessing and Using the Internet, 271 J.A.M.A. 1934 (1994); Douglas D. Bradham, Sheron Morgan, and Margaret E. Dailey, The Information Superhighway: A Critical Discussion of Its Possibilities and Legal Implications, 30 Wake Forest L. Rev. 145, 147 (1995) (discussing existing telemedicine projects around the United States). See also Daniel McCarthy, The Virtual Health Economy: Telemedicine and the Supply of Primary Care Physicians in Rural America, 21 Am. J.L. & Med. 111 (1995); Robin Elizabeth Margolis, Law and Policy Barriers Hamper Growth of Telemedicine, 11 No. 10 HealthSpan 14 (1994) (noting among other problems complicated conflict-of-law problems that might arise with a out-of-state physician giving a telemedicine consultation). See also Second Invitational Consensus Conference on Telemedicine and the National Information Infrastructure, 1 Telemedicine J. 321 et seq. (1995).

2. *Expert Testimony*

The standard of practice in the defendant doctor's specialty or area of practice is normally established through the testimony of medical experts. The cases above illustrate the burden that the plaintiff bears. In any jurisdiction, plaintiffs, to withstand a motion for a directed verdict, must 1) qualify their medical witnesses as experts; 2) satisfy the court that the expert's testimony will assist the trier of fact; and 3) have the witnesses testify based upon facts that support their expert opinions. The requirement that the expert be of the same specialty as the defendant typically governs the qualifying of the expert for testifying at trial.

A plaintiff must offer proof that the defendant physician breached the legally required standard of care and was thus negligent. Expert testimony is needed to establish both the standard of proper professional skill or care and a failure by the defendant to conform. The expert does not have to testify explicitly that the conduct was "malpractice." "In medical malpractice cases, it is proper for the trier of fact to draw inferences and reach conclusions from facts that are found to be proved." Campbell v. Palmer, 20 Conn.App. 544, 568 A.2d 1064, 1067 (1990) (radiologist testified for plaintiff that the defendant's barium enema procedure was inadequate to exclude pathology and that it should have been repeated and a sigmoidoscopy suggested to the patient; he testified that the defendant's procedure was not the way he would have done it and "not the way most of the people [he knew] would have acted.").

The plaintiff's expert must testify that the standard of care breached by the defendant is a national one. The standard of care may be based upon the expert's own practice and education. Practice guidelines or parameters, particularly statements by medical societies as to good practice, will provide a ready-made particularized standard that an expert can use as a benchmark against which to test a defendant's conduct. Some courts are becoming more demanding, requiring that an expert needs "published medical standards, manuals, or protocols" to support the expert opinion, rather than just the expert's own opinion or casual conversation with a few colleagues. Travers v. District of Columbia, 672 A.2d 566 (D.C.App.1996).

The abolition of the locality rule has been one way to ease the plaintiff's burden of proof, broadening the plaintiff's choices of available experts. Many states still require that the expert at least be familiar with the standard of practice in a similar locality, and some testimony is required as to the similarities between the two localities. See, e.g., First Commercial Trust Company v. Rank, 323 Ark. 390, 915 S.W.2d 262 (1996) (family practitioner was sued for medical negligence and failure to report suspected child abuse; held that Florida emergency room physician should have been allowed to testify on the standard of care for diagnosing child abuse).

Plaintiff's experts normally must be in the same specialty as the defendant. Under some circumstances, however, courts have allowed physicians in other specialties to testify, so long as the alleged negligence involved matters within the knowledge of every physician. A general surgeon can testify as to the standard of care of a plastic surgeon performing elective surgery, as to general surgical issues as to whether nerves in the forehead should have been protected, Hauser v. Bhatnager, 537 A.2d 599 (Me.1988); a cardiologist can testify in a case involving a family practice physician, Fiedler v. Spoelhof, 483 N.W.2d 486 (Minn.App.1992); a psychiatrist has been allowed to testify as to the standard of post-operative care for a breast implant procedure, Miller v. Silver, 181 Cal.App.3d 652, 226 Cal.Rptr. 479 (1986). See also Searle v. Bryant, 713 S.W.2d 62 (Tenn.1986) (expert in infectious diseases could testify as to the standard of care for a surgeon, where the patient developed an abdominal infection following surgery.) Contra, see Melville v. Southward, 791 P.2d 383 (Colo.1990) (orthopedic surgeon could not offer expert testimony on the standard of care applicable to a podiatrist).

An expert need not be board certified in the subject of the suit, so long as he has the appropriate education and experience. Hanson v. Baker, 534 A.2d 665 (Me.1987). The liberal view is that an expert need not possess a medical degree so long as he has the medical knowledge. "* * * [B]efore one may testify as an expert, that person must be shown to know a great deal regarding the subject of his testimony." Thompson v. Carter, 518 So.2d 609 (Miss.1987) (toxicologist allowed to testify as to side effects of a drug prescribed by defendant physician). See also Pratt v. Stein, 298 Pa.Super. 92, 444 A.2d 674 (1982); Cornfeldt v. Tongen, 262 N.W.2d 684 (Minn.1977) (nurse anesthetist competent to testify); Hudgins v. Serrano, 186 N.J.Super. 465, 453 A.2d 218 (1982); Glover v. Ballhagen, 232 Mont. 427, 756 P.2d 1166 (Mont. 1988)(expert does not have to be a board certified family practitioner to testify as to practice).

Some jurisdictions adopt a narrower view, requiring that the expert have practiced in the same area as the defendant. See Lundgren v. Eustermann, 370 N.W.2d 877 (Minn.1985) (licensed psychologist could not testify as to standard of a physician); Bell v. Hart, 516 So.2d 562 (Ala.1987) (pharmacist and toxicologist testimony disallowed).

Expert testimony is often based upon clinical literature, FDA statements, and other evidence of the standard of practice and of side-effects of treatments and drugs. Several sources of reliable and authoritative statements may be used by experts in professional liability cases, or relied upon by the trial judge as definitive.

a. pharmaceutical package insert instructions and warnings. Package inserts may be used to establish the standard of care for use of the particular drug. In Thompson v. Carter, 518 S.2d 609 (Miss.1987), the physician used Bactrim, a sulfonamide antibiotic, to treat the plaintiff's kidney infection. She developed Stevens Johnson Syndrome, a severe allergic reaction associated with use of Bactrim. The court allowed the admission of the package insert, holding that the package insert was prima facie proof of the proper method of use of Bactrim, an "authoritative published compilation by a pharmaceutical manufacturer."

Accord, Garvey v. O'Donoghue, 530 A.2d 1141 (D.C.App.1987) (relevant evidence of the medical standard of care). But see Tarter v. Linn, 396 Pa.Super. 155, 578 A.2d 453 (Pa.Super 1990) (sustaining trial court's refusal to allow plaintiff to establish the standard of care by introducing information on adverse drug reactions to the drug Diamox from the Physician's Desk Reference); Craft v. Peebles, 78 Hawai'i 287, 893 P.2d 138 (1995)("some evidence"); Mozer v. Kerth, 224 Ill.App.3d 525, 166 Ill.Dec. 801, 586 N.E.2d 759 (1992)(while package insert may establish the standard of care, "plaintiff must still show by expert testimony that physician failed to follow explicit instructions of the manufacturer").

The Physicians Desk Reference is allowed by most courts as some evidence of the standard of care, if an expert witness relies on it. See, e.g., Morlino v. Medical Center, 152 N.J. 563, 706 A.2d 721 (N.J.1998), where a pregnant patient whose fetus died after she took an antibiotic brought action against prescribing physician, medical center, and obstetrician. The court held that Physicians' Desk Reference (PDR) entries alone did not establish standard of care, but the trier of fact can consider package inserts and parallel PDR references when they are supported by expert testimony. "When supported by expert testimony, PDR entries and package inserts may provide useful information of the standard of care. Physicians frequently rely on the PDR when making decisions concerning the administration and dosage of drugs."

b. judicial notice. When the defendant physician's clinical decisions violate a clearly articulated practice within the specialty, courts are willing to make a finding of per se negligence. See Deutsch v. Shein, 597 S.W.2d 141 (Ky.1980), where the defendant was negligent per se in ordering radiology and other tests on the pregnant plaintiff, injuring the fetus. In United States v. Zwick, 413 F.Supp. 113, 115 (N.D.Ohio 1976), the court considered an action for injunctive relief brought by the United States against a physician who had prescribed over 3,800,000 doses of anorectic controlled substances in a three year period. The court issued an injunction, declaring that minimum standards of medical practice for physicians in bariatric practice require that such drugs not be used as a routine part of treatment of obesity. "* * * [I]t is not proper for the physician dispensing and prescribing anorectic controlled drugs to adopt a unitary approach to the treatment of obesity in that no standard approach to treatment exists." The court cited, as support for its per se finding, a monograph by the National Institutes of Health; a New England Journal of Medicine article; two treatises; Food and Drug Administration regulations; and standards set forth by the American Society of Bariatric Physicians, "Standards of Bariatric Practice".

c. substantive use of a learned treatise. At the common law, a treatise could be used only to impeach the opponent's experts during cross-examination. It could only undercut the expert's testimony, not build the plaintiff's case. The concern was hearsay, since the author of the treatise was not available for cross-examination as to statements contained in the treatise. Federal Rule of Evidence (FRE) 803(18) creates an exception to the hearsay rule, so that the learned treatise can be used for substantive purposes, so long as the treatise is accepted as reliable. Jacober v. St. Peter's Med. Ctr., 128 N.J. 475, 608 A.2d 304 (N.J. 1992). An expert must be on the stand to explain and assist in the application of the treatise. Tart v. McGann, 697 F.2d 75 (2d Cir.1982). The treatise must be declared reliable by the trial court, after a motion by the moving lawyer to use the treatise substantively under FRE 803(18) or its state equivalent. Maggipinto v. Reichman, 481 F.Supp. 547 (E.D.Pa.1979).

d. expert reliance on research findings. Experts in malpractice cases base their testimony on their knowledge, education and experience. They may also rely on outside studies in the research literature. On rare occasions, courts have allowed such research material into evidence in a malpractice suit. In Young v. Horton, 259 Mont. 34, 855 P.2d 502 (Mont. 1993), the court allowed into evidence four medical journal articles that had concluded that a majority of patients forget that they gave informed consent to their doctors prior to surgery. The medical expert then testified based both on his experience with informed consent and on the articles' conclusions.

The admissibility of "novel" scientific evidence is often a thorny issue in environmental and toxic tort cases, although rarely in malpractice cases. The standard for evaluating such evidence had long been held to be established by the Court in Frye v. United States, 54 App.D.C. 46, 293 Fed. 1013 (1923), where the Supreme Court considered the polygraph test and its limitations. The Court held that expert opinion based on a scientific technique is inadmissible unless the technique is "generally accepted" as reliable in the relevant scientific community. In Daubert v. Merrell Dow Pharmaceuticals, Inc., 509 U.S. 579, 113 S.Ct. 2786, 125 L.Ed.2d 469 (1993), the Court again considered the admissibility of scientific evidence, in this case epidemiological and other evidence of birth defects caused by mothers' ingestion of Bendectin. The Court rejected the *Frye* test of "general acceptability" as a threshold test of admissibility of novel scientific evidence, holding that the Federal Rules of Evidence, particularly Rule 702, make the trial judge the gatekeeper of such evidence, with the responsibility to assess the reliability of an expert's testimony, its relevance, and the underlying reasoning or methodology. Expert testimony must have a valid scientific connection to the issues in the case, and be based on "scientifically valid principles". The scientific evidence must pertain to scientific knowledge defined as falsifiable scientific theories capable of empirical testing.

The Supreme Court has extended the Daubert factors to all expert testimony, not just scientific testimony. In Kumho v. Carmichael, 526 U.S. 137, 119 S.Ct. 1167, 143 L.Ed.2d 238 (1999), the Court held that Daubert's gatekeeping role for federal courts, requiring an inquiry into both relevance and reliability, applies not only to scientific testimony but to all expert testimony. The Court noted that this was a flexible test, not a checklist, and it is tied to the particular facts of the case. But "some of these factors may be helpful in evaluating the reliability even of experience-based expert testimony ... " Id. At 1176. The use of the Daubert test is "make certain that an expert, whether basing testimony upon professional studies or personal experience employs in the courtroom the same level of intellectual rigor that characterizes the practice of an expert in the relevant field." Id. This would seem to impose a higher level of scrutiny on the typical malpractice expert, particularly in cases involving institutional liability, where the expert may testify about a system design in a hospital or a salary incentive system in a managed care system. It remains to be seen how the Kumho case will affect judicial screening of malpractice experts. In some state courts, so-called "Kumho" motions challenging experts have become common, asking the trial court to evaluate the reliability of the bases of the expert's testimony.

In Reese v. Stroh, 128 Wash.2d 300, 907 P.2d 282 (Wash. 1995), the Washington Supreme Court considered the use of Prolastin, protein replacement therapy, for emphysema. The treatment, while FDA-approved, lacked statistical proof of efficacy. The court held that "[a]n expert opinion regarding application of an accepted theory or methodology to a particular medical condition does not implicate *Frye*." They also declined to accept the *Daubert* test, finding that it was unnecessary to do so. They held that an expert's practical experience and acquired knowledge is sufficient without further proof of statistical efficacy. Since the defendant did not argue that the theory or methodology involved in Prolastin therapy lacked acceptance in the scientific community, an expert opinion regarding application of an accepted theory to a particular medical condition does not implicate Frye. Id. at 286. See generally Katherine M. Atikian, Note and Comment, Nasty Medicine: Daubert v. Merrell Dow Pharmaceuticals, Inc. Applied to a Hypothetical Medical Malpractice Case, 27 Loy. L.A. L. Rev. 1513 (1994).

e. evidentiary uses of clinical practice guidelines. Clinical practice guidelines, so long as they are developed by an expert witness as a testamentary anchor, will be allowed in evidence to help establish the standard of care. They can also be used to impeach the opinion of an expert witness. In Roper v. Blumenfeld, 309 N.J.Super. 219, 706 A.2d 1151, 1156 (N.J.Super.A.D.1998), the defendant used 1992 Parameters of Care for Oral and Maxillofacial Surgery: A Guide of Practice, Monitoring and Evaluation in order to cross examine plaintiff's expert and to examine his expert. As used to impeach, it was permissible to counter the doctor's opinion that because plaintiff was injured during defendant's failed attempt at extraction, defendant must have deviated from the standard of care because the injury is not a medically accepted risk of the procedures he performed. "As to this claim, the article is quite relevant for it lists as a known risk and complication of 'erupted' teeth '[o]ral-facial neurologic dysfunction.' "

B. PRACTICE GUIDELINES AS CODIFIED STANDARDS OF CARE

A national standard of practice does not exist for many procedures and tools, and the "highest and best" practice may not be the safest or most effective in the long run. Substantial regional variations exist in the use of many procedures, with no apparent differences in outcome (life expectancy, morbidity, days missed from work). See generally John Wennberg and A. Gittlesohn, Small Area Variations in Health Care Delivery, 182 Science 1102 (1973); Pamela Paul–Shaheen, Jane Deane Clark, and Daniel Williams, "Small Area Analysis: A Review and Analysis of the North American Literature," 12 J. Health Politics, Policy and Law 741 (1987).

Different practice styles exist in different regions, and even within states, based on a local concept of good practice, as the locality rule litigation demonstrates. Practices may continue to be used by physicians out of sheer inertia, or because reimbursement reinforces their use, or because it makes a physician at least feel like she is doing something for a patient.

American physicians have in recent years put forth substantial efforts toward standard setting, specifying treatments for particular diseases, under pressure from the government, insurers and managed care organizations looking for ways to reduce variation and "trim the fat" out of clinical practice. Clinical practice guidelines (also referred to as practice parameters and clinical pathways) have been developed by specialty societies such as the American Academy of Pediatrics; by the government, through the Agency for Health Care Policy and Research (AHCPR); and by individual hospitals in the clinical setting. Such guidelines are sets of suggestions, described in decision rules, based on current medical consensus on how to treat a certain illness or condition. The Institute of Medicine has defined clinical guidelines as "systematically developed statements to assist practitioner and patient decisions about appropriate health care for specific clinical circumstances." They are standardized specifications for using a procedure or managing a particular clinical problem. In Hall v. Hilbun, the central issue was the value of such guidelines in directing the nursing staff. Such guidelines may be quality-oriented, reducing variations in practice with improving patient care; they may also be cost-reducing, promoting a lower cost approach to care. The Agency for Health Care Policy and Research (AHCPR) within the Public Health Service, a subdivision of the Department of Health and Human Services (DHHS), has the responsibility for the Department's Medical Treatment Effectiveness Program. This program supports research, data development, and other activities to develop and review clinically relevant guidelines, standards of quality, performance measures, and medical review criteria, in order to improve the quality and effectiveness of health care services.

Clinical pathways share many common attributes with practice guidelines. They are interdisciplinary plans of care that outline the ideal sequence and timing of interventions for patients with a particular diagnosis, procedure, or symptom. They are designed to reduce delays and resource use while maintaining quality of care. They guide care of patients with a highly predictable course of illness, and have been developed for high-volume, high-cost or high-risk diagnoses or procedures. Pathways are intended for use in hospitals or for cases as they move from hospital to home. They cover longer periods of treatment, presenting a kind of map of treatment to guide physicians and support staff, while also educating patients as to the sequence of treatment. They also allow a way to track patient outcomes and document whether or not a patient's outcomes were achieved.

Critical pathways are specific: they describe what will happen to a patient every day that the patient is in the hospital. This specificity includes not only traditional nursing functions, but also medication and treatments that can be ordered only by a physician. An example of such a critical pathway is one developed by University Hospitals of Cleveland for patients chronically dependent on a ventilator, to reduce the costs of caring for this population, based on a retrospective chart review of ventilator-dependent patients and projected reimbursement by third-party payers to the hospital for the patients. The pathway is developed with the patient's physician to fit the patient's needs. Other pathways include one developed by Johns Hopkins Hospital for patients undergoing a radical, retropubic prostatectomy (removal of the prostate gland).

See generally Donna D. Ignatavicius and Kathy A. Hausman, Clinical Pathways for Collaborative Practice 10 (1995); Karen Butler, Health Care Quality Revolution: Legal Landmines for Hospitals and the Rise of the Critical Pathway, 58 Alb. L. Rev. 843 (1995).

Clinical guidelines raise difficult legal questions, since they potentially offer an authoritative and settled statement of what the standard of care should be for a given treatment or illness. A court has several choices when such guidelines are offered in evidence. Such a guideline might be evidence of the customary practice in the medical profession. A doctor practicing in conformity with a guideline would be shielded from liability to the same extent as one who can establish that she or he followed professional custom. The guideline acts like an authoritative expert witness or a well-accepted review article. Using guidelines as evidence of professional custom, however, is problematic if they are ahead of prevailing medical practice. A guideline could also serve as evidence of a "respectable" minority practice. See generally Andrew L. Hyams, David W. Shapiro, and Troyen A. Brennan, Medical Practice Guidelines in Malpractice Litigation: An Early Retrospective, 21 J.Health Pol., Pol'cy & Law 289 (1996).

Guidelines have already had an effect on settlement patterns, according to surveys of malpractice lawyers. Id. Plaintiffs have used such guidelines to their advantage in malpractice cases, particularly the guidelines of the American College of Obstetricians and Gynecologists (ACOG). See, e.g., Miles v. Edward O. Tabor, M.D. 387 Mass. 783, 443 N.E.2d 1302 (1982) (obstetrician's failure to initiate resuscitation of infant immediately after delivery violated ACOG guidelines); Green v. Goldberg, 630 So.2d 606 (Fla.Dist.Ct.App. 1993)(ACOG bulletin on breast cancer treatment used to support expert testimony); Basten v. United States, 848 F.Supp. 962 (M.D.Ala.1994)(ACOG guidelines requiring that alpha-fetoprotein screening be offered and that acceptance or rejection be documented.) See generally Andrew L. Hyams et al., id. at 296–299.

Such guidelines provide a particularized source of standards against which to judge the conduct of the defendant physician. A widely accepted clinical standard may be presumptive evidence of due care, but expert testimony will still be required to introduce the standard and establish its sources and its relevancy. A guideline could thus be treated as negligence per se or at least a rebuttable presumption that could then be countered with evidence.

Professional societies often attach disclaimers to their guidelines, thereby undercutting their defensive use in litigation. The American Medical Association, for instance, calls its guidelines "parameters" instead of protocols to indicate a large sphere of physician discretion, and further suggests that all guidelines contain disclaimers stating that they are not intended to displace physician discretion. Such guidelines therefore cannot be treated as conclusive.

Might medical societies that develop guidelines expose themselves to liability if poorly crafted guidelines lead to injury, or if they fail to keep the guidelines up-to-date as medical knowledge advances? See Mark R. Chassin, Standards of Care in Medicine, 25 Inquiry 437 (1988).

What effect will this development of standards in many areas of medicine have on the proof of a malpractice case? Will it move all medical practice toward a national standard?

A outpouring of writing on practice guidelines has occurred over the past several years. See generally Arnold J. Rosoff, The Role of Clinical Practice Guidelines in Health Care Reform, 5 Health Matrix 369 (1995); Institute of Medicine, Clinical Practice Guidelines: Directions For A New Program 8 (Marilyn J. Field & Kathleen N. Lohr eds., 1990); John Ayres, The Use and Abuse of Medical Practice Guidelines, 15 J. Legal Med. 421, 436–38 (1994); Office of Technology Assessment, U.S. Congress, OTA–H–608, Identifying Health Technologies That Work: Searching For Evidence 145–47 (1994).

C. OTHER METHODS OF PROVING NEGLIGENCE

The plaintiff will usually use his own experts to establish a standard of care, defendant's deviation from it, and causation, as was done in *Hall*. As discussed above, practice guidelines also provide evidence of the standard of care. A physician's negligence can also be established in several other ways.

1. Examination of defendant's expert witnesses. The plaintiff may establish the standard of care through defense witnesses, leaving the issue of breach within the province of the fact finder, not the trial court on summary disposition. Porter v. Henry Ford Hospital, 181 Mich.App. 706, 450 N.W.2d 37 (1989).

2. An admission by the defendant that he or she was negligent. In Grindstaff v. Tygett, 698 S.W.2d 33 (Mo.App.1985), the defendant described a delivery in the hospital records as a "tight midforceps rotation". In his deposition, when asked what this phrase meant, he described the rotation as "[o]ne in which you would have to apply excessive pressure to effect the maneuver." This was held to be sufficient to submit the case to the jury. See also Bro v. Glaser, 22 Cal.App.4th 1398, 27 Cal.Rptr.2d 894 (1994)(suit for negligent infliction of emotional distress; defendant admitted in a written

interrogatory that the baby he delivered sustained a small cut from the scalpel on her left cheek).

An implicit admission of culpability can be found through evidence of intimidation by defendant of plaintiff's expert witnesses, which a jury is allowed to consider as defendant's consciousness of the weakness of his case. "This, in conjunction with the other evidence in the case, may lead to the further inference that appellee considers his case to be weak because he, in fact, is guilty of the negligence which appellant asserts he committed. Such inferences are, of course, merely permissible * * *." Meyer v. McDonnell, 40 Md.App. 524, 392 A.2d 1129 (Md.App. 1978)(defendant surgeon had message relayed through other physicians to plaintiff's medical experts to the effect that their testimony would be transcribed and disseminated to their local medical societies and the American Academy of Orthopedic Surgeons). But see McCool v. Gehret, 657 A.2d 269 (Del.1995), where the plaintiff's expert had felt threatened by the defendant during a telephone conversation and decided not to testify, only to change his mind out of feelings of guilt when plaintiff again asked that he testify; the court held that "even though the doctor's conduct was reprehensible", the plaintiff suffered no injury from Dr. Gehret's efforts to intimidate because the expert did testify.

3. Testimony by the plaintiff, in the rare case where he or she is a medical expert qualified to evaluate the doctor's conduct. Lamont v. Brookwood Health Services, Inc., 446 So.2d 1018 (Ala.1983).

4. Common knowledge in situations where a layperson could understand the negligence without the assistance of experts. See Gannon v. Elliot, 19 Cal.App.4th 1, 23 Cal.Rptr.2d 86 (1993)(plastic cap from a surgical instrument left in plaintiff's hip socket after a hip joint replacement); Seippel–Cress v. Lackamp, 23 S.W.3d 660 (Mo.C.A.2000)(evidence showed that patient became unusually fatigued during barium swallow test; average person knows that a provider in such a case must determine the cause of the change in condition, without expert testimony).

A physician's obvious or admitted ignorance of an illness or a procedure may create a duty to investigate and consult another physician. In Largess v. Tatem, 130 Vt. 271, 291 A.2d 398 (1972), the defendant, a general practitioner in Vermont, treated the plaintiff, a 77 year old woman, for a fracture of her left hip. He called in a specialist in orthopedic surgery, who implanted a Jewett nail. This fixation device was not designed to permit full early weight bearing. Dr. Tatem was not familiar with the postoperative instructions for such a device and released the patient without instructions. The device broke and a second surgery was required. The court held that expert testimony was not required, since the violation of the standard of care was obvious to a lay trier of fact.

5. Use of res ipsa loquitur, as discussed infra.

Note: The Role of the Internet

The Internet enables a doctor to stay current through bulletin boards, physician-directed online services, and both commercial and government-sponsored Websites. Doctors are increasingly expected to seek and use the data. Medical knowledge about evidence-based medicine has accumulated at a staggering rate. Between 1966 and 1995, the number of clinical research articles based on randomized clinical trials jumped from about 100 per year to 10,000 annually. Mark R. Chassin, Is Health Care Ready for Six Sigma Quality? 76 the Milbank Quarterly 565, 574 (1998). Web-based databases have proliferated to sort and promote access by physicians to the newest clinical practice guidelines and other medical developments. The goal has been to help physicians handle the information overload in an efficient and user-friendly way.

The National Guideline Clearinghouse, *http://www.guideline.gov*, offers free access by physicians and others to the current clinical practice guidelines, with instantaneous searches of the database. A search produces all guidelines on a given subject, along with an appropriateness analysis of each guideline. The Clearinghouse provides a standardized abstract of each guideline, and grades the scientific basis of its recommendations and the development process for each. Full text or links to sites with the guidelines are provided. Readers are given synopses to produce a side-by-side comparison of guidelines, outlining where those agree and disagree, and physicians can access electronic mail groups to discuss development and implementation. These guidelines must pass certain entry criteria to be included: they must be current, contain systematically developed statements to guide physician decisions, have been produced by a medical or other professional group, government agency, health care organization or other private or public organization; and they must show that they were developed through systematic search of peer-reviewed scientific evidence. The benefits: easy search features, database comprehensiveness and Internet location make this the most powerful tool to date. Various appropriateness tests have been developed to evaluate guidelines. See Paul G Shekelle and David L. Schriger, Evaluating the Use of the Appropriateness Method in the Agency for Health Care Policy and Research Clinical Practice Guideline Development Process, 31 Health Services Research (1996)

Other Internet based services are available on a commercial basis. One example is MDConsult, a commercial database available by subscription that makes available hundreds of medical textbooks and treatises, as well as easy access to clinical practice guidelines. Subscribership in such commercial sites, designed to be user-friendly, has grown geometrically over the past few years, as physicians look for easy research access to data about patient problems. A survey by MDConsult of physician subscribers found that physicians were accessing the website for a fast and easy way to check the literature while treating patients, allowing for immediate answers; to keep up and to expand a physician's knowledge base about particular conditions. Physicians felt that the immediacy of access to a comprehensive website improved their informational base and therefore their quality of practice.

Medscape is another commercial site that provides a full range of online resources for physicians. It offers a journal scan on the newest research findings, free access to abstracts on MEDLINE, access to drug searching through First DataBank, the largest Web-based drug and disease database, access to clinical practice guidelines, treatment updates, full text articles in many journals, and a clinical management series n the form of interactive e-med texts. A subscriber can also set up an email account to get specific information sent on a regular basis on specific topics. These commercial services in particular offer a busy physician quick and painless access, to both journals and guidelines, as well as to new literature and comments by experts. The location of current information on the Internet facilitates its ease of access to physicians, and its link to other commercial sites makes it easy to connect to, no matter what portal a physician uses to access medical information databases on the Web. Failure to access such data bases is likely to become an important piece of evidence in a malpractice suit, since it is evidence that a physician has failed to stay current in his or her field of practice.

Computer technologies pose other liability risks for physicians. As patient records are computerized, it becomes easier to gain access to a full patient history. Patient records can be easily stored on CDROM or other media, so that access is virtually instantaneous. Patient drug records and possible interactions can therefore be researched effortlessly. For a physician to fail to make such a search and miss a possible problem or drug interaction leads to liability. Another liability risk created by reliance on computer record keeping is the failure to protect such computerized patient records. Computer storage raises issues of security, privacy and integrity of computer records. Breaches of security and unauthorized access to patient information can lead to a range of tort suits, from invasion of privacy to negligence in record maintenance. A physician or institution also has a duty to detect and cripple viruses. Physicians who fail to properly protect patient and other files from corruption may be as negligent as physicians who fail to keep proper paper records.

Problem: Evidentiary Hurdles

You have been approached by Clinton Scott, whose wife Diane died of toxemia at the end of pregnancy. The facts are as follows. Clinton tells you that Diane had experienced symptoms of blurred vision, headaches, chest pains and swelling in the second half of pregnancy, with worsening symptoms in early February. She had had long-standing severe hypertension, as her medical record indicated. Diane had described these symptoms to her obstetrician, Dr. Fowles, during her January examination. He had told her not to worry, that this was normal in first pregnancies, and that everything would be fine. He did not test her urinary protein excretion or her platelet count. Early in February her symptoms got markedly worse. Dr. Fowles then tested her urinary protein excretion and her platelet count and concluded that she had pre-eclampsia (toxemia). He admitted her to the hospital and drugs were administered to control Diane's condition, but she went into convulsions a few hours later. Later that day the staff failed to detect fetal heart tones and a C-section was promptly performed. A stillborn baby girl was delivered. Six days later, Diane's brain had ceased to function. She was taken off life-support with Clinton's approval, and died.

In your preliminary discovery, you have had trouble finding a local obstetrician to testify against Dr. Fowles, who is the president of the local medical society and is quite well-respected among his peers. Your jurisdiction follows the *Hall* rule, so you could hire an expert from elsewhere in the state or region, but you would prefer to use someone who can claim familiarity with local practices and who would cost you less in discovery costs as well.

Consider the following evidence issues. Will you be successful in getting this evidence admitted? In getting the case to the jury? In winning a jury trial?

1. You took the deposition of Dr. Fowles, who was forthright and candid during the examination. The following questions and answers are particularly interesting.

> Q. Is the standard of care when managing a pregnant patient that where you have a condition of persistent headaches, blurred vision, fatigue, significant epigastric pain, and developing edema of the feet, that the physician managing the woman should suspect pre-eclampsia as a cause?

A. Yes, those symptoms should put a doctor on notice of the potential of toxemia. When you suspect this, you should promptly treat the patient, since immediate treatment increases the likelihood of a cure without the development of any adverse complications.

Q. Would earlier diagnosis and treatment of Diane have prevented her brain death and the loss of the infant?

A. That is impossible to say.

2. A review article in the New England Journal of Medicine stated as follows:

> Hypertensive disorders are the most common medical complications of pregnancy and are an important cause of maternal and perinatal morbidity and mortality worldwide. * * *
>
> * * *
>
> Pregnant women with chronic hypertension are at increased risk for superimposed preeclampsia and abruptio placentae, and their babies are at increased risk for perinatal morbidity and mortality. * * *
>
> Women with preeclampsia require close observation because the disorder may worsen suddenly. The presence of symptoms (such as headache, epigastric pain, and visual abnormalities) and proteinuria increase the risk of both eclampsia and abruptio placentae; women with these findings require close observation in the hospital. * * * The management should include close monitoring of the mother's blood pressure, weight, urinary protein excretion, and platelet count, as well as of fetal status. In addition, the woman must be informed about the symptoms of worsening preeclampsia. If there is evidence of disease progression, hospitalization is indicated.

Baha M. Sibai, Drug Therapy: Treatment of Hypertension in Pregnant Women, 335 New Eng. J. Med. 257 (1996).

3. You have interviewed a nurse-practitioner in obstetrics in the area, who examined the medical records and talked with Clinton. She is willing to testify that based upon her experience as an obstetric nurse for over 10 years, Dr. Fowles was negligent in failing to immediately treat Diane when her symptoms were first related to him in January.

4. **Williams on Obstetrics**, a leading textbook used in many medical schools, states the following:

> Since eclampsia is preceded in most cases by premonitory signs and symptoms, its prophylaxis is in many ways more important than its cure and is identical with the treatment of pre-eclampsia. Indeed, a major aim in treating of pre-eclampsia is to prevent convulsions. The necessity of regular and frequent blood pressure measurements thus becomes clear, as well as the importance of detection of rapid gain of weight and of proteinuria, and the immediate institution of appropriate dietary and medical treatment as soon as the earliest signs and symptoms appear. By the employment of these precautionary measures and by prompt termination of pregnancy in those cases that do not improve or that become progressively worse under treatment, frequency of eclampsia will be greatly diminished and many lives will be saved. Prophylaxis, while valuable, is not invariably successful. * * *

5. You have learned during discovery that two hospital committees, the Morbidity Committee and the Obstetrics Committee, have investigated Dr.

Fowles' past performance in dealing with patients with eclampsia. You would like to obtain hospital incident reports and committee minutes to find out whether the medical staff has described his performance as substandard. Consider the note below in analyzing this issue.

6. You have decided to seek an out-of-state expert to testify about toxemia. You are considering hiring Dr. Matthew Berkle, an obstetrician in practice in Pennsylvania. Dr. Berkle has strong opinions on the importance of early and accurate diagnosis of toxemia, formed as the result of his delivery of over a thousand babies in his career and his own study of his patients, over fifty of whom manifested symptoms of toxemia during their pregnancies. He has kept careful records and has determined that several subtle warning signs can be detected by a properly trained physician who follows his methods. Dr. Berkle is not a trained researcher, but rather a highly intelligent and thoughtful physician who cares about his patients.

The relevant rules of evidence in your jurisdiction are identical to the Federal Rules of Evidence below. These rules were amended to reflect the scientific evidence concerns raised in *Daubert* and *Kumho* by the Supreme Court and were effective December 1, 2000.

Federal Rule of Evidence 701 (Opinion testimony by lay witnesses)

If the witness is not testifying as an expert, the witness' testimony in the form of opinions or inferences is limited to those opinions or inferences which are (a) rationally based on the perception of the witness, (b) helpful to a clear understanding of the witness' testimony or the determination of a fact in issue, and (c) not based on scientific, technical, or other specialized knowledge within the scope of Rule 702.

Federal Rule of Evidence 702 (Testimony by experts)

If scientific, technical, or other specialized knowledge will assist the trier of fact to understand the evidence or to determine a fact in issue, a witness qualified as an expert by knowledge, skill, experience, training, or education, may testify thereto in the form of an opinion or otherwise, if (1) the testimony is based upon sufficient facts or data, (2) the testimony is the product of reliable principles and methods, and (3) the witness has applied the principles and methods reliably to the facts of the case.

Federal Rule of Evidence 703 (Bases of opinion testimony by experts)

The facts or data in the particular case upon which an expert bases an opinion or inference may be those perceived by or made known to the expert at or before the hearing. If of a type reasonably relied upon by experts in the particular field in forming opinions or inferences upon the subject, the facts or data need not be admissible in evidence in order for the opinion or inference to be admitted. Facts or data that are otherwise inadmissible shall not be disclosed to the jury by the proponent of the opinion or inference unless the court determines that their probative value in assisting the jury to evaluate the expert's opinion substantially outweighs their prejudicial effect.

Federal Rule of Evidence 803(6) (Records of Regularly Conducted Activity)

A memorandum, report, record, or data compilation, in any form, of acts, events, conditions, opinions, or diagnoses, made at or near the time by, or from information transmitted by, a person with knowledge, if kept in the course of a regularly conducted business activity, and if it was the regular practice of that business activity to make the memorandum, report, record or data compilation, all as shown by the testimony of the custodian or other qualified witness, or by certification that complies with Rule 902(11), Rule 902(12), or a statute permitting certification, unless the source of information or the method or circumstances of preparation indicate lack of trustworthiness. The term "business" as used in this paragraph includes business, institution, association, profession, occupation, and calling of every kind, whether or not conducted for profit.

Note: Discovery of Hospital Committee Proceedings and Incident Reports

A hospital's risk management and quality assurance functions can figure in a variety of legal problems. The most important of these is whether a hospital is liable in tort for injuries caused by its failure to oversee adequately the quality of care provided by its employees or medical staff. A second issue is when and how a hospital may exclude a high risk, poor quality physician. A third issue is when hospital records can be used against a physician sued for malpractice.

Hospital Committee Proceedings. Plaintiffs in malpractice actions frequently seek discovery of the proceedings of hospital quality assurance committees. They may request production of a committee's minutes or reports, propound interrogatories about the committee process or outcome, or ask to depose committee members concerning committee deliberations. If the plaintiff is suing a health care professional whose work was reviewed by the committee, the discovery may seek to confirm the negligence of the professional or to uncover additional evidence substantiating the plaintiff's claim. If the suit is against the hospital on a theory of corporate liability (i.e., claiming that the hospital itself was negligent in appointing or failing to supervise a professional), evidence of committee proceedings may prove vital to establishing the hospital's liability.

These discovery requests are usually met with a claim that information generated within or by hospital committees is not discoverable. In Coburn v. Seda, 101 Wash.2d 270, 677 P.2d 173 (1984), the court considered the plaintiff's discovery requests for the records of the hospital quality review committees.

> * * * The discovery protection granted hospital quality review committee records, like work product immunity, prevents the opposing party from taking advantage of a hospital's careful self-assessment. The opposing party must utilize his or her own experts to evaluate the facts underlying the incident which is the subject of suit and also use them to determine whether the hospital's care comported with proper quality standards.
>
> The discovery prohibition, like an evidentiary privilege, also seeks to protect certain communications and encourage the quality review process. Statutes bearing similarities to RCW 4.24.250 prohibit discovery of records on the theory that external access to committee investigations stifles candor and inhibits constructive criticism thought necessary to effective quality review. Courts determining that hospital quality review records should be subject to a common law privilege have advanced this same rationale. As the court stated in Bredice v. Doctors Hosp., Inc., 50 F.R.D. 249, 250 (D.D.C.1970), aff'd, 479 F.2d 920 (D.C.Cir.1973):
>
>> Confidentiality is essential to effective functioning of these staff meetings; and these meetings are essential to the continued improvement in the care and treatment of patients. Candid and conscientious evaluation

of clinical practices is a *sine qua non* of adequate hospital care * * *. Constructive professional criticism cannot occur in an atmosphere of apprehension that one doctor's suggestion will be used as a denunciation of a colleague's conduct in a malpractice suit.

Most states have statutes affording hospital quality assurance proceedings some degree of protection from discovery. Critics of discovery immunity, on the other hand, argue that immunity deprives plaintiffs, particularly those claiming hospital corporate negligence, of necessary evidence. Moreover, they argue, JCAHO and licensing requirements, plus the threat of tort liability, provide ample incentives for hospital quality assurance efforts so that immunity is unnecessary. See, arguing the immunity question, James F. Flanagan, Rejecting a General Privilege for Self-Critical Analysis, 51 Geo.Wash.L.Rev. 551 (1983); Arthur F. Southwick & Debra A. Slee, Quality Assurance in Health Care: Confidentiality of Information and Immunity for Participants, 5 J.Leg.Med. 343 (1984).

Statutes protecting committee proceedings from discovery are often subject to exceptions, either explicitly or through judicial interpretation. One common exception affords discovery to physicians challenging the results of committee action against them. Thus a physician whose staff privileges were revoked may discover information from the credentialing committee, Schulz v. Superior Court, 66 Cal.App.3d 440, 446, 136 Cal.Rptr. 67, 70 (1977). This seems to be required by notions of fair process. On the other hand, do statutes that grant physicians access to information that is denied to malpractice plaintiffs violate equal protection? See Jenkins v. Wu, 102 Ill.2d 468, 82 Ill.Dec. 382, 386–88, 468 N.E.2d 1162, 1166–68 (1984). If a court in a public proceeding grants a physician access to the transcript of a committee hearing under such an exception, must it subsequently grant a patient access to further information regarding the same proceeding? See Henry Mayo Newhall Memorial Hospital v. Superior Court, 81 Cal.App.3d 626, 146 Cal.Rptr. 542 (1978).

In the absence of a statute providing immunity from discovery, a few courts have refused discovery of peer review committee proceedings under the court's inherent power to control discovery. See Bredice v. Doctors Hospital, Inc., 50 F.R.D. 249, 250 (D.D.C.1970), affirmed, 479 F.2d 920 (D.C.Cir.1973); Dade County Med. Ass'n v. Hlis, 372 So.2d 117 (Fla.App.1979). More courts have rejected common law immunity, holding that the plaintiff's need for evidence outweighs the defendant's claim to protection. See State ex rel. Chandra v. Sprinkle, 678 S.W.2d 804 (Mo.1984); Wesley Medical Center v. Clark, 234 Kan. 13, 669 P.2d 209 (1983).

A number of statutes immunizing committee proceedings from discovery do not explicitly render information from those committees privileged from admission into evidence if the plaintiff can obtain it otherwise. But would such information be otherwise admissible? Would it be hearsay? If so, would it be subject to the business records exception? See Fed.R.Evid. 803(6). Might committee records indicating that a hospital was concerned about the performance of a physician be admissible as an admission in a subsequent corporate negligence action against the hospital? See Fed.R.Evid. 801(d)(2)(D). Might a plaintiff's expert be permitted to testify on the basis of information gleaned from committee records, even though those records were themselves hearsay? See Fed.R.Evid. 703. In a suit brought by one particular patient, would committee records documenting errors made by a physician in the treatment of other patients be relevant? Might opinions concerning a physician's negligence found in committee records or reports invade the province of the jury? See, addressing these questions, Robert F.

Holbrook & Lee J. Dunn, Medical Malpractice Litigation: The Discoverability and Use of Hospitals' Quality Assurance Records, 16 Washburn L.J. 54, 68–70 (1976).

Hospital Incident Reports. When a plaintiff seeks discovery of incident reports rather than committee proceedings, policy considerations are somewhat different. Hospitals have greater incentives to investigate untoward events than they have to carry on continuing quality review, and are less dependent on voluntary participation. The incident report would usually be more directly relevant to a single claim for malpractice than would general committee investigations. Possibly for these reasons, immunity statutes that protect committee proceedings less often protect incident reports, and courts have been less willing to immunize incident reports from discovery. On the other hand, since incident reports are more directly related to litigation of specific mishaps, two privileges can be asserted to protect them that would seldom apply to committee proceedings: the work product immunity and attorney client privilege.

The work product immunity protects materials prepared in anticipation of litigation. See Federal Rules of Civil Procedure 56. Courts look to the nature and purpose of incident reports. If they are regularly prepared and distributed for future loss prevention, they are not considered to be documents prepared in anticipation of litigation so as to invoke application of the work product exception to discovery. See St. Louis Little Rock Hospital, Inc. v. Gaertner, 682 S.W.2d 146, 150–51 (Mo.App.1984).

The attorney-client privilege protects communications, even if the attorney is not yet representing a client, provided that the communication was made between the client as an insured to his liability insuror during the course of an existing insured-insuror relationship. To be privileged, a communication between a client and his attorney, or between an insured and his insuror, must be within the context of the attorney-client relationship, with a purpose of securing legal advice from the client's attorney. If an incident report is used for loss prevention, the mere fact that it was later used by an attorney is irrelevant.

See Kay Laboratories, Inc. v. District Court, 653 P.2d 721 (Colo.1982); but see Sierra Vista Hospital v. Superior Ct., 248 Cal.App.2d 359, 56 Cal.Rptr. 387 (1967).

D. ALTERING THE BURDEN OF PROOF

In the typical malpractice case, the plaintiff must introduce expert testimony as to the standard of care or face a nonsuit. The courts have developed several doctrines that ease the plaintiff's burden of proof, shifting either the burden of production of evidence or the burden of persuasion onto the defendant.

1. Res Ipsa Loquitur

The best known of these evidentiary devices is the doctrine of *res ipsa loquitur* (Latin for "The thing speaks for itself"), which eliminates the plaintiff's need to present expert testimony as to negligence of the defendant. *Ybarra* is the classic statement of the justifications for the doctrine in a medical malpractice case.

YBARRA v. SPANGARD

Supreme Court of California, 1944.
25 Cal.2d 486, 154 P.2d 687.

[The plaintiff underwent an appendectomy. His primary physician, the surgeon and a variety of hospital personnel were present during the operation. Afterwards the plaintiff complained of pain in his right arm and shoulder, which he had first felt when he awoke from the surgery. The pain spread down his arm and grew worse until he was unable to rotate or lift his arm. His medical experts testified that the injury was a paralysis of traumatic origin, probably caused by pressure.]

Plaintiff's theory is that the foregoing evidence presents a proper case for the application of the doctrine of res ipsa loquitur, and that the inference of negligence arising therefrom makes the granting of a nonsuit improper. Defendants take the position that, assuming that plaintiff's condition was in fact the result of an injury, there is no showing that the act of any particular defendant, nor any particular instrumentality, was the cause thereof. They attack plaintiff's action as an attempt to fix liability "en masse" on various defendants, some of whom were not responsible for the acts of others; and they further point to the failure to show which defendants had control of the instrumentalities that may have been involved. * * * We are satisfied, however, that these objections are not well taken in the circumstances of this case.

The doctrine of res ipsa loquitur has three conditions: "(1) the accident must be of a kind which ordinarily does not occur in the absence of someone's negligence; (2) it must be caused by an agency or instrumentality within the exclusive control of the defendant; (3) it must not have been due to any voluntary action or contribution on the part of the plaintiff." [ ] It is applied in a wide variety of situations, including cases of medical or dental treatment and hospital care. [ ]

* * *

The present case is of a type which comes within the reason and spirit of the doctrine more fully perhaps than any other. * * * [I]t is difficult to see how the doctrine can, with any justification, be so restricted in its statement as to become inapplicable to a patient who submits himself to the care and custody of doctors and nurses, is rendered unconscious, and receives some injury from instrumentalities used in his treatment. Without the aid of the doctrine a patient who received permanent injuries of a serious character, obviously the result of some one's negligence, would be entirely unable to recover unless the doctors and nurses in attendance voluntarily chose to disclose the identity of the negligent person and the facts establishing liability. [ ] If this were the state of the law of negligence, the courts, to avoid gross injustice, would be forced to invoke the principles of absolute liability, irrespective of negligence, in actions by persons suffering injuries during the course of treatment under anesthesia. But we think this juncture has not yet been reached, and that the doctrine of res ipsa loquitur is properly applicable to the case before us.

The condition that the injury must not have been due to the plaintiff's voluntary action is of course fully satisfied under the evidence produced herein; and the same is true of the condition that the accident must be one which ordinarily does not occur unless some one was negligent. We have here no problem of negligence in treatment, but of distinct injury to a healthy part of the body not the subject of treatment, nor within the area covered by the operation. The decisions in this state make it clear that such circumstances raise the inference of negligence and call upon the defendant to explain the unusual result. [ ]

* * *

We have no doubt that in a modern hospital a patient is quite likely to come under the care of a number of persons in different types of contractual and other relationships with each other. For example, in the present case it appears that Drs. Smith, Spangard and Tilley were physicians or surgeons commonly placed in the legal category of independent contractors; and Dr. Reser, the anesthetist, and defendant Thompson, the special nurse, were employees of Dr. Swift and not of the other doctors. But we do not believe that either the number or relationship of the defendants alone determines whether the doctrine of res ipsa loquitur applies. * * *

* * *

It may appear at the trial that, consistent with the principles outlined above, one or more defendants will be found liable and others absolved, but this should not preclude the application of the rule of res ipsa loquitur. The control at one time or another, of one or more of the various agencies or instrumentalities which might have harmed the plaintiff was in the hands of every defendant or of his employees or temporary servants. This, we think, places upon them the burden of initial explanation. Plaintiff was rendered unconscious for the purpose of undergoing surgical treatment by the defendants; it is manifestly unreasonable for them to insist that he identify any one of them as the person who did the alleged negligent act.

The other aspect of the case which defendants so strongly emphasize is that plaintiff has not identified the instrumentality any more than he has the particular guilty defendant. Here, again, there is a misconception which, if carried to the extreme for which defendants contend, would unreasonably limit the application of the res ipsa loquitur rule. It should be enough that the plaintiff can show an injury resulting from an external force applied while he lay unconscious in the hospital; this is as clear a case of identification of the instrumentality as the plaintiff may ever be able to make.

An examination of the recent cases, particularly in this state, discloses that the test of actual exclusive control of an instrumentality has not been strictly followed, but exceptions have been recognized where the purpose of the doctrine of res ipsa loquitur would otherwise be defeated. * * *

In the face of these examples of liberalization of the tests for res ipsa loquitur, there can be no justification for the rejection of the doctrine in the instant case. As pointed out above, if we accept the contention of defendants herein, there will rarely be any compensation for patients injured while unconscious. A hospital today conducts a highly integrated system of activities, with many persons contributing their efforts. There may be, e.g., preparation for surgery by nurses and interns who are employees of the hospital, administering of an anesthetic by a doctor who may be an employee of the hospital, an employee of the operating surgeon, or an independent contractor; performance of an operation by a surgeon and assistants who may be his employees, employees of the hospital, or independent contractors; and post surgical care by the surgeon, a hospital physician, and nurses. The number of those in whose care the patient is placed is not a good reason for denying him all reasonable opportunity to recover for negligent harm. It is rather a good reason for re-examination of the statement of legal theories which supposedly compel such a shocking result.

We do not at this time undertake to state the extent to which the reasoning of this case may be applied to other situations in which the doctrine of res ipsa loquitur is invoked. We merely hold that where a plaintiff receives unusual injuries while unconscious and in the course of medical treatment, all those defendants who had any control over his body or the instrumentalities which might have caused the injuries may properly be called upon to meet the inference of negligence by giving an explanation of their conduct.

The judgment is reversed.

Notes and Questions

1. What justifications did the court cite in favor of applying res ipsa loquitur? Does *res ipsa loquitur* operate here purely as a recognition of the probability of negligence, or as something more?

2. In most states, res ipsa loquitur operates as an inference of negligence. That is, the jury may infer that the defendant was in some way negligent, but it is not compelled to conclude negligence. It can reject the inference as well as accepting it. A few states treat res ipsa as a presumption, so that a plaintiff who proves a res ipsa case should win unless the defendant comes forward with some evidence to rebut the presumed negligence. See generally Dan Dobbs, The Law of Torts § 249 (2000).

The doctrine continues to be applied in medical malpractice cases where the injury is to a part of the body outside the scope of an operation. See, e.g., Zumwalt v. Koreckij, 24 S.W.3d 166 (Mo.C.A. 2000)(patient suffered nerve injury to her right hand, arm and shoulder during a knee replacement operation); Adams v. Family Planning Associates Medical Group, Inc., 315 Ill.App.3d 533, 248 Ill.Dec. 91, 733 N.E.2d 766 (Ill.C.A.2000)(patient died during abortion under general anesthesia; res ipsa applied).

The doctrine has become increasingly unpopular, with many jurisdictions reluctant to apply the doctrine in medical malpractice cases out of concern that doctors might be held liable for rare bad outcomes, whether or not they were related to any negligence by the defendant. As Justice Gibson, author of *Ybarra,* wrote in Siverson v. Weber, 57 Cal.2d 834, 22 Cal.Rptr. 337, 372 P.2d 97 (1962), "* * * this would place too great a burden upon the medical profession and might result in an undesirable limitation on the use of operations or new procedures involving an inherent risk of injury even when due care is used."

See also Jackson v. Oklahoma Memorial Hospital, 909 P.2d 765 (Okl.1995); Hoven v. Rice Memorial Hospital, 396 N.W.2d 569 (Minn.1986).

Many states have eliminated the availability of res ipsa loquitur by statute as part of malpractice reform packages.

2. Shifting the Burden of Persuasion

Courts have in special situations used a variety of burden-shifting devices to ease the plaintiff's burden of proof. Res ipsa loquitur, as applied in *Ybarra, supra,* obviated the plaintiff's need to prove a specific error by the defendants. In rare cases, courts have gone even further, shifting the burden of persuasion onto the defendants, requiring that they present evidence to exonerate themselves or face liability.

Consider the case of Anderson v. Somberg, 67 N.J. 291, 338 A.2d 1 (N.J. 1975). The plaintiff underwent a laminectomy. During surgery, the tip of a pituitary rongeur, a surgical implement, broke off in the plaintiff's spinal canal. The surgeon, unable to retrieve the metal fragment, terminated the operation. The fragment caused medical complications and necessitated further surgical interventions. The rongeur had been used five times a year, or in about twenty previous surgical procedures. The rongeur had been purchased from the distributor about four years before; the distributor obtained it from the manufacturer.

The plaintiff sued the surgeon for medical malpractice, the hospital for negligently furnishing a defective surgical instrument, the medical supply distributor on a warranty theory, and the manufacturer of the rongeur, on a strict liability in tort claim. The surgeon testified that he had not examined the rongeur prior to the day of surgery but that day had inspected it visually, and had not twisted it while performing the laminectomy. Other testimony stated that the rongeur was a delicate instrument that might break if twisted. A metallurgist found neither structural defects nor faulty workmanship, but only a small crack of unknown origin. He concluded that the instrument had been strained, probably because of "an improper 'twisting' " of the tool.

The court noted that "[t]he plaintiff was left with multiple defendants, a range of hypothetical causes for the rongeur's failure, and an inability to prove either the cause of the defect or the source of it." The court then continued:

> In the ordinary case, the law will not assist an innocent plaintiff at the expense of an innocent defendant. However, in the type of case we consider here, where an unconscious or helpless patient suffers an admitted mishap not reasonably foreseeable and unrelated to the scope of the surgery (such as cases where foreign objects are left in the body of the patient), those who had custody of the patient, and who owed him a duty of care as to medical treatment, or not to furnish a defective instrument for use in such treatment can be called to account for their default. They must prove their nonculpability, or else risk liability for the injuries suffered.

The court noted that their rule was not the application of *res ipsa loquitur*. It was limited only to those cases where the injury fell outside the scope of the surgical procedure, where the burden of proof should shift to multiple defendants to "prove their freedom from liability."

A "missing witness" instruction has been upheld in a few jurisdictions, allowing the jury to presume negligence and causation from the mere absence of a crucial piece of evidence. In Welsh v. United States, 844 F.2d 1239 (6th Cir.1988), the court shifted the burden of persuasion to the defendants, holding that "acts by the hospital surgeons in this case create a rebuttable presumption of negligence and proximate causation against the defendant—the negligent destruction of a skull bone flap after the second [of two] operations, and the consequent failure at that time to undertake a pathological examination of this evidence * * * ". Id. at 1239–40. See also C. McCormick, McCormick on Evidence, § 273, at 810 at n. 20 (3rd Ed.1984). Rejecting "missing evidence" as substantive proof that shifts the burden, see Battocchi v. Washington Hospital Center, 581 A.2d 759 (D.C.App.1990) (limiting the effect of a showing of missing evidence to an instruction allowing the jury to draw an adverse inference against the defendants, upon a showing of gross indifference to or reckless disregard for the relevance of the evidence to a possible claim).

3. *Strict Liability*

Courts have generally resisted applying strict liability (or implied warranty) to a health care professional or institution. Medicine is usually distinguished from "commercial" enterprises. As the Wisconsin Supreme Court notes in Hoven v. Kelble, 79 Wis.2d 444, 256 N.W.2d 379 (1977):

> There are differences between the rendition of medical services and transactions in goods (or perhaps other types of services as well). Medical and many other professional services tend often to be experimental in nature, dependent on factors beyond the control of the professional, and devoid of certainty or assurance of results. Medical services are an absolute necessity to society, and they must be readily available to the people. It is said that strict liability will inevitably increase the cost for medical services, which might make them beyond the means of many consumers, and that imposition of strict liability might hamper progress in developing new medicines and medical techniques.

Does this distinction seem as convincing in light of the growth of modern corporate health care and the increased blend of professional judgment and medical tools and devices? A medical intervention often requires the use of medical products: knee joints, bone graft material, pig heart valves. Breast implant prostheses are a common example of such a service-product intervention. Courts apply strict liability to the distributors of such products but are reluctant to extend strict liability to a health care provider using the product in a way incidental to the primary function of providing medical services. See, e.g., Cafazzo v. Central Medical Health Services, 430 Pa.Super. 480, 635 A.2d 151 (Pa.Super.1993)(mandibular prosthesis); Hoff v. Zimmer, 746 F.Supp. 872 (W.D.Wis.1990)(hip prosthesis); Budding v. SSM Healthcare System, 19 S.W.3d 678 (Mo.2000)(mandibular implant).

In Porter v. Rosenberg, 650 So.2d 79, 83 (Fla.App. 4 Dist.1995), the court considered a strict liability claim against the physician for a breast implant. The court rejected strict liability in the case but opened the door slightly to a judicial "essence of the transaction" test for future cases.

> ... we conclude that whether or not a plaintiff may bring an action against a physician, hospital, or other health care provider for strict liability depends upon the essence of the physician-patient relationship for the particular transaction. If the medical services could not have been rendered without utilizing the product, then strict liability does not apply. If the predominant purpose of the physician-patient relationship for that transaction is the provision of medical services based upon the physician's medical judgment, skill, or expertise, the malpractice statute applies and strict liability is inapplicable.

> The fact that the physician or health care provider is not solely or primarily in the business of distributing products is not the determinative factor for application of strict liability as long as distributing products is part of its business. [ ] Therefore, if distributing products is part of the health care provider's business and the sales or distribution aspect in the particular transaction between the health care provider and the patient predominates over the services aspect an action instinct liability may lie against the health care provider.[1]

The court however rejected the action in this case on the grounds that the plaintiff had sued several other defendants from the manufacturers to distributors. "We perceive of no overriding public policy argument which would justify an obvious circumvention of the medical malpractice statute and an extension of strict liability to physicians under the circumstances presented here."

For a detailed analysis that rejects strict liability for both physicians and hospitals, see Tanuz v. Carlberg, 122 N.M. 113, 921 P.2d 309 (App.1996) (surgical insertion of temporomandibular joint implants); Parker v. St. Vincent Hospital, 122 N.M. 39, 919 P.2d 1104 (App.1996)(hospitals not distributors or suppliers of product); Parker v. E.I. DuPont de Nemours & Co., 121 N.M. 120, 909 P.2d 1 (App.1995)(analysis of strict liability principles and medical devices). For a proposal to apply strict liability to a particular medical specialty based on a statistical outcomes analysis, see Barry R. Furrow, Defective Mental Treatment: A Proposal for the Application of Strict Liability to Psychiatric Services, 58 B.U.L.Rev. 391 (1978).

Problem: Breathing Hard

Sam had chronic obstructive pulmonary disease and his doctor, Dr. Donahue, recommended treatment with the Intermittent Positive Pressure Breathing ventilator (IPPB). Sam had severe side-effects from the treatment and died. Dr. Donahue used the IPPB ventilator properly, but an alternative device, the nebulizer, is cheaper and safer than IPPB for all IPPB uses. Despite this, IPPB is still reimbursed by most third party payers and continues to be used by some physicians in the hospital setting for obstructive pulmonary disease.

Your research uncovers the following information about IPPB. Intermittent Positive Pressure Breathing is a technology that diffused into use in spite of evidence that it did not work. Research studies have confirmed that it is no better than the cheaper and less dangerous nebulizer. While its use has declined, it has not disappeared and reimbursement is still available for its use from Medicare and private insurers. Doctors continue to use such a technology in the face of clear evidence and authoritative declarations that it is both ineffective and dangerous. The reasons may include habit; clinical impressions that it gives patients short-term relief; and financial benefits to physicians. The medical director of the respiratory therapy department, the primary source of service orders, often receives a cut of the department's income. As long as third party payors still pay for IPPB, cash will flow for its use.

1. Such examples might include a nutrition doctor selling diet products or a dentist selling electric toothbrushes. Some manufacturers may rely solely or mainly on utilizing health care professionals for distribution of their products and the health care professional may rely on selling the product as part of its business as additional profit separate from provision of other medical services.

Sam's family has asked you to consider the merits of a lawsuit against Dr. Donahue. What are your options, and what defenses will the defendant raise if you file suit?

See generally Duffy, S.Q., and Farley, D.E., Intermittent Positive Pressure Breathing: Old Technologies Rarely Die, AHCPR Pub. 94–0001, Div. Provider Studies Research Note 18, Agency for Health Care Policy and Research (1993).

II. JUDICIAL RISK—BENEFIT BALANCING

HELLING v. CAREY

Supreme Court of Washington, 1974.
83 Wash.2d 514, 519 P.2d 981.

HUNTER, ASSOC. JUSTICE.

The plaintiff suffers from primary open angle glaucoma. Primary open angle glaucoma is essentially a condition of the eye in which there is an interference in the ease with which the nourishing fluids can flow out of the eye. Such a condition results in pressure gradually rising above the normal level to such an extent that damage is produced to the optic nerve and its fibers with resultant loss in vision. The first loss usually occurs in the periphery of the field of vision. The disease usually has few symptoms and, in the absence of a pressure test, is often undetected until the damage has become extensive and irreversible.

The defendants (respondents), Dr. Thomas F. Carey and Dr. Robert C. Laughlin, are partners who practice the medical specialty of ophthalmology. Ophthalmology involves the diagnosis and treatment of defects and diseases of the eye.

The plaintiff first consulted the defendants for myopia, nearsightedness, in 1959. At that time she was fitted with contact lenses. She next consulted the defendants in September, 1963, concerning irritation caused by the contact lenses. Additional consultations occurred in October, 1963; February, 1967; September, 1967; October, 1967; May, 1968; July, 1968; August, 1968; September, 1968; and October, 1968. Until the October 1968 consultation, the defendants considered the plaintiff's visual problems to be related solely to complications associated with her contact lenses. On that occasion, the defendant, Dr. Carey, tested the plaintiff's eye pressure and field of vision for the first time. This test indicated that the plaintiff had glaucoma. The plaintiff, who was then 32 years of age, had essentially lost her peripheral vision and her central vision was reduced to approximately 5 degrees vertical by 10 degrees horizontal.

Thereafter, in August of 1969, after consulting other physicians, the plaintiff filed a complaint against the defendants alleging, among other things, that she sustained severe and permanent damage to her eyes as a proximate result of the defendants' negligence. During trial, the testimony of the medical experts for both the plaintiff and the defendants established that the standards of the profession for that specialty in the same or similar circumstances do not require routine pressure tests for glaucoma upon patients under 40 years of age. The reason the pressure test for glaucoma is not given as a regular practice to patients under the age of 40 is that the disease rarely occurs in this age group. Testimony indicated, however, that the standards of the profession do require pressure tests if the patient's complaints and symptoms reveal to the physician that glaucoma should be suspected.

The trial court entered judgment for the defendants following a defense verdict. The plaintiff thereupon appealed to the Court of Appeals, which affirmed the judgment of the trial court. [ ] The plaintiff then petitioned this Court for review, which we granted.

* * * [T]he plaintiff contends * * * that she was unable to argue her theory of the case to the jury that the standard of care for the specialty of ophthalmology was inadequate to protect the plaintiff from the incidence of glaucoma, and that the defendants, by reason of their special ability, knowledge and information, were negligent in failing to give the pressure test to the plaintiff at an earlier point in time which, if given, would have detected her condition and enabled the defendants to have averted the resulting substantial loss in her vision.

We find this to be a unique case. The testimony of the medical experts is undisputed concerning the standards of the profession for the specialty of ophthalmology. It is not a question in this case of the defendants having any greater special ability, knowledge and information than other ophthalmologists which would require the defendants to comply with a higher duty of care than that "degree of care and skill which is expected of the average practitioner in the class to which he belongs, acting in the same or similar circumstances." [ ] The issue is whether the defendants' compliance with the standard of the profession of ophthalmology, which does not require the giving of a routine pressure test to persons under 40 years of age, should insulate them from liability under the facts in this case where the plaintiff has lost a substantial amount of her vision due to the failure of the defendants to timely give the pressure test to the plaintiff.

The defendants argue that the standard of the profession, which does not require the giving of a routine pressure test to persons under the age of 40, is adequate to insulate the defendants from liability for negligence because the risk of glaucoma is so rare in this age group. * * *

The incidence of glaucoma in one out of 25,000 persons under the age of 40 may appear quite minimal. However, that one person, the plaintiff in this instance, is entitled to the same protection, as afforded persons over 40, essential for timely detection of the evidence of glaucoma where it can be arrested to avoid the grave and devastating result of this disease. The test is a simple pressure test, relatively inexpensive. There is no judgment factor involved, and there is no doubt that by giving the test the evidence of glaucoma can be detected. The giving of the test is harmless if the physical condition of the eye permits. The testimony indicates that although the condition of the plaintiff's eyes might have at times prevented the defendants from administering the pressure test, there is an absence of evidence in the record that the test could not have been timely given.

Justice Holmes stated [ ] in Texas & Pac.Ry. v. Behymer,[ ]:

> What usually is done may be evidence of what ought to be done, but what ought to be done is fixed by a standard of reasonable prudence, whether it usually is complied with or not.

In The T.J. Hooper, 60 F.2d 737 * * *, Justice Hand stated:

> [I]n most cases reasonable prudence is in fact common prudence; but strictly it is never its measure; a whole calling may have unduly lagged in the adoption of new and available devices. It never may set its own tests, however persuasive be its usages. *Courts must in the end say what is required; there are precautions so imperative that even their universal disregard will not excuse their omission.*

(Italics ours.)

Under the facts of this case reasonable prudence required the timely giving of the pressure test to this plaintiff. The precaution of giving this test to detect the incidence of glaucoma to patients under 40 years of age is so imperative that irrespective of its disregard by the standards of the ophthalmology profession, it is the duty of the courts to say what is required to protect patients under 40 from the damaging results of glaucoma.

We therefore hold, as a matter of law, that the reasonable standard that should have been followed under the undisputed facts of this case was the timely giving of this simple, harmless pressure test to this plaintiff and that, in failing to do so, the defendants were negligent, which proximately resulted in the blindness sustained by the plaintiff for which the defendants are liable.

* * *

Notes and Questions

1. Is the court correct in imposing its own risk-benefit result on the specialty of ophthalmology? Certainly its view of the tradeoff between blindness and a low-cost test seems to lead inevitably to the *Helling* conclusion. A survey of Washington ophthalmologists subsequent to the *Helling* decision found that they did test for glaucoma with some regularity before *Helling,* with 20.3% reporting that they tested "quite often", and 30.1% testing "virtually always". Jerry Wiley, "The Impact of Judicial Decisions on Professional Conduct: An Empirical Study", 55 S.Cal.L.Rev. 345, 383 (1981). Yet the expert testimony in the case was that testing was not the practice for patients under forty.

The court assumed that the test was harmless as well as low in cost: "the giving of the test is harmless if the physical condition of the eye permits." This view ignores both the costs of false-positives and the merits of treatment when a true positive result is found. It has been estimated that more than 15 patients per one million population go blind from glaucoma annually. Screening for glaucoma using tonometry (the pressure test in *Helling*) is recommended on the theory that early treatment will stop the progression of glaucoma into blindness.

The value of tonometry is limited by its imprecision. First, it has a high false positive rate. Only one percent of those patients who test abnormally high using tonometry actually have glaucoma. Ninety-nine percent of those who test positive therefore have to undergo further testing and are subjected to considerable worry for a disease they do not have. Second, patients who are correctly diagnosed as having glaucoma or at least elevated intraocular pressure may not gain much from this knowledge, since drug treatments often do not produce significant improvements, nor does current evidence support the theory that early treatment will halt the progression of glaucoma. See generally Eliot Robin, Matters of Life & Death: Risks v. Benefits of Medical Care 147 (1984); Eric E. Fortess and Marshall B. Kapp, Medical Uncertainty, Diagnostic Testing, and Legal Liability, 13 Law,

Medicine & Health Care 213 (1985) (because of high false-positive rate, follow-up testing would cost a great deal, and patients who tested positive falsely would also suffer unnecessary anxiety about incipient glaucoma.)

A new screening device, the GDX Access, can now directly test the presence and extent of damage to the nerve fiber layer at the back of the eye: This allows early and accurate diagnosis of glaucoma. See "New Device Helps to Diagnose Glaucoma More Reliably", N.Y. Times (March 5, 2001.)

2. Do these opinions change your view of the rightness of the court's position in *Helling*? Why didn't the defendant ophthalmologists make these arguments to justify the conservative non-testing approach? Why did the defense fail to prove that a significant minority, or even a majority of Washington ophthalmologists, used the pressure test routinely? Should we be reluctant to encourage courts to move beyond the customary practice, given the complexity inherent in medical practice? Or should courts be aggressive in judging the community standard, so long as the parties present full evidence as to the pros and cons of the procedure at issue?

3. *Helling v. Carey* is one of a small number of cases rejecting a customary medical practice. See also Lundahl v. Rockford Memorial Hospital Association, 93 Ill.App.2d 461, 465, 235 N.E.2d 671, 674 (1968) ("what is usual or customary procedure might itself be negligence"); Favalora v. Aetna Casualty & Surety Company, 144 So.2d 544 (La.App.1962); Toth v. Community Hospital at Glen Cove, 22 N.Y.2d 255, 263, 292 N.Y.S.2d 440, 447–48, 239 N.E.2d 368, 373 (1968) ("evidence that the defendant followed customary practice is not the sole test of professional malpractice"). These cases involve a readily understandable therapy or diagnostic procedure, and the courts have allowed the trier of fact to weigh without expert testimony the relative risks of using the procedure or omitting it. Most jurisdictions have been reluctant to follow *Helling* in replacing the established medical standard of care with a case-by-case judicial balancing.

For an interesting judicial discussion of the limits of a customary practice defense, see Nowatske v. Osterloh, 198 Wis.2d 419, 543 N.W.2d 265 (1996). The court considered the standard Wisconsin jury instruction on the standard of care applicable to physicians. Upholding the instruction, they wrote:

> We agree with the parties and the Medical Society that while evidence of the usual and customary conduct of others under similar circumstances is ordinarily relevant and admissible as an indication of what is reasonably prudent, customary conduct is not dispositive and cannot overcome the requirement that physicians exercise ordinary care.
>
> * * *
>
> We recognize that in most situations there will be no significant difference between customary and reasonable practices. In most situations physicians, like other professionals, will revise their customary practices so that the care they offer reflects a due regard for advances in the profession. An emphasis on reasonable rather than customary practices, however, insures that custom will not shelter physicians who fail to adopt advances in their respective fields and who consequently fail to conform to the standard of care which both the profession and its patients have a right to expect.

It has been argued that the customary practice standard of care, protective of physician behavior, is gradually eroding in favor of a general negligence standard. See Philip G. Peters, Jr., The Quiet Demise of Deference to Custom: Malpractice Law at the Millennium, 57 Wash. & Lee L.Rev. 163 (2000).

Note: The Effects of Tort Suits on Provider Behavior

Are tort suits likely to change potentially dangerous patterns of medical practice? Malpractice litigation in theory operates as a quality control mechanism. From the economist's perspective, tort doctrine should be designed to achieve an optimal prevention policy, reducing the sum total of the costs of medical accidents and the costs of preventing them. In theory, the tort system deters accident producing behavior. How? The existence of a liability rule and the resulting threat of a lawsuit and judgment encourages health care providers to reduce error and patient injury in circumstances where patients themselves lack the information (and ability) to monitor the quality of care they receive. Potential defendants will take precautions to avoid error and will buy insurance to cover any errors that injure patients. By finding fault and assessing damages against a defendant, a court sends a signal to health care providers that if they wish to avoid similar damages in the future they may need to change their behavior. See Michelle J. White, The Value of Liability in Medical Malpractice, 13 Health Affairs 75 (1994); Ann G. Lawthers, et al., Physicians' Perceptions of the Risk of Being Sued, 17 J. Health Pol., Policy & L. 463, 479 (1992); Mark I. Taragin, et al., The Influence of Standard of Care and Severity of Injury on the Resolution of Medical Malpractice Claims, 117 Ann. Int. Med. 780 (1992); and Frederick W. Cheney, et al., Standard of Care and Anesthesia Liability, 261 JAMA 1599 (1989). Other critics have noted the limitations on physician understanding of how the negligence system works and what their liability exposure really is. See, e.g., Bryan A. Liang, Medical Malpractice: Do Physicians Have Knowledge of Legal Standards and Assess Cases as Juries Do? 3 U. Chi. L. Sch. Roundtable 59 (1996).

How does the existence of malpractice insurance alter this analysis? If the insurer does not employ experience rating to distinguish the litigation-prone providers from their colleagues, it is in effect causing an inaccurate signal to be sent, since all physicians in a practice area pay the same premiums regardless of their level of malpractice claims. The existence of insurance therefore dilutes or eliminates the financial incentives for physicians or other providers to change their behavior.

Malpractice insurers, particularly the physician-owned companies in many states, now engage in aggressive review of claims. These companies insure about 40% of physicians in active patient care. They routinely use physicians to review applications for insurance and to review the competence of those sued. Physicians with claims due to negligence, as assessed by the peer reviews, may be terminated, may be surcharged, or have restrictions on practice imposed. William B. Schwartz and Daniel N. Mendelson, The Role of Physician–Owned Insurance Companies in the Detection and Deterrence of Negligence, 262 J.A.M.A. 1342 (1989). If a physician loses his malpractice insurance, he may quit, switch jobs, or go without insurance. He may also go to a surplus-lines insurance company that charges much higher premiums for coverage. Claims exposure thus can lead to a direct financial impact on the physician forced to carry such expensive insurance. See William B. Schwartz and Daniel N. Mendelson, Physicians Who Have Lost Their Malpractice Insurance, 262 J.A.M.A. 1335 (1989).

What is the likely effect on a physician of being named a defendant? How might a provider modify her behavior to avoid or reduce negligent behavior? She may spend more time on exams or patient histories, invest in further training, increase support staff or stop doing procedures that she does not do well. The few available studies have found that physicians who have been malpractice defendants often alter their practice as a reaction, even if they win the litigation. They also suffer chronic stress until the trial is over. See, for example, Charles, Wilbert, and Kennedy, Physicians' Self–Reports of Reactions to Malpractice Litigation, 141 Am.J.Psychiatry 563, 565 (1984) ("A malpractice suit was considered a serious and often a devastating event in the personal and professional lives of the respondent physicians").

Malpractice litigation does affect medical practice, making anxious providers either overestimate the risks of a suit or at least adjust their practice to a new assessment of the risk of suit, regardless of the incentive effects of judgments and premium increases. Physicians perceive a threat from the system, judging their risk of being sued as much higher than it actually is. The Harvard New York Study, surveying New York physicians, found that physicians who had been sued were more likely to explain risks to patients, to restrict their scope of practice, and to order more tests and procedures. Patients, Doctors, and Lawyers: Medical Injury, Malpractice Litigation, and Patient Compensation in New York 9–29 (1990). Physicians surveyed in the New York study felt that the malpractice threat was important in maintaining standards of care. Id. at 9–24. The Report notes that "* * * the perception of incentives largely shapes the behavior that ultimately affects patient care." Id. at 3–19. Perceived risk is thus important to physician conduct. See Peter A. Bell, Legislative Intrusions in the Common Law of Medical Malpractice: Thoughts About the Deterrent Effect of Tort Liability, 35 Syracuse L.Rev. 939, 973–90 (1984). Hospitals have instituted risk management offices and quality assurance programs; informed consent forms have become ubiquitous; medical record-keeping with an eye toward proof at trial has become the rule. One economist has estimated (based upon admittedly limited data) that "* * * the current non-trivial incidence of injury due to negligence would be at least 10 percent higher, were it not for the incentives for injury prevention created by the one in ten incidents of malpractice that result in a claim." Patricia Danzon, An Economic Analysis of the Medical Malpractice System, 1 Behavioral Sciences & the Law 39 (1983). See also Patricia M. Danzon, Medical Malpractice 10 (1984); Guido Calabresi, The Costs of Accidents (1970); William B. Schwartz and Neil K. Komesar, Doctors, Damages and Deterrence: An Economic View of Medical Malpractice, 298 New Eng.J.Med. 1282 (1978); The Economics of Medical Malpractice (S. Rottenberg, ed. 1978). For a skeptical view of the signalling effect of tort litigation generally, see Stephen D. Sugarman, Doing Away with Tort Law, 73 Cal.L.Rev. 555 (1985); critiquing Sugarman's view, see Howard A. Latin, Problem–Solving Behavior and Theories of Tort Liability, 73 Cal.L.Rev. 677, 740 (1985).

It can be argued that courts should be willing to articulate clear standards for practice. Such standards are more likely to be heeded by health care professionals in their practice where the rule is a relatively simple one. Daniel J. Givelber, William J. Bowers, and Carolyn L. Blitch, Tarasoff, Myth and Reality: An Empirical Study of Private Law In Action, 1984 Wisc.L.Rev. 443, 485–486. Givelber et al. concluded, after surveying 2875 psychotherapists nationwide, that therapists now warn third parties when a patient utters a threat. They feel bound by *Tarasoff,* even though the case is binding only on California therapists. Therapists feel capable of assessing dangerousness and were comfortable with warning victims.

The authors argued that

> "* * * [I]f an appellate court desires to change behavior, it should use judicially established standards of behavior, not jury determined standards.

The judicially determined rule of *Tarasoff I,* protect through warning, appears to have affected therapist attitudes, knowledge and behavior to a far greater degree than *Tarasoff II.* Id. at 487."

What other forces and incentives affect the quality of health care delivery by physicians, other professionals, and institutions? If you were a physician or a nurse who conscientiously wanted to reduce medical errors in your own practice, what steps would you consider? A technological innovation for example may reduce both the level of medical injury for a procedure and the risks of being sued. Consider the pulse oximeter, which monitors a patient's blood oxygen to indicate when his oxygen level drops due to breathing problems or overuse of anesthesia. This can give physicians three or four minutes to correct a problem before brain damage results. In 1984, no hospital operating room had such a device, but by 1990 all operating rooms did. Patients under anesthesia now suffer fewer injuries as a result.

III. OTHER THEORIES

A. NEGLIGENT INFLICTION OF MENTAL DISTRESS

Most medical malpractice suits are negligence suits for physical injury and lost wages suffered by the patient, or in a wrongful death action, for damages that include harm to the deceased's relatives. Recent cases however have allowed plaintiffs to sue a health care provider for the negligent infliction of emotional distress under particularly egregious circumstances.

OSWALD v. LeGRAND

Supreme Court of Iowa, 1990.
453 N.W.2d 634.

NEUMAN, JUSTICE.

This appeal challenges a grant of summary judgment for medical professionals in a case involving the spontaneous abortion of a 19–22 week-old fetus. The trial court barred the plaintiffs from introducing expert testimony due to their failure to timely designate an expert in accordance with Iowa Code section 668.11(2) (1987). Accordingly, the district court determined that plaintiffs could not generate a material issue of fact concerning the defendants' negligence. Because we conclude that expert testimony is crucial to some but not all of plaintiffs' claims, we affirm in part, reverse in part, and remand for further proceedings.

I. * * *

To establish a prima facie case of medical malpractice, a plaintiff must produce evidence that (1) establishes the applicable standard of care, (2) demonstrates a violation of this standard, and (3) develops a causal relationship between the violation and the injury sustained. [ ] Ordinarily, evidence of the applicable standard of care—and its breach—must be furnished by an expert. [ ] This court has recognized two exceptions to this rule:

> One is where the physician's lack of care is so obvious as to be within the comprehension of a lay[person] and requires only common knowledge and experience to understand. The other exception is really an example of the

first situation. It arises when the physician injures a part of the body not being treated.

[ ] It is the "common knowledge" exception upon which plaintiffs base their argument for reversal in the present case.

II. * * * [W]e accept the following facts as established for purposes of this appeal.

Plaintiffs Susan and Larry Oswald have been married for ten years and are the parents of two healthy sons. During Susan's third pregnancy, she began experiencing bleeding and painful cramping just prior to her five-month checkup. At that time, she was under the care of a family practice physician, defendant Barry Smith. He ordered an ultrasound test and Susan was then examined in his office by one of his colleagues, defendant Larry LeGrand, an obstetrician. Neither the test nor the examination revealed an explanation for the bleeding and Susan was instructed to go home and stay off her feet. Later that day, however, Susan began to bleed heavily. She was taken by ambulance to defendant Mercy Health Center. The bleeding eventually stopped, Dr. Smith's further examination failed to yield a cause of the problem, and Susan was discharged the following day with directions to take it easy.

The following day, Susan's cramping and bleeding worsened. Susan thought she was in labor and feared a miscarriage. She was unable to reach Dr. Smith by telephone and so Larry drove her to the emergency room at Mercy. There Dr. Christopher Clark, another physician in association with Smith and LeGrand, examined her. He advised her there was nothing to be done and she should go home. Larry was angered by this response and insisted Susan be admitted to the hospital. Dr. Clark honored this request and Susan was transferred to the labor and delivery ward.

In considerable pain and anxious about her pregnancy, Susan's first contact on the ward was with a nurse who said, "What are you doing here? The doctor told you to stay home and rest." Susan felt like "a real pest." A short while later, while attached to a fetal monitor, Susan was told by another nurse that if she miscarried it would not be a baby, it would be a "big blob of blood." Susan was scared.

The next morning, an argument apparently ensued over which physician was responsible for Susan's care. Standing outside Susan's room, Dr. Clark yelled, "I don't want to take that patient. She's not my patient and I am sick and tired of Dr. Smith dumping his case load on me." At the urging of Larry and a nurse, Dr. Clark apologized to Susan for this outburst. He assured her that he would care for her until he left for vacation at noon that day when he was scheduled to go "off call" and Dr. LeGrand would take over.

Around 9:00 a.m. Susan began experiencing a great deal of pain that she believed to be labor contractions. Dr. Clark prescribed Tylenol and scheduled her for an ultrasound and amniocentesis at 11:00 a.m. By that time, Susan was screaming in pain and yelling that she was in labor. Dr. Clark arrived in the x-ray department halfway through the ultrasound procedure and determined from viewing the sonogram that there was insufficient fluid in the amniotic sac to perform an amniocentesis. He told the Oswalds that the situation was unusual but did not reveal to them his suspicion that there was an infection in the uterus. He examined Susan abdominally but did not do a pelvic exam. By all accounts, Susan was hysterical and insisting she was about to deliver. Dr. Clark wanted her transferred upstairs for further monitoring. He told Larry to calm her down. Then he left on vacation, approximately one-half hour before the end of his scheduled duty.

Within minutes, Susan began delivering her baby in the hallway outside the x-ray lab. When Larry lifted the sheet covering Susan and "saw [his] daughter hanging from her belly" he kicked open a glass door to get the attention of hospital personnel. Susan was quickly wheeled to the delivery room where two nurses delivered her one-pound baby girl at 11:34 a.m.

After visually observing neither a heartbeat nor any respiratory activity, one of the nurses announced that the baby was stillborn. The nurse wrapped the infant in a towel and placed her on an instrument tray. Ten minutes later, Dr. LeGrand arrived and delivered the placenta. At Susan's request, he checked the fetus for gender. He made no further examination of the infant, assuming it to be a nonviable fetus. After assuring himself that Susan was fine, and offering his condolences to the disappointed parents, he returned to his office.

Meanwhile, Larry called relatives to advise them of the stillbirth. Upon his return to Susan's room, he touched the infant's finger. Much to his surprise, his grasp was returned. Larry told a nurse in attendance that the baby was alive but the nurse retorted that it was only a "reflex motion." The nurses subsequently determined that the baby *was* alive. After having left her on an instrument tray for nearly half an hour, the nurses rushed the infant to the neonatal intensive care unit. The infant, registered on her birth certificate as Natalie Sue, received comfort support measures until she died about twelve hours later. Further facts will be detailed as they become pertinent to the issues on appeal.

III. In January 1987, the Oswalds sued the hospital and doctors Clark, Smith and LeGrand on theories of negligence, negligent loss of chance of survival, breach of implied contract and breach of implied warranty. As to Dr. LeGrand and the hospital, Oswalds additionally alleged gross negligence. Factually, these causes of action were premised on violation of the standard of prenatal care owed to Susan Oswald and alleged negligence in the examination and treatment of Natalie Sue including failure to recognize signs of an imminent premature birth, failure to properly prepare for such delivery, and delaying timely and vital treatment to the infant upon her birth. The Oswalds claimed damages for Natalie Sue's lost chance to live, their loss of society and companionship flowing from Natalie Sue's death, severe emotional distress and anxiety resulting from the defendants' negligence in the care of both Susan and Natalie Sue, and severe emotional distress and mental anguish caused by witnessing the negligent treatment of their newborn infant.

* * *

IV. * * *

A. *Evidence not within common knowledge.* To begin, there is no evidence in this record that more prompt or heroic efforts to sustain Natalie Sue's life would have been successful. * * *

Similarly, the record contains no evidence that the doctors' or hospital's treatment of Susan in any way prompted Susan's premature delivery or could have, in any way, prevented it. * * *

B. *Evidence within the "common knowledge" exception.* Beyond these fundamental treatment issues, however, lie plaintiffs' claims that the care provided by defendants Clark, LeGrand, and Mercy Hospital fell below the standard of medical professionalism understood by laypersons and expected by them. Into this category fall Nurse Slater's unwelcoming remarks upon Susan's arrival at the birthing area; Nurse Gardner's deprecating description of a fetus as a "big blob of blood"; Dr. Clark's tirade outside Susan's door; Dr. Clark's insensitivity to Susan's insistence that she was in the final stage of labor, leaving her in a hysterical state minutes before her delivery in a hospital corridor while he went "off call"; Nurse Flynn's determination that the fetus was stillborn, only to discover it gasping for breath half-an-hour later; and Dr. LeGrand's admitted failure to make an independent determination of the viability of the fetus, conceding it was his obligation to do so. Larry and Susan contend that they have suffered severe emotional distress as a result of these alleged breaches of professional conduct.

We note preliminarily that because the Oswalds can sustain no claim of physical injury, they would ordinarily be denied recovery in a negligence action for emotional distress. [ ] An exception exists, however, where the nature of the relationship between the parties is such that there arises a duty to exercise ordinary care to avoid causing emotional harm. [ ] Such claims have been recognized in the negligent performance of contractual services that carry with them deeply emotional responses in the event of breach as, for example, in the transmission and delivery of telegrams announcing the death of a close relative, [ ] and services incident to a funeral and burial. [ ] Under the comparable circumstances demonstrated by this record, we think liability for emotional injury should attach to the delivery of medical services. As we observed by way of analogy in *Meyer*, the birth of a child involves a matter of life and death evoking such "mental concern and solicitude" that the breach of a contract incident thereto "will inevitably result in mental anguish, pain and suffering." *Meyer*, 241 N.W.2d at 920 (quoting *Stewart v. Rudner*, 349 Mich. 459, 84 N.W.2d 816). * * * [ ]

Insofar as the sufficiency of damages are concerned, the Oswalds' claim appears undisputed.[2] The question is whether these six incidents, if proven at trial, would demonstrate a breach of professional medical conduct so obvious as to be within the common knowledge of laypersons without the aid of expert testimony; or, in the alternative, whether plaintiffs could prove the standard of care and its breach through defendants' own testimony. In other words, is

2. Because the trial court determined plaintiffs' proof was insufficient on the elements of negligence and causation, it did not reach the question of damages. The record reveals that both Susan and Larry have undergone psychological counseling in an effort to overcome the stress, anxiety, and depression associated with Susan's fear of becoming pregnant again and Larry's anger and guilt over the extraordinary helplessness he felt as a witness to his wife's painful and humiliating experience at Mercy Hospital. To the extent that the trial court considered, and dismissed, any claim of intentional infliction of emotional distress due to a perceived lack of "outrageousness" in defendants' conduct, we note that plaintiffs' emotional distress claim has not been pleaded as an independent tort but rather as an element of damages flowing from the underlying breach of professional conduct. Under such circumstances, the dismissal was not warranted because proof of outrageous conduct need not be shown.

the evidence presented by plaintiffs' resistance to the motion sufficient to overcome summary judgment on defendants' claim that no material dispute exists with respect to the issues of negligence and causation? We are persuaded that it is.

The first three incidents described above raise commonly understood issues of professional courtesy in communication regarding a patient's care and treatment. No expert testimony is needed to elaborate on whether the statements by the nurses and Dr. Clark were rude and uncaring; a lay fact finder could easily evaluate the statements in light of the surrounding circumstances to determine whether the language used or message conveyed breached the standard of care expected of medical professionals, and determine the harm, if any, resulting to the plaintiffs. In reaching this conclusion we hasten to emphasize that our decision in this case is closely limited to its facts. We in no way suggest that a professional person must ordinarily answer in tort for rudeness, even in a professional relationship. In order for liability to attach there must appear a combination of the two factors existing here: extremely rude behavior or crass insensitivity coupled with an unusual vulnerability on the part of the person receiving professional services.

We are similarly convinced that a lay jury is also capable of evaluating the professional propriety of Dr. Clark's early departure from the hospital, knowing that he had left Susan Oswald unattended in a hospital corridor screaming hysterically that she was about to give birth. * * *

* * *

C. *Evidence demonstrable through defendants' admissions.* * * *

* * *

Defendants argue that because Natalie Sue's death was inevitable, the emotional distress suffered by the Oswalds is understandable but not compensable. What defendants overlook is the colorable claim of severe emotional distress proximately caused by the equivocation of these health care professionals on the very question of her life or death. Under this record, we think the plaintiffs have produced evidence minimally sufficient to overcome summary judgment on this claim of malpractice.

* * *

In conclusion, we affirm in part, reverse in part, and remand this case for further proceedings not inconsistent with this opinion.

Affirmed in part, reversed in part, and remanded.

Notes and Questions

1. *Oswald* focuses on the vulnerability of the plaintiffs, coupled with the "crass insensitivity" of the medical staff. Consider, as a companion case, Wargelin v. Sisters of Mercy Health Corporation, 149 Mich.App. 75, 385 N.W.2d 732 (1986). In *Wargelin,* a series of obstetric disasters befell the plaintiffs. The obstetrician made only two visits during labor, even though a Caesarean section was indicated due to the plaintiff's lopsided uterus; the fetal monitor indicated distress, but the staff failed to react; an intern subsequently delivered the plaintiff's child, not breathing and blue in color, and placed it on her stomach as if it were a healthy

child; the obstetrician then grabbed the child and began to pound on its chest and administer electrical shocks to revive it; a call for a pediatrician to help went unanswered; and after fifteen minutes the rescue attempt was abandoned.

The Michigan court applied the bystander rule, which allows that a member of the family witnessing an injury to a third person may recover if they are present or suffer shock "fairly contemporaneous" with the accident. The court held that the series of events related above, including negligent acts, were sufficient. "* * * [T]he cumulative effect of all the events surrounding the stillbirth of the child, if proven to be negligent at trial, are sufficient to cause a parent to suffer emotional and mental distress."

Do *Oswald* and *Wargelin,* read together, expand the applicability of the tort of negligent infliction of mental distress? They indicate judicial sensitivity to hospital failures to provide sensitive, well-trained health care, and willingness to extend the bystander doctrine to allow recovery in these highly charged situations.

2. Negligent infliction of mental distress cases typically involve "bystanders" who witness injury to a loved one. Dillon v. Legg, 68 Cal.2d 728, 69 Cal.Rptr. 72, 441 P.2d 912 (1968) was the first case to articulate a general test of foreseeability of harm, a primary guideline being whether the distress resulted from the "sensory and contemporaneous observance of the accident." Parents would thus need to "observe" the accident or trauma in jurisdictions following the *Dillon* approach.

The California Supreme Court limited the *Dillon* "foreseeability" approach in Thing v. La Chusa, 48 Cal.3d 644, 257 Cal.Rptr. 865, 771 P.2d 814 (1989). The court noted that "* * * [t]he emotional distress for which monetary damages may be recovered * * * ought not to be that form of acute emotional distress or the transient emotional reaction to the occasional gruesome or horrible incident to which every person may potentially be exposed in an industrial and sometimes violent society." The court then said that a plaintiff could recover only if he:

> (1) is closely related to the injury victim; (2) is present at the scene of the injury producing event at the time it occurs and is then aware that it is causing injury to the victim; and (3) as a result suffers serious emotional distress—a reaction beyond that which would be anticipated in a disinterested witness and which is not an abnormal response to the circumstances.

Observation of the disturbing events is generally required before courts will allow recovery. Johnson v. Ruark Obstetrics and Gynecology Associates, P.A., 327 N.C. 283, 395 S.E.2d 85 (1990) (expectant parents of a stillborn fetus sued the physicians for the negligent infliction of mental distress, alleging that they had observed events surrounding the death of the fetus; the North Carolina Supreme Court allowed negligent infliction of emotional distress based on a test of reasonably foreseeable consequences). "Observation" has been liberally construed by some state courts. See, for example, Frame v. Kothari, 212 N.J.Super. 498, 515 A.2d 810 (1985)(defendant physician's misdiagnosis of a cerebellar hemorrhage and acute hydrocephalus due to blunt trauma to the skull was held to be an event perceived by the parents; first, the parents' discussion with the defendant about their son's deteriorating condition was an "observation;" and second, their distress was foreseeable after the doctor was informed of the condition and failed to properly treat it.) See also Ochoa v. Superior Court of Santa Clara County, 39 Cal.3d 159, 216 Cal.Rptr. 661, 703 P.2d 1 (1985), where a mother suffered distress after visiting her son who was receiving "woefully inadequate" medical care in a juvenile detention home.

In Estate of Davis v. Yale–New Haven Hospital, 2000 WL 157921 (Conn.Super.2000), the court allowed a bystander emotional distress claim against the doctor and hospital where the decedent underwent cardiac surgery, became paranoid and detached from reality, was discharged without an anti-pyschotic drug prescription or a treatment plan, and killed himself. The court held that in an appropriate case, which would be rare in misdiagnosis cases, an action for bystander emotional disturbance would be allowed.

Most courts require some direct observation of the events causing the bad outcome, not just observation of the bad outcome itself. See, for example, Smelko v. Brinton, 241 Kan. 763, 740 P.2d 591 (1987)(parents waiting outside the operating room for their baby to undergo surgery; he is negligently burned during the surgery and they discover the burn when he is brought out; held that merely seeing the bad result is not sufficient for recovery). Contra, see Martinez v. Long Island Jewish Hillside Medical Center, 70 N.Y.2d 697, 518 N.Y.S.2d 955, 512 N.E.2d 538 (1987) (physician negligently diagnoses a pregnant woman's condition as requiring an abortion; the woman aborts the fetus and then discovers the abortion was not needed; recovery allowed).

3. If a contractual relationship forms the basis for liability for emotional distress, some jurisdictions have held that the injured party need not have observed the disaster, as foreseeability is not required. In Newton v. Kaiser Foundation Hospitals, 184 Cal.App.3d 386, 228 Cal.Rptr. 890 (1986) the plaintiffs' baby was born partially paralyzed as the result of the doctor's failure to perform a caesarian section. The father was not present and the mother was unconscious, but both were allowed to sue for their emotional distress. The court held that "[t]he mother had a contract with Kaiser by which it undertook, for consideration, to provide care and treatment for the delivery of a healthy fetus. Kaiser's contract was the source of its duty and a determination of foreseeability is unnecessary to establish a duty of care". (Id. at 894). For a discussion of the tortuous California jurisprudence on the negligent infliction of emotional distress in the health care setting, see Schwarz v. Regents of the University of California, 226 Cal.App.3d 149, 276 Cal.Rptr. 470 (1990).

This "direct victim" concept, developed in Molien v. Kaiser Foundation Hospitals, 27 Cal.3d 916, 167 Cal.Rptr. 831, 616 P.2d 813 (1980), requires a preexisting relationship between defendant and plaintiff and foreseeability of injury. See Mercado v. Leong, 43 Cal.App.4th 317, 50 Cal.Rptr.2d 569 (C.A.3d Dist. 1996).

In Rowe v. Bennett, 514 A.2d 802 (Me.1986), a lesbian psychotherapist continued to treat her lesbian patient even though she had developed an emotional relationship with the patient's lover. The Maine Supreme Court held that the nature of the therapist-patient relationship could provide the basis for a claim of emotional distress. The court wrote:

> Given the fact that a therapist undertakes the treatment of a patient's mental problems and that the patient is encouraged to divulge his innermost thoughts, the patient is extremely vulnerable to mental harm if the therapist fails to adhere to the standards of care recognized by the profession. Any psychological harm that may result from such negligence is neither speculative nor easily feigned. Unlike evidence of mental distress occurring in other situations, objective proof of the existence vel non of a psychological injury in these circumstances should not be difficult to obtain. (Id. at 819–20).

Are the courts in *Newton* and *Rowe* expanding notions of fiduciary obligations arising out of professional relationships to justify emotional distress damages? What theme ties these cases together?

4. The AIDS epidemic has given rise to public fears of infection, and the health care setting has not escaped this anxiety. Patients exposed to providers or blood materials in the health care setting have sued for the negligent infliction of emotional distress, based on their fear of contagion of the HIV virus. Courts have resisted such claims. In K.A.C. v. Benson, 527 N.W.2d 553 (Minn.1995), the plaintiff sued a physician who had performed two gynecological examinations of her during a period when he suffered from AIDS and had open sores on his hands and forearms as a result of dermatitis. Shortly after the second examination, the Minnesota Department of Health contacted 336 patients on whom Dr. Benson had performed one or more invasive procedures while gloved, but while suffering from exudative dermatitis. None of the patients tested HIV positive, but over 50 sued him and the Clinic where he worked. The plaintiff argued that she was in the "zone of danger" for purposes of a claim of negligent infliction of emotional distress. The court wrote:

> This court has long recognized that a person within the zone of danger of physical impact who reasonably fears for his or her own safety during the time of exposure, and who consequently suffers severe emotional distress with resultant physical injury may recover emotional distress damages whether or not physical impact results. [ ] However, a remote possibility of personal peril is sufficient to place plaintiff within a zone of danger for purposes of a claim of negligent infliction of emotional distress. Consequently, we hold that a plaintiff who fails to allege actual exposure to HIV is not, as a matter of law, in personal physical danger of contracting HIV, and thus not within a zone of danger for purposes of establishing a claim for negligent infliction of emotional distress. Id. at 559.

The majority of jurisdictions considering this issue have agreed that the plaintiff must allege actual exposure to HIV to recover emotional distress damages. See, e.g., Burk v. Sage Products, Inc., 747 F.Supp. 285 (E.D.Pa.1990); Ordway v. County of Suffolk, 154 Misc.2d 269, 583 N.Y.S.2d 1014(1992); Carroll v. Sisters of St. Francis Health Serv., Inc., 868 S.W.2d 585 (Tenn.1993); Johnson v. West Virginia Univ. Hosps., 186 W.Va. 648, 413 S.E.2d 889 (1991). See also John R. Austin, HIV/AIDS and the Health Care Industry Liability: An Annotated Bibliography, 27 J. Marshall L.Rev. 513 (1994).

B. DUTIES TO CONTEST REIMBURSEMENT LIMITS

Solo practice, once the norm in American medical practice, is rapidly disappearing. By 1996, more than a third of physicians were located in group practices of three or more and another third were employees or contractors. The reorganization of the health care industry has pushed physicians into group practices and employment with health care institutions or managed care organizations or alliances with hospitals in integrated delivery systems. Health care is more constrained by explicit financial limits. Institutions that provide health care—such as hospitals or nursing homes—and entities that pay for health care—including insurers and self-insured employers—now oversee the work of the medical professionals who practice within them or whose care they purchase. The emergence of managed care organizations that both pay for and provide care gives lay managers even greater control over medical practice, in the name of both cost containment and quality of care.

The use of prospective payment systems and the expansion of managed care organizations have imposed substantial constraints on the formerly open ended fee-for-service system of American health care. Physicians in the past could order tests, referrals and hospitalization for patients with little resistance from either insurers or employers who may have footed the premium bill. Cost-constrained systems now create tensions between cost control and quality of care. Heavy pressure is put on physicians to reduce diagnostic tests, control lengths of stay in hospitals, and trim the fat out of medical practice. As physicians experience outside utilization review, limits in drug formularies as to what may be prescribed, and constraints on specialist and hospital referrals, they feel caught between duties to patients and duties to the institutions in which they now operate.

A physician may have an obligation to assist patients in obtaining payment for health care. At a minimum, this means that the doctor must be aware of reimbursement constraints, so that he can promptly advise the patient or direct him to an appropriate institutional office for further information. Must a physician actively assist a patient in obtaining funding for a procedure that the physician feels is necessary? No court would require a physician to pay out of his own pocket for a treatment that a patient needs; there is no "duty to rescue" in the sense of a physician's financial obligation to support his patient. However, the *Wickline* case and others support the argument that a physician operating within a constrained reimbursement structure and an institutional bureaucracy is expected to be familiar with limits on payment.

WICKLINE v. STATE

Court of Appeal, Second District, Division 5, California, 1986.
192 Cal.App.3d 1630, 239 Cal.Rptr. 810.

ROWEN, ASSOCIATE JUSTICE.

This is an appeal from a judgment for plaintiff entered after a trial by jury. For the reasons discussed below, we reverse the judgment.

Principally, this matter concerns itself with the legal responsibility that a third party payor, in this case, the State of California, has for harm caused to a patient when a cost containment program is applied in a manner which is alleged to have affected the implementation of the treating physician's medical judgment.

The plaintiff, respondent herein, Lois J. Wickline (plaintiff or Wickline) sued defendant, appellant herein, State of California (State or Medi–Cal). The essence of the plaintiff's claim is found in paragraph 16 of her second amended complaint which alleges: "Between January 6, 1977, and January 21, 1977, Doe I an employee of the State of California, while acting within the scope of employment, negligently discontinued plaintiff's Medi–Cal eligibility, causing plaintiff to be discharged from Van Nuys Community Hospital prematurely and whil [sic] in need of continuing hospital care. As a result of said negligent act, plaintiff suffered a complete occlusion of the right infrarenoaorta, necessitating an amputation of plaintiff's right leg."

I

Responding to concerns about the escalating cost of health care, public and private payors have in recent years experimented with a variety of cost containment mechanisms. We deal here with one of those programs: The prospective utilization review process.

At the outset, this court recognizes that this case appears to be the first attempt to tie a health care payor into the medical malpractice causation chain and that it, therefore, deals with issues of profound importance to the health care community and to the general public. For those reasons we have permitted the filing of amicus curiae briefs in support of each of the respective parties in the matter to assure that due consideration is given to the broader issues raised before this court by this case.

Traditionally, quality assurance activities, including utilization review programs, were performed primarily within the hospital setting under the general control of the medical staff. * * * The principal focus of such quality assurance review schema was to prevent overutilization due to the recognized financial incentives to both hospitals and physicians to maximize revenue by increasing the amount of service provided and to insure that patients were not unnecessarily exposed to risks as a result of unnecessary surgery and/or hospitalization.

Early cost containment programs utilized the retrospective utilization review process. In that system the third party payor reviewed the patient's chart after the fact to determine whether the treatment provided was medically necessary. If, in the judgment of the utilization reviewer, it was not, the health care provider's claim for payment was denied.

In the cost containment program in issue in this case, prospective utilization review, authority for the rendering of health care services must be obtained before medical care is rendered. Its purpose is to promote the well recognized public interest in controlling health care costs by reducing unnecessary services while still intending to assure that appropriate medical and hospital services are provided to the patient in need. However, such a cost containment strategy creates new and added pressures on the quality assurance portion of the utilization review mechanism. The stakes, the risks at issue, are much higher when a prospective cost containment review process is utilized than when a retrospective review process is used.

A mistaken conclusion about medical necessity following retrospective review will result in the wrongful withholding of payment. An erroneous decision in a prospective review process, on the other hand, in practical consequences, results in the withholding of necessary care, potentially leading to a patient's permanent disability or death.

II

[A summary of the facts follows. Mrs. Wickline, a woman in her 40s, was treated in 1976 by Dr. Daniels, a physician in general family practice. She failed to respond to physical therapy and was admitted to Van Nuys Community Hospital and examined by Dr. Polonsky, a specialist in peripheral vascular surgery. He diagnosed Leriche's Syndrome, a condition caused by obstruction of the terminal aorta due to arteriosclerosis. He recommended surgery. Ms. Wickline was eligible for Medi–Cal, California's medical assistance program. Dr. Daniels submitted a treatment authorization request to Medi–Cal, which authorized the surgery and 10 days of hospitalization. Dr. Polonsky then performed the surgery, which involved removing a part of Ms.

Wickline's artery and substituting a synthetic artery. She then developed a clot and a second operation was required. Her recovery after these two procedures was described as "stormy".

Ms. Wickline was to leave the hospital on January 17, 1977. Dr. Polonsky decided on January 16 however that it was "medically necessary" for her to remain in the hospital for another eight days beyond the scheduled discharge date. He was worried about infection, and also about his ability to respond quickly to any emergency that might develop in her legs. He therefore filed a Medi–Cal form 180. The physician puts on this form the patient's diagnosis, significant history, clinical status and treatment plan, in order to permit the Medi–Cal representative—either an "on-site" nurse and/or the Medi–Cal physician consultant—to evaluate the request. The form as filled out by Dr. Polonsky was complete and accurate, and was signed off by Dr. Daniels and submitted to the nurse responsible for completing such forms. The nurse, Doris Futerman, felt that she should not approve the entire eight-day extension. She therefore telephoned the Medi–Cal consultant, Dr. Glassman, a board certified surgeon. Dr. Glassman rejected Wickline's physician's request and authorized only four days beyond the original discharge date.

Doctors Polonsky and Daniels each then wrote discharge orders based on the limited four day extension. As the court described their actions, "[w]hile all three doctors were aware that they could attempt to obtain a further extension of Wickline's hospital stay by telephoning the Medi–Cal Consultant to request such an extension, none of them did so."

Ms. Wickline was discharged. At the time of her departure from the hospital, her condition appeared stable, with no evidence that her leg was in danger. Dr. Polonsky testified that he felt his hands were tied as to further appeals on his part. In the words of the court,

> Dr. Polonsky testified that at the time in issue he felt that Medi–Cal Consultants had the State's interest more in mind than the patient's welfare and that that belief influenced his decision not to request a second extension of Wickline's hospital stay. In addition, he felt that Medi–Cal had the power to tell him, as a treating doctor, when a patient must be discharged from the hospital. Therefore, while still of the subjective, non-communicated, opinion that Wickline was seriously ill and that the danger to her was not over, Dr. Polonsky discharged her from the hospital on January 21, 1977. He testified that had Wickline's condition, in his medical judgment, been critical or in a deteriorating condition on January 21, he would have made some effort to keep her in the hospital beyond that day even if denied authority by Medi–Cal and even if he had to pay her hospital bill himself.

The medical experts in the case agreed that Dr. Polonsky was within the standard of practice in discharging Wickline on January 21. Within a few days of her arrival home, Ms. Wickline had problems with her right leg. She was ordered back to the hospital on January 30, nine days after her last discharge. Attempts to save the leg were unsuccessful, and on February 8 Dr. Polonsky amputated Wickline's leg below the knee, to save her life. On February 17, because of the failure to heal, her leg was amputated above the knee. Dr. Polonsky testified that if she had remained in the hospital, he would have observed the leg's change in color, realized that a clot had formed, and ordered her back into surgery to reopen the graft to remove the clot. He testified to a reasonable medical certainty that she would not have lost her leg if she had remained in the hospital. He further testified, in the court's words, that the "Medi–Cal Consultant's rejection of the requested eight-day extension of acute care hospitalization and his authorization of a four-day extension in its place did not conform to the usual medical standards as they existed in 1977. He stated that, in accordance with those standards, a physician would not be permitted to make decisions regarding the care of a patient without either first seeing the patient, reviewing the patient's chart or discussing the patient's condition with her treating physician or physicians."]

III

From the facts thus presented, appellant takes the position that it was not negligent as a matter of law. Appellant contends that the decision to discharge was made by each of the plaintiff's three doctors, was based upon the prevailing standards of practice, and was justified by her condition at the time of her discharge. It argues that Medi–Cal had no part in the plaintiff's hospital discharge and therefore was not liable even if the decision to do so was erroneously made by her doctors.

* * *

IV

[In this section the court examined the negligence liability rules in California, and concluded that Medi–Cal is absolved from liability in this case.]

Dr. Kaufman, the chief Medi–Cal Consultant for the Los Angeles field office, was called to testify on behalf of the defendant. He testified that in January 1977, the criteria, or standard, which governed a Medi–Cal Consultant in acting on a request to consider an extension of time was founded on title 22 of the California Administrative Code. That standard was "the medical necessity" for the length and level of care requested. That, Dr. Kaufman contended, was determined by the Medi–Cal Consultant from the information provided him in the 180 form. The Medi–Cal Consultant's decision required the exercise of medical judgment and, in doing so, the Medi–Cal Consultant would utilize the skill, knowledge, training and experience he had acquired in the medical field.

Dr. Kaufman supported Dr. Glassman's decision. He testified, based upon his examination of the MC–180 form in issue in this matter, that Dr. Glassman's four-day hospital stay extension authorization was ample to meet the plaintiff's medically necessary needs at that point in time. Further, in Dr. Kaufman's opinion, there was no need for Dr. Glassman to seek information beyond that which was contained in Wickline's 180 form.

Dr. Kaufman testified that it was the practice in the Los Angeles Medi–Cal office for Medi–Cal Consultants not to review other information that might be available, such as the TAR 160 form (request for authorization for initial hospitalization), unless called by the patient's physician and requested to do so and, instead, to rely only on the information contained in the MC–180 form. Dr. Kaufman also stated that Medi–Cal Consultants did not initiate telephone calls to patient's treating doctors because of the volume of work they already had in meeting their prescribed responsibilities. Dr. Kaufman testified that any facts relating to the patient's care and treatment that was not shown on the 180 form was of no significance.

As to the principal issue before this court, i.e., who bears responsibility for allowing a patient to be discharged from the hospital, her treating physicians or the health care payor, each side's medical expert witnesses agreed that, in accordance with the standards of medical practice as it existed in January 1977, it was for the patient's treating physician to decide the course of treatment that was medically necessary to treat the ailment. It was also that physician's responsibility to determine whether or not acute care hospitalization was required and for how long. Finally, it was agreed that the patient's physician is in a better position than the Medi–Cal Consultant to determine the number of days medically necessary for any required hospital care. The decision to discharge is, therefore, the responsibility of the patient's own treating doctor.

Dr. Kaufman testified that if, on January 21, the date of the plaintiff's discharge from Van Nuys, any one of her three treating doctors had decided that in his medical judgment it was necessary to keep Wickline in the hospital for a longer period of time, they, or any of them, should have filed another request for extension of stay in the hospital, that Medi–Cal would expect those physicians to make such a request if they felt it was indicated, and upon receipt of such a request further consideration of an additional extension of hospital time would have been given.

Title 22 of the California Administrative Code section 51110, provided, in pertinent part, at the relevant time in issue here, that: "The determination of need for acute care shall be made in accordance with the usual standards of medical practice in the community."

The patient who requires treatment and who is harmed when care which should have been provided is not provided should recover for the injuries suffered from all those responsible for the deprivation of such care, including, when appropriate, health care payors. Third party payors of health care services can be held legally accountable when medically inappropriate decisions result from defects in the design or implementation of cost containment mechanisms as, for example, when appeals made on a patient's behalf for medical or hospital care are arbitrarily ignored or unreasonably disregarded or overridden. However, the physician who complies without protest with the limitations imposed by a third party payor, when his medical judgment dictates otherwise, cannot avoid his ultimate responsibility for his patient's care. He cannot point to the health care payor as the liability scapegoat when the consequences of his own determinative medical decisions go sour.

There is little doubt that Dr. Polonsky was intimidated by the Medi–Cal program but he was not paralyzed by Dr. Glassman's response nor rendered powerless to act appropriately if other action was required under the circumstances. If, in his medical judgment, it was in his patient's best interest that she remain in the acute care hospital setting for an additional four days beyond the extended time period originally authorized by Medi–Cal, Dr. Polansky should have made some effort to keep Wickline there. He himself acknowledged that responsibility to his patient. It was his medical judgment, however, that Wickline could be discharged when she was. All the plaintiff's treating physicians concurred and all the doctors who testified at trial, for either plaintiff or defendant, agreed that Dr. Polonsky's medical decision to discharge Wickline met the standard of care applicable at the time. Medi–Cal was not a party to that medical decision and therefore cannot be held to share in the harm resulting if such decision was negligently made.

In addition thereto, while Medi–Cal played a part in the scenario before us in that it was the resource for the funds to pay for the treatment sought, and its input regarding the nature and length of hospital care to be provided was of paramount importance, Medi–Cal did not override the medical judgment of Wickline's treating physicians at the time of her discharge. It was given no opportunity to do so. Therefore, there can be no viable cause of action against it for the consequences of that discharge decision.

* * *

[The court, after discussing relevant California statutory law, concluded that "* * * the Medi–Cal Consultant's decision, vis-a-vis the request to extend Wickline's hospital stay, was in accord with then existing statutory law."]

V

This court appreciates that what is at issue here is the effect of cost containment programs upon the professional judgment of physicians to prescribe hospital treatment for patients requiring the same. While we recognize, realistically, that cost consciousness has become a permanent feature of the health care system, it is essential that cost limitation programs not be permitted to corrupt medical judgment. We have concluded, from the facts in issue here, that in this case it did not.

For the reasons expressed herein, this court finds that appellant is not liable for respondent's injuries as a matter of law. That makes unnecessary any discussion of the other contentions of the parties.

The judgment is reversed.

Notes and Questions

1. What are the limits of the duty? Does it require only that a physician engage in bureaucratic infighting, exhausting her procedural rights, when a utilization review process has rejected her recommendation? The Medi–Cal consultant took a rather casual approach to his review, and the treating physicians acted passively in the face of the initial Medi–Cal rejection. Medi–Cal had argued that the decision to discharge was made by each of the plaintiff's three doctors, and Medi–Cal had no part in the discharge. Both sides agreed that "the decision to discharge is . . . the responsibility of the patient's own treating doctor." The chief Medi–Cal consultant testified that if any of the three doctors had filed another request for an extension based upon their determination of medical necessity, such a request would have been granted. The system, in other words, was designed to generate initial denials, which could be reversed with further appeals.

2. California passed legislation in 1994 to protect physicians who "advocate for medically appropriate health care", following the Wickline decision. See Cal. Bus. & Prof. Code § 2056(a) (West Supp. 1998) (prohibiting termination of or retaliation against physicians as a result of patient advocacy). The law states: "It is the public policy of the State of California that a health care practitioner be encouraged to advocate for appropriate health care for his or her patients," and

defines advocacy as "to appeal a payer's decision to deny payment for a service pursuant to the reasonable grievance or appeal procedure established by a [managed care organization] or to protest a decision, policy, or practice that the health care practitioner ... reasonably believes impairs the ... ability to provide appropriate health care.... " Id. § 2056(b); see also id. § 510(b).

In Khajavi v. Feather River Anesthesia Medical Group, 84 Cal.App.4th 32, 100 Cal.Rptr.2d 627 (Cal.App. 3 Dist.2000), the court held that § 2056 is not limited to the facts and issues of Wickline. It protects physicians broadly from retaliation for advocating medically appropriate health care, whether or not the advocacy protests a cost-containment provision.

3. Later cases have held that external utilization review bodies can be held liable for negligent review if a patient suffers harm through denial of care. In Wilson v. Blue Cross of Southern California, 271 Cal.Rptr. 876, 222 Cal.App.3d 660 (1990), the court limited *Wickline* but expanded potential liability of outside reviewers. Howard Wilson suffered from major depression, drug dependency, and anorexia. On March 3, 1983 he entered a hospital for treatment. His insurer contracted with Western Medical, a third party utilization review organization, to make determinations of medical necessity. On March 11, Western Medical decided that Wilson's hospital stay was "not justified or approved." The treating physician felt that Wilson needed 3–4 weeks of care, but did not appeal the utilization review determination. Wilson was discharged, and on March 31 he killed himself. His physician testified that he would have survived if he could have remained longer in the hospital for treatment. The court, in overturning summary judgment for the insurer, held that the test for joint liability for tortious conduct, Restatement, Torts, 2d 431:

> ... actor's negligent conduct is legal cause of harm to another if (a) his conduct is a substantial factor in bringing about the harm, and (b) there is no rule of law relieving the actor from liability because of the manner in which his negligence has resulted in harm.

While the doctor had no obligation to appeal the negative decision in *Wilson*, the court clearly held that under the right facts, the doctor is jointly liable with the utilization reviewer for a denial that leads to a bad patient outcome.

4. Some courts have allowed plaintiffs to plead a duty of a physician to assist patients in finding other sources of funding for expensive procedures. In Wilson v. Chesapeake Health Plan, Inc., Circuit Court, Baltimore, Maryland 1988 (No. 88019032/CL76201), the plaintiff pleaded a variety of theories against the specialist, the managed care plan, and the hospital. The underlying facts of the suit were as follows.[3] The plaintiff Hugh Wilson, a thirty one year old employee of the city of Baltimore, developed liver disease. He was a member of a prepaid health plan, the Chesapeake Health Plan, Inc.(Chesapeake). Dr. Cooper, a Maryland gastroenterologist to whom Wilson was referred by his primary care physician, diagnosed Wilson as having non-alcoholic cirrhosis of the liver. Mr. Wilson and his wife were informed that this condition would be fatal without a liver transplant. Cooper reassured Wilson that a liver transplant would be covered under his HMO coverage. Chesapeake however decided that such a transplant was not a covered service under the subscriber agreement. Dr. Cooper contacted Dr. Starzl, the head of the transplant service at Presbyterian University Hospital (PUH) in Pittsburgh,

3. The facts are taken in part from the court's description in Presbyterian University Hospital v. Wilson, 337 Md. 541, 654 A.2d 1324 (1995), where the Maryland court of appeals held that the trial court was justified in finding that hospital had sufficient contacts with Maryland to justify exercise of specific personal jurisdiction without violating due process.

Pennsylvania. Despite Mr. Wilson's lack of insurance coverage, Dr. Starzl agreed to admit Mr. Wilson and told Dr. Cooper to have Mr. Wilson come to PUH the following Monday. As Dr. Starzl testified: "My honest assessment at the time was ... that Dr. Cooper was laboring under a dictate, a decision by the governance group of this HMO that they would not allow transplantation coverage. And that Dr. Cooper took it upon himself to say to the system, I am not going to go with this, I am going to try to sneak the patient out. That was my impression. And that, on the other end, I told him, Dr. Cooper, I am going to take the patient, and carry on the battle." The Wilsons arrived in Pittsburgh two days later.

Upon his arrival, Mr. Wilson was refused admittance to PUH because Mr. Edward Berkowitz, PUH's credit administrator, had informed the admitting office that coverage for Mr. Wilson's liver transplant had not been confirmed. After being refused admittance, the Wilsons were provided accommodations at a hostel connected with PUH. Mr. Berkowitz participated in protracted discussions with Chesapeake and Mr. Wilson's union, the International Brotherhood of Electrical Workers' (IBEW), to discuss the possibility of providing coverage for Mr. Wilson's liver transplant.

Due to deteriorating health, Mr. Wilson was admitted to the emergency room at PUH under his insurance three days later. At Dr. Starzl's urging, Mrs. Wilson returned to Baltimore to work further on the financing problem, and she then learned that the Maryland Medical Assistance Program would pay for the procedure once the Wilsons had spent down their savings. During this period a second liver became available, but it was also thrown away. Mr. Wilson died before Mrs. Wilson could obtain Maryland MA coverage and despite the fact that two suitable livers had become available to PUH for transplant during the time Mr. Wilson was in Pittsburgh.

The plaintiff's complaint, Count 16, Negligence, alleged that Dr. Cooper and the health plan

> knew or should have known that staff and resources existed ... to assist the Wilsons in determining the scope of coverage provided by their HMO, other insurers, and alternative funding sources, but they failed to utilize such resources, alert plaintiffs to the existence of such resources or advise them of the need to identify a funding source. (Complaint, p. 33).

The trial court refused to dismiss this count in the complaint. The plaintiff then settled with Dr. Cooper and the Chesapeake Health Plan, and the case went to trial against Presbyterian Hospital. The plaintiff obtained a multi-million dollar jury verdict in the case.

What are the limits of the duty pleaded by the plaintiff? Dr. Cooper certainly went out of his way to get Mr. Wilson into the hospital for a transplant. The problem was that he simply wasn't an expert on the Maryland Medical Assistance program and eligibility. Can we expect physicians to be reimbursement experts on their patients' behalf? Shouldn't we expect managed care organizations, even if they don't cover a procedure, to offer financial advice to subscribers as to reimbursement options? Why shouldn't we add such duties to the fiduciary relationship between physician and patient, insurer and subscriber? The central office of the managed care organization should be expected to know in the intricacies of its own coverage of subscribers, as well as other sources for funding if the plan's coverage is limited.

5. Insurance benefit denial cases often impose duties on physicians. Few other cases have considered a duty such as that proposed in *Wilson*. But consider

Ferguson v. New Eng. Mutual Life Insurance Co., 196 Ill.App.3d 766, 143 Ill.Dec. 941, 554 N.E.2d 1013 (1st Dist.1990), where the patient and her husband sued the physician and the insurer where benefits were denied for medically unnecessary and inappropriate services. The physician had assured the plaintiffs through his staff that the prescribed treatment would be covered by their insurance policy. The court extended implied contract law to include physician knowledge of the insurer's rules. Since HMO contracts often prohibit the physician from charging the beneficiary for denied payments, one can argue for an obligation on the physician to advocate for the patient and to have "full knowledge of the scope of the insured's coverage."

An analogous line of caselaw can also be found in the insurance benefit cases, where a plaintiff is denied insurance coverage because a physician neglected to complete benefit forms. In Murphy v. Godwin, 303 A.2d 668 (Del.Super.1973), the plaintiff's family doctor neglected to complete a medical form they needed to obtain health insurance. As a result, their application was declined by the insurance company. The court held:

> Although it is well known that physicians usually accommodate patients by filling in the forms required by them for various reasons connected with insurance, the question of a doctor's legal duty toward his patients with respect to completing insurance forms is apparently novel. The existence of such a duty may be found, however, by reference to established tort theory and recognized incidents of the doctor-patient relationship.
>
> In the absence of special circumstances it was Dr. Godwin's duty to recognize his unique position as the treating physician who alone could comply with the insurance requirement without the expense and delay of a further examination. * * *

A physician who simply examines a person for purposes of employment by a third party and not treatment is generally not obligated to complete insurance forms. See, e.g. Ahnert v. Wildman, 176 Ind.App. 630, 376 N.E.2d 1182 (Ind.App. 1978) (" ... to impose a duty of filling out insurance forms on a doctor who has only consented to examine a patient for a third party, and has not undertaken to treat or advise that patient and is not paid by him, would be inconsistent with the very nature of the limited relationship. No case has gone so far as to saddle an examining physician with such a burden. And neither do we.")

Courts have generally been reluctant to find a hospital or physician negligent for failing to advise patients that they were eligible for government funding. See, e.g., Mraz v. Taft, 85 Ohio App.3d 200, 619 N.E.2d 483 (Ohio App. 8th Dist. 1993)(neither hospital nor nursing home had any duty to advise husband that he qualified for Medicaid). Nor is a physician liable for the financial consequences of a misdiagnosis, for example a patient's cancellation of a life insurance policy upon being erroneously informed that he did not have cancer. See Blacher v. Garlett, 857 P.2d 566, 568 (Colo.C.A., Div.III 1993).

6. A physician may be required to know state law. In Stecker v. First Commercial Trust Company, 331 Ark. 452, 962 S.W.2d 792 (Ark.1998), the administrator of a child's estate sued doctor for medical negligence and failure to report suspected child abuse as required under Arkansas statute. Evidence that the child's life could have been saved if doctor had reported potential abuse presented question for jury on issue of proximate cause for purposes of medical malpractice claim.

Consider the following passage by William Sage, a physician and lawyer, discussing the limits of physicians as advocates.

WILLIAM M. SAGE, PHYSICIANS AS ADVOCATES

35 Houston L. Rev.1529, 1533–34, 1577 (1999)

[P]hysician advocacy should neither be taken for granted nor saddled with expectations which potentially are inconsistent with one another or with normative goals for the health care system. For example, given the undisputed importance of clinical expertise to an efficient health care system, physicians arguably need to direct the provision of care rather than advocate for causes. Nor would patients necessarily accept procedural justice in lieu of substantive entitlements to resources. Moreover, the medical profession's reputation for objective competence might not withstand the adversarial partisanship that accompanies lawyerly advocacy. Because of these and other considerations, I argue that physicians should not aspire to be lawyers when they claim the mantle of "advocate," and the public should not regard them as such.* * *

Should [physicians] accept a new ethic that is population-based? Given the current structure of the health care system, I think not. I believe that intentionally providing minimally acceptable care to some for the benefit of others in an arbitrary group—let alone for the benefit of the bottom line—is wrong. Customizing care on the basis of a patient's insurance coverage is also wrong. When patients are sick and vulnerable, they expect their physicians to be their advocates for optimal care, not for some minimalist standard.... If we capitulate to an ethic of the group rather than the individual, and if we allow market forces to distort our ethical standards, we risk becoming economic agents instead of health care professionals.

* * * [M]anaged care has awakened physicians to the primacy of agency relationships in today's health care system. Health plans claim to represent their shareholders, their customers (usually employers and ERISA plans), and their insurance subscribers as a group. On the other hand, whether health plans have agency obligations to individuals similar to those of physicians remains an open question. Because most physicians are contractually affiliated with or even employed by these organizations, they sometimes struggle to maintain their traditional commitment to serve patient rather than corporate interests.

Managed care has heightened organizational conflicts of interest. As Hall and Berenson note, physicians worry that aggressive advocacy on behalf of patients could jeopardize their relationships with health plans. In addition to financial incentives, the other principal method by which managed care organizations reduce expense is selective contracting. Predictably, most health plans choose to extend network membership to physicians who not only provide high-quality care, but whose style of practice conserves health care resources. Because managed care organizations often control large blocs of patients through their relationships with employers and other group purchasers, physicians increasingly rely on these contracts for their livelihoods. Moreover, many physicians belong to large medical groups, or are affiliated with hospitals or other institutions, all of which have their own economic relationships with health plans to consider.

* * *

Physician advocacy implies a health care system governed more by rules than by incentives. Although financial incentives may taint physician advocacy, managed care organizations that place physicians at financial risk for the overall cost of patient care have less cause to make direct, administrative decisions denying coverage. By contrast, if the use of financial incentives is foreclosed or significantly restricted in the name of advocacy, health plans will be forced to employ more direct mechanisms to review proposed treatments and grant or deny approval. When these decisions are subjected to independent review requirements or other appeal processes, they must be defended—and in any event an ultimate decision must be rendered—based on explicit rules and standards.

Despite its greater transparency, a rule-based health care system is grossly inefficient, if not wholly unmanageable. Certainly, a significant contribution of managed care has been to demand from physicians objective evidence of clinical benefit and cost-effectiveness, rather than meekly deferring to professional habit. Indeed, expert, evidence-based clinical practice guidelines help disseminate useful information about common medical conditions and reduce unwarranted practice variation. Because medical decisions must be customized to the needs of individual patients, however, no compilation of guidelines can feasibly substitute for the clinical judgment of individual physicians. Moreover, physician participation is needed on both ends, describing "best practices" and applying them to specific situations. This is hard to reconcile with advocacy. Having two sets of physicians, one group to treat patients and serve as their advocates and another to rule dispassionately on disputed claims, seems obviously wasteful in the majority of cases. Nor would most members of the medical profession, notwithstanding their theoretical desire to be patient advocates, prefer an externally micromanaged health care system to one that allows physicians to reach decisions using clinical discretion and established patterns of collegial consultation, even if those decisions were subjected to incentive-based financial constraints.

C. FRAUDULENT CONCEALMENT AND SPOLIATION OF EVIDENCE ACTIONS

In a few jurisdictions, courts have allowed a separate intentional tort theory to be pleaded along with a negligence claim where the physician has deliberately altered records to create misleading entries or has knowingly made a false material representation to a plaintiff. The rules allowing these claims have three purposes: (1) to show fraudulent concealment by the physician of obvious negligence, so that the statute of limitations will be tolled; (2) to void the patient's informed consent to a procedure, so that a battery theory may be used; (3) as a separate theory of recovery. See generally D. Louisell and H. Williams, Medical Malpractice, para. 8.11, p. 8–144 (1984). Fraudulent concealment will toll the statute of limitations.

The party seeking to take advantage of a defendant's fraudulent concealment has the burden of proving that the defendant affirmatively concealed the facts upon which the cause of action is based. As one court noted, however, "* * * the close relationship of trust and confidence between patient and physician gives rise to duties of disclosure which may obviate the need for a patient to prove an affirmative act of concealment." Koppes v. Pearson, 384 N.W.2d 381 (Iowa 1986). But see Simcuski v. Saeli, 44 N.Y.2d 442, 406 N.Y.S.2d 259, 265, 377 N.E.2d 713 (1978)("clear and convincing evidence must be shown as to material misrepresentation and likelihood of cure absent fraud.")

An action for deceit requires proof that a false representation of a material fact was made and was relied upon by the patient in ignorance of the true facts, and that damage resulted. The representation must be made fraudulently, since an intention to deceive by the physician is needed. See Harris v. Penninger, 613 S.W.2d 211 (Mo.App.1981); Hart v. Browne, 103 Cal.App.3d 947, 163 Cal.Rptr. 356 (1980)(physician advised the lawyer for a surgeon's patient that the surgeon's conduct was not negligent; fraud found); Henry v. Deen, 310 N.C. 75, 310 S.E.2d 326 (1984) (civil conspiracy and a punitive damages claim allowed); Krueger v. St. Joseph's Hospital, 305 N.W.2d 18 (N.D.1981) (a claim in fraud allowed based upon the physician's false representations.)

A separate action for spoliation is allowed in some jurisdictions. Spoliation of evidence may consist of altering the medical record or adding to it after an initial entry, deleting, substituting, or destroying x-rays, laboratory reports, or physical evidence. One estimate is that up to fifty percent of medical malpractice cases involve altered records and ten percent involve fraudulently altered records. A spoliation claim may allow the plaintiff to circumvent statutory limitations on damages in some states, allowing punitive damages, for example. See Temple Community Hospital v. Superior Ct. of Los Angeles Cty., 51 Cal.Rptr.2d 57 (2d Dist. 1996). For a general discussion, see Robert C. Mathews, Altering the Medical Record, 10 Am. J. Emerg. Med. 162, 162 (1992); Richard F. Gibbs, The Present and Future Medicolegal Importance of Record Keeping in Anesthesia and Intensive Care: The Case for Automation, 5 J. Clinical Monitoring 251, 253 (1989). See also Anthony C. Casamassima, Comment: Spoliation of Evidence and Medical Malpractice, 14 Pace L. Rev. 235 (1994).

Problem: The Hospital Revolving Door

Donna Natoli is a member of U.S. Wellcare, a large managed care organization known for its frugal subscriber benefits. Ms. Natoli's obstetrician, Dr. Omar Benton, arranged with the Plan hospital, Sacred Fegato Hospital, for labor and delivery. Ms. Natoli entered Fegato in active labor. Dr. Benton noted that the baby's heart rate was consistently low, and as he was examining Ms. Natoli, the placenta suddenly separated from the uterus, posing an immediate threat to the life of the mother and the child. He performed an emergency caesarean section. The child, Elena, exhibited signs of hypoxia and cyanosis (lack of oxygen causing a blue appearance) at birth, but was resuscitated and placed in the neonatal intensive care unit (NICU). Within twelve hours, she was transferred to the regular nursery. Elena weighed in excess of five pounds at birth, within the range of normal birth weights.

Two days later, just prior to her discharge under the minimum stay rule of 48 hours required by state law, Elena's bilirubin level in her blood became elevated to 21.3, causing a jaundiced condition. A level above twenty is considered dangerous. This occurs when antigens in the child's blood cause the immune system to destroy its own red blood cells in a process called hemolysis. Bilirubin is a by-product of this process and high levels of it are toxic. The substance is normally extracted from the blood by the liver. In newborns, the liver is often not yet mature enough to perform this function efficiently. If levels of this substance become too high, it can pass between the blood-brain barrier and cause damage to the nervous system, including brain damage. This condition is known as bilirubin encephalopathy or kernicterus.

Dr. Benton called Wellcare to get an authorization for an additional two days in the hospital for Elena to monitor the bilirubin levels. The Wellcare representative would only allow an additional day. Benton then treated Elena's elevated bilirubin level with phototherapy, which acts to neutralize the toxic effects of the bilirubin, and gave her fluids to flush the bilirubin from her system and glycerin suppositories to eliminate excess bilirubin through the stool. He also gave her albumin, which binds with the bilirubin and helps prevent it from damaging the brain.

These measures reduced the bilirubin level at first to 11, a safe level, but it then rose steadily back to 21. Dr. Benton told Ms. Natoli to get Elena and check out; he explained that Wellcare's policy was quite rigid in his experience and he was tired of fighting with them in cases like this. He suggested that she take Elena home and keep an eye on her for a few days. Elena suffered seizures the next day and now has a permanent hearing loss in both ears.

How will you proceed against Dr. Benton?

IV. DEFENSES TO A MALPRACTICE SUIT

A. THE RESPECTABLE MINORITY RULE

CHUMBLER v. McCLURE

United States Court of Appeals, Sixth Circuit, 1974.
505 F.2d 489.

[The plaintiff was injured in an electrical explosion. Dr. McClure diagnosed his illness as cerebral vascular insufficiency and prescribed a female hormone, estrogen, produced and marketed commercially as Premarin. Premarin's known side effects included enlargement of the breasts and loss of libido. The trial court directed a verdict for the defendant on the grounds that the plaintiff failed to show any deviation from accepted medical practice. The testimony in the case was that Dr. McClure was the only neurosurgeon, out of nine in Nashville, using such therapy for cerebral vascular disease. One expert admitted that there was no specific established treatment for the disease.]

> The most favorable interpretation that may be placed on the testimony adduced at trial below is that there is a division of opinion in the medical profession regarding the use of Premarin in the treatment of cerebral vascular insufficiency, and that Dr. McClure was alone among neurosurgeons in Nashville in using such therapy. The test for malpractice and for community standards is not to be determined solely by a plebiscite. Where two or more schools of thought exist among competent members of the medical profession concerning proper medical treatment for a given ailment, each of which is supported by responsible medical authority, it is

not malpractice to be among the minority in a given city who follow one of the accepted schools.

[The court affirmed the directed verdict for the defendant.]

HENDERSON v. HEYER-SCHULTE CORP.

Court of Civil Appeals of Texas, 1980.
600 S.W.2d 844.

[The plaintiff Carol Henderson underwent mammary augmentation operations in which artificial breast implants, consisting of silicone envelopes filled with a soft silicone gel, were inserted. The surgeon then intentionally slit the envelope to allow the gel to escape in to the retro-mammary pockets. The plaintiff experienced pain and inflammation, and developed small lumps under the skin of her chest and abdomen; these were siliconomas caused by accumulations of migrating silicone gel. After twenty operations, the lumps continued to appear and her breasts suffered several deformities in shape and placement. The court, in stating the facts, noted that "[s]he has consulted many other physicians and has undergone subsequent augmentation procedures, some of which were sought to further increase the size of her breasts."

The surgical technique used on the plaintiff had been in common use in Houston at one time but was no longer recognized or accepted. The issue in the case was whether the use of the technique of slitting the silicone implants after implantation was negligent. The jury instructions therefore became critical. The court rejected the trial court's instruction as to recognition by plastic surgeons of more than one method for performing the procedures in question.]

The court continued:

We agree that the instruction should not have been given. The Supreme Court of Texas in *Hood v. Phillips,* [ ] established the proper test for the standard of care in a medical malpractice case where the plaintiff attacks the surgical procedure selected and employed by the doctor. * * * [T]he Court concluded:

> We are of the opinion that the statement of the law most serviceable to this jurisdiction is as follows: A physician who undertakes a mode or form of treatment which a reasonable and prudent member of the medical profession would undertake under the same or similar circumstances shall not be subject to liability for harm caused thereby to the patient. The question which conveys to the jury the standard which should be applicable is as follows: Did the physician undertake a mode or form of treatment which a reasonable and prudent member of the medical profession would not undertake under the same or similar circumstances? [ ]

The court expressly rejected standards which would release doctors from liability when a "respectable minority" or a "considerable number" of physicians adhere to the procedures in question. As Mrs. Henderson points out, the instruction given in this case does not even go that far in establishing a minimal threshold. It simply directs the jury to consider whether "other plastic surgeons" recognized the method used by Dr. Rothenberg. There is no requirement that the "other" surgeons be reasonable or prudent or that they be prepared to employ that method under circumstances similar to those Dr. Rothenberg faced, the two factors most stressed in *Hood.*

[The court concluded that the instruction was harmless error, and that the plaintiff's evidence was insufficient to show that the "rupture method" was no longer in use by reasonable plastic surgeons.]

The judgment is affirmed.

Notes and Questions

1. Can you articulate the difference between the "respectable minority" test and the "reasonable and prudent" physician test? If you were a juror, would you come to a difference conclusion depending on the instruction? In *Chumbler,* the minority of which the defendant was a part seems to have consisted only of himself. Is that sufficiently "respectable"? By what measure should the courts measure a respectable minority practice? Is this doctrine little more than a judicial acknowledgement of the medical profession's uncertainty over how to treat diseases such as cerebral vascular insufficiency?

Some courts reject the idea that counting the number of physicians who follow a particular practice is helpful in establishing a medical standard of care. See United Blood Services v. Quintana, 827 P.2d 509 (Colo.1992).

2. States that instruct on "two schools of thought" often impose restrictions on the defense.

a. Size of the respectable minority. Pennsylvania limits the doctrine to cases involving schools of thought followed by a "considerable number of physicians." Duckworth v. Bennett, 320 Pa. 47, 181 A. 558 (1935), cited with approval by the court in D'Angelis v. Zakuto, 383 Pa.Super. 65, 556 A.2d 431, 433 (1989).

b. Failures to properly diagnose. Where the critical issue is what the diagnosis is, as for example whether the patient had a localized or a generalized infection, then the "two schools of thought" or "alternative means of treatment" instruction may not be appropriate where there is only one agreed approach to each type of infection. See Hutchinson v. Broadlawns Medical Center, 459 N.W.2d 273 (Iowa 1990). In D'Angelis v. Zakuto, 383 Pa.Super. 65, 556 A.2d 431, 433 (1989), the Superior Court held that the instruction is intended for situations where medical experts may disagree among themselves. It is however not appropriately given where "the symptoms of a disease or the effects of an injury are so well known that a reasonably competent and skillful physician or surgeon ought to be able to diagnose the disease or injury * * * " (quoting Morganstein v. House), 377 Pa.Super. 512, 547 A.2d 1180 (1988).

c. Weight given to plaintiff experts as to good practice. In Ourada v. Cochran, 234 Neb. 63, 449 N.W.2d 211 (1989), the court rejected a jury instruction that seemed to give the jury too much leeway to reject the plaintiff's experts' testimony. The rejected instruction read in part: "A physician who is a specialist is not bound to use any particular method of procedure; and if, among physicians of ordinary skill and learning in that specialty, more than one method of procedure is recognized as proper, it is not negligence for a physician to adopt any of such methods.... "

But see DiFilippo v. Preston, 53 Del. 539, 173 A.2d 333 (1961): choice by defendant surgeon of one of two acceptable techniques is not negligence.

4. The "respectable minority" rule allows for variation in clinical judgment: " * * * a physician does not incur liability merely by electing to pursue one of

several recognized courses of treatment." Downer v. Veilleux, 322 A.2d 82, 87 (Me.1974). In the typical case, the minority approach is followed by at least a few doctors, and is often the "best available" for a certain problem. Leech v. Bralliar, 275 F.Supp. 897 (D.Ariz.1967) (prolotherapy for whiplash; 65 doctors in the country used this treatment, with a claimed 85% success rate; the defendant was held liable because he varied the treatment and therefore became a minority of one within the respectable minority.)

5. The "honest error in judgment" doctrine is a corollary of the "respectable minority" rule. The respectable minority rule allows for a choice between alternative approaches to diagnosis or treatment; the honest error in judgment doctrine allows for a range of uncertainty in choosing between alternative treatments. A typical jury instruction reads:

> a [physician] is not a guarantor of a cure or a good result from his treatment and he is not responsible for an honest error in judgment in choosing between accepted methods of treatment.

This was a standard Minnesota instruction, rejected in Ouellette v. Subak, 391 N.W.2d 810 (Minn.1986), where the court found that the instruction is misleading and subjective. The court proposed an instruction that focused the jury's attention on both the diagnostic work-up and its adequacy, and on the accepted nature of the treatment choice:

> A doctor is not negligent simply because his or her efforts prove unsuccessful. The fact a doctor may have chosen a method of treatment that later proves to be unsuccessful is not negligence if the treatment chosen was an accepted treatment on the basis of the information available to the doctor at the time a choice had to be made; a doctor must, however, use reasonable care to obtain the information needed to exercise his or her professional judgment, and an unsuccessful method of treatment chosen because of a failure to use such reasonable care would be negligence.

Is the court's reshaping of the doctrine in its proposed instructions an improvement over the previous "honest error in judgment" instruction? What are the court's concerns? Does their instruction address those concerns? See McKersie v. Barnes Hosp., 912 S.W.2d 562 (Mo.App. E.D.1995) (failure of emergency room intern to diagnose appendicitis was negligence rather than mere honest error of judgment.) Contra, see Haase v. Garfinkel, 418 S.W.2d 108 (Mo.1967)("As long as there is room for an honest difference of opinion among competent physicians, a physician who uses his own best judgment cannot be convicted of negligence, even though it may afterward develop that he was mistaken.)" [ ]

Problem: To Monitor or Not?

You are general counsel for the Columbia Hospital for Women. The head obstetric resident has just walked into your office to get your advice regarding hospital policy. Jane Rudd, pregnant with her second child, has just been admitted to the Obstetrics Ward at term and in labor. The charts reveal that her first delivery of a healthy 7½ pound baby boy had been uncomplicated. Upon admission, she asked not to be given intravenous fluids and stated that she does not want continuous fetal monitoring (EFM). Rather, she wished to be free to walk around with her husband during labor. The nurses told her that hospital policy requires electronic monitoring of all women in labor. The patient responded that she did not need EFM during her first labor, which went well, and expects the same experience again. She has appealed to the resident, who has discussed the request with the staff.

The staff split over the issue. One doctor argued that the policy is a wise measure intended to protect infants. Further, EFM shields staff from accusations that the best care was not provided, if a bad outcome occurs. Another doctor opposed routine EFM, arguing that unmonitored fetuses run an extremely small risk of fetal distress or intrapartum death. Without monitoring the intrapartum death rate was only 1.5 per 1,000 among all labors involving infants who weighed 5½ pounds or more. The mother's risk status is altered, however, since the likelihood of a Caesarean section is increased. This doctor pointed out that a careful British study of low-risk patients revealed that the rate of C-sections doubled, from 4.4 to 9%, when EFM was used. An American study found that the number of Caesareans performed on women hospitalized for delivery between 1980 and 1987 jumped 48%, much of this increase traceable to fetal monitoring.

If Ms. Rudd is allowed to labor with reasonable staff surveillance by auscultation, i.e. use of the stethoscope by staff on a regular basis, and if the obstetric unit can resuscitate her infant if the unexpected occurs, then, this doctor argued, the risks for both mother and child are very low.

You have done some further reading. The conclusions of Karin B. Nelson et al. are striking:

> Electronic fetal monitoring during labor was developed to detect fetal-heart-rate patterns thought to indicate hypoxia. The early recognition of hypoxia would, it was reasoned, alert clinicians to potential problems and enable them to intervene quickly to prevent fetal death or irreversible brain injury.... More than 20 years and 11 randomized trials later, electronic fetal monitoring appears to have little documented benefit over intermittent auscultation with respect to perinatal mortality or long-term neurologic outcome. Furthermore, probably in part because of the widespread use of fetal monitoring, the rate of cesarean section has increased, with a resulting increase in maternal morbidity and costs but without apparent decrease in the incidence of cerebral palsy.

Karin B. Nelson et al., Uncertain Value of Electronic Fetal Monitoring in Predicting Cerebral Palsy, 334 N.E.J.M. 334, 334 (1996). The authors found that cesarean sections did not prevent cerebral palsy in infants born at term, that monitoring did not correlate with reductions in perinatal mortality, nor were low Apgar scores, acidosis, neotal apnea, or need for intubation less frequent among monitored infants.

A second study analyzed the neurologic development of premature infants. The authors compared the early development of children born prematurely whose heart rates were monitored electronically during delivery, compared to children born prematurely whose heart rates were monitored by auscultation. The authors found that not only had the infants' neurologic development not improved with monitoring, compared with auscultation, but there was a 2.9–fold increase in the odds of having cerebral palsy with the monitored infants. Shy et al., Effects of Electronic Fetal–Heart–Rate Monitoring, As Compared with Periodic Auscultation, on the Neurologic Development of Premature Infants, 322 N.Eng.J.Med. 588 (1990). The authors noted, however, that the trials for the study had dedicated nurses assigned to the auscultation group, "a circumstance that is not always possible in a busy clinical setting."

What policies will minimize the hospital's liability exposure while also respecting the patient's wishes whenever it is safe to do so? How do the tort doctrines we have discussed interact?

B. PRACTICE GUIDELINES AS AN AFFIRMATIVE DEFENSE

Medical practice guidelines or practice protocols might be used as an affirmative defense by physicians in a malpractice suit to show compliance with accepted practice. Maine has passed legislation to immunize physicians from suit if they practice in accordance with such standards. Me.Gen.Laws, Ch. 931 (1990). The law was premised on concerns that physicians practiced too much "defensive medicine" in response to liability fears, ordering tests primarily to protect themselves from subsequent suits. If given some protection in the liability area, they could change their practice patterns without fear of liability. The Maine legislation includes physicians in emergency medicine, anesthesia, and obstetrics and gynecology. Physicians who elect to participate can assert compliance with established practice parameters and risk management protocols as an affirmative defense in any malpractice suit brought against them during the five years of the demonstration project. The practice parameters and risk management protocols will be developed by advisory committees in each of the practice areas.

The Maine statute provides:

> * * * in any claims for professional negligence against a physician or the employer of a physician participating in the project in which a violation of standard of care is alleged, only the physician or the physician's employer may introduce into evidence as an affirmative defense the existence of the practice parameters and risk management protocols developed pursuant to the project.

Me. Rev. Stat. Ann., tit. 24, § 2972(1) (West Supp. 1994). Outside experts will not be able to challenge the standard, and the physician is not bound by the standard in a case in which he deviated from the protocol. The project will not take effect until 50% in any specialty elect to participate. See generally General Accounting Office, GAO/HRD–94–8, Medical Malpractice: Maine's Use of Practice Guidelines to Reduce Costs (1993) (describing the Maine demonstration); Professional Liability: Maine's Experiment with Practice Guidelines Produces Little Evidence, 3 Health L. Rep. (BNA) 753, 754 (June 9, 1994).

Minnesota and Kentucky also allow the use of practice parameters by physicians as an affirmative defense. See Ky. Rev. Stat. Ann. § 342.035 (Michie 1995) indicating that "[a]ny provider of medical services under this chapter who has followed the practice parameters or guidelines developed or adopted pursuant to this subsection shall be presumed to have met the appropriate legal standard of care in medical malpractice cases regardless of unanticipated complication that may develop or be discovered after". Id. See Minn. Stat. § 62J.34(3)(a) (1994) (providing an absolute defense for providers). Florida and Vermont also have adopted this approach, and several other states—e.g., Colorado, Pennsylvania, Rhode Island, Virginia, and Hawaii—also have considered or are considering adoption of guidelines legislation. Maryland, by contrast, under Md. Code Ann., [Health–Gen.] § 19–1606 (1995), has mandated that practice parameters are not admissible into evidence in any legal proceeding under the statute.

C. CLINICAL INNOVATION

BROOK v. ST. JOHN'S HICKEY MEMORIAL HOSPITAL

Supreme Court of Indiana, 1978.
269 Ind. 270, 380 N.E.2d 72.

HUNTER, JUSTICE.

This case began as an action by Tracy Lynn Brook and her father (Arthur) against St. John's Hickey Memorial Hospital, Guy E. Ross, M.D., Lawrence Allen, M.D., and Dr. Fischer. The record discloses that Tracy was diagnosed by a specialist as having a possible urological disorder and that X-rays taken with a contrast medium would be necessary to confirm the diagnosis. The Court of Appeals summarized Dr. Fischer's role in Tracy's treatment as follows:

> "Dr. Fischer, a radiologist, injected the contrast medium into the calves of both of Tracy's legs, because he was unable to find a vein which he could use. The package insert, which contained the manufacturer's directions for injecting the contrast medium, recommended that the contrast medium be injected into the gluteal muscles (buttocks). * * *
>
> "A short while [four months later] after being discharged from the hospital Tracy began to have trouble with her right leg. Her leg was stiff and her heel began to lift off the ground. Tracy's problem was later diagnosed as a shortening of the achilles tendon, which *may* have been precipitated by some kind of trauma to her ankle or calf muscle. After two operations and other expensive treatment, including the wearing of a leg brace, Tracy's problem was substantially corrected." 368 N.E.2d 264, 266, 267 [emphasis added].

* * *

* * * [T]he Brooks contended that the trial court erred in refusing to give to the jury plaintiffs' tendered instruction No. 4 which reads as follows:

> "You are instructed that a Radiologist is not limited to the most generally used of several modes of procedure and the use of another mode known and proved by the profession is proper, but every new method of procedure should pass through an experimental stage in its development and a Radiologist is not authorized in trying untested experiments on patients."

The Brooks alleged that Dr. Fischer was negligent in choosing an injection site which had not been specifically recommended by the medical community and that this choice of an unusual injection site was a medical experiment. The trial court refused to give this instruction on the basis that since no substantial evidence of a medical experiment had been introduced, it would be erroneous to give an instruction covering medical experiments. We agree.

The Court of Appeals found that since there was no evidence presented which showed that any other doctors had used the calf muscles as an injection site, Dr. Fischer's use of them may have been a medical experiment. We disagree. The record clearly shows that Dr. Fischer had several compelling, professional reasons for choosing the calf muscles as an injection site for the contrast medium in this case.

First, the record shows that Dr. Fischer had read medical journals which cautioned against the injection of the contrast medium into the buttocks (gluteal area) and thighs of infants and small children. * * *.

Tracy Brook was only twenty-three months old when the injection was given. Dr. Fischer testified that other articles had also warned against the use of the thighs in young children. Because Dr. Fischer was trying to avoid any damage to the sciatic nerve, he chose the next largest muscle mass "away from the trunk" as the site for the injection.

Second, Dr. Fischer had used this injection site successfully on children on prior occasions. He also testified that he had never read or heard anything that proscribed the selection of the calf muscles as an injection site.

Too often courts have confused judgmental decisions and experimentation. Therapeutic innovation has long been recognized as permissible to avoid serious consequences. The everyday practice of medicine involves constant judgmental decisions by physicians as they move from one patient to another in the conscious institution of procedures, special tests, trials and observations recognized generally by their profession as effective in treating the patient or providing a diagnosis of a diseased condition. Each patient presents a slightly different problem to the doctor. A physician is presumed to have the knowledge and skill necessary to use some innovation to fit the peculiar circumstances of each case.

Thus, the choice of the calf muscles as the site for the injection of a contrast medium in a two-year old child, based upon prior successful uses of this same injection site, is not a medical experiment where the use of more common sites had been warned against and where it was reasonably and prudently calculated by the physician [radiologist] to accomplish the intended purpose of diagnosis of the patient's condition.

* * *

The judgment of the trial court is in all respects affirmed.

Notes and Questions

1. If you disagree with the Supreme Court of Indiana, what do you think Dr. Fischer should have done? Should he have refused to treat Tracy? Should he have explained that his treatment was experimental? How would that have helped Tracy? See Chapter 20 for a discussion of legal limitations on human research.

Doctors tend to admire innovators. See, for example, Edenfield v. Vahid, 621 So.2d 1192, 1196 (La.App.1993), where the defendant surgeon attempted to repair the plaintiff's anal fistula with a Prolene suture, and the plaintiff ended up incontinent. Such a suture was an unconventional choice, and the medical panel considered its use below the standard of care. One of the experts stated, however, that trends change through "mavericks" trying different techniques: "Unless this something different is so dramatic that [sic] would result in loss of life or limb then I would say more power to him, somebody has got to try something different and show us that here are other ways of doing things.... the result wasn't ideal, but to consider that a malpractice, no."

2. Should the law allow a defense such as clinical innovation? Are clinicians likely to be trained scientists, keeping careful records and publishing their results for peer review? Medical researchers have criticized such clinical "experiments,"

calling instead for randomized scientifically valid trials. See Gordon Guyatt et al., Determining Optimal Therapy—Randomized Trials in Individual Patients, 314 N.Eng.J.Med. 889 (1986).

3. Experiments are acceptable to the courts when conventional treatments are largely ineffective or where the patient is terminally ill and has little to lose by experimentation with potentially useful treatments. Organ transplantation often involves therapeutic innovation. The classic case is Karp v. Cooley, 493 F.2d 408 (5th Cir.1974), where Dr. Denton Cooley was sued for the wrongful death of Haskell Karp. Dr. Cooley had implanted the first totally mechanical heart in Mr. Karp, who died some 32 hours after the transplant surgery. The court directed a verdict for Dr. Cooley on the issue of experimentation. It held:

> The record contains no evidence that Mr. Karp's treatment was other than therapeutic and we agree that in this context an action for experimentation must be measured by traditional malpractice evidentiary standards. Whether there was informed consent is necessarily linked to the charge of experimentation, and Mr. Karp's consent was expressly to all three stages of the operation actually performed—each an alternative in the event of a preceding failure.

The court excluded testimony by Dr. DeBakey that the heart pump he himself had tested was not ready for use in humans and that he would not have recommended its use. Dr. DeBakey refused however to give his opinion on the pump used by Dr. Cooley, except that it was similar to his pump.

4. New surgical procedures and treatments, other than drugs and medical devices, fall into a regulatory gap. Drugs and medical devices are carefully regulated by the Food and Drug Administration through licensing. See the Federal Food, Drug, and Cosmetic Act, 21 U.S.C.A. § 301 et seq. Human experimentation generally, if the institution is funded by the federal government in whole or part, is governed by regulations of the Department of Health and Human Services. The regulations require the institution sponsoring the research to establish Institutional Review Boards (IRBs). These evaluate the research proposals before any experimentation begins, in order to determine whether human subjects might be "at risk" and if so, how to protect them. See 45 C.F.R. § 46.101(a) and Chapter 20 infra.

It is generally not difficult to determine whether a new drug or device is being used experimentally. It is often very difficult to determine whether a particular surgical procedure is experimental. Surgeons tend to view themselves as artists rather than scientists, custom-tailoring a treatment for a patient's ailment. Such attitudes can produce bad results. In Felice v. Valleylab, 520 So.2d 920 (La.App. 3d Cir.1987), the physician, a third year general surgical resident, used an electrosurgical unit (ESU) to perform a circumcision procedure, although she admitted that she had been taught to perform circumcisions with a scalpel as the standard technique. She testified that the ESU was a new technique that might produce better results. She burned the child's penis so badly that it had to be amputated. The court held that the surgeon's behavior fell below the standard of care in her modification of a familiar technique without knowing the potential risks and by failing to consult with supervising personnel about such risks. In Tramontin v. Glass, 668 So.2d 1252 (La.App.1996), the same surgeon, using the same device, the ESU, burned the breast of a patient on whom she was performing breast augmentation surgery. In this case the use was not experimental, and the jury found for the defendant.

5. Most clinical innovation falls somewhere between standard practice and experimental research. Much of this innovation is unregulated by the government. What kinds of controls, direct or indirect, apply to innovation in medicine? The absence of controls over experimentation has worried some commentators, who have argued that the patient's informed consent is not a sufficient protection against untested procedures. Such experimentation has been termed "nonvalidated practice," since the most salient attribute of a novel practice is the lack of suitable validation of its safety and efficacy. The National Commission for the Protection of Human Subjects of Biomedical and Behavioral Research, discussing innovation, wrote:

> Radically new procedures * * * should * * * be made the object of formal research at an early stage in order to determine whether they are safe and effective. Thus, it is the responsibility of medical practice committees, for example, to insist that a major innovation be incorporated into a formal research project.

For a good discussion of the problem, see Dale H. Cowan and Eva Bertsch, Innovative Therapy: The Responsibility of Hospitals, 5 J.Leg.Med. 219 (1984).

D. GOOD SAMARITAN ACTS

Forty-nine states and the District of Columbia have adopted Good Samaritan legislation to protect health care professionals who render emergency aid from civil liability for damages for any injury they cause or enhance. The statutes take a variety of forms. West's Ann.Cal.Bus. & Prof.Code § 2395, for example, states, in relevant part:

> No licensee, who in good faith renders emergency care at the scene of an emergency, shall be liable for any civil damages as a result of any acts or omissions by such person in rendering the emergency care.
>
> "The scene of an emergency" as used in this section shall include, but not be limited to, the emergency rooms of hospitals in the event of a medical disaster. * * *

The following case applies the California statute in a hospital setting.

McKENNA v. CEDARS OF LEBANON HOSPITAL

Court of Appeal of California, 1979.
93 Cal.App.3d 282, 155 Cal.Rptr. 631.

Mrs. Evangeline McKenna underwent a therapeutic abortion and tubal ligation at Cedars of Lebanon Hospital on January 17, 1974. That afternoon, she had a seizure and was treated by a resident of the hospital. She stopped breathing and went into a coma from which she never recovered. She died over a week later. Her husband and children sued Dr. Margolin, her physician; Dr. Gilman, the anesthesiologist; Dr. Warner, the resident who responded to an alert from his beeper; and Cedars of Lebanon Hospital. The jury verdict was 10–2 in favor of the hospital and Dr. Warner and against plaintiffs. Plaintiffs appeal from the judgment. The primary issue here is whether there can be an emergency, as that term is used in the "Good Samaritan" statute within a hospital, so as to invoke that statute's application as a defense to the malpractice action against the doctor and hospital.

FACTS:

Mrs. McKenna entered Cedars of Lebanon Hospital January 16, 1974. Dr. Margolin, her gynecologist, performed a therapeutic abortion and a tubal sterilization on Mrs. McKenna on the morning of January 17, 1974. She was taken to the recovery room at 9:25 a.m. and stated that she had some difficulty breathing. The recovery room records show that later that morning she stated she felt much better and was returned to her room at about 10:45 a.m. She had lunch at 12:30, and the regular diet was "taken well."

At about 2 p.m., Mrs. McKenna started having seizures. The patient sharing the room with Mrs. McKenna called for assistance. The nurse's notes reveal "Unable to get pulse. Dr. Weirner [sic] called stat * * *." The nurse who originally arrived testified that the patient was "moving her arms and her legs in an uncoordinated, rigid manner which appeared to be some type of seizure activity at that time." Dr. Warner was on the floor above when his beeper sounded. He picked up the phone, spoke to the page operator, and "dashed" to Mrs. McKenna's room. About one minute elapsed from the time he heard his beeper to the time a nurse guided him into Mrs. McKenna's room.

Dr. Warner testified that he observed the patient having a grand-mal type seizure. He observed the patient, asked for Valium from a nurse, and slowly gave the patient approximately five milligrams of Valium into the I.V. tubing in order to stop the convulsions. The patient's convulsions stopped; she had a cardiac arrest and complete cessation of breathing. An anesthesiologist inserted an endotracheal tube; Dr. Warner was giving external cardiac massage, and he called for a Code Blue cardiac pulmonary resuscitation team. The patient was eventually transferred to the intensive care unit where she remained in a coma until her death on January 28, 1974. Appellants claim malpractice by Dr. Warner. As is usual in this type of case, appellants produced a doctor who testified that Dr. Warner's response to the patient's seizure fell below the standard of care and the respondents produced evidence that Dr. Warner's conduct was proper.

* * *

The jury in the case at bench was instructed: "No licensed physician, who in good faith renders emergency care at the scene of the emergency, shall be liable for any civil damages as a result of any of his acts or omissions in rendering the emergency care." * * * Appellants contend that the policy behind the Good Samaritan Statute does not apply to hospital emergencies and that the instruction should not have been given. * * *

Business and Professions Code section 2144 applies to "emergency care at the scene of the emergency * * *." There is no limitation as to the situs of the "scene of the emergency." A 1976 amendment to the statute defined "the scene of the emergency" and included, but did not limit, that phrase to "the emergency rooms of hospitals in the event of a medical disaster." Nothing in the statute itself precludes application of the Good Samaritan Statute to emergency situations in hospitals.

* * *

Dr. Warner in the case at bench was on duty as chief resident the afternoon of the emergency; appellants have failed to demonstrate that he had any legal duty to respond to an emergency call. He was, in essence, a medical volunteer, called to the scene of an emergency from the floor above where he was conducting a routine pelvic examination. Mrs. McKenna was another doctor's patient; there is no showing Dr. Warner had a legal duty to render emergency treatment arising from his contract of employment with Cedars. In such a situation, the legislative intent of encouraging emergency medical care by doctors who have no legal duty to treat a patient is carried out by applying Business and Professions Code section 2144 to Dr. Warner.

* * *

* * * [T]he "need to encourage physicians to render emergency medical care when they otherwise might not" prevails over the policy of vindicating the rights of a malpractice victim.

In the instant case, Dr. Warner proved he was not "on call" for emergencies, was not a member of the hospital team whose job it was to respond to emergencies and did not have a previous physician-patient relationship with Mrs. McKenna. In short, at the time he responded to Mrs. McKenna's emergency, Dr. Warner was truly a volunteer. Since there was evidence showing that Dr. Warner rendered emergency care to Mrs. McKenna in good faith at the place where her emergency occurred, the Good Samaritan statute applied on its face.

Notes and Questions

1. What kinds of situations do the Good Samaritan statutes cover? Suppose a physician walking down the street on Sunday morning to buy her New York Times sees a man fall to the pavement, gasping for breath and turning blue. The physician does not have her black bag, never met the victim before, and is aware of a gathering crowd. If she attempts to help the man and is negligent in administering aid, should she be sued for malpractice? Certainly physicians have worried about such situations. Is the setting of *McKenna* distinguishable from the street rescue situation? In McCain v. Batson, 233 Mont. 288, 760 P.2d 725 (1988), a physician on vacation sutured a hiker's wound at his condominium, using limited medical supplies on hand. The court held that this was an "emergency" within the meaning of statute.

2. The majority of state statutes exclude medical services rendered in the hospital from the coverage of the statutes, either by excluding emergency services provided in the ordinary course of work or services that doctors render to those with whom they have a doctor-patient relationship or to whom they owe a pre-existing duty. Guerrero v. Copper Queen Hospital, 112 Ariz. 104, 537 P.2d 1329 (1975) (statute not applicable to services in hospital); Colby v. Schwartz, 78 Cal.App.3d 885, 144 Cal.Rptr. 624 (1978) (normal course of practice not protected); Gragg v. Neurological Associates, 152 Ga.App. 586, 263 S.E.2d 496 (1979) (crisis during operating procedure is not emergency within meaning of statute).

Hospital-based emergency assistance by a physician is often protected, however, where the physician is not on duty at the time of the call for help. See Gordin v. William Beaumont Hospital, 180 Mich.App. 488, 447 N.W.2d 793 (1989), where the plaintiff's decedent was admitted to the emergency room after a car accident. The ER physician called for the on-call surgeon to assist, but the surgeon was unavailable. He then called Dr. Howard, who was not officially on call. The court held that the Good Samaritan Statute applied. The plaintiff argued that the statute should only be applied in the "biblical" Good Samaritan situation, to a doctor who renders care outside his training, not to a trained surgeon summoned to the hospital to render care for which he was trained and compensated. As in *McKenna,* however, the Michigan statute had been amended to include hospital settings and off-duty physicians. In Kearns v. Superior Court, 204 Cal.App.3d 1325, 252 Cal.Rptr. 4 (2 Dist.1988), a physician happened to be in the hospital treating his own patients when another surgeon asked his help during the course of an operation. The assisting physician was held to be rendering assistance in an "emergency" for purposes of California's Good Samaritan law.

3. Some statutes protect health care professionals, while others protect all Good Samaritans, without regard to their profession. Some states grant statutory immunity from suit to emergency medical personnel unless gross negligence is shown. Mallory v. City of Detroit, 181 Mich.App. 121, 449 N.W.2d 115 (1989). Is there any reason, except for the political power of doctors, to limit the application of such statutes to doctors or health care professionals? See generally Anno., Construction of 'Good Samaritan' Statutes Excusing from Civil Liability One Rendering Care in Emergency, 39 A.L.R.3d 222.

4. The malpractice crisis of 1974 undoubtedly played a role in the push by state legislatures to enact such laws. They are an interesting example of a protective response to a low risk of suit. There is no reason to believe that physicians have any idea as to whether the state in which they practice has a Good Samaritan law, or what its terms might be. Nor can evidence be found to establish that such laws have encouraged emergency treatment. In a study over thirty years ago, the American Medical Association found that the existence of Good Samaritan legislation made no difference to the willingness of physicians to stop and assist. 51.5% said they would stop to furnish emergency aid if the statutes were in effect, and 48.8% if no statute was in effect. Law Dept. of the AMA 1963 Professional Liability Survey, 189 J.A.M.A. 859 (1964). See Hessel, Good Samaritan Laws: Bad Legislation, 2 J.Leg.Med. 40 (1974). For a proposal for a uniform statute, see Comment, Good Samaritan Statutes: Time for Uniformity, 27 Wayne L.Rev. 217 (1980).

5. If the purpose of Good Samaritan statutes is to encourage emergency aid, should they instead impose a civil or criminal penalty on those who fail to offer such assistance? That is the case in many European countries, and—on the books—in Vermont, which imposes a $100 fine for failure to render aid under some circumstances. See 12 Vt.Stat.Ann. § 519. Should we require even more in the way of a duty to rescue? See generally Jean Elting Rowe and Theodore Silver, The Jurisprudence of Action and Inaction in the Law of Tort: Solving the Puzzle of Nonfeasance and Misfeasance from the Fifteenth Through the Twentieth Centuries, 33 Duquesne L.Rev. 807 (1995); Saul Levmore, Waiting for Rescue: An Essay on the Evolution and Incentive Structure of the Law of Affirmative Obligations, 72 Va.L.Rev. 879 (1986).

E. CONTRIBUTORY FAULT OF THE PATIENT

Patients through their own mistakes or lifestyle often enhance, or even cause, their injuries. People don't take their doctor's advice; they fall off their diets, stop exercising, start smoking, or act in a variety of ways counterproductive to their health. Very few tort cases have raised the issue directly, by raising a patient's lifestyle choice as a defense to a malpractice claim. Consider the following case.

OSTROWSKI v. AZZARA

Supreme Court of New Jersey, 1988.
111 N.J. 429, 545 A.2d 148.

O'HERN, J.

This case primarily concerns the legal significance of a medical malpractice claimant's pre-treatment health habits. Although the parties agreed that such habits should not be regarded as evidencing comparative fault for the medical injury at issue, we find that the instructions to the jury failed to draw the line clearly between the normal mitigation of damages expected of any claimant and the concepts of comparative fault that can preclude recovery in a fault-based system of tort reparation. Accordingly, we reverse the judgment below that disallowed any recovery to the diabetic plaintiff who had bypass surgery to correct a loss of circulation in a leg. The need for this bypass was found by the jury to have been proximately caused by the physician's neglect in performing an improper surgical procedure on the already weakened plaintiff.

I

As noted, the parties do not dispute that a physician must exercise the degree of care commensurate with the needs of the patient as she presents herself. This is but another way of saying that a defendant takes the plaintiff as she finds her. The question here, however, is much more subtle and complex. The complication arose from the plaintiff's seemingly routine need for care of an irritated toe. The plaintiff had long suffered from diabetes attributable, in unfortunate part perhaps, to her smoking and to her failure to adhere closely to her diet. Diabetic patients often have circulatory problems. For purposes of this appeal, we shall accept the general version of the events that led up to the operation as they are set forth in defendant-physician's brief.

On May 17, 1983, plaintiff, a heavy smoker and an insulin-dependent diabetic for twenty years, first consulted with defendant, Lynn Azzara, a doctor of podiatric medicine, a specialist in the care of feet. Plaintiff had been referred to Dr. Azzara by her internist whom she had last seen in November 1982. Dr. Azzara's notes indicated that plaintiff presented a sore left big toe, which had troubled her for approximately one month, and calluses. She told Dr. Azzara that she often suffered leg cramps that caused a tightening of the leg muscles or burning in her feet and legs after walking and while lying in bed. She had had hypertension (abnormally high blood pressure) for three years and was taking a diuretic for this condition.

Physical examination revealed redness in the plaintiff's big toe and elongated and incurvated toenails. Incurvated toenails are not ingrown; rather, they press against the skin. Diminished pulses on her foot indicated decreased blood supply to that area, as well as decreased circulation and impaired vascular status. Dr. Azzara made a diagnosis of onychomycosis (a fungous disease of the nails) and formulated a plan of treatment to debride (trim) the incurvated nail. Since plaintiff had informed her of a high blood sugar level, Dr. Azzara ordered a fasting blood sugar test and a urinalysis; she also noted that a vascular examination should be considered for the following week if plaintiff showed no improvement.

Plaintiff next saw Dr. Azzara three days later, on May 20, 1983. The results of the fasting blood sugar test indicated plaintiff's blood sugar was high, with a reading of 306. The urinalysis results also indicated plaintiff's blood sugar was above normal. At this second visit, Dr. Azzara concluded that plaintiff had peripheral vascular disease, poor circulation, and diabetes with a very high sugar elevation. She discussed these conclusions with plaintiff and explained the importance of better sugar maintenance. She also explained that a complication of peripheral vascular disease and diabetes is an increased risk of losing a limb if the diabetes is not controlled. The lack of blood flow can lead to decaying tissue. The parties disagree on whether Dr. Azzara told plaintiff she had to return to her internist to treat her blood sugar and circulation problems, or whether, as plaintiff indicates, Dr. Azzara merely suggested to plaintiff that she see her internist.

In any event, plaintiff came back to Dr. Azzara on May 31, 1983, and, according to the doctor, reported that she had seen her internist and that the internist had increased her insulin and told her to return to Dr. Azzara for further treatment because of her continuing complaints of discomfort about her toe. However, plaintiff had not seen the internist. Dr. Azzara contends that she believed plaintiff's representations. A finger-stick glucose test administered to measure plaintiff's non-fasting blood sugar yielded a reading of 175. A physical examination of the toe revealed redness and drainage from the distal medial (outside front) border of the nail, and the toenail was painful to the touch. Dr. Azzara's proposed course of treatment was to avulse, or remove, all or a portion of the toenail to facilitate drainage.

Dr. Azzara says that prior to performing the removal procedure she reviewed with Mrs. Ostrowski both the risks and complications of the procedure, including nonhealing and loss of limb, as well as the risks involved with not treating the toe. Plaintiff executed a consent form authorizing Dr. Azzara to perform a total removal of her left big toenail. The nail was cut out. (Defendant testified that she cut out only a portion of the nail, although her records showed a total removal.)

Two days later, plaintiff saw her internist. He saw her four additional times in order to check the progress of the toe. As of June 30, 1983, the internist felt the toe was much improved. While plaintiff was seeing the internist, she continued to see Dr. Azzara, or her associate, Dr. Bergman. During this period the toe was healing slowly, as Dr. Azzara said one would expect with a diabetic patient.

During the time plaintiff was being treated by her internist and by Dr. Azzara, she continued to smoke despite advice to the contrary. Her internist testified at the trial that smoking accelerates and aggravates peripheral vascular disease and that a diabetic patient with vascular disease can by smoking accelerate the severity of the vascular disease by as much as fifty percent. By mid-July, plaintiff's toe had become more painful and discolored.

At this point, all accord ceases. Plaintiff claims that it was the podiatrist's failure to consult with the patient's internist and defendant's failure to establish by vascular tests that the blood flow was sufficient to heal the wound, and to take less radical care, that left her with a non-healing, pre-gangrenous wound, that is, with decaying tissue. As a result, plaintiff had to undergo immediate bypass surgery to prevent the loss of the extremity. If left untreated, the pre-gangrenous toe condition resulting from the defendant's nail removal procedure would have spread, causing loss of the leg. The plaintiff's first bypass surgery did not arrest the condition, and she underwent two additional bypass surgeries which, in the opinion of her treating vascular surgeon, directly and proximately resulted from the unnecessary toenail removal procedure on May 31, 1983. In the third operation a vein from her right leg was transplanted to her left leg to increase the flow of blood to the toe.

At trial, defense counsel was permitted to show that during the pre-treatment period before May 17, 1983, the plaintiff had smoked cigarettes and had failed to maintain her weight, diet, and blood sugar at acceptable levels. The trial court allowed this evidence of the plaintiff's pre-treatment health habits to go to the jury on the issue of proximate cause. Defense counsel elicited admissions from plaintiff's internist and vascular surgeon that some doctors believe there is a relationship between poor self-care habits and increased vascular disease, perhaps by as much as fifty percent. But no medical expert for either side testified that the plaintiff's post-treatment health habits could have caused her need for bypass surgery six weeks after defendant's toenail removal. Nevertheless, plaintiff argues that defense counsel was permitted to interrogate the plaintiff extensively on her post-avulsion and post-bypass health habits, and that the court allowed such evidence of plaintiff's health habits during the six weeks after the operation to be considered as acts of comparative negligence that could bar recovery rather than reduce her damages. The jury found that the doctor had acted negligently in cutting out the plaintiff's toenail without adequate consideration of her condition, but found plaintiff's fault (fifty-one percent) to exceed that of the physician (forty-nine percent). She was therefore disallowed any recovery. On appeal the Appellate Division affirmed in an unreported decision. We granted certification to review plaintiff's claims. [ ] We are told that since the trial, the plaintiff's left leg has been amputated above the knee. This was foreseen, but not to a reasonable degree of medical probability at the time of trial.

II

Several strands of doctrine are interwoven in the resolution of this matter. The concepts of avoidable consequences, the particularly susceptible victim, aggravation of preexisting condition, comparative negligence, and proximate cause each play a part. It may be useful to unravel those strands of doctrine for separate consideration before considering them in the composite.

Comparative negligence is a legislative amelioration of the perceived harshness of the common-law doctrine of contributory negligence. [ ] In a fault-based system of tort reparation, the doctrine of contributory negligence served to bar any recovery to a plaintiff whose fault contributed to the accident. Whatever its conceptual underpinnings, its effect was to serve as a "gatekeeper." Epstein, "The Social Consequences of Common Law Rules," 95 *Harv.L.Rev.* 1717, 1736–37 (1982). Any fault kept a claimant from recovering under the system. Fault in that context meant a breach of a legal duty that was comparable to the duty of the other actors to exercise such care in the circumstances as was necessary to avoid the risk of injury incurred. Its prototype was the carriage driver who crossed the train tracks as the train was approaching the crossing. [ ] Harsh, but clear.

Comparative negligence was intended to ameliorate the harshness of contributory negligence but should not blur its clarity. It was designed only to leave the door open to those plaintiffs whose fault was not greater than the defendant's, not to create an independent gate-keeping function. Comparative negligence, then, will qualify the doctrine of contributory negligence when that doctrine would otherwise be applicable as a limitation on recovery. * * *

* * * The doctrine [of avoidable consequences] proceeds on the theory that a plaintiff who has suffered an injury as the proximate result of a tort cannot recover for any portion of the harm that by the exercise of ordinary care he could have avoided. [ ] * * * Avoidable consequences, then, normally comes into action when the injured party's carelessness occurs *after* the defendant's legal wrong has been committed. Contributory negligence, however, comes into action when the injured party's carelessness occurs *before* defendant's wrong has been committed or concurrently with it. [ ]

A counterweight to the doctrine of avoidable consequences is the doctrine of the particularly susceptible victim. This doctrine is familiarly expressed in the maxim that "defendant 'must take plaintiff as he finds him.' " [ ] * * * It is ameliorated by the doctrine of aggravation of a preexisting condition. While it is not entirely possible to separate the doctrines of avoidable consequence and preexisting condition, perhaps the simplest way to distinguish them is to understand that the injured person's conduct is irrelevant to the consideration of the doctrine of aggravation of a preexisting condition. Negligence law generally calls for an apportionment of damages when a plaintiff's antecedent negligence is "found not to contribute in any way to the original accident or injury, but to be a substantial contributing factor in increasing the harm which ensues." *Restatement (Second) of Torts*, § 465 at 510–11, comment c. Courts recognize that a defendant whose acts aggravate a plaintiff's preexisting condition is liable only for the amount of harm actually caused by the negligence. [ ] * * *

Finally, underpinning all of this is that most fundamental of risk allocators in the tort reparation system, the doctrine of proximate cause. * * *

We have sometimes melded proximate cause with foreseeability of unreasonable risk. * * *

We have been candid in New Jersey to see this doctrine, not so much as an expression of the mechanics of causation, but as an expression of line-drawing by courts and juries, an instrument of "overall fairness and sound public policy." [ ] * * * [ ].

III

Each of these principles, then, has some application to this case.[4] Plaintiff obviously had a preexisting condition. It is alleged that she failed to minimize

4. Each principle, however, has limitations based on other policy considerations. For example, the doctrine of avoidable consequences, although of logical application to some instances of professional malpractice, is neutralized by countervailing policy. Thus, a physician who

the damages that she might otherwise have sustained due to mistreatment. Such mistreatment may or may not have been the proximate cause of her ultimate condition.

But we must be careful in reassembling these strands of tort doctrine that none does double duty or obscures underlying threads. In particular, we must avoid the indiscriminate application of the doctrine of comparative negligence (with its fifty percent qualifier for recovery) when the doctrines of avoidable consequences or preexisting condition apply.

The doctrine of contributory negligence bars any recovery to the claimant whose negligent action or inaction *before* the defendant's wrongdoing has been completed has contributed to cause actual invasion of plaintiff's person or property. By contrast,

> "[t]he doctrine of avoidable consequences comes into play at a later stage. Where the defendant has already committed an actionable wrong, whether tort or breach of contract, then this doctrine [avoidable consequences] limits the plaintiff's recovery by disallowing only those items of damages which could reasonably have been averted * * * [.]" "[C]ontributory negligence is to be asserted as a complete defense, whereas the doctrine of avoidable consequences is not considered a defense at all, but merely a rule of damages by which certain particular items of loss may be excluded from consideration * * *." * * *

Hence, it would be the bitterest irony if the rule of comparative negligence, designed to ameliorate the harshness of contributory negligence, should serve to shut out any recovery to one who would otherwise have recovered under the law of contributory negligence. Put the other way, absent a comparative negligence act, it would have never been thought that "avoidable consequences" or "mitigation of damages" attributable to post-accident conduct of any claimant would have included a shutout of apportionable damages proximately caused by another's negligence. * * *

* * *

In this context of post-injury conduct by a claimant, given the understandable complexity of concurrent causation, expressing mitigation of damages as a percentage of fault which reduces plaintiff's damages may aid juries in their just apportionment of damages, provided that the jury understands that neither mitigation of damages nor avoidable consequences will bar the plaintiff from recovery if the defendant's conduct was a substantial factor without which the ultimate condition would not have arisen.

* * * In the field of professional health care, given the difficulty of apportionment, sound public policy requires that the professional bear the burden of demonstrating the proper segregation of damages in the aggravation context. [ ] The same policy should apply to mitigation of damages. [ ] Hence, overall fairness requires that juries evaluating apportionment of damages attributable in substantial part to a faulty medical procedure be given understandable guidance about the use of evidence of post-treatment patient fault that will assist them in making a just apportionment of damages and the burden of persuasion on the issues. This is consistent with our

performed a faulty tubal litigation cannot suggest that the eventual consequences of an unwanted pregnancy could have been avoided by termination of the fetus. [ ]

general view that a defendant bear the burden of proving the causal link between a plaintiff's unreasonable conduct and the extent of damages. [ ] Once that is established, it should be the "defendant who also has the burden of carving out that portion of the damages which is to be attributed to the plaintiff." [ ]

IV

As noted, in this case the parties agree on certain fundamentals. The pre-treatment health habits of a patient are not to be considered as evidence of fault that would have otherwise been pled in bar to a claim of injury due to the professional misconduct of a health professional. This conclusion bespeaks the doctrine of the particularly susceptible victim or recognition that whatever the wisdom or folly of our life-styles, society, through its laws, has not yet imposed a normative life-style on its members; and, finally, it may reflect in part an aspect of that policy judgment that health care professionals have a special responsibility with respect to diseased patients. [ ]

This does not mean, however, that the patient's poor health is irrelevant to the analysis of a claim for reparation. While the doctor may well take the patient as she found her, she cannot reverse the frames to make it appear that she was presented with a robust vascular condition; likewise, the physician cannot be expected to provide a guarantee against a cardiovascular incident. All that the law expects is that she not mistreat such a patient so as to become a proximate contributing cause to the ultimate vascular injury.

However, once the patient comes under the physician's care, the law can justly expect the patient to cooperate with the health care provider in their mutual interests. Thus, it is not unfair to expect a patient to help avoid the consequences of the condition for which the physician is treating her. * * *

Hence, we approve in this context of post-treatment conduct submission to the jury of the question whether the just mitigation or apportionment of damages may be expressed in terms of the patient's fault. If used, the numerical allocation of fault should be explained to the jury as a method of achieving the just apportionment of the damages based on their relative evaluation of each actor's contribution to the end result—that the allocation is but an aspect of the doctrine of avoidable consequences or of mitigation of damages. In this context, plaintiff should not recover more than she could have reasonably avoided, but the patient's fault will not be a bar to recovery except to the extent that her fault caused the damages.

An important caveat to that statement would be the qualification that implicitly flows from the fact that health care professionals bear the burden of proving that their mistreatment did not aggravate a preexisting condition: that the health care professional bear the burden of proving the damages that were avoidable.

Finally, before submitting the issue to the jury, a court should carefully scrutinize the evidence to see if there is a sound basis in the proofs for the assertion that the post-treatment conduct of the patient was indeed a significant cause of the increased damages. Given the short onset between the contraindicated surgery and the vascular incident here, plaintiff asserts that defendant did not present proof, to a reasonable degree of medical probability, that the plaintiff's post-treatment conduct was a proximate cause of the resultant condition. Plaintiff asserts that the only evidence given to support the defense's theory of proximate cause between plaintiff's post-treatment health habits and her damages was her internist's testimony regarding generalized studies showing that smoking increases vascular disease by fifty percent, and her vascular surgeon's testimony that some physicians believe there is a relationship among diabetes, smoking, and vascular impairment. Such testimony did not address with any degree of medical probability a relationship between her smoking or not between May 17, 1983, and the plaintiff's need for bypass surgery in July 1983. Defendant points to plaintiff's failure to consult with her internist as a cause of her injury, but the instruction to the jury gave no guidance on whether this was to be considered as conduct that concurrently or subsequently caused her injuries. [ ]

V

We acknowledge that it is difficult to parse through these principles and policies in the course of an extended appeal. We can well imagine that in the ebb and flow of trial the lines are not easily drawn. There are regrettably no easy answers to these questions.

* * *

[The court noted the factual complexities of the case, and concluded that "the instructions to the jury in this case did not adequately separate or define the concepts that were relevant to the disposition of the plaintiff's case." The case was remanded for a new trial.]

Notes and Questions

1. Do you advocate applying contributory negligence, or comparative negligence (depending upon the jurisdiction), to situations such as that of *Ostrowski*? Such cases raise fundamental questions about the limits of medicine and the role of patients in their own illnesses. Can a smoker easily stop? Is it fair to bar his recovery when his smoking is not a simple, easily abandoned, choice? See Sawka v. Prokopowycz, 104 Mich.App. 829, 306 N.W.2d 354 (1981), where the plaintiff sued the defendant for his failure to diagnose lung cancer. The court rejected the claim that the plaintiff's continued smoking and failure to return for further examination as instructed were contributory negligence.

Would you treat an overzealous jogger who had cardiac arrest while running in the same way as a chain smoking or obese sedentary patient? How much of your decision is based on your desire to punish the smoker or glutton for immoral or irresponsible behavior which may be virtually impossible to control? Blaming the victim, or scapegoating, is a frequent argument used by employers, insurers and the government to reduce obligations to insure, pay benefits, or, as in *Ostrowski*, to pay damages for patient injury. See Robert Schwartz, Life Style, Health Status, and Distributive Justice, 3 Health Matrix 195, 198 (1993) ("If all of those whose life style choices have health consequences were required to bear the full burden of those consequences, there would be few of us (and few diseases or injuries) that would not be implicated.")

2. Consider the case of Smith v. Hull, 659 N.E.2d 185 (Ind.App.1995). Michael Smith was bald. He underwent hair implants over several years from Dr. Hull, who used human hair obtained from women in Indonesia. He also underwent scalp reduction to draw his scalp skin together. Becoming dissatisfied with

the scarring on his scalp, he went back to wearing a hairpiece and sued Dr. Hull for malpractice. Dr. Hull raised contributory negligence as a defense. Smith had signed several consent forms and had been told to wait on scalp reduction until his hair implants fell out, but insisted on proceeding with further surgery. The court found that "Smith's desire to sport a full head of hair motivated him to pursue remedies that he knowingly undertook at his own peril." It upheld the trial court's instructions on contributory negligence.

A finding of contributory negligence was upheld in Ray v. Wagner, 286 Minn. 354, 176 N.W.2d 101, 104 (1970), where the physician performed a pap smear on the plaintiff, got back a positive test result, but was unable to reach the plaintiff by telephone for five months. The court noted:

> Ordinarily, a patient can rely on a doctor's informing her if the results of a test are positive. Here, however, plaintiff gave the doctor somewhat misleading information as to her status, she had no phone at the address where she lived, and she did not live at the address where she had a phone.

See also Harlow v. Chin, 405 Mass. 697, 545 N.E.2d 602 (1989) (plaintiff failed to return for further treatment when pain got worse; plaintiff held to be 13% comparatively negligent.)

3. The theory is typically invoked when a patient failed to follow a physician's instructions after a procedure was performed, or while in the hospital. Thus in Butler v. Berkeley, 25 N.C.App. 325, 213 S.E.2d 571 (1975), the plaintiff removed the nasogastric tube that had been inserted to prevent wounds from being contaminated by food after plastic surgery. This action might have caused the infection that the patient then developed, and the court granted summary judgment for the surgeon on grounds of contributory negligence. In Musachia v. Rosman, 190 So.2d 47 (Fla.App.1966), the decedent left the hospital over the objections of, and contrary to the advice of, the defendants. He drank liquor and ignored instructions to eat only baby food. He then died from fecal peritonitis due to small perforations in the bowel, and his recovery was barred on the basis of contributory negligence. See also Faile v. Bycura, 297 S.C. 58, 374 S.E.2d 687 (App.1988) (patient refused to wear a medically prescribed postoperative orthotic device after foot surgery).

The failure of a patient to follow a treating physician's warnings about behavior can also be considered by the jury under contributory negligence instructions. In Cobo v. Raba, 347 N.C. 541, 495 S.E.2d 362 (N.C.1998), a physician who suffered from depression was treated by the defendant Dr. Raba. Dr. Cobo refused drug treatment for chronic depression, refused to allow the defendant to take notes, and insisted on psychoanalysis as the only mode of treatment. During this period he engaged regularly in unprotected homosexual intercourse with prostitutes, in spite of regular admonitions by the defendant as to the risks, including unprotected sex with a drug-addicted prostitute in a San Francisco bathhouse; he abused alcohol and drugs, and when he became HIV-positive, he substantially delayed his treatment. The court held that the plaintiff's conduct was "clearly active and related directly to his physical complaint," and the jury should be allowed to evaluate it through a contributory negligence instruction.

4. Comparative fault is rarely applied against a patient. In Weil v. Seltzer, 873 F.2d 1453 (D.C.Cir.1989), the defendant argued that the patient was contributorily negligent in failing to discover that the medication given him over a twenty year period was steroids rather than antihistamines as told by the defendant; the court strongly rejected this argument, holding that while a patient must cooperate with her physician, "[i]t is a quantum leap * * * to permit a duty to be placed on

a patient * * * ". The court also rejected the assumption of the risk defense, since there was no evidence that the plaintiff knew of the danger of prolonged steroid use and voluntarily accepted the risks. Physicians are expected to consider the needs and limitations of their patients. Bryant v. Calantone, 286 N.J.Super. 362, 669 A.2d 286 (N.J.Super.A.D.1996).

In Windisch v. Weiman, 161 A.D.2d 433, 555 N.Y.S.2d 731 (1990), the court held that the failure of a physician to properly follow-up a patient, resulting in a missed diagnosis of lung cancer, may provide the basis for imposing liability even when the patient is partially responsible for the delay in diagnosis. See also Jensen v. Archbishop Bergan Mercy Hospital, 236 Neb. 1, 459 N.W.2d 178 (1990) (the court held that a patient's failure to lose weight may have been causally related to his pulmonary embolism, but it was not contributory negligence with respect to a subsequent malpractice claim against the hospital for treatment of the embolism.)

A patient's lack of compliance with treatment instructions may be submitted to the jury under comparative negligence statutes for comparison with the malpractice of the treating physician. In Cox v. Lesko, 263 Kan. 805, 953 P.2d 1033 (Kan.1998), the physician performed shoulder surgery for traumatic posterior subluxation in the left shoulder. The plaintiff then missed most of her physical therapy sessions over several months, which were aimed to strengthen her muscles and increase her shoulder's range of motion. Her condition failed to improve. Plaintiff's lack of compliance with therapy instructions was properly submitted to the jury under the comparative negligence statute as fault to be compared with the malpractice of the physician who performed the surgery.

5. Almost all American jurisdictions have adopted comparative fault, simplifying the issue by eliminating the harsh all-or-nothing effect of contributory negligence. Courts in comparative fault jurisdictions are likely to be more willing to allow evidence of plaintiffs' contributions to their injuries. See generally Victor Schwartz, Comparative Negligence (2nd ed. 1986). The court in McIntyre v. Balentine, 833 S.W.2d 52 (Tenn.1992), lists only four states remaining without comparative fault: Alabama, Maryland, North Carolina, and Virginia.

6. Assumption of the risk. The doctrine of assumption of the risk is a viable defense even in many comparative fault jurisdictions. In Schneider v. Revici, 817 F.2d 987, 995 (2d Cir.1987), the Second Circuit considered whether a patient undergoing unconventional treatment for breast cancer after signing a consent form had waived all her rights to sue or assumed the risk of injury from the treatment. The court held that the consent form was not clear and unequivocal as a covenant not to sue, but that the doctrine of assumption of risk was available:

> * * * we see no reason why a patient should not be allowed to make an informed decision to go outside currently approved medical methods in search of an unconventional treatment. While a patient should be encouraged to exercise care for his own safety, we believe that an informed decision to avoid surgery and conventional chemotherapy is within the patient's right to "determine what shall be done with his own body," [ ]

The court held that the jury could consider assumption of the risk as a total bar to recovery, based on the language of the signed consent form and the patient's general awareness of the risks of treatment.

Assumption of the risk is rarely argued except in cases of obvious defects of which the patient should have been aware, such as hazards in the hospital room. See, e.g., Charrin v. Methodist Hospital, 432 S.W.2d 572 (Tex.Civ.App.1968) (plaintiff tripped over television cord in hospital room; she knew it was there, having previously pointed it out to the staff.) The problem of assumption of the risk, in the sense of a conscious explicit assumption of medical risks, blends into the issues of informed consent and waivers of liability, discussed in Chapter 5, below.

Problem: The Eyes Have It

Dr. Guerra was an ophthalmologist who specialized in corneal surgery. He used a laser procedure—photorefractive keratectomy—to correct nearsightedness in his patients. The procedure involves first peeling off the epithelium, the skin covering the cornea; then the computer-controlled laser, set and positioned by the doctor, shoots pulses of cool ultraviolet light to reshape the cornea. Finally, a contact lens is placed over the eye.

Dr. Guerra had developed his own laser device to allow him more accuracy and control than the machines commercially available (manufactured by Summit Technology and VISX Inc.) for this procedure. He had custom-built his device and used the prototype on several dozen patients with success and with few side effects. This year Dr. Guerra operated on Eva Hendrix, who was nearsighted. He had told her that his machine was built to his own design and was more accurate than the devices on the market. She agreed to go ahead with the procedure, signing all consent forms. Unfortunately, the device malfunctioned; the laser shifted slightly in its mount and improperly shaped her cornea, so that her vision was made much worse. Even with contacts she cannot now be corrected to her previous level of vision.

Does Ms. Hendrix have any recourse against Dr. Guerra for the impairment of her vision?

F. ERISA PREEMPTION

ERISA preemption, discussed in Chapter 9 infra, has been held to preempt common law malpractice actions against managed care organizations, although a variety of exceptions are emerging. Whether ERISA preempts an action against treating physicians for their malpractice is a different issue. The following case provides a first look at this issue.

NEALY v. U.S. HEALTHCARE HMO

Court of Appeals of New York, 1999.
93 N.Y.2d 209, 689 N.Y.S.2d 406, 711 N.E.2d 621.

KAYE, CHIEF JUDGE:

The novel question presented by this appeal is whether the Employee Retirement Income Security Act (ERISA) preempts plaintiff's medical malpractice, breach of contract and breach of fiduciary duty claims against a primary care physician who allegedly delayed in submitting a specialist's referral form for approval by a health maintenance organization (HMO) governed by ERISA. Concluding that ERISA does not preempt plaintiff's claims, we reverse the Appellate Division's dismissal order and reinstate the complaint against the doctor.

In January 1992, plaintiff's husband, Glenn Nealy, then 37 years old, was diagnosed with coronary arteriosclerosis and a coronary artery lesion. As a result, Mr. Nealy took disability leave from his job at Photocircuits Corporation and was treated for his condition by a cardiologist, Dr. Stephen Green. His treatment, which included an angioplasty performed by Dr. Green in March 1992, was in large part covered by Blue Cross/Massachusetts Mutual, the carrier selected by Photocircuits to provide employee medical insurance. Around the time of Mr. Nealy's angioplasty, Photocircuits replaced its carrier with a choice of three HMOs, including U.S. Healthcare, and informed its employees that coverage would become effective April 1, 1992. Mr. Nealy promptly enrolled in the U.S. Healthcare Versatile Plus HMO, which allowed its members to see non-participating physicians, and paid his first monthly premium.

On April 2, and again on April 3, Mr. Nealy visited the offices of defendant, Dr. Ralph Yung, whom he had selected as his primary care provider under the U.S. Healthcare HMO.[5] He experienced renewed chest pain and also required follow-up care as a result of the angioplasty. On his first visit, Mr. Nealy was denied an appointment because he had not yet received a U.S. Healthcare identification number. The next day, he spoke with a U.S. Healthcare representative who told him that a copy of his enrollment form could be presented in lieu of an identification number, and he made a second attempt to visit Dr. Yung. Again he was turned away—this time because his enrollment form bore the wrong primary physician number.

On April 10, 1992—having received his U.S. Healthcare identification card the previous day—Mr. Nealy was examined by Dr. Yung. During that visit, Dr. Yung took a patient history that noted a history of angina and angioplasty, performed a routine new-patient physical examination, and renewed all the medications that had been prescribed by Dr. Green. At Dr. Yung's request, Mr. Nealy returned on April 13 to provide blood and urine samples for laboratory analysis. When Dr. Yung informed him during one or both of these visits that he should see a cardiologist, Mr. Nealy requested a referral to Dr. Green, who was not a participating U.S. Healthcare provider. Dr. Yung allegedly assured his patient that he would submit a request to U.S. Healthcare to approve an out-of-plan referral and do what he could to secure approval of the request. It was not until approximately April 20, however, that Dr. Yung completed a non-participating provider request form and submitted it for approval to U.S. Healthcare.[6]

On May 4th, Mr. Nealy received a copy of a letter from U.S. Healthcare addressed to Dr. Yung denying the request for a referral to Dr. Green. The reason given was that U.S. Healthcare had a participating provider in the area. After the referral to Dr. Green was denied, Mr. Nealy decided to accept a referral to Dr. Carl Spivak, a participating U.S. Healthcare cardiologist. He obtained the referral to Dr. Spivak on May 18 and promptly made an

5. Dr. Yung disputes plaintiff's allegation that Mr. Nealy visited his offices on April 2 and 3, admitting only that he first saw Mr. Nealy on or about April 10.

6. The parties dispute whether the non-participating referral form—instead of a "Versatile" form—was submitted to U.S. Healthcare at Mr. Nealy's request or the result of Dr. Yung's error. A "Versatile" referral would have allowed treatment by a non-participating doctor but required Mr. Nealy to pay a $250 deductible. Plaintiff maintains that Mr. Nealy never expressed a desire to avoid payment of the deductible and was motivated only by a desire to see his cardiologist as soon as possible. Dr. Yung claims that Mr. Nealy did not want to pay the deductible, which is why the non-participating referral form was submitted.

appointment for the next day. Tragically, however, on May 18 Mr. Nealy suffered a massive myocardial infarction and died.

Seeking to recover damages for her husband's death, plaintiff commenced this action in Supreme Court asserting breach of contract, breach of fiduciary duty, wrongful death, negligence and other claims against defendants Dr. Yung, Dr. Richard H. Bernstein (Vice President and Director of U.S. Healthcare), U.S. Healthcare and two subsidiaries. Plaintiff also asserted medical malpractice claims against Dr. Yung and Dr. Bernstein. Dr. Bernstein and U.S. Healthcare successfully sought removal of the case to Federal court, where the claims were dismissed on the ground that they were preempted by ERISA (844 F.Supp. 966 [SDNY]), and no appeal was taken to determine the correctness of that decision. Because Dr. Yung—who had not yet been served with the summons and complaint—did not take part in the removal motion, the Federal court remanded the case against him, as the sole remaining defendant, to Supreme Court.

After service of process and discovery, Dr. Yung moved for summary judgment seeking dismissal of the complaint, alleging that ERISA preempted plaintiff's claims against him as well. Supreme Court denied the motion. The Appellate Division, however, reversed and dismissed the complaint, concluding that ERISA preempted plaintiff's claims. We disagree and now reinstate plaintiff's complaint against Dr. Yung.

Discussion

Concerned with employee pension plan abuses and mismanagement, Congress in 1974 enacted ERISA, a comprehensive statute "designed to promote the interests of employees and their beneficiaries in employee benefit plans" (Aetna Life Ins. v. Borges, 869 F.2d 142, 144 [2d Cir], cert. denied 493 U.S. 811, 110 S.Ct. 57, 107 L.Ed.2d 25; see also, 29 USC §§ 1001, 1001a, 1001b). ERISA subjects employee benefit plans to participation, funding and vesting requirements as well as rules regarding reporting, disclosure and fiduciary responsibility [ ]. By imposing these requirements, Congress sought "to insure against the possibility that the employee's expectation of * * * benefit[s] would be defeated through poor management by the plan administrator" (Massachusetts v. Morash, 490 U.S. 107, 115, 109 S.Ct. 1668, 104 L.Ed.2d 98). In aid of its goal of protecting plan participants and their beneficiaries, ERISA facilitates the development of a uniform national law governing employee benefit plans, and a standard system to guide the processing of claims and disbursement of benefits (New York State Conference of Blue Cross & Blue Shield Plans v. Travelers Ins. Co., 514 U.S. 645, 656–657, 115 S.Ct. 1671, 131 L.Ed.2d 695 [Travelers]).

ERISA's preemption provision is central to achievement of its statutory purposes. The provision reads that ERISA "shall supersede any and all State laws insofar as they * * * relate to any employee benefit plan" covered by ERISA, and it applies to both State statutes and common law (§ 514[a], 29 USC § 1144[a]; id., at § 514[c][1], 29 USC § 1144[c][1]; Pilot Life Ins. Co. v. Dedeaux, 481 U.S. 41, 46, 107 S.Ct. 1549, 95 L.Ed.2d 39). Although the language of the preemption clause is "deliberately expansive," there is a presumption that Congress does not intend to supplant State law, and a claim traditionally within the domain of State law will not be superseded by Federal law "unless that was the clear and manifest purpose of Congress" (Travelers, 514 US, at 654–655).

The issue before us is whether ERISA's preemption clause bars plaintiff's medical malpractice, breach of contract and breach of fiduciary duty claims against her husband's primary care physician, Dr. Yung. All of these claims fall within the traditional domain of State regulation. Dr. Yung, therefore, bears the "considerable burden" of overcoming the presumption that Congress did not intend to preempt them [ ]. In an attempt to surmount that formidable hurdle, Dr. Yung alleges that ERISA preempts these claims because they "relate to" the administration of the U.S. Healthcare HMO. The Appellate Division agreed, holding that he was protected by ERISA preemption because he had acted in a "purely administrative" capacity, and not as an "actual provider of medical care" (___ A.D.2d ___, ___). We conclude that plaintiff's claims against Dr. Yung do not "relate to" an employee benefit plan.

The simple statutory words "relate to" have been the subject of significant scholarly comment and litigation, including considerable attention from the United States Supreme Court [ ] On the one hand, virtually any State law may be said to "relate to" an employee benefit plan, for "universally, relations stop nowhere" (Travelers, supra, 514 US, at 655). On the other hand, application of the preemption clause to "the furthest stretch of its indeterminancy" would render Congress' words of limitation a "mere sham" and nullify the presumption against preemption (id.). Plainly, there is tension between the "deliberately expansive" language of the preemption clause—which, applied literally, would operate to shield benefit plans—and ERISA's goal of protecting employees from abuses at the hands of such entities.

After many years of broadly interpreting ERISA's preemption clause, in 1995 the United States Supreme Court adopted a more pragmatic approach, noting that its prior efforts to define "relate to" did not always afford "much help drawing the line" (Travelers, 514 US, at 655–656). Whereas the Court had previously explained that a law "relates to" an employee benefit plan if it has a connection with or makes reference to such a plan, in Travelers the Court acknowledged that even that definition of the phrase failed to provide adequate guidance (id., at 656). Thus, the Court concluded, in determining whether a State law relates to an employee benefit plan, it is often necessary to "go beyond the unhelpful text and the frustrating difficulty of defining its key term, and look instead to the objectives of the ERISA statute as a guide to the scope of the state law that Congress understood would survive" (Travelers, 514 US, at 656; see also, DeBuono, supra, 117 S.Ct., at 1751 [where there is no clear "connection with or reference to" an ERISA benefit plan, consideration must be given to the objectives of ERISA to determine whether the presumption against preemption has been overcome]).

In Travelers itself, the Supreme Court concluded that a State statute imposing surcharges on hospital bills paid by certain employee benefit plans, but exempting Blue Cross/Blue Shield plans, was not preempted by ERISA. Arguing for preemption, the commercial insurers asserted that the surcharges had an indirect economic effect on choices made by insurance buyers, including ERISA plans, and as such, the State statute had a "connection with" those plans. The Supreme Court, however, held that the indirect economic influence of the surcharges did not interfere with the congressional goal of uniform standards of plan administration. The statute did not "bind plan administrators to any particular choice and thus function as a regulation of an ERISA plan itself," nor did it "preclude uniform administrative practice or the provision of a uniform interstate benefit package" (514 US, at 659–660). The effect of the law bore only on "the costs of benefits and the relative costs of competing insurance to provide them," and the law was therefore not preempted by ERISA [ ]

Here, plaintiff alleges that Dr. Yung, as a direct provider of medical services, violated the duties and standard of care owed to his patient by improperly assessing the nature and extent of his condition and by failing to take reasonable steps to provide for his timely treatment by a specialist. Viewed pragmatically, those claims are not preempted by ERISA. Plaintiff's allegations of negligent medical care do not "relate to" the administration of an ERISA plan merely because they refer to Dr. Yung's delay in submitting the U.S. Healthcare form seeking a referral to Dr. Green. Plaintiff does not allege that Dr. Yung is responsible for delay caused by U.S. Healthcare's decision-making process with respect to coverage or benefits. Her claim against Dr. Yung is that he failed to take timely action to treat her husband.

Provision of medical treatment under an HMO or other managed care plan often requires reference to that plan's administrative procedures or requirements. In this case, for example, under the terms of the U.S. Healthcare HMO plan, Mr. Nealy's primary care physician was required to complete and submit a referral form in order to obtain treatment by a specialist for his patient. That alone, however, does not transform Dr. Yung into an ERISA plan administrator, or plaintiff's State law action charging violations of a physician's duty of care into claims that "relate to" ERISA plan administration. While plaintiff's claims make reference to U.S. Healthcare's administrative framework, any effect those claims may have on an employee benefit plan is "too tenuous, remote or peripheral" to warrant a finding that they "relate to" such a plan (Shaw, supra, 463 US, at 100 n. 21).

Moreover, considering the objectives of the ERISA statute, it is clear that Congress did not intend to preempt claims such as those now before us. Plaintiff's claims do not bind an employee plan to any particular choice of benefits, do not dictate the administration of such a plan and do not interfere with a uniform administrative scheme [ ]. Indeed, plaintiff does not challenge any administrative determination relating to an employee benefit plan or the extent of rights and benefits under such a plan. In short, there is nothing about plaintiff's claims that "conflicts with the provisions of ERISA or operates to frustrate its [objectives]" (Boggs, supra, 117 S.Ct., at 1760). To the contrary, plaintiff's claims are consistent with ERISA's "principal object": the protection of plan participants and beneficiaries (id., at 1762).

Finally, the Appellate Division would have dismissed plaintiff's complaint on the independent ground that she failed to demonstrate that any deviation from professional standards was a proximate cause of Mr. Nealy's demise. At this juncture in the litigation, however, we cannot agree with that conclusion as a matter of law.

Notes and Questions

1. Can you make a case that the design of the health plan in fact narrowed the treating physicians' choice? The requirement of approval before referring a patient to a non-participating specialist constrains the treating physician, does it not? And the time delay in denying the request for the referral to a non-participating cardiologist was arguably a causal factor in the ultimate death of the plaintiff. These arguments go to a suit against the Plan, which will risk preemption by ERISA in most jurisdictions. See Chapter 9 infra. But what about the argument that these elements of the plan's operation were intended to do exactly what happened in this case–deter the treating physician from making referrals expeditiously?

2. The application of ERISA preemption to the individual physician does not make much sense from a policy perspective. ERISA was designed to govern pension plan administration, not individual medical treatment decisions. Using the "relate to" language, the Court properly rejects ERISA preemption as a defense.

V. CAUSATION PROBLEMS: DELAYED, UNCERTAIN, OR SHARED RESPONSIBILITY

A. THE DISCOVERY RULE

MASTRO v. BRODIE

Supreme Court of Colorado, 1984.
682 P.2d 1162.

NEIGHBORS, JUSTICE.

* * *

On February 5, 1977, Mastro surgically removed a small nodule from the back of Brodie's shoulder. He obtained Brodie's consent to the surgery after explaining that she would have a scar, "but it wouldn't be a bad one." Several months later, however, the scar from the surgery became "large, unsightly and uncomfortable." Brodie returned to Mastro in July 1977, but received no further treatment and no explanation of what had happened. He told her only that "there was nothing else he could do about [the scar]." Since that time, Brodie has had no contact with Mastro. She received treatment, including a series of injections into the scar, from two other physicians during the next two years. She also discussed the scar with at least two attorneys for whom she worked during this time period. Her scar, however, has remained approximately the same in size and appearance as when she first became aware of it. In August 1979, a physician at the University of Colorado Medical Center informed Brodie that she had developed a "keloid"[3] on her shoulder. Further, he told her that a surgical procedure on the shoulder of young, dark-skinned individuals frequently results in the formation of a keloid, which, while

3. *Dorland's Illustrated Medical Dictionary* 695 (26th ed. 1981) defines "keloid" as "a sharply elevated, irregularly-shaped, progressively enlarging scar due to the formation of excessive amounts of collagen [fibrous tissue] * * * during connective tissue repair."

unpredictable, does occur in a percentage of such patients. He indicated to Brodie's attorney that "the risk of keloid should have been anticipated" and that Mastro should have warned Brodie of such a risk before operating on her shoulder.[4]

Three months later, in November 1979, Brodie filed a complaint against Mastro * * * alleging medical malpractice. She claimed that, when she consulted him about the nodule on her shoulder, Mastro knew or should have know of the inherent risk of keloid development in a person with her physical characteristics, and that he knew or should have known that disclosure of this risk "would be of great significance to a person in [Brodie's] position in deciding to submit to surgery." Since Mastro was "under a duty to inform [Brodie] of any substantial or special risks inherent in the procedure," his failure to mention keloid scarring before the surgery prevented her from making "an intelligent choice as to alternative treatments consonant with the underlying premise of informed consent." As a result, Brodie suffered "a serious, permanent disfiguring injury" in the form of "a large, unsightly growth" that was "plainly visible on her shoulder." While admitting that she was aware of the scar by July 1977, Brodie concluded by alleging that she was not aware and could not reasonably have been aware of "[Mastro's] negligence in failing to inform her" of the high risk of keloid formation until she consulted the physician at the medical center in August 1979, at the direction of her attorney.

After depositions of the parties were taken, Mastro filed a motion for summary judgment, claiming that the two-year statute of limitations for medical malpractice actions based on lack of informed consent barred Brodie's claim. [ ] Under this provision, the two-year period begins to run when the injured person discovers or in the exercise of reasonable diligence should have discovered "the injury." Mastro claimed that there was no genuine issue of material fact since Brodie "has admitted that she knew of the injury (unsightly scar) more than two years prior to initiation of her Complaint."

* * *

We conclude that the pivotal question in this case is whether Brodie filed suit within two years after she "discovered, or in the exercise of reasonable diligence and concern should have discovered, the *injury*." Section 13–80–105(1) (emphasis added). Therefore, we must interpret the word "injury" as it appears in the statute of limitations governing medical malpractice cases.

* * *

C.

There are at least three possible interpretations of the word "injury": (1) the alleged negligent act or omission; (2) the physical damage or manifestation resulting from the act or omission; or (3) the legal injury, i.e., all the essential elements of a claim for medical malpractice.

At least two courts have adopted the first definition. [ ] We reject this interpretation of the word. * * *

4. She described her racial background in her deposition as "half black and half Mexican." Brodie's father had been a patient of Mastro's before her surgery.

Likewise, we reject the interpretation that the "injury" occurs for purposes of the statute of limitations on the date that the injury manifests itself in a physically objective and ascertainable manner. The physical damage test fails to account adequately for all relevant factors. In some cases, such as the discovery of a sponge left in the patient during surgery * * * the discovery of the physical injury may occur simultaneously with the discovery of the only possible cause, i.e., the doctor's negligence. However, where the injury is consistent with post-operative recovery and treatment is continued by the treating doctor who reassures the patient that there is no permanent damage, the patient who reasonably trusts the doctor and relies upon the physician's advice would be unfairly barred from bringing suit. In addition, the physical injury standard requires a claimant to immediately file suit against a physician, even though the plaintiff has no knowledge of any wrongful conduct on the part of the doctor. Courts should not adopt a construction of a statute which may encourage the filing of frivolous claims. * * *

* * *

We hold that the statute of limitations begins to run when the claimant has knowledge of facts which would put a reasonable person on notice of the nature and extent of an injury and that the injury was caused by the wrongful conduct of another. The overwhelming majority of state appellate courts which have addressed the issue here have adopted the "legal injury" construction of the word "injury" used in statutes of limitation governing medical malpractice actions. The focus is on the plaintiff's knowledge of facts, rather than on discovery of applicable legal theories. * * *

The judgment of the court of appeals is affirmed.

Notes and Questions

1. Has the discovery rule simplified or complicated malpractice litigation? The older cases generally held that a cause of action accrued when the right to bring an action arose, i.e. when the medical error had occurred. Shearin v. Lloyd, 246 N.C. 363, 98 S.E.2d 508 (1957). See also Goldsmith v. Howmedica, Inc., 67 N.Y.2d 120, 500 N.Y.S.2d 640, 491 N.E.2d 1097 (1986) (plaintiff received a total hip replacement in 1973; in 1981 the hip broke and plaintiff sued in 1983. Held: action accrued in 1973 and was barred by the statute of limitations.)

This older rule has the advantage of a bright line approach to the statute of limitation. The newer discovery rule like that adopted in *Brodie* was created to be fair to patients who suffered latent injuries. What does such a rule cost? Can the malpractice insurance crisis be traced in some small way to the uncertainties bred by such a rule? The discovery rule makes it actuarially difficult for a malpractice insurer to predict losses, by creating a long period of time after a medical intervention during which a claim can be "discovered." As a result, insurers must raise premiums to compensate for the uncertainty of future unknown claims not barred by a rigid statute of limitations rule. Or they might change the design of policies to a claims-made basis to eliminate this uncertainty about future claims.

2. The modern discovery rule creates difficult problems. Does the statute begin to run when the initial harm surfaces or when the injury matures or worsens? See Burns v. Hartford Hosp., 192 Conn. 451, 472 A.2d 1257 (1984) (patient had infection due to contaminated IV tube. Court held that "* * * the

harm need not have reached its fullest manifestation before the statute begins to run.")

3. In suits against the federal government, the statute of limitations begins to run when the plaintiff learns of an injury's existence and cause, rather than when he learns the injury was negligently inflicted. Once the injury and its causes are known, the plaintiff can "protect himself by seeking advice in the medical and legal community." United States v. Kubrick, 444 U.S. 111, 100 S.Ct. 352, 62 L.Ed.2d 259 (1979) (suit against government under Tort Claims Act).

B. MULTIPLE DEFENDANTS

1. *Joint Tortfeasor Doctrine*

In the typical malpractice case in which the parties acted together to commit the wrong, or the parties' acts, if independent, unite to cause a single injury, multiple defendants are considered joint rather than separate tortfeasors. In determining whether to assess liability jointly, the courts have considered factors such as whether each defendant has a similar duty; whether the same evidence will support an action against each; the indivisible nature of the plaintiff's injury; and identity of the facts as to time, place or result. See Riff v. Morgan Pharmacy, 353 Pa.Super. 21, 508 A.2d 1247 (1986).

What if a doctor fails to diagnose a patient's problem, and subsequently another doctor is negligent in treating it? The first negligent treating doctor might be liable to the injured plaintiff for all foreseeable injuries resulting from the later negligent medical treatment of a second doctor. Two or more physicians who fail to make a proper diagnosis on successive occasions are co-tortfeasors under contribution statutes. Foote v. United States, 648 F.Supp. 735 (N.D.Ill.1986). See, e.g., Gilson v. Mitchell, 131 Ga.App. 321, 205 S.E.2d 421 (1974):

> "* * * if the separate and independent acts of negligence of several persons combine naturally and directly to produce a single indivisible injury, and a rational basis does not exist for an apportionment of damages, the actors are joint tortfeasors."

Where an existing injury is aggravated by malpractice, the innocent plaintiffs are not required to establish that share of expenses, pain, suffering, disability or impairment attributable solely to malpractice. The burden of proof shifts to the culpable defendant, who is responsible for all damages unless he can demonstrate that the damages for which he is responsible are capable of some reasonable apportionment.

Concurrent causation instructions are required to help the trier of fact sort out the causation complexities. In Zigman v. Cline, 664 So.2d 968 (Fla.App. 4 Dist.1995), the plaintiff was rendered a paraplegic after an complicated surgery "to correct the severe and normally fatal injuries ... suffered in an automobile accident". Without the surgery he would have died; but a possibility existed that the surgeon erred in his choice of technique in repairing the plaintiff's torn aorta. The court held that the jury should have been instructed as to concurrent causation where a defendant's negligence combines with plaintiff's physical condition.

For the physician who knows that his patients see alternative practitioners, or who offers such treatments as an option, what are his or her liabilities?

Joint and several liability is likely to hook the physician firmly if injury is the end result of a continuum of care that includes alternative practitioners. For example, in Samuelson v. McMurtry, 962 S.W.2d 473 (Tenn.1998), the plaintiff was treated by physicians and a chiropractor. His problems began with a boil under his arm, treated by Dr. Holland. The next day he returned to the hospital with a fever and inflammation around the boil and was treated by Dr. McMurty. 8 days later, he went to the hospital emergency room with complaints of back pain. The next day he twice returned to the emergency room. On the first visit he was seen by Dr. Holland but on the second visit he was discouraged by hospital personnel from seeing a physician. The next day, he went to see Dr. Totty, a chiropractor, with complaints of intense back and chest pain and he was treated twice that day by Dr. Totty. The next day he died of pneumonia, "which had not been diagnosed by any of the health care providers." He could have been treated within 6–12 hours of his death. This case presents an apportionment of fault issue, since Dr. Totty was severed as a defendant. The court held that it was an error to sever the claim against him. The general rule will bind all practitioners who treat a patient for the same ailment:

> There can be little doubt that the participation of all potentially responsible persons as parties in the original action would have resulted in a fuller and fairer presentation of the relevant evidence and would have enabled the jury to make a more informed and complete determination of liability.

2. *Multiple Defendants and Burden Shifting*

Where only one of several defendants could have caused the plaintiff's injuries, but the plaintiff cannot adduce evidence as to which defendant is responsible, the courts have developed special rules to protect the obviously deserving plaintiff. Cases like Ybarra v. Spangard, and Anderson v. Somberg, supra, reflect judicial attempts to use doctrines like *res ipsa loquitur* to cover multiple defendant/uncertain proof situations. An equitable doctrine of burden shifting is derived from the exception in the Restatement (Second) Torts, § 433B(3) (1965):

> Where the conduct of two or more actors is tortious, and it is proved that harm has been caused to the plaintiff by only one of them, but there is uncertainty as to which one has caused it, the burden is upon each actor to prove that he has not caused the harm.

The reason for this burden shift is "* * * the injustice of permitting proved wrongdoers, who among them have inflicted an injury upon the entirely innocent plaintiff, to escape liability merely because the nature of their conduct and the resulting harm has made it impossible to prove which of them has caused the harm." Id., comment f.

The DES cases, involving the marketing of drugs and multiple defendants, have taken burden shifting well beyond the common law precedents, with the courts developing a variety of special tests. In Hymowitz v. Eli Lilly and Co., 73 N.Y.2d 487, 541 N.Y.S.2d 941, 539 N.E.2d 1069 (1989), New York's highest court chronicled the efforts by other courts to come to grips with the difficulties inherent in identifying the manufacturer of the particular DES that injured the plaintiff. The court noted the rationale behind burden-shifting generally, to force defendants to come forward or else be held jointly and severally liable.

See Sindell v. Abbott Labs., 26 Cal.3d 588, 163 Cal.Rptr. 132, 607 P.2d 924 (1980). The law review article that gave rise to market share liability is Naomi Sheiner, Comment, DES and a Proposed Theory of Enterprise Liability, 46 Fordham L.Rev. 963 (1978). The best articles on the subject, with full citations to other literature, are David Rosenberg, The Causal Connection in Mass Exposure Cases: A "Public Law" Vision of the Tort System, 97 Harv. L.Rev. 851 (1984), and Richard Wright, Causation in Tort Law, 73 Cal.L.Rev. 1735 (1985). For a useful analysis of the trauma experienced by DES daughters, see R. Apfel and S. Fisher, To Do No Harm: DES and the Dilemmas of Modern Medicine (1984).

The market share theories, while developed in the DES cases, have often been disallowed in vaccine cases. In Shackil v. Lederle Laboratories, 116 N.J. 155, 561 A.2d 511 (N.J.1989), New Jersey rejected a risk-modified market share approach to manufacturers of the pertussis antigen component of a diphtheria, pertussis and tetanus toxoid vaccine (DPT). The court in a long and thoughtful analysis of market share approaches held that such an approach in the vaccine context might discourage a highly valuable activity.

C. ALTERNATIVE CAUSAL TESTS

Proximate cause instructions continue to be given in most states, often confusing jurors just as the doctrine has confused generations of law students. Courts worry that jurors will be misled, particularly where multiple sources of causation are involved. In Peterson v. Gray, 137 N.H. 374, 628 A.2d 244 (N.H. 1993), the plaintiff suffered from arthritis in her hand, and the defendant, a hand surgeon, performed a trapexiectomy that later required wrist fusion. The plaintiff's preexisting condition was clearly implicated in the harm that resulted. The court observed that " ... if the jury determined that the plaintiff's arthritis was '*a* proximate cause' of her wrist fusion, then the defendant's actions could not possibly have been '***the*** proximate cause' ". Id. at 246. At least one state, California, has rejected instructions on proximate cause as unduly confusing to the jury, adopting instead the "substantial factor" test. In Mitchell v. Gonzales, 54 Cal.3d 1041, 1 Cal.Rptr.2d 913, 819 P.2d 872 (Cal. 1991) the California Supreme Court in effect mandated a jury instruction that asks the jury to determine where the defendant's conduct was a "substantial factor" in bringing about harm, allowing a jury to find against the defendant even if their conduct was only a contributing factor. This "substantial factor" test has been around for 25 years, but the influence of California on tort law evolution is likely to push other states to replace the confusing proximate cause instructions with the "substantial factor" test.

The "substantial factor" has come to be used in lieu of the "but for" test in jury instructions where multiple medical actors and concurrent causation are involved. See Vincent by Staton v. Fairbanks Mem. Hosp., 862 P.2d 847 (Alaska 1993).

VI. DAMAGE INNOVATIONS

A. THE "LOSS OF A CHANCE" DOCTRINE

HERSKOVITS v. GROUP HEALTH COOPERATIVE OF PUGET SOUND

Supreme Court of Washington, 1983.
99 Wash.2d 609, 664 P.2d 474.

DORE, JUSTICE.

This appeal raises the issue of whether an estate can maintain an action for professional negligence as a result of failure to timely diagnose lung cancer, where the estate can show probable reduction in statistical chance for survival but cannot show and/or prove that with timely diagnosis and treatment, decedent probably would have lived to normal life expectancy.

Both counsel advised that for the purpose of this appeal we are to *assume* that the respondent Group Health Cooperative of Puget Sound and Dr. William Spencer negligently failed to diagnose Herskovits' cancer on his first visit to the hospital and *proximately* caused a 14 percent reduction in his chances of survival. It is undisputed that Herskovits had less than a 50 percent chance of survival at all times herein.

The main issue we will address in this opinion is whether a patient, with less than a 50 percent chance of survival, has a cause of action against the hospital and its employees if they are negligent in diagnosing a lung cancer which reduces his chances of survival by 14 percent.

* * *

I

The complaint alleged that Herskovits came to Group Health Hospital in 1974 with complaints of pain and coughing. In early 1974, chest x-rays revealed infiltrate in the left lung. Rales and coughing were present. In mid-1974, there were chest pains and coughing, which became persistent and chronic by fall of 1974. A December 5, 1974 entry in the medical records confirms the cough problem. Plaintiff contends that Herskovits was treated thereafter only with cough medicine. No further effort or inquiry was made by Group Health concerning his symptoms, other than an occasional chest x-ray. In the early spring of 1975, Mr. and Mrs. Herskovits went south in the hope that the warm weather would help. Upon his return to the Seattle area with no improvement in his health, Herskovits visited Dr. Jonathan Ostrow on a private basis for another medical opinion. Within 3 weeks, Dr. Ostrow's evaluation and direction to Group Health led to the diagnosis of cancer. In July of 1975, Herskovits' lung was removed, but no radiation or chemotherapy treatments were instituted. Herskovits died 20 months later, on March 22, 1977, at the age of 60.

At hearing on the motion for summary judgment, plaintiff was unable to produce expert testimony that the delay in diagnosis "probably" or "more likely than not" caused her husband's death. The affidavit and deposition of plaintiff's expert witness, Dr. Jonathan Ostrow, construed in the most favorable light possible to plaintiff, indicated that had the diagnosis of lung cancer been made in December 1974, the patient's possibility of 5–year survival was 39 percent. At the time of initial diagnosis of cancer 6 months later, the possibility of a 5–year survival was reduced to 25 percent. Dr. Ostrow testified he felt a diagnosis perhaps could have been made as early as December 1974, or January 1975, about 6 months before the surgery to remove Mr. Herskovits' lung in June 1975.

Dr. Ostrow testified that if the tumor was a "stage 1" tumor in December 1974, Herskovits' chance of a 5–year survival would have been 39 percent. In June 1975, his chances of survival were 25 percent assuming the tumor had progressed to "stage 2". Thus, the delay in diagnosis may have reduced the chance of a 5–year survival by 14 percent.

Dr. William Spencer, the physician from Group Health Hospital who cared for the deceased Herskovits, testified that in his opinion, based upon a reasonable medical probability, earlier diagnosis of the lung cancer that afflicted Herskovits would not have prevented his death, nor would it have lengthened his life. He testified that nothing the doctors at Group Health could have done would have prevented Herskovits' death, as death within several years is a virtual certainty with this type of lung cancer regardless of how early the diagnosis is made.

Plaintiff contends that medical testimony of a reduction of chance of survival from 39 percent to 25 percent is sufficient evidence to allow the proximate cause issue to go to the jury. Defendant Group Health argues conversely that Washington law does not permit such testimony on the issue of medical causation and requires that medical testimony must be at least sufficiently definite to establish that the act complained of "probably" or "more likely than not" caused the subsequent disability. It is Group Health's contention that plaintiff must prove that Herskovits "probably" would have survived had the defendant not been allegedly negligent; that is, the plaintiff must prove there was at least a 51 percent chance of survival.

II

* * *

This court heretofore has not faced the issue of whether, under § 323(a), [of the Restatement (Second) of Torts (1965)] proof that the defendant's conduct increased the risk of death by decreasing the chances of survival is sufficient to take the issue of proximate cause to the jury. Some courts in other jurisdictions have allowed the proximate cause issue to go to the jury on this type of proof. [ ] These courts emphasized the fact that defendants' conduct deprived the decedents of a "significant" chance to survive or recover, rather than requiring proof that with absolute certainty the defendants' conduct caused the physical injury. The underlying reason is that it is not for the wrongdoer, who put the possibility of recovery beyond realization, to say afterward that the result was inevitable. [ ]

Other jurisdictions have rejected this approach, generally holding that unless the plaintiff is able to show that it was *more likely than not* that the harm was caused by the defendant's negligence, proof of a decreased chance of survival is not enough to take the proximate cause question to the jury. [ ]

These courts have concluded that the defendant should not be liable where the decedent more than likely would have died anyway.

The ultimate question raised here is whether the relationship between the increased risk of harm and Herskovits' death is sufficient to hold Group Health responsible. Is a 36 percent (from 39 percent to 25 percent) reduction in the decedent's chance for survival sufficient evidence of causation to allow the jury to consider the possibility that the physician's failure to timely diagnose the illness was the proximate cause of his death? We answer in the affirmative. To decide otherwise would be a blanket release from liability for doctors and hospitals any time there was less than a 50 percent chance of survival, regardless of how flagrant the negligence.

III

[The court then discusses at length the case of *Hamil v. Bashline,* [481 Pa. 256, 392 A.2d 1280 (1978)], where the plaintiff's decedent, suffering from severe chest pains, was negligently treated in the emergency unit of the hospital. The wife, because of the lack of help, took her husband to a private physician's office, where he died. If the hospital had employed proper treatment, the decedent would have had a substantial chance of surviving the attack, stated by plaintiff's medical expert as a 75 percent chance of survival. The defendant's expert witness testified that the patient would have died regardless of any treatment provided by the defendant hospital.]

* * *

* * * In *Hamil* and the instant case, however, the defendant's act or omission failed in a *duty* to protect against harm from *another source.* Thus, as the *Hamil* court noted, the fact finder is put in the position of having to consider not only what *did* occur, but also what *might have* occurred.

* * *

The *Hamil* court held that once a plaintiff has demonstrated that the defendant's acts or omissions have increased the risk of harm to another, such evidence furnishes a basis for the jury to make a determination as to whether such increased risk was in turn a substantial factor in bringing about the resultant harm.

* * *

Under the *Hamil* decision, once a plaintiff has demonstrated that defendant's acts or omissions in a situation to which § 323(a) applies have increased the risk of harm to another, such evidence furnishes a basis for the fact finder to go further and find that such increased risk was in turn a substantial factor in bringing about the resultant harm. The necessary proximate cause will be established if the jury finds such cause. It is not necessary for a plaintiff to introduce evidence to establish that the negligence resulted in the injury or death, but simply that the negligence increased the *risk* of injury or death. The step from the increased risk to causation is one for the jury to make.

* * *

Where percentage probabilities and decreased probabilities are submitted into evidence, there is simply no danger of speculation on the part of the jury. More speculation is involved in requiring the medical expert to testify as to what would have happened had the defendant not been negligent.

Conclusion

* * * We reject Group Health's argument that plaintiffs *must show* that Herskovits "probably" would have had a 51 percent chance of survival if the hospital had not been negligent. We hold that medical testimony of a reduction of chance of survival from 39 percent to 25 percent is sufficient evidence to allow the proximate cause issue to go to the jury.

Causing reduction of the opportunity to recover (loss of chance) by one's negligence, however, does not necessitate a total recovery against the negligent party for all damages caused by the victim's death. Damages should be awarded to the injured party or his family based only on damages caused directly by premature death, such as lost earnings and additional medical expenses, etc.

We reverse the trial court and reinstate the cause of action.

PEARSON, J., concurring.

* * *

* * * I am persuaded * * * by the thoughtful discussion of a recent commentator. King, *Causation, Valuation, and Chance in Personal Injury Torts Involving Preexisting Conditions and Future Consequences,* 90 Yale L.J. 1353 (1981).

* * *

Under the all or nothing approach, typified by *Cooper v. Sisters of Charity of Cincinnati, Inc.,* 27 Ohio St.2d 242, 272 N.E.2d 97 (1971), a plaintiff who establishes that but for the defendant's negligence the decedent had a 51 percent chance of survival may maintain an action for that death. The defendant will be liable for all damages arising from the death, even though there was a 49 percent chance it would have occurred despite his negligence. On the other hand, a plaintiff who establishes that but for the defendant's negligence the decedent had a 49 percent chance of survival recovers nothing.

This all or nothing approach to recovery is criticized by King on several grounds, 90 Yale L.J. at 1376–78. First, the all or nothing approach is arbitrary. Second, it

> subverts the deterrence objectives of tort law by denying recovery for the effects of conduct that causes statistically demonstrable losses * * *. A failure to allocate the cost of these losses to their tortious sources * * * strikes at the integrity of the torts system of loss allocation.

90 Yale L.J. at 1377. Third, the all or nothing approach creates pressure to manipulate and distort other rules affecting causation and damages in an attempt to mitigate perceived injustices. [ ] Fourth, the all or nothing approach gives certain defendants the benefit of an uncertainty which, were it not for their tortious conduct, would not exist. * * * Finally, King argues that the loss of a less than even chance is a loss worthy of redress.

These reasons persuade me that the best resolution of the issue before us is to recognize the loss of a less than even chance as an actionable injury. Therefore, I would hold that plaintiff has established a prima facie issue of proximate cause by producing testimony that defendant probably caused a substantial reduction in Mr. Herskovits' chance of survival. * * *

Finally, it is necessary to consider the amount of damages recoverable in the event that a loss of a chance of recovery is established. Once again, King's discussion provides a useful illustration of the principles which should be applied.

> To illustrate, consider a patient who suffers a heart attack and dies as a result. Assume that the defendant-physician negligently misdiagnosed the patient's condition, but that the patient would have had only a 40% chance of survival even with a timely diagnosis and proper care. Regardless of whether it could be said that the defendant caused the decedent's death, he caused the loss of a chance, and that chance-interest should be completely redressed in its own right. Under the proposed rule, the plaintiff's compensation for the loss of the victim's chance of surviving the heart attack would be 40% of the compensable value of the victim's life had he survived (including what his earning capacity would otherwise have been in the years following death). The value placed on the patient's life would reflect such factors as his age, health, and earning potential, including the fact that he had suffered the heart attack and the assumption that he had survived it. The 40% computation would be applied to that base figure.

(Footnote omitted.) 90 Yale L.J. at 1382.

I would remand to the trial court for proceedings consistent with this opinion.

BRACHTENBACH, JUSTICE (dissenting).

I dissent because I find plaintiff did not meet her burden of proving proximate cause. While the statistical evidence introduced by the expert was relevant and admissible, it was not alone sufficient to maintain a cause of action.

Neither the majority nor Justice Dolliver's dissent focus on the key issue. Both opinions focus on the significance of the 14 percent differentiation in the patient's chance to survive for 5 years and question whether this statistical data is sufficient to sustain a malpractice action. The issue is not so limited. The question should be framed as whether all the evidence amounts to sufficient proof, rising above speculation, that the doctor's conduct was a proximate cause of the patient's death. While the relevancy and the significance of the statistical evidence is a subissue bearing on the sufficiency of the proof, such evidence alone neither proves nor disproves plaintiff's case.

II

Furthermore, the instant case does not present evidence of proximate cause that rises above speculation and conjecture. The majority asserts that evidence of a statistical reduction of the chance to survive for 5 years is sufficient to create a jury question on whether the doctor's conduct was a proximate cause of the death. I disagree that this statistical data can be interpreted in such a manner.

Use of statistical data in judicial proceedings is a hotly debated issue. [ ] Many fear that members of the jury will place too much emphasis on statistical evidence and the statistics will be misused and manipulated by expert witnesses and attorneys. [ ]

Such fears do not support a blanket exclusion of statistical data, however. Our court system is premised on confidence in the jury to understand complex concepts and confidence in the right of cross examination as protection against the misuse of evidence. Attorneys ought to be able to explain the true significance of statistical data to keep it in its proper perspective.

Statistical data should be admissible as evidence if they are relevant, that is, if they have

> any tendency to make the existence of any fact that is of consequence to * * * the action more probable or less probable than it would be without the evidence.

ER 401. The statistics here met that test; they have some tendency to show that those diagnosed at stage one of the disease may have a greater chance to survive 5 years than those diagnosed at stage two.

The problem is, however, that while this statistical fact is relevant, it is not sufficient to prove causation. There is an enormous difference between the "any tendency to prove" standard of ER 401 and the "more likely than not" standard for proximate cause.

* * *

Thus, I would not resolve the instant case simply by focusing on the 14 percent differentiation in the chance to survive 5 years for the different stages of cancer. Instead, I would accept this as an admissible fact, but not as proof of proximate cause. To meet the proximate cause burden, the record would need to reveal other facts about the patient that tended to show that he would have been a member of the 14 percent group whose chance of 5 years' survival could be increased by early diagnosis.

Such evidence is not in the record. Instead, the record reveals that Mr. Herskovits' cancer was located such that corrective surgery "would be more formidable". This would tend to show that his chance of survival may have been less than the statistical average. Moreover, the statistics relied on did not take into consideration the location of the tumor, therefore their relevance to Mr. Herskovits' case must be questioned. Clerk's Papers, at 41.

In addition, as the tumor was relatively small in size when removed (2 to 3 centimeters), the likelihood that it would have been detected in 1974, even if the proper test were performed, was less than average. This uncertainty further reduces the probability that the doctor's failure to perform the tests was a proximate cause of a reduced chance of survival.

Other statistics admitted into evidence also tend to show the inconclusiveness of the statistics relied on by the majority. One study showed the *two*-year survival rate for this type of cancer to be 46.6 percent for stage one and 39.8 percent for stage two. Mr. Herskovits lived for 20 months after surgery, which was 26 months after defendant allegedly should have discovered the cancer. Therefore, regardless of the stage of the cancer at the time Mr. Herskovits was examined by defendant, it cannot be concluded that he survived significantly less than the average survival time. Hence, it is pure speculation to suppose that the doctor's negligence "caused" Mr. Herskovits to die sooner than he would have otherwise. Such speculation does not rise to the level of a jury question on the issue of proximate cause. Therefore, the trial court correctly dismissed the case. [ ]

The apparent harshness of this conclusion cannot be overlooked. The combination of the loss of a loved one to cancer and a doctor's negligence in diagnosis seems to compel a finding of liability. Nonetheless, justice must be dealt with an even hand. To hold a defendant liable without proof that his actions *caused* plaintiff harm would open up untold abuses of the litigation system.

Cases alleging misdiagnosis of cancer are increasing in number, perhaps because of the increased awareness of the importance of early detection. These cases, however, illustrate no more than an inconsistency among courts in their treatment of the problems of proof. *See* Annot., *Malpractice in Connection with Diagnosis of Cancer,* 79 A.L.R.3d 915 (1977). Perhaps as medical science becomes more knowledgeable about this disease and more sophisticated in its detection and treatment of it, the balance may tip in favor of imposing liability on doctors who negligently fail to promptly diagnose the disease. But, until a formula is found that will protect doctors against liability imposed through speculation as well as afford truly aggrieved plaintiffs their just compensation, I cannot favor the wholesale abandonment of the principle of proximate cause. For these reasons, I dissent.

Notes and Questions

1. How would damages be figured under the majority's approach? Under the Pearson/King theory? What is the relationship between causation and damages in these cases? The majority and Pearson opinions would effectively permit recovery but reduce damages as the causation link weakens. Is this a reasonable approach?

2. Judicial approaches to the loss of a chance can be grouped into four categories.

a. All or nothing. The traditional rule allows the plaintiff no recovery unless survival was more likely than not. A less than 51% chance of survival receives nothing. Borowski v. Von Solbrig, 60 Ill.2d 418, 328 N.E.2d 301 (1975). Plaintiff who proves a chance of survival greater than 50% can receive judgment with no discount for the chance that the loss would have occurred without negligence. This award is based on the physical injury suffered and not the lost chance to avoid it. See Cooper v. Sisters of Charity, Inc., 27 Ohio St.2d 242, 272 N.E.2d 97 (1971).

Texas rejected the loss of a chance doctrine in Kramer v. Lewisville Memorial Hospital, 858 S.W.2d 397, 405 (Tex.1993). "Below reasonable probability, however, we do not believe that a sufficient number of alternative explanations and hypotheses for the cause of the harm are eliminated to permit a judicial determination of responsibility.... The more likely than not standard is thus not some arbitrary, irrational benchmark for cutting off malpractice recoveries, but rather a fundamental prerequisite of an ordered system of justice." See also Pillsbury–Flood v. Portsmouth Hospital, 128 N.H. 299, 512 A.2d 1126 (1986) (doctrine rejected; "causation is a matter of probability, not possibility"); Gooding v.

University Hosp. Bldg., Inc., 445 So.2d 1015 (Fla.1984) ("Health care providers could find themselves defending cases simply because a patient fails to improve or where serious disease processes are not arrested because another course of action could possibly bring a better result.")

b. Loss of an appreciable or substantial chance of recovery. Jeanes v. Milner, 428 F.2d 598 (8th Cir.1970). This approach does not give proportional recovery based on the percentage of harm attributable to the defendant, instead manipulating the burden of proof rather than acknowledging the lost chance as the real injury. See Hicks v. United States, 368 F.2d 626 (4th Cir.1966). Defining "substantial possibility" has troubled some courts. Borgren v. United States, 716 F.Supp. 1378 (D.Kan.1989).

c. Increased risk of harm. This approach, found in the Restatement (Second), Torts, section 323(a) and adopted by the majority in *Herskovits*, lowers causation requirements to allow causes of action for those who have a less than 50% chance of survival. Hamil v. Bashline, 481 Pa. 256, 392 A.2d 1280 (Pa. 1978). Compensation is for the increased risk of harm rather than loss of a chance, and damage awards are not discounted for the percentage of harm caused by the physician, death is typically the compensable injury. Any percentage is enough to get to the jury. See Thompson v. Sun City Community Hospital, Inc., 141 Ariz. 597, 688 P.2d 605 (Ariz. 1984) (linking Restatement (Second), Torts, section 323A to the interest seen as "the chance itself"); Mayhue v. Sparkman, 653 N.E.2d 1384 (Ind.1995)(rejects lost chance but lightens plaintiff's burden of proving causation.) For further discussion, see Beth Clemens Boggs, Lost Chance of Survival Doctrine: Should Courts Ever Tinker With Chance? 16 So. Ill. Univ. L. U. 421 (1992).

d. Compensation for the loss of a chance. This looks at damages that include the value of the patient's life reduced in proportion to the lost chance. This approach was developed by Joseph King in his seminal article, Causation, Valuation and Chance in Personal Injury Torts Involving Pre-existing Conditions and Future Consequences, 90 Yale L.J. 1353 (1981). The approach requires a percentage probability test, with the value of the patient's life determined and damages decreased accordingly. This approach was considered in Pearson's concurring opinion in *Herskovits*. Iowa adopted the approach in DeBurkarte v. Louvar, 393 N.W.2d 131 (Iowa 1986). Ohio adopted it in Roberts v. Ohio Permanente Medical Group, Inc., 76 Ohio St.3d 483, 668 N.E.2d 480 (1996), and South Dakota in Jorgenson v. Vener, 616 N.W.2d 366 (S.D.2000).

Loss of a chance and increased risk are grounded in the same justifications of deterring negligent conduct and compensating for real harms that happen to fall below the fifty percent threshold of traditional tort doctrine. Increased risk allows recovery for harm that has not yet occurred, while loss of a chance requires the plaintiff to wait until the condition occurs and then sue. See generally United States v. Anderson, 669 A.2d 73 (Del.1995).

2. What problems do you foresee with the application of the "loss of a chance" doctrine to medical practice? Note that the evidence as to risk must be put in probabilistic form for the jury to consider. What about Judge Brachtenbach's concerns about the weight to be given statistical evidence? Would his concerns always prevent the use of statistics in litigation? Or can you offer some solutions to his problems?

3. Ultimate outcome instructions. Lost chance cases require calculations that assume a probability of loss and an ultimate outcome if the defendant's treatment had been faultless. One example of an "ultimate outcome" charge is

found in the New Jersey Model Jury Charges (Civil)(4th ed.) § 5.36E (emphasis added):

> If you find that defendant has sustained his/her burden of proof, then you must determine based on the evidence what is the likelihood, on a percentage basis, that the plaintiff's ultimate injuries (*condition*) would have occurred even if defendant's treatment was proper. When you are determining the amount of damages to be awarded to the plaintiff, you should award the total amount of damage. Your award should not be reduced by your allocation of harm. The adjustment in damages which may be required will be performed by the Court.

See generally Fischer v. Canario, M.D., 143 N.J. 235, 670 A.2d 516, 524–526 (1996).

4. A judicial illustration of the calculation process for loss of a chance is found in McKellips v. St. Francis Hospital, Inc., 741 P.2d 467 (Okl.1987):

> "To illustrate the method in a case where the jury determines from the statistical findings combined with the specific facts relevant to the patient, the patient originally had a 40% chance of cure and the physician's negligence reduced the chance of cure to 25%, (40%–25%) 15% represents the patient's loss of survival. If the total amount of damages proved by the evidence is $500,000, the damages caused by defendant is 15% x $500,000 or $75,000 * * *."

This has come to be called the percentage apportionment of damages method. A detailed application of the percentage apportionment approach is found in Boody v. United States, 706 F.Supp. 1458 (D.Kan.1989). See also Mays v. United States, 608 F.Supp. 1476 (D.Colo.1985).

5. Another judicial approach to these calculations is to treat the loss of a chance as a wrong separate from wrongful death, and allow the jury to set a dollar amount based on all the evidence, without mechanically applying a percentage to a total damage award. See Smith v. State of Louisiana, 676 So.2d 543 (1996), where the court held that

> * * * the method we adopt today in this decision, is for the factfinder—judge or jury—to focus on the chance of survival lost on account of malpractice as a distinct compensable injury and to value the lost chance as a lump sum award based on all the evidence in the record, as is done for any other item of general damages.

A third approach is simply to recognize the full survival or wrongful death damages, without regard to the lost chance of survival.

6. Can a person recover for the loss of a chance if a physician negligently fails to diagnose AIDS or improperly performs the tests for the HIV virus? In Morton v. Mutchnick, 904 S.W.2d 14 (Mo.App.1995), the court held that if doctors negligently fail to diagnose AIDS, the doctrine does not apply. Their reasoning was that with AIDS, death is inevitable, so that a decedent does not suffer "loss of life, but rather, a shortening of life." Isn't death inevitable for everyone? Why would the court carve out AIDS as a special case? Given new drug therapies for AIDS, life expectancy has increased substantially.

7. One author has described the "loss of a chance" doctrine as one of the "ethereal" torts. See Nancy Levit, Ethereal Torts, 61 Geo. Wash. L. Rev. 136 (1992), arguing that such torts should be taken seriously: "The individual expectancy, dignity, and autonomy interests that ethereal torts protect are intrinsically

valuable." Other useful articles discussing the "loss of a chance" problem include: Joseph King, Causation, Valuation and Chance in Personal Injury Torts Involving Preexisting Conditions and Future Consequences, 90 Yale L.J. 1353 (1981); Darrell L. Keith, Loss of Chance: A Modern Proportional Approach to Damages in Texas, 44 Baylor L. Rev. 759 (1992); Lisa Perrochet, Sandra J. Smith and Ugo Colella, Lost Chance Recovery and the Folly of Expanding Medical Malpractice Liability, 27 Tort & Ins. L.J. 615 (1992) (50–state survey of the doctrine's acceptance or rejection in the courts; the authors attack the doctrine because it may have "an adverse impact on the cost and quality of health care.")

Problem: The Patient's Choice?

Jane Rogers was a fair complected woman in her early thirties. She had worked every summer during high school and college as a lifeguard at the beach. While she was in graduate school, one of her sisters was diagnosed as having melanoma, a deadly cancer that is often fatal if not detected and treated early. Melanoma is more prevalent in people who have fair complexions, and prolonged exposure to the sun over time, particularly severe sun burns, are a risk factor for the cancer.

Ms. Roger's sister died. The family physician, Dr. James, told the family members that they should all get a thorough physical to check for signs of skin tumors that might be precancerous. Ms. Rogers went to the University Student Clinic and requested a physical examination. She explained why she was worried. Dr. Gillespie, an older physician who had retired from active practice and now helped out part-time at the Clinic, examined her. He observed a nodule on her upper back, but incorrectly diagnosed it as a birthmark. He told her not to worry. She continued her lifeguarding and water safety instruction activities during the summer, to pay for her graduate education.

At a party one Friday night, Ms. Rogers met a young physician who was a resident at the University hospital. She was wearing a shoulderless dress, and the resident, Dr. Wunch, noted a mole on her shoulder. He recognized it as a melanoma. He pointed it out to her, and told her that she really ought to get it checked. He gave her his card, with his phone number, and said he would be glad to set her up with an appointment with a good cancer specialist at the hospital. Ms. Rogers called, made an appointment, and filled out the forms required by the University Hospital, but then missed her appointment. She never went back.

A year later, during a routine physical as part of an employment application, the examining physician found several large growths on Ms. Roger's back. She was diagnosed as having melanoma, which had spread into her blood and had metastasized into her lymph nodes. She was dead within a year.

What problems do you see with the suit by her estate against the available defendants?

B. INCREASED RISKS AND FEAR OF THE FUTURE

PETRIELLO v. KALMAN

Supreme Court of Connecticut, 1990.
215 Conn. 377, 576 A.2d 474.

[The court considered two issues on appeal. First, plaintiff alleged that the defendant hospital had a duty to ensure that the plaintiff had given her informed consent to surgery before she was medicated. The court held no such duty existed. Second, the defendant physician contended that the plaintiff could not be rewarded damages for increased risk of future injury.]

SHEA, ASSOC. J.

* * *

The jury could reasonably have found the following facts from the evidence. On April 13, 1984, the plaintiff, who was sixteen weeks pregnant, was seen by the defendant Kalman regarding her complaints of low back pain and vaginal bleeding. Kalman, a specialist in obstetrics,[1] had been treating the plaintiff throughout her pregnancy. As a result of his examination, Kalman diagnosed a possible missed abortion or threatened abortion and, therefore, admitted the plaintiff to the Griffin Hospital later that evening. On the basis of his belief that the plaintiff's child had died, an ultrasound examination was performed the next morning. This test revealed that the child had in fact died in utero. Kalman was advised of the ultrasound results and he then telephoned the plaintiff, who remained at the hospital, informing her that the results of the test indicated fetal death and that he intended to perform, later that afternoon, a surgical procedure known as a dilatation and curettage to remove the fetus from the plaintiff's womb.

* * *

That afternoon, during the procedure to remove the fetus, Kalman, utilizing a suction device, perforated the plaintiff's uterus and drew portions of her small intestine through the perforation, through her uterus and into her vagina. The plaintiff's expert, Phillip Sullivan, an obstetrician, testified that Kalman had used excessive force in the operation of the suction device and that the perforation had resulted from a deviation from the prevailing standard of care. Kalman, in an attempt to repair the damage to the uterine wall, made a transverse incision on the plaintiff's abdomen and requested the assistance of Jose Flores, a general surgeon. Because he could not adequately explore the plaintiff's abdomen, Flores made another incision perpendicular to the one made by the defendant. Flores repaired the injury to the plaintiff's intestine by means of a bowel resection, removing approximately one foot of the intestine and connecting the two ends of the remaining intestine.

Flores, testifying for the plaintiff, stated that, as a result of the bowel resection, adhesions had more probably than not formed in the plaintiff's abdomen. He also testified that the plaintiff faces an increased risk of future bowel obstruction as a result of these adhesions, but that he thought the risk was remote. Flores stated that, in his experience, adhesions were a prominent cause of small bowel obstruction and that he had advised the plaintiff, after the surgery, that adhesions would form in her abdomen and that they could result in a future bowel obstruction. The plaintiff testified that she was also advised of this increased risk of future bowel obstruction by Flores' partner, who was also a physician. The plaintiff's expert, Sullivan, also testified that the plaintiff was subject to an increased risk of future bowel obstruction and that, based on literature he had consulted, she had an 8 to 16 percent chance of developing such an obstruction.

1. The defendant was not employed by the hospital, but, rather, was an independent physician possessing privileges at the hospital.

The plaintiff brought her revised complaint in two counts, alleging that Kalman was negligent in that he: (1) performed the dilatation and curettage without first attempting other nonsurgical methods; (2) perforated the plaintiff's uterus during the surgical procedure; (3) suctioned out portions of the plaintiff's small intestine during the surgical procedure; and (4) made an improper incision in the plaintiff's abdomen during his attempt to repair the plaintiff's small intestine. * * *

I

* * *

II

In his appeal, the defendant claims that the trial court erred by: (1) allowing expert testimony concerning the plaintiff's increased risk of a bowel obstruction; (2) charging the jury that the plaintiff could be compensated for her fear that such an obstruction will occur; and (3) charging the jury that the plaintiff could be compensated for the increased risk that she will suffer a future bowel obstruction. We conclude that the expert testimony was admissible and that the court correctly instructed the jury.

A

The defendant claims that the plaintiff should not have been permitted to present any testimony regarding her increased susceptibility to a future bowel obstruction resulting from the defendant's actions. * * * During a hearing conducted as a result of the defendant's motion in limine, the plaintiff argued that the evidence concerning her increased risk of bowel obstruction was admissible for three reasons: (1) as evidence of her fear of future disability; (2) as evidence that her fear was rational; and (3) as evidence of a presently compensable injury. We conclude that the evidence was admissible for all three purposes.

The defendant has chosen to ignore the fact that the plaintiff, in her revised complaint, alleged that as a result of the defendant's actions she "experienced extreme emotional distress." At trial, she sought to prove that her emotional distress was caused, at least in part, by her fear of suffering an obstruction of her bowel at some later date and that she should be compensated for that fear. We have previously held that evidence concerning an increased risk of injury, although insufficient to justify an award of damages based upon the occurrence of that injury in the future, may, nevertheless, be presented to the jury as evidence of emotional distress. * * * [T]he jury was entitled, in this case, to hear testimony that the plaintiff had been informed of the increased risk of future bowel obstruction, as well as testimony regarding any anxiety this information produced in the plaintiff's mind.

The expert testimony, regarding the plaintiff's increased risk of suffering a future bowel obstruction, was also admissible on the issue of whether the plaintiff's anxiety was rationally based. Although "[s]ome courts have permitted recovery where there is not even a possibility that the feared disability will develop * * * [m]ore often there is a requirement that the plaintiff's anxiety have some reasonable basis." D. Faulkner & K. Woods, "Fear of Future Disability—An Element of Damages in a Personal Injury Action," 7

W.New Eng.L.Rev. 865, 877–78 (1985). [ ] Thus, the evidence objected to by the defendant was admissible to show that the plaintiff's anxiety regarding the possibility of a future bowel obstruction was both subjectively held and objectively reasonable.

Finally, given that we resolve the question of the compensability of an increased risk of future injury in favor of the plaintiff, the expert testimony, regarding the extent of that risk in this case, was also admissible for the purpose of showing how likely it was that the plaintiff would experience a bowel obstruction at some later date.

B

The defendant also claims that, even if the expert testimony was admissible, the court erred in allowing the jury to award the plaintiff compensation for her fear of a future bowel obstruction, since the evidence established that there was only a possibility that the plaintiff would develop a bowel obstruction and this possibility was too speculative to support the inclusion in the verdict of damages for such a fear. The defendant argues that "the Plaintiff's [chance] of incurring a bowel obstruction is 'so remote' that it is not a proper element of damages." We conclude that the evidence presented was sufficient to establish a reasonable basis for the plaintiff's fear that she will suffer from a future bowel obstruction and, therefore, was also sufficient to support compensation for that fear. Although one of the plaintiff's expert witnesses, Flores, testified that there was a "very remote" chance that such a blockage would occur, the testimony of another expert, Sullivan, presented to the jury the results of research conducted by him which indicated that, according to two studies he consulted, there was between an 8 and 16 percent chance that the plaintiff would suffer a future bowel obstruction as a result of the bowel resection necessitated by the defendant's actions. Thus, even if Flore's [sic] testimony was insufficient to establish a reasonable ground for the plaintiff's anxiety, we conclude that the jury could have found a sufficient basis in the opinion rendered by Sullivan. [ ] We conclude, therefore, that the court correctly instructed the jury that it might award the plaintiff damages for her fear of the increased risk that she will someday suffer from a bowel obstruction.

C

The defendant's principal claim on appeal is that the court erred by instructing the jury that the plaintiff could be awarded compensation for the increased risk that the defendant's negligence would cause her to experience a bowel obstruction at some future date. The defendant excepted to this instruction at trial upon the ground that the "intestinal blockage [was] purely speculation" and had not been shown to be "reasonably probable." He raises essentially the same claim on appeal.

The defendant contends that the evidence in this case established no reasonable probability that the plaintiff would suffer a bowel obstruction at some future date, and, therefore, the trial court incorrectly instructed the jury that the plaintiff should be compensated for whatever risk there was of some future injury. The jury heard expert testimony that the risk of the plaintiff suffering a future bowel obstruction was somewhere between 8 and 16 percent. There is no question that such a degree of probability of the occurrence of future injury would not support an award of damages to the same extent as if that injury had in fact occurred. In *Healy v. White,* supra, at 444, 378 A.2d 540, we reasoned that in order to be awarded full compensation for an injury that has not yet manifested itself, a plaintiff must show that there exists a reasonable probability that the injury will in fact occur. * * *

In *Healy,* we affirmed our adherence to the prevailing all or nothing standard for compensating those who have either suffered present harm and seek compensation as if the harm will be permanent, or have suffered present harm and seek compensation for possible future consequences of that harm. * * * By denying any compensation unless a plaintiff proves that a future consequence is more likely to occur than not, courts have created a system in which a significant number of persons receive compensation for future consequences that never occur and, conversely, a significant number of persons receive no compensation at all for consequences that later ensue from risks not rising to the level of probability. This system is inconsistent with the goal of compensating tort victims fairly for all the consequences of the injuries they have sustained, while avoiding, so far as possible, windfall awards for consequences that never happen.

In seeking to enforce their right to individualized compensation, plaintiffs in negligence cases are confronted by the requirements that they must claim all applicable damages in a single cause of action; [ ] and must bring their actions no "more than three years from the date of the act or omission complained of." General Statutes § 52–584. Under these circumstances, no recovery may be had for future consequences of an injury when the evidence at trial does not satisfy the more probable than not criterion approved in *Healy,* despite a substantial risk of such consequences. Conversely, a defendant cannot seek reimbursement from a plaintiff who may have recovered for a future consequence, which appeared likely at the time of trial, on the ground that subsequent events have made that consequence remote or impossible. Our legal system provides no opportunity for a second look at a damage award so that it may be revised with the benefit of hindsight. * * *

If the plaintiff in this case had claimed that she was entitled to compensation to the extent that a future bowel obstruction was a certainty, she would have been foreclosed from such compensation solely on the basis of her experts' testimony that the likelihood of the occurrence of a bowel obstruction was either very remote or only 8 to 16 percent probable. Her claim, however, was for compensation for the increased risk that she would suffer such an obstruction sometime in the future. If this increased risk was more likely than not the result of the bowel resection necessitated by the defendant's actions, we conclude that there is no legitimate reason why she should not receive present compensation based upon the likelihood of the risk becoming a reality. When viewed in this manner, the plaintiff was attempting merely to establish the extent of her present injuries. She should not be burdened with proving that the occurrence of a future event is more likely than not, when it is a present risk, rather than a future event for which she claims damages. In our judgment, it was fairer to instruct the jury to compensate the plaintiff for the increased risk of a bowel obstruction based upon the likelihood of its occurrence rather than to ignore that risk entirely. The medical evidence in this case concerning the probability of such a future consequence provided a sufficient basis for estimating that likelihood and compensating the plaintiff for it.

This view is consistent with the Second Restatement of the Law of Torts, which states, in § 912, that "[o]ne to whom another has tortiously caused harm is entitled to compensatory damages for the harm if, but only if, he establishes by proof the extent of the harm and the amount of money representing adequate compensation with as much certainty as the nature of the tort and the circumstances permit." Damages for the future consequences of an injury can never be forecast with certainty. With respect to awards for permanent injuries, actuarial tables of average life expectancy are commonly used to assist the trier in measuring the loss a plaintiff is likely to sustain from the future effects of an injury. Such statistical evidence does, of course, satisfy the more likely than not standard as to the duration of a permanent injury. Similar evidence, based upon medical statistics of the average incidence of a particular future consequence from an injury, such as that produced by the plaintiff in this case, may be said to establish with the same degree of certitude the likelihood of the occurrence of the future harm to which a tort victim is exposed as a result of a present injury. Such evidence provides an adequate basis for measuring damages for the risk to which the victim has been exposed because of a wrongful act.

The probability percentage for the occurrence of a particular harm, the risk of which has been created by the tortfeasor, can be applied to the damages that would be justified if that harm should be realized. We regard this system of compensation as preferable to our present practice of denying any recovery for substantial risks of future harm not satisfying the more likely than not standard. We also believe that such a system is fairer to a defendant, who should be required to pay damages for a future loss based upon the statistical probability that such a loss will be sustained rather than upon the assumption that the loss is a certainty because it is more likely than not. We hold, therefore, that in a tort action, a plaintiff who has established a breach of duty that was a substantial factor in causing a present injury which has resulted in an increased risk of future harm is entitled to compensation to the extent that the future harm is likely to occur. [ ]

Applying this holding to the facts of this case, we conclude that the trial court correctly instructed the jury that the plaintiff could be awarded compensation for the increased likelihood that she will suffer a bowel obstruction some time in the future. The court's instruction was fully in accord with our holding today. * * *

The judgment of the trial court is affirmed.

* * *

Notes and Questions

1. *Petriello* allows a plaintiff to recover for the risk of future harm, and for the fear that such a risk will materialize. Is this double recovery? *Herskovits* and other "loss of a chance" cases involve missed diagnoses, usually in oncology situations. *Petriello* involves a botched procedure, leaving the plaintiff at an enhanced risk of future injury. What kind of evidence may the plaintiff produce as to the fear of future harm? How do *Petriello* and *Herskovits* differ?

2. Recovery for fear of future harm, based on increased risk, is relatively rare in American case law. See Ferrara v. Galluchio, 5 N.Y.2d 16, 176 N.Y.S.2d 996, 152 N.E.2d 249 (1958); Howard v. Mt. Sinai Hospital, Inc., 63 Wis.2d 515, 217 N.W.2d 383 (1974).

C. PUNITIVE DAMAGES

In the normal malpractice case, damages typically include special damages, such as costs of treating a condition and loss of earning capacity; and general damages, primarily pain and suffering. Punitive damages are extremely rare. See Chapter 5, Section III.D. for a discussion of such punitive damages in informed consent cases. Impatience and inattention to a patient's condition can however lead to punitive damage awards in egregious cases. In Dempsey v. Phelps, 700 So.2d 1340 (Ala.1997), the parents of a two year old child sued, after the child was treated for a clubfoot condition caused by spina bifida and got an infection after surgery, ultimately losing his big toe. The central issue was whether the physician's conduct rose to the level of wantonness, meriting punitive damages. After the surgery, Dr. Dempsey told the mother to bring the boy back a month later, even though postoperative wound healing infections are a common complication that need to be monitored more frequently. The mother testified that "on the top of the foot all the toes were purple and blue and red on the side some. And the top of the foot had kind of a mushy looking place on it that it was draining. It had some drainage on it there and it was—a little black around the edges and it was red. It was just 'real inflamed looking' ". The boy also had diarrhea and fever and wouldn't eat. Dr. Dempsey's response to Mrs. Phelps was that these were common conditions, nothing to worry about, and he did nothing for the fever or anything else. She came back the next day and Dr. Dempsey wouldn't even see the boy at first, and then he said it was just cast blisters, even though, in the mother's words, "[i]t was starting to smell." She came back again the next day and he was very annoyed, and failed to take the boy's temperature, check his lungs or do anything else. The jury awarded $125,000 punitive damage award, on top of other damages, in light of Dr. Dempsey's failures to properly follow-up the child's care.

Problem: The Toxic Dentist

You have been approached by the family of a young woman, Kim Brennan, to explore the possibilities of a tort suit. Kim, a twenty-one year old college student, recently underwent oral surgery and had several wisdom teeth extracted by Dr. James, a local oral surgeon.

Kim has recently learned that Dr. James is now hospitalized with AIDS. She has been tested for the HIV virus and her last test was negative. She has been reading up on AIDS, however, and learned that a small percentage of individuals can carry the HIV virus and not seroconvert (become HIV positive) for an extended period of time, so that they will not test positive (95% of exposed individuals will seroconvert within six months after exposure). She is terrified of entering into romantic relationships now and feels constantly anxious.

Can Kim sue Dr. James? What theories of recovery are possible? Is there any merit to such a suit?

Chapter 5

THE PROFESSIONAL–PATIENT RELATIONSHIP

INTRODUCTION

Health care today is delivered within institutions, whether hospitals, ambulatory care clinics, or offices of managed care organizations, but the individual physician still sees the patient, diagnoses the problem, and prescribes the treatment. Professional liability, discussed in Chapter 4, supra, focuses upon a breach of duty of care owed by the physician to a particular patient. The threshold question is whether the doctor had a relationship with the patient sufficient to create a duty of care.

A physician-patient relationship is usually a prerequisite to a professional malpractice suit against a doctor. When for example a doctor employed by an insurance company examines an individual for the purpose of qualifying him for insurance coverage, most courts considering the issue have held that a doctor owes no duty to the individual to treat or to disclose problems discovered during the examination. See Ervin v. American Guardian Life Assur., 376 Pa.Super. 132, 545 A.2d 354 (1988) (no duty owed by doctor employed by an insurance company to the plaintiff, where doctor examined the plaintiff for purposes of insurance and failed to discover or disclose his cardiac abnormalities to him; plaintiff died a month after the examination from his heart condition); Ney v. Axelrod, 723 A.2d 719 (Pa.Super.1999). But see Ranier v. Frieman, 294 N.J.Super. 182, 682 A.2d 1220 (1996)(social security claimant sued ophthalmologist retained by the government to examine claimant, who failed to diagnose a brain tumor; the court held that the physician had a duty to make a professionally reasonable and competent diagnosis, in spite of the lack of privity of contract); Smith v. Welch, 265 Kan. 868, 967 P.2d 727 (Kan.1998)(Where a physician is retained to provide an expert medical opinion by performing a physical examination, he has a duty to use reasonable and ordinary care in the examination).

Workplace examinations of employees may give rise to a physician-patient relationship. See Green v. Walker, 910 F.2d 291 (5th Cir.1990) (physician-patient relationship should include employees examined by a company physician for employment purposes; "[t]his relationship imposes upon the examining physician a duty to conduct the requested tests and diagnose the results thereof, exercising the level of care consistent with the doctor's professional training and expertise, and to take reasonable steps to make information available timely to the examinee of any findings that pose an imminent danger to the examinee's physical or mental well-being.")

The threshold duty continues to evolve in the setting of independent or workplace physician examinations of employees or potential insureds. In Webb v. T.D., 287 Mont. 68, 951 P.2d 1008 (Mont.1997), the court articulated a compound duty on physicians retained by third parties to do independent medical examinations:

1. to exercise ordinary care to discover those conditions which pose an imminent danger to the examinee's physical or mental well-being and take reasonable steps to communicate to the examinee the presence of any such condition;

2. to exercise ordinary care to assure that when he or she advises an examinee about her condition following an independent examination, the advice comports with the standard of care for the health care provider's profession.

I. THE CONTRACT BETWEEN PATIENT AND PHYSICIAN

A. EXPRESS AND IMPLIED CONTRACT

DINGLE v. BELIN

Court of Appeals of Maryland, 2000.
358 Md. 354, 749 A.2d 157.

The issue before us was characterized by the Court of Special Appeals in this case as one of "ghost surgery." The more precise question is whether a surgeon who is employed by a patient to perform certain surgery and who agrees, as part of that employment, to do the actual cutting, leaving to assisting residents a subordinate role, may be held liable for breach of contract, distinct from negligence in the performance of the surgery or negligence associated with the failure to obtain informed consent from the patient, if the surgeon attends and participates in the surgery but permits a resident to do that cutting.

* * *

Background

On June 29, 1993, Ms. Belin, employed petitioner, Lenox Dingle, a general surgeon with operating privileges at Mercy Hospital in Baltimore, to perform a laparoscopic cholecystectomy—the removal of her gall bladder through a small incision in her abdomen. In brief, the surgery involves making the incision and inserting at least three ports into the abdomen. Carbon dioxide is introduced into the abdomen to expand the area and make it more visible. A camera, inserted through one of the ports, displays the interior on two high-definition television monitors. Observing the monitor, one physician, through another port, retracts the organs and tissues in order to isolate the gall bladder and the structures that connect it to other organs and tissues, and a second physician, also observing the monitor, cuts and clips those connecting structures and removes the gall bladder through a port.

The surgery occurred at Mercy on July 2. Dr. Dingle was assisted by a medical student and by a resident, Dr. Magnuson, who was just beginning her fourth year of residency training. The student was responsible for operating the camera, which was done properly. Dr. Dingle did the retractions, exposing the field. Dr. Magnuson dissected the gall bladder and removed it. She and Dr. Dingle regarded the surgery as routine, without incident. There was, however, a problem. One of the connecting structures that needed to be dissected was the cystic duct, which runs from the gall bladder to the common bile duct. The common bile duct runs from the liver to the intestines. Instead of dissecting the cystic duct, Dr. Magnuson dissected and clipped the common bile duct, which resulted in the drainage of bile into Ms. Belin's abdomen. That, in turn, led to a great deal of pain and discomfort and to the need for extensive corrective surgery at Johns Hopkins Hospital.

In November, 1996, after having waived arbitration pursuant to Maryland Code, § 3–2A–06(b) of the Courts and Judicial Proceedings Article, respondent filed suit against Dr. Dingle, Dr. Magnuson, and Mercy Hospital in the Circuit Court for Baltimore City. The amended complaint now before us contained four counts—negligence based on the lack of informed consent, battery, negligence in the performance of the surgery, and breach of contract. Aside from the negligence alleged as part of the lack of informed consent, Dr. Dingle was not charged with any separate negligence in delegating duties or responsibilities to Dr. Magnuson. The claim of general negligence focused solely on the actual conduct of the surgery.

* * *

The claims for breach of contract and lack of informed consent were both based on the assertion that, when Ms. Belin employed Dr. Dingle, she insisted, and he agreed, that, although he would be assisted in the surgery by one or more residents, he would do the actual cutting and removal of the gall bladder. In Count One—lack of informed consent—she alleged that "[b]ecause Belin was aware that Mercy was a university affiliated hospital and often used for teaching inexperienced residents in various surgical techniques, Belin requested and received assurances from Dingle that he would perform the surgical procedure in the cholecystectomy and only use a resident to assist him as was absolutely necessary." The thrust of Count One was the assertion that, without Belin's knowledge or consent, the resident Magnuson "played a very active role in the surgery" and "did the cutting, clamping and stapling that should have been performed by [Dingle]" and that, by failing to inform Belin of the scope of responsibilities that would be performed by Magnuson, Dingle and Magnuson "breached their duty to secure the fully informed consent of Belin prior to commencing operating upon her." Had she been aware of the active role to be played by Magnuson, Belin asserted, she would not have consented to having the surgery performed at Mercy or by Drs. Dingle and Magnuson. For that breach of duty, Ms. Belin sought compensation for all injuries and losses, past, present, and future, sustained by her, all of which, she claimed, were caused by the defendants' negligence in failing to obtain her informed consent.

Count Four, alleging the breach of contract, incorporated all of the allegations stated in the other counts. It added that Dingle had entered into an oral contract with Belin under which he had agreed "that he would do the identification of the anatomy and the cutting and clipping required during the [surgery] and not a resident or other assistant," and that, in consideration of that agreement, she agreed to allow Dingle to perform the surgery. Dingle breached that contract, she averred, by permitting Dr. Magnuson to perform the cutting and clipping of the gall bladder and related structures. The same measure of damages was asserted—"compensation for all injuries, damages and losses, past, present and future, which she has sustained, is sustaining and will sustain in the future, all of which were caused by the breach of contract."

It was undisputed that Drs. Dingle and Magnuson both participated in the surgery, that Dr. Dingle did the necessary retractions, and that Dr. Magnuson performed the dissections and removed the gall bladder. It was also undisputed that Ms. Belin had no contact whatever with Dr. Magnuson before the surgery, although she was aware that one or more residents would be assisting Dr. Dingle.

The evidence regarding the alleged contract and what Dr. Dingle said and agreed to do was in sharp dispute. Ms. Belin testified that she told Dingle "that I wanted him to be the one that was going to cut me and identify the gall bladder and take it out," that he advised her that he could not do the surgery by himself, and that she said she understood "but if you have a resident in there, I just want that person to maybe suture me up." She added, "I want you to be the one to do my surgery. And he agreed." Ms. Belin informed the jury that, as a surgical technician who worked at Mercy, she was aware that it was a teaching hospital and that surgeons often allowed residents to play a major role in surgery, and she did not want her surgery to be used for training purposes.

The written consent that Ms. Belin signed authorized Dr. Dingle "and/or such assistants as may be selected and supervised by him" to perform the laparoscopic cholecystectomy. The form has a place for "Special remarks or comments by patient," which was left blank. There was no indication on the written consent form, in other words, of any allocation between Dr. Dingle and the assistants selected and supervised by him as to what, precisely, each was to do during the surgery. Dr. Dingle denied that he ever had the conversation testified to by Ms. Belin and stated that he never would have agreed to the conditions she alleged. Although at one point he said that, to satisfy those conditions, the surgery would have to have been performed at another hospital, Dr. Dingle indicated that, if faced with that demand, he would have offered Ms. Belin only two options—"allow me to do what I thought was best unrestricted, or to get another surgeon."

The evidence was essentially undisputed that the particular surgery requires three medical participants—one to operate the camera, one to do the necessary retractions, and one to do the dissection and removal. It would thus not have been possible for Dr. Dingle to do both the retraction and the dissection and removal, as Ms. Belin said he agreed to do. Dr. Dingle and the defense experts opined that the retraction and exposure of the field was often the more difficult and demanding aspect of this kind of laparoscopic surgery.

One of Dr. Dingle's expert witnesses, Dr. Bailey, testified that in most instances the attending surgeon does the retracting and the resident does the dissecting and clipping. The reason, he said, was that the retraction requires a high hand-to-eye skill level, to be able to manipulate and maneuver the gall bladder and keep it properly exposed. Ms. Belin's expert witness, Dr. Goldstone, agreed that it would not breach the standard of care for the resident to do the cutting and clipping and the attending surgeon to do the retracting, "[p]rovided there isn't some previous agreement that this would not occur."

All of the experts agreed that, when one surgeon does the retraction and another does the clipping and cutting, both consult and agree on where the clips are to be put and where the cuts are to be made. They both have the benefit of the television monitors. Dr. Goldstone testified that "not one clip is applied until you both agree where it is to be put" and "not one cut is made with the scissors until you both agree that the cut is being made in the proper place." The evidence indicated that that procedure was followed in Ms. Belin's case—that Drs. Dingle and Magnuson consulted and agreed on where the cuts were to be made and the clips applied.

* * *

In its instructions to the jury, the court essentially merged the two claims of negligence on the part of Dr. Dingle—negligence in the performance of the surgery and negligence in failing to obtain an informed consent. It informed the jury that a health care provider is negligent if the provider "does not use that degree of care and skill which a reasonably competent health care provider engaged in a similar practice and acting in similar circumstances would use" or, "[p]ut another way, a health care provider is negligent if he or she breached or deviated from the applicable standard of care." The court immediately followed that instruction with the statements that "[a] surgeon must obtain consent from the patient to perform a surgery" and "[t]o obtain the required consent, the surgeon must explain the surgery to the patient and warn of all material risks or dangers in the surgery." A material risk, the court continued, "is one which a physician knows or ought to know would be significant to a reasonable person in the patient's position in deciding whether or not to submit to a particular medical treatment or procedure." The surgeon is negligent, it added, "if the surgeon fails to disclose to the patient all the material information, risks, and warnings."

* * *

We granted certiorari principally to consider whether a physician who, as part of his or her contractual undertaking with a patient, agrees to an allocation of tasks between the physician and other physicians, may be liable for breach of contract if that agreement is violated.

Discussion

* * *

Sorting Out Causes of Action

Ms. Belin urges that there is a proper cause of action for breach of contract when a physician promises to fulfill a particular surgical function but fails to do so, resulting in harm, and that that action is independent of any negligence on anyone's part. Her point is that Dr. Magnuson made a mistake in cutting and clipping the common bile duct which, even if not negligent, might not have been made had the cutting and clipping been done by Dr. Dingle, a more experienced surgeon. Dr. Dingle contends that Maryland should not recognize, under any theory, "a claim for 'ghost surgery' against a physician arising out of an alleged agreement regarding the role a resident is to play during a surgical procedure." At the very least, he contends, such a claim should not be permitted as part of an action for lack of informed consent or breach of contract. Creating a duty to disclose a resident's precise role, he warns, "would permit patients to choreograph how an operation is to be performed negating all possibility of informed medical judgment occurring during the operation."

The courts, in proper cases, have recognized a number of different causes of action that might lie against a health care provider when a medical procedure or course of therapy produces unintended and harmful results or fails to produce the positive results reasonably anticipated by the patient. These actions, often bearing the common appellation of "malpractice," differ in their underlying theory, in some of the elements that must be proved, and in the kind of damages that may be recovered. Most are tort-based, sounding either in battery or in negligence of one kind or another, and, occasionally, in misrepresentation or fraud; some are contract-based. When they are pursued either alternatively or in combination, care must be taken to keep the actions separate and not to allow the theories, elements, and recoverable damages to become improperly intertwined.

We have long recognized, as have most courts, that, except in those unusual circumstances when a doctor acts gratuitously or in an emergency situation, recovery for malpractice "is allowed only where there is a relationship of doctor and patient as a result of a contract, express or implied, that the doctor will treat the patient with proper professional skill and the patient will pay for such treatment, and there has been a breach of professional duty to the patient." Hoover v. Williamson, 236 Md. 250, 253, 203 A.2d 861, 862 (1964). The relationship that spawns the malpractice claim is thus ordinarily a contractual one. Largely because of the greater facility offered by tort-based actions for recovering damages for non-economic loss—predominantly pain, suffering, and disfigurement—malpractice actions have traditionally been tort-based, the tort arising from the underlying contractual relationship. [ ]

The traditional action has been for negligence in the performance (or non-performance) of a course of therapy or a medical procedure. [ ] The negligence consists of the breach of the duty that a physician has "to use that degree of care and skill which is expected of a reasonably competent practitioner in the same class to which [the physician] belongs, acting in the same or similar circumstances." Shilkret v. Annapolis Emergency Hosp., 276 Md. 187, 200, 349 A.2d 245, 252 (1975). To recover in such an action, the plaintiff must show that the doctor's conduct—the care given or withheld by the doctor—was not in accordance with the standards of practice among members of the same health care profession with similar training and experience situated in the same or similar communities at the time of the act (or omission) giving rise to the cause of action. [ ] That action necessarily focuses on the manner in which the physician diagnosed and treated the patient's medical problem and, except as it may bear on other issues, such as contributory negligence, causation, or damages, not so much on what was told to the patient or what the patient's expectations may have been.

* * *

Unlike the traditional action of negligence, a claim for lack of informed consent focuses not on the level of skill exercised in the performance of the procedure itself but on the adequacy of the explanation given by the physician in obtaining the patient's consent. * * *

Although, as in Sard v. Hardy, claims based on lack of informed consent usually involve allegations that the physician failed to make adequate disclosure of a material risk or collateral effect of the contemplated procedure or of an available alternative not carrying that risk or effect, the duty is not so limited. Risks, benefits, collateral effects, and alternatives normally must be disclosed routinely, but other considerations, at least if raised by the patient, may also need to be discussed and resolved. See Aaron D. Twerski & Neil B. Cohen, The Second Revolution in Informed Consent: Comparing Physicians to Each Other, 94 NW. U.L.REV. 1 (1999); Johnson v. Kokemoor, 199 Wis.2d 615, 545 N.W.2d 495 (1996). One of those considerations, in an expanding era of more complex medical procedures, group practices, and collaborative efforts among health care providers, may be who, precisely, will be conducting or superintending the procedure or therapy. This may be especially important with respect to surgical procedures, which usually involve collaboration between the chosen surgeon and other medical professionals who may be unknown to the patient. The physician, as Dr. Dingle indicated was the case here, may be unwilling to accept limitations on the actual performance of the surgery, but, if the identity of the persons who will be performing aspects of the surgery is important to the patient, the matter must be discussed and resolved.

Despite Dr. Dingle's protestation to the contrary, a physician who agrees to a specific allocation of responsibility or a specific limitation on his or her discretion in order to obtain the consent of the patient to the procedure and then, absent some emergency or other good cause, proceeds in contravention of that allocation or limitation has not obtained the informed consent of the patient. We do not see this result as having the pernicious effects suggested by Dr. Dingle, of permitting patients to "choreograph" surgery and unduly restrict the flexibility that the surgeon must retain. Precisely as Dr. Dingle stated was the case here, the surgeon does not have to agree to any such limitations, and, presumably, few, if any, of them will so agree. The issue is raised only when there is a claim that such an agreement was made and, without good cause, violated.

Notwithstanding the existence of these tort-based actions, courts have universally recognized that, except in emergency or gratuitous situations, the relationship between doctor and patient is a contractual one, either expressly or by implication, and, from that premise, many have held that, as an alternative to tort-based actions, a separate action for breach of the contract may lie when the doctor acts in contravention of a contractual undertaking, at least in some settings. Those actions are often founded either on a breach of warranty theory, alleging a warranty by the physician of a particular result, or on a promise independent of a medical procedure. * * * [ ]

* * *

Actions for breach of contract have been founded on a variety of alleged promises and commitments. Most have alleged a promise to cure, or to cure within a certain period of time, or of some other particular result. [ ] Others * * * have been based on a commitment to do a certain procedure, to deliver a child by means of a Caesarean section. [ ]

We are unaware of any case precisely like this one, where the dispute is over an alleged allocation of specific functions between or among surgeons, all of whom were expressly authorized to participate and perform some role in the procedure. There have, however, been a number of cases in which a patient was informed that Dr. A would do the procedure, consented to Dr. A's performing the procedure, and later learned that the procedure was performed entirely or predominantly by Dr. B, with little or no participation by Dr. A. Liability has been found in those situations, but on different theories. * * *

* * *

[The court discusses the law of other states, and several cases that have allowed a breach of contract claim when a physician has agreed to do a procedure and then does not.]

We draw a number of conclusions from this judicial landscape. Because the doctor-patient relationship is normally a contractual one, it is permissible for the parties, if they choose to do so, to define with some precision the role that the doctor is to play. The parties may well have conflicting interests in that regard—the doctor wanting as much flexibility and discretion as possible and the patient, if choosing the physician because of some special confidence in that physician's particular abilities, desiring that the selected physician oversee and personally perform the most difficult part of the procedure. As noted in footnote 3 above, the medical community itself recognizes the interest that the patient has in the matter and the need for disclosure and agreement if there is likely to be a significant participation by other persons. The lack of a clear understanding prior to the procedure may well engender a later finding that informed consent was not obtained. A violation of an understanding so reached may constitute the lack of informed consent, negligent delegation, and a breach of the contract, not to mention the risk of a claim of misrepresentation or fraud. It would be prudent, of course, for the written consent form presented to the patient either to set forth any special understanding in this regard or note affirmatively that there is no such understanding.

The scenarios in which these claims can arise are too varied to attempt any complete analysis of how they all may relate, one to another. In the context of this case, it will suffice to say that a doctor who partially abandons his or her patient by improperly delegating to others professional tasks that the doctor was engaged personally to do and agreed personally to do may be liable for traditional professional negligence, lack of informed consent, and breach of contract, depending in part on the nature of the consequences that flow from that abandonment.

The problem for Ms. Belin in this case is that the one issue, common and central to both her claim of lack of informed consent and her claim for breach of contract was, in fact, submitted to the jury, which necessarily found against her. There was no question as to how the surgery proceeded—what Dr. Dingle did and what Dr. Magnuson did; nor was there any claim by Ms. Belin that Dr. Dingle failed to advise her of material risks, of collateral consequences, or of alternative therapies. [ ] The only issue, as to both the informed consent and breach of contract claims, was whether Dr. Dingle ever agreed to the allocation of functions claimed by Ms. Belin. As noted, plaintiff's counsel made clear to the jury, in the context of the informed consent claim, that, to render a defendants' verdict, the jury would have to disbelieve Ms. Belin's version of her conversation with Dr. Dingle. It obviously did so. The breach of contract claim asserted by Ms. Belin could not survive in the face of that finding.

JUDGMENT OF COURT OF SPECIAL APPEALS VACATING JUDGMENT OF CIRCUIT COURT ON BREACH OF CONTRACT CLAIM REVERSED; CASE REMANDED TO COURT OF SPECIAL APPEALS WITH INSTRUCTIONS TO AFFIRM JUDGMENT OF CIRCUIT COURT; COSTS IN THIS COURT AND IN COURT OF SPECIAL APPEALS TO BE PAID BY RESPONDENT.

Notes and Questions

1. The physician-patient relationship can be considered initially as a contractual one. Physicians in private practice may contract for their services as they see fit, and retain substantial control over the extent of their contact with patients. Physicians may limit their specialty, their scope of practice, their geographic area, and the hours and conditions under which they will see patients. They have no obligation to offer services that a patient may require that are outside the physician's competence and training; or services outside the scope of the original physician-patient agreement, where the physician has limited the contract to a type of procedure, to an office visit, or to consultation only. They may transfer responsibility by referring patients to other specialists. They may refuse to enter into a contract with a patient, or to treat patients, even under emergency conditions. Hiser v. Randolph, 126 Ariz. 608, 617 P.2d 774, 776 (1980).

2. Physicians may also expressly contract with a patient for a specific result. Stewart v. Rudner, 349 Mich. 459, 84 N.W.2d 816, 822–23 (1957) (couple contracted with physician to have wife's child delivered by Caesarian section, as she had had two stillbirths and was worried about normal vaginal delivery; the court held that "a doctor and his patient * * * have the same general liberty to contract with respect to their relationship as other parties entering into consensual relationship with one another, and a breach thereof will give rise to a cause of action."). Courts will sometimes allow parol evidence to fill in the terms of these contracts, where the patient has signed other consent forms. Murray v. University of Penn. Hospital, 340 Pa.Super. 401, 490 A.2d 839 (1985) (court allowed parol evidence to show the existence of an oral agreement to guarantee the prevention of future pregnancies by a tubal ligation).

3. Once the physician-patient relationship has been created, however, physicians are subject to an obligation of "continuing attention." Ricks v. Budge, 91 Utah 307, 64 P.2d 208 (1937). Termination of the physician-patient relationship, once created, is subject in some jurisdictions to a "continuous treatment" rule to determine when the statute of limitations is tolled. Treatment obligations cease if

the physician can do nothing more for the patient, or ceases to attend the patient. See Jewson v. Mayo Clinic, 691 F.2d 405 (8th Cir.1982).

4. An express written contract is rarely drafted for specific physician-patient interactions. An implied contract is usually the basis of the relationship between a physician and a patient. A physician who talks with a patient by telephone may be held to have an implied contractual obligation to that patient. Bienz v. Central Suffolk Hospital, 163 A.D.2d 269, 557 N.Y.S.2d 139 (2d Dept., 1990). Likewise, a physician, such as a pathologist, who renders services to a patient but has not contracted with him, is nonetheless bound by certain implied contractual obligations. When the physician evaluates information provided by a nurse and makes a medical decision as to a patient's status, a doctor-patient relationship may be established. Wheeler v. Yettie Kersting Memorial Hospital, 866 S.W.2d 32 (Tex. App.1993).

5. When a physician treating a patient consults by telephone or otherwise with another physician, some courts are reluctant to find a doctor-patient relationship created by such a conversation. The concern is that such informal conferences will be deterred by the fear of liability. See Reynolds v. Decatur Memorial Hosp., 277 Ill.App.3d 80, 214 Ill.Dec. 44, 49, 660 N.E.2d 235, 240 (4th Dist.1996) ("It would have a chilling effect upon practice of medicine. It would stifle communication, education and professional association, all to the detriment of the patient.") Others find a duty in such a consultation. See e.g. Diggs v. Arizona Cardiologists, Ltd., 198 Ariz. 198, 8 P.3d 386 (Ariz.App. Div. 1 2000), where a cardiologist informally consulting with a physician about a patient has a duty to that patient, even though no contractual relationship exists.

6. When a patient goes to a doctor's office with a particular problem, he is offering to enter into a contract with the physician. When the physician examines the patient, she accepts the offer and an implied contract is created. The physician is free to reject the offer and send the patient away, relieving herself of any duty to that patient. See, e.g., Childs v. Weis, 440 S.W.2d 104 (Tex.Civ.App.1969). Some courts state as a starting principle that "* * * [a]s a practical matter, health professionals cannot be required to obtain express consent before each touch or test they perform on a patient. Consent may be express or implied; implied consent may be inferred from the patient's action or seeking treatment or some other act manifesting a willingness to submit to a particular course of treatment * * *." Jones v. Malloy, 226 Neb. 559, 412 N.W.2d 837, 841 (Neb. 1987). But see Tisdale v. Pruitt, infra, for judicial difficulties with contextual consent.

7. The apparent voluntariness of the physician-patient relationship and its reciprocity, i.e., a fee for a service, or consideration, make the relationship look like a traditional contract. In other ways, however, the analogy to a contract is limited. First, the terms of the contract are largely fixed in advance of any bargaining, by standard or customary practices that the physician must follow at the risk of liability for malpractice. The exact nature of the work to be done by the physician is usually left vaguely defined at best. The relationship seems closer to quasi-contract, where we impute to both the physician and the patient standard intentions and reasonable expectations. See Robert Goodin, Protecting the Vulnerable 63, 64–65 (1985).

Second, professional ethics impose fiduciary obligations on physicians in a variety of ways, as the cases in Section II reveal. Courts often look outside the parameters of contract law analysis in judging the obligations of a physician to treat a patient. The courts stress that the physician's obligation to his patient, while having its origins in contract, is governed also by fiduciary obligations and other public considerations "inseparable from the nature and exercise of his calling * * *." Norton v. Hamilton, 92 Ga.App. 727, 89 S.E.2d 809, 812 (1955) (doctor withdrew from case at time when wife was in premature labor; while husband searched for a substitute, wife delivered child). See Chatman v. Millis, 257 Ark. 451, 453 517 S.W.2d 504, 505 (1975) (malpractice action requires a doctor-patient relationship, a duty owed from doctor to patients, although "[w]e do not flatly state that a cause for malpractice must be predicated upon a contractual agreement between a doctor * * * and patient * * *."). For a history of this fiduciary duty, see Michelle Oberman, Mothers and Doctors' Orders: Unmasking the Doctor's Fiduciary Role in Maternal–Fetal Conflicts, 94 N.W.Univ. L.Rev. 451 (2000).

Third, professionals are constrained in their ability to withdraw from their contracts by judicial caselaw defining patient abandonment. A doctor who withdraws from the physician-patient relationship before a cure is achieved or the patient is transferred to the care of another may be liable for abandonment. To escape liability, the physician must give the patient time to find alternative care. See Norton v. Hamilton, 92 Ga.App. 727, 89 S.E.2d 809 (1955). Implied abandonment is a negligence-based theory judged by the overall conduct of the physician. See Meiselman v. Crown Heights Hosp., 285 N.Y. 389, 34 N.E.2d 367 (1941); Ascher v. Gutierrez, 533 F.2d 1235 (D.C.Cir.1976).

B. PHYSICIANS IN INSTITUTIONS

Physicians who practice in institutions must provide health care within the limits of the health plan coverage or their employment contracts with the institution. In this case, the contact between the physician and the patient is preceded by an express contract spelling out the details of the relationship. Physicians who are members of a health maintenance organization or a health plan have a duty to treat plan members as a result of their contractual obligation to the HMO. In these situations, the express contract is between the physician and the health plan, and the subscriber and the plan, with an implied contract between the subscriber and the treating physician.

HAND v. TAVERA

Court of Appeal of Texas, San Antonio, 1993.
864 S.W.2d 678.

OPINION

In this medical malpractice case, plaintiff Lewis Hand appeals from a take-nothing summary judgment rendered on the sole ground that defendant Dr. Robert Tavera owed him no duty because the two never had a physician-patient relationship. We conclude that Tavera did not refute the existence of a physician-patient relationship as a matter of law, and therefore we reverse and remand for further proceedings.

* * * Hand went to the Humana Hospital (Village Oaks) emergency room complaining of a three-day headache. The emergency-room physician (Dr. Boyle) was told that Hand had a personal history of high blood pressure and that his father had died of an aneurism. Boyle observed that Hand's symptoms rose and fell with his blood pressure, which Boyle was able to reduce periodically with medication. After two or three hours of observation, Boyle decided that Hand should be admitted to the hospital, a decision that required

approval from another doctor. Hand had presented a Humana Health Care Plan card, and the front desk told Boyle that defendant Tavera was the doctor responsible that evening for authorizing such admissions. Boyle briefed Tavera by telephone and recommended hospitalization, but ultimately Tavera disagreed with Boyle and concluded that Hand could be treated as an outpatient. Boyle said Tavera told him that Hand's problems "should be controlled by outpatient medication and follow-up in the office" and he also "recommended something for pain." Hand was sent home, where he suffered a stroke a few hours later. He and his wife brought this lawsuit against the hospital, Tavera, and Boyle. Eventually Hand nonsuited Boyle and settled with the hospital.

Tavera moved for summary judgment on the sole ground that he and Hand never established a physician-patient relationship and therefore he owed Hand no duty. Thus this appeal does not present the question whether Tavera's conduct constituted negligence that proximately caused Hand's damages.

Hand argues first that as a member in the Humana Health Care Plan, Tavera owed him a duty of care. There is summary judgment evidence that Hand had Humana Health Care Plan coverage and that Tavera was designated as the doctor acting for the Humana plan that night. The following clauses in the contract between Humana and Southwest Medical Group (which employed Tavera) obligated its doctors to treat Humana enrollees as they would treat their other patients:

> PHYSICIAN agrees to provide or arrange for covered health care services for ENROLLEES in accordance with Attachment B. [Attachment B specifies various physician responsibilities, including "emergency care of a covered ENROLLEE who has been assigned to PHYSICIAN."]
>
> . . . .
>
> PHYSICIAN agrees to provide ENROLLEES with medical services which are within the normal scope of PHYSICIAN's medical practice. These services shall be made available to ENROLLEES without discrimination and in the same manner as provided to PHYSICIAN's other patients. PHYSICIAN agrees to provide medical services to ENROLLEES in accordance with the prevailing practices and standards of the profession and community.

Thus the contracts in the record show that the Humana plan brought Hand and Tavera together just as surely as though they had met directly and entered the physician-patient relationship. Hand paid premiums to Humana to purchase medical care in advance of need; Humana met its obligation to Hand and its other enrollees by employing Tavera's group to treat them; and Tavera's medical group agreed to treat Humana enrollees in exchange for the fees received from Humana. In effect, Hand had paid in advance for the services of the Humana plan doctor on duty that night, who happened to be Tavera, and the physician-patient relationship existed. We hold that when the health-care plan's insured shows up at a participating hospital emergency room, and the plan's doctor on call is consulted about treatment or admission, there is a physician-patient relationship between the doctor and the insured.

* * *

Tavera also argues that Hand is a third party who cannot assert rights under the Tavera–Humana contract, which expressly provides that it creates no third-party beneficiaries. But Hand does not assert rights under the Humana–Tavera contract in isolation or seek to recover for breach of contract; instead he contends that the entire health-care plan arrangement establishes that Tavera had a physician-patient relationship with him and therefore owed him a duty of care. He argues in essence that when the Hand–Humana contract is read together with the Humana–Tavera contract, he has a right to care from the doctor on call when his medical condition falls within his coverage with Humana. We agree and hold that when a patient who has enrolled in a prepaid medical plan goes to a hospital emergency room and the plan's designated doctor is consulted, the physician-patient relationship exists and the doctor owes the patient a duty of care.

* * *

We reverse the summary judgment and remand this cause for further proceedings on Hand's negligence action based on the physician-patient relationship created by the Humana Health Care Plan.

Notes and Questions

1. A physician who has staff privileges at a hospital also agrees to abide by hospital bylaws and policies and has therefore agreed to a doctor-patient relationship with whomever comes into the hospital, according to most courts that have considered the issue. Physicians on call to treat emergency patients are under a duty to treat patients. See Noble v. Sartori, 799 S.W.2d 8 (Ky.1990); Hastings v. Baton Rouge Gen. Hosp., 498 So.2d 713 (La.1986). Texas requires some further affirmative step by the physician to establish the relationship. Merely volunteering to be "on call" at a hospital is not sufficient. Ortiz v. Shah, 905 S.W.2d 609, 611 (Tex.App.—Houston[14th Dist.] 1995). See also Anderson v. Houser, 240 Ga.App. 613, 523 S.E.2d 342 (Ga.App. 1999)(physician scheduled to be on call when patient admitted to emergency room, who never met or treated patient and was out of town during her hospitalization, owed no duty). However, the on-call physician owes a duty to foreseeable emergency room patients to provide reasonable notice to hospital personnel when he or she will not be able to respond to calls, and this duty exists independent of any physician-patient relationship. Oja v. Kin, 229 Mich.App. 184, 581 N.W.2d 739 (Mich.App.1998)(implied consent to doctor-patient relationship may be found only where the physician has done something such as participate in the patient's diagnosis and treatment).

2. Physician contract obligations bind them to treat individual subscribers. And the traditional scope of the contractual relationship may also include obligations such as completing a variety of benefit forms for a patient. If these forms are not properly and timely completed, and a patient suffers an economic detriment, courts have held that a suit for breach of contract will lie. Chew v. Meyer, M.D., P.A., 72 Md.App. 132, 527 A.2d 828 (1987).

C. SPECIFIC PROMISES AND WARRANTIES OF CURE

A contract claim may have several advantages for the plaintiff. The statute of limitations is typically longer than for a tort action. The plaintiff need not establish the medical standard of care and thus may not need to present expert testimony. A contract claim may be viable even when the doctor has made the proper risk disclosure, satisfying the requirements of the tort doctrine of informed consent. Finally, a contract claim offers a remedy to the plaintiff who underwent the procedure because of the enticements of the physician.

The contract between physician and patient can be breached in a variety of ways. The physician may promise to use a certain procedure and then use an alternative procedure. See Stewart v. Rudner, 349 Mich. 459, 84 N.W.2d 816 (1957) (breached promise by physician to perform Caesarean section); Moser v. Stallings, 387 N.W.2d 599 (Iowa 1986) (plastic surgeon did not perform chin implant as part of cosmetic surgery on plaintiff, after telling patient that implant would be a part of the procedure; court in dicta suggested that patient might have had a contract claim). Contra, see Labarre v. Duke University, 99 N.C.App. 563, 393 S.E.2d 321 (1990), where the pregnant plaintiff had been assured that if, during delivery she needed an epidural anesthetic, the Director of Obstetric Anesthesia or another fully-trained faculty anesthesiologist would administer it. Instead, a resident administered the anesthesia, causing the plaintiff to suffer injury. The court held that the promise was not supported by consideration and was therefore unenforceable.

Breach of warranty claims have been rare against health care providers. A breach may also be found where the doctor promises a particular result which fails to occur. The classic case is Guilmet v. Campbell, 385 Mich. 57, 188 N.W.2d 601 (1971), where the physician treated the patient for a bleeding ulcer. The doctor had allegedly told the patient prior to the operation:

> Once you have an operation it takes care of all your troubles. You can eat as you want to, you can drink as you want to, you can go as you please. Dr. Arena and I are specialists, there is nothing to it at all—it's a very simple operation. You'll be out of work three to four weeks at most. There is no danger at all in this operation. After the operation you can throw away your pill box. 385 Mich. 57, 68, 188 N.W.2d 601, 606 (1971).

The patient suffered serious after-effects, and the jury found for the plaintiff on a breach of contract theory. Michigan then added a provision to their Statute of Frauds that covered "[a]n agreement, promise, contract, or warranty of cure relating to medical care or treatment". MCL s.566.132(g).

One emerging area in which warranties are being offered is that of fertility treatment. Fertility clinics in Minnesota and California have begun to offer a guarantee that their patients become pregnant, or they will get their money back. See Stephen L. Cohen, Should Health Care Come With a Warranty? The New York Times 12 (November 10, 1996).

The remedial options for a breach by a physician of a warranty of good results are discussed in Sullivan v. O'Connor, 363 Mass. 579, 296 N.E.2d 183 (1973), where the surgeon promised the plaintiff, a professional entertainer, that he would improve the appearance of her nose. He failed, and her nose ended up bulbous and asymmetrical. Justice Kaplan noted the problems with the application of a contract theory to the medical enterprise:

> It is not hard to see why the courts should be unenthusiastic or skeptical about the contract theory. Considering the uncertainties of medical science and the variations in the physical and psychological conditions of individual patients, doctors can seldom in good faith promise

specific results. Therefore it is unlikely that physicians of even average integrity will in fact make such promises. Statements of opinion by the physician with some optimistic coloring are a different thing, and may indeed have therapeutic value. But patients may transform such statements into firm promises in their own minds, especially when they have been disappointed in the event, and testify in that sense to sympathetic juries. If actions for breach of promise can be readily maintained, doctors, so it is said, will be frightened into practicing "defensive medicine." On the other hand, if these actions were outlawed, leaving only the possibility of suits for malpractice, there is fear that the public might be exposed to the enticements of charlatans, and confidence in the profession might ultimately be shaken.

The measure of damages in a breach of contract suit might be "expectancy" damages, that amount sufficient to place the plaintiff in the position he would be in if the contract had been performed, or "restitution" damages, an amount equivalent to the benefit conferred by the plaintiff upon the defendant. In *Sullivan,* the Massachusetts Supreme Judicial Court considered an intermediate position, a "reliance" basis, a more lenient standard for breach of an agreement "to effect a cure, attain a stated result, or employ a given medical method: * * * the substance is that the plaintiff is to recover any expenditures made by him and for other detriment * * * following proximately and foreseeably upon the defendant's failure to carry out his promise." The Court allowed pain and suffering as an item of damages, as a foreseeable consequence of a surgical operation which fails.

See also Stewart v. Rudner, supra, where the court noted that ordinarily damages are not recoverable for mental anguish or disappointment. "Yet not all contracts are purely commercial in their nature. Some involve rights we cherish, dignities we respect, emotions recognized by all as both sacred and personal. In such cases the award of damages for mental distress and suffering is a commonplace, even in actions ex contractu."

Courts will sometimes allow contract claims, but then define the "contract" restrictively. Courts typically distinguish "therapeutic assurances" from express warranties to effect a cure. In Anglin v. Kleeman, 140 N.H. 257, 665 A.2d 747 (N.H. 1995), the court found that the statement by a physician to patient upon whom knee surgery was performed—that the operation could make the knee stronger than before—did not give rise to contract or warranty claim. See also Ferlito v. Cecola, 419 So.2d 102 (La.App.1982), where the court held that a dentist's statement that crown work would make the plaintiff's teeth "pretty" did not constitute a guarantee. Other courts have imposed evidentiary burdens, requiring proof by clear and convincing evidence. See Burns v. Wannamaker, 281 S.C. 352, 315 S.E.2d 179 (App.1984). Even if the burden of proof is not elevated from the preponderance test to clear and convincing evidence, the jury will be instructed that they must find that the physician "clearly and unmistakably [gave] a positive assurance [that he or she would] produce or * * * avoid a particular result * * *." Scarzella v. Saxon, 436 A.2d 358 (D.C.App.1981). In some states, the Statute of Frauds specifically requires that for agreements guaranteeing therapeutic results to be enforceable, they must be in writing and signed. See, e.g., West's Ann.Ind. Code 16–915–1–4. What effect might such a requirement have?

D. EXCULPATORY CLAUSES

TUNKL v. REGENTS OF UNIV. OF CALIFORNIA

Supreme Court of California, 1963.
60 Cal.2d 92, 32 Cal.Rptr. 33, 383 P.2d 441.

TOBRINER, JUSTICE.

This case concerns the validity of a release from liability for future negligence imposed as a condition for admission to a charitable research hospital. For the reasons we hereinafter specify, we have concluded that an agreement between a hospital and an entering patient affects the public interest and that, in consequence, the exculpatory provision included within it must be invalid under Civil Code section 1668.

Hugo Tunkl brought this action to recover damages for personal injuries alleged to have resulted from the negligence of two physicians in the employ of the University of California Los Angeles Medical Center, a hospital operated and maintained by the Regents of the University of California as a nonprofit charitable institution. Mr. Tunkl died after suit was brought, and his surviving wife, as executrix, was substituted as plaintiff.

The University of California at Los Angeles Medical Center admitted Tunkl as a patient on June 11, 1956. The Regents maintain the hospital for the primary purpose of aiding and developing a program of research and education in the field of medicine; patients are selected and admitted if the study and treatment of their condition would tend to achieve these purposes. Upon his entry to the hospital, Tunkl signed a document setting forth certain "Conditions of Admission." The crucial condition number six reads as follows: "RELEASE: The hospital is a nonprofit, charitable institution. In consideration of the hospital and allied services to be rendered and the rates charged therefor, the patient or his legal representative agrees to and hereby releases The Regents of the University of California, and the hospital from any and all liability for the negligent or wrongful acts or omissions of its employees, if the hospital has used due care in selecting its employees."

Plaintiff stipulated that the hospital had selected its employees with due care. The trial court ordered that the issue of the validity of the exculpatory clause be first submitted to the jury and that, if the jury found that the provision did not bind plaintiff, a second jury try the issue of alleged malpractice. When, on the preliminary issue, the jury returned a verdict sustaining the validity of the executed release, the court entered judgment in favor of the Regents.[1] Plaintiff appeals from the judgment.

We shall first set out the basis for our prime ruling that the exculpatory provision of the hospital's contract fell under the proscription of Civil Code section 1668; we then dispose of two answering arguments of defendant.

We begin with the dictate of the relevant Civil Code section 1668. The section states: "All contracts which have for their object, directly or indirectly, to exempt anyone from responsibility for his own fraud, or willful injury to

1. Plaintiff at the time of signing the release was in great pain, under sedation, and probably unable to read. At trial plaintiff contended that the release was invalid, asserting that a release does not bind the releasor if at the time of its execution he suffered from so weak a mental condition that he was unable to comprehend the effect of his act. [ ]

the person or property of another, or violation of law, whether willful or negligent, are against the policy of the law."

* * *

In one respect, as we have said, the decisions are uniform. The cases have consistently held that the exculpatory provision may stand only if it does not involve "the public interest."

* * *

If, then, the exculpatory clause which affects the public interest cannot stand, we must ascertain those factors or characteristics which constitute the public interest. * * *

* * * It concerns a business of a type generally thought suitable for public regulation. The party seeking exculpation is engaged in performing a service of great importance to the public, which is often a matter of practical necessity for some members of the public. The party holds himself out as willing to perform this service for any member of the public who seeks it, or at least for any member coming within certain established standards. As a result of the essential nature of the service, in the economic setting of the transaction, the party invoking exculpation possesses a decisive advantage of bargaining strength against any member of the public who seeks his services. In exercising a superior bargaining power the party confronts the public with a standardized adhesion contract of exculpation, and makes no provision whereby a purchaser may pay additional reasonable fees and obtain protection against negligence. Finally, as a result of the transaction, the person or property of the purchaser is placed under the control of the seller, subject to the risk of carelessness by the seller or his agents.

* * *

In the light of the decisions, we think that the hospital-patient contract clearly falls within the category of agreements affecting the public interest. To meet that test, the agreement need only fulfill some of the characteristics above outlined; here, the relationship fulfills all of them. Thus the contract of exculpation involves an institution suitable for, and a subject of, public regulation. [ ] That the services of the hospital to those members of the public who are in special need of the particular skill of its staff and facilities constitute a practical and crucial necessity is hardly open to question.

The hospital, likewise, holds itself out as willing to perform its services for those members of the public who qualify for its research and training facilities. While it is true that the hospital is selective as to the patients it will accept, such selectivity does not negate its public aspect or the public interest in it. The hospital is selective only in the sense that it accepts from the public at large certain types of cases which qualify for the research and training in which it specializes. But the hospital does hold itself out to the public as an institution which performs such services for those members of the public who can qualify for them.

In insisting that the patient accept the provision of waiver in the contract, the hospital certainly exercises a decisive advantage in bargaining. The would-be patient is in no position to reject the proffered agreement, to bargain with the hospital, or in lieu of agreement to find another hospital.

The admission room of a hospital contains no bargaining table where, as in a private business transaction, the parties can debate the terms of their contract. As a result, we cannot but conclude that the instant agreement manifested the characteristics of the so-called adhesion contract. Finally, when the patient signed the contract, he completely placed himself in the control of the hospital; he subjected himself to the risk of its carelessness.

* * *

We turn to a consideration of the * * * arguments urged by defendant to save the exemptive clause. Defendant contends that while the public interest may possibly invalidate the exculpatory provision as to the paying patient, it certainly cannot do so as to the charitable one. * * *

* * *

In substance defendant here asks us to modify our decision in *Malloy*, which removed the charitable immunity; defendant urges that otherwise the funds of the research hospital may be deflected from the real objective of the extension of medical knowledge to the payment of claims for alleged negligence. Since a research hospital necessarily entails surgery and treatment in which fixed standards of care may not yet be evolved, defendant says the hospital should in this situation be excused from such care. But the answer lies in the fact that possible plaintiffs must *prove negligence;* the standards of care will themselves reflect the research nature of the treatment; the hospital will not become an insurer or guarantor of the patient's recovery. To exempt the hospital completely from any standard of due care is to grant it immunity by the side-door method of a contractual clause exacted of the patient. We cannot reconcile that technique with the teaching of *Malloy*.

* * *

The judgment is reversed.

Notes and Questions

1. Why shouldn't a patient be able to waive the right to sue in exchange for lower cost or free treatment? Is there something special about medical care in general, or Tunkl's situation in particular, that makes such a choice by a patient suspect? Do the court's arguments convince you as to the reasons for invalidating such attempts by health care institutions to limit their liability? Short of a complete waiver of a right to sue, how else might hospitals or doctors protect themselves? Can a patient be asked to waive the right to sue for punitive damages? Could the parties agree on liquidated damages? Could the parties agree that an action would be brought in the local state court? Could treatment be conditioned on the patient submitting any malpractice claim to an administrative body, or to arbitration?

Courts continue to follow *Tunkl*'s analysis, rejecting exculpatory agreements signed by patients. See, e.g., Cudnik v. William Beaumont Hospital, 207 Mich.App. 378, 525 N.W.2d 891 (Mich.App. 1994)(patient receiving radiation therapy for prostate cancer signed agreement; court held it to be "invalid and unenforceable as against public policy."); Ash v. New York Univ. Dental Center, 164 A.D.2d 366, 564 N.Y.S.2d 308(1990). The only exception courts find acceptable is an exculpatory agreement for treatments involving experimental procedures as the patient's last hope for survival. See Colton v. New York Hospital, 98 Misc.2d 957, 414 N.Y.S.2d 866 (1979).

For a thoughtful analysis of *Tunkl,* and a proposal to allocate medical risks by contract, see Glen Robinson, Rethinking the Allocation of Medical Malpractice Risks Between Patients and Providers, 49 Law & Contemp.Probs. 173 (1986). See also Emory University v. Porubiansky, 248 Ga. 391, 282 S.E.2d 903 (1981) (dental clinic could not ask patients to waive right to sue for negligence; the court noted however that the clinic could enter into binding contracts with patients, asking patients for example to waive the right to insist on complete treatment.).

E. PARTIAL LIMITATIONS ON THE RIGHT TO SUE

SHORTER v. DRURY

Supreme Court of Washington, 1985.
103 Wash.2d 645, 695 P.2d 116.

DOLLIVER, JUSTICE.

This is an appeal from a wrongful death medical malpractice action arising out of the bleeding death of a hospital patient who, for religious reasons, refused a blood transfusion. Plaintiff, the deceased's husband and personal representative, appeals the trial court's judgment on the verdict in which the jury reduced plaintiff's wrongful death damages by 75 percent based on an assumption of risk by the Shorters that Mrs. Shorter would die from bleeding. The defendant doctor appeals the judgment alleging that a plaintiff-signed hospital release form completely barred the wrongful death action. Alternatively, defendant asks that we affirm the trial court's judgment on the verdict. Defendant does not appeal the special verdict in which the jury found the defendant negligent.

The deceased, Doreen Shorter, was a Jehovah's Witness, as is her surviving husband, Elmer Shorter. Jehovah's Witnesses are prohibited by their religious doctrine from receiving blood transfusions.

Doreen Shorter became pregnant late in the summer of 1979. In October of 1979, she consulted with the defendant, Dr. Robert E. Drury, a family practitioner. Dr. Drury diagnosed Mrs. Shorter as having had a "missed abortion". A missed abortion occurs when the fetus dies and the uterus fails to discharge it.

When a fetus dies, it is medically prudent to evacuate the uterus in order to guard against infection. To cleanse the uterus, Dr. Shorter recommended a "dilation and curettage" (D and C). There are three alternative ways to perform this operation. The first is with a curette, a metal instrument which has a sharp-edged hoop on the end of it. The second, commonly used in an abortion, involves the use of a suction device. The third alternative is by use of vaginal suppositories containing prostaglandin, a chemical that causes artificial labor contractions. Dr. Drury chose to use curettes.

Although the D and C is a routine medical procedure there is a risk of bleeding. Each of the three principal methods for performing the D and C presented, to a varying degree, the risk of bleeding. The record below reflects that the curette method which Dr. Drury selected posed the highest degree of puncture-caused bleeding risk due to the sharpness of the instrument. The record also reflects, however, that no matter how the D and C is performed, there is always the possibility of blood loss.

Dr. Drury described the D and C procedure to Mr. and Mrs. Shorter. He advised her there was a possibility of bleeding and perforation of the uterus. Dr. Drury did not discuss any alternate methods in which the D and C may be performed. Examination of Mr. Shorter at trial revealed he was aware that the D and C posed the possibility, albeit remote, of internal bleeding.

The day before she was scheduled to receive the D and C from Dr. Drury, Mrs. Shorter sought a second opinion from Dr. Alan Ott. Mrs. Shorter advised Dr. Ott of Dr. Drury's intention to perform the D and C. She told Dr. Ott she was a Jehovah's Witness. Although he confirmed the D and C was the appropriate treatment, Dr. Ott did not discuss with Mrs. Shorter the particular method which should be used to perform it. He did, however, advise Mrs. Shorter that "she could certainly bleed during the procedure" and at trial confirmed she was aware of that possibility. Dr. Ott testified Mrs. Shorter responded to his warning by saying "she had faith in the Lord and that things would work out. * * * "

At approximately 6 a.m. on November 30, Mrs. Shorter was accompanied by her husband to Everett General Hospital. At the hospital the Shorters signed the following form (underlining after heading indicates blanks in form which were completed in handwriting):

GENERAL HOSPITAL OF EVERETT

REFUSAL TO PERMIT BLOOD TRANSFUSION

Date November 30, 1979 Hour 6:15 a.*m.*

I request that no blood or blood derivatives be administered to

Doreen v. Shorter

during this hospitalization. I hereby release the hospital, its personnel, and the attending physician from any responsibility whatever for unfavorable reactions or any untoward results due to my refusal to permit the use of blood or its derivatives and I fully understand the possible consequences of such refusal on my part.

[/s/Doreen Shorter]
Patient]

[/s/ Elmer Shorter]
Patient's Husband or Wife

The operation did not go smoothly. Approximately 1 hour after surgery, Mrs. Shorter began to bleed internally and go into shock. Emergency exploratory surgery conducted by other surgeons revealed Dr. Drury had severely lacerated Mrs. Shorter's uterus when he was probing with the curette.

Mrs. Shorter began to bleed profusely. She continued to refuse to authorize a transfusion despite repeated warnings by the doctors she would likely die due to blood loss. Mrs. Shorter was coherent at the time she refused to accept blood. While the surgeons repaired Mrs. Shorter's perforated uterus and abdomen, Dr. Drury and several other doctors pleaded with Mr. Shorter to permit them to transfuse blood into Mrs. Shorter. He likewise refused. Mrs.

Shorter bled to death. Doctors for both parties agreed a transfusion in substantial probability would have saved Doreen Shorter's life.

Mr. Shorter thereafter brought this wrongful death action alleging Dr. Drury's negligence proximately caused Mrs. Shorter's death; the complaint did not allege a survival cause of action. The release was admitted into evidence over plaintiff's objection. Plaintiff took exception to jury instructions numbered 13 and 13A which dealt with assumption of the risk.

The jury found Dr. Drury negligent and that his negligence was "a proximate cause of the death of Doreen Shorter". Damages were found to be $412,000. The jury determined, however, that Mr. and/or Mrs. Shorter "knowingly and voluntarily" assumed the risk of bleeding to death and attributed 75 percent of the fault for her death to her and her husband's refusal to authorize or accept a blood transfusion. Plaintiff was awarded judgment of $103,000. Both parties moved for judgment notwithstanding the verdict. The trial court denied both motions. Plaintiff appealed and defendant cross-appealed to the Court of Appeals, which certified the case pursuant to RCW 2.06.030(d).

The three issues before us concern the admissibility of the "Refusal to Permit Blood Transfusion" (refusal); whether assumption of the risk is a valid defense and if so, whether there is sufficient evidence for the jury to have found the risk was assumed by the Shorters; and whether the submission of the issue of assumption of the risk to the jury violated the free exercise clause of the First Amendment. The finding of negligence by Dr. Drury is not appealed by defendant.

I

Plaintiff argues the purpose of the refusal was only to release the defendant doctor from liability for not transfusing blood into Mrs. Shorter had she required blood during the course of a nonnegligently performed operation. He further asserts the refusal as it applies to the present case violates public policy since it would release Dr. Drury from the consequences of his negligence.

Defendant concedes a survival action filed on behalf of Mrs. Shorter for her negligently inflicted injuries would not be barred by the refusal since enforcement would violate public policy. Defendant argues, however, the refusal does not release the doctor for his negligence but only for the consequences arising out of Mrs. Shorter's voluntary refusal to accept blood, which in this case was death.

While the rule announced by this court is that contracts against liability for negligence are valid except in those cases where the public interest is involved [ ], the refusal does not addrEss the negligence of Dr. Drury. This being so it cannot be considered as a release from liability for negligence. * * *

Plaintiff categorizes the refusal as an all or nothing instrument. He claims that if it is a release of liability for negligence it is void as against public policy and if it is a release of liability where a transfusion is required because of nonnegligent treatment then it is irrelevant. We have already stated the document cannot be considered as a release from liability for negligence. The document is more, however, than a simple declaration that the signer would refuse blood only if there was no negligence by Dr. Drury. * * *

We find the refusal to be valid. There was sufficient evidence for the jury to find it was not signed unwittingly but rather voluntarily. * * *

We also hold the release was not against public policy. We emphasize again the release did not exculpate Dr. Drury from his negligence in performing the surgery. Rather, it was an agreement that Mrs. Shorter should receive no blood or blood derivatives. The cases cited by defendant, Tunkl v. Regents of Univ. of Cal.; Colton v. New York Hosp., 98 Misc.2d 957, 414 N.Y.S.2d 866 (1979); Olson v. Molzen, 558 S.W.2d 429 (Tenn.1977), all refer to exculpatory clauses which release a physician or hospital from all liability for negligence. The Shorters specifically accepted the risk which might flow from a refusal to accept blood. Given the particular problems faced when a patient on religious grounds refuses to permit necessary or advisable blood transfusions, we believe the use of a release such as signed here is appropriate. [ ] Requiring physicians or hospitals to obtain a court order would be cumbersome and impractical. Furthermore, it might subject the hospital or physician to an action under 42 U.S.C. § 1983. [ ] The alternative of physicians or hospitals refusing to care for Jehovah's Witnesses is repugnant in a society which attempts to make medical care available to all its members.

We believe the procedure used here, the voluntary execution of a document protecting the physician and hospital and the patient is an appropriate alternative and not contrary to the public interest.

If the refusal is held valid, defendant asserts it acts as a complete bar to plaintiff's wrongful death claim. We disagree. While Mrs. Shorter accepted the consequences resulting from a refusal to receive a blood transfusion, she did not accept the consequences of Dr. Drury's negligence which was, as the jury found, a proximate cause of Mrs. Shorter's death. Defendant was not released from his negligence. We next consider the impact of the doctrine of assumption of the risk on this negligence.

II

[In Part II the court considered assumption of the risk as a defense.]

* * * Defendant argues, and we agree, that the Shorters could be found by the jury to have assumed the risk of death from an operation which had to be performed without blood transfusions and where blood could not be administered under any circumstances including where the doctor made what would otherwise have been correctable surgical mistake. The risk of death from a failure to receive a transfusion to which the Shorters exposed themselves was created by, and must be allocated to, the Shorters themselves.

* * *

III

[The court in Part III rejected the argument that the submission of the issue of assumption of the risk to the jury violated the free exercise clause of the First Amendment, since no state action was present.]

* * *

Affirmed.

Notes and Questions

1. Jehovah's Witnesses rarely sue physicians who respect their decisions not to receive blood. A decision to vitiate the partial release in Shorter might have discouraged surgeons from agreeing to treat Jehovah's Witnesses consistent with their religious beliefs.

The refusal by Jehovah's Witnesses to accept blood transfusions has its origins in their interpretation of the Bible. Their religious doctrine mandates that they "abstain from blood":

> A human is not to sustain his life with the blood of another creature. (Genesis 9:3, 4) When an animal's life is taken, the blood representing that life is to be 'poured out,' given back to the Life–Giver. (Leviticus 17:13, 14) And as decreed by the apostolic council, Christians are to 'abstain from blood,' which applies to human blood as well as to animal blood. (Acts 15:28, 29.)

Jehovah's Witnesses and the Question of Blood 17 (1977).

Jehovah's Witnesses make no distinction between taking blood in by mouth and into the blood vessels, and treat the issue of blood as involving "the most fundamental principles on which they as Christians base their lives. Their relationship with their Creator and God is at stake." Id. at 19. The Jehovah's Witnesses have prepared brochures for health care professionals that explain these beliefs, stating that they will sign consent forms that relieve doctors of any responsibility for possible adverse consequences of blood refusal.

2. How does the court support its allowance of the partial release? What does the court fear might happen to patients with particular religious beliefs? Can you think of any other methods by which a hospital or doctor might protect against the risk of lawsuits by patients who refuse certain kinds of medical interventions? Is the contract an adhesion contract, as were the contracts in *Tunkl* or *Porubianksy?*

3. *Shorter* offers a defense of a partial waiver, under a special set of circumstances. The issue is important for two reasons. First, providers would like to limit their liability exposure in order to keep malpractice premiums under control. Second, economists and other reformers of the tort system advocate the use of contracts that allocate risk by agreement.

Several states have already adopted contract approaches, such as elective arbitration contracts that allow the provider and the patient to change the forum for resolving the dispute. Similarly, living wills and durable powers of attorney allow a patient to control the extent of treatment, while protecting the treating doctor from liability for complying with the patient's refusal of treatment.

4. The contract approach to allocating the risks of health care has been advocated by many commentators. See William Ginsburg et al., Contractual Revisions to Medical Malpractice Liability, 49 Law & Contemp.Probs. 253 (1986); Clark Havighurst, Reforming Malpractice Law Through Consumer Choice, 3 Health Affairs 63 (1984).

Reliance on provider-patient contracts has also been criticized. See Maxwell Mehlman, Fiduciary Contracting: Limitations on Bargaining Between Patients and Health Care Providers, 51 Univ.Pitt.L.Rev. 365 (1990); P.S. Atiyah, Medical Malpractice and the Contract/Tort Boundary, 49 Law & Contemp.Probs. 287, 302 (1986) ("So American reformers turn, as a last resort, to the law of contract, however unsatisfactory this may be as an instrument of legal change compared with legislation or appropriate changes in common law doctrine."); Sylvia Law, A Consumer Perspective on Medical Malpractice, 49 Law & Contemp.Probs. 305 (1989).

Problem: Arbitrating Disaster

Rhoda Cumin went to the Gladstone Clinic in Las Vegas, Nevada to get a prescription for an oral contraceptive. Her medical history put her at a higher risk of a stroke from use of birth control pills. She did not know this, but her medical records and history would have alerted an obstetrician to the risk. She obtained a prescription for the pills, and began taking them. Six months later she suffered a cerebral incident that left her partially paralyzed.

Ms. Cumin has asked you to handle her suit against the clinic. Your investigation determines that the clinic was negligent in prescribing the contraceptive in light of Ms. Cumin's history. You file a negligence action. The clinic then moves to stay the lawsuit pending arbitration, and for a court order to compel arbitration. Its affidavit states that the clinic requires all patients to sign an arbitration agreement before receiving treatment. This agreement provides that all disputes must be submitted to binding arbitration and that the parties expressly waive their right to a trial. The clinic's standard procedure is to have the receptionist hand the patient the agreement along with two information sheets, informing her that any questions will be answered. The patient must sign the agreement before receiving treatment; the physician signs later. If the patient refuses to sign, the clinic refuses treatment. The agreement, signed by Rhoda Cumin, is attached to the affidavit.

Ms. Cumin tells you that she does not remember either signing the agreement or having it explained to her, and you file an affidavit to that effect. Prepare a memorandum of law in support of your motion in opposition to arbitration.

II. CONFIDENTIALITY AND DISCLOSURE IN THE PHYSICIAN–PATIENT RELATIONSHIP

A. BREACHES OF CONFIDENCE

One of the most important obligations owed by a professional to a patient is the protection of confidences revealed by the patient to the professional. There is also an emerging trend to impose on professionals a duty to disclose to the patient information which the professional has regarding the patient. These obligations are discussed in this section.

HUMPHERS v. FIRST INTERSTATE BANK OF OREGON

Supreme Court of Oregon, In Banc, 1985.
298 Or. 706, 696 P.2d 527.

LINDE, JUSTICE.

We are called upon to decide whether plaintiff has stated a claim for damages in alleging that her former physician revealed her identity to a daughter whom she had given up for adoption.

In 1959, according to the complaint, plaintiff, then known as Ramona Elwess or by her maiden name, Ramona Jean Peek, gave birth to a daughter in St. Charles Medical Center in Bend, Oregon. She was unmarried at the time, and her physician, Dr. Harry E. Mackey, registered her in the hospital as "Mrs. Jean Smith." The next day, Ramona consented to the child's adoption by Leslie and Shirley Swarens of Bend, who named her Leslie Dawn. The hospital's medical records concerning the birth were sealed and marked to show that they were not public. Ramona subsequently remarried and raised a family. Only Ramona's mother and husband and Dr. Mackey knew about the daughter she had given up for adoption.

Twenty-one years later the daughter, now known as Dawn Kastning, wished to establish contact with her biological mother. Unable to gain access to the confidential court file of her adoption (though apparently able to locate the attending physician), Dawn sought out Dr. Mackey, and he agreed to assist in her quest. Dr. Mackey gave Dawn a letter which stated that he had registered Ramona Jean Peek at the hospital, that although he could not locate his medical records, he remembered administering diethylstilbestrol to her, and that the possible consequences of this medication made it important for Dawn to find her biological mother. The latter statements were untrue and made only to help Dawn to breach the confidentiality of the records concerning her birth and adoption. In 1982, hospital personnel, relying on Dr. Mackey's letter, allowed Dawn to make copies of plaintiff's medical records, which enabled her to locate plaintiff, now Ramona Humphers.

Ramona Humphers was not pleased. The unexpected development upset her and caused her emotional distress, worry, sleeplessness, humiliation, embarrassment, and inability to function normally. She sought damages from the estate of Dr. Mackey, who had died, by this action against defendant as the personal representative. After alleging the facts recounted above, her complaint pleads for relief on five different theories: First, that Dr. Mackey incurred liability for "outrageous conduct";[1] second, that his disclosure of a professional secret fell short of the care, skill and diligence employed by other physicians in the community and commanded by statute; third, that his disclosure wrongfully breached a confidential or privileged relationship; fourth, that his disclosure of confidential information was an "invasion of privacy" in the form of an "unauthorized intrusion upon plaintiff's seclusion, solitude, and private affairs;" and fifth, that his disclosures to Dawn Kastning breached a contractual obligation of secrecy. The circuit court granted defendant's motion to dismiss the complaint on the grounds that the facts fell short of each theory of relief and ordered entry of judgment for defendant. On appeal, the Court of Appeals affirmed the dismissal of the first, second, and fifth counts but reversed on the third, breach of a confidential relationship, and the fourth, invasion of privacy. [ ] We allowed review. We hold that if plaintiff has a claim, it arose from a breach by Dr. Mackey of a professional duty to keep plaintiff's secret rather than from a violation of plaintiff's privacy.

A physician's liability for disclosing confidential information about a patient is not a new problem. In common law jurisdictions it has been more

1. This court has attempted, so far unsuccessfully, to discourage the idea that there is a general tort of "outrageous conduct," partly because the phrase misleadingly suggests potential recovery of damages whenever someone's conduct could be said to deserve this epithet. [ ] Plaintiff in this case actually alleged the factual elements of intentional or reckless infliction of severe emotional distress as well as "outrageous" conduct.

discussed than litigated throughout much of this century.[2] There are precedents for damage actions for unauthorized disclosure of facts conveyed in confidence, although we know of none involving the disclosure of an adoption. Because such claims are made against a variety of defendants besides physicians or other professional counselors, for instance against banks [ ], and because plaintiffs understandably plead alternative theories of recovery, the decisions do not always rest on a single theory.

Sometimes, defendant may have promised confidentiality expressly or by factual implication, in this case perhaps implied by registering a patient in the hospital under an assumed name. Plaintiffs were allowed to proceed on implied contract claims in *Horne v. Patton,* 291 Ala. 701, 287 So.2d 824 (1973), in *Hammonds v. Aetna Casualty & Surety Company,* 243 F.Supp. 793 (N.D.Ohio 1965), and in *Doe v. Roe,* 93 Misc.2d 201, 400 N.Y.S.2d 668 (1977) (psychiatrist). * * * A contract claim may be adequate where the breach of confidence causes financial loss, and it may gain a longer period of limitations; but contract law may deny damages for psychic or emotional injury not within the contemplation of the contracting parties, [ ] though perhaps this is no barrier when emotional security is the very object of the promised confidentiality. A contract claim is unavailable if the defendant physician was engaged by someone other than the plaintiff [ ] and it would be an awkward fiction at best if age, mental condition, or other circumstances prevent the patient from contracting; yet such a claim might be available to someone less interested than the patient, for instance her husband, [ ].

Malpractice claims, based on negligence or statute, in contrast, may offer a plaintiff professional standards of conduct independent of the defendant's assent. * * * Finally, actions for intentional infliction of severe emotional distress, *see supra* note 1, fail when the defendant had no such intention or * * * when a defendant was not reckless or did not behave in a manner that a factfinder could find to transcend "the farthest reaches of socially tolerable behavior." [ ] Among these diverse precedents, we need only consider the counts of breach of confidential relationship and invasion of privacy on which the Court of Appeals allowed plaintiff to proceed. Plaintiff did not pursue her other theories * * * and we express no view whether the dismissal of those counts was correct.

Privacy

Although claims of a breach of privacy and of wrongful disclosure of confidential information may seem very similar in a case like the present, which involves the disclosure of an intimate personal secret, the two claims depend on different premises and cover different ground. Their common denominator is that both assert a right to control information, but they differ in important respects. Not every secret concerns personal or private information; commercial secrets are not personal, and governmental secrets are neither personal nor private. Secrecy involves intentional concealment. * * *

For our immediate purpose, the most important distinction is that only one who holds information in confidence can be charged with a breach of

2. *See, e.g.,* Hanning and Brady, *Extra-judicial Truthful Disclosure of Medical Confidences: A Physician's Civil Liability,* 44 Den. L.J. 463 (1967) (citing the earlier literature); Boyle, *Medical Confidence—Civil Liability for Breach,* 24 N.Ire.Leg.Q. 19 (1973).

confidence. If an act qualifies as a tortious invasion of privacy, it theoretically could be committed by anyone. In the present case, Dr. Mackey's professional role is relevant to a claim that he breached a duty of confidentiality, but he could be charged with an invasion of plaintiff's privacy only if anyone else who told Dawn Kastning the facts of her birth without a special privilege to do so would be liable in tort for invading the privacy of her mother.

Whether "privacy" is a usable legal category has been much debated in other English-speaking jurisdictions as well as in this country, especially since its use in tort law, to claim the protection of government against intrusions by others, became entangled with its use in constitutional law, to claim protection against rather different intrusions by government. No concept in modern law has unleashed a comparable flood of commentary, its defenders arguing that "privacy" encompasses related interests of personality and autonomy, while its critics say that these interests are properly identified, evaluated, and protected below that exalted philosophical level. Indeed, at that level, a daughter's interest in her personal identity here confronts a mother's interest in guarding her own present identity by concealing their joint past. But recognition of an interest or value deserving protection states only half a case. Tort liability depends on the defendant's wrong as well as on the plaintiff's interest, or "right," unless some rule imposes strict liability. One's preferred seclusion or anonymity may be lost in many ways; the question remains who is legally bound to protect those interests at the risk of liability.

* * *

In this country, Dean William L. Prosser and his successors, noting that early debate was more "preoccupied with the question whether the right of privacy existed" than "what it would amount to if it did," concluded that invasion of privacy "is not one tort but a complex of four" * * * Prosser and Keeton, Torts 851, § 117 (5th ed. 1984). They identify the four kinds of claims grouped under the "privacy" tort as, first, appropriation of the plaintiff's name or likeness; second, unreasonable and offensive intrusion upon the seclusion of another; third, public disclosure of private facts; and fourth, publicity which places the plaintiff in a false light in the public eye. *Id.* at 851–66. The same classification is made in the Restatement (Second) Torts §§ 652A to 652E. * * *

This court has not adopted all forms of the tort wholesale. * * *

* * *

* * * The Court of Appeals concluded that the complaint alleges a case of tortious intrusion upon plaintiff's seclusion, not by physical means such as uninvited entry, wiretapping, photography, or the like, but in the sense of an offensive prying into personal matters that plaintiff reasonably has sought to keep private. *See* Prosser and Keeton, *supra* at 854–55, § 117.[11] We do not believe that the theory fits this case.

11. Hospital patients have recovered on a variety of theories for what courts recognized as an injury to privacy when the patient, without knowing consent, was exposed to nonmedical personnel, beginning with *DeMay v. Roberts,* 46 Mich. 160, 9 N.W. 146 (1881) (finding the nonmedical stranger's touch to be a battery). *See* LeBlang, *Invasion of Privacy: Medical Practice and the Tort of Intrusion,* 18 Washburn L.J. 205, 219–39 (1979). This court recognized that intrusive surveillance could be a tort, though not made out on the facts, in

Doubtless plaintiff's interest qualifies as a "privacy" interest. That does not require the judgment of a court or a jury; it is established by the statutes that close adoption records to inspection without a court order. ORS 7.211, 432.420. * * * But as already stated, to identify an interest deserving protection does not suffice to collect damages from anyone who causes injury to that interest. Dr. Mackey helped Dawn Kastning find her biological mother, but we are not prepared to assume that Ms. Kastning became liable for invasion of privacy in seeking her out. Nor, we think, would anyone who knew the facts without an obligation of secrecy commit a tort simply by telling them to Ms. Kastning.

Dr. Mackey himself did not approach plaintiff or pry into any personal facts that he did not know; indeed, if he had written or spoken to his former patient to tell her that her daughter was eager to find her, it would be hard to describe such a communication alone as an invasion of privacy. The point of the claim against Dr. Mackey is not that he pried into a confidence but that he failed to keep one. If Dr. Mackey incurred liability for that, it must result from an obligation of confidentiality beyond any general duty of people at large not to invade one another's privacy. We therefore turn to plaintiff's claim that Dr. Mackey was liable for a breach of confidence, the third count of the complaint.

Breach of Confidence

It takes less judicial innovation to recognize this claim than the Court of Appeals thought. A number of decisions have held that unauthorized and unprivileged disclosure of confidential information obtained in a confidential relationship can give rise to tort damages. *See, e.g., Horne v. Patton, supra; MacDonald v. Clinger,* 84 A.D.2d 482, 446 N.Y.S.2d 801 (1982); * * *.

* * *

In the case of the medical profession, courts in fact have found sources of a nonconsensual duty of confidentiality. Some have thought such a duty toward the patient implicit in the patient's statutory privilege to exclude the doctor's testimony in litigation, enacted in this state in OEC 504–1(2). *See, e.g., Berry v. Moench,* 8 Utah 2d 191, 331 P.2d 814 (1958); *Hammonds v. Aetna Cas. & Sur. Co., supra;* [ ]. More directly in point are legal duties imposed as a condition of engaging in the professional practice of medicine or other occupations.[15]

[The court noted that medical licensing statutes and professional regulations have been used as sources of a duty.]

This strikes us as the right approach to a claim of liability outside obligations undertaken expressly or implied in fact in entering a contractual relationship. [ ] The contours of the asserted duty of confidentiality are determined by a legal source external to the tort claim itself.

* * *

McLain v. Boise Cascade Corp., 271 Or. 549, 533 P.2d 343 (1975).

15. *See, e.g., In re Lasswell,* 296 Or. 121, 124–26, 673 P.2d 855 (1983) (sustaining professional constraints on disclosure if disclosure is incompatible with professional function and sanction is limited to the professional role or relationship). * * *

Because the duty of confidentiality is determined by standards outside the tort claim for its breach, so are the defenses of privilege or justification. Physicians, like members of many ordinary confidential professions and occupations, also may be legally obliged to report medical information to others for the protection of the patient, of other individuals, or of the public. *See, e.g.*, ORS 418.750 (physician's duty to report child abuse); ORS 433.003, 434.020 (duty to report certain diseases). * * * Even without such a legal obligation, there may be a privilege to disclose information for the safety of individuals or important to the public in matters of public interest. [ ] Some cases have found a physician privileged in disclosing information to a patient's spouse, *Curry v. Corn,* 52 Misc.2d 1035, 277 N.Y.S.2d 470 (1966) or perhaps an intended spouse, *Berry v. Moench, supra.* In any event, defenses to a duty of confidentiality are determined in the same manner as the existence and scope of the duty itself. They necessarily will differ from one occupation to another and from time to time. A physician or other member of a regulated occupation is not to be held to a noncontractual duty of secrecy in a tort action when disclosure would not be a breach or would be privileged in direct enforcement of the underlying duty.

A physician's duty to keep medical and related information about a patient in confidence is beyond question. It is imposed by statute. ORS 677.190(5) provides for disqualifying or otherwise disciplining a physician for "wilfully or negligently divulging a professional secret." * * *

It is less obvious whether Dr. Mackey violated ORS 677.190(5) when he told Dawn Kastning what he knew of her birth. She was not, after all, a stranger to that proceeding. * * * If Ms. Kastning needed information about her natural mother for medical reasons, as Dr. Mackey pretended, the State Board of Medical Examiners likely would find the disclosure privileged against a charge under ORS 677.190(5); but the statement is alleged to have been a pretext designed to give her access to the hospital records. If only ORS 677.190(5) were involved, we do not know how the Board would judge a physician who assists at the birth of a child and decades later reveals to that person his or her parentage. But as already noted, other statutes specifically mandate the secrecy of adoption records. * * * Given these clear legal constraints, there is no privilege to disregard the professional duty imposed by ORS 677.190(5) solely in order to satisfy the curiosity of the person who was given up for adoption.

For these reasons, we agree with the Court of Appeals that plaintiff may proceed under her claim of breach of confidentiality in a confidential relationship. The decision of the Court of Appeals is reversed with respect to plaintiff's claim of invasion of privacy and affirmed with respect to her claim of breach of confidence in a confidential relationship, and the case is remanded to the circuit court for further proceedings on that claim.

* * *

BIDDLE v. WARREN GENERAL HOSPITAL

Supreme Court of Ohio, 1999.
86 Ohio St.3d 395, 715 N.E.2d 518.

[The following facts are drawn from the court's opinion. ED. Sometime prior to 1993, appellant and cross-appellee Robert L. Heller, a shareholder in appellant and cross-appellee Elliott, Heller, Maas, Moro & Magill Co., L.P.A. ("the law firm"), attended a legal seminar, where he got the idea that the law firm could assist a hospital in determining whether unpaid medical bills could be submitted to the Social Security Administration for payment. Upon his return, Heller proposed this idea to Rush Elliott, president of the law firm and, at that time, a trustee of Warren General Hospital Foundation and president of Warren General Hospital Health Systems. Elliott asked Mark Tierney, then chief financial officer of appellant and cross-appellee Warren General Hospital ("the hospital"), to meet with Heller.]

In early 1993, a meeting was held resulting in an unwritten agreement under which, according to Tierney, "[t]he law firm would screen potential candidates for SSI [Supplemental Security Income] eligibility and contact those patients on the hospital's behalf as to their rights to apply for SSI Disability, thus having their medical claim covered under SSI and the hospital could, therefore, receive payment for services that it provided that it would otherwise have to write-off [sic] as an uncollect[i]ble account, and in return for those services, upon payment from SSI, the hospital would pay a contingency fee to Elliott, Heller & Maas."

Heller informed the hospital that in order for the law firm to perform this service, it would be necessary for the hospital to provide four pieces of information with regard to each patient to be screened: name, telephone number, age, and medical condition. Accordingly, a joint decision was made to provide the law firm with the hospital's patient registration forms.

Over the next two and one-half years, the hospital released all of its patient registration forms to the law firm without obtaining any prior consent or authorization from its patients to do so, and without prescreening or sorting them in any way. The law firm sent a courier to the hospital on a weekly basis to retrieve the forms and bring them back to its office, where they were reviewed by Heller and Sharyn Jacisin, a legal assistant employed by the law firm, and separated according to potential SSI eligibility. The forms of those patients whom the law firm determined not to be eligible for disability benefits were put in a cardboard box and eventually placed in storage, and nothing further was done on those accounts.

Those patients who were considered potential candidates for SSI were telephoned by either Jacisin or Melanie Sutton, who at that time was Heller's secretary. According to the law firm, neither Jacisin nor Sutton indicated where they worked, but instead stated that they were calling on behalf of the hospital and that "you might be entitled to Social Security benefits that might help you pay your medical bill." Those patients who showed interest were referred to Heller. Jacisin testified at deposition that she made approximately one hundred of these phone calls, the purpose of which was to make an appointment to see if those patients were eligible for Social Security benefits.

Heller testified that he met with only "[p]robably 5" individuals, that he "absolutely [did] not" tell them that he or his law firm would represent them in making application for benefits, but that these individuals did retain him, without any discussion of compensation, "to help them get their benefits so their medical bills could get paid." However, Elliott testified that it "was more or less the understood agreement * * * between the firm and the hospital" that the hospital was the initial client of the law firm, but "at some point in time" the law firm may come to represent individual patients with regard to their Social Security benefits.

One patient stated by way of affidavit that Sutton telephoned her in July 1993, indicated that she was Heller's secretary, "and stated that the law firm worked closely with Warren General Hospital and * * * was trying to help Warren General Hospital patients obtain SSI benefits." She stated that "Sutton asked me to come into the office of Attorney Heller and engage Attorney Heller to represent me regarding a potential Social Security claim." She also stated that she met with Heller, that neither he nor Sutton said anything regarding her hospital bill or whether it would be paid by SSI, and that she was a Medicaid recipient and her bill had already been paid prior to the communications from the law firm. Lastly, she stated that even though she never retained the services of Heller or the law firm, "Heller's name appears as my representative on my Social Security denial of benefits letter dated Sept. 29, 1993."

On May 12, 1994, Sutton learned that the law firm was going to terminate her employment and began photocopying the patient registration forms. It appears that Sutton later sent copies of these registration forms to WFMJ–TV in Youngstown, Ohio, and when a reporter for the station confronted the law firm in June 1995, as part of an investigation into breach of patient confidentiality, the relationship between the law firm and the hospital was terminated.

On July 10, 1995, appellees and cross-appellants, Cheryl A. Biddle, individually and as surviving spouse of Robert A. Biddle, and Gary Ball, filed a class action complaint against the hospital, the law firm, Heller, and appellant and cross-appellee Kevin Andrews, who at all pertinent times was the administrator, executive director, and chief executive officer of the hospital. The complaint seeks compensatory and punitive damages and injunctive relief on behalf of appellees and approximately twelve thousand other patients whose patient registration forms were provided by the hospital to the law firm without prior authorization. Appellees allege several causes of action, all of which are based on the premise that the arrangement between the hospital and the law firm constituted a breach of patient confidentiality. These include claims for invasion of privacy, intentional infliction of emotional distress, and negligence against the hospital and Andrews, and similar claims for inducement against the law firm and Heller. Appellees also assert claims for breach of implied contract and various statutory violations against the hospital and Andrews, and an improper solicitation claim against the law firm and Heller.[ ]

ALICE ROBIE RESNICK, J.

Aside from the procedural and evidentiary questions, these appeals present five general issues for our determination. The first issue is whether a physician or hospital can be held liable for the unauthorized, out-of-court disclosure of confidential information obtained in the course of the physician-patient relationship.

This issue is easily resolved. "In Ohio, a physician can be held liable for unauthorized disclosures of medical information...." [ ]

However, Littleton does not specify the basis or legal theory under which a physician can be held liable for unauthorized disclosures of medical information ..... [ ] The second issue, therefore, is whether this court should recognize an independent common-law tort of breach of confidence in the physician-patient setting. Since appellants raise no serious argument against the recognition of such an action, this issue need not detain us long either.

* * *

* * *[C]ourts in Ohio and elsewhere have faced common metamorphic disturbances in attempting to provide a legal identity for an actionable breach of patient confidentiality. In their efforts to devise a civil remedy "for so palpable a wrong," many of these courts have endeavored to fit a breach of confidence into a number of traditional or accepted legal theories. In much the same way as trying to fit a round peg into a square hole, courts have utilized theories of invasion of privacy, defamation, implied breach of contract, intentional and negligent infliction of emotional distress, implied private statutory cause of action, breach of trust, detrimental reliance, negligence, and medical malpractice. Invariably, these theories prove ill-suited for the purpose, and their application contrived, as they are designed to protect diverse interests that only coincidentally overlap that of preserving patient confidentiality. These courts, therefore, often find themselves forced to stretch the traditional theories beyond their reasonable bounds, or ignore or circumvent otherwise sound doctrinal limitations, in order to achieve justice within the parameters they have set for themselves. In so doing, they rely on various sources of public policy favoring the confidentiality of communications between a physician and a patient, including state licensing or testimonial privilege statutes, or the Principles of Medical Ethics of the American Medical Association (1957), Section 9, or the Oath of Hippocrates. Some note that while public policy considerations are a sound enough basis to support liability, a more appropriate basis can be found in the nature of the physician-patient relationship itself, either because of its fiduciary character or because it is customarily understood to carry an obligation of secrecy and confidence. Slowly and unevenly, through various gradations of evolution, courts have moved toward the inevitable realization that an action for breach of confidence should stand in its own right, and increasingly courts have begun to adopt it as an independent tort in their respective jurisdictions. [ ] We hold that in Ohio, an independent tort exists for the unauthorized, unprivileged disclosure to a third party of nonpublic medical information that a physician or hospital has learned within a physician-patient relationship.

The third issue, as framed by the law firm, "is whether the duty to hold this patient information confidential is absolute, as the Court of Appeals has held, or, whether, and under what circumstances the hospital may disclose the confidential information to others and for what purpose." In particular, appellants and their amici argue that a privilege should attach in this case under which a hospital may disclose confidential medical information to its attorney without obtaining prior patient authorization to do so.

We do not interpret the court of appeals' decision to provide for an absolute duty of confidentiality, but it does contain some language suggesting that a disclosure may be privileged only if mandated by statute. Disclosures of otherwise confidential medical information made pursuant to statutory mandate are certainly privileged, such as occupational diseases [ ]. diseases which are infectious, contagious, or dangerous to public health [ ] , medical conditions indicative of child abuse or neglect [ ] , and injuries indicative of criminal conduct [ ]. Otherwise, a physician would be forced into the dilemma of violating a statute for failing to report a medical condition to the appropriate state agency or incurring civil liability for disclosing it. Thus, when a physician's report "is made in the manner prescribed by law, he of course has committed no breach of duty toward his patient and has betrayed no confidence, and no liability could result." [ ]

The physician also has certain duties under the common law to disclose otherwise confidential medical information concerning the public health or safety to third persons, the breach of which can result in civil liability. [ ] If a privilege to disclose were held not to attach under these circumstances, the physician would be placed in the untenable position of incurring civil liability for breaching one of two opposing common-law duties.

More important, the privilege to disclose is not necessarily coextensive with a duty to disclose. "Even without such a legal obligation, there may be a privilege to disclose information for the safety of individuals or important to the public in matters of public interest." Humphers, supra, 298 Ore. at 720, 696 P.2d at 535. * * * Thus, special situations may exist where the interest of the public, the patient, the physician, or a third person are of sufficient importance to justify the creation of a conditional or qualified privilege to disclose in the absence of any statutory mandate or common-law duty. [ ]

We hold that in the absence of prior authorization, a physician or hospital is privileged to disclose otherwise confidential medical information in those special situations where disclosure is made in accordance with a statutory mandate or common-law duty, or where disclosure is necessary to protect or further a countervailing interest which outweighs the patient's interest in confidentiality.

[The court discusses the arguments raised by the law firm and the amicus briefs.]

* * *

The main thrust of these arguments is to focus our attention on the nature of the relationship between attorney and client, rather than between physician and patient. From this perspective, the physician's duty to keep patient confidences is irrelevant, and the action itself is viewed as an attack on the viability of the attorney-client relationship. Nevertheless, we are being asked to recognize a privilege under which a hospital can release thousands of patient registration forms without consent or authorization so that a law firm can search for potential Social Security claimants, on the sole basis that the medical bill of one or more of these patients may thereby be paid. Placed in its proper perspective, such a privilege would also protect the individual medical practitioner who releases the bulk of his or her office files without authorization so that a lawyer can search through them for potential workers' compensation or personal injury claimants.

In Neal, supra, 745 F.Supp. at 1297, the court recognized a conditional privilege under which a patient's physician can disclose medical information to another treating physician. * * *

The privilege recognized in Neal applies only to disclosures made to a third party who owes a duty of confidentiality to the patient, i.e., "a physician also bound by O.R.C. § 4731.22(B)'s mandate of confidentiality." It does not extend to disclosures made to a third party who owes a duty of confidentiality to the patient's physician, but not the patient.

* * *

Contrary to the assertions of appellants and OSBA, a refusal to recognize a privilege in this case will not sound the death knell of the attorney-client relationship. By withholding a privilege in this case, we do no more than recognize that there are some circumstances under which a hospital can be held liable for the unauthorized disclosure of confidential medical information to its attorney.

It is appropriate at this point to step back for a moment and review the facts of this case. A hospital hands over to a law firm thousands of patient registration forms containing information about the medical condition of each patient, including diagnoses of alcohol and drug abuse, mental illness, and sexually transmitted diseases. The law firm reviews these forms for the sole purpose of finding amongst them potential Social Security claimants. The firm then calls these potential claimants and gives them unsolicited advice that they should take legal action in the form of obtaining SSI. In so doing, the law firm either conceals its legal identity or, according to one account, directly asked the potential claimant to engage Attorney Heller to represent her regarding a potential Social Security claim. Those who show interest are scheduled for an appointment with Heller, which is the admitted purpose of making the calls, and the law firm ultimately accepts employment (which Elliott testified was contemplated from the outset).

We can find no interest, public or private, that would justify the recognition of a privilege under these circumstances.[ ] Thus, we agree with the court of appeals that "[i]f hospitals wish to engage in this type of procedure in the future, liability can be avoided [only] by obtaining clear patient consent for this type of informational release."

This brings us to the fourth issue presented in this case, which is whether the hospital did in fact obtain such consent. The hospital contends that its general authorization for release of information form was sufficient to permit it to disclose the patient registration forms to its attorney. The form provides:

> Authorization is hereby granted to release to my insurance company and/or third party payor such information including medical records as may be necessary for the completion of my hospitalization claims. I understand that the information released upon authority of this authorization may contain information concerning treatment for alcohol, drug abuse, a psychiatric condition, or HIV test results, an AIDS diagnosis, or AIDS-related condition.

By its express terms, this form authorizes the hospital to release medical information only "to my insurance company and/or third party payor," and then only "as may be necessary for the completion of my hospitalization claims." It does not authorize the release of medical information to the hospital's lawyer, and certainly not for the purpose of determining the patient's status as a potential Social Security claimant.

* * *

In this case, the hospital's general consent form did not provide the authority to release medical information to the law firm and, therefore, the disclosures were unauthorized.

The fifth and final substantive issue is whether a third party can be held liable for inducing the unauthorized, unprivileged disclosure of nonpublic medical information. Those courts that have considered this issue have answered in the affirmative, and, for the reasons expressed in those decisions, we now do the same. [ ]

* * *

* * *[T]here may be special situations where the interests of the patient will justify the creation of a privilege to disclose. However, the only interest that has been recognized in this regard is the patient's interest in obtaining medical care and treatment, and disclosure is limited to those who have a legitimate interest in the patient's health. [ ] Otherwise, it is for the patient—not some medical practitioner, lawyer, or court—to determine what the patient's interests are with regard to personal confidential medical information.

We hold that a third party can be held liable for inducing the unauthorized, unprivileged disclosure of nonpublic medical information that a physician or hospital has learned within a physician-patient relationship. "To establish liability the plaintiff must prove that: (1) the defendant knew or reasonably should have known of the existence of the physician-patient relationship; (2) the defendant intended to induce the physician to disclose information about the patient or the defendant reasonably should have anticipated that his actions would induce the physician to disclose such information; and (3) the defendant did not reasonably believe that the physician could disclose that information to the defendant without violating the duty of confidentiality that the physician owed the patient." [ ]

* * *

For all the foregoing reasons, the judgment of the court of appeals is affirmed, and the cause is remanded to the trial court for further proceedings consistent with this opinion.

Notes and Questions

1. What harms were the plaintiffs exposed to by the disclosure of their medical information to the law firm? Wasn't this practice one that could primarily accrue to the benefit of patients who might have claims?

2. Every time a person consults a medical professional, is admitted to a health care institution, or receives a medical test, a medical record is created or an

entry is made in an existing record. Billions of such records exist in the United States, most of which will be retained from 10 to 25 years. Many of these records contain very personal information—revelations to psychotherapists or documentation of treatment for alcoholism or venereal disease, for example—the disclosure of which could prove devastating to the patient. Yet most records are available to many users for a variety of legitimate and more questionable purposes. The conflict between the need for confidentiality and various claims to access have traditionally been resolved by professional ethics and institutional management practices, but is increasingly being litigated in legal forums.

3. Who uses medical information? Professional and non-professional medical staff must have access to records of patients in medical institutions for treatment purposes. Consent to such access is commonly presumed. Third party payors are the most common requestors of medical records outside the treatment setting. Access to records also is sought routinely for a variety of medical evaluation and support purposes. For example, in-house quality assurance committees, JCAHO accreditation inspection teams, and state institutional licensure reviewers all must review medical records to assess the quality of hospital care. Medical researchers frequently use information from medical records. If researchers are affiliated with the institution holding the records, access is routinely granted; if they are external to the institution, a request to review records may be reviewed more carefully, but will often be granted. State public health laws require medical professionals and institutions to report a variety of medical conditions and incidents: venereal disease, contagious diseases, wounds inflicted by violence, poisonings, industrial accidents, abortions, and child abuse.

Access to medical records is also sought for secondary, nonmedical, purposes. Law enforcement agencies, for example, often seek access to medical information. A moderate-size Chicago hospital reported that the FBI requested information about patients as often as twice a month. Attorneys seek medical records to establish disability, personal injury, or medical malpractice claims for their clients. Though they most commonly will ask for records of their own clients, they may also want to review records of other patients to establish a pattern of knowing medical abuse by a physician or the culpability of a hospital for failing to supervise a negligent practitioner. Life, health, disability and liability insurers often seek medical information, as do employers and credit investigators. Disclosure of information from medical records may occur without a formal request. Though secondary users of medical information commonly receive information pursuant to patient record releases, they have been known to seek and compile information surreptitiously. See Privacy Protection Study Commission, Personal Privacy in an Information Society, 285, 286 (1977) [hereafter Personal Privacy]. Another study found that 51% of doctors and 70% of medical students discuss confidential information at parties. Obviously these secondary disclosures of medical information are of great import to patients, as disclosure can result in loss of employment or denial of insurance or credit, or, at least, severe embarrassment.

4. What legal devices protect the confidentiality of medical information? The physician-patient privilege comes first to mind, but in fact it plays a very limited role. First, and most important, it is only a testimonial privilege, not a general obligation to maintain confidentiality: though it may permit a doctor to refuse to disclose medical information in court, it does not require the doctor to keep information from employers or insurers. Second, it is a statutory privilege or one created through judicial rulemaking and does not exist in all jurisdictions. According to the Privacy Protection Study Commission 43 states have some form of testimonial privilege, yet some of these are only applicable to psychiatrists. Third,

as a privilege created by state statute, it does not apply in non-diversity federal court proceedings, Personal Privacy, supra, at 284. Fourth, the privilege is in most states subject to many exceptions. In California, it is subject to twelve exceptions, including cases where the patient is a litigant, criminal proceedings, will contests, and physician licensure proceedings. State privilege statutes often cover physicians only, who today deliver only about 5% of health care. Finally, the privilege applies only to confidential disclosures made to a physician in the course of treatment and is easily waived.

5. Several federal and state statutes protect the confidentiality of medical information. Most notable among these are amendments to the Drug Abuse and Treatment Acts and Comprehensive Alcohol Abuse and Alcoholism Prevention, Treatment, and Rehabilitation Act, 42 U.S.C.A. §§ 290dd–3, 390ee–3 (West 1982 & Supp.1986), and implementing regulations, 42 C.F.R. Part 2 (1985), which impose rigorous requirements on the disclosure of information from alcohol and drug abuse treatment programs. Some state statutes provide civil penalties for disclosure of confidential information. See Ill.Rev.Stat. ch. 91½, § 815; West's Fla.Stat.Ann. § 395.018.

6. State courts have imposed liability on doctors for violating a duty of confidentiality expressed or implied in state licensure or privilege statutes. See Berry v. Moench, 8 Utah 2d 191, 331 P.2d 814 (1958); Felis v. Greenberg, 51 Misc.2d 441, 273 N.Y.S.2d 288 (1966). Others have rejected such a duty. See Moses v. McWilliams, 379 Pa.Super. 150, 549 A.2d 950 (1988). Several common law theories have also been advanced to impose liability on professionals who disclose medical information. Two of these, invasion of privacy and breach of confidential relationship, are discussed in Humphers. See Berger v. Sonneland, 101 Wash.App. 141, 1 P.3d 1187 (Wash.App.2000)(allowing action for unauthorized disclosure of confidential information, including emotional distress damages.)

Where the doctor breaches a confidence in reporting a plaintiff's health problem to a third party, and the plaintiff arguably had an obligation to report directly, courts have refused to allow a suit for breach of confidentiality. See Alar v. Mercy Memorial Hospital, 208 Mich.App. 518, 529 N.W.2d 318 (Mich.App.1995)(psychiatrist informed Air Force Academy about suicide attempt of high school student who had been accepted to the Academy; the court held that there was no causal link between the defendant's disclosure and the harm suffered by plaintiff, since he had an independent obligation to inform.) Absent a compelling public interest or other justification, however, an action typically will life for a physician's breach of the duty to maintain patient confidences. See McCormick v. England, 328 S.C. 627, 494 S.E.2d 431 (S.C.App.1997); Marek v. Ketyer, 733 A.2d 1268 (Pa.Super.1999).

Other theories that have been argued, some of which are mentioned in Humphers, include breach of contract, Hammonds v. Aetna Casualty and Surety Co., 3 Ohio Misc. 83, 237 F.Supp. 96 (N.D.Ohio 1965) and 7 Ohio Misc. 25, 243 F.Supp. 793 (N.D.Ohio 1965); Doe v. Roe, 93 Misc.2d 201, 400 N.Y.S.2d 668 (1977); medical malpractice, Clark v. Geraci, 29 Misc.2d 791, 208 N.Y.S.2d 564 (1960) (rejecting argument); defamation, Gilson v. Knickerbocker Hospital, 280 App.Div. 690, 116 N.Y.S.2d 745 (1952) (rejecting argument). Where an accurate disclosure of information is made in good faith for a legitimate purpose, courts are generally reluctant to impose liability. See, discussing liability theories, Joseph G. White, Physicians' Liability for Breach of Confidentiality: Beyond the Limitations of the Privacy Tort, 49 S.C.L.Rev. 1271 (1998).

7. Does a patient have a right to review his or her own records? Since access to medical information is commonly granted pursuant to patient consent, it would seem that the answer to this question would obviously be yes. Surprisingly, however, a provider may still deny a patient access to medical records in a number of jurisdictions. Medical records are the property of the institution or practitioner that creates them, McGarry v. J.A. Mercier Co., 272 Mich. 501, 262 N.W. 296 (1935), though some courts have recognized a property right of the patient in the information the records contain, Pyramid Life Insurance Co. v. Masonic Hospital Association, 191 F.Supp. 51 (W.D.Okl.1961). Many (though certainly not all) doctors argue that patients should not have access to their records, or should have access only under tight controls. They contend that patients cannot understand the information found in the records, may become anxious and upset by what they find, and may rely on medical information to engage in harmful self-treatment. They argue that patient access to medical information may violate confidences of third parties and discourage physician frankness in recording, and will impose administrative costs on institutions. Patient advocates argue that greater access will improve patient understanding of and compliance with treatment, physician-patient relations, and continuity of care. They also contend that patients cannot give informed authorization for disclosure of records to others if they do not know the contents of their own records, and thus access is important. Most of the evidence available supports the arguments for greater access—there is little evidence that patients are harmed by disclosure, some that they are helped. See Hayley Rosenman, Patients' Right to Access Their Medical Records: An Argument for Uniform Recognition of a Right of Access in the United States and Australia, 21 Fordham Int'l L.J. 1500(1998); Paul V. Stearns, Access To and Cost of Reproduction of Patient Medical Records: A Comparison of State Laws, 21 J.Leg.Med. 79 (2000).

Several states have enacted statutes permitting patients access to their medical records, though these are often subject to exceptions. Some statutes, for example, only provide access subsequent to discharge, West's Colo.Rev.Stat.Ann. §§ 25–1–801 & 802; Conn.Gen.Stat.Ann. § 4–104; 22 Me.Rev.Stat.Ann. § 1711; others permit the institution to provide only a summary of the records; West's Ann.Cal.Health & Safety Code § 25256; Or.Rev.Stat. 192.525; Minn.Stat.Ann. § 144.335; and others require the patient to show good cause for access, Tenn. Code Ann. § 53–1322(A); Miss.Code 1981, § 41–9–65. Absent statutory authority, a number of courts have permitted patients access to records under a property theory, Wallace v. University Hospitals of Cleveland, 164 N.E.2d 917 (Ohio Com.Pl.1959), modified, 170 N.E.2d 261 (1960), appeal dismissed, 171 Ohio St. 487, 172 N.E.2d 459 (1961); or fiduciary theory, Hutchins v. Texas Rehabilitation Commission, 544 S.W.2d 802 (Tex.Civ.App.1976); Emmett v. Eastern Dispensary and Casualty Hospital, 396 F.2d 931 (D.C.Cir.1967). Some courts, however, have denied patients access to their records, Gotkin v. Miller, 379 F.Supp. 859 (E.D.N.Y.1974).

8. Medical records often play a pivotal role in medical malpractice cases. By the time a malpractice action comes to trial memories may have dimmed as to what actually occurred at the time negligence is alleged to have taken place, leaving the medical record as the most telling evidence. Medical records, if properly authenticated, will usually be admitted under the business records exception to the hearsay rule. Because either documentation of inadequate care or inadequate documentation of care may result in liability, physicians are sometimes tempted to destroy records or to alter them to reflect the care they wish in retrospect they had rendered. There is nothing wrong with correcting records, so

long as corrections are made in such a way as to leave the previous entry clearly readable and the new entry clearly identified as a corrected entry. Conscious concealment, fabrication, or falsification of records may result in an inference of awareness of guilt, Pisel v. Stamford Hospital, 180 Conn. 314, 340, 430 A.2d 1, 15 (1980); Thor v. Boska, 38 Cal.App.3d 558, 113 Cal.Rptr. 296 (1974); or punitive damages. It may also toll the statute of limitations. Finally, premature disposition of records could result in negligence liability, Fox v. Cohen, 84 Ill.App.3d 744, 40 Ill.Dec. 477, 406 N.E.2d 178 (1980).

9. The duty to maintain confidentiality occasionally comes in conflict with a duty to disclose information. Such a duty to disclose may be based on a statute, such as a child abuse or venereal disease reporting act, or on the common law duty of psychotherapists to warn identifiable persons threatened by their patients. See section B, infra.

B. FEDERAL MEDICAL PRIVACY STANDARDS

Concerns about the privacy of patient medical information have intensified with the growth of both electronic recordkeeping and the Internet. The federal government studied this problem for several years before developing a highly detailed set of standards for health care providers.

Standards for Privacy of Individually Identifiable Health Information

Department of Health and Human Services
Office of the Secretary

65 FR 82462
45 CFR Parts 160 and 164
Thursday, December 28, 2000

This regulation has three major purposes: (1) To protect and enhance the rights of consumers by providing them access to their health information and controlling the inappropriate use of that information; (2) to improve the quality of health care in the U.S. by restoring trust in the health care system among consumers, health care professionals, and the multitude of organizations and individuals committed to the delivery of care; and (3) to improve the efficiency and effectiveness of health care delivery by creating a national framework for health privacy protection that builds on efforts by states, health systems, and individual organizations and individuals.

* * *

In enacting HIPAA, Congress recognized the fact that administrative simplification cannot succeed if we do not also protect the privacy and confidentiality of personal health information. The provision of high-quality health care requires the exchange of personal, often-sensitive information between an individual and a skilled practitioner. Vital to that interaction is the patient's ability to trust that the information shared will be protected and kept confidential. Yet many patients are concerned that their information is not protected. Among the factors adding to this concern are the growth of the number of organizations involved in the provision of care and the processing of claims, the growing use of electronic information technology, increased efforts to market health care and other products to consumers, and the increasing ability to collect highly sensitive information about a person's current and future health status as a result of advances in scientific research.

Rules requiring the protection of health privacy in the United States have been enacted primarily by the states. While virtually every state has enacted one or more laws to safeguard privacy, these laws vary significantly from state to state and typically apply to only part of the health care system. Many states have adopted laws that protect the health information relating to certain health conditions such as mental illness, communicable diseases, cancer, HIV/AIDS, and other stigmatized conditions. An examination of state health privacy laws and regulations, however, found that "state laws, with a few notable exceptions, do not extend comprehensive protections to people's medical records." Many state rules fail to provide such basic protections as ensuring a patient's legal right to see a copy of his or her medical record. See Health Privacy Project, "The State of Health Privacy: An Uneven Terrain," Institute for Health Care Research and Policy, Georgetown University (July 1999) (http://www.healthprivacy.org) (the "Georgetown Study").

Until now, virtually no federal rules existed to protect the privacy of health information and guarantee patient access to such information. This final rule establishes, for the first time, a set of basic national privacy standards and fair information practices that provides all Americans with a basic level of protection and peace of mind that is essential to their full participation in their care. The rule sets a floor of ground rules for health care providers, health plans, and health care clearinghouses to follow, in order to protect patients and encourage them to seek needed care. The rule seeks to balance the needs of the individual with the needs of the society. It creates a framework of protection that can be strengthened by both the federal government and by states as health information systems continue to evolve.

Need for a National Health Privacy Framework

The Importance of Privacy

Privacy is a fundamental right. As such, it must be viewed differently than any ordinary economic good. The costs and benefits of a regulation must, of course, be considered as a means of identifying and weighing options. At the same time, it is important not to lose sight of the inherent meaning of privacy: it speaks to our individual and collective freedom.

* * *

Increasing Public Concern About Loss of Privacy

Today, it is virtually impossible for any person to be truly "let alone." The average American is inundated with requests for information from potential employers, retail shops, telephone marketing firms, electronic marketers, banks, insurance companies, hospitals, physicians, health plans, and others. In a 1998 national survey, 88 percent of consumers said they were "concerned" by the amount of information being requested, including 55 percent who said they were "very concerned." See Privacy and American Business, 1998 Privacy Concerns & Consumer Choice Survey (http://www.pandab.org). These worries are not just theoretical. Consumers who use the Internet to make purchases or request "free" information often are asked for personal and financial information. Companies making such requests routinely promise to protect the confidentiality of that information.

Yet several firms have tried to sell this information to other companies even after promising not to do so.

Americans' concern about the privacy of their health information is part of a broader anxiety about their lack of privacy in an array of areas. * * *

This growing concern stems from several trends, including the growing use of interconnected electronic media for business and personal activities, our increasing ability to know an individual's genetic make-up, and, in health care, the increasing complexity of the system. Each of these trends brings the potential for tremendous benefits to individuals and society generally. At the same time, each also brings new potential for invasions of our privacy.

Increasing Use of Interconnected Electronic Information Systems

Until recently, health information was recorded and maintained on paper and stored in the offices of community-based physicians, nurses, hospitals, and other health care professionals and institutions. In some ways, this imperfect system of record keeping created a false sense of privacy among patients, providers, and others. Patients' health information has never remained completely confidential. Until recently, however, a breach of confidentiality involved a physical exchange of paper records or a verbal exchange of information. Today, however, more and more health care providers, plans, and others are utilizing electronic means of storing and transmitting health information. In 1996, the health care industry invested an estimated $10 billion to $15 billion on information technology. See National Research Council, Computer Science and Telecommunications Board, "For the Record: Protecting Electronic Health Information," (1997). The electronic information revolution is transforming the recording of health information so that the disclosure of information may require only a push of a button. In a matter of seconds, a person's most profoundly private information can be shared with hundreds, thousands, even millions of individuals and organizations at a time. While the majority of medical records still are in paper form, information from those records is often copied and transmitted through electronic means.

This ease of information collection, organization, retention, and exchange made possible by the advances in computer and other electronic technology affords many benefits to individuals and to the health care industry. Use of electronic information has helped to speed the delivery of effective care and the processing of billions of dollars worth of health care claims. Greater use of electronic data has also increased our ability to identify and treat those who are at risk for disease, conduct vital research, detect fraud and abuse, and measure and improve the quality of care delivered in the U.S. The National Research Council recently reported that "the Internet has great potential to improve Americans" health by enhancing communications and improving access to information for care providers, patients, health plan administrators, public health officials, biomedical researchers, and other health professionals. See "Networking Health: Prescriptions for the Internet," National Academy of Sciences (2000).

At the same time, these advances have reduced or eliminated many of the financial and logistical obstacles that previously served to protect the confidentiality of health information and the privacy interests of individuals. And they have made our information available to many more people. The shift from paper to electronic records, with the accompanying greater flows of sensitive health information, thus strengthens the arguments for giving legal protection to the right to privacy in health information. In an earlier period where it was far more expensive to access and use medical records, the risk of harm to individuals was relatively low. In the potential near future, when technology makes it almost free to send lifetime medical records over the Internet, the risks may grow rapidly. It may become cost-effective, for instance, for companies to offer services that allow purchasers to obtain details of a person's physical and mental treatments. In addition to legitimate possible uses for such services, malicious or inquisitive persons may download medical records for purposes ranging from identity theft to embarrassment to prurient interest in the life of a celebrity or neighbor. The comments to the proposed privacy rule indicate that many persons believe that they have a right to live in society without having these details of their lives laid open to unknown and possibly hostile eyes. These technological changes, in short, may provide a reason for institutionalizing privacy protections in situations where the risk of harm did not previously justify writing such protections into law.

The growing level of trepidation about privacy in general, noted above, has tracked the rise in electronic information technology. Americans have embraced the use of the Internet and other forms of electronic information as a way to provide greater access to information, save time, and save money. For example, 60 percent of Americans surveyed in 1999 reported that they have a computer in their home; 82 percent reported that they have used a computer; 64 percent say they have used the Internet; and 58 percent have sent an e-mail. Among those who are under the age of 60, these percentages are even higher. See "National Survey of Adults on Technology," Henry J. Kaiser Family Foundation (February, 2000). But 59 percent of Americans reported that they worry that an unauthorized person will gain access to their information. A recent survey suggests that 75 percent of consumers seeking health information on the Internet are concerned or very concerned about the health sites they visit sharing their personal health information with a third party without their permission. Ethics Survey of Consumer Attitudes about Health Web Sites, California Health Care Foundation, at 3 (January, 2000).

Unless public fears are allayed, we will be unable to obtain the full benefits of electronic technologies. The absence of national standards for the confidentiality of health information has made the health care industry and the population in general uncomfortable about this primarily financially-driven expansion in the use of electronic data. Many plans, providers, and clearinghouses have taken steps to safeguard the privacy of individually identifiable health information. Yet they must currently rely on a patchwork of State laws and regulations that are incomplete and, at times, inconsistent. States have, to varying degrees, attempted to enhance confidentiality by establishing laws governing at least some aspects of medical record privacy. This approach, though a step in the right direction, is inadequate. These laws fail to provide a consistent or comprehensive legal foundation of health information privacy. For example, there is considerable variation among the states in the type of information protected and the scope of the protections provided. See Georgetown Study, at Executive Summary; Lawrence O. Gostin, Zita Lazzarrini, Kathleen M. Flaherty, Legislative Survey of State Confidentiality Laws, with Specific Emphasis on HIV and Immunization, Report to Centers for Disease Control, Council of State and Territorial Epidemiologists, and Task Force for Child Survival and Development, Carter Presidential Center (1996) (Gostin Study).

Moreover, electronic health data is becoming increasingly "national"; as more information becomes available in electronic form, it can have value far beyond the immediate community where the patient resides. Neither private action nor state laws provide a sufficiently comprehensive and rigorous legal structure to allay public concerns, protect the right to privacy, and correct the market failures caused by the absence of privacy protections (see discussion below of market failure under section V.C). Hence, a national policy with consistent rules is necessary to encourage the increased and proper use of electronic information while also protecting the very real needs of patients to safeguard their privacy.

Advances in Genetic Sciences

Recently, scientists completed nearly a decade of work unlocking the mysteries of the human genome, creating tremendous new opportunities to identify and prevent many of the leading causes of death and disability in this country and around the world. Yet the absence of privacy protections for health information endanger these efforts by creating a barrier of distrust and suspicion among consumers. A 1995 national poll found that more than 85 percent of those surveyed were either "very concerned" or "somewhat concerned" that insurers and employers might gain access to and use genetic information. See Harris Poll, 1995 #34. Sixty-three percent of the 1,000 participants in a 1997 national survey said they would not take genetic tests if insurers and employers could gain access to the results. See "Genetic Information and the Workplace," Department of Labor, Department of Health and Human Services, Equal Employment Opportunity Commission, January 20, 1998. "In genetic testing studies at the National Institutes of Health, thirty-two percent of eligible people who were offered a test for breast cancer risk declined to take it, citing concerns about loss of privacy and the potential for discrimination in health insurance." Sen. Leahy's comments for March 10, 1999 Introduction of the Medical Information Privacy and Security Act.

The Changing Health Care System

The number of entities who are maintaining and transmitting individually identifiable health information has increased significantly over the last 10 years. In addition, the rapid growth of integrated health care delivery systems requires greater use of integrated health information systems. The health care industry has been transformed from one that relied primarily on one-on-one interactions between patients and clinicians to a system of integrated health care delivery networks and managed care providers. Such a system requires the processing and collection of information about patients and plan enrollees (for example, in claims files or enrollment records), resulting in the creation of databases that can be easily transmitted. This dramatic change in the practice of medicine brings with it important prospects for the improvement of the quality of care and reducing the cost of that care. It also, however, means that increasing numbers of people have access to health information. And, as health plan functions are increasingly outsourced, a growing number of organizations not affiliated with our physicians or health plans also have access to health information.

According to the American Health Information Management Association (AHIMA), an average of 150 people "from nursing staff to x-ray technicians, to billing clerks" have access to a patient's medical records during the course of a typical hospitalization. While many of these individuals have a legitimate need to see all or part of a patient's records, no laws govern who those people are, what information they are able to see, and what they are and are not allowed to do with that information once they have access to it. According to the National Research Council, individually identifiable health information frequently is shared with:

— Consulting physicians;

— Managed care organizations;

— Health insurance companies

— Life insurance companies;

— Self-insured employers;

— Pharmacies;

— Pharmacy benefit managers;

— Clinical laboratories;

— Accrediting organizations;

— State and Federal statistical agencies; and

— Medical information bureaus.

Much of this sharing of information is done without the knowledge of the patient involved. While many of these functions are important for smooth functioning of the health care system, there are no rules governing how that information is used by secondary and tertiary users. For example, a pharmacy benefit manager could receive information to determine whether an insurance plan or HMO should cover a prescription, but then use the information to market other products to the same patient. Similarly, many of us obtain health insurance coverage though our employer and, in some instances, the employer itself acts as the insurer. In these cases, the employer will obtain identifiable health information about its employees as part of the legitimate health insurance functions such as claims processing, quality improvement, and fraud detection activities. At the same time, there is no comprehensive protection prohibiting the employer from using that information to make decisions about promotions or job retention.

* * *

Concerns about the lack of attention to information privacy in the health care industry are not merely theoretical. In the absence of a national legal framework of health privacy protections, consumers are increasingly vulnerable to the exposure of their personal health information. Disclosure of individually identifiable information can occur deliberately or accidentally and can occur within an organization or be the result of an external breach of security. Examples of recent privacy breaches include:

— A Michigan-based health system accidentally posted the medical records of thousands of patients on the Internet (The Ann Arbor News, February 10, 1999).

— A Utah-based pharmaceutical benefits management firm used patient data to solicit business for its owner, a drug store (Kiplingers, February 2000).

— An employee of the Tampa, Florida, health department took a computer disk containing the names of 4,000 people who had tested positive for HIV, the virus that causes AIDS (USA Today, October 10, 1996).

— The health insurance claims forms of thousands of patients blew out of a truck on its way to a recycling center in East Hartford, Connecticut (The Hartford Courant, May 14, 1999).

— A patient in a Boston-area hospital discovered that her medical record had been read by more than 200 of the hospital's employees (The Boston Globe, August 1, 2000).

— A Nevada woman who purchased a used computer discovered that the computer still contained the prescription records of the customers of the pharmacy that had previously owned the computer. The pharmacy data base included names, addresses, social security numbers, and a list of all the medicines the customers had purchased. (The New York Times, April 4, 1997 and April 12, 1997).

— A speculator bid $4000 for the patient records of a family practice in South Carolina. Among the businessman's uses of the purchased records was selling them back to the former patients. (New York Times, August 14, 1991).

— In 1993, the Boston Globe reported that Johnson and Johnson marketed a list of 5 million names and addresses of elderly incontinent women. (ACLU Legislative Update, April 1998).

— A few weeks after an Orlando woman had her doctor perform some routine tests, she received a letter from a drug company promoting a treatment for her high cholesterol. (Orlando Sentinel, November 30, 1997).

No matter how or why a disclosure of personal information is made, the harm to the individual is the same. In the face of industry evolution, the potential benefits of our changing health care system, and the real risks and occurrences of harm, protection of privacy must be built into the routine operations of our health care system.

Privacy Is Necessary To Secure Effective, High Quality Health Care

While privacy is one of the key values on which our society is built, it is more than an end in itself. It is also necessary for the effective delivery of health care, both to individuals and to populations. The market failures caused by the lack of effective privacy protections for health information are discussed below (see section V.C below). Here, we discuss how privacy is a necessary foundation for delivery of high quality health care. In short, the entire health care system is built upon the willingness of individuals to share the most intimate details of their lives with their health care providers.

The need for privacy of health information, in particular, has long been recognized as critical to the delivery of needed medical care. More than anything else, the relationship between a patient and a clinician is based on trust. The clinician must trust the patient to give full and truthful information about their health, symptoms, and medical history. The patient must trust the clinician to use that information to improve his or her health and to respect the need to keep such information private. In order to receive accurate and reliable diagnosis and treatment, patients must provide health care professionals with accurate, detailed information about their personal health, behavior, and other aspects of their lives. The provision of health information assists in the diagnosis of an illness or condition, in the development of a treatment plan, and in the evaluation of the effectiveness of that treatment. In the absence of full and accurate information, there is a serious risk that the treatment plan will be inappropriate to the patient's situation.

Patients also benefit from the disclosure of such information to the health plans that pay for and can help them gain access to needed care. Health plans and health care clearinghouses rely on the provision of such information to accurately and promptly process claims for payment and for other administrative functions that directly affect a patient's ability to receive needed care, the quality of that care, and the efficiency with which it is delivered.

Accurate medical records assist communities in identifying troubling public health trends and in evaluating the effectiveness of various public health efforts. Accurate information helps public and private payers make correct payments for care received and lower costs by identifying fraud. Accurate information provides scientists with data they need to conduct research. We cannot improve the quality of health care without information about which treatments work, and which do not.

Individuals cannot be expected to share the most intimate details of their lives unless they have confidence that such information will not be used or shared inappropriately. Privacy violations reduce consumers' trust in the health care system and institutions that serve them. Such a loss of faith can impede the quality of the health care they receive, and can harm the financial health of health care institutions.

Patients who are worried about the possible misuse of their information often take steps to protect their privacy. Recent studies show that a person who does not believe his privacy will be protected is much less likely to participate fully in the diagnosis and treatment of his medical condition. A national survey conducted in January 1999 found that one in five Americans believe their health information is being used inappropriately. See California HealthCare Foundation, "National Survey: Confidentiality of Medical Records" (January, 1999) (http://www.chcf.org). More troubling is the fact that one in six Americans reported that they have taken some sort of evasive action to avoid the inappropriate use of their information by providing inaccurate information to a health care provider, changing physicians, or avoiding care altogether. Similarly, in its comments on our proposed rule, the Association of American Physicians and Surgeons reported 78 percent of its members reported withholding information from a patient's record due to privacy concerns and another 87 percent reported having had a patient request to withhold information from their records. [ ]

* * *

Breaches of Health Privacy Harm More Than Our Health Status

A breach of a person's health privacy can have significant implications well beyond the physical health of that person, including the loss of a job, alienation of family and friends, the loss of health insurance, and public humiliation. For example:

— A banker who also sat on a county health board gained access to patients' records and identified several people with cancer and called in their mortgages. See the National Law Journal, May 30, 1994.

— A physician was diagnosed with AIDS at the hospital in which he practiced medicine. His surgical privileges were suspended. See Estate of Behringer v. Medical Center at Princeton, 249 N.J.Super. 597, 592 A.2d 1251 (1991).

— A candidate for Congress nearly saw her campaign derailed when newspapers published the fact that she had sought psychiatric treatment after a suicide attempt. See New York Times, October 10, 1992, Section 1, page 25.

— A 30–year FBI veteran was put on administrative leave when, without his permission, his pharmacy released information about his treatment for depression. (Los Angeles Times, September 1, 1998) Consumer Reports found that 40 percent of insurers disclose personal health information to lenders, employers, or marketers without customer permission. "Who's reading your Medical Records," Consumer Reports, October 1994, at 628, paraphrasing Sweeny, Latanya, "Weaving Technology and Policy Together to Maintain Confidentiality," The Journal Of Law Medicine and Ethics (Summer & Fall 1997) Vol. 25, Numbers 2,3.

The answer to these concerns is not for consumers to withdraw from society and the health care system, but for society to establish a clear national legal framework for privacy. By spelling out what is and what is not an allowable use of a person's identifiable health information, such standards can help to restore and preserve trust in the health care system and the individuals and institutions that comprise that system. As medical historian Paul Starr wrote: "Patients have a strong interest in preserving the privacy of their personal health information but they also have an interest in medical research and other efforts by health care organizations to improve the medical care they receive. As members of the wider community, they have an interest in public health measures that require the collection of personal data." (P. Starr, "Health and the Right to Privacy," American Journal of Law & Medicine, 25, nos. 2 & 3 (1999) 193–201). The task of society and its government is to create a balance in which the individual's needs and rights are balanced against the needs and rights of society as a whole.

National standards for medical privacy must recognize the sometimes competing goals of improving individual and public health, advancing scientific knowledge, enforcing the laws of the land, and processing and paying claims for health care services. This need for balance has been recognized by many of the experts in this field. Cavoukian and Tapscott described it this way: "An individual's right to privacy may conflict with the collective rights of the public * * *. We do not suggest that privacy is an absolute right that reigns supreme over all other rights. It does not. However, the case for privacy will depend on a number of factors that can influence the balance—the level of harm to the individual involved versus the needs of the public."

The Federal Response

There have been numerous federal initiatives aimed at protecting the privacy of especially sensitive personal information over the past several years—and several decades. While the rules below are likely the largest single federal initiative to protect privacy, they are by no means alone in the field. Rather, the rules arrive in the context of recent legislative activity to grapple with advances in technology, in addition to an already established body of law granting federal protections for personal privacy.

* * *

As described in more detail in the next section, Congress recognized the importance of protecting the privacy of health information by enacting the Health Insurance Portability and Accountability Act of 1996. The Act called on Congress to enact a medical privacy statute and asked the Secretary of Health and Human Services to provide Congress with recommendations for protecting the confidentiality of health care information. The Congress further recognized the importance of such standards by providing the Secretary with authority to promulgate regulations on health care privacy in the event that lawmakers were unable to act within the allotted three years.

Finally, it also is important for the U.S. to join the rest of the developed world in establishing basic medical privacy protections. In 1995, the European Union (EU) adopted a Data Privacy Directive requiring its 15 member states to adopt consistent privacy laws by October 1998. The EU urged all other nations to do the same or face the potential loss of access to information from EU countries.

* * *

Subpart E—Privacy of Individually Identifiable Health Information

§ 164.104 Applicability.

Except as otherwise provided, the provisions of this part apply to covered entities: health plans, health care clearinghouses, and health care providers who transmit health information in electronic form in connection with any transaction referred to in section 1173(a)(1) of the Act.

* * *

Subpart E—Privacy of Individually Identifiable Health Information

* * *

§ 164.501 Definitions.

As used in this subpart, the following terms have the following meanings:

* * *

Individually identifiable health information is information that is a subset of health information, including demographic information collected from an individual, and:

(1) Is created or received by a health care provider, health plan, employer, or health care clearinghouse; and

(2) Relates to the past, present, or future physical or mental health or condition of an individual; the provision of health care to an individual; or the past, present, or future payment for the provision of health care to an individual; and

(i) That identifies the individual; or

(ii) With respect to which there is a reasonable basis to believe the information can be used to identify the individual.

* * *

Marketing means to make a communication about a product or service a purpose of which is to encourage recipients of the communication to purchase or use the product or service.

(1) Marketing does not include communications that meet the requirements of paragraph (2) of this definition and that are made by a covered entity:

(i) For the purpose of describing the entities participating in a health care provider network or health plan network, or for the purpose of describing if and the extent to which a product or service (or payment for such product or service) is provided by a covered entity or included in a plan of benefits; or

(ii) That are tailored to the circumstances of a particular individual and the communications are:

(A) Made by a health care provider to an individual as part of the treatment of the individual, and for the purpose of furthering the treatment of that individual; or

(B) Made by a health care provider or health plan to an individual in the course of managing the treatment of that individual, or for the purpose of directing or recommending to that individual alternative treatments, therapies, health care providers, or settings of care.

(2) A communication described in paragraph (1) of this definition is not included in marketing if:

(i) The communication is made orally; or

(ii) The communication is in writing and the covered entity does not receive direct or indirect remuneration from a third party for making the communication.

* * *

Protected health information means individually identifiable health information:

(1) Except as provided in paragraph (2) of this definition, that is:

(i) Transmitted by electronic media;

(ii) Maintained in any medium described in the definition of electronic media at § 162.103 of this subchapter; or

(iii) Transmitted or maintained in any other form or medium.

* * *

Treatment means the provision, coordination, or management of health care and related services by one or more health care providers, including the coordination or management of health care by a health care provider with a third party; consultation between health care providers relating to a patient; or the referral of a patient for health care from one health care provider to another.

Use means, with respect to individually identifiable health information, the sharing, employment, application, utilization, examination, or analysis of such information within an entity that maintains such information.

§ 164.502 Uses and disclosures of protected health information: general rules.

(a) Standard. A covered entity may not use or disclose protected health information, except as permitted or required by this subpart or by subpart C of part 160 of this subchapter.

(1) Permitted uses and disclosures. A covered entity is permitted to use or disclose protected health information as follows:

(i) To the individual;

(ii) Pursuant to and in compliance with a consent that complies with § 164.506, to carry out treatment, payment, or health care operations;

(iii) Without consent, if consent is not required under § 164.506(a) and has not been sought under § 164.506(a)(4), to carry out treatment, payment, or health care operations, except with respect to psychotherapy notes;

(iv) Pursuant to and in compliance with a valid authorization under § 164.508;

(v) Pursuant to an agreement under, or as otherwise permitted by, § 164.510; and

(vi) As permitted by and in compliance with this section, § 164.512, or § 164.514(e), (f), and (g).

(2) Required disclosures. A covered entity is required to disclose protected health information:

(i) To an individual, when requested under, and required by § 164.524 or § 164.528; and

(ii) When required by the Secretary under subpart C of part 160 of this subchapter to investigate or determine the covered entity's compliance with this subpart.

(b) Standard: Minimum necessary. (1) Minimum necessary applies. When using or disclosing protected health information or when requesting protected health information from another covered entity, a covered entity must make reasonable efforts to limit protected health information to the minimum necessary to accomplish the intended purpose of the use, disclosure, or request.

(2) Minimum necessary does not apply. This requirement does not apply to:

(i) Disclosures to or requests by a health care provider for treatment;

(ii) Uses or disclosures made to the individual, as permitted under paragraph (a)(1)(i) of this section, as required by paragraph (a)(2)(i) of this section, or pursuant to an authorization under § 164.508, except for authorizations requested by the covered entity under § 164.508(d), (e), or (f);

(iii) Disclosures made to the Secretary in accordance with subpart C of part 160 of this subchapter;

(iv) Uses or disclosures that are required by law, as described by § 164.512(a); and

(v) Uses or disclosures that are required for compliance with applicable requirements of this subchapter.

(c) Standard: Uses and disclosures of protected health information subject to an agreed upon restriction. A covered entity that has agreed to a restriction pursuant to § 164.522(a)(1) may not use or disclose the protected health information covered by the restriction in violation of such restriction, except as otherwise provided in § 164.522(a).

* * *

(h) Standard: Confidential communications. A covered health care provider or health plan must comply with the applicable requirements of § 164.522(b) in communicating protected health information.

(i) Standard: Uses and disclosures consistent with notice. A covered entity that is required by § 164.520 to have a notice may not use or disclose protected health information in a manner inconsistent with such notice. A covered entity that is required by § 164.520(b)(1)(iii) to include a specific statement in its notice if it intends to engage in an activity listed in § 164.520(b)(1)(iii)(A)-(C), may not use or disclose protected health information for such activities, unless the required statement is included in the notice.

* * *

§ 164.506 Consent for uses or disclosures to carry out treatment, payment, or health care operations.

(a) Standard: Consent requirement. (1) Except as provided in paragraph (a)(2) or (a)(3) of this section, a covered health care provider must obtain the individual's consent, in accordance with this section, prior to using or disclosing protected health information to carry out treatment, payment, or health care operations.

(2) A covered health care provider may, without consent, use or disclose protected health information to carry out treatment, payment, or health care operations, if:

(i) The covered health care provider has an indirect treatment relationship with the individual; or

(ii) The covered health care provider created or received the protected health information in the course of providing health care to an individual who is an inmate.

(3)(i) A covered health care provider may, without prior consent, use or disclose protected health information created or received under paragraph (a)(3)(i)(A)-(C) of this section to carry out treatment, payment, or health care operations:

(A) In emergency treatment situations, if the covered health care provider attempts to obtain such consent as soon as reasonably practicable after the delivery of such treatment;

(B) If the covered health care provider is required by law to treat the individual, and the covered health care provider attempts to obtain such consent but is unable to obtain such consent; or

(C) If a covered health care provider attempts to obtain such consent from the individual but is unable to obtain such consent due to substantial barriers to communicating with the individual, and the covered health care provider determines, in the exercise of professional judgment, that the individual's consent to receive treatment is clearly inferred from the circumstances.

(ii) A covered health care provider that fails to obtain such consent in accordance with paragraph (a)(3)(i) of this section must document its attempt to obtain consent and the reason why consent was not obtained.

(4) If a covered entity is not required to obtain consent by paragraph (a)(1) of this section, it may obtain an individual's consent for the covered entity's own use or disclosure of protected health information to carry out treatment, payment, or health care operations, provided that such consent meets the requirements of this section.

(5) Except as provided in paragraph (f)(1) of this section, a consent obtained by a covered entity under this section is not effective to permit another covered entity to use or disclose protected health information.

(b) Implementation specifications: General requirements. (1) A covered health care provider may condition treatment on the provision by the individual of a consent under this section.

(2) A health plan may condition enrollment in the health plan on the provision by the individual of a consent under this section sought in conjunction with such enrollment.

(3) A consent under this section may not be combined in a single document with the notice required by § 164.520.

(4)(i) A consent for use or disclosure may be combined with other types of written legal permission from the individual (e.g., an informed consent for treatment or a consent to assignment of benefits), if the consent under this section:

(A) Is visually and organizationally separate from such other written legal permission; and

(B) Is separately signed by the individual and dated.

(ii) A consent for use or disclosure may be combined with a research authorization under § 164.508(f).

(5) An individual may revoke a consent under this section at any time, except to the extent that the covered entity has taken action in reliance thereon. Such revocation must be in writing.

(6) A covered entity must document and retain any signed consent under this section as required by § 164.530(j).

* * *

§ 164.508 Uses and disclosures for which an authorization is required.

(a) Standard: Authorizations for uses and disclosures. (1) Authorization required: General rule. Except as otherwise permitted or required by this subchapter, a covered entity may not use or disclose protected health information without an authorization that is valid under this section. When a covered entity obtains or receives a valid authorization for its use or disclosure of protected health information, such use or disclosure must be consistent with such authorization.

* * *

§ 164.510 Uses and disclosures requiring an opportunity for the individual to agree or to object.

A covered entity may use or disclose protected health information without the written consent or authorization of the individual as described by ss 164.506 and 164.508, respectively, provided that the individual is informed in advance of the use or disclosure and has the opportunity to agree to or prohibit or restrict the disclosure in accordance with the applicable requirements of this section. The covered entity may orally inform the individual of and obtain the individual's oral agreement or objection to a use or disclosure permitted by this section.

* * *

§ 164.512 Uses and disclosures for which consent, an authorization, or opportunity to agree or object is not required.

A covered entity may use or disclose protected health information without the written consent or authorization of the individual as described in §§ 164.506 and 164.508, respectively, or the opportunity for the individual to agree or object as described in § 164.510, in the situations covered by this section, subject to the applicable requirements of this section. When the covered entity is required by this section to inform the individual of, or when the individual may agree to, a use or disclosure permitted by this section, the covered entity's information and the individual's agreement may be given orally.

(a) Standard: Uses and disclosures required by law. (1) A covered entity may use or disclose protected health information to the extent that such use or disclosure is required by law and the use or disclosure complies with and is limited to the relevant requirements of such law.

(2) A covered entity must meet the requirements described in paragraph (c), (e), or (f) of this section for uses or disclosures required by law.

* * *

§ 164.514 Other requirements relating to uses and disclosures of protected health information.

(a) Standard: de-identification of protected health information. Health information that does not identify an individual and with respect to which there is no reasonable basis to believe that the information can be used to identify an individual is not individually identifiable health information.

(b) Implementation specifications: requirements for de-identification of protected health information. A covered entity may determine that health information is not individually identifiable health information only if:

(1) A person with appropriate knowledge of and experience with generally accepted statistical and scientific principles and methods for rendering information not individually identifiable:

(i) Applying such principles and methods, determines that the risk is very small that the information could be used, alone or in combination with other reasonably available information, by an anticipated recipient to identify an individual who is a subject of the information; and

(ii) Documents the methods and results of the analysis that justify such determination; * * *

(d)(1) Standard: minimum necessary requirements. A covered entity must reasonably ensure that the standards, requirements, and implementation specifications of s 164.502(b) and this section relating to a request for or the use and disclosure of the minimum necessary protected health information are met.

* * *

(3) Implementation specification: Minimum necessary disclosures of protected health information. (i) For any type of disclosure that it makes on a routine and recurring basis, a covered entity must implement policies and procedures (which may be standard protocols) that limit the protected health information disclosed to the amount reasonably necessary to achieve the purpose of the disclosure.

(ii) For all other disclosures, a covered entity must:

(A) Develop criteria designed to limit the protected health information disclosed to the information reasonably necessary to accomplish the purpose for which disclosure is sought; and

(B) Review requests for disclosure on an individual basis in accordance with such criteria.

* * *

(e)(1) Standard: Uses and disclosures of protected health information for marketing. A covered entity may not use or disclose protected health information for marketing without an authorization that meets the applicable requirements of s 164.508, except as provided for by paragraph (e)(2) of this section.

(2) Implementation specifications: Requirements relating to marketing. (i) A covered entity is not required to obtain an authorization under s 164.508 when it uses or discloses protected health information to make a marketing communication to an individual that:

(A) Occurs in a face-to-face encounter with the individual;

(B) Concerns products or services of nominal value; or

(C) Concerns the health-related products and services of the covered entity or of a third party and the communication meets the applicable conditions in paragraph (e)(3) of this section.

(ii) A covered entity may disclose protected health information for purposes of such communications only to a business associate that assists the covered entity with such communications.

(3) Implementation specifications: Requirements for certain marketing communications. For a marketing communication to qualify under paragraph (e)(2)(i) of this section, the following conditions must be met:

(i) The communication must:

(A) Identify the covered entity as the party making the communication;

(B) If the covered entity has received or will receive direct or indirect remuneration for making the communication, prominently state that fact; and

(C) Except when the communication is contained in a newsletter or similar type of general communication device that the covered entity distributes to a broad cross-section of patients, enrollees, or other broad groups of individuals, contain instructions describing how the individual may opt out of receiving future such communications.

(ii) If the covered entity uses or discloses protected health information to target the communication to individuals based on their health status or condition:

(A) The covered entity must make a determination prior to making the communication that the product or service being marketed may be beneficial to the health of the type or class of individual targeted; and

(B) The communication must explain why the individual has been targeted and how the product or service relates to the health of the individual.

(iii) The covered entity must make reasonable efforts to ensure that individuals who decide to opt out of receiving future marketing communications, under paragraph (e)(3)(i)(C) of this section, are not sent such communications.

* * *

§ 164.520 Notice of privacy practices for protected health information.

(a) Standard: notice of privacy practices. (1) Right to notice. Except as provided by paragraph (a)(2) or (3) of this section, an individual has a right to adequate notice of the uses and disclosures of protected health information that may be made by the covered entity, and of the individual's rights and the covered entity's legal duties with respect to protected health information.

* * *

§ 164.522 Rights to request privacy protection for protected health information.

(a)(1) Standard: Right of an individual to request restriction of uses and disclosures. (i) A covered entity must permit an individual to request that the covered entity restrict:

(A) Uses or disclosures of protected health information about the individual to carry out treatment, payment, or health care operations; and

(B) Disclosures permitted under s 164.510(b).

(ii) A covered entity is not required to agree to a restriction.

(iii) A covered entity that agrees to a restriction under paragraph (a)(1)(i) of this section may not use or disclose protected health information in violation of such restriction, except that, if the individual who requested the restriction is in need of emergency treatment and the restricted protected health information is needed to provide the emergency treatment, the covered entity may use the restricted protected health information, or may disclose such information to a health care provider, to provide such treatment to the individual.

(iv) If restricted protected health information is disclosed to a health care provider for emergency treatment under paragraph (a)(1)(iii) of this section, the covered entity must request that such health care provider not further use or disclose the information.

(v) A restriction agreed to by a covered entity under paragraph (a) of this section, is not effective under this subpart to prevent uses or disclosures permitted or required under ss 164.502(a)(2)(i), 164.510(a) or 164.512.

* * *

§ 164.524 Access of individuals to protected health information.

(a) Standard: Access to protected health information. (1) Right of access. Except as otherwise provided in paragraph (a)(2) or (a)(3) of this section, an individual has a right of access to inspect and obtain a copy of protected health information about the individual in a designated record set, for as long as the protected health information is maintained in the designated records * * *

* * *

§ 164.526 Amendment of protected health information.

(a) Standard: Right to amend. (1) Right to amend. An individual has the right to have a covered entity amend protected health information or a record about the individual in a designated record set for as long as the protected health information is maintained in the designated record set.

* * *

§ 164.528 Accounting of disclosures of protected health information.

(a) Standard: Right to an accounting of disclosures of protected health information. (1) An individual has a right to receive an accounting of disclosures of protected health information made by a covered entity in the six years prior to the date on which the accounting is requested, except for disclosures:

(i) To carry out treatment, payment and health care operations as provided in § 164.502;

(ii) To individuals of protected health information about them as provided in § 164.502;

* * *

§ 164.530 Administrative requirements.

(a)(1) Standard: Personnel designations. (i) A covered entity must designate a privacy official who is responsible for the development and implementation of the policies and procedures of the entity.

Notes and Questions

1. These rules step into a vacuum created by erratic state regulation and little federal regulation. Do they strike an appropriate balance between patient privacy and provider and insurer needs for information? Do they impose substantial new compliance costs on health care providers as a by-product of protecting privacy?

Are the rules open to criticism as not being protective enough in some ways? Consider the marketing sections 164.514, particularly standard (e)(1). "A covered entity is not required to obtain an authorization under § 164.508 when it uses or discloses protected health information to make a marketing communication to an individual that: (A) Occurs in a face-to-face encounter with the individual; (B) Concerns products or services of nominal value; or (C) Concerns the health-related products and services of the covered entity or of a third party and the communication meets the applicable conditions in paragraph (e)(3) of this section."

Does this mean a tremendous increase in the medical equivalent of junk mail targeted to your particular medical problems? How do you feel about having your health information available for such use? A pregnant woman, for example, could receive sales pitches about vitamins or infant health care products; a patient treated for sexually transmitted diseases could receive telemarketing calls offering condoms or new medicines; a patient treated for depression could receive pharmaceutical advertisements for the latest anti-depressants. The medical record becomes a marketing tool. Is this offensive, or is it just American-style capitalism in action, extending options to consumers as a by-product of their medical treatment. The rules provide for opt-out provisions to avoid such marketing. How easy will it be to notify hundreds of suppliers of medical products that you do not want to be bothered?

2. The portions of the Medical Privacy Standards quoted above in a highly abbreviated form give some sense of the scope and detail of the rules. They have several laudatory goals. First and foremost, they aim to give consumers control over their own health information. Health providers must inform patients about how their information is being used and to whom it is disclosed. The rules create a "disclosure history" for individuals. Most important, the release of private health information without consent is limited. Doctors treating patients, and hospitals, must obtain the patient's written consent to use their health information even for routine purposes such as treatment and payment. Other nonroutine disclosure requires specific patient authorization. Patients may access their own health files and request correction of potentially harmful errors.

Second, the rules set boundaries on medical record use and release. The amount of information to be disclosed is restricted to the "minimum necessary", in contrast to prevailing practice of releasing a patient's entire health record even if an entity needs very specific information.

Third, the rules attempt to ensure the security of personal health information. The rules are very specific in their mandates on providers and others who might access health information. They require privacy-conscious business practices, with internal procedures and privacy officers to protect the privacy of medical records. The rules create a whole new category of compliance officer within health care institutions as a result of the mandates in the rules.

Fourth, the rules create accountability for medical record use and release, with new criminal and civil penalties for improper use or disclosure. This rule applies the standards included in HIPAA to create new criminal penalties for intentional disclosure, up to $50,000 and up to a year in prison, with new civil penalties of $100 per person for unintentional disclosure and other violations, up to $25,000 per person per year. The rules do not however create a private cause of action for damages for harm that is suffered through intentional or negligent release of information.

Fifth, the rules attempt to balance public responsibility with privacy protections, requiring that information be disclosed only limited public purposes such as public health and research. They attempt to limit disclosure of information without sacrificing public safety.

See generally James G.Hodge, The Intersection of Federal Health Information Privacy and State Administrative Law: The Protection of Individual Health Data and Workers' Compensation, 51 Adm.L. Rev. 117(1999); (Health Privacy Project, The State of Health Privacy: An Uneven Terrain, Institute for Health Care Research and Policy, Georgetown University (July 1999) http://www.healthprivacy.org)

3. The urgency underlying the new federal medical privacy rules is understandable. Computer recordkeeping is increasingly common in storing and retrieving medical records. Indiana, for example, has expressly authorized retention of medical records in computer files. See West's Ann. Ind. Code §§ 34–3–15.5–1 et seq. Sensitive health care data are stored, transferred and used with the ease that only modern computers could allow. Given the sheer volume of data collected on each patient, the movement to computerize patient records is being pushed along by pressures from the federal and state governments as well as hospital desires for efficiency. As health care has blossomed into a complex industry, the organizations involved, from employers to drug companies and managed organizations, have a compelling interest in data to control their costs, increase revenues and improve performance. Information has as a result become a central aspect of the health care enterprise. Paul Starr, Health and the Right to Privacy, 25 Am.J.L. & Med. 194, 196(1999); Committee on Maintaining Privacy & Security in Health Care Applications of the National Information Infrastructure, National Research Council, For the Record: Protecting Electronic Health Information 25 (1997) (noting that more than half of hospitals were investing in electronic medical records and the market would grow into a $$1.5 billion industry by 2000); Lawrence O. Gostin, Health Information Privacy, 80 Cornell L.Rev. 451(1995); David M. Studdert, Direct Contracts, Data Sharing and Employee Risk Selection: New Stakes for Patient Privacy in Tomorrow's Health Insurance Markets, 25 Am.J.Law & Med. 233(1999).

4. Violations of health information privacy fall into three major categories. First, medical record information is abused or misappropriated. Legal protections for the alteration of the computerized medical record are less stringent than those for release of medical records generally. New computer development may add confidential information to these porous patient files. For example, the increased use of e-mail messages from patients to their physicians can lead to the storage of these messages in the file, allowed the patient's own words to be easily accessed. Patients may reveal too much in light of the casual and conversational attributes of e-mail messaging. Hackers may also gain access to hospital medical record systems. See,e.g., Ann Carrns, Hacker's Break–In at University Hospital Heats UP Debate on Security Standards, Wall St.J., December 2000. Data security measures and sanctions against misuse can reduce this problem.

Second, health information may be used by institutions for marketing and other commercial purposes, for example by selling patient prescription information to direct mail companies. Some of these uses may be valuable and the costs to patients small.

Third, organizations may abuse confidential patient health information in substantial and serious ways that result in discrimination, loss of employment, insurance or other welfare benefits. Alissa R. Spielberg, Online Without a Net: Physician–Patient Communication by Electronic Mail, 25 Am.J.Law & Med 267, 274 (1999); Latanya Sweeney, Weaving Technology and Policy Together to Maintain Confidentiality, 25 J.Law, Med & Ethics 98 (1997).

5. The Institute of Medicine has recommended that all providers adopt a computer-based patient record as the standard. Personally identifiable health information about individuals is available in electronic form in health databases and online networks. Such computerization of records aims to improve efficiency in health care delivery. It is likely that a standardized on-line database for all patients will become the national norm. This movement toward medical record computerization creates serious computer security and confidentiality issues. A third party with a modem and a computer can in theory download confidential patient information, opening the door to even wider proliferation of sensitive information about individuals. This raises privacy concerns about individually identifiable health information and the quality and reliability of that information. A computer security system can offer substantial confidentiality protections compared to traditional medical records because fewer access points are available to a computer; each person's access can be restricted to limited information; and information can be monitored through individual access codes. Computer storage can be designed with safeguards such as passwords, access codes, and selective "need to know" requirements for certain portions of a patient's file. Unauthorized access to computer files can also be traced through audit systems more easily than can such access to paper records. Informed consent doctrine could be redefined to require both the physician and the institution to discuss some of these informational risks with patients.

Institute of Medicine, The Computer–Based Patient Record: An Essential Technology for Health Care (Richard S. Dick and Elaine B. Steen, eds. 1991); see also, General Accounting Office, Committee on Governmental Affairs, U.S. Senate, Medical ADP Systems: Automated Medical Records Hold Promise to Improve Patient Care (January 1991). See generally, Lawrence O. Gostin, Joan Turek–Brezina, Madison Powers, and Rene Kozloff, Privacy and Security of Health Information in the Emerging Health Care System, 5 Health Matrix 1 (1995); Wendy E. Parmet, Public Health Protection and the Privacy of Medical Records, 16 Harv.C.R.–C.L. L.Rev. 265 (1981); Diane B. Lawrence, Strict Liability Computer Software and Medicine: Public Policy at the Crossroads, 23 Tort & Ins.L.J. 1 (1991); Health Privacy Working Group, Principles for Health Privacy (1999)(www.healthprivacy.org).

6. The obvious benefits of computerized record keeping have propelled medical records to a central position in health care delivery. A standardized database of patient information has the potential to promote efficiency, further competition, and allow providers to better track patient outcomes. Only a computerized record, in spite of its confidentiality dimensions, can further such goals. The new Medical Privacy Standards offer considerable protection to patients; they also require substantial expenditures by providers to achieve compliance by 2003 with the complex requirements.

See generally, James G. Hodge, National Health Information Privacy and New Federalism, 14 Notre Dame J.L.Ethics & Pub. Pol'y 791(2000); James G. Hodge, Lawrence O. Gostin, and Peter D. Jacobson, Legal Issues Concerning Electronic Health Information: Privacy, Quality, and Liability, 282 J.A.M.A. 1466(1999); Off. of Tech. Assessment, U.S. Congress, Protecting Privacy in Computerized Medical Information (1993); John D. Rootenberg, Computer–Based Patient Records: The Next Generation of Medicine?, 267 J.A.M.A. 168 (1992); Off. of Tech. Assessment, U.S. Congress, Policy Implications of Medical Information Systems 50–51 (1997). Institute of Medicine, The Computer-Based Patient Record: An Essential Technology for Health Care (1997)(www.nap.edu/readingroom/); Janlori Goldman, Protecting Privacy to Improve Health Care, 17 Health Affairs 47(1998).

C. DUTIES TO PROTECT THIRD PARTIES

The obligations of health professionals normally extend only to the patients with whom they have a legal relationship, either under an implied or an express contract. They are not under an obligation to enter into a relationship with a patient, and cannot be compelled to treat someone outside the boundaries of this contractual relationship. The Good Samaritan laws, discussed supra in Chapter 4, reflect legislative reinforcement of the absence of a duty to rescue at the common law. But what if doctors have information about a patient which if disclosed might prevent harm to others? Requirements of confidentiality of the physician-patient relationship militate against disclosure generally, and disclosure may expose the physician to potential liability, as the *Humphers* case indicates.

Physicians and other health professionals have in many jurisdictions an affirmative obligation to protect third parties against hazards created by their patients. Consider the limits on such a duty in *Pate* and *Bradshaw*, below.

PATE v. THRELKEL

Supreme Court of Florida, 1995.
661 So.2d 278.

WELLS, JUSTICE.

We have for review the following question certified to be of great public importance: DOES A PHYSICIAN OWE A DUTY OF CARE TO THE CHILDREN OF A PATIENT TO WARN THE PATIENT OF THE GENETICALLY TRANSFERABLE NATURE OF THE CONDITION FOR WHICH THE PHYSICIAN IS TREATING THE PATIENT? . . . [ ]

In March 1987, Marianne New received treatment for medullary thyroid carcinoma, a genetically transferable disease. In 1990, Heidi Pate, New's adult daughter, learned that she also had medullary thyroid carcinoma. Consequently, Pate and her husband filed a complaint against the physicians who initially treated New for the disease as well as the physicians' respective employers. Pate and her husband alleged that the physicians knew or should have known of the likelihood that New's children would have inherited the condition genetically; that the physicians were under a duty to warn New that her children should be tested for the disease; that had New been warned in 1987, she would have had her children tested at that time; and if Pate had been tested in 1987, she would have taken preventative action, and her condition, more likely than not, would have been curable. Pate claimed that as a direct and proximate cause of the physicians' negligence, she suffers from advanced medullary thyroid carcinoma and its various damaging effects.

The respondent health care providers moved to dismiss the complaint for failure to state a cause of action. Specifically, the respondents alleged that Pate did not demonstrate the existence of a professional relationship between her and respondents and thus failed to establish that respondents owed her a duty of care. The trial court granted the motion and dismissed the Pates' complaint with prejudice, finding that the plaintiffs were not patients of the respondents and that they did not fit within any exception to the requirement that there be a physician-patient relationship between the parties as a condition precedent to bringing a medical malpractice action.

The district court affirmed the trial court's dismissal. The court rejected the Pates' argument that it should, based upon past decisions recognizing a doctor's duty to inform others of a patient's contagious disease, [ ] extend a physician's duty to cover the child of a patient who suffers from an inheritable disease. The court also rejected the Pates' reliance on Schroeder v. Perkel, 87 N.J. 53, 432 A.2d 834 (1981), in which the parents of a four-year-old child brought suit against the child's pediatricians for failing to diagnose the child with cystic fibrosis early enough to prevent the parents from having a second diseased child. The New Jersey court in Schroeder recognized that due to the special nature of the family relationship, a physician's duty may extend beyond a patient to members of the patient's immediate family. [ ]

In rejecting the Pates' claim, the district court focused upon the legal issue of duty. . . . [T]he district court recognized the existence of a physician's duty. The court, however, declined to extend the boundaries of that duty to include Heidi Pate. . . . [ ]

We agree with the district court's focus on duty. We conclude that to answer the certified question we must consider two questions related to duty. First, we must determine whether New's physicians had a duty to warn New of the genetically transferable nature of her disease. We find that to make this determination we must apply section 766.102, Florida Statutes (1989), which defines the legal duty owed by a health care provider in a medical malpractice case. . . . [ ] In applying this statute to the instant case, we conclude that a duty exists if the statutory standard of care requires a reasonably prudent health care provider to warn a patient of the genetically transferable nature of the condition for which the physician was treating the patient.

In medical malpractice cases, the standard of care is determined by a consideration of expert testimony. . . . [ ] . . . [W]e must accept as true the Pates' allegations that pursuant to the prevailing standard of care, the health care providers were under a duty to warn New of the importance of testing her children for medullary thyroid carcinoma. . . . [ ]

The second question we must address in answering the certified question is to whom does the alleged duty to warn New of the nature of her disease run? The duty obviously runs to the patient who is in privity with the physician. In the past, courts have held that in order to maintain a cause of action against a physician, privity must exist between the plaintiff and the physician. [ ] In other professional relationships, however, we have recognized the rights of identified third party beneficiaries to recover from a professional because that party was the intended beneficiary of the prevailing standard of care. In such cases, we have determined that an absence of privity does not necessarily foreclose liability. [ ]. . . . [ ] We conclude that this analysis recognizing that privity is not always needed to establish liability should apply to the professional relationship between a patient's child and a health care provider.

Here, the alleged prevailing standard of care was obviously developed for the benefit of the patient's children as well as the patient. We conclude that when the prevailing standard of care creates a duty that is obviously for the benefit of certain identified third parties and the physician knows of the existence of those third parties, then the physician's duty runs to those third parties. Therefore, in accord with our decision in Baskerville–Donovan Engineers, we hold that privity does not bar Heidi Pate's pursuit of a medical malpractice action. Our holding is likewise in accord with McCain because under the duty alleged in this case, a patient's children fall within the zone of foreseeable risk.

Though not encompassed by the certified question, there is another issue which should be addressed in light of our holding. If there is a duty to warn, to whom must the physician convey the warning? Our holding should not be read to require the physician to warn the patient's children of the disease. In most instances the physician is prohibited from disclosing the patient's medical condition to others except with the patient's permission. [ ] Moreover, the patient ordinarily can be expected to pass on the warning. To require the physician to seek out and warn various members of the patient's family would often be difficult or impractical and would place too heavy a burden upon the physician. Thus, we emphasize that in any circumstances in which the physician has a duty to warn of a genetically transferable disease, that duty will be satisfied by warning the patient.

Accordingly, we conclude that the trial court erred by dismissing the complaint with prejudice. . . .

Notes and Questions

1. Define the limits imposed in *Pate*. Is there any reason for the duty to disclose to be so limited? The court in *Pate* uses existing medical customary practice as a limit, but isn't that too limited a duty in cases where no custom exists or the existing custom fails to protect third parties? After all, is a medical specialty likely to willingly and broadly define a standard of care to expand their obligations to third parties not their patients? See Jeffrey W. Burnett, A Physician's Duty to Warn a Patient's Relatives of a Patient's Genetically Inheritable Disease, 36 Hous.L.Rev.559 (1999); Lawrence O. Gostin and James G. Hodge, Genetic Privacy and the Law: An End to Genetics Exceptionalism, 40 Jurimetrics J.21 (1999); Angela Liang, The Argument Against a Physician's Duty To Warn for Genetic Diseases: The Conflicts Created by Safer v. Pack, 1 J.Health Care L. & Pol'y 437 (1998).

2. In Bradshaw v. Daniel, 854 S.W.2d 865 (Tenn.1993), the court considered whether a physician had a duty to warn a non-patient, the wife of his patient, of her risk of exposure to his patient's non-contagious disease, Rocky Mountain Spotted Fever. The plaintiff's expert had testified that the ticks carrying the disease "clustered", so that people hiking together would be exposed to the disease vector, the ticks. A physician treating a patient with symptoms of Rocky Mountain Spotted Fever should advise the family of the patient as to the incubation period, the symptoms of the disease, and the need for immediate medical attention upon manifestation of the symptoms. The disease, untreated, has a 40 percent mortality rate, but only 4 percent mortality rate if treatment is given promptly.

> We, therefore, conclude that the existence of the physician-patient relationship is sufficient to impose upon a physician an affirmative duty to warn identifiable third persons in the patient's immediate family against foreseeable risks emanating from a patient's illness.

In *Bradshaw*, the risk was self-limiting. What is the unifying factor in these cases, and in most of the duty to disclose cases?

3. Duties to warn patients of medical risks may arise out of medical knowledge of how diseases are communicated. In Tenuto v. Lederle Laboratories, 90 N.Y.2d 606, 665 N.Y.S.2d 17, 687 N.E.2d 1300 (N.Y.1997), aff'd 276 A.D.2d 550, 714 N.Y.S.2d 448 (N.Y.A.D. 2 Dept.2000), Dr. Schwartz gave a second dose of oral poliomyelitis vaccine manufactured by Lederle to a five month old girl. He did not ask the girl's father Mr. Tenuto whether he had previously been vaccinated against polio, nor did he advise the parents of the risk for contact polio and precautions to avoid exposure, particularly in light of surgical wound from surgery that Mr. Tenuto was about to undergo. It was a rare but predictable risk that live viruses in an infant recipient's gastrointestinal tract may grow and revert to virulent form. When these wild viruses are excreted from the infant's bowel in feces or from the mouth in saliva, contact with feces or saliva may result in infection and in vulnerable adults in paralytic polio. These risks, known since 1961, were found since 1977 in the package inserts and the Physician Desk Reference (PDR).

The court held that plaintiffs fell within a determinate and identified class of immediate family members whose relationships to the "person acted upon have traditionally been recognized as a means of extending and yet limiting the scope of liability for injuries caused by a party's negligent acts or omissions."

> Moreover, existence of a special relationship sufficient to supply the predicate for extending the duty to warn and advise plaintiffs of their peril and the need to employ precautions is especially pointed where, as here, the physician is a pediatrician engaged by the parents to provide medical services to their infant, and whose services, by necessity, require advising the patient's parents. Thus, the special relationship factor is triangulated here, involving interconnections of reliance running directly between plaintiffs and Dr. Schwartz, and indirectly from their status and responsibility as the primary caretakers of his infant patient.
>
> ... it would be inferable that in administering the vaccine and advising plaintiffs, as parents of his infant patient, Dr. Schwartz knew or should have known that his comprehensive services necessarily brought into play the protection of the health of plaintiffs, who relied upon his professional expertise in providing advice and other forms of medical services.

What about a day care teacher, an au pair caring for the infant, a visiting grandmother? Is warning the parents sufficient? Is this duty, like the duty imposed on the physician in Bradshaw, supra at n. 2, self-limiting?

4. Genetically transmissible risks elevate a physician's duty to warn beyond imminent contagious diseases to latent genetic defects that may or may not materialize over a long period of time. Consider the breast cancer gene. A woman who possesses the gene might want to step up self-monitoring, mammograms and other early detection approaches. When physicians err in analyzing patients' genetic histories, the consequences can be serious.

Many of the wrongful birth/wrongful life cases involve negligence by a genetic counselor or physician in advising parents as to their risks in having genetically impaired children. See Chapter 16 infra. Courts have split in their willingness to impose duties on physicians for such errors. In Richardson v. Rohrbaugh, 857 S.W.2d 415 (Mo.App. E.D.1993) the Richardson's son Cody was a patient of Dr. Rohrbaugh, a pediatric neurologist. Cody was severely retarded and suffered from club foot. He told them that Cody's condition was not genetic and there was no reason they should not have another child. Their second child was born with the same condition as Cody, Fahr's Syndrome. The court struggled to avoid pinning responsibility on the doctor for his obvious ignorance. It held that no doctor-patient relationship existed. In a curious holding, the court wrote:

> To allow discussions between pediatricians and the parents of the child patient to spawn a factual issue of whether a physician/patient relationship exists with the parents * * * grows dangerously close to birthing an offspring of liability that would chill communications between pediatricians and parents. We are not willing to breath life into such a claim.

5. A long line of cases involve risks of contagious diseases. In Shepard v. Redford Community Hospital, 151 Mich.App. 242, 390 N.W.2d 239 (1986) the court held that the treating physicians were negligent in part for failing to warn the mother about the risk of transmission of spinal meningitis to her young son, who ultimately died from the disease; the duty created by the physician-patient relationship extended to the patient's child. Physicians have been held liable for failing to warn the daughter of a patient with scarlet fever, a wife about the danger of infection from a patient's wounds, a neighbor about the patient's smallpox. Family members are foreseeable third parties, as are neighbors. See Skillings v. Allen, 143 Minn. 323, 173 N.W. 663 (1919); Edwards v. Lamb, 69 N.H. 599, 45 A. 480 (1899); Freese v. Lemmon, 210 N.W.2d 576 (Iowa 1973).

6. The courts have moved beyond family members to include then unknown third parties, imposing on treating physicians a duty to inform patients or to warn third parties when deadly illnesses such as AIDS or highly contagious ones such as hepatitis are involved. In Reisner v. Regents of the University of California, 31 Cal.App.4th 1195, 37 Cal.Rptr.2d 518 (2d Dist. 1995), the patient of Dr. Fonklesrud, 12-year old Jennifer Lawson, received a transfusion contaminated with HIV antibodies during surgery. Dr. Fonkelsrud learned of the contamination, continued to treat Jennifer but never told her or her parents about the tainted blood. Three years later, she started to date Daniel Reisner and they had sexual relations. Two years later, the doctor finally told Jennifer she had AIDS and Jennifer told Daniel. Jennifer died a month later. Daniel then learned he was HIV positive.

The defendants argued they owed no duty to Daniel, who was an unidentified third party at the time Jennifer was infected with HIV. The court cited *Tarasoff* and other cases that had imposed a duty to warn either the patient or third parties about risks, holding that the defendants had a duty to warn a contagious patient to take steps to protect others.

> Once the physician warns the patient of the risk to others and advises the patient how to prevent the spread of the disease, the physician has fulfilled his duty—and no more (but no less) is required....
>
> ... We need not decide in this case what the result would be if someone infected by Daniel sued the doctor who failed to warn Jennifer, and the fact that a duty is owed to Daniel does not mean it will be extended without limitation. However, the possibility of such an extension does not offend us, legally or morally. Viewed in the abstract ... we believe that a doctor who knows he is dealing with the 20th Century version of Typhoid Mary ought to

> have a very strong incentive to tell his patient what she ought to do and not do and how she ought to comport herself in order to prevent the spread of her disease.

In DiMarco v. Lynch Homes—Chester County, 525 Pa. 558, 583 A.2d 422 (1990), the sexual partner of a patient sued her physicians, who had assured her that she would not contract hepatitis. The plaintiff Janet Viscichini, a blood technician, went to the Lynch Home to take a blood sample from one of the residents. During the procedure, her skin was accidentally punctured by the needle she had used to extract blood. When she learned that the patient had hepatitis, she sought treatment from Doctors Giunta and Alwine. They told her that if she remained symptom free for six weeks, she would not be infected by the hepatitis virus. She was not told to refrain from sexual relations for any period of time following her exposure to the disease, but she practiced sexual abstinence until eight weeks after the exposure. Since she had remained symptom-free during that time, she then resumed sexual relations with the plaintiff. She was later diagnosed as suffering from hepatitis B in September; in December, the plaintiff was similarly diagnosed.

The court cited Restatement (Second) Torts, s. 324A, which provided in part that one who provides services to another may be liable to a third person for harm resulting from his failure to exercise reasonable care, if the "the harm is suffered because of reliance of the other or the third person upon the undertaking." The court allowed the action, concluding that the class of persons at risk included any one who is physically intimate with the patient.

> When a physician treats a patient who has been exposed to or who has contracted a communicable and/or contagious disease, it is imperative that the physician give his or her patient the proper advice about preventing the spread of the disease. ... Physicians are the first line of defense against the spread of communicable diseases, because physicians know what measures must be taken to prevent the infection of others.

7. Medication Side–effects. Caselaw requires physicians to warn third parties about, or take steps to protect them from, patients who are taking medication. These steps might include warning the patient about the effects of medication, or even refusing to prescribe the medication if the patient might still drive. See Welke v. Kuzilla, 144 Mich.App. 245, 375 N.W.2d 403 (1985); Myers v. Quesenberry, 144 Cal.App.3d 888, 193 Cal.Rptr. 733 (1983)(physician failed to warn his patient, a diabetic, of the dangers of driving). Contra, see Lester ex rel. Mavrogenis v. Hall, 126 N.M. 404, 970 P.2d 590 (N.M. 1998)(physician exercised no direct control over patient's ingestion of medication, and owed no duty to third parties).

8. Psychiatric Dangerousness. In Tarasoff v. Regents of the Univ. of Cal., 17 Cal.3d 425, 131 Cal.Rptr. 14, 551 P.2d 334 (1976), a psychotherapist at the University of California was treating a patient, Poddar, who had uttered explicit threats toward his former girlfriend during the therapy sessions. No one, including the defendant, attempted to warn the young woman, and Poddar ultimately killed her. The parents sued, alleging negligence in the therapist's failure to warn. The California Supreme Court held that a therapist treating a mentally ill patient owes a duty of reasonable care to warn threatened persons against foreseeable danger created by the patient's condition. The relationship between the physician or therapist and the patient is sufficient to create a duty to protect others.

The *Tarasoff* duty has been accepted by most states. See e.g. O'Keefe v. Orea, 731 So.2d 680 (Fla.App.1998); Turner v. Jordan, 957 S.W.2d 815 (Tenn.1997), with only Texas and Virginia explicitly rejecting *Tarasoff*. See Nasser v. Parker,

249 Va. 172, 455 S.E.2d 502 (Va. 1995); Thapar v. Zezulka, 994 S.W.2d 635 (Tex.1999).

Cases involving epileptics or others with conditions that might impair driving occur frequently. Courts are reluctant to require a physician to notify the state as to a patient's condition. See Crosby v. Sultz, 405 Pa.Super. 527, 592 A.2d 1337 (Pa.Super.1991) (no duty to report patient to Department of Transportation, since type of diabetes did not impose duty to warn); Estate of Witthoeft v. Kiskaddon, 557 Pa. 340, 733 A.2d 623 (Pa.1999)(Physician owed no duty to third party for injuries suffered in a car accident caused by a patient; he was ophthalmologist who did not notify the Pennsylvania Department of Transportation of the patient's poor visual acuity); Praesel v. Johnson, 967 S.W.2d 391 (Tex.1998).

Problem: The Stubborn Patient

You represent Dr. Will Toma, a physician specializing in gerontology. He regularly examines and treats elderly patients, and has come to you for advice. One of his patients, Harry Glint, 86 years old, has a mild neurological disorder that causes blurred or double vision at times. Harry complains that his double vision is worst when he drives at night, when, he says, "The middle line becomes double and I have trouble staying on my side of the road." The problem is not treatable and it will worsen over time (although changes in prescriptions of eyeglasses may reduce the problem at times). Dr. Toma has admonished Mr. Glint never to drive at night, and to stop driving during the day as soon as possible. Mr. Glint is adamant about the importance of his driving, which he says keeps him young and active.

Dr. Toma is worried about his potential liability if Mr. Glint has a car accident that injures others. What are his liability risks, and what steps can he take to minimize them?

Problem: The Tour Bus

A physician, Dr. Vivian Hayes, has been treating a patient, Steven Moore, who just returned from a bus tour of Germany. Moore has a illness caused by the bite of a small tick found on deer in the Black Forest of Germany. Dr. Hayes has successfully treated the illness. Moore took a bus tour of Germany and the Black Forest with a group put together by a travel agency, Rathskeller Travel, which declared bankruptcy shortly after the trip was over. What further obligations does Dr. Hayes have? Should she notify the state division of public health? The tour members were from twenty different states. Should she call everyone on the roster of the tour?

D. CONFIDENTIALITY AND DISCLOSURE OF AIDS–RELATED INFORMATION

DOE v. MARSELLE

Supreme Court of Connecticut, 1996.
236 Conn. 845, 675 A.2d 835.

KATZ, ASSOCIATE JUDGE.

The dispositive issue on appeal is whether in order to state a cause of action under General Statutes § 19a–590[1] for a violation of General Statutes

1. General Statutes § 19a–590 provides: "Liability for violations. Any person, except as otherwise provided in this chapter, who wilfully violates any provision of this chapter shall

§ 19a–583 (AIDS statute)[2], the confidentiality provision of chapter 368x, entitled "AIDS Testing and Medical Information," a plaintiff must allege that the person who violated that provision intended to engage in the prohibited conduct and intended to produce the resulting injury. We conclude that a wilful violation of § 19a–583 requires only a knowing disclosure of confidential human immunodeficiency virus (HIV) related information.

The following facts are undisputed. The plaintiff, Jane Doe, was a patient of the defendant Dionisio C. Flores, a surgeon, to whom, during the course of her treatment, she disclosed that she was infected with HIV. A surgical assistant employed by Flores, the named defendant Doris Marselle, after learning of the plaintiff's condition from her medical chart and from personal discussions with the plaintiff, consulted Flores regarding her intention to disclose the plaintiff's HIV status to Marselle's sons who were illegal drug users and who had friends in common with the plaintiff. Flores authorized Marselle to make the disclosures provided that she not identify the plaintiff by name.

When the plaintiff learned that Marselle had told at least three other individuals in the community that she was HIV positive, the plaintiff, who had never authorized the disclosures, brought a multicount complaint against Flores and Marselle alleging that they each had: (1) violated the confidentiality provisions of § 19a–583 by intentionally disclosing her HIV status (first count); (2) violated the Connecticut Unfair Trade Practices Act (CUTPA); General Statutes § 42–110b; based upon a breach of confidentiality and Flores' false representations to her that her HIV status would be kept confidential (third and fourth counts); and (3) negligently inflicted emotional distress by disclosing her HIV status (sixth count). Additionally, the plaintiff alleged that Flores had been negligent in failing to instruct his employees regarding their obligation to comply with General Statutes § 19a–581 et seq. (second count), and that Marselle had intentionally inflicted emotional distress by wilfully disclosing the confidential medical information (fifth count).

* * *

In her appeal to the Appellate Court, the plaintiff argued that the term "wilful" in § 19a–590 means "intentionally" as opposed to "accidentally" and that the trial court improperly had defined the term to mean intending to injure. [ ] The Appellate Court disagreed * * *

Thereafter, the plaintiff petitioned this court for certification. We granted certification limited to the following questions: (1) "Did the Appellate Court

be liable in a private cause of action for injuries suffered as a result of such violation. Upon a finding that an individual has been injured as a result of such violation, damages shall be assessed in the amount sufficient to compensate said individual for such injury."

2. General Statutes § 19a–583 provides in relevant part: "Limitations on disclosure of HIV-related information. (a) No person who obtains confidential HIV-related information may disclose or be compelled to disclose such information. . . ."

General Statutes § 19a–581 (8) defines "confidential HIV-related information" as "any information pertaining to the protected individual or obtained pursuant to a release of confidential HIV-related information, concerning whether a person has been counseled regarding HIV infection, has been the subject of an HIV-related test, or has HIV infection, HIV-related illness or AIDS, or information which identifies or reasonably could identify a person as having one or more of such conditions, including information pertaining to such individual's partners. . . ."

correctly conclude that the second amended complaint did not allege a wilful violation of General Statutes § 19a–583 (a)?"; and (2) "Did the Appellate Court properly decide that the plaintiff's negligence, negligent infliction of emotional distress and Connecticut Unfair Trade Practices Act (CUTPA) counts had been properly stricken?" Doe v. Marselle, 235 Conn. 915, 665 A.2d 606 (1995). Because we answer both certified questions in the negative, we reverse.

* * *

The AIDS statute was designed and intended to combat the AIDS epidemic, beginning with protecting confidentiality. The legislation imposes certain requirements on the testing and treatment of persons who may be HIV positive or who have AIDS. These requirements relate principally to the areas of informed consent for HIV testing and confidential treatment of HIV-related information, and are aimed at helping health care providers to identify those people with the disease, to treat them and to educate them in an attempt to put an end to the epidemic in our state, which, at the time this legislation was under consideration, had the ninth highest number of AIDS cases per capita in the nation and the highest percentage of AIDS cases in children. [ ] As one of the bill's sponsors, Representative Benjamin N. DeZinno, Jr., explained, * * * the bill was intended to "protect the confidentiality of data related to AIDS, requires informed consent for tests for the AIDS virus, and allows for notification of partners of those that are so infected." [ ] He explained that in order to "wipe out or hope to wipe [out] this horrible epidemic disease in our lifetime ... [w]e have to start with protecting the confidentiality ... [b]ecause people will not step forward for testing and treatment of AIDS unless they know that a positive result will not become public information. I think that's very important. Now unfortunately, there is widespread discrimination against the AIDS victim, and many people would rather [forgo] treatment, than risk being stigmatized."[10] [ ]

Beth Weinstein, chief of the AIDS section for the then department of health services, now the department of public health and addiction services (department), along with James Hadler, a physician and the chief of the epidemiology section of the department, testified that the department had proposed "this critical legislation ... [to] provide us with the tools to continue fighting the AIDS epidemic in Connecticut. If passed, it will protect the confidentiality of AIDS information and will require informed consent for the test for the virus which causes AIDS.... The AIDS epidemic has magnified many problems in the existing health care system. Among the most glaring is the lack of protection [in] current Connecticut statutes for informed consent and disclosure of information. Although this problem goes beyond AIDS, we

10. Studies in the medical literature indicate that fear of discrimination discourages people from seeking appropriate care. See K. Siegel, M. Levine, C. Brooks & R. Kern, "The Motives of Gay Men for Taking or Not Taking the HIV Antibody Test," 36 Social Problems 368, 378–79 (1989) (people avoid HIV testing in part because they fear discrimination if their illness or sexual behavior become known); R. Weitz, "Anonymity in Testing for HIV Antibodies Desired Option," 81 Am.J.Pub. Health 1213 (1991) (fear of discrimination based on illness or on having been tested). As one recent nationwide study found, people are more likely to undergo HIV testing if they believe that their test results will remain private. K. Phillips, "The Relationship of 1988 State HIV Testing Policies to Previous and Planned Voluntary Use of HIV Testing," 7 J. Acquired Immune Deficiency Syndromes 403, 405 (1994).

feel it is most important to solve it for AIDS because of the sensitivities regarding the disease." Conn. Joint Standing Committee Hearings, Public Health, Pt. 3, 1989 Sess., p. 766. Weinstein explained how this legislation was necessary to encourage confidential testing and to allow medical providers to provide proper follow-up treatment. "In most of the sites that the department funds for counseling and testing for the AIDS virus, anonymous testing is done, largely because we don't have confidentiality protection. However, anonymous testing has limitations. Counselors have no ability to follow-up with clients to provide support for behavior change, additional counseling, public health services, social services or medical assistance. Voluntary testing in which the identity of the person tested [is] known will only be widely accepted if there is specific protection in the statutes." Id., p. 767. Weinstein concluded her testimony by emphasizing that confidentiality is essential "to protect people from the discrimination that often comes with the knowledge that a person has AIDS or HIV infection" and to help eliminate the stigma that often accompanies AIDS. Id., pp. 768–69.

In order to accomplish the aforementioned goals, disclosure of confidential HIV-related information is prohibited except in very limited and discrete circumstances. [ ][11] Even health care providers or persons who engage in

11. General Statutes § 19a–583 provides in relevant part: "Limitations on disclosure of HIV-related information. (a) No person who obtains confidential HIV-related information may disclose or be compelled to disclose such information, except to the following:

"(1) The protected individual, his legal guardian or a person authorized to consent to health care for such individual;

"(2) Any person who secures a release of confidential HIV-related information;

"(3) A federal, state or local health officer when such disclosure is mandated or authorized by federal or state law;

"(4) A health care provider or health facility when knowledge of the HIV-related information is necessary to provide appropriate care or treatment to the protected individual or a child of the individual or when confidential HIV-related information is already recorded in a medical chart or record and a health care provider has access to such record for the purpose of providing medical care to the protected individual;

"(5) A medical examiner to assist in determining the cause or circumstances of death;

"(6) Health facility staff committees or accreditation or oversight review organizations which are conducting program monitoring, program evaluation or service reviews;

"(7) A health care provider or other person in cases where such provider or person in the course of his occupational duties has had a significant exposure to HIV infection, provided the following criteria are met: (A) The worker is able to document significant exposure during performance of his occupation, (B) the worker completes an incident report within forty-eight hours of exposure, identifying the parties to the exposure, witnesses, time, place and nature of the event, (C) the worker submits to a baseline HIV test within seventy-two hours of the exposure and is negative on that test for the presence of the AIDS virus, (D) the patient's or person's physician or, if the patient or person does not have a personal physician or if the patient's or person's physician is unavailable, another physician or health care provider has approached the patient or person and sought voluntary consent to disclosure and the patient or person refuses to consent to disclosure, except in an exposure where the patient or person is deceased, (E) the worker would be able to take meaningful immediate action as defined in regulations adopted pursuant to section 19a–589 which could not otherwise be taken, (F) an exposure evaluation group determines that the criteria specified in subparagraphs (A), (B), (C), (D) and (E) of this subdivision are met and that a worker has a significant exposure to the blood of a patient or person and the patient or person or the patient's or person's legal guardian refuses to consent to release of the information. No member of the exposure evaluation group who determines that a worker has sustained a significant exposure and authorizes the disclosure of confidential HIV-related information nor the health facility, correctional facility or other institution nor any person in a health facility, correctional facility or other institution who relies in good faith on the group's determination and discloses the result shall have any liability as a result of his action carried out under this section, unless such persons acted in bad faith. If the information is not held by a health facility, correctional facility or other institution, a physician not directly involved in

occupational therapy who have had significant exposure to HIV infection are not entitled to this information unless they satisfy the rigid criteria listed in § 19a–583(a)(7). See footnote 11. Similarly, employees of mental health hospitals operated by the department of mental health and correctional facilities operated by the department of correction are not entitled to this information even when the patient or inmate poses a significant risk of transmission unless the infection control committee of the hospital or the medical director and chief administrator of the correctional facility first determine that such disclosure is likely to prevent or reduce the risk of transmission and that no reasonable alternatives exist that will achieve the same goal and preserve the confidentiality of the information. [ ]

A person who does not fall within these exceptions may petition the court for disclosure, however, a court order may be issued only when the moving party demonstrates a clear and imminent danger to the health of another or the public health and further demonstrates a compelling need for the test results that cannot be accommodated by other means. In assessing compelling need, the court must weigh, among other things, the need for disclosure against the privacy interest of the test subject and the public interest that may be disserved by disclosure that deters future testing or that may lead to discrimination. [ ] Finally, even when disclosure is authorized, the AIDS statute strictly limits the terms of that disclosure. See General Statutes § 19a–585. In short, the drafters of this legislation "crafted the bill very carefully to give protection while also enabling those who care for people with AIDS and HIV infection to have access to information needed for the patient's care."[14] [ ]

Keeping this legislative history in mind, coupled with the elaborate statutory safeguards imposed against disclosure of HIV-related information, it is difficult to presume a definition of wilful that would make permissible the

the exposure has certified in writing that the criteria specified in subparagraphs (A), (B), (C), (D) and (E) of this subdivision are met and that a significant exposure has occurred;

"(8) Employees of hospitals for mental illness operated by the department of mental health * * *;

"(9) Employees of facilities operated by the department of correction * * *;

"(11) Life and health insurers, government payers and health care centers and their affiliates, reinsurers, and contractors, except agents and brokers, in connection with underwriting and claim activity for life, health, and disability benefits; and

"(12) Any health care provider specifically designated by the protected individual to receive such information received by a life or health insurer or health care center pursuant to an application for life, health or disability insurance.

"(b) No person, except the protected individual, his legal guardian or a person authorized to consent to health care for such individual, to whom confidential HIV-related information is disclosed may further disclose such information, except as provided in this section and sections 19a–584 and 19a–585."

14. The legislature's concern for discrimination against people with AIDS is well founded. In a 1993 poll, 35.7 percent of the respondents said they were "afraid" of people with AIDS, 27.7 percent were "disgusted" and 27.1 percent were "angry." G. Herek & J. Capitanio, "Public Reactions to AIDS in the United States: A Second Decade of Stigma," 83 Am. J.Pub.Health 574, 575 (1993). More than one in five Americans (20.4 percent) would avoid an office job if they had to work with a man with AIDS, and nearly one half (47.1 percent) would avoid a neighborhood grocery store if the owner had AIDS. Id. Feelings of hostility translate into acts of discrimination against people infected with HIV. In lawsuits across the country, people have alleged discrimination based on HIV status in housing, employment and access to public accommodations, as well as in education and health care. See L. Gostin, Jr., "A National Review of Court and Human Rights Commission Decisions, Part II: Discrimination," 263 J.Am.Med.Assn. 2086 (1990) (listing nearly 150 lawsuits and other complaints stemming from such alleged discrimination).

unauthorized disclosure of a person's HIV-related information except in the extreme situation where the person disclosing the information actually intends to injure the protected individual. We have noted that as part of its attempt to foster an increase in medical treatment for people with AIDS and HIV infection, the legislature created the AIDS statute to correct the problems, such as the lack of confidentiality, that have stood in the way of this goal. A definition of wilful that would require a plaintiff to prove that confidentiality was breached with the intent to cause injury would do nothing to advance the laudable goals of the legislation's sponsors. Indeed, were we to apply the definition of wilful proposed by Flores and adopted by the Appellate Court, a patient who is HIV positive, knowing that he or she could obtain redress for a violation of the confidentiality provisions in only the most egregious circumstances, would have no confidence that his or her status or test results would be zealously protected. This lack of confidence, in turn, would create a disincentive for that person to submit to testing. Additionally, because General Statutes § 19a–582(b)(4) requires that pretest counseling include "an explanation of the confidentiality protections afforded confidential HIV-related information, including the circumstances under which and classes of persons to whom disclosure of such information may be required, authorized or permitted by law," the lack of protection resulting from a definition of wilful that requires an evil intent would be more likely to eviscerate the purpose of the statute and consequently undermine the public health strategy against AIDS that prompted the legislation. It is not our practice to construe a statute in a way to thwart its purpose or lead to absurd results; [ ] or in a way "that fails to attain a rational and sensible result that bears directly on the purpose the legislature sought to achieve." Consequently, we cannot endorse a definition of wilful that would allow virtually any disclosure of confidential HIV-related information.

Moreover, to limit the definition of wilful to the case of a medical provider who intended to cause the patient injury, as Flores argues, would be to provide a cure for which there is no disease. No one speaking on behalf of the legislation identified a problem with medical providers seeking to sabotage the ability of their AIDS patients to obtain good medical care. Nor has Flores argued that such a problem exists. Because we do not presume that the legislature enacted legislation that was devoid of purpose; we will not interpret wilful as Flores has proposed.

Rather, we interpret wilful to mean a knowing disclosure of confidential HIV-related information. Contrary to the Appellate Court's assertion, this interpretation does not render the term superfluous. Had the term wilful not been used, persons would be liable for inadvertent disclosures or nonvolitional acts. By establishing liability only for wilful violations, the legislature indicated that inadvertent violations would not be actionable.

* * *

The judgment is reversed and the case is remanded for further proceedings according to law.

Notes and Questions

1. Consider the exceptions to nondisclosure specified in the statute in footnote 11. Do you see any problems with some of these exceptions? How about

exception 7? Does it provide adequate safeguards for patients, in the face of provider anxiety about exposure to the HIV/AIDS virus? In Doe v. Protective Life Ins. Co., 1998 WL 568326 (Conn.Super.1998), the court allowed disclosure under protective orders (limited to named defendants in case).

2. Special characteristics of AIDS and of the AIDS epidemic present new and unique challenges to health care workers trying to understand their general duty to keep confidences and their specific obligations, under some circumstances, to disclose medical information. First, widespread continuing fear of AIDS and ignorance about how it is spread, combined with a history of prejudice and discrimination against gay men among whom AIDS has been most common, have made concerns of privacy and confidentiality even more urgently important. If information about a person's AIDS infection or HIV positivity reaches employers, insurers, schools, family, or acquaintances it may have disastrous consequences. It is widely believed, therefore, that maintenance of the strictest confidentiality is essential if voluntary AIDS testing programs are to succeed—that any risk of disclosure will discourage persons who may possibly be HIV infected or who have AIDS or ARC from seeking testing and counseling.

Second, the fact that the HIV virus cannot be spread through casual contact, unlike many other contagious diseases, limits the need for disclosure of information about infection. The fact that the rate of infection through heterosexual genital intercourse is very low (about .001 per exposure) may argue against a duty to warn heterosexual partners, since it is unlikely that casual heterosexual partners will be infected, or may argue in favor of a warning, since it is possible that longer term partners may have not yet been infected. The possibility of transmission to unborn children may also argue for warning potentially infected persons who may potentially bear children.

Third, the fact that AIDS is presently incurable makes prevention all the more essential. Does this argue for maintaining strict confidentiality, so that persons who may be infected will come forward to be tested and thereafter modify their behavior voluntarily to avoid infecting others? Or does it argue for limited disclosure to protect persons who may be exposed to possible infection? Does the emergence of new treatment modalities like AZT, which may slow the infection process, argue for greater confidentiality or broader disclosure?

What is the relevance to questions of confidentiality and disclosure of the fact that HIV testing results in a significant number of false positives in low-risk populations? Of what significance is the fact that HIV positivity may not show up in testing until months, perhaps years, after a person becomes HIV infected?

3. Should medical records or laboratory specimens of patients in health care institutions who are HIV positive be specially marked to permit special precautions to protect against infection? Might doing so unduly risk further disclosure of confidential information, while offering little additional protection to health care workers who should be observing universal precautions against infection in any event? Might such special identification lull health care workers into unwarranted complacency in dealing with patients and specimens not so identified, despite the fact that patients may be infected but untested or that tests may have resulted in false negatives? Should infected medical personnel be reported to licensure agencies? What action, if any, should licensure agencies take based upon this information?

4. Health care workers should certainly counsel HIV-infected patients to take special precautions to avoid infecting others and to tell their sexual or needle-sharing partners to seek testing, counseling, and treatment. If patients indicate,

however, that they will not do so, does the health care worker have an obligation to warn others? Should the health care worker rather notify the state health department of the patient's infected status and of persons who may have been infected by the patient, to permit contact tracing? Even if the health care worker has no duty to warn, is the worker permitted to do so, or does the health care worker face liability for violating confidentiality requirements if she or he proceeds to warn potentially infected persons?

Consider the AMA position on this question:

> Where there is no statute that mandates or prohibits reporting of seropositive individuals to public health authorities and it is clear that the seropositive individual is endangering an identified third party, the physician should (1) attempt to persuade the infected individual to cease endangering the third party; (2) if persuasion fails, notify authorities; and (3) if authorities take no action, notify and counsel the endangered third party.

HIV Blood Test Counseling: A.M.A. Physician Guidelines (1988)

5. The states have adopted a variety of legislative and administrative approaches to confidentiality and disclosure of information regarding HIV-positivity, ARC, and AIDS status. All states now require physicians to report AIDS cases to the state health department. A number also require reporting of cases of asymptomatic HIV infection. Several states have adopted statutes mandating strict confidentiality of AIDS-related information. See Cal.Health & Safety Code, § 199.21; West's Fla.Stat.Ann. § 14A § 381.609(2)(f); Mass.Gen.L. Ch. 111 § 70F. Other states have adopted laws permitting disclosure of HIV test results to certain persons or under certain circumstances. See Vernon's Ann.Tex.Rev.Civ.Stat. art. 4419b–1, § 9.03, (disclosure to spouse permitted); Ga.Code Ann. § 38–723(g) (disclosure to spouse, sexual partner or child permitted under some circumstances); McKinney's–N.Y.Pub.Health Law § 2782(4)(a) & (b) (physician may disclose information to persons in significant risk of infection if already infected person will not do so after counseling and physician warns that person of the physician's intention to disclose.) The identity of the infected person cannot be disclosed. (The physician is protected from liability whether he discloses or chooses not to disclose the information.) For an excellent recent review of state statutes, see David P.T. Price, Between Scylla and Charybdis: Charting A Course to Reconcile The Duty of Confidentiality and the Duty to Warn in the AIDS Context, 94 Dick.L.Rev. 435 (1990). See also *www.unaids.org/hivaidsinfo/documents.html#wad* and Report on the Global HIV/AIDS Epidemic, June 2000.

6. A number of states permit public health authorities to engage in contact tracing or partner notification with respect to persons with AIDS or who are HIV infected. Five different approaches to contact tracing have been identified: 1) solicitation of the names of all sexual and needle-sharing contacts of AIDS-and HIV-infected persons with subsequent notification of all identified contacts (with offers for testing and counseling); 2) limited contact tracing focusing on high risk or especially vulnerable groups who are likely to be unaware of the risk of infection (heterosexual contacts of individuals with AIDS); 3) voluntary contact tracing: infected persons are asked to notify potentially infected persons voluntarily and assistance is offered to those who want help in notifying others; 4) notification in special circumstances, as to rescue or emergency personnel potentially infected in the line of duty; 5) notification of specific persons in specific situations, such as those exposed to infected blood. See Karen Rothenberg, et al. The AIDS Project: Creating a Public Health Policy—Rights and Obligations of Health Care Workers, 48 Md.L.Rev. 94, 181–183 (1989). Colorado has been

particularly active in contact tracing, and claims that its program has resulted in the identification and treatment of a number of individuals who would not otherwise have been aware of their HIV positive status. See Partner Notification for Preventing Immunodeficiency Virus (HIV) Infection—Colorado, Idaho, South Carolina, Virginia, 260 J.A.M.A. 613 (1988). Does the fact that contact tracing usually depends on voluntary disclosure of sexual and needle-sharing partners by the infected person render it ineffective in situations where the infected person refuses to notify others voluntarily? See generally Lawrence O. Gostin and James G. Hodge, Piercing the Veil of Secrecy in HIV/AIDS and Other Sexually Transmitted Diseases: Theories of Privacy and Disclosure in Partner Notification, 5 Duke J. Gender L. & Pol'y 9 (1998).

7. One particular situation in which the disclosure of the identify of HIV-infected persons has been frequently sought is where a person who has become HIV infected through tainted blood seeks disclosure of the identity of the donor who donated the infected blood, either to assist in establishing negligence on the part of the blood service or to permit a suit against the donor. These cases have tended to deny discovery, relying on various privacy, physician patient privilege, or discovery protection theories and on the importance of protecting the identity of blood donors to encourage voluntary blood donations. See Krygier v. Airweld, Inc., 137 Misc.2d 306, 520 N.Y.S.2d 475 (1987); Rasmussen v. South Florida Blood Service, Inc., 500 So.2d 533 (Fla.1987); contra, see Gulf Coast Regional Blood Center v. Houston, 745 S.W.2d 557 (Tex.App.1988). See Kevin Hopkins, Blood, Sweat, and Tears: Toward a New Paradigm for Protecting Donor Privacy, 7 Va.J.Soc.Pol'y & L. 141(2000).

Problem: The HIV–Positive Physician

One of your established clients, Joel Feinberg, an internist, has consulted you concerning a problem that has arisen in his practice. Two weeks ago one of his patients, Dr. Alan Miller, a resident at Mercy hospital where Dr. Feinberg is on staff, came in for a physical. Dr. Feinberg met Dr. Miller last year when Dr. Miller did an internal medicine rotation under Dr. Feinberg's supervision, and they have seen each other socially from time to time since. After his blood had been drawn for routine blood work, Dr. Miller requested that an HIV test be done on the blood. The test results came back positive for HIV antibodies. Dr. Feinberg immediately called Dr. Miller to tell him of the results. Dr. Miller, however, told Dr. Feinberg not to worry, the test was undoubtedly a false positive, and assured him that he would follow up with further testing later when he could find the time.

Dr. Feinberg has been deeply troubled by the test and by Dr. Miller's response to it. First, Dr. Feinberg knows that Dr. Miller is scheduled for orthopedic surgery to correct an old knee injury next month. He wonders whether he should inform the surgeon who will be doing the surgery, a colleague, of the test results. He also wonders whether nurses, surgical assistants, laboratory personnel and others who may be exposed to body fluids from the surgery should be informed. Second, he knows that Dr. Miller has applied for permanent staff privileges at Mercy hospital. Should the hospital medical staff or administration be informed of the test results? Does Dr. Feinberg have any obligation under state law to inform the public health department of the results? Should he inform the state medical licensure board? Finally, he knows that Dr. Miller is planning to marry another intern, Dr. Anne Bowen, early next year. When he asked Dr. Miller whether he would inform Anne of the test results, however, Dr. Miller said he would rather not bother her with results that were probably wrong in any event.

Dr. Feinberg wants to know whether he should tell Dr. Bowen himself, ask the Department of Health to contact her through its contact-tracing program, or say nothing? Dr. Feinberg is well aware of his general obligation to keep patient confidences, but wonders whether any exceptions apply in this situation or whether, in fact, he has any obligations to disclose.

III. INFORMED CONSENT: THE PHYSICIAN'S OBLIGATION

A. ORIGINS OF THE INFORMED CONSENT DOCTRINE

Informed consent has developed out of strong judicial deference toward individual autonomy, reflecting a belief that an individual has a right to be free from nonconsensual interference with his or her person, and a basic moral principle that it is wrong to force another to act against his or her will. This principle was articulated in the medical context by Justice Cardozo in Schloendorff v. Society of New York Hospital, 211 N.Y. 125, 105 N.E. 92 (1914): "Every human being of adult years and sound mind has a right to determine what shall be done with his own body * * * ". Informed consent doctrine has guided medical decisionmaking by setting boundaries for the doctor-patient relationship and is one of the forces altering the attitudes of a new generation of doctors toward their patients. It has provided the starting point for federal regulations on human experimentation, and is now reflected in consent forms that health care institutions require all patients to sign upon admission and before various procedures are performed.

Professor Alexander Capron has argued that the doctrine can serve six salutory functions. It can:

1) protect individual autonomy;

2) protect the patient's status as a human being;

3) avoid fraud or duress;

4) encourage doctors to carefully consider their decisions;

5) foster rational decision-making by the patient; and

6) involve the public generally in medicine.

Alexander Capron, "Informed Consent in Catastrophic Disease Research and Treatment," 123 U.Penn.L.Rev. 340, 365–76 (1974).

This chapter will examine how the doctrine developed and how it now functions as a litigation tool in American jurisdictions.

Informed consent has been an unnatural graft onto medical practice. As Jay Katz wrote in The Silent World of Doctor and Patient 1 (1984), "* * * disclosure and consent, except in the most rudimentary fashion, are obligations alien to medical thinking and practice." The function of disclosure historically has been to get patients to agree to what the doctors wanted. In ancient Greece, patients' participation in decision-making was considered undesirable, since the doctor's primary task was to inspire confidence. Medieval medical writing likewise viewed conversations between doctors and patients as an opportunity for the former to offer comfort and hope, but emphasized the need for the doctor to be manipulative and even deceitful. Authority needed to be coupled with obedience to create a patient's faith in the cure. By the Enlightenment, the view had emerged that patients had a capacity to listen to the doctor, but that deception was still needed to facilitate patient management. By the nineteenth century, the profession was split over such issues as disclosure of a dire prognosis, although the majority of doctors still argued against disclosure. The beginnings of the twentieth century showed no progress in the evolution of the doctor-patient relationship toward collaboration.

The judicial development of informed consent into a distinct doctrine can be roughly divided into three periods, according to Katz. During the first period, up to the mid-twentieth century, courts built upon the law of battery and required little more than disclosure by doctors of their proposed treatment. The second period saw an emerging judicial feeling that doctors should disclose the alternatives to a proposed treatment and their risks, as well as of risks of the proposed treatment itself. The third period, from 1972 to the present, has seen legislative retrenchment and judicial inertia.

During the first period of doctrinal development, the doctrine of battery provided the theoretical underpinnings for a cause of action. The doctrine of battery protects a patient's physical integrity from harmful contacts and her personal dignity from unwanted bodily contact, requiring a showing only that the patient was not informed of the very nature of the medical touching, typically a surgical procedure. Physical injury is not necessary. When a surgeon, in the course of surgery, removes or operates upon an organ other than the one he and the patient discussed, a battery action lies. The most obvious medical battery cases, e.g., where a surgeon amputates the wrong leg, can be readily brought as a negligence case.

The procedural and other advantages of a battery-based action tip the scales substantially in the favor of the patient. First, the focus is on the patient's right to be free from a touching different from that to which she consented. The physician has few defenses to a battery. Second, the plaintiff need not prove through expert testimony what the standard of care was; the proof is only that the particular physician failed to explain to the patient the nature and character of the particular procedure. Third, to prove causation, the plaintiff need only show that an unconsented-to touching occurred. Under a negligence theory the plaintiff must show that he would have declined a procedure if he had known all the details and risks. See generally Kohoutek v. Hafner, 383 N.W.2d 295 (Minn.1986). In Chouinard v. Marjani, 21 Conn.App. 572, 575 A.2d 238 (1990), the plaintiff sued the defendant surgeon, claiming that the surgeon had performed bilateral breast surgery although the plaintiff had consented only to surgery on her left breast. She admitted that if the surgeon had asked, she would have consented to the surgery on her right breast. The court applied battery doctrine, holding that plaintiff did not need to present either expert testimony nor testify that she would not have consented if the surgeon had asked.

Use of a battery theory therefore reduces the need for medical testimony, restricting the scope of physicians' beliefs about what patients should know and might want as therapy. A judicial sense that medical judgment should be allowed more leeway has led to a movement from battery to negligent nondisclosure over the years. Malpractice reform in the states has often included abrogation of the battery basis of informed consent. See Rubino v.

DeFretias, 638 F.Supp. 182 (D.Ariz.1986) (holding statute unconstitutional on grounds that the Arizona constitution establishes a fundamental right to bring an action against a physician based on common law theory of battery.)

As you read the cases in this section, ask how far the courts have gone toward permitting patients to control treatment decisions that affect them. Consider also what a plaintiff must show to make out an informed consent case in various jurisdictions. Finally, ask if any other processes are likely to serve the purposes of informed consent more efficiently, and with less adverse effect on the doctor-patient relationship.

B. THE LEGAL FRAMEWORK OF INFORMED CONSENT

1. *Negligence as a Basis for Recovery*

CANTERBURY v. SPENCE

United States Court of Appeals, District of Columbia Circuit, 1972.
464 F.2d 772.

SPOTTSWOOD W. ROBINSON, III, CIRCUIT JUDGE:

This appeal is from a judgment entered in the District Court on verdicts directed for the two appellees at the conclusion of plaintiff-appellant Canterbury's case in chief. His action sought damages for personal injuries allegedly sustained as a result of an operation negligently performed by appellee Spence, a negligent failure by Dr. Spence to disclose a risk of serious disability inherent in the operation, and negligent post-operative care by appellee Washington Hospital Center. On close examination of the record, we find evidence which required submission of these issues to the jury. We accordingly reverse the judgment as to each appellee and remand the case to the District Court for a new trial.

I

The record we review tells a depressing tale. A youth troubled only by back pain submitted to an operation without being informed of a risk of paralysis incidental thereto. A day after the operation he fell from his hospital bed after having been left without assistance while voiding. A few hours after the fall, the lower half of his body was paralyzed, and he had to be operated on again. Despite extensive medical care, he has never been what he was before. Instead of the back pain, even years later, he hobbled about on crutches, a victim of paralysis of the bowels and urinary incontinence. In a very real sense this lawsuit is an understandable search for reasons.

At the time of the events which gave rise to this litigation, appellant was nineteen years of age, a clerk-typist employed by the Federal Bureau of Investigation. In December, 1958, he began to experience severe pain between his shoulder blades. He consulted two general practitioners, but the medications they prescribed failed to eliminate the pain. Thereafter, appellant secured an appointment with Dr. Spence, who is a neurosurgeon.

Dr. Spence examined appellant in his office at some length but found nothing amiss. On Dr. Spence's advice appellant was x-rayed, but the films did not identify any abnormality. Dr. Spence then recommended that appellant undergo a myelogram—a procedure in which dye is injected into the spinal column and traced to find evidence of disease or other disorder—at the Washington Hospital Center.

Appellant entered the hospital on February 4, 1959. The myelogram revealed a "filling defect" in the region of the fourth thoracic vertebra. Since a myelogram often does no more than pinpoint the location of an aberration, surgery may be necessary to discover the cause. Dr. Spence told appellant that he would have to undergo a laminectomy—the excision of the posterior arch of the vertebra—to correct what he suspected was a ruptured disc. Appellant did not raise any objection to the proposed operation nor did he probe into its exact nature.

Appellant explained to Dr. Spence that his mother was a widow of slender financial means living in Cyclone, West Virginia, and that she could be reached through a neighbor's telephone. Appellant called his mother the day after the myelogram was performed and, failing to contact her, left Dr. Spence's telephone number with the neighbor. When Mrs. Canterbury returned the call, Dr. Spence told her that the surgery was occasioned by a suspected ruptured disc. Mrs. Canterbury then asked if the recommended operation was serious and Dr. Spence replied "not any more than any other operation." He added that he knew Mrs. Canterbury was not well off and that her presence in Washington would not be necessary. The testimony is contradictory as to whether during the course of the conversation Mrs. Canterbury expressed her consent to the operation. Appellant himself apparently did not converse again with Dr. Spence prior to the operation.

Dr. Spence performed the laminectomy on February 11 at the Washington Hospital Center. Mrs. Canterbury traveled to Washington, arriving on that date but after the operation was over, and signed a consent form at the hospital. The laminectomy revealed several anomalies: a spinal cord that was swollen and unable to pulsate, an accumulation of large tortuous and dilated veins, and a complete absence of epidural fat which normally surrounds the spine. A thin hypodermic needle was inserted into the spinal cord to aspirate any cysts which might have been present, but no fluid emerged. In suturing the wound, Dr. Spence attempted to relieve the pressure on the spinal cord by enlarging the dura—the outer protective wall of the spinal cord—at the area of swelling.

For approximately the first day after the operation appellant recuperated normally, but then suffered a fall and an almost immediate setback. Since there is some conflict as to precisely when or why appellant fell, we reconstruct the events from the evidence most favorable to him. Dr. Spence left orders that appellant was to remain in bed during the process of voiding. These orders were changed to direct that voiding be done out of bed, and the jury could find that the change was made by hospital personnel. Just prior to the fall, appellant summoned a nurse and was given a receptacle for use in voiding, but was then left unattended. Appellant testified that during the course of the endeavor he slipped off the side of the bed, and that there was no one to assist him, or side rail to prevent the fall.

Several hours later, appellant began to complain that he could not move his legs and that he was having trouble breathing; paralysis seems to have been virtually total from the waist down. Dr. Spence was notified on the night of February 12, and he rushed to the hospital. Mrs. Canterbury signed another consent form and appellant was again taken into the operating room. The surgical wound was reopened and Dr. Spence created a gusset to allow the spinal cord greater room in which to pulsate.

Appellant's control over his muscles improved somewhat after the second operation but he was unable to void properly. As a result of this condition, he came under the care of a urologist while still in the hospital. In April, following a cystoscopic examination, appellant was operated on for removal of bladder stones, and in May was released from the hospital. He reentered the hospital the following August for a 10–day period, apparently because of his urologic problems. For several years after his discharge he was under the care of several specialists, and at all times was under the care of a urologist. At the time of the trial in April, 1968, appellant required crutches to walk, still suffered from urinal incontinence and paralysis of the bowels, and wore a penile clamp.

In November, 1959 on Dr. Spence's recommendation, appellant was transferred by the F.B.I. to Miami where he could get more swimming and exercise. Appellant worked three years for the F.B.I. in Miami, Los Angeles and Houston, resigning finally in June, 1962. From then until the time of the trial, he held a number of jobs, but had constant trouble finding work because he needed to remain seated and close to a bathroom. The damages appellant claims include extensive pain and suffering, medical expenses, and loss of earnings.

II

* * *

At the close of appellant's case in chief, each defendant moved for a directed verdict and the trial judge granted both motions. The basis of the ruling, he explained, was that appellant had failed to produce any medical evidence indicating negligence on Dr. Spence's part in diagnosing appellant's malady or in performing the laminectomy; that there was no proof that Dr. Spence's treatment was responsible for appellant's disabilities; and that notwithstanding some evidence to show negligent post-operative care, an absence of medical testimony to show causality precluded submission of the case against the hospital to the jury. The judge did not allude specifically to the alleged breach of duty by Dr. Spence to divulge the possible consequences of the laminectomy.

We reverse. The testimony of appellant and his mother that Dr. Spence did not reveal the risk of paralysis from the laminectomy made out a prima facie case of violation of the physician's duty to disclose which Dr. Spence's explanation did not negate as a matter of law. * * *

III

* * *

* * * True consent to what happens to one's self is the informed exercise of a choice, and that entails an opportunity to evaluate knowledgeably the options available and the risks attendant upon each. The average patient has little or no understanding of the medical arts, and ordinarily has only his physician to whom he can look for enlightenment with which to reach an intelligent decision. From these almost axiomatic considerations springs the

need, and in turn the requirement, of a reasonable divulgence by physician to patient to make such a decision possible.[15]

A physician is under a duty to treat his patient skillfully but proficiency in diagnosis and therapy is not the full measure of his responsibility. The cases demonstrate that the physician is under an obligation to communicate specific information to the patient when the exigencies of reasonable care call for it. Due care may require a physician perceiving symptoms of bodily abnormality to alert the patient to the condition. It may call upon the physician confronting an ailment which does not respond to his ministrations to inform the patient thereof. It may command the physician to instruct the patient as to any limitations to be presently observed for his own welfare, and as to any precautionary therapy he should seek in the future. It may oblige the physician to advise the patient of the need for or desirability of any alternative treatment promising greater benefit than that being pursued. Just as plainly, due care normally demands that the physician warn the patient of any risks to his well-being which contemplated therapy may involve.

The context in which the duty of risk-disclosure arises is invariably the occasion for decision as to whether a particular treatment procedure is to be undertaken. To the physician, whose training enables a self-satisfying evaluation, the answer may seem clear, but it is the prerogative of the patient, not the physician, to determine for himself the direction in which his interests seem to lie. To enable the patient to chart his course understandably, some familiarity with the therapeutic alternatives and their hazards becomes essential.

A reasonable revelation in these respects is not only a necessity but, as we see it, is as much a matter of the physician's duty. It is a duty to warn of the dangers lurking in the proposed treatment, and that is surely a facet of due care. It is, too, a duty to impart information which the patient has every right to expect. The patient's reliance upon the physician is a trust of the kind which traditionally has exacted obligations beyond those associated with

15. The doctrine that a consent effective as authority to form therapy can arise only from the patient's understanding of alternatives to and risks of the therapy is commonly denominated "informed consent." See, *e.g.*, Waltz & Scheuneman, Informed Consent to Therapy, 64 Nw.U.L.Rev. 628, 629 (1970). The same appellation is frequently assigned to the doctrine requiring physicians, as a matter of duty to patients, to communicate information as to such alternatives and risks. See, *e.g.*, Comment, Informed Consent in Medical Malpractice, 55 Calif.L.Rev. 1396 (1967). While we recognize the general utility of shorthand phrases in literary expositions, we caution that uncritical use of the "informed consent" label can be misleading. See, *e.g.*, Plante, An Analysis of "Informed Consent," 36 Ford.L.Rev. 639, 671–72 (1968).

In duty-to-disclose cases, the focus of attention is more properly upon the nature and content of the physician's divulgence than the patient's understanding or consent. Adequate disclosure and informed consent are, of course, two sides of the same coin—the former a *sine qua non* of the latter. But the vital inquiry on duty to disclose relates to the physician's performance of an obligation, while one of the difficulties with analysis in terms of "informed consent" is its tendency to imply that what is decisive is the degree of the patient's comprehension. As we later emphasize, the physician discharges the duty when he makes a reasonable effort to convey sufficient information although the patient, without fault of the physician, may not fully grasp it. See text *infra* at notes 82–89. Even though the factfinder may have occasion to draw an inference on the state of the patient's enlightenment, the factfinding process on performance of the duty ultimately reaches back to what the physician actually said or failed to say. And while the factual conclusion on adequacy of the revelation will vary as between patients—as, for example, between a lay patient and a physician-patient—the fluctuations are attributable to the kind of divulgence which may be reasonable under the circumstances.

arms-length transactions. His dependence upon the physician for information affecting his well-being, in terms of contemplated treatment, is well-nigh abject. As earlier noted, long before the instant litigation arose, courts had recognized that the physician had the responsibility of satisfying the vital informational needs of the patient. More recently, we ourselves have found "in the fiducial qualities of [the physician-patient] relationship the physician's duty to reveal to the patient that which in his best interests it is important that he should know." We now find, as a part of the physician's overall obligation to the patient, a similar duty of reasonable disclosure of the choices with respect to proposed therapy and the dangers inherently and potentially involved.

* * *

IV

Duty to disclose has gained recognition in a large number of American jurisdictions, but more largely on a different rationale. The majority of courts dealing with the problem have made the duty depend on whether it was the custom of physicians practicing in the community to make the particular disclosure to the patient. If so, the physician may be held liable for an unreasonable and injurious failure to divulge, but there can be no recovery unless the omission forsakes a practice prevalent in the profession. We agree that the physician's noncompliance with a professional custom to reveal, like any other departure from prevailing medical practice, may give rise to liability to the patient. We do not agree that the patient's cause of action is dependent upon the existence and nonperformance of a relevant professional tradition.

There are, in our view, formidable obstacles to acceptance of the notion that the physician's obligation to disclose is either germinated or limited by medical practice. To begin with, the reality of any discernible custom reflecting a professional concensus [sic] on communication of option and risk information to patients is open to serious doubt. We sense the danger that what in fact is no custom at all may be taken as an affirmative custom to maintain silence, and that physician-witnesses to the so-called custom may state merely their personal opinions as to what they or others would do under given conditions. We cannot gloss over the inconsistency between reliance on a general practice respecting divulgence and, on the other hand, realization that the myriad of variables among patients makes each case so different that its omission can rationally be justified only by the effect of its individual circumstances. Nor can we ignore the fact that to bind the disclosure obligation to medical usage is to arrogate the decision on revelation to the physician alone. Respect for the patient's right of self-determination on particular therapy demands a standard set by law for physicians rather than one which physicians may or may not impose upon themselves.

* * * The caliber of the performance exacted by the reasonable-care standard varies between the professional and non-professional worlds, and so also the role of professional custom. * * *

We have admonished, however, that "[t]he special medical standards are but adaptations of the general standard to a group who are required to act as reasonable men possessing their medical talents presumably would." There is, by the same token, no basis for operation of the special medical standard where the physician's activity does not bring his medical knowledge and skills peculiarly into play. And where the challenge to the physician's conduct is not to be gauged by the special standard, it follows that medical custom cannot furnish the test of its propriety, whatever its relevance under the proper test may be. The decision to unveil the patient's condition and the chances as to remediation, as we shall see, is ofttimes a non-medical judgment and, if so, is a decision outside the ambit of the special standard. Where that is the situation, professional custom hardly furnishes the legal criterion for measuring the physician's responsibility to reasonably inform his patient of the options and the hazards as to treatment.

The majority rule, moreover, is at war with our prior holdings that a showing of medical practice, however probative, does not fix the standard governing recovery for medical malpractice. Prevailing medical practice, we have maintained, has evidentiary value in determinations as to what the specific criteria measuring challenged professional conduct are and whether they have been met, but does not itself define the standard. That has been our position in treatment cases, where the physician's performance is ordinarily to be adjudicated by the special medical standard of due care. We see no logic in a different rule for nondisclosure cases, where the governing standard is much more largely divorced from professional considerations. And surely in nondisclosure cases the factfinder is not invariably functioning in an area of such technical complexity that it must be bound to medical custom as an inexorable application of the community standard of reasonable care.

Thus we distinguished, for purposes of duty to disclose, the special-and general-standard aspects of the physician-patient relationship. When medical judgment enters the picture and for that reason the special standard controls, prevailing medical practice must be given its just due. In all other instances, however, the general standard exacting ordinary care applies, and that standard is set by law. In sum, the physician's duty to disclose is governed by the same legal principles applicable to others in comparable situations, with modifications only to the extent that medical judgment enters the picture. We hold that the standard measuring performance of that duty by physicians, as by others, is conduct which is reasonable under the circumstances.

V

Once the circumstances give rise to a duty on the physician's part to inform his patient, the next inquiry is the scope of the disclosure the physician is legally obliged to make. The courts have frequently confronted this problem but no uniform standard defining the adequacy of the divulgence emerges from the decisions. Some have said "full" disclosure, a norm we are unwilling to adopt literally. It seems obviously prohibitive and unrealistic to expect physicians to discuss with their patients every risk of proposed treatment—no matter how small or remote—and generally unnecessary from the patient's viewpoint as well. Indeed, the cases speaking in terms of "full" disclosure appear to envision something less than total disclosure, leaving unanswered the question of just how much.

The larger number of courts, as might be expected, have applied tests framed with reference to prevailing fashion within the medical profession. Some have measured the disclosure by "good medical practice," others by what a reasonable practitioner would have bared under the circumstances, and still others by what medical custom in the community would demand. We have explored this rather considerable body of law but are unprepared to follow it. The duty to disclose, we have reasoned, arises from phenomena apart from medical custom and practice. The latter, we think, should no more establish the scope of the duty than its existence. Any definition of scope in terms purely of a professional standard is at odds with the patient's prerogative to decide on projected therapy himself. That prerogative, we have said, is at the very foundation of the duty to disclose, and both the patient's right to know and the physician's correlative obligation to tell him are diluted to the extent that its compass is dictated by the medical profession.

In our view, the patient's right of self-decision shapes the boundaries of the duty to reveal. That right can be effectively exercised only if the patient possesses enough information to enable an intelligent choice. The scope of the physician's communications to the patient, then, must be measured by the patient's need, and that need is the information material to the decision. Thus the test for determining whether a particular peril must be divulged is its materiality to the patient's decision: all risks potentially affecting the decision must be unmasked. And to safeguard the patient's interest in achieving his own determination on treatment, the law must itself set the standard for adequate disclosure.

Optimally for the patient, exposure of a risk would be mandatory whenever the patient would deem it significant to his decision, either singly or in combination with other risks. Such a requirement, however, would summon the physician to second-guess the patient, whose ideas on materiality could hardly be known to the physician. That would make an undue demand upon medical practitioners, whose conduct, like that of others, is to be measured in terms of reasonableness. Consonantly with orthodox negligence doctrine, the physician's liability for nondisclosure is to be determined on the basis of foresight, not hindsight; no less than any other aspect of negligence, the issue on nondisclosure must be approached from the viewpoint of the reasonableness of the physician's divulgence in terms of what he knows or should know to be the patient's informational needs. If, but only if, the fact-finder can say that the physician's communication was unreasonably inadequate is an imposition of liability legally or morally justified.

Of necessity, the content of the disclosure rests in the first instance with the physician. Ordinarily it is only he who is in position to identify particular dangers; always he must make a judgment, in terms of materiality, as to whether and to what extent revelation to the patient is called for. He cannot know with complete exactitude what the patient would consider important to his decision, but on the basis of his medical training and experience he can sense how the average, reasonable patient expectably would react. Indeed, with knowledge of, or ability to learn, his patient's background and current condition, he is in a position superior to that of most others—attorneys, for example—who are called upon to make judgments on pain of liability in damages for unreasonable miscalculation.

From these considerations we derive the breadth of the disclosure of risks legally to be required. The scope of the standard is not subjective as to either the physician or the patient; it remains objective with due regard for the patient's informational needs and with suitable leeway for the physician's situation. In broad outline, we agree that "[a] risk is thus material when a reasonable person, in what the physician knows or should know to be the patient's position, would be likely to attach significance to the risk or cluster of risks in deciding whether or not to forego the proposed therapy."

The topics importantly demanding a communication of information are the inherent and potential hazards of the proposed treatment, the alternatives to that treatment, if any, and the results likely if the patient remains untreated. The factors contributing significance to the dangerousness of a medical technique are, of course, the incidence of injury and the degree of the harm threatened. A very small chance of death or serious disablement may well be significant; a potential disability which dramatically outweighs the potential benefit of the therapy or the detriments of the existing malady may summon discussion with the patient.

There is no bright line separating the significant from the insignificant; the answer in any case must abide a rule of reason. Some dangers—infection, for example—are inherent in any operation; there is no obligation to communicate those of which persons of average sophistication are aware. Even more clearly, the physician bears no responsibility for discussion of hazards the patient has already discovered, or those having no apparent materiality to patients' decision on therapy. The disclosure doctrine, like others marking lines between permissible and impermissible behavior in medical practice, is in essence a requirement of conduct prudent under the circumstances. Whenever nondisclosure of particular risk information is open to debate by reasonable-minded men, the issue is for the finder of the facts.

Notes and Questions

1. Although states are almost equally divided, a slight majority has adopted the professional disclosure standard, measuring the duty to disclose by the standard of the reasonable medical practitioner similarly situated. Expert testimony is required to establish the content of a reasonable disclosure. The *Canterbury* rule, using the "reasonable patient" as the measure of the scope of disclosure, has won over several states in the last few years. See Carr v. Strode, 79 Hawai'i 475, 904 P.2d 489 (1995). Georgia finally recognized the informed consent doctrine in Ketchup v. Howard, 247 Ga.App. 54, 543 S.E.2d 371 (2000)(with full appendix surveying other states' laws).

This professional standard is justified by three arguments. First, it protects good medical practice—the primary duty of physicians is to advance their patients' best interests, and they should not have to concern themselves with the risk that an uninformed lay jury will later decide they acted improperly. Woolley v. Henderson, 418 A.2d 1123 (Me.1980). Second, a patient-oriented standard would force doctors to spend unnecessary time discussing every possible risk with their patients, thereby interfering with the flexibility that they need to decide on the best form of treatment. Third, only physicians can accurately evaluate the psychological and other impact that risk would have on particular patients.

These jurisdictions ordinarily require the plaintiff to offer medical testimony to establish 1) whether a reasonable medical practitioner in the same or similar community would make this disclosure, and 2) that the defendant did not comply with this community standard. Fuller v. Starnes, 268 Ark. 476, 597 S.W.2d 88

(1980). Expert testimony is essential, since determination of what information needs to be disclosed is viewed as a medical question.

2. Judge Robinson suggests that the *Canterbury* standard is nothing more than the uniform application of the negligence principle to medical practice. However, the negligence principle normally evaluates the conduct of a reasonable actor—not the expectations of a reasonable victim. The values served by the doctrine—patient autonomy and dignity—are unrelated to the values served by the doctrine of negligence. Informed consent really serves the values we otherwise identify with the doctrine of battery. It is ironic that a doctrine developed to foster and recognize individual choice should be measured by an objective standard.

3. The effect of a patient-oriented disclosure standard is to ease the plaintiff's burden of proof, since the trier of fact could find that a doctor acted unreasonably in failing to disclose, in spite of unrebutted expert medical testimony to the contrary. The question of whether a physician disclosed risks which a reasonable person would find material is for the trier of fact, and technical expertise is not required. Pedersen v. Vahidy, 209 Conn. 510, 552 A.2d 419 (1989). In Savold v. Johnson, 443 N.W.2d 656 (S.D.1989), the South Dakota Supreme Court held that expert testimony as to informed consent information was not needed, where a factual dispute exists as to whether any information of the material risks was given at all. Expert testimony is still needed, however, to clarify the treatments and their probabilities of risks. Thus in Cross v. Trapp, 170 W.Va. 459, 294 S.E.2d 446, 455 (1982), the court held that experts were needed to establish "* * * (1) the risks involved concerning a particular method of treatment, (2) alternative methods of treatment, (3) the risks relating to such alternative methods of treatment and (4) the results likely to occur if the patient remains untreated." Accord, Festa v. Greenberg, 354 Pa.Super. 346, 511 A.2d 1371 (Pa.Super.1986); Sard v. Hardy, 281 Md. 432, 379 A.2d 1014 (Md.1977).

4. *Information to be disclosed.* The doctor must consider disclosure of a variety of factors:

a. Diagnosis. This includes the medical steps preceding diagnosis, including tests and their alternatives. The right of informed refusal, as established in Truman v. Thomas, 27 Cal.3d 285, 165 Cal.Rptr. 308, 611 P.2d 902 (1980), requires disclosure of the risks of foregoing a diagnostic procedure.

b. Nature and purpose of the proposed treatment.

c. Risks of the treatment. Risks that are remote can be omitted. The threshold of disclosure, as the *Canterbury* court suggests, varies with the product of the probability and the severity of the risk. Thus a five percent risk of lengthened recuperation might be ignored, while a one percent risk of paralysis, as in *Canterbury,* or an even smaller risk of death, should be disclosed. Cobbs v. Grant, 8 Cal.3d 229, 104 Cal.Rptr. 505, 502 P.2d 1 (1972). In Hartke v. McKelway, 707 F.2d 1544, 1549 (D.C.Cir.1983) the doctor performed a laparoscopic cauterization to prevent pregnancy of the plaintiff, who later became pregnant and had a healthy child. "In this case, the undisclosed risk was a .1% to .3% chance of subsequent pregnancy. For most people this risk would be considered very small, but this patient was in a particularly unusual position. In view of the very serious expected consequences of pregnancy for her—possibly including death—as well as the ready availability of ways to reduce the risk * * * a jury could conclude that a reasonable person in what Dr. McKelway knew to be plaintiff's position would be likely to attach significance to the risk here."

The difference between a temporary and permanent risk can be critical, and even mention in a consent form of the general risk, but characterized as temporary, will be insufficient to constitute full disclosure. See, e.g., Johnson v. Brandy, 1995 WL 29230 (Ohio App.1995)(risk of scalp numbness after scalp-reduction surgery for baldness not described as permanent risk, but only temporary; consent form held to be inadequate disclosure).

Where a drug or injectable substance is part of treatment, a patient is entitled to know whether that drug or substance has been tested or approved by Federal authorities such as the Food and Drug Administration. Gaston v. Hunter, 121 Ariz. 33, 588 P.2d 326 (Ariz.App.1978)(investigational procedure must be disclosed); Retkwa v. Orentreich, 154 Misc.2d 164, 584 N.Y.S.2d 710 (S.C., N.Y.Cty. 1992)(patient entitled to information about FDA status of liquid injectable silicone).

d. Treatment alternatives. Doctors should disclose those alternatives that are generally acknowledged within the medical community as feasible, Martin v. Richards, 192 Wis.2d 156, 531 N.W.2d 70, 78 (Wisc. 1995), their risks and consequences, and their probability of success. Even if the alternative is more hazardous, some courts have held that it should be disclosed. Logan v. Greenwich Hospital Association, 191 Conn. 282, 465 A.2d 294 (1983). In Wenger v. Oregon Urology Clinic, P.C., 102 Or.App. 665, 796 P.2d 376 (1990), the court held that defendants failed to properly inform plaintiff of several treatment alternatives to treat Peyonie's disease, a male genital condition which can impair sexual function. The procedure used by the defendant caused an infection, ultimately leading to the amputation of the plaintiff's penis. In Stover v. Surgeons, 431 Pa.Super. 11, 635 A.2d 1047 (1993), the court upheld a duty of disclosure of alternative replacement heart valves and their merits.

A physician must disclose medical information even if the procedure is noninvasive, considering that observation rather than more aggressive treatments may entail significant risks. Martin v. Richards, 192 Wis.2d 156, 531 N.W.2d 70, 79 (Wisc. 1995)(physician failed to disclose to parents the risks of intracranial bleeding and the need for a CT scan or transfer to another facility in that case).

If the alternative is not a legitimate treatment option, it need not be disclosed to the patient. See Morris v. Ferriss, 669 So.2d 1316 (La.App. 4 Cir.1996)(physician did not have to advise patient that psychiatric treatment was an alternative treatment for epileptic partial complex seizures, since it was not accepted as feasible); Lienhard v. State, 431 N.W.2d 861 (Minn.1988) (managing pregnancy at home rather than in hospital not a choice between alternative methods of treatment; disclosure therefore not required).

e. Doing nothing as an option. In a health care environment of managed care, conservative practice is the goal and doing nothing and "watchful waiting" are desirable clinical approaches to patient care. In Wecker v. Amend, 22 Kan.App.2d 498, 918 P.2d 658 (C.A. Kansas 1996), the plaintiff contended that Dr. Amend failed to obtain her informed consent before performing laser surgery on her cervix. She had a human papilloma virus wart on her cervix. Since this might be precancerous, Dr. Amend recommended laser surgery to remove it. She watched a video about laser surgery, which stated that "Laser surgery involves the same risks as with any surgical procedure. There is a small risk of excessive bleeding and possible infection, but those cases are not common and can be treated". Following the surgery, she suffered excessive bleeding and he had to perform a total hysterectomy to control the bleeding. She underwent further surgeries and injections to control her pain. She argue that he failed to inform her of alternatives including the option of no treatment at all.

One expert testified that it was reasonable to do nothing and see if the wart disappeared. In the court's words,

> ... how can a patient give an informed consent to treatment for a condition if the patient is not informed that the condition might resolve itself without any treatment at all? The court held that the jury must be instructed that a physician has a duty to advise a patient of the option of choosing no treatment at all. (Italics mine).

The definition of treatment has been construed broadly to include diagnostic options and choices of hospitals for performing a procedure. Physicians must disclose diagnostic procedures that might assist patients in making an informed decision about treatment. In Martin v. Richards, 176 Wis.2d 339, 500 N.W.2d 691 (Wis.App.1993), the court held that it was for the jury to decide whether the physicians' failure to inform the parents of a minor patient of the availability of a CAT scan to detect intracranial bleeding and the unavailability of a neurosurgeon at the hospital to operate caused the patient's brain damage. In Vachon v. Broadlawns Medical Foundation, 490 N.W.2d 820 (Iowa 1992), the plaintiff suffered severe multiple trauma injuries and the issue was whether his transfer to a university hospital two hours away instead of to closer trauma hospitals was reasonable. The court held that the decision to transfer was part of treatment and raised an issue of reasonable care.

5. *The patient's state of mind.* Courts do not usually consider whether the patient comprehended the risk discussion. If the patient is competent, the focus is typically on the content of the physician's disclosure and whether the risks and alternatives were discussed. However, when a patient might lack the state of mind to objectively evaluate treatment alternatives, at least one court has allowed the jury to consider factors that might cause a patient to disregard the discussion. In Macy v. Blatchford, 330 Or. 444, 8 P.3d 204, 211 (Or.2000), the court held that evidence of a sexual relationship between a physician and patient might be relevant to prove that the physician failed to obtain the patient's informed consent. "* * * [A] reasonable juror might believe that a sexual relationship between defendant and Macy would undermine Macy'[s] ability to listen objectively to and utilize information provided by the physician, in making an independent and informed decision about her health care."

2. *Disclosure of Physician–Specific Risk Information*

As medical knowledge grows and institutional tracking of physician performance becomes the norm, much more information is available in theory to patients not only about a particular disease and its treatment, but also about the particular physician's skill and track record. Consider the following case.

JOHNSON v. KOKEMOOR

Supreme Court of Wisconsin, 1996.
199 Wis.2d 615, 545 N.W.2d 495.

SHIRLEY S. ABRAHAMSON, JUSTICE.

* * *

Donna Johnson (the plaintiff) brought an action against Dr. Richard Kokemoor (the defendant) alleging his failure to obtain her informed consent to surgery as required by Wis.Stat. § 448.30 (1993–94). The jury found that the defendant failed to adequately inform the plaintiff regarding the risks associated with her surgery. The jury also found that a reasonable person in the plaintiff's position would have refused to consent to surgery by the defendant if she had been fully informed of its attendant risks and advantages.

This case presents the issue of whether the circuit court erred in admitting evidence that the defendant, in undertaking his duty to obtain the plaintiff's informed consent before operating to clip an aneurysm, failed (1) to divulge the extent of his experience in performing this type of operation; (2) to compare the morbidity and mortality rates[1] for this type of surgery among experienced surgeons and inexperienced surgeons like himself; and (3) to refer the plaintiff to a tertiary care center staffed by physicians more experienced in performing the same surgery. The admissibility of such physician-specific evidence in a case involving the doctrine of informed consent raises an issue of first impression in this court and is an issue with which appellate courts have had little experience.

* * *

We conclude that all three items of evidence were material to the issue of informed consent in this case. As we stated in Martin v. Richards, 192 Wis.2d 156, 174, 531 N.W.2d 70 (1995), "a patient cannot make an informed, intelligent decision to consent to a physician's suggested treatment unless the physician discloses what is material to the patient's decision, i.e., all of the viable alternatives and risks of the treatment proposed." In this case information regarding a physician's experience in performing a particular procedure, a physician's risk statistics as compared with those of other physicians who perform that procedure, and the availability of other centers and physicians better able to perform that procedure would have facilitated the plaintiff's awareness of "all of the viable alternatives" available to her and thereby aided her exercise of informed consent. We therefore conclude that under the circumstances of this case, the circuit court did not erroneously exercise its discretion in admitting the evidence.

I.

We first summarize the facts giving rise to this review, recognizing that the parties dispute whether several events occurred, as well as what infer-

1. As used by the parties and in this opinion, morbidity and mortality rates refer to the prospect that surgery may result in serious impairment or death.

ences should be drawn from both the disputed and the undisputed historical facts.

On the advice of her family physician, the plaintiff underwent a CT scan to determine the cause of her headaches. Following the scan, the family physician referred the plaintiff to the defendant, a neurosurgeon in the Chippewa Falls area. The defendant diagnosed an enlarging aneurysm at the rear of the plaintiff's brain and recommended surgery to clip the aneurysm.[9] The defendant performed the surgery in October of 1990.

The defendant clipped the aneurysm, rendering the surgery a technical success. But as a consequence of the surgery, the plaintiff, who had no neurological impairments prior to surgery, was rendered an incomplete quadriplegic. She remains unable to walk or to control her bowel and bladder movements. Furthermore, her vision, speech and upper body coordination are partially impaired.

At trial, the plaintiff introduced evidence that the defendant overstated the urgency of her need for surgery and overstated his experience with performing the particular type of aneurysm surgery which she required. According to testimony introduced during the plaintiff's case in chief, when the plaintiff questioned the defendant regarding his experience, he replied that he had performed the surgery she required "several" times; asked what he meant by "several," the defendant said "dozens" and "lots of times."

In fact, however, the defendant had relatively limited experience with aneurysm surgery. He had performed thirty aneurysm surgeries during residency, but all of them involved anterior circulation aneurysms. According to the plaintiff's experts, operations performed to clip anterior circulation aneurysms are significantly less complex than those necessary to clip posterior circulation aneurysms such as the plaintiff's.[10] Following residency, the defendant had performed aneurysm surgery on six patients with a total of nine aneurysms. He had operated on basilar bifurcation aneurysms only twice and had never operated on a large basilar bifurcation aneurysm such as the plaintiff's aneurysm.[11]

The plaintiff also presented evidence that the defendant understated the morbidity and mortality rate associated with basilar bifurcation aneurysm surgery. According to the plaintiff's witnesses, the defendant had told the plaintiff that her surgery carried a two percent risk of death or serious impairment and that it was less risky than the angiogram procedure she would have to undergo in preparation for surgery. The plaintiff's witnesses also testified that the defendant had compared the risks associated with the plaintiff's surgery to those associated with routine procedures such as tonsillectomies, appendectomies and gall bladder surgeries.[12]

9. The defendant acknowledged at trial that the aneurysm was not the cause of the plaintiff's headaches.

10. The plaintiff's aneurysm was located at the bifurcation of the basilar artery. According to the plaintiff's experts, surgery on basilar bifurcation aneurysms is more difficult than any other type of aneurysm surgery.

11. The defendant testified that he had failed to inform the plaintiff that he was not and never had been board certified in neurosurgery and that he was not a subspecialist in aneurysm surgery.

12. The defendant testified at trial that he had informed the plaintiff that should she decide to forego surgery, the risk that her unclipped aneurysm might rupture was two percent per annum, cumulative. Since he informed the plaintiff that the risk accompanying surgery was two percent, a reasonable person in

The plaintiff's neurosurgical experts testified that even the physician considered to be one of the world's best aneurysm surgeons, who had performed hundreds of posterior circulation aneurysm surgeries, had reported a morbidity and mortality rate of ten-and-seven-tenths percent when operating upon basilar bifurcation aneurysms comparable in size to the plaintiff's aneurysm. Furthermore, information in treatises and articles which the defendant reviewed in preparation for the plaintiff's surgery set the morbidity and mortality rate at approximately fifteen percent for a basilar bifurcation aneurysm. The plaintiff also introduced expert testimony that the morbidity and mortality rate for basilar bifurcation aneurysm operations performed by one with the defendant's relatively limited experience would be between twenty and thirty percent, and "closer to the thirty percent range."[13]

Finally, the plaintiff introduced into evidence testimony and exhibits stating that a reasonable physician in the defendant's position would have advised the plaintiff of the availability of more experienced surgeons and would have referred her to them. The plaintiff also introduced evidence stating that patients with basilar aneurysms should be referred to tertiary care centers—such as the Mayo Clinic, only 90 miles away—which contain the proper neurological intensive care unit and microsurgical facilities and which are staffed by neurosurgeons with the requisite training and experience to perform basilar bifurcation aneurysm surgeries.

In his testimony at trial, the defendant denied having suggested to the plaintiff that her condition was urgent and required immediate care. He also denied having stated that her risk was comparable to that associated with an angiogram or minor surgical procedures such as a tonsillectomy or appendectomy. While he acknowledged telling the plaintiff that the risk of death or serious impairment associated with clipping an aneurysm was two percent, he also claims to have told her that because of the location of her aneurysm, the risks attending her surgery would be greater, although he was unable to tell her precisely how much greater.[14] In short, the defendant testified that his disclosure to the plaintiff adequately informed her regarding the risks that she faced.

The defendant's expert witnesses testified that the defendant's recommendation of surgery was appropriate, that this type of surgery is regularly undertaken in a community hospital setting, and that the risks attending anterior and posterior circulation aneurysm surgeries are comparable. They placed the risk accompanying the plaintiff's surgery at between five and ten percent, although one of the defendant's experts also testified that such statistics can be misleading. The defendant's expert witnesses also testified

the plaintiff's position might have concluded that proceeding with surgery was less risky than non-operative management.

13. The plaintiff introduced into evidence as exhibits articles from the medical literature stating that there are few areas in neurosurgery where the difference in results between surgeons is as evident as it is with aneurysms. One of the plaintiff's neurosurgical experts testified that experience and skill with the operator is more important when performing basilar tip aneurysm surgery than with any other neurosurgical procedure.

14. The defendant maintained that characterizing the risk as two percent was accurate because the aggregate morbidity and mortality rate for all aneurysms, anterior and posterior, is approximately two percent. At the same time, however, the defendant conceded that in operating upon aneurysms comparable to the plaintiff's aneurysm, he could not achieve morbidity and mortality rates as low as the ten-and-seven-tenths percent rate reported by a physician reputed to be one of the world's best aneurysm surgeons.

that when queried by a patient regarding their experience, they would divulge the extent of that experience and its relation to the experience of other physicians performing similar operations.[14]

II.

[In Part II The court discussed Wisconsin's approach to informed consent, essentially the Canterbury position. The court noted that significant potential risks must be disclosed, as part of all information material to a patient's decision.]

III.

[In Part III the court discussed the standard of review in informed consent cases.]

IV.

[In Part IV, the court considered whether a physician's experience with a procedure should be considered by the trier of fact. It held that information as to such experience could be important to the plaintiff's decision as to whether to proceed with a medical procedure.]

In this case, the plaintiff introduced ample evidence that had a reasonable person in her position been aware of the defendant's relative lack of experience in performing basilar bifurcation aneurysm surgery, that person would not have undergone surgery with him. According to the record the plaintiff had made inquiry of the defendant's experience with surgery like hers. In response to her direct question about his experience he said that he had operated on aneurysms comparable to her aneurysm "dozens" of times. The plaintiff also introduced evidence that surgery on basilar bifurcation aneurysms is more difficult than any other type of aneurysm surgery and among the most difficult in all of neurosurgery. We conclude that the circuit court did not erroneously exercise its discretion in admitting evidence regarding the defendant's lack of experience and the difficulty of the proposed procedure. A reasonable person in the plaintiff's position would have considered such information material in making an intelligent and informed decision about the surgery.

* * *

V.

The defendant next argues that the circuit court erred in allowing the plaintiff to introduce evidence of morbidity and mortality rates associated

14. The defendant's expert witness Dr. Patrick R. Walsh testified: In my personal practice, I typically outline my understanding of the natural history of aneurysms, my understanding of the experience of the neurosurgical community in dealing with aneurysms and then respond to specific questions raised by the patient. If a patient asks specifically what my experience is, I believe it is mandatory that I outline that to him as carefully as possible.

Dr. Walsh also stated that "[i]t certainly is reasonable for [the defendant] to explain to [the plaintiff] that other surgeons are available."

Dr. Douglas E. Anderson, who also testified for the defense, stated that "if the patient is asking issues about prior experience, it is reasonable ... to proceed with a discussion of your prior experience." Dr. Anderson also stated that "if the patient asks a surgeon if there is someone who has performed more surgeries than he, it is reasonable to tell the truth."

with the surgery at issue. The defendant particularly objects to comparative risk statistics purporting to estimate and compare the morbidity and mortality rates when the surgery at issue is performed, respectively, by a physician of limited experience such as the defendant and by the acknowledged masters in the field. Expert testimony introduced by the plaintiff indicated that the morbidity and mortality rate expected when a surgeon with the defendant's experience performed the surgery would be significantly higher than the rate expected when a more experienced physician performed the same surgery.

The defendant asserts that admission of these morbidity and mortality rates would lead the jury to find him liable for failing to perform at the level of the masters rather than for failing to adequately inform the plaintiff regarding the risks associated with her surgery. Furthermore, contends the defendant, statistics are notoriously inaccurate and misleading.

As with evidence pertaining to the defendant's prior experience with similar surgery, the defendant requests that the court fashion a bright line rule as a matter of law that comparative risk evidence should not be admitted in an informed consent case. For many of the same reasons which led us to conclude that such a bright line rule of exclusion would be inappropriate for evidence of a physician's prior experience, we also reject a bright line rule excluding evidence of comparative risk relating to the provider.

The medical literature identifies basilar bifurcation aneurysm surgery as among the most difficult in neurosurgery. As the plaintiff's evidence indicates, however, the defendant had told her that the risks associated with her surgery were comparable to the risks attending a tonsillectomy, appendectomy or gall bladder operation. The plaintiff also introduced evidence that the defendant estimated the risk of death or serious impairment associated with her surgery at two percent. At trial, however, the defendant conceded that because of his relative lack of experience, he could not hope to match the ten-and-seven-tenths percent morbidity and mortality rate reported for large basilar bifurcation aneurysm surgery by very experienced surgeons.

The defendant also admitted at trial that he had not shared with the plaintiff information from articles he reviewed prior to surgery. These articles established that even the most accomplished posterior circulation aneurysm surgeons reported morbidity and mortality rates of fifteen percent for basilar bifurcation aneurysms. Furthermore, the plaintiff introduced expert testimony indicating that the estimated morbidity and mortality rate one might expect when a physician with the defendant's relatively limited experience performed the surgery would be close to thirty percent.

Had a reasonable person in the plaintiff's position been made aware that being operated upon by the defendant significantly increased the risk one would have faced in the hands of another surgeon performing the same operation, that person might well have elected to forego surgery with the defendant. Had a reasonable person in the plaintiff's position been made aware that the risks associated with surgery were significantly greater than the risks that an unclipped aneurysm would rupture, that person might well have elected to forego surgery altogether. In short, had a reasonable person in the plaintiff's position possessed such information before consenting to surgery, that person would have been better able to make an informed and intelligent decision.

The defendant concedes that the duty to procure a patient's informed consent requires a physician to reveal the general risks associated with a particular surgery. The defendant does not explain why the duty to inform about this general risk data should be interpreted to categorically exclude evidence relating to provider-specific risk information, even when that provider-specific data is geared to a clearly delineated surgical procedure and identifies a particular provider as an independent risk factor. When different physicians have substantially different success rates, whether surgery is performed by one rather than another represents a choice between "alternate, viable medical modes of treatment" under § 448.30.

For example, while there may be a general risk of ten percent that a particular surgical procedure will result in paralysis or death, that risk may climb to forty percent when the particular procedure is performed by a relatively inexperienced surgeon. It defies logic to interpret this statute as requiring that the first, almost meaningless statistic be divulged to a patient while the second, far more relevant statistic should not be. Under Scaria and its progeny as well as the codification of Scaria as Wis.Stat. § 448.30, the second statistic would be material to the patient's exercise of an intelligent and informed consent regarding treatment options. A circuit court may in its discretion conclude that the second statistic is admissible.

The doctrine of informed consent requires disclosure of "all of the viable alternatives and risks of the treatment proposed" which would be material to a patient's decision. [ ] We therefore conclude that when different physicians have substantially different success rates with the same procedure and a reasonable person in the patient's position would consider such information material, the circuit court may admit this statistical evidence.[32]

We caution, as did the court of appeals, that our decision will not always require physicians to give patients comparative risk evidence in statistical terms to obtain informed consent.[33] Rather, we hold that evidence of the morbidity and mortality outcomes of different physicians was admissible under the circumstances of this case.

In keeping with the fact-driven and context-specific application of informed consent doctrine, questions regarding whether statistics are sufficient-

32. See Aaron D. Twerski & Neil B. Cohen, Comparing Medical Providers: A First Look at the New Era of Medical Statistics, 58 Brook. L.Rev. 5 (1992). Professors Twerski and Cohen note that the development of sophisticated data regarding risks of various procedures and statistical models comparing the success rates of medical providers signal changes in informed consent law. Specifically, they state:

> The duty to provide information may require more than a simple sharing of visceral concerns about the wisdom of undertaking a given therapeutic procedure. Physicians may have a responsibility to identify and correlate risk factors and to communicate the results to patients as a predicate to fulfilling their obligation to inform. Id. at 6.

See also Douglas Sharrott, Provider–Specific Quality-of-Care Data: A Proposal for Limited Mandatory Disclosure, 58 Brook L.Rev. 85 (1992) (stating that it is difficult to refute the argument that provider-specific data, once disclosed to the public by the government, should also be disclosed to patients because the doctrine of informed consent requires a physician to inform a patient of both material risks and alternatives to a proposed course of treatment).

33. For criticisms of medical performance statistics and cautions that provider-specific outcome statistics must be carefully evaluated to insure their reliability and validity when used as evidence, see, e.g., Jesse Green, Problems in the Use of Outcome Statistics to Compare Health Care Providers, 58 Brook.L.Rev. 55 (1992); Paul D. Rheingold, The Admissibility of Evidence in Malpractice Cases: The Performance Records of Practitioners, 58 Brook. L.Rev. 75, 78–79 (1992); Sharrott, supra, at 92–94, 120; Twerski & Cohen, supra, at 8–9.

ly material to a patient's decision to be admissible and sufficiently reliable to be non-prejudicial are best resolved on a case-by-case basis. The fundamental issue in an informed consent case is less a question of how a physician chooses to explain the panoply of treatment options and risks necessary to a patient's informed consent than a question of assessing whether a patient has been advised that such options and risks exist.

As the court of appeals observed, in this case it was the defendant himself who elected to explain the risks confronting the plaintiff in statistical terms. He did this because, as he stated at trial, "numbers giv[e] some perspective to the framework of the very real, immediate, human threat that is involved with this condition." Because the defendant elected to explain the risks confronting the plaintiff in statistical terms, it stands to reason that in her effort to demonstrate how the defendant's numbers dramatically understated the risks of her surgery, the plaintiff would seek to introduce other statistical evidence. Such evidence was integral to her claim that the defendant's nondisclosure denied her the ability to exercise informed consent.

VI.

The defendant also asserts that the circuit court erred as a matter of law in allowing the plaintiff to introduce expert testimony that because of the difficulties associated with operating on the plaintiff's aneurysm, the defendant should have referred her to a tertiary care center containing a proper neurological intensive care unit, more extensive microsurgical facilities and more experienced surgeons. While evidence that a physician should have referred a patient elsewhere may support an action alleging negligent treatment, argues the defendant, it has no place in an informed consent action.

* * *

When faced with an allegation that a physician breached a duty of informed consent, the pertinent inquiry concerns what information a reasonable person in the patient's position would have considered material to an exercise of intelligent and informed consent. [ ] Under the facts and circumstances presented by this case, the circuit court could declare, in the exercise of its discretion, that evidence of referral would have been material to the ability of a reasonable person in the plaintiff's position to render informed consent.

The plaintiff's medical experts testified that given the nature and difficulty of the surgery at issue, the plaintiff could not make an intelligent decision or give an informed consent without being made aware that surgery in a tertiary facility would have decreased the risk she faced. One of the plaintiff's experts, Dr. Haring J.W. Nauta, stated that "it's not fair not to bring up the subject of referral to another center when the problem is as difficult to treat" as the plaintiff's aneurysm was. Another of the plaintiff's experts, Dr. Robert Narotzky, testified that the defendant's "very limited" experience with aneurysm surgery rendered reasonable a referral to "someone with a lot more experience in dealing with this kind of problem." Dr. Fredric Somach, also testifying for the plaintiff, stated as follows:

> [S]he should have been told that this was an extremely difficult, formidable lesion and that there are people in the immediate geographic vicinity

that are very experienced and that have had a great deal of contact with this type of aneurysm and that she should consider having at least a second opinion, if not going directly to one of these other [physicians].

Articles from the medical literature introduced by the plaintiff also stated categorically that the surgery at issue should be performed at a tertiary care center while being "excluded" from the community setting because of "the limited surgical experience" and lack of proper equipment and facilities available in such hospitals.

* * * Hence under the materiality standard announced in Scaria, we conclude that the circuit court properly exercised its discretion in admitting evidence that the defendant should have advised the plaintiff of the possibility of undergoing surgery at a tertiary care facility.

The defendant asserts that the plaintiff knew she could go elsewhere. This claim is both true and beside the point. Credible evidence in this case demonstrates that the plaintiff chose not to go elsewhere because the defendant gave her the impression that her surgery was routine and that it therefore made no difference who performed it. The pertinent inquiry, then, is not whether a reasonable person in the plaintiff's position would have known generally that she might have surgery elsewhere, but rather whether such a person would have chosen to have surgery elsewhere had the defendant adequately disclosed the comparable risks attending surgery performed by him and surgery performed at a tertiary care facility such as the Mayo Clinic, only 90 miles away.

* * *

Finally, the defendant argues that if his duty to procure the plaintiff's informed consent includes an obligation to disclose that she consider seeking treatment elsewhere, then there will be no logical stopping point to what the doctrine of informed consent might encompass. We disagree with the defendant. As the plaintiff noted in her brief to this court, "[i]t is a rare exception when the vast body of medical literature and expert opinion agree that the difference in experience of the surgeon performing the operation will impact the risk of morbidity/mortality as was the case here," thereby requiring referral. Brief for Petitioner at 40. At oral argument before this court, counsel for the plaintiff stated that under "many circumstances" and indeed "probably most circumstances," whether or not a physician referred a patient elsewhere would be "utterly irrelevant" in an informed consent case. In the vast majority of significantly less complicated cases, such a referral would be irrelevant and unnecessary.

Moreover, we have already concluded that comparative risk data distinguishing the defendant's morbidity and mortality rate from the rate of more experienced physicians was properly before the jury. A close link exists between such data and the propriety of referring a patient elsewhere. A physician who discloses that other physicians might have lower morbidity and mortality rates when performing the same procedure will presumably have access to information regarding who some of those physicians are. When the duty to share comparative risk data is material to a patient's exercise of informed consent, an ensuing referral elsewhere will often represent no more than a modest and logical next step.[37]

Given the difficulties involved in performing the surgery at issue in this case, coupled with evidence that the defendant exaggerated his own prior experience while downplaying the risks confronting the plaintiff, the circuit court properly exercised its discretion in admitting evidence that a physician of good standing would have made the plaintiff aware of the alternative of lower risk surgery with a different, more experienced surgeon in a better-equipped facility.

For the reasons set forth, we conclude that the circuit court did not erroneously exercise its discretion in admitting the evidence at issue, and accordingly, we reverse the decision of the court of appeals and remand the cause to the circuit court for further proceedings consistent with this opinion.

The decision of the court of appeals is reversed and the cause is remanded to the circuit court with directions.

Notes and Questions

1. Do you see any problems with the duty to disclose articulated in *Johnson*? Can a surgeon manage to disguise poor results or repackage the data to confuse the patient? Or is this likely to represent the future, in which patients peruse batting averages before choosing their providers? Is there anything wrong with a consumer-driven model of medicine?

Consumer advocates have lobbied with success for disclosure of hospital and physician performance data in a variety of formats, including report cards and other rankings. Studies of the effects of disclosure of such data have not been encouraging. See for example Eric C. Schneider, Arnold M. Epstein, Use of Public Performance Reports: A Survey of Patients Undergoing Cardiac Surgery, 279 J.A.M.A. 1638, 1642(1998). The authors concluded that "... public reporting of mortality outcomes in Pennsylvania has had virtually no direct impact on patients' selection of hospitals or surgeons. Nevertheless, a substantial number of patients expressed interest in data on mortality outcomes and claimed that they would use such reports in their decision making ... [w]ithout a tailored and intensive program for dissemination and patient education, efforts to aid patient decision making with performance reports are unlikely to succeed." See also Judith H. Hibbard, Paul Slovic, and Jacquelyn J. Jewett, Informing Consumer Decisions in Health Care: Implications from Decision–Making Research, 75 Milbank Q. 395, 411–412 (1997) (finding little congruence between current report card strategies and decision-making research.); Stephen T. Mennemeyer, Michael A. Morrisey, and Leslie Z. Howard, Death and Reputation: How Consumers Acted Upon HCFA Mortality Information, 34 Inquiry 117 (1997) (quality measures aimed at the public must be very simply designed and described; complex measures are largely ignored).

2. Most courts resist requirements that specific percentages of risks be disclosed, arguing that medicine is an inexact science. In Ditto v. McCurdy, 86

37. The Canterbury court included a duty to refer among its examples of information which, under the facts and circumstances of a particular case, a physician might be required to disclose in order to procure a patient's informed consent. The court stated: "The typical situation is where a general practitioner discovers that the patient's malady calls for specialized treatment, whereupon the duty generally arises to advise the patient to consult a specialist." Canterbury, 464 F.2d at 781 n. 22.

Hawai'i 84, 947 P.2d 952 (1997) two patients underwent breast implant procedures and had complications, and sued the cosmetic surgeon. They argued among other claims that the surgeon's experience should have been disclosed to them, since he was not certified as a plastic surgeon, but only as an otolaryngologist, facial surgeon, and cosmetic surgeon. The court concluded that "[u]nder the circumstances of the present case, we decline to hold that a physician has a duty to affirmatively disclose his or her qualifications or the lack thereof to a patient. Id at 958. The court preferred to leave such disclosure requirements to the legislature."

See also Kennedy v. St. Charles General Hospital Auxiliary, 630 So.2d 888, 892 (La.App.1993). But see Hales v. Pittman, 118 Ariz. 305, 576 P.2d 493 (Ariz.1978) (discussing the battery count of the plaintiff's complaint; the court proposed that the doctor should disclose both the general statistical success rate for a given procedure, and his particular experience with that procedure.) See also Hidding v. Williams, 578 So.2d 1192 (La.Ct.App.1991) (plaintiff sued on an informed consent theory, alleging in part that the physician had failed to disclose that he was a chronic alcoholic; held, such a failure to inform violated Louisiana informed consent requirements); contra, Ornelas v. Fry, 151 Ariz. 324, 727 P.2d 819 (Ariz.Ct.App.1986) (court refused to allow evidence as to alcoholism of anesthesiologist as a separate claim of negligence, absent a showing that the physician was impaired at the time of the procedure.)

3. Suppose that a surgeon in his late fifties is aware that his skill level—his vision, his fine motor skills—is diminishing. His success rate is dropping, which means that his patient survival statistics are worsening. The odds of an iatrogenic injury with this surgeon have increased from 1 in 1,000 to 1 in 750. His record is still excellent. Should he disclose to his patients that he is beginning to suffer the inevitable results of aging? Or just that his success rate is a certain percentage? Institutional peer review is likely to restrict the surgeon's practice to those procedures he is competent to perform, with regular proctoring to guarantee good results, when he falls below a reasonable norm. We might also expect a physician with integrity to recognize his limits and begin to cut back on procedures. The role of the institution and peers in controlling these practices is central to reducing risks, backstopped by the ever present threat of a tort suit for damages. Hospital medical staff law has focused on provider competency in articulating the limits of negligent staff selection. Hospitals screen their medical staff to reduce the level of risk of injury to their patient population, refusing to credential high risk physicians, defining risk by a competency/quality definition.

For good general discussions of contemporary informed consent issues, see Robert Gatter, Informed Consent and the Forgotten Duty of Physician Inquiry, 1 Loy. U. Chi. L.J. 557 (2000); Arnold J. Rosoff, Informed Consent in the Electronic Age, 25 Am.J.L. & Med.367(1999); Frances H. Miller, Health Care Information Technology and Informed Consent: Computers and the Doctor–Patient Relationship, 31 Ind. L. Rev. 1019 (1998).

4. The disclosure of a contagious status that exposes a patient to a risk of death is arguably different from performance-based risks. A competent physician may expose a patient to the HIV virus, while the risks discussed above are created by performance failures. The distinction is however not compelling. From the patient's perspective, the source of the risk is less important than the risk itself, whether death or impairment. From a patient's perspective, if the low risk of transmission of the HIV-virus must be disclosed, then surely so must alcoholism in a surgeon. A provider's performance can be affected by fatigue, depression,

anger, and other psychological states with potentially lethal results for the patient. We don't presently require disclosure of the various forces that affect providers, and it is hard to imagine how this could be done. If a court is to avoid singling out AIDs as presenting unique risks to a patient, then vastly expanded disclosure obligations may well be next.

The courts have not often agreed with these arguments. In Behringer v. The Medical Center at Princeton, 249 N.J.Super. 597, 592 A.2d 1251 (1991), the plaintiff, a surgeon at the medical center, was diagnosed as having AIDS. The information leaked out in the hospital, and he lost most of his patients. The court held that informed consent doctrine mandated disclosure of the doctor's contagious status in spite of evidence that the risk of transmission of the HIV virus from provider to patient was extremely low. The court wrote:

> If there is to be an ultimate arbiter of whether the patient is to be treated invasively by an AIDS-positive surgeon, the arbiter will be the fully-informed patient. The ultimate risk to the patient is so absolute—so devastating—that it is untenable to argue against informed consent combined with a restriction on procedures which present "any risk" to the patient.

While the theory and application of informed consent doctrine by the courts seems to justify disclosure of HIV positive status, the efficacy of the doctrine in actually inducing providers to so act is unclear at best. HIV status does not pose unique risks: the risk of either contagion or death is inherent in a range of provider-created risks. A better way to frame the risks for the courts is to think of such status risks as better regulated by both threshold screening of providers for staff privileges, by institutional policies to promote safer health care delivery, and by use of tort law to set a standard of unreasonable risk creation. A provider who fails to protect residents or medical staff may be liable for negligence. See, e.g., Doe v. Yale University, 252 Conn. 641, 748 A.2d 834 (2000)(noting that a physician employee may be limited to Workers' Compensation).

Methods of achieving such threshold screening to protect patients against high-risk providers include staff privilege limitations, the threat of a negligence suit against a provider who is truly a "typhoid surgeon", and professional self-restraint by physicians who become aware that they are high-risk providers. Informed consent doctrine seems ill-suited to carry such additional baggage—it is unfair to providers, moves doctrine into an area of risk disclosure that lacks a clear stopping point or bright line, and is simply not justified by a risk analysis.

See generally Lawrence O. Gostin, A Proposed National Policy on Health Care Workers Living With HIV/AIDS and Other Blood–Borne Pathogens, 284 JAMA 1965 (2000); Anthony L. Osterlund, The Unequal Balancing Act Between HIV–Positive Patients and Physicians, 25 Ohio N.U. L. Rev. 149 (1999); Mara E. Zazzali, HIV–Infected Health Care Workers Who Perform Invasive, Exposure–Prone Procedures: Defining the Risk and Balancing the Interests of Health Care Workers and Patients, 28 Seton Hall L. Rev. 1000 (1998); American Bar Association Aids Coordinating Committee, (Edited by Eric N. Richardson and Salvatore J. Russo), Calming AIDS Phobia: Legal Implications of the Low Risk of Transmitting HIV in the Health Care Setting, 28 U. Mich. J.L. Ref. 733 (1995); Leonard H. Glantz et al., Risky Business: Setting Public Health Policy for HIV-infected Health Care Professionals, 70 The Milbank Quart. 43, 72–73 (1992); Norman Daniels, HIV–Infected Health Care Professionals: Public Threat or Public Sacrifice?, 70 Milbank Quart. 3(1992).

5. The American Medical Association (AMA) and the American Dental Association (ADA) have taken the position that HIV infected professionals should

abstain from performing risky invasive procedures, or should disclose their seropositive status to their patients. The burden is placed on the individual professional. The calculation of the professional organizations appears to be that some patients will stick with the provider because they will take on the low risks of infection, valuing their relationship with the professional, or the professional's reputation for quality. But why should the professional disclose his status, if he knows it? He may see his practice diminish or disappear as patients spread the word. If a hospital or managed care organization finds out, they may restrict his practice and cut his income. It is more likely that they will restrict his privileges, or in the case of a managed care organization, remove him from panel membership. The infected provider therefore has little incentive to disclose and substantial incentives to remain silent.

Disclosure of a provider's HIV status to a patient, particularly prior to invasive surgery, is often required. In Doe v. Noe No. 1, 293 Ill.App.3d 1099, 228 Ill.Dec. 937, 690 N.E.2d 1012 (Ill.App. 1 Dist.1997), the court followed Maryland's approach in Faya v. Almaraz, 329 Md. 435, 620 A.2d 327 (1993), finding that a physician should disclose his or her HIV-positive status to a patient who is going to submit to an invasive surgery.

6. The studies to date have found no evidence of transmission from provider to patient, with the possible exception of the Bergalis case. See Jeffrey J. Sacks, AIDS in a Surgeon, 313 New Eng. J. Med. 1017 (1985) (study of 400 Florida patients of surgeon); Frances P. Armstrong et al, Investigation of a Health Care Worker with Symptomatic Immunodeficiency Virus Infection: An Epidemiologic Approach, 152 Military Medicine 414 (1987) (1004 patients of military surgeon); John D. Porter et al, Management of Patients Treated by Surgeon with HIV Infection, The Lancet, January 1990, at 113 (339 patients of British surgeon); Ban Mishu et al, A Surgeon with AIDS: Lack of Evidence of Transmission to Patients, 264 JAMA 467 (1990) (study of 2160 patients of Nashville surgeon).

7. The perils of 3rd party disclosure. Disclosure of HIV-positive status to third parties, where the patients have not faced risks of exposure, can lead to liability by the party disclosing this status information. In Tolman v. Doe, 988 F.Supp. 582 (D.C.E.D.Va. 1997), the HIV-positive physician sued another physician in state court, alleging causes of action including defamation and intentional infliction of emotional distress based on a letter by defendant to plaintiff's patients informing them that plaintiff had Acquired Immune Deficiency Syndrome (AIDS) and that defendant would not want plaintiff as his cardiologist.

The plaintiff Dr.Tolman was a physician. He was also gay. He has not kept this fact secret from family, close friends, or acquaintances. In 1994, he learned that he had AIDS. Dr. Tolman was in compliance with the Center for Disease Control ("CDC") guidelines while treating patients and, specifically, performing cardiology procedures. Recommendations For Preventing Transmission Of Human Immunodeficiency Virus and Hepatitis B Virus To Patients During Exposure–Prone Invasive Procedures MMWR, Vol. 40/No. RR–8 ("CDC Rec."), at 1.

Defendant Dr. Doe was a physician who practiced with Dr. Tolman until 1996, when he left to take a position out of state. In September or October of 1995, Dr. Doe learned that Dr. Tolman had AIDS. Dr. Doe stated that his "personal opinion" is to disagree with the CDC's determination that a physician with AIDS who complies with the CDC's guidelines may safely perform the procedures that Dr. Tolman was performing. In May 1996 Dr. Doe had a conversation with a patient, during which the patient expressly asked Dr. Doe if Dr. Tolman had AIDS. The patient also asked what Dr. Doe recommended regarding the patient's continued treatment by Dr. Tolman. Dr. Doe told the patient that Dr. Tolman had AIDS and that he (Dr. Doe) would not want a physician with AIDS treating him if he were a patient.

In December 1996, Dr. Doe wrote a letter to between ten and fifteen patients. The letter stated in relevant part:

> I would like to tell you that I left the program for personal reasons and because my personal career at . . . was not going anywhere, and also because I could not work any more with Dr. Tolman, especially when I learned that he had AIDS and continues to perform invasive procedres [sic] on the [cardiology] patients.
>
> (Unfortunately, he never told me any thing about it himself, maybe because he did not want me to know that he was homosexual.)
>
> I don't realy [sic] know what to tell you regarding your heart transplant care after you learn this fact. Howevr [sic], I will leave this to your personal judgment. I personally will not want somebody with AIDS to be my physcian [sic], let alone being my [cardiologist]. You may want to think of an alternative that will beter [sic] serve you.

The court held that the plaintiff, for purposes of a motion for summary judgment, had established that a defamatory publication was false. The letter reasonably implied that Dr. Tolman was unfit to practice as a physician, specifically to perform invasive procedures, and that he was placing his patients at an inappropriate risk by continuing these procedures while having contracted AIDS. The court noted the CDC report described the procedures done by the plaintiffs as not "exposure prone" procedures. The court further found that the "CDC has determined that physicians with AIDS, such as Dr. Tolman, are fit to practice medicine and to perform the procedures at issue." He was also in compliance with CDC guidelines in treating patients.

> The evidence offered by Defendant consists of the type of speculative inferences, glancing statistics, and unsupported conclusions that Abbott warns against. Indeed, Doe's effort to rebut the consensus of public health officials is much weaker than the effort that was rejected on summary judgment by the Abbott trial court and affirmed on appeal. No reasonable jury could disagree that Defendant's insinuations that Plaintiff was unfit to be a physician, and more specifically, to perform the procedures in question, were false.

Problem: Impaired Physicians

Mercy Hospital employs Dr. Frank Tehr, a surgeon who in the past has sexually assaulted female patients. Suppose that he sees a thousand patients a year, half of them women, and has only assaulted two women over five years, making the risk for the individual female patient 2/2500, or .0008, or .08%. Should every female patient be informed of the low risk of sexual assault, in light of Behringer? What else might the hospital do?

Boosier City Memorial Hospital has a staff surgeon, Dr. Williams, who is an alcoholic. He is an excellent surgeon when he is not impaired by drinking, but because he is a chronic alcoholic it is hard to predict when he may be impaired. Should Dr. Williams be required to disclose to patients that he is an alcoholic, so they can choose whether to continue with him?

3. Disclosure of Statistical Mortality Information

Patients with diseases such as cancer usually face a reduced life expectancy even with the best medical treatment. Such patients would presumably like to know as much as possible about their life expectancy for a variety of reasons—estate planning, goodbyes to family and friends, fortifying themselves to face death for personal and religious reasons. Must the doctor inform the patient of his life expectancy based on statistical tables?

ARATO v. AVEDON

Supreme Court of California, 1993.
5 Cal.4th 1172, 23 Cal.Rptr.2d 131, 858 P.2d 598.

ARABIAN, JUSTICE.

A physician's duty to disclose to a patient information material to the decision whether to undergo treatment is the central constituent of the legal doctrine known as "informed consent." In this case, we review the ruling of a divided Court of Appeal that, in recommending a course of chemotherapy and radiation treatment to a patient suffering from a virulent form of cancer, the treating physicians breached their duty to obtain the patient's informed consent by failing to disclose his statistical life expectancy.

* * *

I

A

Miklos Arato was a successful 42–year–old electrical contractor and part-time real estate developer when, early in 1980, his internist diagnosed a failing kidney. On July 21, 1980, in the course of surgery to remove the kidney, the operating surgeon detected a tumor on the "tail" or distal portion of Mr. Arato's pancreas. After Mrs. Arato gave her consent, portions of the pancreas were resected, or removed, along with the spleen and the diseased kidney. A follow-up pathological examination of the resected pancreatic tissue confirmed a malignancy. Concerned that the cancer could recur and might have infiltrated adjacent organs, Mr. Arato's surgeon referred him to a group of oncology practitioners for follow-up treatment.

During his initial visit to the oncologists, Mr. Arato filled out a multipage questionnaire routinely given new patients. Among the some 150 questions asked was whether patients "wish[ed] to be told the truth about [their] condition" or whether they wanted the physician to "bear the burden" for them. Mr. Arato checked the box indicating that he wished to be told the truth.

The oncologists discussed with Mr. and Mrs. Arato the advisability of a course of chemotherapy known as "F.A.M.," a treatment employing a combination of drugs which, when used in conjunction with radiation therapy, had shown promise in treating pancreatic cancer in experimental trials. The nature of the discussions between Mr. and Mrs. Arato and the treating physicians, and in particular the scope of the disclosures made to the patient by his doctors, was the subject of conflicting testimony at trial. By their own admission, however, neither the operating surgeon nor the treating oncologists specifically disclosed to the patient or his wife the high statistical mortality rate associated with pancreatic cancer.

Mr. Arato's oncologists determined that a course of F.A.M. chemotherapy was indicated for several reasons. According to their testimony, the high statistical mortality of pancreatic cancer is in part a function of what is by far the most common diagnostic scenario—the discovery of the malignancy well after it has metastasized to distant sites, spreading throughout the patient's body. As noted, in Mr. Arato's case, the tumor was comparatively localized, having been discovered in the tail of the pancreas by chance in the course of surgery to remove the diseased kidney.

Related to the "silent" character of pancreatic cancer is the fact that detection in such an advanced state usually means that the tumor cannot as a practical matter be removed, contributing to the high mortality rate. In Mr. Arato's case, however, the operating surgeon determined that it was possible to excise cleanly the tumorous portion of the pancreas and to leave a margin of about one-half centimeter around the surgical site, a margin that appeared clinically to be clear of cancer cells. Third, the mortality rate is somewhat lower, according to defense testimony, for pancreatic tumors located in the distal part of the organ than for those found in the main body. Finally, then-recent experimental studies on the use of F.A.M. chemotherapy in conjunction with therapeutic radiation treatments had shown promising response rates—on the order of several months of extended life—among pancreatic cancer patients.

Mr. Arato's treating physicians justified not disclosing statistical life expectancy data to their patient on disparate grounds. According to the testimony of his surgeon, Mr. Arato had exhibited great anxiety over his condition, so much so that his surgeon determined that it would have been medically inappropriate to disclose specific mortality rates. The patient's oncologists had a somewhat different explanation. As Dr. Melvin Avedon, his chief oncologist, put it, he believed that cancer patients in Mr. Arato's position "wanted to be told the truth, but did not want a cold shower." Along with the other treating physicians, Dr. Avedon testified that in his opinion the direct and specific disclosure of extremely high mortality rates for malignancies such as pancreatic cancer might effectively deprive a patient of any hope of cure, a medically inadvisable state. Moreover, all of the treating physicians testified that statistical life expectancy data had little predictive value when applied to a particular patient with individualized symptoms, medical history, character traits and other variables.

According to the physicians' testimony, Mr. and Mrs. Arato were told at the outset of the treatment that most victims of pancreatic cancer die of the disease, that Mr. Arato was at "serious" or "great" risk of a recurrence and that, should the cancer return, his condition would be judged incurable. This information was given to the patient and his wife in the context of a series of verbal and behavioral cues designed to invite the patient or family member to follow up with more direct and difficult questions. Such follow-up questions, on the order of "how long do I have to live?," would have signaled to his doctors, according to Dr. Avedon's testimony, the patient's desire and ability to confront the fact of imminent mortality. In the judgment of his chief oncologist, Mr. Arato, although keenly interested in the clinical significance of the most minute symptom, studiously avoided confronting these ultimate issues; according to his doctors, neither Mr. Arato nor his wife ever asked for information concerning his life expectancy in more than 70 visits over a period of a year. Believing that they had disclosed information sufficient to enable him to make an informed decision whether to undergo chemotherapy, Mr. Arato's doctors concluded that their patient had as much information regarding his condition and prognosis as he wished.

Dr. Avedon also testified that he told Mr. Arato that the effectiveness of F.A.M. therapy was unproven in cases such as his, described its principal adverse side effects, and noted that one of the patient's options was not to undergo the treatment. In the event, Mr. Arato consented to the proposed course of chemotherapy and radiation, treatments that are prolonged, difficult and painful for cancer patients. Unfortunately, the treatment proved ineffective in arresting the spread of the malignancy. Although clinical tests showed him to be free of cancer in the several months following the beginning of the F.A.M. treatments, beginning in late March and into April of 1981, the clinical signs took an adverse turn.[1] By late April, the doctors were convinced by the results of additional tests that the cancer had returned and was spreading. They advised the patient of their suspicions and discontinued chemotherapy. On July 25, 1981, a year and four days following surgery, Mr. Arato succumbed to the effects of pancreatic cancer.

B

Not long after his death, Mr. Arato's wife and two children brought this suit against the physicians who had treated their husband and father in his last days, including the surgeon who performed the pancreas resection and the oncologists who had recommended and administered the chemotherapy/radiation treatment. As presented to the jury, the gist of the lawsuit was the claim that in discussing with their patient the advisability of undergoing a course of chemotherapy and radiation, Mr. Arato's doctors had failed to disclose adequately the shortcomings of the proposed treatment in light of the diagnosis, and thus had failed to obtain the patient's informed consent. Specifically, plaintiffs contended that the doctors were aware that, because early detection is difficult and rare, pancreatic cancer is an especially virulent malignancy, one in which only 5 to 10 percent of those afflicted live for as long as five years, and that given the practically incurable nature of the disease, there was little chance Mr. Arato would live more than a short while, even if the proposed treatment proved effective.

Such mortality information, the complaint alleged—especially the statistical morbidity rate of pancreatic cancer—was material to Mr. Arato's decision whether to undergo postoperative treatment; had he known the bleak truth concerning his life expectancy, he would not have undergone the rigors of an unproven therapy, but would have chosen to live out his last days at peace with his wife and children, and arranging his business affairs. Instead, the complaint asserted, in the false hope that radiation and chemotherapy treatments could effect a cure—a hope born of the negligent failure of his

1. Around this time—on March 12, 1981, according to the record—an article appeared in the Los Angeles Times stating that only 1 percent of males and 2 percent of females diagnosed as having pancreatic cancer live for five years. According to his wife's testimony, Mr. Arato read the Times article and brought it to the attention of his oncologists. One of his oncologists confirmed such a discussion but denied that he told Mr. Arato that the statistics did not apply to his case, as Mrs. Arato testified. Mr. Arato continued to undergo chemotherapy treatment after reading the article and evidently made no changes in his estate planning or business and real estate affairs.

physicians to disclose the probability of an early death—Mr. Arato failed to order his affairs in contemplation of his death, an omission that, according to the complaint, led eventually to the failure of his contracting business and to substantial real estate and tax losses following his death.

As the trial neared its conclusion and the court prepared to charge the jury, plaintiffs requested that several special instructions be given relating to the nature and scope of the physician's duty of disclosure. Two proffered instructions in particular are pertinent to this appeal. In the first, plaintiffs asked the trial court to instruct the jury that "A physician has a fiduciary duty to a patient to make a full and fair disclosure to the patient of all facts which materially affect the patient's rights and interests." The second instruction sought by plaintiffs stated that "The scope of the physician's duty to disclose is measured by the amount of knowledge a patient needs in order to make an informed choice. All information material to the patient's decision should be given."

The trial judge declined to give the jury either of the two instructions sought by plaintiffs. Instead, the court read to the jury a modified version of BAJI No. 6.11, the so-called "reality of consent" instruction drawn from our opinion in Cobbs v. Grant [ ]. * * *

After concluding its deliberations, the jury returned two special verdicts—on a form approved by plaintiffs' counsel—finding that none of the defendants was negligent in the "medical management" of Mr. Arato, and that defendants "disclosed to Mr. Arato all relevant information which would have enabled him to make an informed decision regarding the proposed treatment to be rendered him." Plaintiffs appealed from the judgment entered on the defense verdict, contending that the trial court erred in refusing to give the jury the special instructions requested by them. As noted, a divided Court of Appeal reversed the judgment of the trial court, and ordered a new trial. We granted defendants' ensuing petition for review and now reverse the judgment of the Court of Appeal.

C

[The court in section C discusses the Court of Appeal decision, which required that Mr. Arato's doctors disclose numerical life expectancy information so that he could reduce the risks of financial loss; and found that the trial court instructions were defective in several regards].

II

A

[The court discusses Cobbs v. Grant at length, and the duty it imposed on a treating physician "of reasonable disclosure of the available choices with respect to proposed therapy and of the dangers inherently and potentially involved in each." [ ] It also considered both Truman v. Thomas and Moore v. Board of Regents, and their refinement of California's informed consent law.]

B

* * *

Despite the critical standoff between these extremes of "patient sovereignty" and "medical paternalism," indications are that the Cobbs-era decisions helped effect a revolution in attitudes among patients and physicians alike regarding the desirability of frank and open disclosure of relevant medical information. The principal question we must address is whether our holding in Cobbs v. Grant, [ ] as embodied in BAJI No. 6.11, accurately conveys to juries the legal standard under which they assess the evidence in determining the adequacy of the disclosures made by physician to patient in a particular case or whether, as the Court of Appeal here appeared to conclude, the standard instruction should be revised to mandate specific disclosures such as patient life expectancy as revealed by mortality statistics.

In our view, one of the merits of the somewhat abstract formulation of BAJI No. 6.11 is its recognition of the importance of the overall medical context that juries ought to take into account in deciding whether a challenged disclosure was reasonably sufficient to convey to the patient information material to an informed treatment decision. The contexts and clinical settings in which physician and patient interact and exchange information material to therapeutic decisions are so multifarious, the informational needs and degree of dependency of individual patients so various, and the professional relationship itself such an intimate and irreducibly judgment-laden one, that we believe it is unwise to require as a matter of law that a particular species of information be disclosed.... [ ]

* * *

This sensitivity to context seems all the more appropriate in the case of life expectancy projections for cancer patients based on statistical samples. Without exception, the testimony of every physician-witness at trial confirmed what is evident even to a nonprofessional: statistical morbidity values derived from the experience of population groups are inherently unreliable and offer little assurance regarding the fate of the individual patient; indeed, to assume that such data are conclusive in themselves smacks of a refusal to explore treatment alternatives and the medical abdication of the patient's well-being. Certainly the jury here heard evidence of articulable grounds for the conclusion that the particular features of Mr. Arato's case distinguished it from the typical population of pancreatic cancer sufferers and their dismal statistical probabilities—a fact plaintiffs impliedly acknowledged at trial in conceding that the oncologic referral of Mr. Arato and ensuing chemotherapy were not in themselves medically negligent.

* * *

Rather than mandate the disclosure of specific information as a matter of law, the better rule is to instruct the jury that a physician is under a legal duty to disclose to the patient all material information—that is, "information which the physician knows or should know would be regarded as significant by a reasonable person in the patient's position when deciding to accept or reject a recommended medical procedure"—needed to make an informed decision regarding a proposed treatment. That, of course, is the formulation embodied in BAJI No. 6.11 and the instruction given in this case. Having been properly instructed, the jury returned a defense verdict—on a form approved by plaintiffs' counsel—specifically finding that defendants had "disclosed to

Mr. Arato all relevant information which would have enabled him to make an informed decision regarding the proposed treatment to be rendered him."

We decline to intrude further, either on the subtleties of the physician-patient relationship or in the resolution of claims that the physician's duty of disclosure was breached, by requiring the disclosure of information that may or may not be indicated in a given treatment context. Instead, we leave the ultimate judgment as to the factual adequacy of a challenged disclosure to the venerable American jury, operating under legal instructions such as those given here and subject to the persuasive force of trial advocacy.

Here, the evidence was more than sufficient to support the jury's finding that defendants had reasonably disclosed to Mr. Arato information material to his decision whether to undergo the proposed chemotherapy/radiation treatment. There was testimony that Mr. and Mrs. Arato were informed that cancer of the pancreas is usually fatal; of the substantial risk of recurrence, an event that would mean his illness was incurable; of the unproven nature of the F.A.M. treatments and their principal side effects; and of the option of forgoing such treatments. Mr. Arato's doctors also testified that they could not with confidence predict how long the patient might live, notwithstanding statistical mortality tables.

In addition, the jury heard testimony regarding the patient's apparent avoidance of issues bearing upon mortality; Mrs. Arato's testimony that his physicians had assured her husband that he was "clear" of cancer; and the couple's common expectation that he had been "cured," only to learn, suddenly and unexpectedly, that the case was hopeless and life measurable in weeks. The informed consent instructions given the jury to assess this evidence were an accurate statement of the law, and the Court of Appeal in effect invaded the province of the trier of fact in overturning a fairly litigated verdict.[ ]

C

In addition to their claim that his physicians were required to disclose statistical life expectancy data to Mr. Arato to enable him to reach an informed treatment decision, plaintiffs also contend that defendants should have disclosed such data because it was material to the patient's nonmedical interests, that is, Mr. Arato's business and investment affairs and the potential adverse impact of his death upon them. In support of this proposition, plaintiffs rely on the following statement in Bowman v. McPheeters [ ]: "As fiduciaries it was the duty of defendants [physicians] to make a full and fair disclosure to plaintiff of all facts which materially affected his rights and interests." Plaintiffs contend that since Mr. Arato's contracting and real estate affairs would suffer if he failed to make timely changes in estate planning in contemplation of imminent death, and since these matters are among "his rights and interests," his physicians were under a legal duty to disclose all material facts that might affect them, including statistical life expectancy information. We reject the claim as one founded on a premise that is not recognized in California.

The short answer to plaintiffs' claim is our statement in *Moore* [ ] that a "physician is not the patient's financial adviser."[ ] From its inception, the rationale behind the disclosure requirement implementing the doctrine of informed consent has been to protect the patient's freedom to "exercise ... control over [one's] own body" by directing the course of medical treatment.[ ] We recently noted that "the principle of self-determination ... embraces all aspects of medical decisionmaking by the competent adult...."[ ] Although an aspect of personal autonomy, the conditions for the exercise of the patient's right of self-decision presuppose a therapeutic focus, a supposition reflected in the text of BAJI No. 6.11 itself. The fact that a physician has "fiducial" obligations ... which ... prohibit misrepresenting the nature of the patient's medical condition, does not mean that he or she is under a duty, the scope of which is undefined, to disclose every contingency that might affect the patient's nonmedical "rights and interests." Because plaintiffs' open-ended proposed instruction—that the physician's duty embraces the "disclosure ... of all facts which materially affect the patient's rights and interests"—failed to reflect the therapeutic limitation inherent in the doctrine of informed consent, it would have been error for the trial judge to give it to the jury.

Finally, plaintiffs make much of the fact that in his initial visit to Dr. Avedon's office, Mr. Arato indicated in a lengthy form he was requested to complete that he "wish[ed] to be told the truth about [his] condition." In effect, they contend that as a result of Mr. Arato's affirmative answer, defendants had an absolute duty to make specific life expectancy disclosures to him. Whether the patient has filled out a questionnaire indicating that he or she wishes to be told the "truth" about his or her condition or not, however, a physician is under a legal duty to obtain the patient's informed consent to any recommended treatment. Although a patient may validly waive the right to be informed, we do not see how a request to be told the "truth" in itself heightens the duty of disclosure imposed on physicians as a matter of law.

III.

The final issue we must resolve concerns the use of expert testimony at trial. As noted, the Court of Appeal concluded that expert testimony offered on behalf of defendants went beyond what was appropriate in support of the so-called "therapeutic exception" to the physician's duty of disclosure, misleading the jury and prejudicing plaintiffs' case. Resolution of this issue requires an understanding of the proper, albeit limited, role of expert testimony in informed consent cases.

Over plaintiffs' objection, the trial court admitted the testimony of two medical experts, Drs. Plotkin and Wellisch, the former a professor of clinical medicine and the latter an expert in the psychological management of cancer patients. Both testified that the standard of medical practice cautioned against disclosing to pancreatic cancer patients specific life expectancy data unless the patient directly requested such information and that, in effect, defendants complied with that standard in not disclosing such information to Mr. Arato under the circumstances. Plaintiffs offered expert medical testimony of their own to counter this evidence; their expert testified that there are a number of indirect and compassionate ways to approach the issue of imminent mortality in dealing with patients with terminal cancer and that the standard of professional practice required that a patient in Mr. Arato's circumstances be given specific numerical life expectancy information.

Plaintiffs now complain that it was error for the trial court to admit expert defense testimony, relying on our statement in Cobbs v. Grant, supra, 8 Cal.3d at page 243, 104 Cal.Rptr. 505, 502 P.2d 1, that the weighing of the risks accompanying a given therapy "against the individual subjective fears and hopes of the patient is not an expert skill." Plaintiffs fail to distinguish between the two kinds of physician disclosure discussed in Cobbs. Our formulation of the scope of the duty of disclosure encompassed "the potential of death or serious harm" known to be inherent in a given procedure and an explanation "in lay terms [of] the complications that might possibly occur." [ ] In addition to these disclosures, which we termed the "minimal" ones required of a physician to insure the patient's informed decisionmaking, we said that the physician must also reveal to the patient "such additional information as a skilled practitioner of good standing would provide under similar circumstances." [ ]

As its verbatim presence in BAJI No. 6.11 testifies, the quoted language, including the reference to the standard of professional practice as the benchmark for measuring the scope of disclosure beyond that implicated by the risks of death or serious harm and the potential for complications, has become an integral part of the legal standard in California for measuring the adequacy of a physician's disclosure in informed consent cases. [ ]

In reckoning the scope of disclosure, the physician will for the most part be guided by the patient's decisional needs * * * [ ] A physician, however, evaluates the patient's decisional needs against a background of professional understanding that includes a knowledge of what information beyond the significant risks associated with a given treatment would be regarded by the medical community as appropriate for disclosure under the circumstances.

* * * [S]ituations will sometimes arise in which the trier of fact is unable to decide the ultimate issue of the adequacy of a particular disclosure without an understanding of the standard of practice within the relevant medical community. For that reason, in an appropriate case, the testimony of medical experts qualified to offer an opinion regarding what, if any, disclosures—in addition to those relating to the risk of death or serious injury and significant potential complications posed by consenting to or declining a proposed treatment—would be made to the patient by a skilled practitioner in the relevant medical community under the circumstances is relevant and admissible.

We underline the limited and essentially subsidiary role of expert testimony in informed consent litigation. * * * Nevertheless, as explained above, there may be a limited number of occasions in the trial of informed consent claims where the adequacy of disclosure in a given case may turn on the standard of practice within the relevant medical community. In such instances, expert testimony will usually be appropriate.

Because statistical life expectancy data is information that lies outside the significant risks associated with a given treatment * * * it falls within the scope of the "additional information ... a skilled practitioner ... would provide...." [ ] And since the question of whether a physician should disclose such information turns on the standard of practice within the medical community, the trial court did not err in permitting expert testimony directed at that issue.

* * *

CONCLUSION

The judgment of the Court of Appeal is reversed and the cause is remanded with directions to affirm the judgment of the trial court.

Notes and Questions

1. The California Supreme Court says it is simply applying the *Cobbs* analysis to the facts of the *Arato* case. It refuses to impose as a matter of law any requirement that a physician disclose to the patient his life expectancy. Why? Is it a desire to leave the lay jury some "wriggle" room, empowering it as the trier of fact? Or a desire to give physicians the flexibility to avoid difficult disclosures? Is life expectancy data so inherently untrustworthy that patients should not be told?

2. Does *Arato* in effect expand the defense of "therapeutic privilege", giving professional standards undue weight in both the instructions and the expert testimony? If a patient has a cancer that is often lethal in a short time, how much more terrifying is specific knowledge as to life expectancy?

3. To what extent should a health care provider's informational power expand its obligations to protect a patient's financial interests? A middle-aged patient, facing imminent death, might pursue several alternatives to protect assets for his or her family: he or she might declare personal bankruptcy to wipe out debts; might undertake estate planning to protect assets for the family; might restructure a small business to bring in new administrators. *Arato* seems to blame the plaintiff for not asking, letting the physicians off the hook. Should we let them off so easily? Physicians historically had to discuss treatment costs with patients. In the early days of fee-for-service medicine, patients had to choose between expensive treatments and their other needs, since insurance was not readily available. Today, patients seeking organ transplantation or experimental therapies need to know about their insurance coverage or the availability of Medicaid or other government sources. The health care provider clearly has some role in helping a patient sort out payment sources and costs.

4. Courts have generally refused to find a hospital or physician negligent for failing to advise patients that they were eligible for government funding. See, e.g., Mraz v. Taft, 85 Ohio App.3d 200, 619 N.E.2d 483 (8 Dist.1993) (neither hospital nor nursing home had any duty to advise husband that he qualified for Medicaid). Nor is a physician liable for the financial consequences of a misdiagnosis, for example a patient's cancellation of a life insurance policy upon being erroneously informed that he did not have cancer. See Blacher v. Garlett, 857 P.2d 566, 568 (Colo.App.Div.III 1993). But see the discussion in Chapter 3 of the *Wickline* and *Wilson* cases.

5. One study suggests that the defendants' approach in Arato can create problems. Physician failures to help cancer patients understand their survival odds may lead patients to overestimate their odds of survival, and may influence their preference for medical therapies that are highly toxic and unproductive, in light of the prognosis of a short life expectancy. This describes the facts of Arato. See Jane C. Weeks et al., Relationship Between Cancer Patients' Predictions of Prognosis and Their Treatment Preferences, 279 J.A.M.A. 1709 (1998).

4. *Disclosure of Risks of Non-Treatment*

TRUMAN v. THOMAS

Supreme Court of California, 1980.
27 Cal.3d 285, 165 Cal.Rptr. 308, 611 P.2d 902.

BIRD, C.J.

This court must decide whether a physician's failure to inform a patient of the material risks of not consenting to a recommended pap smear, so that the patient might make an informed choice, may have breached the physician's duty of due care to his patient, who died from cancer of the cervix.

I

Respondent, Dr. Claude R. Thomas, is a family physician engaged in a general medical practice. He was first contacted in April 1963 by appellants' mother, Rena Truman, in connection with her second pregnancy. He continued to act as the primary physician for Mrs. Truman and her two children until March 1969. During this six-year period, Mrs. Truman not only sought his medical advice, but often discussed personal matters with him.

In April 1969, Mrs. Truman consulted Dr. Casey, a urologist, about a urinary tract infection which had been treated previously by Dr. Thomas. While examining Mrs. Truman, Dr. Casey discovered that she was experiencing heavy vaginal discharges and that her cervix was extremely rough. Mrs. Truman was given a prescription for the infection and advised to see a gynecologist as soon as possible. When Mrs. Truman did not make an appointment with a gynecologist, Dr. Casey made an appointment for her with a Dr. Ritter.

In October 1969, Dr. Ritter discovered that Mrs. Truman's cervix had been largely replaced by a cancerous tumor. Too far advanced to be removed by surgery, the tumor was unsuccessfully treated by other methods. Mrs. Truman died in July 1970 at the age of 30.

Appellants are Rena Truman's two children. They brought this wrongful death action against Dr. Thomas for his failure to perform a pap smear test on their mother. At the trial, expert testimony was presented which indicated that if Mrs. Truman had undergone a pap smear at any time between 1964 and 1969, the cervical tumor probably would have been discovered in time to save her life. There was disputed expert testimony that the standard of medical practice required a physician to explain to women patients that it is important to have a pap smear each year to "pick up early lesions that are treatable rather than having to deal with [more developed] tumor[s] that very often aren't treatable. * * * "[1]

Although Dr. Thomas saw Mrs. Truman frequently between 1964 and 1969, he never performed a pap smear test on her. Dr. Thomas testified that he did not "specifically" inform Mrs. Truman of the risk involved in any failure to undergo the pap smear test. Rather, "I said, 'You should have a pap

1. Dr. Thomas conceded at the trial that it is the accepted standard of practice for physicians in his community to recommend that women of child-bearing age undergo a pap smear each year. His records indicate that during the period in which he acted as Mrs. Truman's family physician he performed between 10 and 20 pap smears per month.

smear.' We don't say by now it can be Stage Two [in the development of cervical cancer] or go through all of the different lectures about cancer. I think it is a widely known and generally accepted manner of treatment and I think the patient has a high degree of responsibility. We are not enforcers, we are advisors." However, Dr. Thomas' medical records contain no reference to any discussion or recommendation that Mrs. Truman undergo a pap smear test.

For the most part, Dr. Thomas was unable to describe specific conversations with Mrs. Truman. For example, he testified that during certain periods he "saw Rena very frequently, approximately once a week or so, and I am sure my opening remark was, 'Rena, you need a pap smear,' . . . I am sure we discussed it with her so often that she couldn't [have] fail[ed] to realize that we wanted her to have a complete examination, breast examination, ovaries and pap smear." Dr. Thomas also testified that on at least two occasions when he performed pelvic examinations of Mrs. Truman she refused him permission to perform the test, stating she could not afford the cost. Dr. Thomas offered to defer payment, but Mrs. Truman wanted to pay cash.

Appellants argue that the failure to give a pap smear test to Mrs. Truman proximately caused her death. Two instructions requested by appellants described alternative theories under which Dr. Thomas could be held liable for this failure. First, they asked that the jury be instructed that it "is the duty of a physician to disclose to his patient all relevant information to enable the patient to make an informed decision regarding the submission to or refusal to take a diagnostic test. [¶] Failure of the physician to disclose to his patient all relevant information including the risks to the patient if the test is refused renders the physician liable for any injury legally resulting from the patient's refusal to take the test if a reasonably prudent person in the patient's position would not have refused the test if she had been adequately informed of all the significant perils." Second, they requested that the jury be informed that "as a matter of law . . . a physician who fails to perform a Pap smear test on a female patient over the age of 23 and to whom the patient has entrusted her general physical care is liable for injury or death proximately caused by the failure to perform the test." Both instructions were refused.

The jury rendered a special verdict, finding Dr. Thomas free of any negligence that proximately caused Mrs. Truman's death. This appeal followed.

II

The central issue for this court is whether Dr. Thomas breached his duty of care to Mrs. Truman when he failed to inform her of the potentially fatal consequences of allowing cervical cancer to develop undetected by a pap smear.

* * *

* * * The scope of a physician's duty to disclose is measured by the amount of knowledge a patient needs in order to make an informed choice. All information material to the patient's decision should be given. [ ]

Material information is that which the physician knows or should know would be regarded as significant by a reasonable person in the patient's position when deciding to accept or reject the recommended medical procedure. [ ] To be material, a fact must also be one which is not commonly appreciated. [ ] If the physician knows or should know of a patient's unique concerns or lack of familiarity with medical procedures, this may expand the scope of required disclosure. [ ]

Applying these principles, the court in *Cobbs* stated that a patient must be apprised not only of the "risks inherent in the procedure [prescribed, but also] the risks of a decision not to undergo the treatment, and the probability of a successful outcome of the treatment." [ ] This rule applies whether the procedure involves treatment or a diagnostic test. On the one hand, a physician recommending a risk-free procedure may safely forego discussion beyond that necessary to conform to competent medical practice and to obtain the patient's consent. [ ] If a patient indicates that he or she is going to *decline* the risk-free test or treatment, then the doctor has the additional duty of advising of all material risks of which a reasonable person would want to be informed before deciding not to undergo the procedure. On the other hand, if the recommended test or treatment is itself risky, then the physician should always explain the potential consequences of declining to follow the recommended course of action.

Nevertheless, Dr. Thomas contends that *Cobbs* does not apply to him because the duty to disclose applies only where the patient *consents* to the recommended procedure. He argues that since a physician's advice may be presumed to be founded on an expert appraisal of the patient's medical needs, no reasonable patient would fail to undertake further inquiry before rejecting such advice. Therefore, patients who reject their physician's advice should shoulder the burden of inquiry as to the possible consequences of their decision.

This argument is inconsistent with *Cobbs*. The duty to disclose was imposed in *Cobbs* so that patients might meaningfully exercise their right to make decisions about their own bodies. [ ] The importance of this right should not be diminished by the manner in which it is exercised. Further, the need for disclosure is not lessened because patients reject a recommended procedure. Such a decision does not alter "what has been termed the 'fiducial qualities' of the physician-patient relationship," since patients who reject a procedure are as unskilled in the medical sciences as those who consent. [ ] To now hold that patients who reject their physician's advice have the burden of inquiring as to the potential consequences of their decisions would be to contradict *Cobbs*. It must be remembered that Dr. Thomas was not engaged in an arms-length transaction with Mrs. Truman. Clearly, under *Cobbs,* he was obligated to provide her with all the information material to her decision.

Dr. Thomas next contends that, as a matter of law, he had no duty to disclose to Mrs. Truman the risk of failing to undergo a pap smear test because "the danger [is] remote and commonly appreciated to be remote." (*Cobbs, supra,* 8 Cal.3d at p. 245, 104 Cal.Rptr. at p. 516, 502 P.2d at p. 12.) The merit of this contention depends on whether a jury could reasonably find that knowledge of this risk was material to Mrs. Truman's decision.

The record indicates that the pap smear test is an accurate detector of cervical cancer. Although the probability that Mrs. Truman had cervical cancer was low, Dr. Thomas knew that the potential harm of failing to detect the disease at an early stage was death. This situation is not analogous to one which involves, for example, "relatively minor risks inherent in [such] common procedures" as the taking of blood samples. [ ] These procedures are not central to the decision to administer or reject the procedure. In contrast, the risk which Mrs. Truman faced from cervical cancer was not only significant, it was the principal reason why Dr. Thomas recommended that she undergo a pap smear.

Little evidence was introduced on whether this risk was commonly known. Dr. Thomas testified that the risk would be known to a reasonable person. Whether such evidence is sufficient to establish that there was no general duty to disclose this risk to patients is a question of fact for the jury. Moreover, even assuming such disclosure was not generally required, the circumstances in this case may establish that Dr. Thomas did have a duty to inform Mrs. Truman of the risks she was running by not undergoing a pap smear.

Dr. Thomas testified he never specifically informed her of the purpose of a pap smear test. There was no evidence introduced that Mrs. Truman was aware of the serious danger entailed in not undergoing the test. However, there was testimony that Mrs. Truman said she would not undergo the test on certain occasions because of its cost or because "she just didn't feel like it." Under these circumstances, a jury could reasonably conclude that Dr. Thomas had a duty to inform Mrs. Truman of the danger of refusing the test because it was not reasonable for Dr. Thomas to assume that Mrs. Truman appreciated the potentially fatal consequences of her conduct. Accordingly, this court cannot decide as a matter of law that Dr. Thomas owed absolutely no duty to Mrs. Truman to make this important disclosure that affected her life.

* * *

Refusal to give the requested instruction meant that the jury was unable to consider whether Dr. Thomas breached a duty by not disclosing the danger of failing to undergo a pap smear. Since this theory finds support in the record, it was error for the court to refuse to give the requested instruction. [ ] If the jury had been given this instruction and had found in favor of the appellants, such a finding would have had support in the record before us. Reversal is therefore required. [ ]

* * *

The judgment is reversed.

* * *

Notes and Questions

1. Is there such a thing as a "risk-free test or treatment," as the *Truman* court characterizes the choice? Think back to Helling v. Carey and the notes following the case. Why did Mrs. Truman persist in refusing the Pap smear? Was it just the cost, an aversion to the procedure, generalized anxiety over the thought of cancer, or her sense that it wasn't necessary? What if Mrs. Truman had third-party health insurance that covered the full costs of a pap smear? Do you think that Dr. Thomas would have tried harder to convince her of the necessity of the test?

2. Dr. Thomas argued that a patient who rejects her physician's advice has the burden of inquiring as to the consequences of this decision. Isn't this a reasonable position for a physician to take? The court says the "fiducial qualities" of the physician-patient relationship mandate disclosure, given patient ignorance. How far does this fiduciary obligation extend?

Justice Clark, dissenting, worried about an "intolerable burden" of explanation about every procedure and the risks if it is foregone. He feared that the burden would extend beyond pap smears to "all diagnostic procedures allegedly designed to detect illness which could lead to death or serious complication if not timely treated." Id. at 910.

3. The dissent in *Truman* also talks about "how far a doctor should go in selling his services without alienating the patient from all medical care." Id. at 910. Must the doctor do a "hard sell" in order to avoid the application of the *Truman* rule, manipulating information in order to get the patient to do what he thinks is best therapeutically?

4. Some courts are uncomfortable with the potential scope of Truman. In Farina v. Kraus, 333 N.J.Super. 165, 754 A.2d 1215 (N.J.Sup., App. 1999), the plaintiff claimed negligent diagnosis and treatment of bladder cancer. His wife Marie Farina died as a result of a claimed failure to diagnose and treat a "transitional cell carcinoma" of the bladder. She had been diagnosed with cancer, underwent surgery that removed her bladder and uterus. Her diagnosis was metastatic cancer. She underwent chemotherapy and radiation therapy in a futile attempt to control the spread of the disease. She died of the advanced spread of cancer. The court said: "This case before us is not about options for a course of treatment or for surgery but about suitable diagnostic testing. If the doctor wrongly failed to use the cytology test and this led to a diagnostic mistake which adversely affected the outcome, the doctor can be liable. If the standard of reasonable care did not require using the cytology test to aid a diagnosis, then there is no liability here. There is either a deviation, or there is not. A malpractice defendant does not have a duty to discuss every possible non-invasive, risk-free diagnostic or laboratory test with a patient and secure a consent to or waiver thereof. The doctor must, of course, use reasonable care and skill in choosing the diagnostic tests and interpreting the results. If he does not, he is vulnerable."

5. Are physicians exposed to conflicting incentives with regard to testing patients? Consider emerging genetic diagnostic technologies. The adoption of such diagnostics by physicians will be driven by both clinical and economic motivations. Genetic testing will proliferate if third party payers reimburse such testing. Providers paid on a fee-for-service basis will adopt them if they are profitable. Malpractice fears will also cause physicians to use new tests if there is any chance of detecting a predisposition to disease. And of course some providers will want the information even if it is of marginal value. Blumenthal and Zeckhauser, Genetic Diagnosis: Implications for Medical Practice, 5 Intl.J.Tech.Assess. in Health Care 579, 585 (1989). See Hillman et al., Frequency and Costs of Diagnostic Imaging in Office Practice—A Comparison of Self–Referring and Radiologist–Referring Physicians, 323 N.Eng.J.Med. 1604 (1990) (finding that physicians who self-referred patients for diagnostic imaging performed imaging from 2½ to 11 times as often as the physician who referred patients to outside radiologists).

6. What is best for the patient therapeutically? Consider new techniques of genetic diagnosis, performed on adults to see if they might be carriers of the gene for Huntington's disease, cystic fibrosis, manic-depressive illness and other neuro-

logical disorders. The purpose of these tests is to assess whether the patient will develop a particular condition. However, the presence of particular genetic structures and the development of clinically relevant disease is not straightforward for diseases such as heart disease, hypertension, mental illness, or cancer. An abnormal gene may not result in clinical disease. In Huntington's chorea, for example, the time of onset varies from early childhood to the seventies. Thus, a patient needs to know a great deal about the likelihood of a disease developing, before it is useful to face the anxiety produced by a positive test result indicating the presence of a genetic marker for a disease.

The very existence of techniques for prenatal diagnosis also produces stress in potential parents. Negative results give relief, alleviating anxiety that the very existence of the tests created. The tests' availability "sharpens what might otherwise be low-level, diffuse concerns that surface only, as one woman put it, 'on bad days,' and turns them into real and dreaded possibilities." Kolker, Advances in Prenatal Diagnosis: Social–Psychological and Policy Issues, 5 Intl.J.Tech.Assess. in Health Care 601, 608 (1989). For further discussion of genetic counseling and screening, see Chapter 16.

See generally Joan H. Krause, Reconceptualizing Informed Consent in an Era of Health Care Cost Containment, 85 Iowa L.Rev. 261 (1999).

Problem: Information Overload

You have been asked by one of your clients, the Gladstone Womens Clinic, to draft some guidelines to help staff physicians handle disclosures to patients who are reluctant to discuss risks of tests or procedures or who are uninsured and therefore careful about medical costs. What are the safe outer limits of physician silence about diagnostic options and their risks? Consider the kinds of tests that might be available to women who come to the clinic:

1. Pap Smears and mammograms to detect cancer;

2. Amniocentesis, chorionic villus sampling (CVS) and ultrasound imaging for evaluating fetal development and health;

3. HIV tests to look for the possibility of the AIDS virus in a woman who may want to get pregnant;

4. Genetic diagnostic technologies used to assess whether a patient will develop a given condition such as breast cancer.

5. *Disclosure of Physician Conflicts of Interest*

Medical professionals are in a position of dominance with regard to their patients. The relationship is inherently unequal. The physician has superior knowledge produced by long years of training and practice, expertise the patient cannot have; the physician is less concerned about the patient's health than is the patient; the patient is often anxious and ill-equipped to process complex medical information; and the physician can usually get another patient more easily than the patient can obtain another doctor. Patients are thus vulnerable, and this vulnerability imposes on physicians a "trust", a fiduciary obligation justified by the physician's dominant position in the relationship.

MOORE v. REGENTS OF THE UNIVERSITY OF CALIFORNIA

Supreme Court of California, 1990.
51 Cal.3d 120, 271 Cal.Rptr. 146, 793 P.2d 479.

[The plaintiff John Moore underwent treatment for hairy-cell leukemia at the Medical Center of the University of California at Los Angeles (UCLA Medical Center). The defendants were Dr. David Golde, the attending physician; the Regents of the University of California, who own and operate the university; Shirley Quan, a researcher at the University; Genetics Institute; and Sandoz Pharmaceuticals Corporation. The Supreme Court granted review to determine whether Moore had stated a cause of action for breach of the physician's disclosure obligations and for conversion. The Court rejected the conversion cause of action.]

* * *

II. Facts

* * *

Moore first visited UCLA Medical Center on October 5, 1976, shortly after he learned that he had hairy-cell leukemia. After hospitalizing Moore and "withdr[awing] extensive amounts of blood, bone marrow aspirate, and other bodily substances," Golde confirmed that diagnosis. At this time all defendants, including Golde, were aware that "certain blood products and blood components were of great value in a number of commercial and scientific efforts" and that access to a patient whose blood contained these substances would provide "competitive, commercial, and scientific advantages."

On October 8, 1976, Golde recommended that Moore's spleen be removed. Golde informed Moore "that he had reason to fear for his life, and that the proposed splenectomy operation * * * was necessary to slow down the progress of his disease." Based upon Golde's representations, Moore signed a written consent form authorizing the splenectomy.

Before the operation, Golde and Quan "formed the intent and made arrangements to obtain portions of [Moore's] spleen following its removal" and to take them to a separate research unit. Golde gave written instructions to this effect on October 18 and 19, 1976. These research activities "were not intended to have * * * any relation to [Moore's] medical * * * care." However, neither Golde nor Quan informed Moore of their plans to conduct this research or requested his permission. Surgeons at UCLA Medical Center, whom the complaint does not name as defendants, removed Moore's spleen on October 20, 1976.

Moore returned to the UCLA Medical Center several times between November 1976 and September 1983. He did so at Golde's direction and based upon representations "that such visits were necessary and required for his health and well-being, and based upon the trust inherent in and by virtue of the physician-patient relationship. * * * "On each of these visits Golde withdrew additional samples of "blood, blood serum, skin, bone marrow aspirate, and sperm." On each occasion Moore travelled to the UCLA Medical Center from his home in Seattle because he had been told that the procedures were to be performed only there and only under Golde's direction.

"In fact, [however,] throughout the period of time that [Moore] was under [Golde's] care and treatment, * * * the defendants were actively involved in a number of activities which they concealed from [Moore]. * * * "Specifically, defendants were conducting research on Moore's cells and planned to "benefit financially and competitively * * * [by exploiting the cells] and [their] exclusive access to [the cells] by virtue of [Golde's] on-going physician-patient relationship. * * * "

Sometime before August 1979, Golde established a cell line from Moore's T-lymphocytes. On January 30, 1981, the Regents applied for a patent on the cell line, listing Golde and Quan as inventors. "[B]y virtue of an established policy * * *, [the] Regents, Golde, and Quan would share in any royalties or profits * * * arising out of [the] patent." The patent issued on March 20, 1984, naming Golde and Quan as the inventors of the cell line and the Regents as the assignee of the patent. (U.S. Patent No. 4,438,032 (Mar. 20, 1984).)

The Regent's patent also covers various methods for using the cell line to produce lymphokines. Moore admits in his complaint that "the true clinical potential of each of the lymphokines * * * [is] difficult to predict, [but] * * * competing commercial firms in these relevant fields have published reports in biotechnology industry periodicals predicting a potential market of approximately $3.01 Billion Dollars by the year 1990 for a whole range of [such lymphokines]. * * * "

With the Regents' assistance, Golde negotiated agreements for commercial development of the cell line and products to be derived from it. Under an agreement with Genetics Institute, Golde "became a paid consultant" and "acquired the rights to 75,000 shares of common stock." Genetics Institute also agreed to pay Golde and the Regents "at least $330,000 over three years, including a pro-rata share of [Golde's] salary and fringe benefits, in exchange for * * * exclusive access to the materials and research performed" on the cell line and products derived from it. On June 4, 1982, Sandoz "was added to the agreement," and compensation payable to Golde and the Regents was increased by $110,000. "[T]hroughout this period, * * * Quan spent as much as 70 [percent] of her time working for [the] Regents on research" related to the cell line.

* * *

III. Discussion

A. *Breach of Fiduciary Duty and Lack of Informed Consent*

Moore repeatedly alleges that Golde failed to disclose the extent of his research and economic interests in Moore's cells before obtaining consent to the medical procedures by which the cells were extracted. These allegations, in our view, state a cause of action against Golde for invading a legally protected interest of his patient. This cause of action can properly be characterized either as the breach of a fiduciary duty to disclose facts material to the patient's consent or, alternatively, as the performance of medical procedures without first having obtained the patient's informed consent.

Our analysis begins with three well-established principles. First, "a person of adult years and in sound mind has the right, in the exercise of control over his own body, to determine whether or not to submit to lawful medical treatment." [ ] Second, "the patient's consent to treatment, to be effective, must be an informed consent." [ ] Third, in soliciting the patient's consent, a physician has a fiduciary duty to disclose all information material to the patient's decision. * * * [ ]

These principles lead to the following conclusions: (1) a physician must disclose personal interests unrelated to the patient's health, whether research or economic, that may affect the physician's professional judgment; and (2) a physician's failure to disclose such interests may give rise to a cause of action for performing medical procedures without informed consent or breach of fiduciary duty.

To be sure, questions about the validity of a patient's consent to a procedure typically arise when the patient alleges that the physician failed to disclose medical risks, as in malpractice cases, and not when the patient alleges that the physician had a personal interest, as in this case. The concept of informed consent, however, is broad enough to encompass the latter. "The scope of the physician's communication to the patient * * * must be measured by the patient's need, and that need is whatever information is material to the decision." (*Cobbs v. Grant,* supra, 8 Cal.3d at p. 245, 104 Cal.Rptr. 505, 502 P.2d 1.)

Indeed, the law already recognizes that a reasonable patient would want to know whether a physician has an economic interest that might affect the physician's professional judgment. As the Court of Appeal has said, "[c]ertainly a sick patient deserves to be free of any reasonable suspicion that his doctor's judgment is influenced by a profit motive." (*Magan Medical Clinic v. Cal. State Bd. of Medical Examiners* (1967) 249 Cal.App.2d 124, 132, 57 Cal.Rptr. 256.) The desire to protect patients from possible conflicts of interest has also motivated legislative enactments. Among these is Business and Professions Code section 654.2. Under that section, a physician may not charge a patient on behalf of, or refer a patient to, any organization in which the physician has a "significant beneficial interest, unless [the physician] first discloses in writing to the patient, that there is such an interest and advises the patient that the patient may choose any organization for the purposes of obtaining the services ordered or requested by [the physician]." (Bus. & Prof.Code, § 654.2, subd. (a). See also Bus. & Prof.Code, § 654.1 [referrals to clinical laboratories].) Similarly, under Health and Safety Code section 24173, a physician who plans to conduct a medical experiment on a patient must, among other things, inform the patient of "[t]he name of the sponsor or funding source, if any, * * * and the organization, if any, under whose general aegis the experiment is being conducted." (Health & Saf.Code, § 24173, subd. (c)(9).)

It is important to note that no law prohibits a physician from conducting research in the same area in which he practices. Progress in medicine often depends upon physicians, such as those practicing at the university hospital where Moore received treatment, who conduct research while caring for their patients.

Yet a physician who treats a patient in whom he also has a research interest has potentially conflicting loyalties. This is because medical treatment decisions are made on the basis of proportionality—weighing the *benefits* to the patient against the *risks* to the patient. As another court has said, "the determination as to whether the burdens of treatment are worth enduring for any individual patient depends upon the facts unique in each case," and "the patient's interests and desires are the key ingredients of the decision-making process." (*Barber v. Superior Court* (1983) 147 Cal.App.3d 1006, 1018–1019, 195 Cal.Rptr. 484.) A physician who adds his own research interests to this balance may be tempted to order a scientifically useful procedure or test that offers marginal, or no, benefits to the patient. The possibility that an interest extraneous to the patient's health has affected the physician's judgment is something that a reasonable patient would want to know in deciding whether to consent to a proposed course of treatment. It is material to the patient's decision and, thus, a prerequisite to informed consent. [ ]

Golde argues that the scientific use of cells that have already been removed cannot possibly affect the patient's medical interests. The argument is correct in one instance but not in another. If a physician has no plans to conduct research on a patient's cells at the time he recommends the medical procedure by which they are taken, then the patient's medical interests have not been impaired. In that instance the argument is correct. On the other hand, a physician who does have a preexisting research interest might, consciously or unconsciously, take that into consideration in recommending the procedure. In that instance the argument is incorrect: the physician's extraneous motivation may affect his judgment and is, thus, material to the patient's consent.

We acknowledge that there is a competing consideration. To require disclosure of research and economic interests may corrupt the patient's own judgment by distracting him from the requirements of his health. But California law does not grant physicians unlimited discretion to decide what to disclose. Instead, "it is the prerogative of the patient, not the physician, to determine for himself the direction in which he believes his interests lie." (*Cobbs v. Grant,* supra, 8 Cal.3d at p. 242, 104 Cal.Rptr. 505, 502 P.2d 1.) * * *

Accordingly, we hold that a physician who is seeking a patient's consent for a medical procedure must, in order to satisfy his fiduciary duty[10] and to obtain the patient's informed consent, disclose personal interests unrelated to the patient's health, whether research or economic, that may affect his medical judgment.

10. In some respects the term "fiduciary" is too broad. In this context the term "fiduciary" signifies only that a physician must disclose all facts material to the patient's decision. A physician is not the patient's financial adviser. As we have already discussed, the reason why a physician must disclose possible conflicts is not because he has a duty to protect his patient's financial interests, but because certain personal interests may affect professional judgment.

1. Dr. Golde

We turn now to the allegations of Moore's third amended complaint to determine whether he has stated such a cause of action. We first discuss the adequacy of Moore's allegations against Golde, based upon the physician's disclosures prior to the splenectomy.

Moore alleges that, prior to the surgical removal of his spleen, Golde "formed the intent and made arrangements to obtain portions of his spleen following its removal from [Moore] in connection with [his] desire to have regular and continuous access to, and possession of, [Moore's] unique and rare Blood and Bodily Substances." Moore was never informed prior to the splenectomy of Golde's "prior formed intent" to obtain a portion of his spleen. In our view, these allegations adequately show that Golde had an undisclosed research interest in Moore's cells at the time he sought Moore's consent to the splenectomy. Accordingly, Moore has stated a cause of action for breach of fiduciary duty, or lack of informed consent, based upon the disclosures accompanying that medical procedure.

We next discuss the adequacy of Golde's alleged disclosures regarding the postoperative takings of blood and other samples. In this context, Moore alleges that Golde "expressly, affirmatively and impliedly represented * * * that these withdrawals of his Blood and Bodily Substances were necessary and required for his health and well-being." However, Moore also alleges that Golde actively concealed his economic interest in Moore's cells during this time period. "[D]uring each of these visits * * *, and even when [Moore] inquired as to whether there was any possible or potential commercial or financial value or significance of his Blood and Bodily Substances, or whether the defendants had discovered anything * * * which was or might be * * * related to any scientific activity resulting in commercial or financial benefits * * *, the defendants repeatedly and affirmatively represented to [Moore] that there was no commercial or financial value to his Blood and Bodily Substances * * * and in fact actively discouraged such inquiries."

Moore admits in his complaint that defendants disclosed they "were engaged in strictly academic and purely scientific medical research. * * * "However, Golde's representation that he had no financial interest in this research became false, based upon the allegations, at least by May 1979, when he "began to investigate and initiate the procedures * * * for [obtaining] a patent" on the cell line developed from Moore's cells.

In these allegations, Moore plainly asserts that Golde concealed an economic interest in the postoperative procedures. Therefore, applying the principles already discussed, the allegations state a cause of action for breach of fiduciary duty or lack of informed consent.

We thus disagree with the superior court's ruling that Moore had not stated a cause of action because essential allegations were lacking. We discuss each such allegation. First, in the superior court's view, Moore needed but failed to allege that defendants knew his cells had potential commercial value *on October 5, 1976* (the time blood tests were first performed at UCLA Medical Center) and had *at that time* already formed the intent to exploit the cells. We agree with the superior court that the absence of such allegations precludes Moore from stating a cause of action based upon the procedures undertaken on October 5, 1976. But, as already discussed, Moore clearly alleges that Golde had developed a research interest in his cells by October 20, 1976, when the splenectomy was performed. Thus, Moore can state a cause of action based upon Golde's alleged failure to disclose that interest before the splenectomy.

The superior court also held that the lack of essential allegations prevented Moore from stating a cause of action based on the splenectomy. According to the superior court, Moore failed to allege that the operation lacked a therapeutic purpose or that the procedure was totally unrelated to therapeutic purposes. In our view, however, neither allegation is essential. Even if the splenectomy had a therapeutic purpose,[11] it does not follow that Golde had no duty to disclose his additional research and economic interests. As we have already discussed, the existence of a motivation for a medical procedure unrelated to the patient's health is a potential conflict of interest and a fact material to the patient's decision.

Notes and Questions

1. In *Moore,* the court explicitly uses both fiduciary duty and informed consent doctrine in order to impose an obligation on the physicians to disclose their research and economic interests. Does a claim of breach of fiduciary duty add anything to an informed consent claim? If so, what? What worries the California Supreme Court? Is it that the patient's medical interests will somehow be impaired, since the physician's judgment during treatment may be corrupted by the promise of financial gain? Or is the court concerned about the patient's economic interests?

Judge Mosk, dissenting, argues that the nondisclosure cause of action is inadequate on three grounds. First, a damage remedy will not give physician-researchers an incentive to disclose conflicts of interest prior to treatment, since it is hard to establish the causal connection between injury and the failure to inform. The patient must show he would have declined, if given full information. Even if the patient claims that he would have refused, he must prove that "no reasonably prudent" person so situated would have declined. Id. at 519. Second, "* * * it gives the patient only the right to refuse consent, i.e., the right to prohibit the commercialization of his tissue; it does not give him the right to grant consent to that commercialization on the condition that he share in its proceeds." Id. at 520. Third, the cause of action "* * * fails to reach a major class of potential defendants: all those who are outside the strict physician-patient relationship with the plaintiff." Id. at 521. This may include other researchers and corporations exploiting the tissue.

Judge Broussard, concurring and dissenting, disagrees with Judge Mosk as to the efficacy of the nondisclosure action. He argues that the breach of fiduciary duty encompasses the postoperative conduct of defendants as well as the presurgical failure to disclose, so that the plaintiff can recover by "establishing that he would not have consented to some or all of the extensive postoperative medical procedures if he had been fully aware of defendants' research and economic interests and motivations." Id. at 500. He also observes that the fiduciary duty, unlike an informed consent cause of action, requires "* * * only that the doctor's wrongful failure to disclose information proximately caused the plaintiff some type

11. The record shows that the splenectomy did have a therapeutic purpose. The Regents' patent application, which the superior court and the Court of Appeal both accepted as part of the record, shows that Moore had a grossly enlarged spleen and that its excision improved his condition.

of compensable damage." Id. at 500. Punitive as well as compensatory damages will be available.

2. Does the normal treatment setting pose any comparable conflicts of interest, in which the physician's treatment decision may be affected by his financial interests in treating a particular patient? Suppose a physician examines a boy brought into the emergency room of a small community hospital after an auto accident. The boy has an injured leg and foot. The x-ray suggests a dislocated foot. The doctor can either try to reduce the dislocation in the hospital, or he can refer the boy to an orthopedic specialist in a large city a hundred miles away. If the physician chooses to treat, he gets a fee, while the referral generates no further income for him. What should the physician choose to disclose to the boy's parents? The medical risks in either approach? The economic issue that may color his judgment? See David Hilifiker, Facing Our Mistakes, 310 N.Eng.J.Med. 118, 119 (1984). Ison v. McFall, 55 Tenn.App. 326, 400 S.W.2d 243 (1964); Larsen v. Yelle, 310 Minn. 521, 246 N.W.2d 841 (1976) (physician in general practice liable for failing to refer patient with fractured wrist to orthopedic specialist). See Principles of Medical Ethics of the American Medical Association § 8 (requiring doctor to seek consultation "whenever it appears that the quality of medical services may be enhanced thereby.")

3. Physicians may at times want to try a new or innovative approach to a patient's problems. What are their obligations to disclose that they are in effect "experimenting" on the patient? In Estrada v. Jaques, 70 N.C.App. 627, 321 S.E.2d 240 (1984), the surgeons treated the plaintiff for a gunshot wound to his leg. They tried a new technique, inserting a small steel coil into his weakened artery upstream from his aneurysm to cut off the flow of blood. Plaintiff signed a consent form prior to surgery. The surgery failed, and Estrada had to have his leg amputated. He argued that his consent was not "informed" since neither the surgeons nor the radiologists told him the procedure was experimental. The court held that the patient had a right to know that the embolization procedure was experimental.

> * * * [W]e hold that where the health care provider offers an experimental procedure or treatment to a patient, the health care provider has a duty, in exercising reasonable care under the circumstances, to inform the patient of the experimental nature of the proposed procedure. With experimental procedures the "most frequent risks and hazards" will remain unknown until the procedure becomes established. If the health care provider has a duty to inform of *known* risks for *established* procedures, common sense and the purposes of the statute equally require that the health care provider inform the patient of any *uncertainty* regarding the risks associated with *experimental* procedures. This includes the experimental nature of the procedure and the *known or projected most likely risks.* The evidence presented in this case illustrates the logic of our holding perfectly: taken in Estrada's favor, it shows that the surgeons presented a full picture of the risks of the surgical procedure and simply advised him that the embolization might not work, without informing him of its experimental nature and their consequent lack of knowledge of the risks of whether it would fail or not. Not surprisingly, Estrada chose the experimental procedure. * *
>
> * * *
>
> Our decision that health care providers must inform their patients that proposed procedures are experimental accords with the majority of courts and commentators which have considered the problem. * * * [ ] The psychology of

the doctor-patient relation, and the rewards, financial and professional, attendant upon recognition of experimental success, increase the potential for abuse and strengthen the rationale for uniform disclosure. We have found little authority supporting a contrary rule. Accordingly, we reaffirm our holding that reasonable standards of informed consent to an experimental procedure require disclosure to the patient that the procedure is experimental.

How does the court in *Estrada* define "experimental" for purposes of disclosure to patients? They mention the fact that the surgeons and radiologists were aware of only one previous operation and one article, and that the surgeons had no personal experience. Does the court have the same attitude toward such clinical experimentation as the court did in *Brook,* in Chapter 3, supra?

What should be disclosed to a patient about to undergo an experimental procedure? That this is the first time this team has attempted this procedure? That the literature lacks support at present for it? That the surgeons and radiologists will benefit financially or in career recognition if the procedure succeeds? Must the motivations of the team be clearly disclosed to the patient? Should the physicians' motivations even matter, so long as the patient and the physicians believe that the new procedure offers a better chance for the patient?

* * *

NEADE v. PORTES

Supreme Court of Illinois, 2000.
193 Ill.2d 433, 250 Ill.Dec. 733, 739 N.E.2d 496.

JUSTICE MCMORROW delivered the opinion of the court:

Plaintiff filed a three-count complaint in the circuit court of Lake County, two counts of which were directed against defendants Steven Portes and Primary Care Family Center. In count I, plaintiff alleged that defendants were liable for medical negligence, and in count II, plaintiff charged defendants with a breach of fiduciary duty. The principle issue in this appeal is whether, in a complaint alleging medical negligence, a patient has a cause of action for breach of fiduciary duty against a physician for that physician's failure to disclose incentives that exist under the physician's arrangement with the patient's health maintenance organization (HMO). We hold that a patient may not bring a breach of fiduciary duty claim against a physician under these circumstances.

BACKGROUND

According to the allegations in plaintiff Therese Neade's complaint, plaintiff's husband, Anthony Neade, had a family history of heart disease, suffered from hypertension and a high cholesterol count, smoked heavily and was overweight. In 1990, at age 37, Mr. Neade began to exhibit symptoms of coronary artery blockage. Specifically, Mr. Neade experienced chest pain extending into his arm and shortness of breath. Mr. Neade's primary care physician, Steven Portes, M.D., hospitalized Mr. Neade from August 10 through August 13, 1990. During this hospitalization, Mr. Neade received several tests, including a thallium stress test and an electrocardiogram (EKG). Dr. Thomas Engel (not a party to this appeal) found the results of the tests to be normal and diagnosed Mr. Neade with hiatal hernia and/or esophagitis. Mr. Neade was thereafter discharged.

After his hospitalization, Mr. Neade visited Dr. Portes on August 17, August 28 and September 24, 1990, at the Primary Care Family Center (Primary Care), complaining of continued chest pain radiating to his neck and arm. Relying on the results of the thallium stress test and EKG taken during Mr. Neade's hospitalization, Dr. Portes informed Mr. Neade that his chest pain was not cardiac related. In October 1990, Mr. Neade returned to Dr. Portes, this time complaining of stabbing chest pain. At the request of Dr. Portes, his associate, Dr. Huang, examined Mr. Neade. Dr. Huang recommended that Mr. Neade undergo an angiogram-a test that is more specific for diagnosing coronary artery disease than a thallium stress test. Dr. Huang was employed on a part-time basis at Primary Care and had no hospital privileges. Dr. Portes, as Mr. Neade's primary care physician, was responsible for ordering any necessary hospitalization or additional tests. Despite Dr. Huang's recommendation, Dr. Portes did not authorize an angiogram for Mr. Neade.

Mr. Neade again returned to Primary Care in June 1991, complaining of chest pain. Dr. Portes asked Dr. Schlager, another part-time physician at Primary Care, to examine Mr. Neade. After this examination, Dr. Schlager also recommended that Mr. Neade undergo an angiogram, but Dr. Portes, relying on the thallium stress test, did not authorize the angiogram and advised Dr. Schlager that Mr. Neade's chest pain was not cardiac related. Subsequently, on September 16, 1991, Mr. Neade suffered a massive myocardial infarction caused by coronary artery blockage. Nine days later, Mr. Neade died.

Plaintiff's complaint alleges that Dr. Portes was the president of Primary Care and, as such, negotiated contracts with various organizations on behalf of himself and the clinic. Chicago HMO, of which Mr. Neade was a member, was one of the organizations with which Dr. Portes had contracted for the provision of services. According to plaintiff's complaint, Dr. Portes personally negotiated with Chicago HMO in 1990 and 1991 and agreed that Dr. Portes and his group would receive from Chicago HMO, inter alia, $75,000 annually. The $75,000 was to be used by Dr. Portes and his group to cover costs for patient referrals and outside medical tests prescribed for Chicago HMO members. This fund was termed the "Medical Incentive Fund."

Pursuant to the contract between Dr. Portes, Primary Care and Chicago HMO, any portion of the Medical Incentive Fund that was not used for referrals or outside tests would be divided at the end of each year between Primary Care's full time physicians and Chicago HMO, with the physicians receiving 60% of the remaining money and Chicago HMO receiving 40%. If the Medical Incentive Fund was exhausted prior to the end of the year, Dr. Portes and his group would be required to fund any additional consultant fees and outside tests. Plaintiff and Mr. Neade were not informed of this arrangement between Dr. Portes, Primary Care and Chicago HMO.

Count I of plaintiff's amended complaint alleges that Dr. Portes' reliance on the thallium stress test and EKG and his failure to authorize an angiogram constituted medical negligence which proximately resulted in Mr. Neade's death. In count I, plaintiff alleged facts regarding the Medical Incentive Fund.

Count II of plaintiff's amended complaint alleges that Dr. Portes had a fiduciary duty to act in good faith and in the best interest of Mr. Neade, and that he breached that duty by refusing to authorize further testing, by refusing to refer Mr. Neade to a specialist and by refusing to disclose to the Neades Dr. Portes' financial relationship (including the Medical Incentive Fund) with Chicago HMO. Count II further alleges that Dr. Portes breached his fiduciary duty by entering into a contract with Chicago HMO that put his financial well-being in direct conflict with Mr. Neade's physical well-being.

The trial court agreed with defendants' argument that financial motive was not relevant to whether Dr. Portes violated the applicable standard of care in treating Mr. Neade. The trial court therefore struck the allegations relating to the Medical Incentive Fund from count I. With respect to count II, the trial court found that there existed no cause of action against a physician for breach of fiduciary duty and granted defendants' motion to dismiss. Plaintiff thereafter filed a motion to reconsider, to which she attached her own affidavit and portions of the deposition of plaintiff's expert, Dr. Jay Schapira. Plaintiff's affidavit stated that, if she had known of the Medical Incentive Fund, she would have sought a second opinion from a physician outside of Dr. Portes' group concerning the necessity of an angiogram. In his deposition, Dr. Schapira stated that both the applicable standard of care and ethical considerations obligate a doctor to disclose his financial interest in withholding care. According to Dr. Schapira, a patient can then make an informed decision concerning the quality of care he is receiving and his doctor's motivations in treating him. Defendants filed a motion to strike the affidavit and deposition excerpts from plaintiff's motion to reconsider. The trial court denied defendants' motion to strike and also denied plaintiff's motion to reconsider.

On appeal, plaintiff argued that allegations concerning the Medical Incentive Fund are relevant to count I of plaintiff's complaint, in which plaintiff alleged medical negligence, to show that Dr. Portes deviated from the standard of care. The appellate court determined that allegations relating to financial motive are not appropriate in a medical negligence claim, and affirmed the trial court's holding on this issue. However, the appellate court held that evidence relating to the Medical Incentive Fund may be relevant at trial to attack Dr. Portes' credibility if he testifies. The appellate court reversed the trial court's dismissal of count II and held that plaintiff stated a cause of action for breach of fiduciary duty against Dr. Portes for Dr. Portes' failure to disclose the Medical Incentive Fund. [ ]

On appeal to this court, defendants argue for reversal of the appellate court's finding that: (1) a cause of action for breach of fiduciary duty exists for Dr. Portes' failure to disclose the Medical Incentive Fund; and (2) evidence of the Medical Incentive Fund is relevant in plaintiff's medical negligence action if Dr. Portes testifies at trial. We allowed the Illinois Trial Lawyers Association to file an amicus curiae brief in support of plaintiff and the Illinois State Medical Society and American Medical Association to file an amicus curiae brief in support of defendant.

ANALYSIS

* * *

I. Breach of Fiduciary Duty

The primary issue in this appeal is whether plaintiff can state a cause of action for breach of fiduciary duty against Dr. Portes for Dr. Portes' failure to disclose his interest in the Medical Incentive Fund. A fiduciary relationship imposes a general duty on the fiduciary to refrain from "seeking a selfish benefit during the relationship." Kurtz v. Solomon, 275 Ill.App.3d 643, 651, 212 Ill.Dec. 31, 656 N.E.2d 184 (1995), citing Collins v. Nugent, 110 Ill.App.3d 1026, 1036, 66 Ill.Dec. 594, 443 N.E.2d 277 (1982). Illinois courts have recognized a fiduciary relationship between a physician and his patient [ ] but Illinois courts have never recognized a cause of action for breach of fiduciary duty against a physician.

Though Illinois courts have never addressed the issue of whether a plaintiff can state a cause of action for breach of fiduciary duty against a physician, courts have rejected breach of fiduciary duty claims brought against attorneys on the basis that they are duplicative of negligence or malpractice claims. For example, our appellate court has held that where a claim for legal malpractice and a claim for breach of fiduciary duty are based on the same operative facts and result in the same injury to the plaintiff, the breach of fiduciary duty claim should be dismissed as duplicative. [ ]

Courts in other jurisdictions have dismissed claims for breach of fiduciary duty when those claims are duplicative of medical negligence claims. Such claims for breach of fiduciary duty have also been dismissed where they constitute an impermissible recasting of a medical negligence claim, even though plaintiff's complaint did not include a medical negligence claim. The appellate court in the case at bar discussed decisions from Minnesota, Colorado, Arizona and New Mexico. Each of these jurisdictions held that a breach of fiduciary duty claim is duplicative of a negligence claim. [ ] * * *

In a case involving facts similar to the case at bar, the United States Supreme Court recently refused to recognize a breach of fiduciary duty under ERISA. Pegram v. Herdrich, 530 U.S. 211, 120 S.Ct. 2143, 147 L.Ed.2d 164 (2000). In Herdrich, the plaintiff, a member of the Carle Clinic Association, P.C., Health Alliance Medical Plans, Inc., and Carle Health Insurance Management Co., Inc. (collectively Carle), an HMO, visited her primary care physician complaining of groin pain. The following week, the physician found an inflamed mass in the plaintiff's abdomen. The physician required the plaintiff to wait eight days to receive an ultrasound at a Carle facility over 50 miles away. In the interim, the plaintiff's appendix ruptured, causing peritonitis. The plaintiff filed a suit for both medical malpractice against her physician and breach of fiduciary duty against Carle. The breach of fiduciary duty claim alleged that Carle's act of providing incentives for its physicians to limit medical care and procedures constituted a breach of fiduciary duty under ERISA. Herdrich, 530 U.S. at ___, 120 S.Ct. at 2147, 147 L.Ed.2d at 173. The Supreme Court reversed the Seventh Circuit's determination that the plaintiff stated a cause of action for breach of fiduciary duty under ERISA. Herdrich, 530 U.S. at ___, 120 S.Ct. at 2158–59, 147 L.Ed.2d at 186. The Supreme Court noted the nature of a breach of fiduciary claim against an HMO physician. The Court stated:

> [T]he defense of any HMO would be that its physician did not act out of financial interest but for good medical reasons, the plausibility of which

> would require reference to standards of reasonable and customary medical practice in like circumstances. That, of course, is the traditional standard of the common law. [Citation.] Thus, for all practical purposes, every claim of fiduciary breach by an HMO physician making a mixed decision [about a patient's eligibility for treatment under an HMO and the appropriate treatment for the patient] would boil down to a malpractice claim, and the fiduciary standard would be nothing but the malpractice standard traditionally applied in actions against physicians. Herdrich, 530 U.S. at ___, 120 S.Ct. at 2157, 147 L.Ed.2d at 185.

See also B. Furrow, Managed Care Organizations and Patient Injury: Rethinking Liability, 31 Ga. L.Rev. 419, 484 (1997).

We find the reasoning in the foregoing cases persuasive in analysis of the case at bar and decline to uphold plaintiff's breach of fiduciary duty claim. The appellate court held that because plaintiff pled different facts in support of her breach of fiduciary duty claim from those facts pled in her medical negligence claim, she stated two separate causes of action. Though many of the facts pled in counts I and II are identical, in her breach of fiduciary duty claim, plaintiff did plead the additional fact that Dr. Portes failed to disclose the Medical Incentive Fund. However, as our appellate court in Majumdar stated, it is operative facts together with the injury that we look to in order to determine whether a cause of action is duplicative. In the case at bar, the operative fact in both counts is Dr. Portes' failure to order an angiogram for Mr. Neade. Plaintiff alleges in both counts that Mr. Neade's failure to receive an angiogram is the ultimate reason for his subsequent death. Plaintiff also alleges the same injury in both her medical negligence claim and her breach of fiduciary duty claim, namely, Mr. Neade's death and its effect on plaintiff and her family. We determine that plaintiff's breach of fiduciary duty claim is a re-presentment of her medical negligence claim.

An examination of the elements of a medical negligence claim and breach of fiduciary duty claim illustrates the way in which a breach of fiduciary duty claim would "boil down to a malpractice claim." Herdrich, 530 U.S. at ___, 120 S.Ct. at 2157, 147 L.Ed.2d at 185. To sustain an action for medical negligence, plaintiff must show: (1) the standard of care in the medical community by which the physician's treatment was measured; (2) that the physician deviated from the standard of care; and (3) that a resulting injury was proximately caused by the deviation from the standard of care. [ ] Thus, the standard of care is the relevant inquiry by which we judge a physician's actions in a medical negligence case. Under a standard of care analysis, a defendant will be held to "the reasonable skill which a physician in good standing in the community would use in a similar case." Newell v. Corres, 125 Ill.App.3d 1087, 1094, 81 Ill.Dec. 283, 466 N.E.2d 1085 (1984). If a physician deviates from the standard of care and that deviation proximately causes injury to a patient, the physician is liable for damages caused by his medical negligence.

In contrast to an action for medical negligence, in order to state a claim for breach of fiduciary duty, it must be alleged that a fiduciary duty exists, that the fiduciary duty was breached, and that such breach proximately caused the injury of which the plaintiff complains. [ ] In the case at bar, plaintiff alleged in her complaint that "as a direct and proximate result of

Defendant's breach of fiduciary duty * * *, Anthony Neade suffered a massive myocardial infarction." The appellate court agreed, holding that "[i]t is conceivable that a trier of fact could find * * * that Dr. Portes did breach his fiduciary duty in not disclosing his financial incentive arrangement and, as a proximate result thereof, Neade did not obtain a second opinion, suffered a massive coronary infarction, and died." 303 Ill.App.3d at 814, 237 Ill.Dec. 788, 710 N.E.2d 418.

In order to sustain a breach of fiduciary duty claim against Dr. Portes, plaintiff would have to allege, inter alia, that: (1) had she known of the Medical Incentive Fund she would have sought an opinion from another physician; (2) that the other physician would have ordered an angiogram for Mr. Neade; (3) that the angiogram would have detected Mr. Neade's heart condition; and (4) that treatment could have prevented his eventual myocardial infarction and subsequent death. [ ] In order to prove the second element, plaintiff would have been required to present expert testimony that the expert, after examining Mr. Neade and considering his history, would have ordered an angiogram. This requirement relates to the standard of care consideration-the first prong in a traditional medical negligence claim-under which a physician is held to "the reasonable skill which a physician in good standing in the community would use." Newell, 125 Ill.App.3d at 1094, 81 Ill.Dec. 283, 466 N.E.2d 1085. That is precisely what plaintiff must prove to support her breach of fiduciary duty claim. As the Supreme Court stated in Herdrich, the breach of fiduciary duty claim "would boil down to a malpractice claim, and the fiduciary standard would be nothing but the malpractice standard traditionally applied in actions against physicians." Herdrich, 530 U.S. at ___, 120 S.Ct. at 2157, 147 L.Ed.2d at 185. Thus, we need not recognize a new cause of action for breach of fiduciary duty when a traditional medical negligence claim sufficiently addresses the same alleged misconduct. The breach of fiduciary duty claim in the case at bar would be duplicative of the medical negligence claim.

An examination of the damages pled in plaintiff's complaint further supports our conclusion that a medical negligence claim sufficiently addresses plaintiff's injuries. While pleading in the alternative is generally permitted [ ] duplicate claims are not permitted in the same complaint. Count I of plaintiff's amended complaint sounds in medical negligence committed by Dr. Portes. In count I, plaintiff alleges that Mr. Neade's death deprived plaintiff and her children of Mr. Neade's "companionship as well as other attributes that they would normally receive as wife and children respectively, now and in the future, as well as the support of money and valuable services which he had provided." Plaintiff requests $50,000 in addition to costs of the law suit in damages under count I. Count II of plaintiff's amended complaint attempts to state a cause of action for Dr. Portes' breach of fiduciary duty. The damages alleged in count II are identical to those alleged in count I. Here, though attempting to couch the claim in different terms, plaintiff is essentially pleading the same cause of action which caused the same damages.

Our decision to refrain from permitting the creation of this new cause of action finds additional support in statutory law. The Illinois legislature has placed the burden of disclosing HMO incentive schemes on HMOs themselves. The Illinois General Assembly recently enacted the Managed Care Reform and Patient Rights Act (hereinafter, the Managed Care Act), which states: "Upon written request, a health care plan shall provide to enrollees a description of the financial relationships between the health care plan and any health care provider * * *." 215 ILCS 134/15(b) (West Supp.1999). The Managed Care Act, effective on January 1, 2000, requires that managed care organizations disclose physician incentive plans to patients. Thus, the legislature has chosen to put the burden of disclosing any financial incentive plans on the HMO, rather than on the physician. The legislature has put the burden of disclosure on the entities that create financial incentive plans and require physicians to adhere to them. If the legislature had wished to place the burden of disclosing financial incentives on physicians, it could have done so.

Moreover, the outcome that would result if we were to allow the creation of a new cause of action for breach of fiduciary duty against a physician in these circumstances may be impractical. For example, physicians often provide services for numerous patients, many of whom may be covered by different HMOs. In order to effectively disclose HMO incentives, physicians would have to remain cognizant at all times of every patient's particular HMO and that HMO's policies and procedures. See, e.g., M. Hall, A Theory of Economic Informed Consent, 31 Ga. L.Rev. 511, 525–26 (1997) ("[A] typical primary care physician in a metropolitan city may have a dozen or more contracts with managed care networks, while specialists may have several dozen or even a hundred. It is not feasible to ask physicians to keep track of the payment incentives and treatment rules for each of these many different plans, nor is this necessarily good public policy"). If we were to recognize a breach of fiduciary duty claim in the context of the case at bar, we fear the effects of such a holding may be unworkable.

Plaintiff and the appellate court rely on Current Opinions of the Council on Ethical and Judicial Affairs of the American Medical Association (AMA) in support of the argument that plaintiff can state a cause of action for breach of fiduciary duty against Dr. Portes for his failure to disclose the Medical Incentive Fund. Specifically, they rely on Opinion 8.132 entitled "Referral of Patients: Disclosure of Limitations," which states:

> Physicians must assure disclosure of any financial inducements that may tend to limit the diagnostic and therapeutic alternatives that are offered to patients or that may tend to limit patients' overall access to care. Physicians may satisfy this obligation by assuring that the managed care plan makes adequate disclosure to patients enrolled in the plan. AMA Council on Ethical and Judicial Affairs, Current Op. 8.132 (1995–2000).

As previously noted in this opinion, the Illinois legislature determined that disclosure to patients is to be made by managed care plans.

In addition to AMA opinions, plaintiff and the appellate court also rely on Herdrich v. Pegram, 154 F.3d 362 (7th Cir.1998), Shea v. Esensten, 107 F.3d 625 (8th Cir.1997), and Moore v. Regents of the University of California, 51 Cal.3d 120, 271 Cal.Rptr. 146, 793 P.2d 479 (1990), to support the establishment of a cause of action for breach of a fiduciary duty by medical professionals. As discussed, the United States Supreme Court has reversed Herdrich and held that, under ERISA, a physician's "mixed" decisions about HMO eligibility and patient treatment is not a fiduciary decision. Herdrich, 530 U.S. at ___, 120 S.Ct. at 2158, 147 L.Ed.2d at 186. Shea held that a plaintiff could state a cause of action against an HMO for breach of fiduciary duty under ERISA for the HMO's failure to disclose physician incentive schemes. Shea, 107 F.3d at 629. The Shea court, like the Illinois General Assembly, placed the burden of disclosing financial incentive plans on the entity that both creates those plans and is more equipped to make those disclosures-the HMO. However, the issue of whether an HMO breaches its fiduciary duty in failing to disclose incentive schemes is not before us today. As our appellate court pointed out, both Herdrich, before it was reversed, and Shea "recognize that patients should be informed of financial arrangements that may negatively impact their health care." 303 Ill.App.3d at 808, 237 Ill.Dec. 788, 710 N.E.2d 418. While we may agree that patients should be told of financial considerations which may negatively impact their healthcare, we will not place the burden of that disclosure on physicians.

Moreover, plaintiff's reliance on Moore is misplaced. Moore involved a plaintiff who alleged that his doctor breached his fiduciary duty when the doctor used portions of the plaintiff's spleen and other cells, which he recommended be removed, to conduct research and benefit financially without informing the plaintiff. Moore, 271 Cal.Rptr. at 148, 793 P.2d at 481. The California appellate court held that the plaintiff could state a cause of action for either breach of fiduciary duty or for the performance of medical procedures without informed consent. [ ] However, a physician's failure to disclose HMO incentive plans is significantly unlike the egregious nature of the alleged behavior at issue in Moore. Further, in Moore, the plaintiff had no way of discovering the physician's research plans unless disclosed by his physician. In Illinois, a patient can obtain information about the relationship and payment practices between her physician and her HMO by contacting the HMO.

Plaintiff also cites numerous cases that allow breach of fiduciary duty claims against professionals other than physicians. [ ] These cases are inapposite, as the plaintiffs in those cases did not bring causes of action sounding in both breach of fiduciary duty and negligence. Thus, the courts in the cited cases did not determine whether the plaintiffs' injuries were sufficiently addressed by traditional negligence claims.

* * *

We decline to recognize a new cause of action for breach of fiduciary duty against a physician for the physician's failure to disclose HMO incentives in a suit brought against the physician for medical negligence. We hold that, under the facts in the case at bar, a breach of fiduciary duty claim is duplicative of a medical negligence claim. The injuries suffered by plaintiff as a result of Dr. Portes' medical care are sufficiently addressed by application of traditional concepts of negligence.

II. Evidence of Financial Incentives at Trial

The appellate court held that evidence of the Medical Incentive Fund may be relevant in the event that Dr. Portes testifies in the medical negligence trial. [ ] The appellate court noted that, in general, a witness may be cross-examined on issues relating to interest and bias, and found that "issues concerning Dr. Portes' financial gain go to his credibility." We agree. Therefore, we hold that evidence of the Medical Incentive Fund may be relevant if

Dr. Portes testifies at trial. The relevance and admission of such evidence is for the discretion of the trial court.

CONCLUSION

For the foregoing reasons, we hold that plaintiff may not state a cause of action for breach of fiduciary duty against Dr. Portes. Therefore, we reverse the appellate court's reinstatement of count II. The judgment of the circuit court is affirmed, and the cause is remanded to that court for further proceedings.

[The opinion of the dissenting justice is omitted.]

Notes and Questions

1. The Illinois Supreme Court sees the fiduciary claim as adding nothing to a basic negligence claim. They argue that plaintiff would end up having to show that she would have chosen differently with knowledge of the salary incentive system, and that another physician would have offered the test, and the test would have detected the plaintiff's condition. What would a physician have to say to a patient? And how much would a patient have to know about the incentives that operate on other physicians that she might choose over Dr. Portes? Isn't it sufficient that a physician will always face the threat of a malpractice suit for breaching the standard of care, and this is a powerful counterforce to the subtle effects of salary incentives operating on physicians? How would you go about studying these questions?

2. Can you make an argument that a right to information in such cases does add something to a plaintiff's rights? Isn't this claim similar to the underlying goals of a battery-based informed consent claim? Is it in the same category as claimed rights to know about a physician's performance record, mental status, and substance abuse?

3. Is the court right that any meaningful disclosure of how physicians are paid should be done at the level of the managed care plan itself at the time the subscriber selects the plan. They distinguish the 8th Circuit Shea case on the grounds that it required disclosure only at the plan level. See generally Chapter 8 for a discussion of managed care regulation and liability, and Chapter 9 for a discussion of disclosure obligations under ERISA.

C. CAUSATION COMPLEXITIES

CANTERBURY v. SPENCE

United States Court of Appeals, District of Columbia Circuit, 1972.
464 F.2d 772.

VII

No more than breach of any other legal duty does nonfulfillment of the physician's obligation to disclose alone establish liability to the patient. An unrevealed risk that should have been made known must materialize, for otherwise the omission, however unpardonable, is legally without consequence. Occurrence of the risk must be harmful to the patient, for negligence unrelated to injury is nonactionable. And, as in malpractice actions generally, there must be a causal relationship between the physician's failure to adequately divulge and damage to the patient.

A causal connection exists when, but only when, disclosure of significant risks incidental to treatment would have resulted in a decision against it. The patient obviously has no complaint if he would have submitted to the therapy notwithstanding awareness that the risk was one of its perils. On the other hand, the very purpose of the disclosure rule is to protect the patient against consequences which, if known, he would have avoided by foregoing the treatment. The more difficult question is whether the factual issue on causality calls for an objective or a subjective determination.

It has been assumed that the issue is to be resolved according to whether the factfinder believes the patient's testimony that he would not have agreed to the treatment if he had known of the danger which later ripened into injury. We think a technique which ties the factual conclusion on causation simply to the assessment of the patient's credibility is unsatisfactory. To be sure, the objective of risk-disclosure is preservation of the patient's interest in intelligent self-choice on proposed treatment, a matter the patient is free to decide for any reason that appeals to him. When, prior to commencement of therapy, the patient is sufficiently informed on risks and he exercises his choice, it may truly be said that he did exactly what he wanted to do. But when causality is explored at a post-injury trial with a professedly uninformed patient, the question whether he actually would have turned the treatment down if he had known the risks is purely hypothetical: "Viewed from the point at which he had to decide, would the patient have decided differently had he known something he did not know?" And the answer which the patient supplies hardly represents more than a guess, perhaps tinged by the circumstance that the uncommunicated hazard has in fact materialized.

In our view, this method of dealing with the issue on causation comes in second-best. It places the physician in jeopardy of the patient's hindsight and bitterness. It places the factfinder in the position of deciding whether a speculative answer to a hypothetical question is to be credited. It calls for a subjective determination solely on testimony of a patient-witness shadowed by the occurrence of the undisclosed risk.

Better it is, we believe, to resolve the causality issue on an objective basis: in terms of what a prudent person in the patient's position would have decided if suitably informed of all perils bearing significance. If adequate disclosure could reasonably be expected to have caused that person to decline the treatment because of the revelation of the kind of risk or danger that resulted in harm, causation is shown, but otherwise not. The patient's testimony is relevant on that score of course but it would not threaten to dominate the findings. And since that testimony would probably be appraised congruently with the factfinder's belief in its reasonableness, the case for a wholly objective standard for passing on causation is strengthened. Such a standard would in any event ease the fact-finding process and better assure the truth as its product.

* * *

Notes and Questions

1. Causation can only be established if there is a link between the failure of a doctor to disclose and the patient's injury. Two tests of causation have emerged: the objective reasonable patient test and the subjective particular patient test. The

former asks what a reasonable patient would have done. The latter asks what the particular patient would have done. *Canterbury* adopted the objective test, after a good deal of vacillation. The court was concerned with patient hindsight testimony that he or she would have foregone the treatment, testimony which the court feared would be "* * * hardly * * * more than a guess, perhaps tinged by the circumstance that the uncommunicated hazard has in fact materialized." The fear is of self-serving testimony.

The risk must be "material" to a reasonable patient in the shoes of the plaintiff. Under this standard, a patient's testimony is not needed to get the issue of causation to the jury. The testimony may be admissible and relevant on causation, but not dispositive. The jury can decide without it "what a reasonable person in that position would have done." Hartke v. McKelway, 707 F.2d 1544 (D.C.Cir.1983). See also Sard v. Hardy, 281 Md. 432, 450, 379 A.2d 1014, 1025 (1977).

Even if the plaintiff can establish that a reasonable patient would not have consented if properly informed, evidence that the plaintiff would have consented if fully informed may be presented to the jury. Bourgeois v. McDonald, 622 So.2d 684 (La.App. 4 Cir.1993).

2. Is it easy for a jury to put themselves in the shoes of a particular plaintiff? To some extent, that is what the jury is always asked to do in tort cases, particularly as to pain and suffering awards. In that sense, therefore, the courts' rejection of the particular patient test seems unreasonable. Is, however, the jury's empathetic attempt to understand the plaintiff's pain in a personal injury case the same as the jury's collective attempt to second guess the plaintiff's decision whether or not to undergo the diagnosis or treatment proposed by the doctor? Consider the following argument:

> "Interferences with self-determination occur in all situations in which a person's dignitary interests have been violated. They are not limited to those in which physical harm has occurred. Lack of informed consent is itself a violation. It is the harm. The additional presence of physical harm only adds injury to insult * * * As citizens, patients are wronged when physicians begin treatment without fulfilling their disclosure obligation. What patients might or might not have agreed to, if properly informed, is beside the point."

Jay Katz, The Silent World of Doctor and Patient 79 (1984). Adoption of an objective standard on causation takes away most of what the *Canterbury* court granted as to risk disclosure. It asks the jury to put themselves in the place of a reasonable person, rather than the particular person. Is a jury likely to find causation in these cases, unless (1) the doctor was clearly negligent, so no reasonable person would have agreed to the treatment; (2) the doctor offered an experimental procedure which a person might refuse in spite of the doctor's urging; (3) the jury ignores its instructions and applies a subjective standard?

In Cheung v. Cunningham, 214 N.J.Super. 649, 520 A.2d 832, 834 (Sup.Ct., A.D. N.J. 1987), the court held that the subjective test for causation was preferable to Canterbury's objective test. " ... [T]he totally objective standard used in the court's charge denies the individual's right to decide what is to be done with his or her body and may deny the individual the right to base consent on proper information in light of their individual fears, apprehensions, religious beliefs and the like."

3. The majority of American jurisdictions have adopted the objective test of causality. See Fain v. Smith, 479 So.2d 1150 (Ala.1985) and cases cited.

D. DAMAGE ISSUES

1. *The "Benefits" Doctrine*

In a typical informed consent case, the plaintiff is not informed of a certain risk, undergoes treatment, and suffers a bad result. The plaintiff then argues that if the risks had been disclosed, he would not have undergone the procedure and would have avoided the risk that materialized, either by choosing another alternative or doing nothing. Damages are then measured by comparing the bad outcome with the probable result if an alternative procedure were performed, or nothing was done. What if the procedure achieves the success promised by the physician and no alternatives to the treatment were available, but an undisclosed side-effect does occur? Some states apply the benefits doctrine in such a situation. In Gracia v. Meiselman, 220 N.J.Super. 317, 531 A.2d 1373 (1987), the plaintiff who underwent jaw reconstruction contended that the surgeon did not advise him of the risk of medial nerve damage inherent in the operation. The plaintiff claimed that if he had known that there was any risk in the proposed operation, he would have withheld his consent. He suffered a loss of feeling in the area of his chin, about three centimeters in length and two centimeters in width. The plaintiff alleged that "he has had post-operative marital problems because he does not want to be kissed by his wife because of the numbness, and that he is angry in general because he is left with the numbness above described."

> The condition to be compared in an informed consent case is (where the risk is the only complication of surgery) the condition that the patient would have been in without having the operation and the condition that the patient is in after having had the operation. * * * In an informed consent case, where there are no alternatives of treatment, the operation could not have been performed without the inherent risk. Therefore, the comparison is between plaintiff's condition without having the operation and plaintiff's condition after having the operation.

The Court therefore offset the complications of surgery and its benefits, holding that "if an operation is properly performed, of overall benefit to the patient, and there are no alternative options for treatment, there should be no compensable damages awarded against the physician." Isn't non-treatment always an option for any medical procedure?

2. *Punitive Damages*

TISDALE v. PRUITT, JR., M.D.

Court of Appeals of South Carolina, 1990.
302 S.C. 238, 394 S.E.2d 857.

LITTLEJOHN, J.

In this medical malpractice action, Plaintiff, Laurel S. Tisdale, Respondent (the patient) sued Defendant A. Bert Pruitt Jr., Appellant (Dr. Pruitt) seeking damages alleged to have grown out of an unauthorized dilation and curettage (D & C). The Complaint alleges assault and battery, negligence, recklessness and willfulness and charges that the D & C was performed by the doctor without the informed consent of the patient. The Answer of Dr. Pruitt amounts to a general denial, asserting a medical emergency as justification and alleging the two-year statute of limitations as a bar to the assault and battery claim.

Among the allegations of the Complaint are found the following:

The Defendant's conduct toward the Plaintiff was negligent, reckless, willful, and in conscious disregard of the Plaintiff's rights in the following particulars:

* * *

b) In failing to read the Plaintiff's chart in order to determine that the sole purpose of her visit to him was for him to render a second opinion to Dr. Murphy concerning her intended hospital stay.

* * *

d) In failing to obtain her consent prior to performing any procedures upon her other than obtaining a biopsy in order to render a second opinion to Dr. Murphy; * * *.

The trial judge granted a directed verdict by reason of the statute of limitations as to the assault and battery cause of action, and submitted the other causes of action to the jury which returned a verdict for $5,000 actual damages plus $25,000 punitive damages. The doctor appeals. We affirm.

FACTS

The patient had been seeing her own family physician, Dr. Murphy, for approximately ten years. She was having problems with a pregnancy and consulted him. He recommended a D & C and arranged for her to be admitted to St. Francis Hospital for a final diagnosis and for treatment under general anesthesia.

Before hospitalization insurance coverage would be afforded, her carrier required a second opinion, and she was referred by the insurance company to Dr. Pruitt. She went to his office and filled out an information sheet and told his receptionist that she was there for a second opinion. The receptionist initiated a patient's chart and indicated on it in two places that the patient was there for the purpose of a second opinion. Dr. Pruitt admitted that he did not read the chart and placed her on the examination table with feet in stirrups and proceeded not only to examine her so as to supply a second opinion but to perform the D & C. It was not completely satisfactory, and a supplemental D & C was required thereafter; it was performed by Dr. Murphy at the hospital under general anesthesia.

It is the testimony of the patient that she preferred not to have an abortion and if the same was to be performed, she wanted it to be performed by her own doctor rather than by the second opinion doctor whom she had never seen before.

She testified as follows:

Q. And Mrs. Tisdale, if Dr. Pruitt had fully informed you, and asked you for permission, or asked you for your consent to perform a D & C in his office that day, would you have given that consent?

A. No sir. No sir.

Q. Tell the jury why not?

A. I had known Dr. Pruitt for about fifteen minutes. I have known my doctor for over ten years, and I would never consent to have something that painful done in an office, whereas you could go to the hospital and be under general anesthesia, and be confident that everything is all right.

Dr. Pruitt does not with specificity testify as to exactly what he told the patient but says "* * * I explained everything to her * * *" He further testified relative to the patient's consent as follows:

Q. * * * [W]hat were the signals? What made you think that she agreed?

A. I don't know how you would even say. What are vibes? You know, you can sometimes sense hostility, sometimes you can sense grief. Sometimes you can sense disapproval or approval. I could well have missed—I obviously misread Mrs. Tisdale's vibes or signals, or things, but when someone is really upset, that's not hard to do.

Issues

While Dr. Pruitt filed thirteen exceptions as appear in the record, the gravamen of his appeal is found in his brief as follows:

* * * Accordingly, the main issue for the Court's decision is whether the evidence presented at trial was sufficient to sustain a verdict based on the doctrine of informed consent. In deciding this issue, the Court is asked to consider the essential elements of *informed consent,* whether the Plaintiff proved causation, and whether the damages awarded were proper. Additionally, the Court is also asked to decide whether consent to a medical procedure may be implied from the patient's conduct and silence, and whether the jury should have been so instructed.

Analysis

* * * Under the doctrine of informed consent, it is generally held that a physician who performs a diagnostic, therapeutic, or surgical procedure has a duty to disclose to a patient of sound mind, in the absence of an emergency that warrants immediate medical treatment, (1) the diagnosis, (2) the general nature of the contemplated procedure, (3) the material risks involved in the procedure, (4) the probability of success associated with the procedure, (5) the prognosis if the procedure is not carried out, and (6) the existence of any alternatives to the procedure.

In a letter (written by Dr. Pruitt to Dr. Murphy after the D & C had been performed) we think that Dr. Pruitt effectively pleads guilty to negligence, recklessness and willfulness. From that letter we quote:

> Again, let me say that I am most distressed that I did not realize Mrs. Tisdale was referred to the office by the Prudential Insurance Co. for a second opinion. Although my receptionist had put this on the chart, I did not notice it, and as I did not realize that D & C's required second opinions, the thought literally never occurred to me. I have been asked on

numerous occasions to give second opinions on hysterectomies and other procedures but never for D & C's, especially for missed abortions.

* * *

I do hope that you will pardon my "goof". I only wish Mrs. Tisdale at the time I was doing the procedure, had mentioned to me more clearly why she was sent to the office. If she did, it fell on deaf ears.

An analysis of Dr. Pruitt's testimony leaves much to be desired in the way of informing a patient of facts upon which an intelligent, informed consent can be made. * * * [W]e hold that the trial judge must be affirmed because of a lack of consent on the part of the patient. The circumstance under which Dr. Pruitt would have us find that the patient consented are relevant in determining whether or not the patient should have ordered Dr. Pruitt to stop what he was doing. She was in the office of a strange doctor recommended by the insurance company. She was greatly disturbed and was crying, experiencing pain. She was on the examining table with her feet in the stirrups. The procedure lasted about five minutes.

Dr. Pruitt's own testimony relative to her acquiescence is relevant. He relies mostly on her silence. He testified as follows:

* * * I just falsely assumed, or incorrectly assumed that this was what she was there for.

* * *

* * * Dewey, just for the record—and this may sound offensive, but I obviously, looking back, misread Mrs. Tisdale's feelings, but when I talked with her during the history taking, she very, very much wanted this pregnancy.

* * * She was just absolutely docile I guess, and I just assumed that she was acquiescing, but I thought I had her consent and her inform—very informed consent * * *

The argument of counsel that the evidence does not make at least a jury issue on whether damages were sustained and proximately caused by Dr. Pruitt's wrongful conduct is without merit. There is testimony that she suffered pain from the procedure without anesthesia; she was deprived of her right to choose the doctor to perform her D & C; in addition, she sustained emotional injury. Both actual and punitive damages are supported by the evidence. We hold that the evidence is not susceptible of the inference that the patient gave an informed consent, expressed or implied. Accordingly, the trial judge properly declined to charge the law of implied consent.

Affirmed.

Notes and Questions

1. The Tisdale court refused to imply consent by the plaintiff, given the context and her passivity. Given the doctor's admissions, the court went further and allowed punitive damages, even though the battery count had been dismissed. Might this kind of award increase a doctor's enthusiasm for conversation with his more quiet patients?

2. Punitive damages are typically awarded as part of the damage claims for an intentional tort such as battery. The focus is on the reprehensible nature of

defendant's conduct, which may be reckless or motivated by malice or fraud. Even gross negligence in a malpractice suit usually will not suffice. The circumstances surrounding a tortious act may however warrant an inference of a wilful or wanton attitude, or reckless disregard of the patient's wishes. In *Tisdale,* the physician's cavalier assumptions about the patient's consent, his lack of a conversation with her, and her obvious vulnerability, together constituted reckless behavior, justifying punitive damages. Battery theory normally applies when the surgery is completely unauthorized. Negligence covers situations where surgery was authorized but the consent was uninformed. Fraud and deceit in obtaining a patient's consent has always sounded in battery. The burden of proving fraudulent inducement is a heavy one. See Tonelli v. Khanna, 238 N.J.Super. 121, 569 A.2d 282 (1990) (plaintiff alleged that defendant surgeon rushed her into surgery for his own financial gain; no intentional tort found.) In *Perna,* the issue of physician deceit is explicitly discussed by the court as justification for the result. One advantage of the battery-based action in informed consent is the possibility of getting punitive damages, even where actual damages are small. Punitive damages have been criticized as unfair and out of control in tort litigation generally. In malpractice cases, courts are not willing to allow such damages except under extreme circumstances. Deceit and breach of fiduciary obligations by a physician are examples of causes of action that may justify such damages.

3. If a material fact is concealed with the intention to mislead a patient, fraud may be found, and the patient's consent to a procedure is vitiated. See Smith v. Wilfong, 218 Ga.App. 503, 462 S.E.2d 163 (1995) (plaintiff claimed that doctor misrepresented the extent of her kidney problem and alternative treatments; there was sufficient evidence to deny defendant's motion for summary judgment.)

For an excellent discussion of punitive damages generally, see Daniel Dobbs, Ending Punishment in "Punitive Damages": Deterrence–Measured Remedies, 40 Ala.L.Rev. 831 (1989).

4. In Strauss v. Biggs, 525 A.2d 992 (Del.Sup.1987), defendant surgeon began to operate on the plaintiff after having worked for sixteen hours straight prior to the surgery; he proposed a procedure that would give only partial relief, when he knew that another procedure would give complete relief, but he was incapable of performing it. He then failed to perform his proposed procedure, but neglected to tell the plaintiff, and continued with surgery after the plaintiff had screamed in pain on the first incision. He finally billed the insurer for procedures both unnecessary and not done. The court found these facts "compelling" for purposes of allowing the jury to find punitive damages. The case seems to add "greed" to "fraud" or "malice" as sufficient to establish physician conduct reprehensible enough for punitive damages.

E. EXCEPTIONS TO THE DUTY TO DISCLOSE

CANTERBURY v. SPENCE

United States Court of Appeals, District of Columbia Circuit, 1972.
464 F.2d 772.

VI

Two exceptions to the general rule of disclosure have been noted by the courts. Each is in the nature of a physician's privilege not to disclose, and the reasoning underlying them is appealing. Each, indeed, is but a recognition that, as important as is the patient's right to know, it is greatly outweighed by the magnitudinous circumstances giving rise to the privilege. The first comes into play when the patient is unconscious or otherwise incapable of consenting, and harm from a failure to treat is imminent and outweighs any harm threatened by the proposed treatment. When a genuine emergency of that sort arises, it is settled that the impracticality of conferring with the patient dispenses with need for it. Even in situations of that character the physician should, as current law requires, attempt to secure a relative's consent if possible. But if time is too short to accommodate discussion, obviously the physician should proceed with the treatment.

The second exception obtains when risk-disclosure poses such a threat of detriment to the patient as to become unfeasible or contraindicated from a medical point of view. It is recognized that patients occasionally become so ill or emotionally distraught on disclosure as to foreclose a rational decision, or complicate or hinder the treatment, or perhaps even pose psychological damage to the patient. Where that is so, the cases have generally held that the physician is armed with a privilege to keep the information from the patient, and we think it clear that portents of that type may justify the physician in action he deems medically warranted. The critical inquiry is whether the physician responded to a sound medical judgment that communication of the risk information would present a threat to the patient's well-being.

The physician's privilege to withhold information for therapeutic reasons must be carefully circumscribed, however, for otherwise it might devour the disclosure rule itself. The privilege does not accept the paternalistic notion that the physician may remain silent simply because divulgence might prompt the patient to forego therapy the physician feels the patient really needs. That attitude presumes instability or perversity for even the normal patient, and runs counter to the foundation principle that the patient should and ordinarily can make the choice for himself. Nor does the privilege contemplate operation save where the patient's reaction to risk information, as reasonably foreseen by the physician, is menacing. And even in a situation of that kind, disclosure to a close relative with a view to securing consent to the proposed treatment may be the only alternative open to the physician.

VIII

In the context of trial of a suit claiming inadequate disclosure of risk information by a physician, the patient has the burden of going forward with evidence tending to establish prima facie the essential elements of the cause of action, and ultimately the burden of proof—the risk of nonpersuasion—on those elements. These are normal impositions upon moving litigants, and no reason why they should not attach in nondisclosure cases is apparent. The burden of going forward with evidence pertaining to a privilege not to disclose, however, rests properly upon the physician. This is not only because the patient has made out a prima facie case before an issue on privilege is reached, but also because any evidence bearing on the privilege is usually in the hands of the physician alone. Requiring him to open the proof on privilege is consistent with judicial policy laying such a burden on the party who seeks shelter from an exception to a general rule and who is more likely to have possession of the facts.

Notes and Questions

1. The common law has long recognized the right of a doctor in a true emergency to act without patient consent, so long as he acts in conformity with customary practice in such emergencies. Jackovach v. Yocom, 212 Iowa 914, 237 N.W. 444 (1931). Some courts hold that consent is presumed in these situations. What constitutes an emergency situation is often unclear; the courts tend to err on the side of permitting arguable emergency treatment without formal consent.

An unconscious or incompetent patient cannot consent, and the physician may turn to a substitute decisionmaker such as a spouse or sibling. Even disorientation may be enough for most courts to allow such substitution. See King v. Our Lady of the Lake Regional Medical Center, 623 So.2d 139 (La.App. 1 Cir.1993).

2. Where the patient has consented to a procedure to remedy his condition, he is presumed to have consented to all steps necessary to correct it, even though the procedure in fact used varies from that authorized specifically. Kennedy v. Parrott, 243 N.C. 355, 90 S.E.2d 754 (1956). Does this make sense? If the alternative procedure is part of the repertoire of treatment for the patient's illness, then shouldn't the doctor have advised the patient of the possibility of this procedure as well as the intended one?

3. The most controversial privilege is the therapeutic privilege. Though this privilege is often discussed in dicta, it has not formed the basis for court rulings. *Canterbury* seems to have defined the privilege narrowly: information may be withheld in some situations, since "patients occasionally become so ill or emotionally distraught on disclosure as to foreclose a rational decision." The court used the word *menacing* to describe the patient reaction, but then it equivocated, suggesting that the privilege would be justified where disclosure would complicate or hinder treatment or pose psychological damage to the patient. Given physician unhappiness with requirements of disclosure generally, the therapeutic privilege exception threatens in theory to swallow the informed consent doctrine whole. See generally Margaret Somerville, "Therapeutic Privilege: Variation on the Theme of Informed Consent," 12 Law, Med. & Health Care 4 (1984). In analyzing risks to be disclosed, some courts talk of the need to avoid scaring a patient away from a "needed" procedure, recognizing the effect of disclosure of risks on the patient's choices. Pedersen v. Vahidy, 209 Conn. 510, 552 A.2d 419 (1989).

4. *Waiver.* Suppose a patient, trusting his doctor to do the best for him, says, "I don't want to know a thing, Doc, just do what you think is best". Should the doctor be able to use this as a defense? It appears that the patient is exercising self-determination in choosing a veil of ignorance. See, e.g., Henderson v. Milobsky, 595 F.2d 654 (D.C.Cir.1978). Alan Meisel, The "Exceptions" to the Informed Consent Doctrine: Striking a Balance Between Competing Values in Medical Decisionmaking, 1979 Wis.L.Rev. 413, 453–60. Should a patient's waiver be readily allowed, or should a duty to converse be imposed, even in the face of a waiver by the patient of his right to information? Should a patient be forced to listen to a full risk disclosure? If an informed consent form is the primary device for risk disclosure, the patient can choose not to read it as a way of avoidance. Should the patient be forced to read it? See Mark Strasser, "Mill and the Right to Remain Uninformed", 11 J.Med. & Philosophy 65 (1986); David E. Ost, The "Right" Not to Know, 9 J.Med. & Philosophy 301, 306–7 (1984).

5. *Statutory Limits.* More than half of the states have enacted legislation dealing with informed consent, largely in response to the "malpractice crisis" of

1974, or more recent perceived crises in their states. The statutes take a variety of forms, from specific to general, but they all share the common thread of moving the informed consent standard toward greater deference to medical judgment. Given the current state and national mood of legislative limitations on common law tort remedies, it may be expected that the common law of informed consent will continue to be affected by legislative action.

Problem: Whose Benefit Is It Anyway?

You represent Croziere Hospital, a small nonprofit hospital in Northeast Washington, D.C. The Chief of Surgery, Dr. Leaf, has just come into your office seeking your advice on a patient problem. A patient, Mrs. Jan Lee, was admitted to the hospital yesterday through the emergency room in the final stages of labor. She gave birth just an hour ago to a baby boy, healthy in all respects except that his right foot is a club foot. The staff surgeon can easily correct this anomaly now so that the child would be able to walk normally. Without surgery now, the risks of failure are progressively greater.

Mrs. Lee and her husband are Asian immigrants recently arrived in the United States. Dr. Leaf knows from past experience in the military in Asia that Asians from the Lee's area of Asia believe that birth defects are an expression of divine anger, punishing the parents for past misdeeds. The Lees are therefore likely to consider any attempts to correct their son's defects to be an insult to their gods. Dr. Leaf is afraid that if he talks with the Lees, they will refuse the surgery and leave the hospital immediately. They have not yet seen their son and are not aware of the club foot. Dr. Leaf would like to operate on the boy without their permission immediately, given what he sees as the clear benefits of an operation now.

What do you advise him to do, in light of informed consent doctrine and its privileges and exceptions?

IV. INFORMED CONSENT: THE INSTITUTION'S OBLIGATION

Consent forms are universally used in institutions, where most health care is provided. Hospitals use them at several points in a patient's progress through the institution—upon admission, when a generic form is signed; and before surgery or anesthesia, when more detailed forms may be offered. These forms have to operate as a legal surrogate for consent, sometimes memorializing an actual physician-patient discussion, sometimes acting simply as a fiction. The courts have had little to say about consent forms.

A consent form, or other written documentation of the patient's verbal consent, is treated in many states as presumptively valid consent to the treatment at issue, with the burden on the patient to rebut the presumption. See West's Florida Statutes Ann. § 766.103(4); Official Code Georgia Ann. § 88–2906.1(b)(2); Idaho Code § 39–4305; Iowa Code Ann. § 147.137; LSA–R.S. 24, Tit. 40, § 1299.40.A; Maine Revised Statutes Ann. § 2905.2; Nevada Revised Statutes § 41A/110; North Carolina G.S., § 90–21.13(b); Ohio Revised Code § 2317.54; Vernon's Ann.Texas Revised Civil Statutes, Art. 4590i, § 6.06; Utah Code Ann. § 78–14–5(2)(e); West's Washington Revised Code Ann. § 7.70.060.

Institutional responsibility to ensure that a patient's informed consent is obtained exists only in two limited areas: documentation of patient consent for the record, and experimental therapies. If a nurse fails to obtain a properly executed consent form and make it part of the patient record, the hospital may be liable for this failure as a violation of its own internal procedures. See, e.g., Butler v. South Fulton Medical Center, Inc., 215 Ga.App. 809, 452 S.E.2d 768, 772 (1994). If a hospital participates in a study of an experimental procedure, it must ensure that the patient is properly informed of the risks of the procedure. See Kus v. Sherman Hospital, 268 Ill.App.3d 771, 206 Ill.Dec. 161, 644 N.E.2d 1214 (1995) (hospital was part of a research study on intraocular lens implantation; the court held that " . . . a hospital, as well as a physician, may be held liable for a patient's defective consent in a case involving experimental intraocular lenses . . .")

Does the hospital have a duty to see that a patient's informed consent to surgery by a nonemployee attending physician is properly obtained? In Petriello v. Kalman, 215 Conn. 377, 576 A.2d 474 (1990), the Connecticut Supreme Court held that a hospital had no duty to obtain a patient's consent to surgery, nor to conduct any kind of inquiry into the quality of the plaintiff's consent. The plaintiff had suffered a miscarriage, and the treating physician scheduled the plaintiff for a dilation and curettage to remove the fetus. A hospital nurse medicated the plaintiff before the procedure, without getting the plaintiff's signature on the consent form. This violated a hospital policy requiring completion of such forms.

The court held that the responsibility lay with the attending physician, rejecting the plaintiff's claims that the hospital had a duty to get her signature on the form: "This contention is unsound, however, because it equates the signing of the form with the actuality of informed consent, which it is the sole responsibility of the attending physician to obtain." 576 A.2d at 478. Most other jurisdictions have agreed with Petriello. See e.g. Johnson v. Sears, Roebuck and Co., 113 N.M. 736, 832 P.2d 797 (App.1992), cert. denied 113 N.M. 744, 832 P.2d 1223 (1992); Goss v. Oklahoma Blood Inst., 856 P.2d 998 (Okla.Ct.App.1990); Howell v. Spokane & Inland Empire Blood Bank, 114 Wash.2d 42, 785 P.2d 815 (1990) (rejecting appellant's "corporate negligence" claim); Kershaw v. Reichert, 445 N.W.2d 16 (N.D.1989); Krane v. St. Anthony Hosp. Systems, 738 P.2d 75 (Colo.App.1987) (hospital assumes no duty by adopting standardized consent form). But see Magana v. Elie, 108 Ill.App.3d 1028, 64 Ill.Dec. 511, 439 N.E.2d 1319 (1982) (hospital has duty to obtain patient's informed consent).

The law of informed consent is highly variable, and at the same time it lacks specificity as a guide to physicians. One commentator has proposed that explicit contracts between providers and patient groups might better serve the doctrine, allowing specific guidelines to be developed by agreement. This would allow the law to be tailor-made to the different settings in which risks arise, contextualizing consent. Contextualization would advance the aim of cost-effectiveness and would also be desirable in its own right. Each goal seeks to improve the informed consent dialogue, and the doctrine that regulates it, by tailoring the law's requirements more carefully to the different settings in which risks arise and are discussed, assessed, and acted upon. Peter H. Schuck, Rethinking Informed Consent, 103 Yale L.J. 899, 906 (1994).

What might be the effect of imposing a duty on the hospital and its staff to ensure that patient consent is properly obtained by attending physicians? Might the hospital not work harder to make sure that consent is properly obtained? Or is deference to physicians too much a part of the hospital-physician relationship? Would it make any difference to the reality of patient consent? See Catherine Jones, Autonomy and Informed Consent in Medical Decisionmaking: Toward a New Self–Fulfilling Prophecy, 47 Wash. & Lee. L.Rev. 379, 429 (1990).

A study by Charles W. Lidz et al., Informed Consent: A Study of Decisionmaking in

Psychiatry 318, 326 (1985) concluded that informed consent forms were not important in the decisionmaking process: they were presented too late, were too complex, were unread by the patients before signed, and were treated by both staff and patients as simply a ritual for confirming a decision already made. How can such forms be improved, so that they will facilitate doctor-patient conversation and risk disclosure?

Problem: Forcing Conversation

You have recently gone to work for the assistant administrator of the Health Care Financing Administration (HCFA) of the Department of Health and Human Services. HCFA is responsible for the Medicare program, which pays physicians for medical services they provide to elderly patients who are Medicare-eligible.

Your superior, Dr. Tuff, has two concerns. First, he is concerned that too many Medicare patients are being treated without much discussion by physicians of the risks of treatment or nontreatment. He reasons that this is due in part to physician attempts to impose their own treatment preferences on patients, thereby maximizing their reimbursement, wherever possible, while also spending as little time as possible with each patient. The proliferation of Medicare HMOs also concerns him, because of the risk of undertreatment by physicians to increase their bonuses. He would like to use informed consent doctrine as a way of gaining further control over the costs of health care, while also giving the elderly a better level of control over their treatments.

Second, he is worried about the salary incentives that many Medicare HMOs use to promote cost-effective practices in their physicians. He fears that such salary incentives, combined with the aversion some physicians already have to treating the demanding and complex health problems of the elderly, will promote undertreatment.

He asks that you consider the following recommendation, to be incorporated into Medicare requirements:

> No Medicare payments for treatments rendered by either individual or institutional health care providers shall be made absent proof that the claimed medical service was consented to by the patient or a suitable surrogate decision maker in a voluntary, competent, and informed manner, or that the risks of nontreatment were fully and completely explained.
>
> Any physician treating a Medicare patient must fully disclose to that patient in advance of treatment all details of his or her salary compensation, including the types of incentive arrangement chosen.

What problems do you foresee with this proposal? What standards for disclosure do you suggest? What modes of proof that consent was obtained? What weight should be given the proof?

Managed care organizations are currently required to provide information on the incentive arrangements affecting an MCO's physicians to any person receiving Medicare or Medicaid benefits who requests the information. Suggested language is found at the Web site of the Health Care Financing Administration, at *http://www.hcfa.gov/medicare/physincp/beneinfo.htm.*

See generally Marshall Kapp, "Enforcing Patient Preferences: Linking Payment for Medical Care to Informed Consent," 261 J.A.M.A. 1935, 1936 (1989). For a critical response to Kapp's proposal, see Ruth Faden, Editorial: Enforcing Informed Consent Requirements: Form or Substance? 261 J.A.M.A. 1948 (1989).

Chapter 6

LIABILITY OF HEALTH CARE INSTITUTIONS

INTRODUCTION

The modern hospital—with its operating theaters, stainless steel equipment, and its large staffs of nurses, doctors, and support personnel—has come to symbolize the delivery of medical care. It was not always so. For centuries, in Europe and in America, hospitals tended the sick and the insane but made no attempt to treat or cure. They were supported by the philanthropy of the wealthy and by religious groups. In the 1870's it could be said that only a small minority of doctors practiced in hospitals, and even they devoted only a small portion of their practice to such work. A person seeking medical care before 1900 did not consider hospitalization, since doctors made house calls and even operated in the home. By the late 1800's, however, developments in medical knowledge moved the hospital toward a central position in health care. The development of antiseptic and aseptic techniques reduced the previously substantial risk of infection within hospitals; the growing scientific content of medicine made hospitals a more attractive place for medical practice.

Therapeutic and diagnostic improvements became identified with hospital doctors. These doctors, the product of the modernization of medicine, discovered that the hospital was well suited to their practice needs. Control over the hospital began to shift from the trustees to the doctors during the early 1900's. As the hospital evolved, physicians became increasingly dependent upon hospital affiliation. By the 1970s, no doctor would consider practicing without the resources that a hospital offered, and 25 percent of active physicians practiced fulltime in a hospital. Today health care delivery has shifted again, from the hospital setting to outpatient settings for many kinds of surgery. The American hospital is moving from the hub of the health care delivery system to a satellite. For an excellent extended discussion of the history of the hospital, see Paul Starr, The Social Transformation of American Medicine (1982), particularly Chapter 4.

Traditionally, the relationship of doctor to hospital was one of independent contractor rather than employee. The hospital was therefore not regularly targeted as a defendant in a malpractice suit. Only if the doctor whose negligence injured a patient was an employee could the hospital be reached through the doctrine of vicarious liability. The hospital was independently liable only if it were negligent in its administrative or housekeeping functions, for example causing a patient to slip and fall on a wet floor. Otherwise, the hospital was often immune from liability.

I. FROM IMMUNITY TO VICARIOUS LIABILITY

A. CHARITABLE AND OTHER IMMUNITIES

Until recently hospitals have been considered as charitable institutions, as such exempted from the general rule that a corporation is responsible for the acts of its employees. The doctrine of charitable immunity protected hospitals from liability in any form through the 1940's. In the 1950's, however, courts began to observe the increasing importance of the hospital in providing health care and supervising their staffs.

BING v. THUNIG

Supreme Court of New York, 1957.
2 N.Y.2d 656, 163 N.Y.S.2d 3, 143 N.E.2d 3.

The doctrine declaring charitable institutions immune from liability was first declared in this country in 1876. McDonald v. Massachusetts Gen. Hosp., 120 Mass. 432. Deciding that a charity patient, negligently operated upon by a student doctor, could not hold the hospital responsible, the court reasoned that the public and private donations that supported the charitable hospital constituted a trust fund which could not be diverted. * * * The second reason which the court advanced was that the principle of *respondeat superior* was not to be applied to doctors and nurses. It was the court's thought that, even though employed by the hospital, they were to be regarded as independent contractors rather than employees because of the skill they exercised and the lack of control exerted over their work—and yet, we pause again to interpolate, the special skill of other employees (such as airplane pilots, locomotive engineers, chemists, to mention but a few) has never been the basis for denying the application of *respondeat superior* and, even more to the point, that very principle has been invoked to render a public hospital accountable for the negligence of its doctors, nurses and other skilled personnel. [ ]

Nor may the exemption be justified by the fear, the major impetus originally behind the doctrine, that the imposition of liability will do irreparable harm to the charitable hospital. At the time the rule originated, in the middle of the nineteenth century, not only was there the possibility that a substantial award in a single negligence action might destroy the hospital, but concern was felt that a ruling permitting recovery against the funds of charitable institutions might discourage generosity and "constrain * * * [them], as a measure of self-protection, to limit their activities." Schloendorff v. New York Hosp., supra, 211 N.Y. 125, 135, 105 N.E. 92, 95, 52 L.R.A.,N.S., 505. Whatever problems today beset the charitable hospital, and they are not to be minimized, the dangers just noted have become less acute. Quite apart from the availability of insurance to protect against possible claims and lawsuits, we are not informed that undue hardships or calamities have overtaken them in those jurisdictions where immunity is withheld and liability imposed. * * * In any event, today's hospital is quite different from its predecessor of long ago; it receives wide community support, employs a large number of people and necessarily operates its plant in businesslike fashion.

The conception that the hospital does not undertake to treat the patient, does not undertake to act through its doctors and nurses, but undertakes instead simply to procure them to act upon their own responsibility, no longer reflects the fact. Present-day hospitals, as their manner of operation plainly demonstrates, do far more than furnish facilities for treatment. They regularly employ on a salary basis a large staff of physicians, nurses and interns, as well as administrative and manual workers, and they charge patients for medical care and treatment, collecting for such services, if necessary, by legal action. Certainly, the person who avails himself of "hospital facilities" expects that the hospital will attempt to cure him, not that its nurses or other employees will act on their own responsibility.

Hospitals should, in short, shoulder the responsibilities borne by everyone else. There is no reason to continue their exemption from the universal rule of *respondeat superior*. The test should be, for these institutions, whether charitable or profit-making, as it is for every other employer, was the person who committed the negligent injury-producing act one of its employees and, if he was, was he acting within the scope of his employment.

The rule of nonliability is out of tune with the life about us, at variance with modern day needs and with concepts of justice and fair dealing. * * *

In sum, then, the doctrine according the hospital an immunity for the negligence of its employees is such a rule, and we abandon it. The hospital's liability must be governed by the same principles of law as apply to all other employers.

The judgment of the Appellate Division should be reversed and a new trial granted, with costs to abide the event.

* * *

Note: Elimination of Immunity

Most hospitals prior to 1940 were protected from suit either by charitable or governmental immunity. The reasons were related to hospital difficulties in obtaining liability insurance and the fiscal fragility of many hospitals in a time before extensive government financing of health care.

The trend over the past few decades in the states have been to abolish charitable immunity. The charitable immunity doctrine disappeared with remarkable speed from American law. Prior to 1942, some form of immunity was recognized by most American jurisdictions. The case of President and Directors of Georgetown College v. Hughes, 130 F.2d 810 (D.C.Cir.1942) was a watershed case eliminating immunity. Since that case, a clear majority of jurisdictions have abrogated charitable immunity, while the remainder retain immunity to the extent of statutory ceilings on recoverable damages, or only up to available insurance coverage, or as to charity care. See Etheridge v. Medical Center Hospitals, 237 Va. 87, 376 S.E.2d 525 (Va.1989)(upholding Virginia $1 million cap on recovery in a malpractice judgment for a single incident); Pulliam v. Coastal Emergency Services of Richmond, Inc., 257 Va. 1, 509 S.E.2d 307 (Va. 1999); Daniel v. Jones, 39 F.Supp.2d 635 (E.D.Va.1999); Cutts v. Fulton–DeKalb Hosp. Auth., 192 Ga.App. 517, 385 S.E.2d 436 (Ga.App.1989).

Governmental immunity has proved more resistant to elimination by the courts. State courts have split on governmental immunity, with some eliminating it, others leaving it to the legislatures, and others retaining immunity in various forms. The Federal Tort Claims Act (FTCA), 28 U.S.C.A. §§ 1346(b) and 2671–2680, defines the extent to which the Federal government can be sued. Section 2680 provides for an exception to the Federal government's waiver of immunity for claims based upon "the exercise or performance or the failure to exercise or perform a discretionary function or duty on the part of a federal agency or an employee of the Government, whether or not the discretion involved be abused." Several states have adopted acts similar to the FTCA, and "discretionary" has been narrowly construed by both the federal courts and state courts to cover primarily policy making of a broad sort. See Hyde v. University of Mich. Board of Regents, 426 Mich. 223, 393 N.W.2d 847 (1986), granting immunity to state hospitals. Municipal and county immunity has likewise seen erosion by the courts.

Judicial and legislative actions have left most hospitals responsible for the torts of their employees, including doctors. Principles of vicarious liability became applicable to health care institutions once charitable and governmental immunities were abrogated. A master-servant relationship, a partnership, or a joint venture could lead to liability. The hospital came to be viewed as an enterprise liable for the acts of its employees, and the physician became liable for the acts of her employees, a partner, or another physician working jointly with her.

B. VICARIOUS LIABILITY DOCTRINE

1. The Captain of the Ship Doctrine

The Captain of the Ship doctrine provides that a physician who exercises control and authority over nurses and other health care professionals should be held liable for their negligence. It is a harsher version of the "borrowed servant" doctrine, which provides that a surgeon borrows nurses or support personnel during surgery. In the typical case, the surgeon is held responsible for an error in a sponge count done by the nursing staff after surgery, even though the surgeon does not participate in such sponge counts. See Johnston v. Southwest Louisiana Ass'n, 693 So.2d 1195 (La.App.1997) (surgeon had nondelegable duty to remove sponges from patient's body). If the surgeon is held liable, of course, the hospital will not be, since the nurses are considered to have been "borrowed" by the physician, so that temporarily the hospital is not vicariously liable for their errors. See Restatement (Second) of Agency § 227.

The Captain of the Ship doctrine is a special application of this agency rule of borrowed servant in the medical context, on the theory that the surgeon is in complete control of the operating room. It is a strict liability theory, often predicated on the surgeon's "right to control", rather than actual control. As the court noted in Truhitte v. French Hospital, 128 Cal.App.3d 332, 348, 180 Cal.Rptr. 152, 160 (1982), "* * * the 'captain of the ship' doctrine arose from the need to assure plaintiffs a source of recovery for malpractice at a time when many hospitals enjoyed charitable immunity." See Stephen H. Price, The Sinking of the "Captain of the Ship": Reexamining the Vicarious Liability of an Operating Surgeon for the Negligence of Assisting Hospital Personnel, 10 J.Leg.Med. 323 (1989).

2. *Stretching Vicarious Liability Doctrine*

Hospitals continued through the sixties to be protected from most litigation for patient injuries by a treating physician, even though charitable immunity was abrogated, since most doctors were independent contractors. The courts then began to articulate doctrines to give the plaintiff a possible defendant, where the hospital had immunity or where vicarious liability would not work. Thus the "borrowed servant" rule and the "Captain of the Ship" doctrine placed the doctor in the position of responsibility in some specialized situations.

In the last four decades the courts have begun to grapple with the independent doctor's connection to the institution, using a number of doctrines to circumvent vicarious liability limitations.

a. The General Rule

SCHLOTFELDT v. CHARTER HOSPITAL OF LAS VEGAS

Supreme Court of Nevada, 1996.
112 Nev. 42, 910 P.2d 271.

YOUNG, JUSTICE:

On Saturday, March 4, 1989, appellant/cross-respondent Debra Schlotfeldt ("Schlotfeldt") presented herself to respondent/cross-appellant Charter Hospital of Las Vegas, a Nevada corporation ("Charter") that specializes in the treatment of alcoholism and drug addiction. Charter personnel observed that Schlotfeldt was extremely depressed and displayed rapid changes in her emotions. Schlotfeldt admitted at trial that she had abused alcohol and ingested methamphetamine prior to her admission to Charter. Schlotfeldt stated during a psychiatric examination that she gambled out of control when under the influence of drugs, was depressed for over a year and a half, and had thoughts of suicide. In a statement revealing the depth of Schlotfeldt's emotional difficulties, Schlotfeldt told Charter staff that "I don't trust myself," "I feel like I'm going crazy," and "I feel like I am at the end of my rope." After this conversation, Schlotfeldt went home to retrieve personal belongings. Escorted by her husband, Schlotfeldt returned to Charter and signed documents requesting voluntary admission and authorizing such care and treatment as ordered by her attending physician.

A Charter psychiatrist prepared an admitting diagnosis of Schlotfeldt that concluded she suffered from major depression and suicidal ideation. Anil Batra, M.D., also examined Schlotfeldt and diagnosed a major depressive disorder. On Sunday morning, March 5, 1989, Gilles M.K. Desmarais, M.D. ("Desmarais") examined Schlotfeldt. According to Charter, Desmarais was an independent doctor who was not assigned by Charter to Schlotfeldt. Instead, Desmarais attended to Schlotfeldt at the request of a Charter psychiatrist who was busy with other patients. Desmarais' examination revealed that Schlotfeldt had marital problems that led to alcohol abuse, drug use and compulsive gambling. Desmarais concluded that Schlotfeldt was a suicide risk because her severe depression of one and a half years was nearing a pinnacle.

Schlotfeldt argues that she made repeated requests to return home after the morning of March 5, 1989. Charter admits that Schlotfeldt requested to return home, but claims that because she was a suicide risk and her husband was out of town, releasing her at the time was imprudent. Desmarais urged her to stay voluntarily until her husband returned. Eventually, Desmarais allowed Schlotfeldt to leave because the effects of the drugs had worn off, she was no longer a suicide risk, and her husband had returned. Schlotfeldt spent a total of sixty-six hours at Charter.

Eighteen months later, Schlotfeldt filed suit against Charter and Desmarais. Schlotfeldt's initial complaint contained numerous claims for relief. However, all claims except the false imprisonment claim were withdrawn prior to trial. Schlotfeldt claimed she was admitted to Charter against her will and that she requested to leave Charter, but Charter and Desmarais continued to hold her against her will. Charter claimed that Schlotfeldt admitted herself voluntarily and it was obligated to urge her to remain until she was no longer a danger to herself or others. The district court excluded evidence showing Schlotfeldt was hospitalized for her psychiatric condition on multiple occasions after her stay at the Charter facility. Also, the district court found, as a matter of law, that Charter was vicariously liable for the acts of Desmarais. At the conclusion of trial, a jury found Charter and Desmarais liable for false imprisonment and awarded Schlotfeldt $50,000.00 in compensatory damages. After the district court entered a second amended judgment on the jury's verdict, Schlotfeldt and Charter appealed.

Discussion

* * *

Agency Relationship

The district court instructed the jury that Charter was vicariously liable, as a matter of law, for the acts of Desmarais.[2] Based on the ostensible agency theory, the district court found that Charter should be held liable for the acts of Desmarais because he was chosen by Charter to examine Schlotfeldt. Charter opposed the instruction because it claimed an issue of fact existed as to whether an agency relationship existed between Charter and Desmarais. The district court's instruction, according to Charter, was improper and materially prejudiced its position by binding its liability to the improper acts of Desmarais.

The existence of an agency relationship is generally a question of fact for the jury if the facts showing the existence of agency are disputed, or if conflicting inferences can be drawn from the facts. [ ] A question of law exists as to whether sufficient competent evidence is present to require that the agency question be forwarded to a jury. [ ]

* * *

Medical malpractice cases also serve as a guide for establishing the presence of agency between a doctor and hospital and evoking vicarious liability. Those cases have found that absent an employment relationship, a

2. The district court instructed the jury as follows:

The law holds an employer responsible for the acts of his employees while acting in the course of their employment. The law also holds a principal liable for the acts of its agent. Therefore, defendant Charter Hospital is legally responsible for the acts and omissions of all its employees and the acts or omissions of defendant Dr. Desmarais.

doctor's mere affiliation with a hospital is not sufficient to hold a hospital vicariously liable for the doctor's negligent conduct. [ ] A physician or surgeon who is on a hospital's staff is not necessarily an employee of the hospital, and the hospital is not necessarily liable for his tortious acts. [ ] A hospital does not generally expose itself to vicarious liability for a doctor's actions by merely extending staff privileges to that doctor. [ ] Further, evidence that a doctor maintains a private practice may tend to dispel any claim of an agency relationship between a doctor and a hospital.

The evidence admitted in this case on the issue of agency was limited. Desmarais testified that he was not an employee of Charter but had staff privileges. Desmarais also testified that he was covering for another doctor the night Schlotfeldt was admitted to Charter. Charter's administrator stated that Desmarais only had staff privileges at Charter and was covering for another Charter doctor during the period in question. Also, evidence indicated that Desmarais may have maintained an independent practice because he billed Schlotfeldt separately for the services he rendered at Charter. Other than the fact that Desmarais went to Schlotfeldt's room to conduct a medical examination, no evidence was presented to show an employment or agency relationship existed between Charter and Desmarais.

* * *

Charter presented evidence suggesting that no employment relationship existed with Desmarais, that Desmarais merely had staff privileges, and that Desmarais operated a private practice. This evidence was sufficiently competent to raise a question of fact for the jury regarding the existence of agency. Further, the district court's use of the ostensible agency theory to find agency as a matter of law was improper because application of the theory required a determination of numerous issues of fact. Accordingly, the jury should have decided the agency issue. Because Charter was materially prejudiced by having its liability linked to the acts of Desmarais, the district court committed reversible error.

CONCLUSION

In considering this case, it is not necessary to resolve the issues raised by Schlotfeldt on appeal. The district court erred by excluding essential evidence and concluding as a matter of law that an agency relationship was present. Accordingly, the district court's judgment against Charter is reversed and this matter is remanded for a new trial.

Notes and Questions

1. The hospital-physician relationship is an unusual one. A typical hospital may have several categories of practicing physicians, but the largest group is comprised of private physicians with staff privileges. Staff privileges include the right of the physicians to admit and discharge their private patients to the hospital and the right to use the hospital's facilities.

The organized medical staff of a hospital, private physicians with privileges, governs the hospital's provision of medical services. The typical medical staff operates under its own bylaws, elects its own officers, and appoints its own committees. It is not simply another administrative component of the hospital, and is subject to only limited authority of the governing board of the hospital. While the hospital board must approve the staff's bylaws and can approve or disapprove particular staff actions, it cannot usually discipline individual physicians directly or appoint administrative officers to exercise direct authority. A hospital's medical staff is therefore a powerful body within the larger organization. See generally Clark C. Havighurst, Doctors and Hospitals: An Antitrust Perspective on Traditional Relationships, 1984 Duke L.J. 1071, 1084–92.

2. What explains this curious structure, where two parallel structures exist side-by-side, with nurses and other allied health professionals operating as hospital employees subject to master-servant rules, and the medical staff operating relatively autonomously as independent contractors? The professional status and power of physicians? See generally Charles E. Rosenberg, The Care of Strangers: The Rise of America's Hospital System 66–68, 262–267 (1987).

b. The Control Test

BEREL v. HCA HEALTH SERVICES OF TEXAS, INC.

Court of Appeals of Texas, 1994.
881 S.W.2d 21.

[Plaintiffs consulted Dr. Robinson in her professional capacity as a psychiatrist. Dr. Robinson recommended that Kristy and Jake Berel, and Beverly Berel and her children Kelly and Brian, be hospitalized in Houston International Hospital for treatment of alleged emotional disturbances. The plaintiffs claimed that Dr. Robinson, as an agent of the hospital, was negligent in admitting them to the hospital on the basis of insufficient observation; recommending inpatient treatment; and negligently treating them. They further alleged that the hospital was negligent because it should have known of the malpractice committed by its agent, Dr. Robinson, and because it did not properly supervise and regulate her. The trial court granted the hospital's motion for summary judgment, in part on the grounds that Dr. Robinson was an independent contractor, and that the hospital had no right to control the details of her medical practice.

The Court of Appeals noted that independent contractor physicians normally transmit no liability to the hospital, but then continued:]

> If, however, a hospital retains the right to control the details of the work to be performed by a contracting party, a master-servant relationship exists that will authorize the application of the doctrine of respondeat superior.[ ] It is the right of control, not actual control, that gives rise to a duty to see that the independent contractor performs his work in a safe manner. [ ] . . .
>
> * * *
>
> The plaintiffs rely on Dr. Robinson's deposition testimony. She testified that the hospital's staff included a "quality assurance person" who "reviewed charts to . . . assure appropriate patient care." The plaintiffs' trial counsel asked Dr. Robinson additional questions regarding the quality assurance person: Q. If that quality assurance person felt like that there had been an over utilization or an under utilization, what would they do? A. As far as I can recall that person would discuss that with the

doctor and also would—would write those recommendations up in a particular form as—as best of my recall and we present that to the particular doctor who's treating the patient and could also possibly—feeling that needed further information or clarification or whatever—talk with the medical director and also possibly the medical director of the—of the hospital and also possibly the utilization review committee. Q. Could the utilization review committee and the medical director of the hospital override the admitting physician's orders? A. Yes. Q. Okay. Did the utilization review committee and the medical director have authority to discharge a patient that they thought was—had been admitted or did not need the services of Houston International Hospital? A. The medical director of the utilization review committee as far as my recall, there were appropriate procedures if they felt that the patient was not being administered appropriate treatment and needed—needed to—which would be if the patient did not need to be there, they could have overruled the admitting physician's order. Q. And have the patient discharged? A. If that was what was indicated that was needed.

We agree with the plaintiffs that Dr. Robinson's own testimony raises a fact question regarding whether the hospital maintained control over Dr. Robinson's treatment to a degree that would make the hospital liable for her negligent acts. We sustain this point of error.

Notes and Questions

1. What are the implications of the *Berel* decision? Does the court mean that a physician's independent contractor status no longer provides a shield for a hospital or a managed care organization, since such institutions now have utilization review and quality assurance activities that exercise substantial oversight over physicians? If this is so, then the more intensive the utilization review, the more control exercised under agency principles. This is a real Catch–22 for the institution.

2. The first approach to determining an agency relationship is to test whether the doctor was an employee or subject to the control of the hospital, applying a number of standard criteria for evaluating the existence of a master-servant relationship. If the contract gave the hospital substantial control over the doctor's choice of patients or if the hospital furnished equipment, then an employee relationship might be found. The caselaw reflects divergent applications of the "control" test, because of the breadth of the factors involved. See Mduba v. Benedictine Hospital, 52 A.D.2d 450, 384 N.Y.S.2d 527 (3d Dept.1976) (doctor failed to give blood to patient, resulting in his death; hospital, in the contract with doctor, had guaranteed doctor's salary and controlled his activities. Held: doctor is an employee); Kober v. Stewart, 148 Mont. 117, 417 P.2d 476 (1966) (contract establishes the method by which hospital hired a doctor as supervisor).

c. The "Ostensible Agency" Test

Some courts have held that in settings such as the emergency room or the radiology labs, the hospital holds itself out as offering services to the patient through a doctor, even though the doctor who renders the service is not an employee. The following case illustrates a modern application of this test to a contemporary contractual relationship between a hospital and a physician.

SWORD v. NKC HOSPITALS, INC.

Supreme Court of Indiana, 1999.
714 N.E.2d 142.

SELBY, J.

* * *

FACTS

The facts taken in the light most favorable to the non-moving party are as follows. Diana Sword lives in southern Indiana. On April 24, 1991, Diana Sword and her husband entered Norton in Louisville, Kentucky for the delivery of their first child. Prior to entering the hospital, Sword consulted with her obstetrician about whether or not to deliver with the help of an anesthetic. Her obstetrician recommended using an epidural; he told Sword that the epidural procedure would numb her from the waist down, and that he used them frequently. Sword decided to have an epidural. She, however, did not know in advance who would administer the epidural.

Sword also made arrangements to go to Norton through her obstetrician's office. Norton aggressively marketed its services to the public. It stated in brochures that its Women's Pavilion is "the most technically sophisticated birthplace in the region." (R. at 228.) Norton also advertised that it offers:

> [I]nstant access to the specialized equipment and facilities, as well as to physician specialists in every area of pediatric medicine and surgery. Every maternity patient has a private room and the full availability of a special anesthesiology team, experienced and dedicated exclusively to OB patients.

Id. (emphasis added). One brochure stated that:

> The Women's Pavilion medical staff includes the only physicians in the region who specialize exclusively in obstetrical anesthesiology. They are immediately available within the unit 24 hours a day and are experts in administering continuous epidural anesthesia.

(R. at 232.) (emphasis added).

At some point during her labor, an anesthesiologist came into Sword's room. He explained the epidural procedure and how it would make her feel. He told her that he would stick the tubing for the epidural in her lower back and then she would feel numbness from the waist down. As the anesthesiologist was preparing to begin the procedure, he was called out of the room.

Five to ten minutes later, a second anesthesiologist, Dr. Luna, came into Sword's room to administer the epidural. The parties do not dispute that Dr. Luna practiced medicine at Norton as an independent contractor. After verifying that the previous anesthesiologist had explained the procedure to Sword, Dr. Luna began the epidural procedure. As Sword sat on the bed and leaned forward, Dr. Luna began inserting the epidural tubing. Dr. Luna first inserted the tubing near the top of Sword's neck. Shortly thereafter, Dr. Luna removed the epidural tubing "because it did not take" and then reinserted it in Sword's lower back. (R. at 181–82.)

Soon after the delivery of her healthy baby, Sword began to have headaches which recur every four to six weeks. When the headaches occur, Sword is very sensitive to light and sound. In addition to the headaches, she also feels a numbness in her back where the second epidural was administered. Sword alleges that these symptoms are a result of Dr. Luna's negligent placement of the epidural tubing and that Norton is liable.

* * *

III. Apparent or Ostensible Agency

The principal issue in this case is whether, under Indiana law, Norton can be held liable for the alleged negligence of an independent contractor anesthesiologist. Sword is seeking to hold Norton liable for the alleged negligence which caused her injuries. There are no allegations of direct corporate negligence, that is, that the hospital itself was negligent. Because the alleged negligence was not committed by Norton, but instead by a physician working at Norton, Sword must present a theory by which a court can find the hospital vicariously liable for the actions of a physician who practices there. After reviewing the basic tort and agency concepts relevant to theories of vicarious liability, as well as the jurisprudence in Indiana and other jurisdictions, in the specific context of this case, we adopt the theory of apparent and ostensible agency formulated in the Restatement (Second) of Torts section 429 (1965). We then conclude that there are genuine issues of material fact in dispute as to the existence of an apparent or ostensible agency relationship here.

A. Vicarious Liability

Vicarious liability is "indirect legal responsibility." BLACK'S LAW DICTIONARY 1404 (5th ed.1979). It is a legal fiction by which a court can hold a party legally responsible for the negligence of another, not because the party did anything wrong but rather because of the party's relationship to the wrongdoer. See KEETON, TORTS § 69. Courts employ various legal doctrines to hold people vicariously liable, including respondeat superior, apparent or ostensible agency, agency by estoppel,[3] and the non-delegable duty doctrine.[4] Some doctrines are based in tort law, some are based in agency law. Courts often discuss the various doctrines as if they are interchangeable; they are not. We will address each applicable doctrine in turn.

3. Courts holding hospitals liable under an agency theory often interchangeably describe the theory as "apparent agency" and "agency by estoppel." See Martin C. McWilliams, Jr. & Hamilton E. Russell, III, Hospital Liability for Torts of Independent Contractor Physicians, 47 S.C.L.REV. 431, 445–46 n. 76 (1996); Diane M. Janulis & Alan D. Hornstein, Damned if You Do, Damned if You Don't: Hospitals' Liability for Physicians' Malpractice, 64 NEB. L.REV. 689, 696 (1985). The distinction, if any, is that agency by estoppel requires both reliance and a change in position. Restatement (Second) of Agency § 8 cmt. d. [ ]

4. While a master is generally not liable for the negligence of an independent contractor, the master may be liable if the independent contractor was performing a non-delegable duty.[ ] A non-delegable duty is one that public policy holds to be so important that one party should not be permitted to transfer the duty (and its resultant liability) to another party.[ ] Sword argues that Norton had a non-delegable duty to provide anesthesiological care because such care is essential and the patient has no choice in the anesthesiologist who provides this care. Given our resolution of the apparent or ostensible agency issue, we need not address the concept of non-delegable duty in this opinion.

Respondeat superior is the applicable tort theory of vicarious liability. Under respondeat superior, an employer, who is not liable because of his own acts, can be held liable "for the wrongful acts of his employee which are committed within the scope of employment." Stropes v. Heritage House Childrens Ctr., 547 N.E.2d 244, 247 (Ind.1989); see also KEETON, TORTS §§ 69, 70; WARREN A. SEAVEY, AGENCY § 83 (1964). In this context, "employer" and "employee" are often stated in broader terms as "master" and "servant." [ ]

One important aspect in applying respondeat superior is differentiating between those who are servants and those who are independent contractors. A servant is defined in the following general manner: one who is employed by a master to perform personal services and whose physical conduct is subject to the right to control by the master. [ ] It is the employer's right to control that generally separates a servant from an independent contractor. [ ] An independent contractor can, therefore, be defined as "a person who contracts with another to do something for him but who is not controlled by the other nor subject to the other's right to control with respect to his physical conduct in the performance of the undertaking." Restatement (Second) of Agency § 2(3).

It is important to distinguish between servants and independent contractors in the tort context because, while a master can be held liable for a servant's negligent conduct under respondeat superior, a master generally cannot be held liable for the negligence of an independent contractor. [ ] The theory behind non-liability for independent contractors is that it would be unfair to hold a master liable for the conduct of another when the master has no control over that conduct. See Restatement (Second) of Torts § 409 cmt. b.

Apparent agency is a doctrine based in agency law. It is most often associated with contracts and the ability of an agent with "apparent authority" to bind the principal to a contract with a third party. [ ] Apparent authority "is the authority that a third person reasonably believes an agent to possess because of some manifestation from his principal." [ ] The manifestation must be made by the principal to a third party and reasonably cause the third party to believe that an individual is an agent of the principal and to act upon that belief. [ ] The manifestations can originate from direct or indirect communication.[ ] They can also originate from advertisements to the community. [ ]

In certain instances, apparent or ostensible agency also can be a means by which to establish vicarious liability. One enunciation of this doctrine is set forth in the Restatement (Second) of Agency section 267, which provides that:

> One who represents that another is his servant or other agent and thereby causes a third person justifiably to rely upon the care or skill of such apparent agent is subject to liability to the third person for harm caused by the lack of care or skill of the one appearing to be a servant or other agent as if he were such.

(emphasis added) [hereinafter "Section 267"]. Under a Section 267 analysis, if, because of the principal's manifestations, a third party reasonably believes that in dealing with the apparent agent he is dealing with the principal's servant or agent and exposes himself to the negligent conduct because of the principal's manifestations, then the principal may be held liable for that negligent conduct. See Restatement (Second) of Agency § 267 cmt. a; see also

Restatement (Second) of Torts § 429; Seavey, Restatement (Second) of AgencyYY §§ 8 cmt. D, 90 cmt. A, 91 cmt. B.

Another similar enunciation of this doctrine is set forth in the Restatement (Second) of Torts section 429 (1965), which is captioned "Negligence in Doing Work Which is Accepted in Reliance on the Employer's Doing the Work Himself" and which provides:

> One who employs an independent contractor to perform services for another which are accepted in the reasonable belief that the services are being rendered by the employer or by his servants, is subject to liability for physical harm caused by the negligence of the contractor in supplying such services, to the same extent as though the employer were supplying them himself or by his servants.

(emphasis added) [hereinafter "Section 429"]. Both Section 267 and Section 429 are estoppel-based. To the extent that Section 429 differs from Section 267 when applied in the hospital context, the primary difference appears to be that the reliance element is less subjective under Section 429.

B. *Indiana Jurisprudence*

In the hospital setting, Indiana courts have long followed the general rule that hospitals could not be held liable for the negligent actions of independent contractor physicians. * * *

* * * [C]ourts no longer allow hospitals to use their inability to practice medicine as a shield to protect themselves from liability.[ ] Moreover, although Indiana law may support a claim of vicarious liability through apparent or ostensible agency in some instances, courts in this jurisdiction rarely have considered this doctrine in a hospital setting and have never applied it to hold a hospital liable for the acts of an independent contractor physician. Rather, Indiana courts have continued to limit hospital liability under the doctrine of respondeat superior and have continued to focus on the question of whether the alleged acts of negligence were committed by an employee of the hospital or by an independent contractor. [ ] If the alleged negligence was committed by an independent contractor physician, the courts generally have held that the hospital cannot be held liable for those actions. [ ]

C. *Evolving Law in Other Jurisdictions*

In the area of hospital liability, there has been an ongoing movement by courts to use apparent or ostensible agency as a means by which to hold hospitals vicariously liable for the negligence of some independent contractor physicians.[ ][10] Many of these cases employ the doctrine of apparent agency when the plaintiff was negligently injured by a physician's actions while visiting the hospital's emergency room. [ ] Courts, however, also have em-

10. See also Seneris v. Haas, 45 Cal.2d 811, 291 P.2d 915 (1955); Paintsville Hosp. Co. v. Rose, 683 S.W.2d 255 (Ky.1985); Grewe v. Mt. Clemens Gen. Hosp., 404 Mich. 240, 273 N.W.2d 429 (1978); Kashishian v. Port, 167 Wis.2d 24, 481 N.W.2d 277 (1992); Pamperin v. Trinity Mem'l Hosp., 144 Wis.2d 188, 423 N.W.2d 848 (1988); Sharsmith v. Hill, 764 P.2d 667 (Wyo.1988). See generally Martin C. McWilliams, Jr. and Hamilton E. Russell, III, Hospital Liability for Torts of Independent Contractor Physicians, 47 S.C.L.REV. 431 (1996); Kenneth S. Abraham and Paul C. Weiler, Enterprise Medical Liability and the Evolution of the American Health Care System, 108 HARV.L.REV. 381, 386–89 (1994); Diane M. Janulis and Alan D. Hornstein, Damned if You Do, Damned if You Don't: Hospitals' Liability for Physician Malpractice, 64 NEB.L.REV. 689 (1985).

ployed the doctrine of apparent agency to hold a hospital liable for assertedly negligent acts committed in non-emergency room settings, including negligent acts committed by anesthesiologists. See Seneris v. Haas, 45 Cal.2d 811, 291 P.2d 915, 917, 926–27 (1955) (discussing negligence of an anesthesiologist during the delivery of a baby); see also Williams v. St. Claire Med. Ctr., 657 S.W.2d 590, 592–93 (Ky.Ct.App.1983) (discussing negligence of an independent contractor nurse anesthetist).[11]

Courts that have held hospitals liable for the negligence of independent contractor physicians under apparent agency have sometimes referred to or adopted Section 267, Section 429, or both, and sometimes have not referred to or adopted either Section 267 or Section 429. While the language employed by these courts sometimes varies, generally they have employed tests which focus primarily on two basic factors. The first factor focuses on the hospital's manifestations and is sometimes described as an inquiry whether the hospital "acted in a manner which would lead a reasonable person to conclude that the individual who was alleged to be negligent was an employee or agent of the hospital." Kashishian, 481 N.W.2d at 284–85; Gilbert, 190 Ill.Dec. 758, 622 N.E.2d at 795–96 (quoting Pamperin v. Trinity Mem'l Hosp., 144 Wis.2d 188, 423 N.W.2d 848, 855–56 (1988)); see also Seneris, 291 P.2d at 927. Courts considering this factor often ask whether the hospital "held itself out" to the public as a provider of hospital care, for example, by mounting extensive advertising campaigns. [ ] In this regard, the hospital need not make express representations to the patient that the treating physician is an employee of the hospital; rather a representation also may be general and implied. [ ]

The second factor focuses on the patient's reliance. It is sometimes characterized as an inquiry as to whether "the plaintiff acted in reliance upon the conduct of the hospital or its agent, consistent with ordinary care and prudence." Kashishian, 481 N.W.2d at 285; Gilbert, 190 Ill.Dec. 758, 622 N.E.2d at 795 (quoting Pamperin, 423 N.W.2d at 855–56); see also Seneris, 291 P.2d at 927. Courts considering this factor sometimes ask whether, because of the hospital's manifestations, the plaintiff believed that the hospital was providing the pertinent medical care as opposed to simply acting as a situs for the physician to provide health care as an independent contractor. [ ] Other courts, however, seem to employ a less subjective form of reliance or even to presume reliance absent any evidence that the patient knew or should have known that the physician was not an employee of the hospital and that it is the physician and not the hospital who is responsible for his medical care. [ ] An example of a situation where a patient might be in a position to know that the physician was an independent contractor may exist if the patient

11. See also Kashishian, 481 N.W.2d at 278 (discussing negligence of a cardiologist arising out of a cardiology consultation). See generally Abraham, supra note 10, at 388 (noting that patients are certainly under the impression that it is the hospital and not the individual physicians that provides such services as emergency, radiology, and anesthesiology, and that patients have maintained successful apparent agency suits against hospitals for the acts of emergency room physicians, anesthesiologists, pathologists, and radiologists); Janulis, supra note 10, at 693 (explaining that hospitals often execute exclusive service contracts with groups of independent contractor physicians to staff areas such as radiology, pathology, and emergency room services and that consequently patients' ability to select physicians becomes limited by the restriction of clinical practice to the contracting physicians); McWilliams, supra note 10, 437 (explaining that hospitals try to utilize the doctrine of respondeat superior to insulate themselves or limit their liability by utilizing independent contractors in many high-risk specialties such as radiology, pathology, anesthesiology, and emergency room services).

establishes an independent relationship with the physician or selects a particular physician in advance of going to the hospital. [ ] Even in such circumstances, however, the courts have reasoned that the patient may not have had reason to know of the contractual arrangements between the physician and the hospital.[ ]

Central to both of these factors—that is, the hospital's manifestations and the patient's reliance—is the question of whether the hospital provided notice to the patient that the treating physician was an independent contractor and not an employee of the hospital. [ ]

D. Adoption of Restatement (Second) of Torts Section 429

In the present case, Sword argues that, under the doctrine of apparent or ostensible agency, Norton is vicariously liable for the actions of its apparent agent Dr. Luna, whom the parties agree was an independent contractor. * * * The Court of Appeals invited us to consider the appropriateness of more clearly defining a test and adopting one of the two formulations of the test set forth in the Restatements. [ ] We agree with the conclusion of the Court of Appeals and now, in the specific context of a hospital setting, expressly adopt the formulation of apparent or ostensible agency set forth in the Restatement (Second) of Tort section 429.

Under Section 429, as we read and construe it, a trier of fact must focus on the reasonableness of the patient's belief that the hospital or its employees were rendering health care. This ultimate determination is made by considering the totality of the circumstances, including the actions or inactions of the hospital, as well as any special knowledge the patient may have about the hospital's arrangements with its physicians. We conclude that a hospital will be deemed to have held itself out as the provider of care unless it gives notice to the patient that it is not the provider of care and that the care is provided by a physician who is an independent contractor and not subject to the control and supervision of the hospital. A hospital generally will be able to avoid liability by providing meaningful written notice to the patient, acknowledged at the time of admission. See Cantrell v. Northeast Georgia Med. Ctr., 235 Ga.App. 365, 508 S.E.2d 716, 719–20 (1998) (concluding that hospital did not hold physician out as its employee as evidenced by conspicuous signs posted in hospital's registration area and express language in the patient consent to treatment form); Valdez v. Pasadena Healthcare Management, Inc., 975 S.W.2d 43, 48 (Tex.App.1998) (finding written notice, signed by the patient, that physician served as an independent contractor was sufficient to release hospital from liability for physician's medical malpractice). Under some circumstances, such as in the case of a medical emergency, however, written notice may not suffice if the patient had an inadequate opportunity to make an informed choice.

As to the meaning and importance of reliance in this specific context, we agree with the cases that hold that if the hospital has failed to give meaningful notice, if the patient has no special knowledge regarding the arrangement the hospital has made with its physicians, and if there is no reason that the patient should have known of these employment relationships, then reliance is presumed. [ ]

Applying this test here, we conclude that there are genuine material issues of fact in dispute as to whether Dr. Luna was an apparent or ostensible agent of Norton and whether Norton may be held liable for any of Dr. Luna's asserted negligent acts. First, there is nothing in this record which indicates that the hospital did anything to put plaintiff on notice that it was her physician, an independent contractor, who was responsible for her medical care and not the hospital.[16] Second, this is clearly not a case where plaintiff selected her own anesthesiologist prior to admission, for she specifically testified that she did not know who would administer the epidural until just before the procedure, and if she had any special knowledge of the hospital's employment arrangement with Dr. Luna or with the hospital's general employment practices with respect to physicians, it is not apparent on this record. Finally, Norton held itself out, through an extensive advertising campaign, as a full-service hospital which specializes in obstetric care.

Based on this record and under Section 429 as we construe it today, there are clearly genuine issues of material fact as to whether Dr. Luna is an apparent agent of Norton. The trial court erred when it entered summary judgment for defendant on this issue.

Notes and Questions

1. What can a hospital do to avoid liability under the court's analysis in Sword? Will explicit notice to the plaintiff at the time of admission be sufficient? How about a large time in the admitting area of the hospital? A brochure handed to each patient? If the hospital advertises aggressively, perhaps the reliance created by such advertising overwhelms all targeted attempts to inform patients about the intricacies of the physicians' employment relationships with the hospital?

2. Some courts have put it more sharply: the patient relies on the reputation of the hospital, not any particular doctor, and for that reason selects that hospital. See e.g., White v. Methodist Hosp. South, 844 S.W.2d 642 (Tenn.App.1992). If the negligence results from emergency room care, most courts have held that a patient may justifiably rely on the physician as an agent unless the hospital explicitly disclaims an agency relationship. Ballard v. Advocate Health and Hospitals Corporations, 1999 WL 498702 (N.D.Ill.1999). A promotional campaign or advertising can create such reliance. Clark v. Southview Hospital & Family Health Center, 68 Ohio St.3d 435, 628 N.E.2d 46 (Ohio 1994)(promotional and marketing campaign stressed the emergency departments); Gragg v. Calandra, 297 Ill.App.3d 639, 231 Ill.Dec. 711, 696 N.E.2d 1282 (A.C.Ill. 1998)(unless patient is put on notice of the independent status of the professionals in a hospital, he or see will reasonably assume they are employees).

To avoid liability, a hospital can try to avoid patient misunderstanding by its billing procedures, the letterhead used, signs , and other clues of the true nature

16. In a deposition colloquy, counsel made a general reference to a document titled "Condition of Admission and Authorization for Treatment," which assertedly informed plaintiff that her physician is not an employee of the hospital, and that the hospital is not liable for any acts of the practicing physician. That document, however, is not in the record, and no witness testified regarding that document. Nevertheless, even assuming the accuracy of counsel's representations during this colloquy, it is far from clear that this document would constitute sufficient notice of the relationship between the hospital and the physician within the meaning of the rule we articulate today. In fact, it is likely insufficient notice if it is the sole source of notice and if plaintiff did not read or sign that form until she arrived at the hospital in active labor.

of the relationship of the physician to the institution. Cantrell v. Northeast Georgia Medical Center, 235 Ga.App. 365, 508 S.E.2d 716 (C.A.Ga. 1998)(sign over registration desk stated that the physicians in the emergency room were independent contracts; consent form repeated this.) The court is likely however to cut through these devices if the reliance on reputation by the patient is strong enough. It appears that a few states allow a clear statement in a consent form that physicians in the hospital are independent contractors and not agents has been held to be sufficient to put a patient on notice. Valdez v. Pasadena Healthcare Management, Inc., 975 S.W.2d 43 (C.A.Tex. 1998); James v. Ingalls Memorial Hospital, 299 Ill.App.3d 627, 233 Ill.Dec. 564, 701 N.E.2d 207 (App.Ct. Ill. 1998); Roberts v. Galen of Virginia, Inc., 111 F.3d 405 (6th Cir. 1997)(statement in outpatient registration and authorization for medical treatment form stated that "physicians, residents, and medical students are independent practitioners and are not employees or agents of the hospital"; even though patient had neither read nor signed this, it is the action of the hospital that governs as to ostensible agency.)

3. The second element—justifiable reliance by the patient to her detriment on the appearance of an apparent agency—has been found by many courts through the context in which health care is delivered. Hospitals are big businesses, spending millions marketing themselves through "expensive advertising campaigns." Kashishian v. Port, 167 Wis.2d 24, 481 N.W.2d 277 (Wis.1992) (noting the substantial sums of money spent by U.S. hospitals on advertising in 1989, and the fact the many people recall such advertising.) They provide a range of health services, and the public expects emergency care and other functions, as a result of hospitals' self-promotion. Hospitals do not actively inform the public about the various statuses of emergency room and other physicians. As the role and image of the hospital have evolved, judicial willingness to stretch agency exceptions has likewise followed suit.

Recent decisions have declined to limit the doctrine to just emergency room services, but rather have left it as a question of fact as to whether the patient knew the physician was an independent contractor. See, e.g., Dahan v. UHS of Bethesda, Inc., 295 Ill.App.3d 770, 230 Ill.Dec. 137, 692 N.E.2d 1303 (A.C. Ill. 1998)(physicians's contract with the hospital required him to see hospital employees free of charge; a reasonable person would conclude that he was an agent of the hospital). Even the fact that a patient had contracted with a private physician as primary surgeon may not be sufficient to block the use of apparent authority doctrine.

d. The Inherent Function Test

A third approach, the inherent function doctrine, is discussed in the following case.

BEECK v. TUCSON GENERAL HOSPITAL

Supreme Court of Arizona, 1972.
18 Ariz.App. 165, 500 P.2d 1153.

[The plaintiff contracted pneumonia as the result of the insertion of a needle into her spine during a lumbar myelogram, due to the collision by the x-ray machine screen with the needle. She brought a malpractice suit against Tucson General and the radiologists who administered the test. The trial court granted the hospital's motion for summary judgment on the ground that Dr. Rente was an independent contractor. Plaintiff appealed.]

Having undertaken one of mankind's most critically important and delicate fields of endeavor, concomitantly therewith the hospital must assume the grave responsibility of pursuing this calling with appropriate care. The care and service dispensed through this high trust, however technical, complex and esoteric its character may be, must meet standards of responsibility commensurate with the undertaking to preserve and protect the health, and indeed, the very lives of those placed in the hospital's keeping. [ ]

* * *

The radiology department of Tucson General was operated virtually on a monopoly basis. Dr. Rente and his colleagues were the only ones authorized to perform x-ray work for the department. Any choice by Mrs. Beeck was eliminated. The hospital had chosen for her. It had placed the "hospital radiologists" in the position of exclusive radiologists for the hospital. Further, the hospital furnished everything. The equipment belonged to the hospital and the radiologist paid no rent for use of the equipment or for space at the hospital. Working hours, vacation time, billing and employment of technicians were all controlled by the hospital. The radiology services were obviously furnished under the auspices of Tucson General. Clearly the hospital could regulate operation of its x-ray department to the extent of requiring that the descent-arresting stop be in place before undertaking the type of procedure in question here. Checklists are commonly used in operating complicated equipment. Furthermore, it is well known that hospitals undertake control of the highly technical service with which they deal through overseeing boards and supervisors and peer group mechanisms of various types. [ ]

* * * Further, the hospital had the right to control the standards of performance of this chosen radiologist. The radiologist was employed by the hospital for an extended period of time (five years) to perform a service which was an inherent function of the hospital, a function without which the hospital could not properly achieve its purpose. All facilities and instrumentalities were provided by the hospital together with all administrative services for the radiology department.

* * * [W]e hold that an employee-employer relationship existed between Dr. Rente and the hospital and the doctrine of respondeat superior applies.

* * *

For the reasons given, the judgment is reversed and the case remanded for further proceedings consistent with this opinion.

Notes and Questions

1. Do the above cases reflect the changing balance of power between health care institutions and physicians? The control test is closest to vicarious liability principles, looking to the terms of the contract and the actual relationship between the hospital and the physician. The evolution of corporate concepts of accountability and control have come to permeate health care delivery, and Berel indicates the willingness of courts to see such control mechanisms as sufficient to override agency defenses.

2. Apparent authority tests look at patient expectations and reasonable, justifiable reliance. Sword describes three different approaches to such apparent

agency. See also Gilbert v. Sycamore Municipal Hospital, 156 Ill.2d 511, 190 Ill.Dec. 758, 622 N.E.2d 788 (1993); Hardy v. Brantley, 471 So.2d 358 (Miss.1985).

3. The inherent function test takes the inquiry one step further, looking at those functions of a hospital that are essential to its operation rather than stopping the inquiry at patient reliance. Radiology labs and emergency rooms are often held to be two such functions. See, e.g., Adamski v. Tacoma General Hospital, 20 Wash.App. 98, 579 P.2d 970 (1978). This notion of "inherent function" overlaps substantially with the "nondelegable duty" rule in agency law, as expressed in corporate negligence cases.

4. Hospitals have been held liable for the acts of radiologists, residents, emergency room physicians, and surgeons, even though these persons were not hospital employees. The number of courts that have adopted exceptions to vicarious liability is increasing. See James by James v. Ingalls Memorial Hospital, 299 Ill.App.3d 627, 233 Ill.Dec. 564, 701 N.E.2d 207 (Ill.App. 1 Dist., 1998); Pamperin v. Trinity Memorial Hospital, 144 Wis.2d 188, 423 N.W.2d 848 (1988) (radiologists); Thompson v. The Nason Hospital, 527 Pa. 330, 591 A.2d 703 (Pa. 1991) (surgeons); Richmond County Hospital Authority v. Brown, 257 Ga. 507, 361 S.E.2d 164 (Ga. 1987) (emergency room physicians); Strach v. St. John Hospital Corp.,160 Mich.App. 251, 408 N.W.2d 441 (Mich.App.1987) (physicians referred to surgery unit as part of hospital's team and surgery team doctors exercised direct authority over hospital employees.); Barrett v. Samaritan Health Services, Inc., 153 Ariz. 138, 735 P.2d 460 (App.1987) (emergency room physicians). Contra, see Baptist Memorial Hospital v. Sampson, 969 S.W.2d 945 (Tex.1998)(rejecting ostensible agency for emergency room physician who failed to diagnose and treat a poisonous spider bite).

Problem: Creating a Shield

You represent Bowsman Hospital, a small rural hospital in Iowa. The hospital has until now relied on Dr. Francke for radiology services. It provides him with space, equipment and personnel for the radiology department, sends and collects bills on his behalf, and provides him with an office. It also pays him $300 a day in exchange for which Dr. Francke agrees to be at the hospital one day a week. Bowsman is one of several small hospitals in this part of Iowa that use Dr. Francke's services. Bowsman advertises in the local papers of several nearby communities. Its advertisements stress its ability to handle trauma injuries, common in farming areas. The ads say in part:

"Bowsman treats patient problems with big league medical talent. Our physicians and nurses have been trained for the special demands of farming accidents and injuries."

What advice can you give as to methods of shielding Bowsman from liability for the negligent acts of Dr. Francke? Must it insist that Dr. Francke operate his own outside laboratory? Or furnish his own equipment? Pay his own bills? Should the hospital hire its own radiologist?

The Chief Executive Officer asks you to develop guidelines to protect the hospital from liability for medical errors of the radiologist. Your research has uncovered the following cases.

Estates of Milliron v. Francke, 243 Mont. 200, 793 P.2d 824 (1990). The plaintiff was referred to the hospital and the radiologist who practiced there by his family physician, for evaluation of prostatis and uropathy. The radiologist used an intravenous pyelogram, to which the plaintiff had a reaction. The patient suffered brain damage. The hospital provided space, equipment and personnel for the radiology department, sent and collected bills on his behalf, and provided him with an office. The court granted summary judgment for the defendant on the ostensible agency claim. The court noted that this was a small hospital in a rural area, and the radiologist rotated between this and several other small hospitals. This was an ordinary practice in smaller communities in Montana.

> Providing these traveling physicians with offices at the hospital simply helps ensure that these smaller and more remote communities will be provided with adequate medical care and is not a sufficient factual basis to establish an agency relationship. Id. at 827.

Gregg v. National Medical Health Care Services, Inc., 145 Ariz. 51, 699 P.2d 925 (1985). Gregg went to the hospital's emergency room at 3 a.m. after having three episodes of crushing substernal chest pain accompanied by nausea and vomiting. The court noted that the hospital's right to control the physician was critical to its liability for the physician's acts, and held that the facts raised a jury question. The physician was paid $300 per week to commute from his office to the hospital clinic to act as a consultant. He was required to be at the hospital at least once a week.

II. HOSPITAL DIRECT LIABILITY

A. NEGLIGENCE

WASHINGTON v. WASHINGTON HOSPITAL CENTER

District of Columbia Court of Appeals, 1990.
579 A.2d 177.

[The Court considered two issues: whether the testimony of the plaintiff's expert was sufficient to create a issue for the jury; and whether the hospital's failure to request a finding of liability of the settling defendants or to file a cross claim for contribution against any of the defendants defeated the hospital's claim for a pro rata reduction in the jury verdict. The discussion of the first issue follows.]

FARRELL, ASSOCIATE JUDGE:

This appeal and cross-appeal arise from a jury verdict in a medical malpractice action against the Washington Hospital Center (WHC or the hospital) in favor of LaVerne Alice Thompson, a woman who suffered permanent catastrophic brain injury from oxygen deprivation in the course of general anesthesia for elective surgery * * *

* * *

I. THE FACTS

On the morning of November 7, 1987, LaVerne Alice Thompson, a healthy 36–year-old woman, underwent elective surgery at the Washington Hospital Center for an abortion and tubal ligation, procedures requiring general anesthesia. At about 10:45 a.m., nurse-anesthetist Elizabeth Adland, under the supervision of Dr. Sheryl Walker, the physician anesthesiologist, inserted an endotracheal tube into Ms. Thompson's throat for the purpose of conveying oxygen to, and removing carbon dioxide from, the anesthetized patient. The tube, properly inserted, goes into the patient's trachea just above the lungs. Plaintiffs alleged that instead Nurse Adland inserted the tube into Thompson's esophagus, above the stomach. After inserting the tube, Nurse Adland "ventilated" or pumped air into the patient while Dr. Walker, by observing physical reactions—including watching the rise and fall of the patient's chest and listening for breath sounds equally on the patient's right and left sides—sought to determine if the tube had been properly inserted.

At about 10:50 a.m., while the surgery was underway, surgeon Nathan Bobrow noticed that Thompson's blood was abnormally dark, which indicated that her tissues were not receiving sufficient oxygen, and reported the condition to Nurse Adland, who checked Thompson's vital signs and found them stable. As Dr. Bobrow began the tubal ligation part of the operation, Thompson's heart rate dropped. She suffered a cardiac arrest and was resuscitated, but eventually the lack of oxygen caused catastrophic brain injuries. Plaintiffs' expert testified that Ms. Thompson remains in a persistent vegetative state and is totally incapacitated; her cardiac, respiratory and digestive functions are normal and she is not "brain dead," but, according to the expert, she is "essentially awake but unaware" of her surroundings. Her condition is unlikely to improve, though she is expected to live from ten to twenty years.

* * *

The plaintiffs alleged that Adland and Walker had placed the tube in Thompson's esophagus rather than her trachea, and that they and Dr. Bobrow had failed to detect the improper intubation in time to prevent the oxygen deprivation that caused Thompson's catastrophic brain injury. WHC, they alleged, was negligent in failing to provide the anesthesiologists with a device known variously as a capnograph or end-tidal carbon dioxide monitor which allows early detection of insufficient oxygen in time to prevent brain injury.

* * *

II. Washington Hospital Center's Claims on Cross-Appeal

A. *Standard of Care*

On its cross-appeal, WHC first asserts that the plaintiffs failed to carry their burden of establishing the standard of care and that the trial court therefore erred in refusing to grant its motion for judgment notwithstanding the verdict.

* * *

In a negligence action predicated on medical malpractice, the plaintiff must carry a tripartite burden, and establish: (1) the applicable standard of care; (2) a deviation from that standard by the defendant; and (3) a causal relationship between that deviation and the plaintiff's injury. [ ] * * *

Generally, the "standard of care" is "the course of action that a reasonably prudent [professional] with the defendant's specialty would have taken under the same or similar circumstances." [ ] With respect to institutions such as hospitals, this court has rejected the "locality" rule, which refers to the standard of conduct expected of other similarly situated members of the profession in the same locality or community, [ ] in favor of a national standard. [ ] Thus, the question for decision is whether the evidence as a whole, and reasonable inferences therefrom, would allow a reasonable juror to find that a reasonably prudent tertiary care hospital,[3] at the time of Ms. Thompson's injury in November 1987, and according to national standards, would have supplied a carbon dioxide monitor to a patient undergoing general anesthesia for elective surgery.

WHC argues that the plaintiffs' expert, Dr. Stephen Steen, failed to demonstrate an adequate factual basis for his opinion that WHC should have made available a carbon dioxide monitor. The purpose of expert opinion testimony is to avoid jury findings based on mere speculation or conjecture. [ ] The sufficiency of the foundation for those opinions should be measured with this purpose in mind. * * *

* * *

* * * [WHC] asserts that * * * Steen gave no testimony on the number of hospitals having end-tidal carbon dioxide monitors in place in 1987, and that he never referred to any written standards or authorities as the basis of his opinion. We conclude that Steen's opinion * * * was sufficient to create an issue for the jury.

Dr. Steen testified that by 1985, the carbon dioxide monitors were available in his hospital (Los Angeles County—University of Southern California Medical Center (USC)), and "in many other hospitals." In response to a question whether, by 1986, "standards of care" required carbon dioxide monitors in operating rooms, he replied, "I would think that by that time, they would be [required]." As plaintiffs concede, this opinion was based in part on his own personal experience at USC, which * * * cannot itself provide an adequate foundation for an expert opinion on a national standard of care. But Steen also drew support from "what I've read where [the monitors were] available in other hospitals." He referred to two such publications: The American Association of Anesthesiology (AAA) Standards for Basic Intra-Operative Monitoring, approved by the AAA House of Delegates on October 21, 1986, which "encouraged" the use of monitors, and an article entitled *Standards for Patient Monitoring During Anesthesia at Harvard Medical School,* published in August 1986 in the Journal of American Medical Association, which stated that as of July 1985 the monitors were in use at Harvard, and that "monitoring end-tidal carbon dioxide is an emerging standard and is strongly preferred."

WHC makes much of Steen's concession on cross-examination that the AAA Standards were recommendations, strongly encouraged but not mandatory, and that the Harvard publication spoke of an "emerging" standard. In its brief WHC asserts, without citation, that "[p]alpable indicia of widespread *mandated* practices are necessary to establish a standard of care" (emphasis added), and that at most the evidence spoke of "recommended" or "encouraged" practices, and "emerging" or "developing" standards as of 1986–87. A standard of due care, however, necessarily embodies what a *reasonably prudent* hospital would do, [ ] and hence care and foresight exceeding the

3. Plaintiffs' expert defined a tertiary care hospital as "a hospital which has the facilities to conduct clinical care management of patients in nearly all aspects of medicine and surgery."

minimum required by law or mandatory professional regulation may be necessary to meet that standard. It certainly cannot be said that the 1986 recommendations of a professional association (which had no power to issue or enforce mandatory requirements), or an article speaking of an "emerging" standard in 1986, have no bearing on an expert opinion as to what the standard of patient monitoring equipment was fully one year later when Ms. Thompson's surgery took place.

Nevertheless, we need not decide whether Dr. Steen's testimony was sufficiently grounded in fact or adequate data to establish the standard of care. The record contains other evidence from which, in combination with Dr. Steen's testimony, a reasonable juror could fairly conclude that monitors were required of prudent hospitals similar to WHC in late 1987. The evidence showed that at least four other teaching hospitals in the United States used the monitors by that time. In addition to Dr. Steen's testimony that USC supplied them and the article reflecting that Harvard University had them, plaintiffs introduced into evidence an article entitled *Anesthesia at Penn,* from a 1986 alumni newsletter of the Department of Anesthesia at the University of Pennsylvania, indicating that the monitors were then in use at that institution's hospital, and that they allowed "instant recognition of esophageal intubation and other airway problems. * * * " Moreover, WHC's expert anesthesiologist, Dr. John Tinker of the University of Iowa, testified that his hospital had installed carbon dioxide monitors in every operating room by early 1986, and that "by 1987, it is certainly true that many hospitals were in the process of converting" to carbon dioxide monitors.[5]

Perhaps most probative was the testimony of WHC's own Chairman of the Department of Anesthesiology, Dr. Dermot A. Murray, and documentary evidence associated with his procurement request for carbon dioxide monitors. In December 1986 or January 1987, Dr. Murray submitted a requisition form to the hospital for end-tidal carbon dioxide units to monitor the administration of anesthesia in each of the hospital's operating rooms, stating that if the monitors were not provided, the hospital would "fail to meet the national standard of care." The monitors were to be "fully operational" in July of 1987.[6] Attempting to meet this evidence, WHC points out that at trial

> Dr. Murray was *never asked to opine,* with a reasonable degree of medical certainty, that the applicable standard of care at the relevant time *required* the presence of CO_2 monitors. Indeed, his testimony was directly to the contrary. Moreover, the procurement process which he had initi-

5. In its reply brief, WHC argues that

> the fact that four teaching hospitals used CO_2 monitors during the relevant time period is almost irrelevant. Institutions with significantly enhanced financial resources and/or government grants which accelerate their testing and implementation of new and improved technologies would naturally have available to them items which, inherently, were not yet required for the general populace of hospitals.

In fact, Dr. Steen, in voir dire examination on his qualification as an expert on the standard required of hospitals in WHC's position in regard to equipment, testified that his review of WHC's President's Report for 1986–87 led him to conclude that WHC was a teaching hospital. Counsel for the hospital could have identified and probed fully before the jury any differences between WHC and the hospitals relied on to establish the standard of care. To the extent the record was not so developed, the jury could credit Steen's testimony that WHC was required to adhere to the standard applicable to teaching hospitals.

6. As supporting documentation for the requisition, Dr. Murray attached a copy of the Journal of the American Medical Association article on standards at Harvard University. The requisitions, with attachments, were exhibits admitted in evidence.

> ated envisioned obtaining the equipment * * * over time, not even beginning until fiscal year 1988, a period ending June 30, 1988. [Emphasis by WHC.]

Dr. Murray opined that in November 1987 there was *no* standard of care relating to monitoring equipment. The jury heard this testimony and Dr. Murray's explanation of the procurement process, but apparently did not credit it, perhaps because the requisition form itself indicated that the equipment ordered was to be operational in July 1987, four months before Ms. Thompson's surgery, and not at some unspecified time in fiscal year 1988 as Dr. Murray testified at trial.

On the evidence recited above, a reasonable juror could find that the standard of care required WHC to supply monitors as of November 1987. The trial judge therefore did not err in denying the motion for judgment notwithstanding the verdict.

* * *

Notes and Questions

1. Does the plaintiff present sufficient evidence that the carbon dioxide monitor is now standard equipment for tertiary care hospitals? Is the Washington Hospital Center stuck in a zone of transition between older precautions and emerging technologies that improve patient care? Why did they not purchase such monitors earlier?

A companion device to the carbon dioxide monitor is the blood-monitoring pulse oximeter, which has become a mandatory device in hospital operating rooms. In 1984 no hospital had them; by 1990 all hospitals used oximeters in their operating rooms. The device beeps when a patient's blood oxygen drops due to breathing problems or overuse of anesthesia. That warning can give a vital three or four minutes warning to physicians, allowing them to correct the problem before the patient suffers brain damage. These devices have so improved patient safety that malpractice insurers have lowered premiums for anesthesiologists. See Appleby, Pulse Oximeters Pump Up Bottom Lines and Patient Safety, Deflate Malpractice Risk, HealthWeek 17–18 (October 9, 1990).

The Joint Commission on Accreditation of Healthcare Organization (JCAHO) now requires hospitals to develop protocols for anesthesia care that mandate pulse oximetry equipment for measuring oxygen saturation. See Revisions to Anesthesia Care Standards Comprehensive Accreditation Manual for Hospitals Effective January 1, 2001 (Standards and Intents for Sedation and Anesthesia Care), *http://www.jcaho.org/standard/aneshap.html.*

2. A health care institution, whether hospital, nursing home, or clinic, is liable for negligence in maintaining its facilities, providing and maintaining medical equipment, hiring, supervising and retaining nurses and other staff, and failing to have in place procedures to protect patients. Basic negligence principles govern hospital liability for injuries caused by other sources than negligent acts of the medical staff. As *Washington* holds, hospitals are generally held to a national standard of care for hospitals in their treatment category. They must provide a safe environment for diagnosis, treatment, and recovery of patients. Bellamy v. Appellate Department, 50 Cal.App.4th 797, 57 Cal.Rptr.2d 894 (Cal.App. 5 Dist. 1996).

a. Hospitals must have minimum facility and support systems to treat the range of problems and side effects that accompany procedures they offer. In Hernandez v. Smith, 552 F.2d 142 (5th Cir.1977), for example, an obstetrical clinic that lacked surgical facilities for caesarean sections was found liable for "* * * the failure to provide proper and safe instrumentalities for the treatment of ailments it undertakes to treat * * *." See also Valdez v. Lyman–Roberts Hosp., Inc., 638 S.W.2d 111 (Tex.App.1982).

b. Staffing must be adequate. Short staffing can be negligence. See Merritt v. Karcioglu, 668 So.2d 469 (La.App. 4th Cir.1996)(hospital ward understaffed in having only three critical care nurses for six patients). If existing staff can be juggled to cover a difficult patient, short staffing is no defense. See Horton v. Niagara Falls Memorial Medical Center, 51 A.D.2d 152, 380 N.Y.S.2d 116 (1976).

c. Equipment must be adequate for the services offered, although it need not be the state of the art. See Emory University v. Porter, 103 Ga.App. 752, 120 S.E.2d 668, 670 (1961); Lauro v. Travelers Ins. Co., 261 So.2d 261 (La.App.1972). If a device such as an expensive CT scanner has come into common use, however, a smaller and less affluent hospital can argue that it should be judged by the standards of similar hospitals with similar resources. This variable standard, reflecting resource differences between hospitals, would then protect a hospital in a situation where its budget does not allow purchase of some expensive devices. If an institution lacks a piece of equipment that has come to be recognized as essential, particularly for diagnosis, it may have a duty to transfer the patient to an institution that has the equipment. In Blake v. D.C. General Hospital (discussed in Maxwell Mehlman, Rationing Expensive Lifesaving Medical Treatments, 1985 Wisc.L.Rev. 239) the trial court allowed a case to go to the jury where the plaintiff's estate claimed that she died because of the hospital's lack of a CT scanner to diagnose her condition. The court found a duty to transfer in such circumstances.

d. A hospital and its contracting physicians may be liable for damages caused by inadequate or defective systems they develop and implement, particularly where emergency care is involved. In the case of Marks v. Mandel, 477 So.2d 1036 (Fla.App.1985), the plaintiff brought a wrongful death action against the hospital, alleging negligence based on the failure of the on-call system to produce a thoracic surgeon and failure of the hospital staff to send the patient to a hospital with a trauma center. The Florida Supreme Court held that the trial court erred in excluding from evidence the hospital's emergency room policy and procedure manual. This manual set out in detail how the on-call system should operate and itemized procedures for responding to calls made from ambulances. The court held that evidence was sufficient to go to the jury on the issue of liability of the hospital and the emergency room supervisor for the failure of the on-call system to produce a thoracic surgeon in a timely fashion. See also Habuda v. Trustees of Rex Hospital, 3 N.C.App. 11, 164 S.E.2d 17 (1968), where the hospital was liable for inadequate rules for handling, storing, and administering medications; Herrington v. Hiller, 883 F.2d 411 (5th Cir.1989) (failure to provide for adequate 24–hour anesthesia service). See also Ball Memorial Hosp. v. Freeman, 245 Ind. 71, 196 N.E.2d 274 (1964).

e. A hospital's own safety rules or internal regulations serve as a source of a standard of care, as would any non-legislative safety standard. They are material and relevant on the issue of quality of care, but are usually not sufficient by themselves to establish the degree of care due. Jackson v. Oklahoma Memorial Hospital, 909 P.2d 765 (Okl.1995).

3. An institution's own internal rules and regulations for medical procedures may be offered as evidence of a standard of care for the trier of fact to consider. In Williams v. St. Claire Medical Center, 657 S.W.2d 590 (Ky.App.1983), the court held that a hospital owes a duty to all patients, including the private patients of staff physicians, to enforce its published rules and regulations pertaining to patient care. The nurse anesthetist was required under hospital rules to work under the direct supervision of a certified registered nurse anesthetist, and he was alone when he administered the anesthesia to the plaintiff. Because of problems with the administration, the plaintiff went into a coma.

The court stated:

> * * * [W]hile the patient must accept all the rules and regulations of the hospital, he should be able to expect that the hospital will follow its rules established for his care. Whether a patient enters a hospital through the emergency room or is admitted as a private patient by a staff physician, the patient is entering the hospital for only one reason * * *
>
> "Indeed, the sick leave their homes and enter hospitals because of the superior treatment there promised them."

There is no rational reason or public policy why a hospital's duty to properly administer its policies should be any less to one patient than another depending upon how the patient initially arrived at the hospital.

See also Adams v. Family Planning Associates Medical Group, Inc., 315 Ill.App.3d 533, 248 Ill.Dec. 91, 733 N.E.2d 766 (Ill.C.A. 2000)(internal policies and procedures of family planning clinic admissible as evidence of standard of care).

B. NEGLIGENCE PER SE

EDWARDS v. BRANDYWINE HOSPITAL

Superior Court of Pennsylvania, 1995.
438 Pa.Super. 673, 652 A.2d 1382.

Opinion By Olszewski

In 1986, Charles Edwards was a 69–year-old retired steel worker with an artificial hip. He arrived at the Brandywine Hospital emergency room on August 25, complaining of hip pain. The hospital admitted him, and the nursing staff installed a heparin lock on his left hand. A heparin lock is a device which allows multiple intravenous fluids to be introduced at a common point.

Mr. Edwards stayed at the hospital for five days. The heparin lock was left in place for either three or four days, in apparent violation of standards promulgated by the Pennsylvania Department of Health.[10] The day after his discharge from the hospital, Mr.Edwards noticed a red spot on the back of his hand where the heparin lock had been. He returned to the hospital that day for physical therapy, and his therapist referred him to the emergency room.

10. 28 Pa.Code § 146.1. The regulation requires hospitals to develop written standards regarding such antiseptic practices as changing intravenous catheter sites. The regulation states that these standards should comply with those described in the American Hospital Association's publication entitled Infection Control in the Hospital (1979), which recommends that intravenous catheter sites be changed every 48 hours in order to avoid infection. The longer the catheter remains in the same site, the greater the risk of infection. [ ]

An ER physician checked Mr. Edwards' hand, took a sample of pus for analysis, and sent him home with a prescription for oral antibiotics. The lab results came back the next day showing a staphylococcus aureus (staph) infection. The ER physician placed the lab results and diagnosis in Mr. Edwards' chart, as required by hospital rules.

A few days later, Mr. Edwards returned to the hospital with leg pains. Somehow, his treating physicians did not notice the recent diagnosis of a staph infection in his chart. After a week, Mr. Edwards' treating physicians ordered a second lab test, which again showed the presence of a staph infection. Now Mr. Edwards' doctors put him on intravenous antibiotics. By the end of September Mr. Edwards' doctors believed they had wiped out the infection, and discharged him. He was back again a week later with pain and a fever. This time his doctors suspected that the obviously-not-yet-defeated staph infection had spread to Mr. Edwards' artificial hip.

Mr. Edwards stayed in the hospital for a month. He claimed he was discharged not for medical reasons, but because his Medicare hospitalization coverage was about to expire. He endured more treatment and hospitalizations over the next two years, until his doctors decided to remove his artificial hip and wipe out the staph infection with massive doses of antibiotics. Without his hip prosthesis, Mr. Edwards now needs crutches or a walker to get around.

Mr. Edwards sued the hospital and the doctors who treated him there for professional negligence. The trial court took notice of the Health Department regulation regarding catheter site changing, and ruled that the hospital's admitted failure to move the heparin lock for at least three days constituted negligence per se. After this ruling, Mr. Edwards' treating physicians settled, leaving only the hospital as a defendant.

At the close of Mr. Edwards' case, the trial court granted the hospital's motion for a directed verdict. The court held that while the negligence per se ruling established the hospital's breach of a duty of care, Mr. Edwards could not prove causation as a matter of law. * * *

* * * Because we disagree with the trial court's analysis that Mr. Edwards failed to establish causation, we must reverse and remand for a new trial.

Before launching into a discussion of causation and the other questions presented, it would be helpful to review the theory of this case, and how it unfolded at trial. Mr. Edwards claimed that his doctors and the hospital made a number of mistakes in treating him which led to his severe bacterial infection and the removal of his hip prosthesis. The big mistake was allowing him to develop a staph infection. Mr. Edwards sought to prove that the hospital was negligent for leaving the heparin lock in his hand for too long, which allowed the staph infection to develop. Mr. Edwards also sought to prove that a series of lesser mistakes exacerbated the initial infection, leading to the ultimate result of his hip loss: the ER doctor should have prescribed intravenous antibiotics, not oral antibiotics; the diagnosis of staph infection should have been noted by his treating physicians immediately upon his return to the hospital; his treating physicians should have consulted with an infectious disease expert early on; and the hospital should not have discharged him so soon, without a prescription for more antibiotics, and without adequate follow up.

The trial court took note of the Department of Health regulation which referred to a rule that intravenous catheter sites should be changed every 48 hours. The hospital was prepared to argue that this standard was never mandatory, and by 1986 was superseded by a 72–hour standard promulgated by the Centers for Disease Control. The trial court held that the Department of Health regulation, even if outdated and superseded, was still the applicable standard. It ruled that the hospital was negligent per se in leaving the heparin lock in the same place for over 48 hours. S.R.R. at 325a–29a.

The trial court then held that while duty and breach were established as a matter of law, Mr. Edwards had failed to prove causation as a matter of law, and that none of the other alleged mistakes by the hospital could constitute negligence. The court therefore directed a verdict in favor of the hospital.

I.

[The court first considered the trial court's ruling on causation. The trial court had held that even if the hospital violated a standard for leaving the heparin lock in longer than appropriate, this breach could not have caused the staph infection. The court applied the causation standard of Hamil v. Bashline, requiring only that the plaintiff introduce evidence that the defendant's negligent act increased the risk of harm, and the harm was in fact sustained, to raise a jury question.]

* * *

III.

This finally brings us to the issue which the hospital has prudently raised in its cross-appeal: did the trial court err in holding that leaving the heparin lock in the same spot for over 48 hours constituted negligence per se?

The trial court arrived at this ruling by examining a Pennsylvania Department of Health regulation: (a) A multidisciplinary committee made up of representatives of the medical staff, the administration, the microbiology laboratory, and the nursing staff shall establish effective measures for the control and prevention of infections. (b) The multidisciplinary committee described in subsection (a) shall do the following: (1) Develop written standards for hospital sanitation and medical asepsis. Copies of the standards shall be made available to all appropriate personnel. Adequate standards should comply with those described in Infection Control in the Hospital, published by the American Hospital Association, Chicago, Illinois. 28 Pa.Code s 146.1 (emphasis added); R.R. 222a. Page 166 of Infection Control states that intravenous catheter sets should be changed and moved to a different site every 48 hours. [ ]

The hospital was prepared to argue at trial that Infection Control in the Hospital (1979) was an outdated publication, and that the 48–hour standard had been superseded by a 72–hour standard promulgated by the Centers for Disease Control. The trial court ruled that even if the 48–hour standard was outdated, the Pennsylvania Department of Health expressly adopted it by reference in its regulation, so the hospital had to follow the 48–hour rule until the Department got around to changing it. [ ]

We see no need to determine whether the 48–hour standard was current or outdated, because the regulation only referenced the standard, and did not require its adoption. The regulation merely states that whatever standards a hospital's infection committee chooses to adopt should be in line with Infection Control. The regulation did not require Brandywine Hospital to follow in lock step with the 48–hour rule, so its decision to adopt a 72–hour rule is not necessarily negligent. We do not express any opinion about what the correct standard should be, or whether the hospital's actions were negligent. We merely hold that the hospital's failure to move Mr. Edwards' heparin lock after 48 hours did not constitute negligence per se.

* * *

Order reversed and remanded for a new trial.

Notes and Questions

1. What is the point of state regulations that specify hour limits, if they are not to be treated as enforceable rules? If elasticity is intended by the regulations, why not spell out the conditions under which deviation from the 48–hour rule is appropriate? If the regulation had required the adoption of the standard, would the court have been comfortable imposing negligence per se on the hospital?

2. The usual American practice in a tort case not involving health care is to treat violation of a statute as negligence per se, giving rise to a rebuttable presumption of negligence. If the defendant fails to rebut the presumption, the trier of fact must find against him on the negligence issue. The classic statement of the rule is found in Martin v. Herzog, 228 N.Y. 164, 126 N.E. 814 (1920). Negligence per se is usually applied in cases where a statute is used to show a standard of care. In malpractice cases, however, standards are typically used to create only a permissive inference of negligence, allowing the plaintiff to get the jury which can then accept or reject the inference of fault.

3. Hospitals are regulated by their states. The majority are also subject generally to the standards of the Joint Commission on Accreditation of Healthcare Organizations (JCAHO). The standard of care that the courts have applied reflects a baseline mandated by JCAHO standards, including peer review through internal committee structures. The court in the *Darling* case, infra, allowed evidence of JCAHO standards, which the trier of fact could accept or reject. The JCAHO Guidelines therefore operated to create a permissive inference of negligence.

This baseline has largely doomed the locality rule for hospitals. See Shilkret v. Annapolis Emergency Hospital Association, 276 Md. 187, 349 A.2d 245 (1975). As to the JCAHO generally, see Timothy S. Jost, The Joint Commission on Accreditation of Hospitals: Private Regulation of Health Care and the Public Interest, 24 B.C.L.Rev. 835 (1983).

4. Courts have proved resistant to the application of negligence per se to health care institutions, even to create an inference of negligence, unless the standard is specific and supported by expert testimony. In Van Iperen v. Van Bramer, 392 N.W.2d 480 (Iowa 1986), the court considered the effect of JCAHO standards on a hospital. The plaintiff had argued that the hospital should have provided drug monitoring services, based on JCAHO accreditation standards requiring that a hospital provide drug monitoring services through its pharmacy,

including a medication record or drug profile and a review of the patient's drug regimen for potential problems. The court rejected the argument, holding that the standards were not sufficiently specific to justify a negligence per se standard.

C. DUTIES TO TREAT PATIENTS

The relationship of the medical staff to the hospital insulates the hospital from liability, while giving physicians substantial autonomy in their treating decisions. What happens when the patient's insurance or other resources are exhausted but the staff physician believes that continued hospitalization is needed?

MUSE v. CHARTER HOSPITAL OF WINSTON–SALEM, INC.

Court of Appeals of North Carolina, 1995.
117 N.C.App. 468, 452 S.E.2d 589.

LEWIS, JUDGE.

This appeal arises from a judgment in favor of plaintiffs in an action for the wrongful death of Delbert Joseph Muse, III (hereinafter "Joe"). Joe was the son of Delbert Joseph Muse, Jr. (hereinafter "Mr. Muse") and Jane K. Muse (hereinafter "Mrs. Muse"), plaintiffs. The jury found that defendant Charter Hospital of Winston–Salem, Inc. (hereinafter "Charter Hospital" or "the hospital") was negligent in that, inter alia, it had a policy or practice which required physicians to discharge patients when their insurance expired and that this policy interfered with the exercise of the medical judgment of Joe's treating physician, Dr. L. Jarrett Barnhill, Jr. The jury awarded plaintiffs compensatory damages of approximately $1,000,000. The jury found that Mr. and Mrs. Muse were contributorily negligent, but that Charter Hospital's conduct was willful or wanton, and awarded punitive damages of $2,000,000 against Charter Hospital. Further, the jury found that Charter Hospital was an instrumentality of defendant Charter Medical Corporation (hereinafter "Charter Medical") and awarded punitive damages of $4,000,000 against Charter Medical.

The facts on which this case arose may be summarized as follows. On 12 June 1986, Joe, who was sixteen years old at the time, was admitted to Charter Hospital for treatment related to his depression and suicidal thoughts. Joe's treatment team consisted of Dr. Barnhill, as treating physician, Fernando Garzon, as nursing therapist, and Betsey Willard, as social worker. During his hospitalization, Joe experienced auditory hallucinations, suicidal and homicidal thoughts, and major depression. Joe's insurance coverage was set to expire on 12 July 1986. As that date neared, Dr. Barnhill decided that a blood test was needed to determine the proper dosage of a drug he was administering to Joe. The blood test was scheduled for 13 July, the day after Joe's insurance was to expire. Dr. Barnhill requested that the hospital administrator allow Joe to stay at Charter Hospital two more days, until 14 July, with Mr. and Mrs. Muse signing a promissory note to pay for the two extra days. The test results did not come back from the lab until 15 July. Nevertheless, Joe was discharged on 14 July and was referred by Dr. Barnhill to the Guilford County Area Mental Health, Mental Retardation and Substance Abuse Authority (hereinafter "Mental Health Authority") for outpatient treatment. Plaintiffs' evidence tended to show that Joe's condition upon discharge was worse than when he entered the hospital. Defendants' evidence, however, tended to show that while his prognosis remained guarded, Joe's condition at discharge was improved. Upon his discharge, Joe went on a one-week family vacation. On 22 July he began outpatient treatment at the Mental Health Authority, where he was seen by Dr. David Slonaker, a clinical psychologist. Two days later, Joe again met with Dr. Slonaker. Joe failed to show up at his 30 July appointment, and the next day he took a fatal overdose of Desipramine, one of his prescribed drugs.

On appeal, defendants present numerous assignments of error. We find merit in one of defendants' arguments.

II.

Defendants next argue that the trial court submitted the case to the jury on an erroneous theory of hospital liability that does not exist under the law of North Carolina. As to the theory in question, the trial court instructed: "[A] hospital is under a duty not to have policies or practices which operate in a way that interferes with the ability of a physician to exercise his medical judgment. A violation of this duty would be negligence." The jury found that there existed "a policy or practice which required physicians to discharge patients when their insurance benefits expire and which interfered with the exercise of Dr. Barnhill's medical judgment." Defendants contend that this theory of liability does not fall within any theories previously accepted by our courts.

* * *

Our Supreme Court has recognized that hospitals in this state owe a duty of care to their patients. Id. In Burns v. Forsyth County Hospital Authority, Inc. [ ] this Court held that a hospital has a duty to the patient to obey the instructions of a doctor, absent the instructions being obviously negligent or dangerous. Another recognized duty is the duty to make a reasonable effort to monitor and oversee the treatment prescribed and administered by doctors practicing at the hospital. [ ] In light of these holdings, it seems axiomatic that the hospital has the duty not to institute policies or practices which interfere with the doctor's medical judgment. We hold that pursuant to the reasonable person standard, Charter Hospital had a duty not to institute a policy or practice which required that patients be discharged when their insurance expired and which interfered with the medical judgment of Dr. Barnhill.

III.

Defendants next argue that even if the theory of negligence submitted to the jury was proper, the jury's finding that Charter Hospital had such a practice was not supported by sufficient evidence. * * * We conclude that in the case at hand, the evidence was sufficient to go to the jury.

Plaintiffs' evidence included the testimony of Charter Hospital employees and outside experts. Fernando Garzon, Joe's nursing therapist at Charter Hospital, testified that the hospital had a policy of discharging patients when their insurance expired. Specifically, when the issue of insurance came up in treatment team meetings, plans were made to discharge the patient. When

Dr. Barnhill and the other psychiatrists and therapists spoke of insurance, they seemed to lack autonomy. For example, Garzon testified, they would state, "So and so is to be discharged. We must do this." Finally, Garzon testified that when he returned from a vacation, and Joe was no longer at the hospital, he asked several employees why Joe had been discharged and they all responded that he was discharged because his insurance had expired. Jane Sims, a former staff member at the hospital, testified that several employees expressed alarm about Joe's impending discharge, and that a therapist explained that Joe could no longer stay at the hospital because his insurance had expired. Sims also testified that Dr. Barnhill had misgivings about discharging Joe, and that Dr. Barnhill's frustration was apparent to everyone. One of plaintiffs' experts testified that based on a study regarding the length of patient stays at Charter Hospital, it was his opinion that patients were discharged based on insurance, regardless of their medical condition. Other experts testified that based on Joe's serious condition on the date of discharge, the expiration of insurance coverage must have caused Dr. Barnhill to discharge Joe. The experts further testified as to the relevant standard of care, and concluded that Charter Hospital's practices were below the standard of care and caused Joe's death. We hold that this evidence was sufficient to go to the jury.

Defendants further argue that the evidence was insufficient to support the jury's finding that Charter Hospital engaged in conduct that was willful or wanton. An act is willful when it is done purposely and deliberately in violation of the law, or when it is done knowingly and of set purpose, or when the mere will has free play, without yielding to reason. [ ] * * * We conclude that the jury could have reasonably found from the above-stated evidence that Charter Hospital acted knowingly and of set purpose, and with reckless indifference to the rights of others. Therefore, we hold that the finding of willful or wanton conduct on the part of Charter Hospital was supported by sufficient evidence.

* * *

For the reasons stated, we find no error in the judgment of the trial court, except for that part of the judgment awarding punitive damages, which is reversed and remanded for proceedings consistent with this opinion.

No error in part, reversed in part and remanded.

Notes and Questions

1. Should the *Muse* duty extend to all situations in which the physician and the hospital administration are in conflict? If the physician always prevails, then how does a hospital control its costs and its bad debts? Why does the court treat health care as special in this case? Surely a grocery store does not have to give us free groceries if we are short of cash as the checkout counter, nor does our landlord have to allow us to stay for free if we cannot cover our next month's rent. Is it simply the advantage of hindsight here that impels the court's allowance of such a duty on hospitals?

2. How does this holding square with the *Wickline* and *Wilson* decisions discussed in Chapter 4, supra. What can a hospital do in such situations? Offer free care?

3. Does such a duty extend as well to managed care organizations, whose very design is premised on mechanisms for containing health care costs? What would happen to the underlying premises of cost control in managed care organizations, if the *Muse* doctrine were held to apply?

D. STRICT LIABILITY

KARIBJANIAN v. THOMAS JEFFERSON UNIVERSITY HOSPITAL

United States District Court, Eastern District of Pennsylvania, 1989.
717 F.Supp. 1081.

LORD.

Plaintiff claims that her husband died as a result of exposure in 1956 to the substance Thorotrast, a form of thorium dioxide, with which he was injected during a diagnostic medical procedure called a cerebral arteriography.[1] She alleges Thorotrast is an inherently unsafe product and that defendants knew or should have known that it is so. Defendant Thomas Jefferson University Hospital ("Hospital") moves to dismiss several paragraphs of the complaint, pursuant to Fed.R.Civ.P. 12(b)(6). * * * [ ]

* * *

Finally, the Hospital asks me to dismiss paragraphs 80 and 81 of the complaint, which allege

> 80. [The Hospital] sold, supplied and/or distributed a defective and dangerous product, Thorotrast, which was administered to plaintiff's decedent substantially unchanged from the form that it was received in.
>
> 81. [The Hospital] is strictly liable to plaintiff's decedent for the injuries and resulting death sustained under §§ 402A and/or 519 and 520 of the *Restatement (Second) of Torts* as adopted in the Commonwealth of Pennsylvania.

Section 402A provides, in part, that

> (1) One who sells any product in a defective condition unreasonably dangerous to the user or consumer * * * is subject to liability * * * if (a) the seller is engaged in the business of selling such a product. * * *

The Hospital cites two Superior Court decisions which hold that a hospital cannot be liable under § 402A when a defective surgical tool injures a patient during an operation. *Podrat v. Codman–Shurtleff,* 384 Pa.Super. 404, 558 A.2d 895 (1989) (forceps); *Grubb v. Albert Einstein Medical Center,* 255 Pa.Super. 381, 387 A.2d 480 (1978) (bone plug cutter).[4] The *Podrat* court reasoned that a hospital is primarily in the business of supplying services, and "supplies" surgical tools only incidentally; and that the medical service (a

1. According to *Stedman's Medical Dictionary,* 5th Ed. (1982), a cerebral arteriography, also called a cerebral angiography, is "visualization of an artery or arteries by x-rays after injection of a radiopaque contrast medium." "[I]njection may be made by percutaneous puncture or after exposure. * * * " It appears from the complaint that Thorotrast was used as the contrast medium.

4. In *Grubb,* the per curiam opinion states that a hospital can be liable under § 402A; however, four of the seven judges dissented from this statement, and the hospital was held liable only under a negligence theory.

back operation) could not have been performed without the use of the instrument. ___ Pa.Super. at ___, 558 A.2d at 898. The Hospital contends that likewise it was not in the "business of selling" Thorotrast; rather that it was in the business of providing services.

Plaintiff seeks to limit the holding in *Podrat* to products which are approved but turn out to be defective; she argues that Thorotrast, because it is alleged to be inherently unsafe, is distinguishable. I do not find this proposed distinction persuasive.

It might be supposed that surgical tools like the forceps in *Podrat* and the bone plug cutter in *Grubb* are different from contrast media because those surgical tools may be reused on a number of patients, while a dose of Thorotrast is completely consumed by a single patient. However, in *Francioni v. Gibsonia,* 472 Pa. 362, 372 A.2d 736, 739 (1977), the court held that lessors of durable products are liable to the same degree as sellers of such products.

A decision of a state's intermediate appellate court "is a datum for ascertaining state law which is not to be disregarded by a federal court unless it is convinced by other persuasive data that the highest court of the state would decide otherwise." [ ] There are, I think, significant data which suggest Pennsylvania's Supreme Court would in some circumstances hold a hospital liable under § 402A as a seller of a product like Thorotrast, if it is the product itself rather than the procedure by which it was administered which is alleged to have been defective.

Comment (f) to § 402A explains what the *Restatement's* authors meant by the "business of selling."

> It is not necessary that the seller be engaged solely in the business of selling such products. Thus the rule applies to the owner of a motion picture theatre who sells popcorn or ice cream, either for consumption on the premises or in packages to be taken home.
>
> The rule does not, however, apply to the occasional seller of food or other such products who is not engaged in that activity as a part of his business. Thus it does not apply to the housewife who, on one occasion, sells to her neighbor a jar of jam. * * *

So long as a hospital *regularly* supplies contrast media to its patients, albeit as an incidental part of its service operations, it seems to fall within § 402A as explained by comment (f). The comment draws no distinction between suppliers of goods who also supply services, and those suppliers who simply supply goods.

* * *

It is not beyond doubt that plaintiff can prove no facts which would establish that the Hospital was a seller of Thorotrast for purposes of § 402A. Unlike the product auctioned in *Musser,* the Thorotrast allegedly came from the Hospital's own inventory, ¶ 33, which I take to mean the Hospital owned it until it supplied it to plaintiff's decedent, via his physician, and that the Hospital regularly supplied Thorotrast to other patients. Plaintiff must be given the opportunity to present evidence concerning the other factors identified in *Musser* and *Francioni.*

I am also influenced by the thoughtful discussion of Judge Pollak in *Villari v. Terminix,* 677 F.Supp. 330, 333–334 (E.D.Pa.1987), in which he held that a professional pesticide application firm could be liable under § 402A even though it provided services as well as the pesticides themselves.[5] Judge Pollak noted that the defendant was the sole "retail" supplier of the pesticide, and that it told its customers that the product was safe. On the other hand, at least one court, in California, has held that hospitals cannot be liable under § 402A for defective drugs, under reasoning similar to that in *Podrat. Carmichael v. Reitz,* 17 Cal.App.3d 958, 95 Cal.Rptr. 381 (1971). *See also Flynn v. Langfitt,* 710 F.Supp. 150, 152 (E.D.Pa.1989) (hospital not liable under § 402A for defective tissue graft).

I will deny the Hospital's motion to dismiss ¶ ¶ 80 and 81 of the complaint. Plaintiff will, however, have to establish the factual bases I outlined above before she can recover against the Hospital under § 402A. Neither party has briefed the question of whether the Hospital can be liable under § 519 and § 520 of the *Restatement (Second) of Torts,* dealing with abnormally dangerous activities. I will leave that imaginative theory of liability for another day.

Notes and Questions

1. The hospital in *Karibjanian* considers Pennsylvania Superior Court cases rejecting the application of Restatement (Second) Torts, section 402A, to hospitals for defective surgical tools. It then rejects these decisions as predictive of what the Pennsylvania Supreme Court might do. In Podrat v. Codman–Shurtleff, Inc., 384 Pa.Super. 404, 558 A.2d 895 (1989) (involving forceps that broke, leaving piece in patient's disc space), the court stressed the hospital's actual function of providing a service to a patient. The instrument's use was simply incidental to the provision of this medical service. In Grubb v. Albert Einstein Medical Center, 255 Pa.Super. 381, 387 A.2d 480 (1978) (defective plug cutter), the per curiam opinion stated that a hospital could be liable under § 402A; however, since four of the seven judges dissented, the hospital was liable only under a negligence theory.

What is the "persuasive data" that leads the court to reject these lower court decisions? The court does not seem impressed by the argument that providers of medical services should be treated specially. It cites as analogous activities auctioneering and pesticide application. What facts must the plaintiff now establish before she can recover against the hospital?

How about the analogy in footnote 5? Is the provision of expensive restaurant food and service an apt comparison to hospital-based care involving drugs and devices? A chef cannot, after all, make a souffle without eggs; neither can a surgeon operate on a patient without medical devices, nor a radiologist do testing without contrast media. A plurality of the Pennsylvania Superior Court in *Grubb,* supra, in dicta, stated that "* * * if a hospital supplies equipment to an operating physician the hospital must appraise themselves of the risks involved and adopt every effort to insure the safety of the equipment chosen."

5. To offer another analogy, a restaurant patron who enjoys an exquisite souffle values the services of the chef more than the eggs with which it is made, since the eggs could be had for less than a dollar at any store. Nonetheless, if fate has it that the eggs are bad, the restaurant would be liable under § 402A as a supplier of eggs, even though the eggs were but an incidental part of what the patron paid for. And this is not to mention the services of the maitre d' who seats her, and the waiter who serves her.

2. The court also suggests, in a tantalizing last paragraph, that the hospital might be liable under sections 519 and 520 of the Restatement (Second) of Torts, Abnormally Dangerous Activities, which the plaintiffs had pleaded. Is the court kidding? Or is there a possible argument to be made against hospital-based health care? See the discussion in Chapter 1 on iatrogenic injury.

3. A medical intervention often requires the use of medical products: knee joints, bone graft material, pig heart valves. Breast implant prostheses are a common example of such a service-product intervention. Courts apply strict liability to the distributors of such products but are reluctant to extend strict liability to a health care provider using the product in a way incidental to the primary function of providing medical services. See, e.g., Cafazzo v. Central Medical Health Services, 430 Pa.Super. 480, 635 A.2d 151 (Pa.Super.1993)(mandibular prosthesis); Hoff v. Zimmer, 746 F.Supp. 872 (W.D.Wis.1990)(hip prosthesis); Hector v. Cedars–Sinai Medical Center, 180 Cal.App.3d 493, 225 Cal.Rptr. 595 (2d Dist.1986) (pacemaker). Contra, see Budding v. SSM Healthcare System, 19 S.W.3d 678 (Mo.2000).

4. The devices that a hospital furnishes its staff and patients, as part of the provision of medical service, must be properly maintained. Strict liability arguments imported from product defects litigation have made some inroads in lawsuits against hospitals. Both implied warranty doctrine and Section 402A of the Restatement, Second, have on rare occasions been applied to devices used in hospitals. The growth of technological medicine has made physicians increasingly dependent upon diagnostic machinery, computer-assisted tests, and drugs and devices. Many of the *res ipsa loquitur* cases, for example, involve medical devices that failed during surgery. These devices are bought by a hospital's purchasing department, subject to the controls imposed by the hospital's administration. The standard use of devices such as fetal monitors and CT scanners implicate the hospital as middleman in a stream of commerce of the sort courts discuss in products liability cases.

In Skelton v. Druid City Hosp. Board, 459 So.2d 818 (Ala.1984), a suture needle broke off in the patient during ventral hernia repair. These needles were reused several times by the hospital, and there was no way to be sure exactly how many times. Section 2–315 of the Uniform Commercial Code, implied warranty of fitness for a particular purpose, was applied to this "hybrid" service-product transaction between hospital and patient. The court held:

> The gist of an action under this section is reliance. Patients are rarely in a position to judge the quality of the medical supplies and other goods sold to them and used in their care; often, those supplies are of an inherently dangerous nature. The complete dependence of patients on the staff of a hospital to choose fit products justifies the imposition of an implied warranty under s. 7–2–315, whether the hospital is a "merchant" or not. Id. at 823.

5. Hospitals often reuse medical devices, such as pulmonary catheters, hemodialyzers, biopsy needles, electrosurgical devices, and endotracheal tubes. The pressure to contain costs is one of the primary reasons for this practice. When a reused device proves defective and a patient is injured as a result, liability may fall on the manufacturer, the retailer, the hospital, and health care professionals. Strict liability and breach of warranty theories, as well as negligence, are likely to be attractive doctrines to apply, by analogy to the products liability area generally. Janice M. Hogan and Thomas E. Cdolonna, 53 Food & Drug L.J. 385 (1998).

6. Drugs are normally prescribed by the treating physician, and are purchased by the patient from third party pharmacies. In the hospital setting,

however, the patient is usually administered a variety of drugs as part of treatment and these drugs come from hospital supplies. Should a duty to warn a patient of possible side-effects of the drug fall on the hospital as well as the treating physician? The court in *Karibjanian* allowed the plaintiff's cause of action claiming a hospital duty to supervise physicians, which included ensuring that informed consent was obtained. This has not been a popular position. See, e.g., Kirk v. Michael Reese Hospital and Medical Center, 117 Ill.2d 507, 111 Ill.Dec. 944, 513 N.E.2d 387 (1987), where the Illinois Supreme Court held that a hospital which had dispensed and administered psychotropic drugs to the plaintiff as an in-patient had no duty to warn him of the drug's side effects upon discharge a few hours later.

7. Hospital administrative and mechanical services have been held to be subject potentially to strict liability, Johnson v. Sears, 355 F.Supp. 1065, 1067 (E.D.Wis.1973), as have hospital operations that are not "integrally related to its primary function of providing medical services", Silverhart v. Mount Zion Hospital, 20 Cal.App.3d 1022, 98 Cal.Rptr. 187 (1971) (gift shop as example of such a nonessential function).

Problem: The Monitor Failed

Jane Rudd has approached you as to the merits of a suit for injuries sustained by her infant during childbirth. Ms. Rudd went into labor at full term and was admitted to the Columbia Hospital. She was examined, placed in a labor room, and attached to a fetal monitor. She objected to the use of the monitor, but the Chief Resident, after a lengthy debate with the staff, strongly urged her to use it. She finally acquiesced. The monitor is manufactured by Rohm Instruments and leased to the hospital by Medex Equipment Ltd. Medex maintains the monitors it leases to hospitals on a monthly basis, or as needed.

The nurse responsible for Ms. Rudd checked the monitor printout several times an hour. The machine has a warning buzzer that sounds if abnormal fetal heart rates are detected. It did not sound at any time. Neither the doctor nor the nurses checked the fetal heart rate with a stethoscope after the first two hours. At 6 a.m. on Sunday morning, the doctor on duty delivered Ms. Rudd's baby. Its umbilical cord was wrapped tightly around its neck and it showed signs of fetal distress at delivery. The child has extensive brain damage due to oxygen deprivation.

Because of comments made by the delivery room nurse, Ms. Rudd believes that the monitor may have malfunctioned and failed to either detect or print out variations in fetal heartrate near the end of labor.

What tort doctrines can you invoke in drafting a complaint? What defendants might you pursue? What further information do you need?

E. THE EMERGENCE OF CORPORATE NEGLIGENCE

The courts' stretching of vicarious liability doctrine to sweep in doctors as conduits to hospital liability led inevitably to the direct imposition of corporate negligence liability on the hospital. The courts effectively made the medical personnel who used the hospital part of this "enterprise", whether they were staff employees or independent contractors.

1. The Duty to Protect Patients From Medical Staff Negligence

The next step was to hold the hospital directly liable for the failure of administrators and staff to properly monitor and supervise the delivery of health care within the hospital. The leading case is *Darling v. Charleston Community Memorial Hospital.*

DARLING v. CHARLESTON COMMUNITY MEMORIAL HOSPITAL

Supreme Court of Illinois, 1965.
33 Ill.2d 326, 211 N.E.2d 253.

This action was brought on behalf of Dorrence Darling II, a minor (hereafter plaintiff), by his father and next friend, to recover damages for allegedly negligent medical and hospital treatment which necessitated the amputation of his right leg below the knee. The action was commenced against the Charleston Community Memorial Hospital and Dr. John R. Alexander, but prior to trial the action was dismissed as to Dr. Alexander, pursuant to a covenant not to sue. The jury returned a verdict against the hospital in the sum of $150,000. This amount was reduced by $40,000, the amount of the settlement with the doctor. The judgment in favor of the plaintiff in the sum of $110,000 was affirmed on appeal by the Appellate Court for the Fourth District, which granted a certificate of importance. 50 Ill.App.2d 253, 200 N.E.2d 149.

On November 5, 1960, the plaintiff, who was 18 years old, broke his leg while playing in a college football game. He was taken to the emergency room at the defendant hospital where Dr. Alexander, who was on emergency call that day, treated him. Dr. Alexander, with the assistance of hospital personnel, applied traction and placed the leg in a plaster cast. A heat cradle was applied to dry the cast. Not long after the application of the cast plaintiff was in great pain and his toes, which protruded from the cast, became swollen and dark in color. They eventually became cold and insensitive. On the evening of November 6, Dr. Alexander "notched" the cast around the toes, and on the afternoon of the next day he cut the cast approximately three inches up from the foot. On November 8 he split the sides of the cast with a Stryker saw; in the course of cutting the cast the plaintiff's leg was cut on both sides. Blood and other seepage were observed by the nurses and others, and there was a stench in the room, which one witness said was the worst he had smelled since World War II. The plaintiff remained in Charleston Hospital until November 19, when he was transferred to Barnes Hospital in St. Louis and placed under the care of Dr. Fred Reynolds, head of orthopedic surgery at Washington University School of Medicine and Barnes Hospital. Dr. Reynolds found that the fractured leg contained a considerable amount of dead tissue which in his opinion resulted from interference with the circulation of blood in the limb caused by swelling or hemorrhaging of the leg against the construction of the cast. Dr. Reynolds performed several operations in a futile attempt to save the leg but ultimately it had to be amputated eight inches below the knee.

The evidence before the jury is set forth at length in the opinion of the Appellate Court and need not be stated in detail here. The plaintiff contends that it established that the defendant was negligent in permitting Dr. Alexander to do orthopedic work of the kind required in this case, and not requiring him to review his operative procedures to bring them up to date; in failing, through its medical staff, to exercise adequate supervision over the case, especially since Dr. Alexander had been placed on emergency duty by the hospital, and in not requiring consultation, particularly after complications had developed. Plaintiff contends also that in a case which developed as this one did, it was the duty of the nurses to watch the protruding toes constantly for changes of color, temperature and movement, and to check circulation every ten to twenty minutes, whereas the proof showed that these things were done only a few times a day. Plaintiff argues that it was the duty of the hospital staff to see that these procedures were followed, and that either the nurses were derelict in failing to report developments in the case to the hospital administrator, he was derelict in bringing them to the attention of the medical staff, or the staff was negligent in failing to take action. Defendant is a licensed and accredited hospital, and the plaintiff contends that the licensing regulations, accreditation standards, and its own bylaws define the hospital's duty, and that an infraction of them imposes liability for the resulting injury.

* * *

The basic dispute, as posed by the parties, centers upon the duty that rested upon the defendant hospital. That dispute involves the effect to be given to evidence concerning the community standard of care and diligence, and also the effect to be given to hospital regulations adopted by the State Department of Public Health under the Hospital Licensing Act (Ill.Rev.Stat. 1963, chap. 111½, pars. 142–157.), to the Standards for Hospital Accreditation of the American Hospital Association, and to the bylaws of the defendant.

As has been seen, the defendant argues in this court that its duty is to be determined by the care customarily offered by hospitals generally in its community. Strictly speaking, the question is not one of duty, for "* * * in negligence cases, the duty is always the same, to conform to the legal standard of reasonable conduct in the light of the apparent risk. What the defendant must do, or must not do, is a question of the standard of conduct required to satisfy the duty." (Prosser on Torts, 3rd ed. at 331.) * * * Custom is relevant in determining the standard of care because it illustrates what is feasible, it suggests a body of knowledge of which the defendant should be aware, and it warns of the possibility of far-reaching consequences if a higher standard is required. [ ] But custom should never be conclusive.

In the present case the regulations, standards, and bylaws which the plaintiff introduced into evidence, performed much the same function as did evidence of custom. This evidence aided the jury in deciding what was feasible and what the defendant knew or should have known. It did not conclusively determine the standard of care and the jury was not instructed that it did.

"The conception that the hospital does not undertake to treat the patient, does not undertake to act through its doctors and nurses, but undertakes instead simply to procure them to act upon their own responsibility, no longer reflects the fact. Present-day hospitals, as their manner of operation plainly demonstrates, do far more than furnish facilities for treatment. They regularly employ on a salary basis a large staff of physicians, nurses and interns, as well as administrative and manual workers, and they charge patients for medical care and treatment, collecting for such services, if necessary, by legal action. Certainly, the person who avails himself of 'hospital facilities' expects that the hospital will attempt to cure him, not that its nurses or other employees will act on their own responsibility." (Fuld, J., in Bing v. Thunig (1957), 2 N.Y.2d 656, 163 N.Y.S.2d 3, 11, 143 N.E.2d 3, 8.) The Standards for Hospital Accreditation, the state licensing regulations and the defendant's bylaws demonstrate that the medical profession and other responsible authorities regard it as both desirable and feasible that a hospital assume certain responsibilities for the care of the patient.

* * * Therefore we need not analyze all of the issues submitted to the jury. Two of them were that the defendant had negligently: "5. Failed to have a sufficient number of trained nurses for bedside care of all patients at all times capable of recognizing the progressive gangrenous condition of the plaintiff's right leg, and of bringing the same to the attention of the hospital administration and to the medical staff so that adequate consultation could have been secured and such conditions rectified; * * * 7. Failed to require consultation with or examination by members of the hospital surgical staff skilled in such treatment; or to review the treatment rendered to the plaintiff and to require consultants to be called in as needed."

We believe that the jury verdict is supportable on either of these grounds. On the basis of the evidence before it the jury could reasonably have concluded that the nurses did not test for circulation in the leg as frequently as necessary, that skilled nurses would have promptly recognized the conditions that signalled a dangerous impairment of circulation in the plaintiff's leg, and would have known that the condition would become irreversible in a matter of hours. At that point it became the nurses' duty to inform the attending physician, and if he failed to act, to advise the hospital authorities so that appropriate action might be taken. As to consultation, there is no dispute that the hospital failed to review Dr. Alexander's work or require a consultation; the only issue is whether its failure to do so was negligence. On the evidence before it the jury could reasonably have found that it was.

[The remainder of the opinion, discussing expert testimony and damages, is omitted.]

Notes and Questions

1. Consider the issues submitted to the jury. It is alleged that both the nurses and the administrators were negligent in not taking steps to curtail Dr. Alexander's handling of the case. How can a nurse "blow the whistle" on a doctor without risking damage to her own career? See the section on labor law in health care institutions, infra. How can a nurse exercise medical judgment in violation of Medical Practice statutes?

In Jensen v. Archbishop Bergan Mercy Hospital, 236 Neb. 1, 459 N.W.2d 178, 183 (1990), the plaintiffs alleged that the nursing staff should have altered the attending physician's orders if they had reason to believe they were wrong. The court disagreed, holding that " * * * hospital staff members lack authority to alter or depart from an attending physician's order for a hospital patient and lack authority to determine what is a proper course of medical treatment for a hospitalized patient. The foregoing is recognition of the realities and practicalities inherent in the physician-hospital nurse relationship."

In Gafner v. Down East Community Hospital, 735 A.2d 969 (Me.1999), the plaintiff's daughter suffered a brachial plexus injury while the defendant physician was trying to deliver the baby. The plaintiff argued that the hospital's lack of written policies regarding consultation constituted corporate negligence. Maine refused to recognize corporate negligence in an action against independent physicians for failing to control their actions. "Creating a duty that would place external controls upon the medical judgments and actions of physicians should not be undertaken without a thorough and thoughtful analysis. We decline to create such a duty from whole cloth and therefore decline to recognize the cause of action.... "

2. *Darling* disclosed the prevailing attitude of hospital administrators toward affiliated doctors, reflecting the earlier concept of the doctor as independent contractor. The hospital administrator was subjected to a prolonged cross-examination by the plaintiff's attorney exploring his obligations to evaluate doctor training and conduct. The administrator testified:

> "As the Board's representative, I did nothing to see that Dr. Alexander reviewed his operating techniques for the handling of broken bones. So far as I know, Dr. Alexander may not have reviewed his operating techniques since he was first licensed to practice in 1928. No examinations were ever given. I never asked questions of the doctor about this matter. The governing board, neither through me nor through any other designated administrative representative, ever checked up on the ability of Dr. Alexander as compared by medical text books. I had access at the hospital to some good orthopedic books. * * * Other than buying these books, I never made any effort to see that Dr. Alexander, or any other physician admitted to practice more than thirty years ago, read them." Darling v. Charleston Community Memorial Hosp., 50 Ill.App.2d 253, 295, 200 N.E.2d 149, 171 (1964).

How can a hospital administrator devise procedures to trigger an alarm when a physician is incompetent? Must the administrator himself be an M.D.? Can you think of methods that would have avoided the *Darling* tragedy? Consider the ideas developed by Leape in Chapter 1. What systems might you implement to prevent such errors?

In Albain v. Flower Hospital, 50 Ohio St.3d 251, 553 N.E.2d 1038, 1046 (1990), the Ohio Supreme Court recognized a hospital's independent duty to exercise due care in granting staff privileges and retaining competent physicians, but qualified the duty. The Court held that an act of physician malpractice does not create a presumption that the hospital negligently granted staff privileges, and that a hospital is not expected "to constantly supervise and second-guess the activities of its physicians, beyond the duty to remove a known incompetent. Most hospital administrators are laypersons with no medical training at all." They added: " * * * the hospital is not an *insurer* of the skills of physicians to whom it has granted staff privileges."

3. See, for a description of the *Darling* case by the plaintiff's lawyer, Appelman, Hospital Liability for Acts of Nonsalaried Staff Physicians, Personal Injury Annual 161 (1964); see also (describing the case), Spero, Hospital Liability, 15 Trial 22 (Sept. 1979). For an older case imposing direct liability for the failure of a hospital to control the use of its facilities, see Hendrickson v. Hodkin, 276 N.Y. 252, 11 N.E.2d 899 (1937) (hospital liable for allowing a quack to treat a patient on its premises).

* * *

THOMPSON v. NASON HOSP.

Supreme Court of Pennsylvania, 1991.
527 Pa. 330, 591 A.2d 703.

ZAPPALA, JUSTICE.

Allocatur was granted to examine the novel issue of whether a theory of corporate liability with respect to hospitals should be recognized in this Commonwealth. For the reasons set forth below, we adopt today the theory of corporate liability as it relates to hospitals. * * *

* * *

Considering this predicate to our analysis, we now turn to the record which contains the facts underlying this personal injury action. At approximately 7 a.m. on March 16, 1978, Appellee, Linda A. Thompson, was involved in an automobile accident with a school bus. Mrs. Thompson was transported by ambulance from the accident scene to Nason Hospital's emergency room where she was admitted with head and leg injuries. The hospital's emergency room personnel were advised by Appellee, Donald A. Thompson, that his wife was taking the drug Coumadin, that she had a permanent pacemaker, and that she took other heart medications.

Subsequent to Mrs. Thompson's admission to Nason Hospital, Dr. Edward D. Schultz, a general practitioner who enjoyed staff privileges at Nason Hospital, entered the hospital via the emergency room to make his rounds. Although Dr. Schultz was not assigned duty in the emergency room, an on-duty hospital nurse asked him to attend Mrs. Thompson due to a prior physician-patient relationship. Dr. Schultz examined Mrs. Thompson and diagnosed her as suffering from multiple injuries including extensive lacerations over her left eye and the back of her scalp, constricted pupils, enlarged heart with a Grade III micro-systolic murmur, a brain concussion and amnesia. X-rays that were taken revealed fractures of the right tibia and right heel.

Following Dr. Schultz's examination and diagnosis, Dr. Larry Jones, an ophthalmologist, sutured the lacerations over Mrs. Thompson's left eye. It was during that time that Dr. Schultz consulted with Dr. Rao concerning orthopedic repairs. Dr. Rao advised conservative therapy until her critical medical condition improved.

Dr. Schultz knew Mrs. Thompson was suffering from rheumatic heart and mitral valve disease and was on anticoagulant therapy. Because he had no specific training in establishing dosages for such therapy, Dr. Schultz called Dr. Marvin H. Meisner, a cardiologist who was treating Mrs. Thompson with an anticoagulant therapy. Although Dr. Meisner was unavailable, Dr. Schultz did speak with Dr. Meisner's associate Dr. Steven P. Draskoczy.

Mrs. Thompson had remained in the emergency room during this time. Her condition, however, showed no sign of improvement. Due to both the multiple trauma received in the accident and her pre-existing heart disease, Dr. Schultz, as attending physician, admitted her to Nason Hospital's intensive care unit at 11:20 a.m.

The next morning at 8:30 a.m., Dr. Mark Paris, a general surgeon on staff at Nason Hospital, examined Mrs. Thompson. He found that she was unable to move her left foot and toes. It was also noted by Dr. Paris that the patient had a positive Babinski—a neurological sign of an intracerebral problem. Twelve hours later, Dr. Schultz examined Mrs. Thompson and found more bleeding in her eye. He also indicated in the progress notes that the problem with her left leg was that it was neurological.

On March 18, 1978, the third day of her hospitalization, Dr. Larry Jones, the ophthalmologist who treated her in the emergency room, examined her in the intensive care unit. He indicated in the progress notes an "increased hematuria secondary to anticoagulation. Right eye now involved". Dr. Schultz also examined Mrs. Thompson that day and noted the decreased movement of her left leg was neurologic. Dr. Paris's progress note that date approved the withholding of Coumadin and the continued use of Heparin.

The following day, Mrs. Thompson had complete paralysis of the left side. Upon examination by Dr. Schultz he questioned whether she needed to be under the care of a neurologist or needed to be watched there. At 10:30 a.m. that day, Dr. Schultz transferred her to the Hershey Medical Center because of her progressive neurological problem.

Linda Thompson underwent tests at the Hershey Medical Center. The results of the tests revealed that she had a large intracerebral hematoma in the right frontal temporal and parietal lobes of the brain. She was subsequently discharged on April 1, 1978, without regaining the motor function of her left side.

* * * The complaint alleged inter alia that Mrs. Thompson's injuries were the direct and proximate result of the negligence of Nason Hospital acting through its agents, servants and employees in failing to adequately examine and treat her, in failing to follow its rules relative to consultations and in failing to monitor her conditions during treatment. * * *

* * *

The first issue Nason Hospital raised is whether the Superior Court erred in adopting a theory of corporate liability with respect to a hospital. This issue had not heretofore been determined by the Court. Nason Hospital contends that it had no duty to observe, supervise or control the actual treatment of Linda Thompson.

Hospitals in the past enjoyed absolute immunity from tort liability. [ ] The basis of that immunity was the perception that hospitals functioned as charitable organizations. [ ] However, hospitals have evolved into highly sophisticated corporations operating primarily on a fee-for-service basis. The corporate hospital of today has assumed the role of a comprehensive health center with responsibility for arranging and coordinating the total health care of its patients. As a result of this metamorphosis, hospital immunity was eliminated. [ ]

Not surprisingly, the by-product of eliminating hospital immunity has been the filing of malpractice actions against hospitals. Courts have recognized several bases on which hospitals may be subject to liability including respondeat superior, ostensible agency and corporate negligence. [ ]

The development of hospital liability in this Commonwealth mirrored that which occurred in other jurisdictions. * * * We now turn our attention to the theory of corporate liability with respect to the hospital, which was first recognized in this Commonwealth by the court below.

Corporate negligence is a doctrine under which the hospital is liable if it fails to uphold the proper standard of care owed the patient, which is to ensure the patient's safety and well-being while at the hospital. This theory of liability creates a nondelegable duty which the hospital owes directly to a patient. Therefore, an injured party does not have to rely on and establish the negligence of a third party.

The hospital's duties have been classified into four general areas: (1) a duty to use reasonable care in the maintenance of safe and adequate facilities and equipment—Candler General Hospital Inc. v. Purvis, 123 Ga.App. 334, 181 S.E.2d 77 (1971); (2) a duty to select and retain only competent physicians—Johnson v. Misericordia Community Hospital, 99 Wis.2d 708, 301 N.W.2d 156 (1981); (3) a duty to oversee all persons who practice medicine within its walls as to patient care—Darling v. Charleston Community Memorial Hospital, supra.; and (4) a duty to formulate, adopt and enforce adequate rules and policies to ensure quality care for the patients–Wood v. Samaritan Institution, 26 Cal.2d 847, 161 P.2d 556 (Cal. Ct. App.1945). [ ]

Other jurisdictions have embraced this doctrine of corporate negligence or corporate liability such as to warrant it being called an "emerging trend". [ ]

* * *

Today, we take a step beyond the hospital's duty of care delineated in Riddle in full recognition of the corporate hospital's role in the total health care of its patients. In so doing, we adopt as a theory of hospital liability the doctrine of corporate negligence or corporate liability under which the hospital is liable if it fails to uphold the proper standard of care owed its patient. In addition, we fully embrace the aforementioned four categories of the hospital's duties. It is important to note that for a hospital to be charged with negligence, it is necessary to show that the hospital had actual or constructive knowledge of the defect or procedures which created the harm. [ ] Furthermore, the hospital's negligence must have been a substantial factor in bringing about the harm to the injured party. [ ].

The final question Nason Hospital raises is did Superior Court err in finding that there was a material issue of fact with respect to the hospital's duty to monitor and review medical services provided within its facilities. Nason Hospital contends that during Linda Thompson's hospitalization, it did not become aware of any exceptional circumstance which would require or justify its intervention into her treatment. The Hospital Association of Pennsylvania, as amicus curiae, argues that it is neither realistic nor appropriate to expect the hospital to conduct daily review and supervision of the independent medical judgment of each member of the medical staff of which it may have actual or constructive knowledge.

Conversely, Appellees argue that Nason Hospital was negligent in failing to monitor the medical services provided Mrs. Thompson. Specifically, Appellees claim that the hospital ignored its Rules and Regulations governing Medical Staff by failing to ensure the patient received adequate medical attention through physician consultations. Appellees also contend that Nason Hospital's medical staff members and personnel treating Mrs. Thompson were aware of her deteriorating condition, brought about by being over anticoagulated, yet did nothing.

It is well established that a hospital staff member or employee has a duty to recognize and report abnormalities in the treatment and condition of its patients. [ ] If the attending physician fails to act after being informed of such abnormalities, it is then incumbent upon the hospital staff member or employee to so advise the hospital authorities so that appropriate action might be taken. [ ] When there is a failure to report changes in a patient's condition and/or to question a physician's order which is not in accord with standard medical practice and the patient is injured as a result, the hospital will be liable for such negligence. [ ]

A thorough review of the record of this case convinces us that there is a sufficient question of material fact presented as to whether Nason Hospital was negligent in supervising the quality of the medical care Mrs. Thompson received, such that the trial court could not have properly granted summary judgment on the issue of corporate liability.

The order of Superior Court is affirmed. Jurisdiction is relinquished.

Notes and Questions

1. What does *Thompson* add to *Darling*'s discussion of the scope of corporate negligence? The fourth duty, "to formulate, adopt and enforce adequate rules and policies to ensure quality care for the patients", moves well beyond monitoring staff, drawing our scrutiny to how the institution operates as a system, and allowing plaintiffs to search for negligence in the very design of the operating framework of the hospital. Is this a useful advance over the caselaw thus far?

2. Selection and retention of medical staff. Probably the most important function of a hospital is to select high quality physicians for its medical staff. A typical hospital has several categories of practicing physicians. The largest category is comprised of private physicians with staff privileges. These privileges include the right of the physicians to admit and discharge their private patients to the hospital and the right to use the hospital's facilities. Hospitals will also have physicians in training present, including interns, residents, and externs. Hospitals will often also have full-time salaried physicians, including teaching hospital faculty, and physicians under contract with the hospital to provide services for an agreed upon price. H. Ward Classen, Hospital Liability for Independent Contractors: Where Do We Go From Here?, 40 Ark.L.Rev. 469, 478 (1987).

The organized medical staff of a hospital, private physicians with privileges, comprises the largest group of hospital-based physicians. The medical staff governs the hospital's provision of medical services. The typical medical staff operates under its own bylaws, elects its own officers, and appoints its own committees. It is not simply another administrative component of the hospital, under the authority of the governing board of the hospital. While the hospital board must approve the staff's bylaws and can approve or disapprove particular staff actions, it cannot usually discipline individual physicians directly or appoint administrative officers to exercise direct authority. A hospital's medical staff is therefore a powerful body within the larger organization. See generally Clark C. Havighurst, Doctors and Hospitals: An Antitrust Perspective on Traditional Relationships, 1984 Duke L.J. 1071, 1084–92. The requirement of staff self-governance under

JCAHO standards maintains and reinforces this physician authority within hospitals.

The process by which the medical staff is selected is of crucial importance. A hospital has an obligation to its patients to investigate the qualifications of medical staff applicants. The Wisconsin Supreme Court elaborated on this obligation in Johnson v. Misericordia Community Hospital, 99 Wis.2d 708, 301 N.W.2d 156 (Wis. 1981).

> In summary, we hold that a hospital owes a duty to its patients to exercise reasonable care in the selection of its medical staff and in granting specialized privileges. The final appointing authority resides in the hospital's governing body, although it must rely on the medical staff and in particular the credentials committee (or committee of the whole) to investigate and evaluate an applicant's qualifications for the requested privileges. However, this delegation of the responsibility to investigate and evaluate the professional competence of applicants for clinical privileges does not relieve the governing body of its duty to appoint only qualified physicians and surgeons to its medical staff and periodically monitor and review their competency. The credentials committee (or committee of the whole) must investigate the qualifications of applicants. The facts of this case demonstrate that a hospital should, at a minimum, require completion of the application and verify the accuracy of the applicant's statements, especially in regard to his medical education, training and experience. Additionally, it should: (1) solicit information from the applicant's peers, including those not referenced in his application, who are knowledgeable about his education, training, experience, health, competence and ethical character; (2) determine if the applicant is currently licensed to practice in this state and if his licensure or registration has been or is currently being challenged; and (3) inquire whether the applicant has been involved in any adverse malpractice action and whether he has experienced a loss of medical organization membership or medical privileges or membership at any other hospital. The investigating committee must also evaluate the information gained through its inquiries and make a reasonable judgment as to the approval or denial of each application for staff privileges. The hospital will be charged with gaining and evaluating the knowledge that would have been acquired had it exercised ordinary care in investigating its medical staff applicants and the hospital's failure to exercise that degree of care, skill and judgment that is exercised by the average hospital in approving an applicant's request for privileges is negligence. This is not to say that hospitals are *insurers* of the competence of their medical staff, for a hospital will not be negligent if it exercises the noted standard of care in selecting its staff. Id. 174–75.

Hospitals are expected to investigate adverse information with regard to possible appointments or reappointments of medical staff. See Elam v. College Park Hospital, 132 Cal.App.3d 332, 183 Cal.Rptr. 156 (1982); Purcell v. Zimbelman, 18 Ariz.App. 75, 500 P.2d 335 (1972); Oehler v. Humana Inc., 105 Nev. 348, 775 P.2d 1271 (Nev.1989).

3. The hospital must also have proper procedures developed to detect impostors. Insinga v. LaBella, 543 So.2d 209 (Fla.1989) (non physician fraudulently obtained an appointment to the medical staff, after having assumed the name of a deceased Italian physician; the court applied corporate negligence.)

4. A hospital should also properly restrict the clinical privileges of staff physicians who are incompetent to handle certain procedures, or detect conceal-

ment by a staff doctor of medical errors. See Cronic v. Doud, 168 Ill.App.3d 665, 119 Ill.Dec. 708, 523 N.E.2d 176 (1988); Corleto v. Shore Memorial Hospital, 138 N.J.Super. 302, 350 A.2d 534 (1975).

5. The medical staff has also been held liable in a few cases independently for its failure to supervise and regulate the activity of its members. *Corleto,* supra.

6. Under the Health Care Quality Improvement Act of 1986 (HCQIA), hospitals must check a central registry, a national database maintained by the Unisys Corporation under contract with the Department of Health and Human Services, before a new staff appointment is made. This National Practitioner Data Bank contains information on individual physicians who have been disciplined, had malpractice claims filed against them, or had privileges revoked or limited. If the hospital fails to check the registry, it is held constructively to have knowledge of any information it might have gotten from the inquiry. See discussion of staff privileges in Chapter 12, infra. The Data Bank has been criticized by the Government Accounting Office as having unreliable and incomplete data. See U.S. Government Accounting Office, National Practitioner Data Bank: Major Improvements are Needed to Enhance Data Bank's Reliability, *http://www.gao.gov.*

Equifax, a major credit reporting entity, operates a physician database to enable subscribers such as hospitals and managed care organizations to instantly verify physician credentials. The database has information on more than 600,000 U.S. physicians, including educational background, registrations for prescribing medications, board certifications and any other disciplinary actions that might have been taken by state or federal bodies. The sources for the database include the Drug Enforcement Administrations, the American Medical Association and state and federal licensing and regulatory agencies. Credentials Verifications Services are also available to hospitals and managed care organizations for a fee. See for example Medirisk at *www.medirisk.com.*

Problem: Proctoring Peers

You have been asked by Hilldale Adventist Hospital to advise them on the implications of their use of proctors for assessing candidates for medical staff privileges. The hospital has used Dr. Hook, a surgeon certified by the American Board of Orthopedic Surgery, as a proctor during two different operations on the plaintiff at two different hospitals during the process of evaluation of Dr. Frank DiBianco for staff privileges. Dr. Hook had been asked to observe ten surgeries by Dr. DiBianco and then file a report. He observed an operation on the plaintiff during one of these observations. Two months later, he was again asked to proctor Dr. DiBianco at another hospital, and he again observed a procedure on the plaintiff. Prior to each procedure, Dr. Hook had reviewed the x-rays and discussed the operative plan, but he otherwise had taken no part in the care and treatment of the plaintiff. He did not participate in the operations, did not scrub in, and always observed from outside the "sterile field". He got no payment for his proctoring efforts, and he had never met the plaintiff nor had any other contact with her.

Can Hilldale be liable for their use of Dr. Hook as a proctor? Can Dr. Hook be directly liable for failing to stop negligent work by Dr. DiBianco?

Problem: The "Love" Surgeon

You have recently been contacted by Ms. Helen Brown as to the merits of a suit against Drs. Ruth and Blue, physicians on staff at St. Helen's Medical Center (SHMC). Ms. Brown had gone to Dr. Blue, a urologist, for bladder infections and difficulties she experienced voiding urine. Blue performed surgery upon Brown but her condition failed to improve. She began to complain of constant bladder pain and of pain during sexual relations with her husband. Blue then referred her to Dr. Ruth for "exploratory pelvic laparotomy with lysis" and "vaginoplasty."

Dr. Ruth met with Brown prior to surgery. He explained to Brown that the pain she experienced during sexual relations was caused by her husband's penis striking her bladder. Ruth explained that he and Dr. Blue would perform surgery to place her bladder upon a "pedestal," and that this procedure would correct her problems voiding urine and alleviate the pain she suffered during intercourse. Ruth also indicated that he would do some "cosmetic things" to improve Brown's sex life.

Ruth and Blue had staff privileges at St. Helen's Medical Center (SHMC). The hospital required that a form letter be given by Dr. Ruth to each of his patients prior to the surgical procedures he did to Ms. Brown. The form letter, which bears the SHMC letterhead, stated:

"Dear Patient:

"The Executive Committee of the Medical Staff of St. Elizabeth Medical Center wishes to inform you that the 'female coital area reconstruction' surgery you are about to undergo is:

"1. Not documented by ordinary standards of scientific reporting and publication.

"2. Not a generally accepted procedure.

"3. As yet not duplicated by other investigators.

"4. Detailed only in non-scientific literature.

"You should be informed that the Executive Committee of the Medical Staff considers the aforementioned procedure an unproven, non-standard practice of gynecology."

Drs. Ruth and Blue performed "vaginal reconstruction surgery" upon Brown at SHMC, purportedly to correct her painful bladder condition. The surgery actually performed upon Brown consisted of an exploratory pelvic laparotomy, vaginal reconstruction, circumcision of the clitoris and insertion of a urinary catheter. The vaginal reconstruction consisted of, among other things, a redirection and elongation of her vagina.

Brown has told you that after her "love surgery," she continued to suffer from bladder infections and developed problems with urinary incontinence. Her bladder infections after the surgery were more frequent than before. Following the surgery, Brown could not engage in sexual relations without extreme pain and difficulties. At some point, she also began to develop severe kidney problems. She underwent further surgery to correct her problems, with the final surgery removing her right kidney. She continued to suffer bladder infections, difficulties voiding, problems during sexual intercourse, and periods of urinary incontinence. She also developed bowel problems sometime during her treatment with Ruth and Blue. She was told by a gynecologist two months before she came to your office that the surgery performed upon her could not be corrected, and that Dr. Ruth "had cut away everything."

Consider any theories you might develop against the hospital in a malpractice action.

2. *The Duty to Protect Non-patients*

Darling for the first time imposed a duty on the hospital administrators to supervise and evaluate care delivered by physicians within the hospital. The court drew on JCAHO standards, the hospital's own bylaws, and other documents in outlining the extent of the responsibility. Later cases refined and limited the concept of corporate negligence.

PEDROZA v. BRYANT

Supreme Court of Washington, 1984.
101 Wash.2d 226, 677 P.2d 166.

The issue before us is whether a hospital may be held liable under a theory of corporate negligence for its action in granting privileges to a nonemployee doctor who allegedly commits malpractice while in private practice off the hospital premises.

In December of 1978, Maria Pedroza was in her 35th week of pregnancy and under the care of Dr. Ben Bryant. During the week of December 3 through 9, Maria became ill and exhibited the classical symptoms of preeclampsia (a toxemia of pregnancy), namely, hypertension, headaches, and edema of the lower extremities. Mrs. Pedroza visited Dr. Bryant's office on December 6 and 7, and telephoned him on December 8. Dr. Bryant prescribed no medicine other than bed rest and aspirin. He did not refer Mrs. Pedroza to another health care provider.

On December 9, 1978, Maria Pedroza was admitted, comatose, to defendant Skagit Valley Hospital. She was admitted to surgery, with a diagnosis of irreversible cerebral death due to intracerebral hemorrhage resulting from eclampsia. Dr. Bryant was neither the admitting nor the treating physician for this hospitalization. Indeed, the hospital had, on April 13, 1977, limited Dr. Bryant's obstetrical and newborn privileges to Class II for the years 1977 and 1978. Dr. Bryant was thus required to consult with a Class I physician on all "seriously ill patients," including pregnancies with "major medical complications" and "[l]ate or severe toxemia of pregnancy." Thus, Dr. Bryant would not have been allowed to treat Maria Pedroza for eclampsia in the hospital.

In surgery, Mrs. Pedroza's child was successfully delivered by emergency cesarean section. After family consent was obtained, respiratory support for Mrs. Pedroza was discontinued on December 15, 1978, whereupon she died.

It should be noted at the outset that plaintiff is not claiming that defendant hospital is vicariously liable for the negligence of Dr. Bryant under the theory of respondeat superior. Dr. Bryant is an independent contractor, not an employee of defendant hospital. Plaintiff is instead relying solely on the doctrine of corporate negligence, which differs from respondeat superior in that it imposes on the hospital a nondelegable duty owed directly to the patient, regardless of the details of the doctor-hospital relationship. Plaintiff contends that defendant hospital owed a duty to Maria Pedroza of carefully selecting and reviewing the competency of its staff physicians. ("Staff physicians" are those doctors who have been given "staff privileges" at the hospital. A physician must be a member of the hospital's medical staff in order to regularly admit patients to the hospital.) Plaintiff alleges that defendant hospital breached this duty by allowing Dr. Bryant to possess staff privileges at the hospital, and that this breach was the proximate cause of Mrs. Pedroza's death.

II.

The first question we must address, then, is whether the doctrine of corporate negligence applies to hospitals in Washington. * * *

[The court adopted the doctrine of corporate negligence in Washington, citing several justifications:

(1) "the public's perception of the modern hospital as a multifaceted health care facility responsible for the quality of medical care and treatment rendered, and the public's subsequent reliance on the hospital";

(2) the hospital's "superior position to monitor and control physician performance", given its opportunities to observe professional practices on a daily basis, to adopt procedures to detect problems, and the use of its medical staff to monitor quality;

(3) incentives on hospitals, created by imposing corporate negligence, "to insure the competency of their medical staffs", thereby reducing their malpractice insurance costs.]

III.

Having adopted the doctrine of corporate negligence, we turn now to the task of defining the standard of care to which hospitals will be held. [The court noted that hospitals are members of national organizations such as the Joint Commission on Accreditation of Healthcare Organizations, subject to accreditation requirements.]

* * *

Also relevant to a hospital's standard of care are the hospital's own bylaws. [ ] Hospitals are required by statute and regulation to adopt bylaws with respect to medical staff activities. [ ] It is "recommended" that the organization and functions of the medical staff under the bylaws be in accord with the JCAH standards. [ ] Bylaws are therefore based on national standards, and their use in defining a standard of care for hospitals is appropriate. * * *

IV.

Our decision to adopt the doctrine of corporate negligence as enunciated by other jurisdictions does not necessarily entitle plaintiff in the case at bar to a reversal of the summary judgment against him. The alleged acts of malpractice committed by Dr. Bryant occurred entirely outside the hospital. Mrs. Pedroza was not a patient of the hospital at the time. For plaintiff to prevail, we must decide that the duty of care owed by hospitals under the corporate negligence doctrine extends not only to hospital patients, but also to patients treated by hospital staff members in those staff members' private office practices, where the hospital is not involved. No other jurisdiction appears to have done this; all the cases involve acts of malpractice committed at the hospital.

Defendant argues that extending a hospital's duty of care to patients outside the hospital would require a hospital to supervise and, if necessary, limit the private medical practices of its staff members outside the hospital. Such intervention could adversely affect the delicate physician-patient relationship. Substantial administrative problems would probably result as well.

This argument appears to be based upon a misconception of the doctrine of corporate negligence. The doctrine does not impose vicarious liability on a hospital for the acts of a medical staff member. The pertinent inquiry is whether the hospital exercised reasonable care in the granting, renewal, and delineation of staff privileges. This inquiry focuses on the procedures for the granting and renewal of staff privileges set forth in the hospital bylaws. In no case adopting corporate negligence premised upon a hospital's independent duty to select and maintain a competent medical staff has there been a suggestion that a hospital, in order to fulfill its duty of reasonable care, must supervise a physician's office practice. Acts of malpractice committed by a staff physician outside the hospital are relevant only if the hospital has actual or constructive notice of them, and where failure to take some action as a result of such notice is negligence. [ ]

Plaintiff argues that defendant hospital's independent duty of care should extend to Maria Pedroza because she was a foreseeable plaintiff. Foreseeability determines the extent and scope of duty. [ ] Plaintiff alleges that Maria Pedroza used Dr. Bryant's services only because Dr. Bryant possessed admitting and obstetrical privileges at defendant hospital (each of Maria Pedroza's seven children had been born at Skagit Valley Hospital), and that it was, therefore, foreseeable that the hospital's alleged negligence in the granting or renewal of Dr. Bryant's staff privileges might result in harm to his obstetrical patients. Plaintiff argues that it should make no difference whether the harm occurred in or out of the hospital, as long as the harm was foreseeable. The doctrine of corporate negligence focuses on the negligence of the hospital in failing to rescind Dr. Bryant's privileges.

The fact remains, however, that every jurisdiction that has adopted corporate negligence has based the hospital's liability on the duty owed by the hospital *to its patients.* * * * The hospital holds itself out to the community as a competent provider of medical care. The hospital does *not* hold itself out as an inspector or insurer of the private office practices of its staff members. The delineation of staff privileges by the hospital can only affect the procedures used by staff members while they are inside hospital walls. The public cannot reasonably expect anything more.

This court has in the past recognized a hospital's independent duty of care only in those situations where the plaintiff was a patient of the hospital. [ ] RCW 70.41, which controls the licensing and regulation of hospitals, supports the limitation of a hospital's duty of care to those who are patients in the hospital. RCW 70.41.010 provides in pertinent part: "The primary purpose of this chapter is to promote safe and adequate care of individuals in hospitals * * *."

Extending the hospital's duty of care to those who are not its patients would be undesirable in that it would likely grant those people a windfall, as any increased hospital costs resulting from such an extension of liability would be spread among hospital patients, rather than those who would benefit from the extended liability.

Accordingly, we hold that a hospital's duty of care under the doctrine of corporate negligence extends only to those who are patients within the hospital. Defendant Skagit Valley Hospital owed no duty to Maria Pedroza under the doctrine because she was not a hospital patient when the harm occurred. The fact that she had been a patient at defendant hospital in years past does not make her a patient for purposes of this case. Each of those prior hospital-patient relationships ended upon her discharge from the hospital; they did not continue indefinitely.

Since there are no allegations of negligence after Mrs. Pedroza was admitted to the hospital, we affirm the trial court's order of summary judgment.

Notes and Questions

1. Washington later applied its new corporate negligence doctrine in Schoening v. Grays Harbor Community Hospital, 40 Wash.App. 331, 698 P.2d 593 (1985). The plaintiff was treated in the emergency room for an infection. The plaintiff's expert, in his affidavit, wrote that the hospital should have been aware of "obvious negligence." The court held that where the care by the attending physician is questionable and the patient's condition is deteriorating, the hospital staff should have continuously monitored and observed the patient and sought additional evaluations. The court held that a fact question was raised by the expert's affidavit as to the hospital's duty to intervene.

See, rejecting the doctrine of corporate negligence, Albain v. Flower Hospital, 50 Ohio St.3d 251, 553 N.E.2d 1038 (1990).

2. Can you make a stronger argument that a hospital should be responsible, under some circumstances, for the negligent acts of physicians in their private practice, so long as they have staff privileges? What if the hospital is on notice of a long history of malpractice claims against one of its staff, resulting from negligence in that physician's private practice? If the physician has performed adequately while treating patients within the hospital, should the hospital have any further responsibility?

3. Some states by statute have adopted corporate negligence for institutional providers. Florida, for example, has by statute incorporated "institutional liability" or "corporate negligence" in its regulation of hospitals. Hospitals and other providers will be liable for injuries caused by inadequacies in the internal programs that are mandated by the statute. West's Fla.Stat.Ann. § 768.60.

4. Consider the case of Copithorne v. Framingham Union Hospital, 401 Mass. 860, 520 N.E.2d 139 (1988). The plaintiff, Copithorne, was a technologist at Framingham Union Hospital who was drugged and sexually assaulted by a physician with staff privileges at the hospital. The Massachusetts Supreme Judicial Court imposed liability on the hospital. The court summarized the facts as follows:

> At the time of the incident, Helfant was a practicing neurosurgeon and a visiting staff member of the hospital. He was not a hospital employee, but had been affiliated with the hospital for about seventeen years, having been reappointed to the visiting staff each year since his initial appointment. Copithorne was a hospital employee. In the course of her employment, she

injured her back, and, aware of Helfant's reputation within the hospital as a good neurosurgeon and a specialist in back injuries, she sought his professional assistance. In the course of treating her, Helfant made a house call to Copithorne's apartment, where he committed the drugging and rape for which he was convicted and which caused the injuries for which Copithorne seeks compensation.

The court assumed, as did the trial court, that the hospital was negligent in retaining Dr. Helfant on staff.

We think that a jury reasonably could find that the hospital owed a duty of care to Copithorne, as an employee who, in deciding to enter a doctor-patient relationship with Helfant, reasonably relied on Helfant's good standing and reputation within the hospital community, and that the hospital violated this duty by failing to take sufficient action in response to previous allegations of Helfant's wrongdoing.

The hospital had received actual notice, prior to the assault on the plaintiff, of at least two prior incidents of sexual assault in which Helfant had caressed and otherwise improperly fondled female patients in the hospital. One of these patients filed a complaint with the Board of Registration in Medicine, copying the complaint to the hospital. The hospital then took action.

* * * Dr. Byrne [Chief of Surgery] met with Helfant, who denied any wrongdoing. Dr. Byrne then instructed Helfant to have a chaperon present in the future when visiting female patients in the hospital. Based on Helfant's "excellent record" at the hospital, Dr. Bryne "felt that no further action was necessary as it was his opinion that he had no need to worry about Dr. Helfant harming a patient. In effect, Dr. Helfant was given an oral warning." Dr. Bryne also told the nurses on the floor to "keep an eye on Dr. Helfant."

The court found that the facts would support a jury finding that

the risk of injury to Copithorne was within the range of foreseeable consequences of the hospital's negligence in continuing Helfant's staff privileges. Where the hospital had received actual notice of allegations that Helfant had sexually assaulted patients, both on the hospital premises and off the premises in his office and in a patient's home, and yet took only the limited measures indicated, it was not unforeseeable that Helfant would continue to act in a consistent, if not worse, manner.

The court also rejected the trial judge's ruling that the withdrawal of Helfant's staff privileges would not have prevented his assault on the plaintiff.

Copithorne asserted that, by reason of her employment, she was aware of Helfant's good reputation within the hospital, and that she relied on this reputation in entering in a doctor-patient relationship with him; that as an employee, any change in Helfant's status would have become known to her; and that, if she had had any reason to know that the hospital has suspended Helfant's staff privileges or imposed any disciplinary sanctions on him, she would not have entered into a doctor-patient relationship with him. A different question would be presented if a member of the general public claimed that the hospital was liable for similar harm simply because Helfant was a staff member and should not have been.

The court reversed the summary judgment in favor of the defendant, and remanded the case for further proceedings.

How broad is the holding in *Copithorne?* Does this case contradict *Pedroza,* or is it distinguishable? Analyze the relationship of the hospital to the plaintiff and the defendant. Is the employer-employee relationship between the hospital and the nurse crucial to the holding? Or does this simply reinforce the reliance by the plaintiff on the defendant's implied representation that its staff is trustworthy? As hospitals devote more attention to staff privileges, driven by their need to avoid liability and achieve the best possible staffs, and as physicians come to restrict their privileges to fewer hospitals, or just one, does the reliance interest of the public increase?

Are your encouraged by the action of the medical disciplinary board of the state, which did nothing? See Doctors Rarely Lose Licenses: Maryland Panel Allowed Rapist to Keep Practicing, Washington Post, Part I, p. 1, January 10, 1988.

Problem: Referrals

You represent Chadds Hospital, a small nonprofit hospital that is trying to increase its patient count. One of the strategies it is contemplating is a physician referral service. The hospital plans to advertise, in local newspapers and on the radio, that individuals should call Chadds Hospital for the name of a doctor for specific problems. The referral service operator will then offer to make the appointment for the caller with the particular doctor, to be seen in his office practice. The draft of the advertising copy that the hospital marketing staff has prepared states: "You can trust the high quality of these doctors because they are members of the medical staff of Chadds Hospital, and our doctors are the best."

What is your advice to the hospital in light of the above cases? Do you foresee any legal risks in this marketing strategy?

Problem: The Birthing Center

You have been approached by Rosa Hernandez to handle a tort suit for damages for the death of her infant during delivery at the Hastings Birthing Center. Discovery reveals the following facts.

The death of the infant is attributable to the negligence of Dr. Jones, the physician who attended Ms. Hernandez at the Center during delivery. The death was caused in part by the infant's aspiration of meconium into the lungs. Although the Center is equipped to suction meconium and other material from a newborn's throat, it is not equipped to perform an intubation and attach the infant to a ventilator. To intubate the infant, it would have to be transferred to the hospital. Even if the infant had been transferred, it would probably have suffered brain damage due to oxygen deprivation before the procedure could have been undertaken.

Dr. Jones has a spotless record, but over the two weeks preceding the incident he had appeared at the hospital smelling of alcohol and evidencing other signs of intoxication. He was apparently having marital problems at the time. Nurses at the hospital had reported this behavior to their supervisor and had watched the physician's work very carefully, calling his attention to things he missed. The nurse supervisor had reported the situation to the head of OB/GYN, who said he would "look into it". Ms. Hernandez noticed the smell of liquor on Dr. Jones' breath during her labor, and was upset by his apparent intoxication. Dr. Jones has also dropped his malpractice insurance coverage, a fact of which the hospital is aware.

Further discovery has revealed that the nurse-midwife had observed that Dr. Jones' acts were questionable, but she had not intervened because she knew of his excellent reputation. She knew that doctors were resentful of the independence of nurse-midwives at the Center, and she believed she could "compensate" for his mistakes during the delivery. By the time she realized the extent of Dr. Jones' intoxication and took over the delivery, it was too late.

Your discovery reveals that there is a complicated relationship between the Birthing Center and the nearby Columbia Hospital. The hospital found that it had needed to increase its patient census, and that neonatology was one of its most profitable services. To increase its census in this area and to better serve the community, Columbia established the Hastings Birthing Center last year. The hospital receives a percentage of the profits of the Center.

The Center is located in a former convent one block from the hospital. The hospital owns the building and rents it to the Center. This particular birthing center, according to its promotional literature, offers "both a home-like setting for the delivery of your child and the security of the availability of back-up physicians and hospital care." The Center is separately incorporated and has its own Board of Directors. It is totally self-governing and is solely responsible for staff, provision of equipment, and policy.

The phone listing in the Yellow Pages describes the Hospital as a "cooperating hospital that will provide hospital care for mother and child if needed." Columbia has a contract with the Center requiring the Center to establish a screening program that will exclude high-risk patients and requiring that doctors attending patients at the Center have privileges at Columbia Hospital. The hospital allows the employees of the Center to participate in the hospital's group health and pension plans. Nurses from the hospital moonlight at the Center. When they do so, they receive a separate paycheck from the Center.

Although the Center's by-laws provide for a committee to review the qualifications of physicians who attend at the Center, it has in fact relied on the hospital's review of qualifications, since the hospital has a better opportunity to review credentials and performance. It is not clear that the hospital is aware of this; while it does notify the Center of the suspension, denial or revocation of privileges, it does not provide the Center with information used in investigations.

If you decide to litigate, should you sue both the Center and the hospital as well as Dr. Jones? Describe your theories, based on the information you have discovered to date, and consider what other facts you would like to know.

Chapter 7

PRIVATE HEALTH INSURANCE AND MANAGED CARE: STATE REGULATION AND LIABILITY

I. INSURANCE AND MANAGED CARE: SOME BASIC CONCEPTS

A. THE CONCEPT OF MANAGED CARE

The United States is unique among modern industrialized nations in the extent to which it relies on private payment for health care services. In 1999 Americans paid $186.5 billion out-of-pocket to health care providers for health care services, 15.4 percent of the $1210.7 billion national health expenditures in that year. Private health insurance, amounting to $401.2 billion, covered 33.1 percent of personal health care costs. The federal and state governments paid $548.5 billion, most of the rest, or 45.3 percent of the total. Government funding, however, goes primarily for financing health care for the elderly and disabled, and indigent families and children. Most working age Americans rely on private health insurance to cover the cost of their health care. Today, of course, private health insurance means managed care.

In previous editions of this book we have had separate sections discussing regulation of health insurance and of managed care. Until recently it was possible, and indeed sensible, to make a distinction between insurance (meaning indemnity or service benefit insurance) and managed care as different approaches to financing health care. In fact, regulatory programs continue even now to treat traditional commercial insurance and some forms of managed care organizations differently. But in general health insurance has become managed care, and it no longer makes sense to consider them as distinct approaches to health care finance, though it continues to be useful to distinguish between the insurance and care management function of managed care.

Health insurance in the United States is of quite recent origin. It did not become truly widespread until the Second World War. Insurance for medical costs was available on a limited basis in the early twentieth century, usually as an adjunct to disability policies. Some employers or unions also offered employee medical care programs quite early on, often through their own contracted physicians or clinics. Prior to the 1930s, however, health insurance was very unusual. Most Americans paid for health care services out of pocket.

During the 1930s, however, hospitals reacted to the extreme financial distress of the Depression by forming hospital-sponsored "service benefit" plans to ensure a more consistent flow of revenues. These "Blue Cross" plans negotiated payment rates with participating hospitals and charged the same "community-rated" premium to the whole community. The states created special incorporation statutes and regulatory programs for these plans, and often exempted them from state taxes as well. In the late 1930s and 1940s, doctors followed on the accomplishment of the Blue Cross plans by creating their own Blue Shield plans, which operated in much the same way.

Observing the success of Blue Cross and Blue Shield plans, commercial insurers began to offer health insurance themselves, providing "indemnity coverage." Commercial insurers, unlike the Blue Cross and Blue Shield plans, did not pay providers directly, but rather indemnified their insureds for services, first for hospital expenses, and later for physicians services and surgery. Commercial insurers were not limited by the community-rating requirements that constrained the Blues, however, and were often able to pick-off less expensive groups, using "experience rating".

During World War II, many employers, limited from raising wages by war time wage controls, began to offer health insurance benefits as an incentive to attract employees. The Internal Revenue Code permitted employers to claim health insurance premiums as business expenses, while not taxing the premiums to employees as income. This created a significant tax subsidy for employment-based health insurance, which encouraged its rapid spread even after the war ended.

The Employee Retirement Income Security Act of 1974 (ERISA, discussed in chapter 9), freed self-insured employee benefit plans from state regulation, thus offering a significant incentive for large employers to self-insure. Self-insured employers often purchase stop-loss insurance and administer their health insurance plans through third-party administrators. Their plans, therefore, are often almost indistinguishable from insured plans, except for their exemption from state regulation.

Throughout the twentieth century there were always prepaid health plans, such as the Kaiser Permanente group in California, the Group Health Association of Washington, D.C., and the Health Insurance Plan of Greater New York. Prepaid medical practice was vigorously opposed by organized medicine, however. Indeed the AMA was convicted of criminal antitrust violations in 1942 for its efforts to suppress it. AMA v. United States, 130 F.2d 233 (D.C.Cir.1942), affirmed, 317 U.S. 519, 63 S.Ct. 326, 87 L.Ed. 434 (1943). In the 1970s, Paul Ellwood renamed prepaid health care "Health Maintenance Organizations", and HMOs became the cornerstone of President Nixon's health reform plan. Federal legislation to encourage the growth of HMOs was adopted in 1973.

It was not federal incentives, however, but the double-digit increases in health insurance premiums in the late 1980s and early 1990s that led to the triumph of "managed care", a term that emerged to describe HMOs and other forms of health insurance that attempted not just to pay for, but also to control the cost of, health care services. At present, private health insurance is managed care—only a trivial number of classical indemnity insurance policies without care management care elements continue to be sold in the

United States. Most of the surviving Blue Cross and Blue Shield plans (and indeed most state Medicaid programs and, to a lesser extent Medicare) now predominantly offer managed care products. Private health care finance in the United States has become managed care. The history of these developments is traced in Paul Starr's Pulitzer Prize winning, The Social Transformation of American Medicine (1982); Eleanor Kinney, Protecting American Consumers of Health Care (2001); and Gail A. Jensen, et al., The New Dominance of Managed Care: Insurance Trends in the 1990s, 16 Health Aff., Jan.-Feb. 1997 at 125.

But what exactly is "managed care"?

JACOB S. HACKER AND THEODORE R. MARMOR, HOW NOT TO THINK ABOUT "MANAGED CARE"

32 U. Mich. J. L. Ref. 661 (1999).

* * * The * * * critical question that [came] to preoccupy health policy analysts [at the end of the twentieth century] was how to make sense of the "managed care revolution" and its future prospects.

The premise of our argument is that this question cannot be answered as currently formulated. The very term "managed care"—much like that ubiquitous reform phrase of the early 1990s, "managed competition"—is a confused assemblage of sloganeering, aspirational rhetoric, and business school jargon that sadly reflects the general state of discourse about American medical institutions. Because "managed care" is an incoherent subject, most claims about it will suffer from incoherence as well. Moreover, to incorporate "managed care" and other similar marketing terms into health policy research is to presuppose answers to some of the most crucial questions about the recent evolution of medical care in the United States.

* * *

Expressions like "managed care," "integrated delivery systems," and "evidence-based medicine" are in some respects all slogans—persuasively defined terms that imply success by their very use. We do not, for example, routinely speak of "unmanaged care," "disintegrated delivery systems," or "non-evidence based medicine." The relative absence of such categories suggests that the purpose of terms like "managed care" is less to clarify than to convince, less to illuminate what an organization is or does than to bolster empirical claims and normative connotations that are neither self-evident nor, in most cases, subject to critical scrutiny.

* * *

The expression "managed care" came into widespread use only in the past decade. * * * The term "managed care" does not appear once in Paul Starr's exhaustive 1982 history of American medical care, The Social Transformation of American Medicine, nor can it be found in other books on American health policy written before the early 1980s, * * *. Because "managed care" has become such a commonly used and widely recognized expression, it is difficult to recognize just how recently it entered the mainstream of American discourse.

From the beginning, "managed care" was a category with a strong ideological edge, employed to imply competence, concern, and, above all, control over a dangerously unfettered health insurance structure. "Managed care," * * * was an alternative "to the unbridled fee-for-service non-system" that sent "blank checks to hospitals, doctors, dentists, etc." and led to "referrals of dubious necessity" and "unmanaged and uncoordinated care ... of poor or dubious quality." As these words indicate, managed care was portrayed less as a means to control patient behavior than as a way to bring doctors and hospitals in line with perceived economic realities. Moreover, managed care promised not only cost-control but also coordination and cooperation, not only better management but also better care. By imposing managerial authority on an anarchic "non-system," managed care would simultaneously restrain costs and rationalize an allegedly archaic structure of medical care finance and delivery.

What exactly constitutes "managed care," however, has never been made clear, even by its strongest proponents. To some, the crucial distinguishing feature is a shift in financing from indemnity-style fee-for-service, in which the insurer is little more than a bill-payer, to capitated payment, in which medical providers are paid a fixed amount to treat an individual patient regardless of the volume of services delivered. However, there is nothing intrinsic in fee-for-service payment that requires open-ended reimbursement or passive insurance behavior. Conversely, many, if not most, health insurance plans labeled "managed care" do not rely primarily on capitation. To other proponents, the distinctive characteristic is the creation of administrative protocols for reviewing and sometimes denying care demanded by patients or medical professionals. Such micro-level managerial controls are likewise not universal among so-called managed care health plans. In fact, such controls may be obviated by particular payment methods, like capitation or regulated fee-for-service reimbursement, that create more diffuse constraints on medical practice. Finally, to some, what distinguishes managed care is its reliance on "integrated" networks of health professionals from which patients are required to obtain care. Yet some self-styled managed care plans have no such networks, and what is called a network by many plans is little more than a list of providers willing to accept discounted fee-for-service payments—hardly the dense coordination and integration that industry insiders routinely celebrate.

Perhaps the most defensible interpretation of "managed care" is that it represents a fusion of two functions that once were regarded as largely separate: the financing of medical care and the delivery of medical services. This interpretation, at least, provides a reasonably accurate description of the most familiar organizational entity that marched under the managed care banner until the late 1980s: the health maintenance organization (HMO), a successor to the pre-paid group practice plans that began in the 1930s. When the vast majority of American health insurers used fee-for-service payment and placed few restrictions on patient or provider discretion, it was at least possible to identify a small subset of renegade health plans that existed outside this insurance mainstream, however poorly the expression "managed care" described the organization of such plans or what they did.

Today, however, that is no longer the case. In 1997, * * * between eighty and ninety-eight percent of today's private health insurers appear to fall into the broad category of managed care. "Managed care" therefore does not offer any guidance as to how to distinguish among the vast majority of contemporary health plans.

The standard response to this problem has been to subdivide the managed care universe into a collage of competing acronyms, most coined by industry executives and marketers: HMOs, Preferred Provider Organizations (PPOs), and Exclusive Provider Organizations (EPOs). This is the approach taken by Jonathan Weiner and Gregory de Lissovoy in their frequently cited 1993 article, Razing a Tower of Babel: A Taxonomy for Managed Care and Health Insurance Plans. [18 J. Health Pol. Pol'y & L. (1993).]

* * *

The central problem with Weiner and de Lissovoy's taxonomy—and, indeed, with most contemporary commentary about health insurance—is the tendency to confuse reimbursement methods, managerial techniques, and organizational forms. For example, fee-for-service, a payment method, is regularly contrasted with "managed care," presumably an organizational form. In Weiner and de Lissovey's taxonomy, MIPs [managed indemnity plans] are distinguished from traditional fee-for-service plans by their reliance on a particular managerial technique, namely utilization review. In contrast, PPOs and EPOs are distinguished from MIPs by their particular organizational form, namely their reliance on a network of participating providers. And HMOs are distinguished from all these plans by their particular payment method, namely capitation.

The practice of conflating organization, technique, and incentives leads to unnecessary confusion. It means that when we contrast health plans we are often comparing them across incommensurable dimensions. So, for instance, an HMO becomes by definition more "managed" than a fee-for-service plan with utilization review even when the latter uses much stricter controls on individual treatment decisions. By conflating distinct characteristics, we also are tempted to presume necessary relationships between particular features of health plans (such as their payment method) and specific outcomes that are claimed to follow from these features (such as the degree of integration of medical finance and delivery). Finally, the desire to describe an assortment of disparate plan features with a few broad labels encourages a wild goose chase of efforts to come up with black-and-white standards for identifying plan types. * * *

* * *

In understanding the structure of health insurance, the crucial relationship is between those who deliver medical care and those who pay for it. Even a passive indemnity insurer stands between the patient and the medical provider as a financial intermediary and an underwriter of risk. Today, with risk shifting from insurers to employers, and with financial intermediaries playing more of an administrative role than in the past, the trilateral relationship is more complex. Nonetheless, it still remains the locus of the insurance contract. To characterize this trilateral relationship, we focus on three of its essential features: first, the degree of risk-sharing between providers and the primary bearer of risk (whether an insurer or a self-insured employer); second, the degree to which administrative oversight constrains clinical decisions; and, third, the degree to which enrollees in a plan are required to receive their care from a specified roster of providers. * * *

* * * Our argument is that health plans differ across at least [these] three principal dimensions * * *. Each dimension crucially affects the trilateral connections among provider, patient, and plan. We also wish to emphasize that there is no simple relationship between plan label and the placement of a plan along these axes. Staff-model HMOs may seem like the quintessence of "managed care," yet because they place financial constraints at the group level they do not necessarily concentrate as much risk on physicians as do other network-based health plans, nor do they not necessarily entail as much clinical regulation at the micro-level. Microregulation may go hand in hand with restrictions on patient choice of provider, but it also may not. Indeed, management of individual clinical decisions and the creation of broad incentives for conservative practice patterns may very well be alternative mechanisms for lowering the cost of medical care. Finally, as recent developments in the health insurance market suggest, greater risk-sharing can co-exist with almost any set of arrangements. It does not require a closed network, much less strict utilization review. Risk sharing is a product of the payment methods and incentive structures that connect risk-bearing agents and medical providers. It does not exclusively occur in HMOs, nor does it require capitation.

Notice, too, that [we make] no mention of those popular buzzwords "integration" and "coordination." Movement toward a closed network, toward greater utilization control, or toward increased risk-sharing can create the conditions under which integration or coordination may occur. They do not imply, however, that such integrative activities actually take place. Getting the right care to the right patient at the right time is a managerial accomplishment, not a product of labels.

Finally, the conventional fee-for-service versus capitation dichotomy does not remain a useful means of distinguishing among different health plans. Instead, the crucial issue is what incentives medical providers actually face. The particular mix of payment methods that create those incentives is less important and will undoubtedly change as health plans experiment with new reimbursement modalities in the future.

Disaggregating health insurance into its constituent features not only helps to clarify what health plans do and how they are structured, but it also makes it easier to identify the specific trends in medical finance and delivery that are carelessly jumbled together when we speak of such grand events as the "managed care revolution." Although we cannot provide a comprehensive empirical survey in this context, our reading of the evidence leads us to believe that the developments of the past decade have not pushed American health insurance in a consistent direction, much less toward any single organized entity that might be labeled "managed care."

Indeed, movement along these axes has been halting and inconsistent. Through roughly the late 1980s, an increasing number of health plans moved toward closed networks. In the 1990s, by contrast, the trend has been toward intermediate levels of compulsion, with formerly closed plans offering opportunities for patients to opt out with a penalty and with new plans shying away from closed-network structures. Utilization review was also fashionable during the 1980s, yet it too has fallen somewhat into disfavor as plans have moved toward greater reliance on plan-provider risk-sharing, which in turn has become more focused at the level of the individual provider and individual service category over time. If there has been any general movement in the past two decades—and surely there has been—it has been [toward imposing all three types of controls]. Even this development, however, has been neither consistent nor evenly paced. In fact, the clearest and most unmistakable trend has been in the direction of straightforward price-discounting, as plans have used their market clout to selectively contract with physicians willing to accept negotiated rates. This is an important development, but in both international and historical perspective, it is hardly as unprecedented as grand phrases like "the managed-care revolution" imply.

* * *

Note

Following the lead of Hacker and Marmor, we will examine the regulation of managed care, not in terms of traditional distinctions between various types of managed care organizations (i.e. HMOs, PPOs, PSOs, etc.), but rather focusing on how the states regulate the various techniques described above for managing care: networks, utilization controls, and provider incentives. Before we do so, however, we must first learn a bit about the nature of insurance, and its regulation.

B. THE CONCEPT OF INSURANCE

Despite the triumph of "managed care" in the United States, it continues to make analytic sense to consider separately the insurance and the health care management functions of private health care financing. Insurance involves by definition the transfer of risk from the insured (called also variously the beneficiary, recipient, member, or enrollee) to a financing entity (the insurer, managed care organization, or self-insured benefits plan). It is invariably the case in health care that a small proportion of all insureds account for a very high proportion of health care costs. Ten percent of the population account for 72 percent of health care costs, 2 percent for 41 percent of costs. Health insurance essentially involves transferring costs from those insureds who account for most of health care costs to those who provide most of the premiums through the medium of the insurer.

Insurers transfer risk by pooling the risks of large numbers of insureds. The insurer, however, must be prudent about the risk it assumes from these insureds, and assure that it has the resources to cover the risk. Obtaining insurance, therefore, customarily involves an assessment of the risk of the insured (underwriting), and the payment of an appropriate premium.

When financing is provided through employment-related group insurance, of course, part of the premium is paid by the employer and the underwriting is of the group as a whole. When an employer self-insures its employee benefits plan, no premium exchanges hands (except insofar as the employee contributes to the cost) and there is no underwriting, except insofar as an person's health status might affect an employer's willingness to take on the person as an employee, or when the employer purchases stop-loss insurance.

Though managed care plans typically include an insurance function, managed care plans have not always been regarded as insurers. Managed care entities that themselves provide care, the classic staff-model HMO or the more recent provider-based integrated delivery system (or provider-sponsored organization), have sometimes been regarded as sellers of services on a prepaid basis (a bit like appliance service agreements) rather than insurers. But managed care organizations in fact do assume, and spread, risk, and are often, though not always, regulated much like insurers. See generally, John S. Conniff, Regulating Managed Health Care Provider Sponsored Organizations, 16 J. Ins. Reg. 377 (1998); Edward Hirshfeld., Provider Sponsored Organizations and Provider Service Networks, 22 Am.J.L. & Med. 263 (1996).

There are a number of concepts that must be mastered to understand health insurance and health insurance law. The excerpt that follows discusses these:

CONGRESSIONAL RESEARCH SERVICE, INSURING THE UNINSURED: OPTIONS AND ANALYSIS

(House Comm. on Education & Labor, Comm. Print, 1988).

II. Principles of Health Insurance

Insurance is a response to risk, to uncertainty about specific outcomes, and to the possibility that those outcomes will be unfavorable. * * * Most people * * * choose to transfer the risk of a financially costly illness to an insurer (or comparable third-party payer). In this way, insurance provides an economic device whereby a person substitutes a certain payment (a premium) for the uncertain financial loss that would occur in the event of an uninsured accident or illness.

* * *

For insurance to operate, there has to be a way to predict the likelihood or probability that a loss will occur as a result of a specific outcome. Such predictions in insurance are based upon probability theory and the law of large numbers. According to probability theory, "while some events appear to be a matter of chance, they actually occur with regularity over a large number of trials." [ ] By examining patterns of behavior over a large number of trials, it is therefore possible for the insurer to infer the likelihood of such behaviors in the future.

* * * Applied to insurance, probability allows the insurer to make predictions on the basis of historical data. In so doing, the insurer " . . . implicitly says, 'if things continue to happen in the future as they happened in the past, and if our estimate of what has happened in the past is accurate, this is what we may expect.' " [ ]

Losses seldom occur exactly as expected, so insurance companies have to make predictions about the extent to which actual experience might deviate from predicted results. For a small group of insured units, there is a high probability that losses will be much greater or smaller than was predicted. For a very large group, the range of probable error diminishes, especially if the insured group is similar in composition to the group upon which the prediction is based. Thus, to predict the probability of a loss, insurers seek to aggregate persons who are at a similar risk for that loss. * * *

In theory all probabilities of loss can be insured. Insurance could cover any risk for a price. As the probability of loss increases, however, the premium will increase to the point at which it approaches the actual potential pay-out.

To keep premiums competitive, there are in practice some risks that insurers will not accept. In general, insurable risks must meet the following criteria:

- There has to be uncertainty that the loss will occur, and that the loss must be beyond the control of the insured. Insurers will not sell hospital insurance to a person who is on his way to a hospital, nor fire insurance to someone holding a lit match. * * *
- The loss produced by the risk must be measurable. The insurer has to be able to determine that a loss has occurred and that it has a specific dollar value.
- There must be a sufficiently large number of similar insured units to make the losses predictable. * * *
- Generally, the loss must be significant, but there should be a low probability that a very high loss will occur. A person does not need to insure against a trivial loss. However, it would not be prudent for an insurer to accept a risk in which there is a high probability that an expensive loss will occur to a large percentage of the insured units at the same time. * * *

* * *

III. Ratemaking

Ratemaking is the "process of predicting future losses and future expenses and allocating those costs among the various classes of insureds." The outcome of the ratemaking process is a "premium" or price of policy. The premium is made up of expected claims against the insurer and the insurer's "administrative expenses." The term "administrative expenses" is used to mean any expense that the insurance company charges that is not for claims (including reserves for potential claims). * * * In the case of employer group coverage, a third part of the premium is set aside in a reserve held against unexpected claims. This reserve is often refundable to the employer if claims do not exceed expectations.

In the textbook descriptions of ratemaking for health insurance, insurers predict losses on the basis of predicted claims costs. This prediction involves an assessment of the likely morbidity (calculated in terms of the number of times the event insured against occurs) and severity (the average magnitude of each loss) of the policyholder or group of policyholders. * * *

* * *

There are different approaches to determining rates. In health insurance, the most frequently used approaches are "experience rating" and "community rating."

Under experience rating, the past experience of the group to be insured is used to determine the premium. For employer groups, experience rating would take into account the company's own history of claims and other expenses. * * *

* * *

The advantage of experience rating is that it adjusts the cost of insurance for a specific group in a manner more commensurate with the expected cost of that particular group than is possible through the exclusive use of manual rates. In addition, the increasingly competitive environment among insurers demands that each one "make every effort to retain groups with favorable experience. Unless an insurer can provide coverage to such groups at a reasonable cost, it runs the risk of losing such policyholders to another insurer which more closely reflects the expected costs of their programs in its rates." [ ]

Under community rating, premium rates are based on the allocation of total costs to all the individuals or groups to be insured, without regard to the past experience of any particular subgroup. * * * Community or class rating has the advantage of allowing an insurer to apply a single rate or set of rates to a large number of people, thus simplifying the process of determining premiums.

* * *

IV. Adverse and Favorable Selection

If everyone in the society purchased health insurance, and if everyone opted for an identical health insurance plan, then insurance companies could adhere strictly to the models of prediction and rate-setting described above. However, everyone does not buy insurance, nor do all the purchasers of insurance choose identical benefits. People who expect to need health services are more likely than others to purchase insurance, and are also likely to seek coverage for the specific services they expect to need. * * *

Insurers use the term "adverse selection" to describe this phenomenon. Adverse selection is defined by the health insurance industry as the "tendency of persons with poorer than average health expectations to apply for, or continue, insurance to a greater extent than do persons with average or better health expectations." [ ]

* * *

Adjusting premiums for adverse selection results in further adverse selection. As the price of insurance goes up, healthier people are less likely to want to purchase insurance. Each upward rate adjustment will leave a smaller and sicker group of potential purchasers. If there were only a single insurance company, it would serve a steadily shrinking market paying steadily increasing premiums. However, because multiple insurance companies are operating in the market, each company may strive to enroll the lower cost individuals or groups, leaving the higher cost cases for its competitors. In this market, adverse selection consists (from the insurer's point of view) of drawing the least desirable cases from within the pool of insurance purchasers. "Favorable" selection occurs if the insurer successfully enrolls lower risk clients than its competitors.

It is thus necessary to distinguish between the more traditional use of "adverse selection," as a term to describe the differences between people who do and do not buy insurance, and the sense in which the term is often used today, to describe the differences among purchasers choosing various insurers or types of coverage. This second type of adverse selection can occur within an insured group, if the individuals in that group are permitted to select from among different insurance options.

Insurers are still concerned about the more traditional type of adverse selection. They use underwriting rules, to exclude or limit the worst risks. Some insurers may also attempt to limit adverse selection by careful selection of where they market and to whom they sell a policy. For example, a company offering a Medicare supplement (Medigap) plan might be more likely to advertise its plan in senior citizen recreation centers, where the patrons tend to be relatively young and healthy, than in nursing homes, where the residents are probably older and have chronic health conditions. Thus, from the perspective of the individual or group applying for insurance, the insurer's attempts to avoid adverse selection may result in lack of availability of coverage, denial of coverage, incomplete coverage or above-average premiums.

* * *

Notes and Questions

The text asserts that the purpose of insurance is to spread risk from individuals to all members of a group. This suggests a vision of distributive justice based on group solidarity. Can you think of other understandings of the purpose of insurance? Should insurance alternatively be based on a principle of actuarial fairness, under which every individual pays for insurance based on his own risks? Which principle best explains the market for health insurance, as it exists in the United States today? See Deborah Stone, The Struggle for the Soul of Health Insurance, 18 J. Health Pol. Pol'y & L. 287 (1993).

Having now introduced the basic concepts of insurance and managed care, we will proceed to examine relevant state law, first considering the liability of insurers and managed care organizations under state contract and tort law, and then looking at state programs that regulate health insurers and managed care organizations.

II. CONTRACT LIABILITY OF PRIVATE INSURERS AND MANAGED CARE ORGANIZATIONS

Insurance companies and insurance contracts have historically been governed primarily by state law, and states continue to have primary responsibility for regulating managed care. In the first instance, insurance and managed care contracts are contracts, and the failure of an insurer or managed care plan to perform to the expectations of the insured may result in contract litigation in state court. Our discussion begins, therefore, with an examination of state insurance contract law.

LUBEZNIK v. HEALTHCHICAGO, INC.

Appellate Court of Illinois, 1994.
268 Ill.App.3d 953, 206 Ill.Dec. 9, 644 N.E.2d 777.

JUSTICE JOHNSON delivered the opinion of the court:

Plaintiff, Bonnie Lubeznik, filed this action in the Circuit Court of Cook County seeking a permanent injunction requiring defendant, Healthchicago, Inc., to pre-certify her for certain medical treatment. Following a hearing, the trial court granted the injunction. Defendant appeals, contending the trial court improperly (1) determined that the requested treatment was a covered benefit under plaintiff's insurance policy; (2) interpreted portions of the Illinois Health Maintenance Organization Act; (3) * * *; and (4) granted the injunction.

We affirm.

The record reveals that in November 1988 plaintiff was diagnosed with Stage III ovarian cancer. At the time of her diagnosis, the cancer had spread through plaintiff's abdomen and liver and she had a 20 percent survival rate over the next five years. * * *

In June 1991, plaintiff was referred to Dr. Patrick Stiff, the director of the bone marrow treatment program at Loyola University Medical Center (hereinafter Loyola). Dr. Stiff sought to determine the prospect of treating plaintiff with high dose chemotherapy with autologous bone marrow transplant (hereinafter HDCT/ABMT). HDCT/ABMT is a procedure where bone marrow stem cells are removed from the patient's body and frozen in storage until after the patient has been treated with high dose chemotherapy. Following chemotherapy, which destroys the cancer, the marrow previously extracted is reinfused to proliferate and replace marrow destroyed by the chemotherapy. HDCT/ABMT had been a state of the art treatment for leukemia and Hodgkin's disease for many years. It began to be used in the late 1980's for women who were in the late stages of breast cancer.

* * *

On October 28, 1991, Dr. Stiff contacted defendant requesting that it pre-certify plaintiff for the HDCT/ABMT, i.e., agree in advance to pay for the treatment. Plaintiff's insurance policy required her to get pre-certified before receiving elective treatment, procedures and therapies. Dr. Wayne Mathy, defendant's medical director, received Dr. Stiff's pre-certification request and telephoned him shortly thereafter. During his conversation with Dr. Stiff, Dr. Mathy stated that the ABMT/HDCT was not a covered benefit under plaintiff's insurance policy because the treatment was considered experimental.

On October 31, 1991, plaintiff filed a two-count complaint against defendant and Loyola. In count one, plaintiff sought a mandatory injunction against defendant to pre-certify her for the HDCT/ABMT. In her second count, plaintiff sought an injunction against Loyola to admit her for medical treatment without a deposit of $100,000. Both defendant and Loyola filed motions to dismiss plaintiff's complaint. Subsequently, plaintiff took a voluntary non-suit against Loyola.

Following a hearing, the trial court denied defendant's motion to dismiss and defendant filed its answer instanter. Thereafter, a hearing on the complaint was held at which Dr. Stiff testified that the HDCT/ABMT was an effective treatment for plaintiff given that all conventional treatments for her had been exhausted. He stated that he had performed 21 HDCT/ABMT procedures on patients with Stage III ovarian cancer and as a result, 75 percent of those patients were in complete remission.

During further testimony, Dr. Stiff opined that the HDCT/ABMT was not experimental and presented documents and literature in support of his testimony. * * *

Dr. Mathy testified at the hearing that his responsibilities as defendant's medical director included determining whether a requested medical treatment is covered under an insurance policy issued by defendant. He stated that after he received plaintiff's request for pre-certification, a member of defendant's benefit analysis staff contacted the National Institute of Health, the National Cancer Institute, and Medicare seeking an assessment as to whether the requested treatment was experimental. According to Dr. Mathy, defendant determined that the HDCT/ABMT was experimental based on information received from those medical assessment bodies. * * *

During cross-examination, Dr. Mathy testified that he first learned on October 29, 1991, that Dr. Stiff was contemplating treating plaintiff with HDCT/ABMT. Dr. Mathy admitted that immediately upon learning of the proposed treatment, he decided that the HDCT/ABMT was experimental and that plaintiff's pre-certification request should be denied. Dr. Mathy stated that he did not consult with the National Institute of Health or the National Cancer Institute before making the decision to deny plaintiff's request.

At the conclusion of the testimony, the parties presented final arguments to the trial court. Subsequently, the trial court issued an injunction against defendant ruling that the ABMT/HDCT is neither an experimental therapy for ovarian cancer, nor a transplant within the meaning of Illinois Health Maintenance Organization Act (Ill.Rev.Stat.1991, ch. 111 1/2, par. 1408.5) (hereinafter the Act). Defendant then filed this appeal.

Defendant initially argues that the trial court erroneously determined that the HDCT/ABMT procedure is a covered benefit under plaintiff's insurance policy. Defendant claims it supported its determination that the procedure is experimental with similar conclusions by appropriate medical technology boards as required by plaintiff's insurance contract. Plaintiff's insurance policy provides that "[e]xperimental medical, surgical, or other procedures as determined by the [Insurance] Plan in conjunction with appropriate medical technology assessment bodies," are excluded from coverage. Defendant contends that the trial court improperly disregarded the terms of the insurance contract, which, defendant argues, were clear and unambiguous.

At the outset, we note that coverage provisions in an insurance contract are to be liberally construed in favor of the insured to provide the broadest possible coverage.[ ] In determining whether a certain provision in an insurance contract is applicable, a trial court must first determine whether the specific provision is ambiguous.[ ] A provision which is clear or unambiguous, i.e., fairly admits but of one interpretation, must be applied as written.[ ]

However, where a provision is ambiguous, its language must be construed in favor of the insured.[ ]

Moreover, where an insurer seeks to deny insurance coverage based on an exclusionary clause contained in an insurance policy, the clause must be clear and free from doubt.[ ] This is so because all doubts with respect to coverage are resolved in favor of the insured. * * *

After carefully reviewing the evidence, we cannot agree with defendant that the trial court improperly determined the HDCT/ABMT to be a covered benefit under plaintiff's insurance policy. First, we disagree with defendant that the exclusionary language was clear and unambiguous. We note that the plaintiff's insurance policy does not define the phrase "appropriate medical technology boards." The plain language of the policy does not indicate who will determine whether a certain medical board is appropriate. Further, the policy fails to outline any standards for determining how a medical board is deemed appropriate. Thus, the phrase, without more, gives rise to a genuine uncertainty about which medical boards are considered appropriate and how and by whom the determination is made.

Second, despite defendant's argument to the contrary, the exclusionary language in plaintiff's insurance contract varies significantly from the language in section 4–5 of the Act which provides as follows:

> "No contract or evidence of coverage issued by a health maintenance organization which provides coverage for health care services shall deny reimbursement for an otherwise covered expense incurred for any organ transplantation procedure solely on the basis that such procedure is deemed experimental or investigational unless supported by the determination of the Office of Health Care Technology Assessment within the Agency for the Health Care Policy and Research within the federal Department of Health and Human Services that such a procedure is either experimental or investigational * * *." (Ill.Rev.Stat.1991, ch. 111 1/2, par. 1408.5.)

Unlike plaintiff's insurance contract, the Act specifically provides which agency has the authority to determine whether a procedure is experimental.

Third, we must note that even if the exclusionary language did apply, defendant failed to follow the terms of the insurance policy. Plaintiff's insurance policy excludes from coverage medical and surgical procedures that are considered experimental by defendant "in conjunction with appropriate technology assessment bodies." At the hearing, Dr. Mathy testified that upon learning of plaintiff's pre-certification request, he had already determined that the HDCT/ABMT was experimental prior to receiving or reviewing any information from the medical assessment boards. Given our careful review of the evidence, including defendant's admitted disregard for the terms of the insurance policy, we hold that the trial court did not err in ruling that the requested treatment was a covered benefit under the policy.

* * *

Lastly, defendant claims that the trial court improperly granted the mandatory injunction because plaintiff failed to meet the requirements for an injunction to issue. An injunction may be granted only after the plaintiff establishes that (1) a lawful right exists; (2) irreparable injury will result if the injunction is not granted; and (3) his or her remedy at law is inadequate.[ ] * * *

* * *

At the hearing, Dr. Stiff testified that given the steady development of plaintiff's disease, it was imperative to begin the HDCT/ABMT treatment as quickly as possible. He opined that delaying the HDCT/ABMT any further might have rendered plaintiff ineligible for such treatment due to further development of the disease. Based on our understanding of Dr. Stiff's testimony, we do not believe, as defendant now posits, that plaintiff was not eligible for the treatment.

Moreover, Dr. Stiff further testified that the HDCT/ABMT was an effective treatment for plaintiff and offered her a "very high chance of a complete disappearance of her disease." In addition, when asked during direct examination to give a prognosis of plaintiff's condition, Dr. Stiff gave the following response:

> "[Plaintiff] has a fatal illness with a zero percent to one percent chance of being alive at five years, let alone alive and disease free."

Given the evidence presented at the hearing, including Dr. Stiff's testimony, we do not agree with defendant that plaintiff failed to show she would suffer irreparable harm without the treatment.[ ] Therefore, we hold that the trial court did not abuse its discretion in granting the requested injunctive relief.

* * *

Notes and Questions

1. Courts have traditionally viewed insurance contracts as adhesion contracts and interpreted them under the doctrine of contra proferentem. This has made it difficult for insurance companies to control their exposure to risk through general clauses that refuse payment for care that is not "medically necessary" or that it "experimental". Usually when such clauses are litigated, as in the principal case, the treating physician testifies that care is standard and is urgently necessary, the insurer's medical director testifies that the care is experimental or unnecessary. What conflicts of interest does each face? Whom should the court believe? Are there more appropriate ways of resolving these disputes? What are the ramifications of these disputes for the cost of medical care? In one recent case a jury returned a verdict for $77 million in punitive damages and $12.1 million in compensatory damaged against an HMO which had denied coverage of ABMT for breast cancer. Fox v. Health Net of California, No. 219692 (Cal.Sup.Ct.1993) cited at 3 Health Law Reporter (BNA) 18, 19 (Jan. 6, 1994). What effect might such a decision have on medical necessity determinations?

On the other hand, a number of courts have upheld insurers who have denied coverage for ABMT. See Fuja v. Benefit Trust Life Insurance Co., 18 F.3d 1405 (7th Cir.1994); Holder v. Prudential Ins. Co. of America 951 F.2d 89 (5th Cir.1992), finding that the language of the policy was sufficiently clear to support denial. Paradoxically, though most insurers eventually came to cover ABMT for breast cancer, the most recent research indicates that its efficacy is highly questionable. See Karen Antman, et al., High Dose Chemotherapy for Breast Cancer, 282 JAMA 1701 (1999).

2. A fascinating empirical study of coverage disputes is reported in Mark Hall, et al., Judicial Protection of Managed Care Consumers: An Empirical Study of Insurance Coverage Disputes, 26 Seton Hall 1055 (1996). Professor Hall found that patients win coverage disputes over half of the time, and that the specificity of the language with which the insurer attempts to exclude coverage does not significantly affect its likelihood of winning. See also, analyzing medical necessity disputes, Peter D. Jacobson, et al., Defining and Implementing Medical Necessity in Washington State and Oregon, 34 Inquiry 143 (1997); and William M. Sage, Judicial Opinions Involving Health Insurance Coverage: Trompe L'Oeil or Window on the World?, 31 Ind. L. Rev. 49 (1998). The issue of how medical necessity should be defined and who should determine it has become an important and controversial issue in managed care reform proposals. See Sara Rosenbaum, David M. Frankford, Brad More & Phyllis Borzi, Who Should Determine When Health Care is Medically Necessary? 340 JAMA 229 (1999). See also, regarding experimental treatment exclusions, J. Gregory Lahr, What is the Method to Their "Madness?" Experimental Treatment Exclusions in Health Insurance Policies, 13 J. Contemp. Health L. & Pol'y 613 (1997).

See discussing the policy issues raised by cases interpreting medical necessity and experimental treatment clauses, Mark A. Hall & Gerard F. Anderson, Health Insurers' Assessment of Medical Necessity, 140 U. Pa. L. Rev. 1637 (1992); Richard S. Saver, Note: Reimbursing New Technologies: Why are the Courts Judging Experimental Medicine?, 44 Stan. L. Rev. 1095 (1992); Frank P. James, The Experimental Treatment Exclusion Clause: A Tool For Silent Rationing of Health Care?, 12 J. Legal Med. 359 (1991).

Insurance and managed care coverage disputes present not only contract interpretation issues, but also issues of tort law, to which we now turn.

III. TORT LIABILITY OF MANAGED CARE

Managed care organizations are increasingly defendants in liability suits, facing the same theories that hospitals face, as well as newer theories related to the cost-conserving functions of managed care. "Managed care" is a phrase often used to describe organizational groupings that attempt to control the utilization of health care services through a variety of techniques, including prepayment by subscribers for services on a contract basis, use of physicians as "gatekeepers" for hospital and specialty services, and others. The groups cover a wide variety of plans—from plans that require little more than preauthorization of patient hospitalization, to staff model HMOs—that focus on utilization and price of services. The goal is reduction of health care costs and maximization of value to both patient and payer. A Managed Care Organization (MCO) is a reimbursement framework combined with a health care delivery system, an approach to the delivery of health care services that contrasts with "fee-for-service" medicine. Managed care is usually distinguished from traditional indemnity plans by the existence of a single entity responsible for integrating and coordinating the financing and delivery of services that were once scattered between providers and payers.

Managed care has rapidly supplanted fee-for-service medicine. The shift from traditional indemnity plans to health maintenance organizations and other network plans has been rapid over the past decade. By 1998 only 14 percent of employees in large firms of more than 200 employees were enrolled in conventional plans, with small firms seeing a similar shift to managed care.

By contrast, in 1980 only five to ten percent of the workforce was enrolled in such plans. By 1999 HMO enrollment had exceeded 81 million members, with almost 30 percent of the U.S. population enrolled in an HMO. Managed care organizations have taken over the financing of American health care primarily because they promise to control costs. And they have in fact contributed to a substantial slowing in health care inflation. Looking at the period from 1960 to 1996, expenditure growth has slowed to 4.4%—the lowest rate in thirty-seven years of measuring health care spending.

See generally Contemporary Managed Care: Readings in Structure, Operations, and Public Policy (Marsha R. Gold, ed.1998); M. Susan Marquis and Stephen H. Long, Trends in Managed Care and Managede Competition, 1993–1997, 18 Health Affairs 75(1999); Robert H. Miller and Harold S. Luft, Managed Care: Past Evidence and Potential Trends, 9 Frontiers of Health Services Management 3 (1993); Robert Shouldice, Introduction to Managed Care: Health Maintenance Organizations, Preferred Provider Organizations, and Competitive Medical Plans (1991); Jonathan P. Weiner and Gregory de Lissovoy, Razing a Tower of Babel: A Taxonomy for Managed Care and Health Insurance Plans, 18 J. Health Pol., Pol'y & Law 75 (1993). See Total HMO Enrollment and Growth Rate, January 1990 to January 1999, 4 On Managed Care 3 (Nov.1999).Katherine R. Levit et al, National Health Spending Trends in 1996, 17 Health Affairs 35(1998).

This growth of "virtual" managed care means less integration and as a result less patient satisfaction and trust. An increase in litigation has resulted, and plaintiff lawyers have borrowed heavily from hospital liability law. David Mechanic and Marsha Rosenthal, Responses of HMO Medical Directors to Trust Building in Managed Care, 77 Milb.Q. 283(1999).

A. VICARIOUS LIABILITY

Health maintenance organizations (HMOs) and Independent Practice Associations (IPAs) in theory face the same vicarious and corporate liability questions as hospitals, since they provide services through physicians, whether the physicians are salaried employees or independent contractors. These medical services can injure patients/subscribers, leading to a malpractice suit for such injuries.

Vicarious liability theories have provided the first wave of successful litigation against managed care organizations.

PETROVICH v. SHARE HEALTH PLAN OF ILLINOIS, INC.

Supreme Court of Illinois, 1999.
188 Ill.2d 17, 241 Ill.Dec. 627, 719 N.E.2d 756.

Justice Bilandic delivered the opinion of the court:

The plaintiff brought this medical malpractice action against a physician and others for their alleged negligence in failing to diagnose her oral cancer in a timely manner. The plaintiff also named her health maintenance organization (HMO) as a defendant. The central issue here is whether the plaintiff's HMO may be held vicariously liable for the negligence of its independent-contractor physicians under agency law. The plaintiff contends that the HMO is vicariously liable under both the doctrines of apparent authority and implied authority.

* * *

FACTS

In 1989, plaintiff's employer, the Chicago Federation of Musicians, provided health care coverage to all of its employees by selecting Share and enrolling its employees therein. Share is an HMO and pays only for medical care that is obtained within its network of physicians. In order to qualify for benefits, a Share member must select from the network a primary care physician who will provide that member's overall care and authorize referrals when necessary. Share gives its members a list of participating physicians from which to choose. Share has about 500 primary care physicians covering Share's service area, which includes the counties of Cook, Du Page, Lake, McHenry and Will. Plaintiff selected Dr. Marie Kowalski from Share's list, and began seeing Dr. Kowalski as her primary care physician in August of 1989. Dr. Kowalski was employed at a satellite facility of Illinois Masonic Medical Center (Illinois Masonic), which had a contract with Share to provide medical services to Share members.

In September of 1990, plaintiff saw Dr. Kowalski because she was experiencing persistent pain in the right sides of her mouth, tongue, throat and face. Plaintiff also complained of a foul mucus in her mouth. Dr. Kowalski referred plaintiff to two other physicians who had contracts with Share: Dr. Slavick, a neurologist, and Dr. Friedman, an ear, nose and throat specialist.

Plaintiff informed Dr. Friedman of her pain. Dr. Friedman observed redness or marked erythema alongside plaintiff's gums on the right side of her mouth. He recommended that plaintiff have a magnetic resonance imaging (MRI) test or a computed tomography (CT) scan performed on the base of her skull. According to plaintiff's testimony at her evidence deposition, Dr. Kowalski informed her that Share would not allow new tests as recommended by Dr. Friedman. Plaintiff did not consult with Share about the test refusals because she was not aware of Share's grievance procedure. Dr. Kowalski gave Dr. Friedman a copy of an old MRI test result at that time. The record offers no further information about this old MRI test.

Nonetheless, Dr. Kowalski later ordered an updated MRI of plaintiff's brain, which was performed on October 31, 1990. Inconsistent with Dr. Friedman's directions, however, this MRI failed to image the right base of the tongue area where redness existed. Plaintiff and Dr. Kowalski discussed the results of this MRI test on November 19, 1990, during a follow-up visit. Plaintiff testified that Dr. Kowalski told her that the MRI revealed no abnormality.

Plaintiff's pain persisted. In April or May of 1991, Dr. Kowalski again referred plaintiff to Dr. Friedman. This was plaintiff's third visit to Dr. Friedman. Dr. Friedman examined plaintiff and observed that plaintiff's tongue was tender. Also, plaintiff reported that she had a foul odor in her mouth and was experiencing discomfort. On June 7, 1991, Dr. Friedman performed multiple biopsies on the right side of the base of plaintiff's tongue and surrounding tissues. The biopsy results revealed squamous cell carcinoma, a cancer, in the base of plaintiff's tongue and the surrounding tissues of the pharynx. Later that month, Dr. Friedman operated on plaintiff to remove the cancer. He removed part of the base of plaintiff's tongue, and portions of her palate, pharynx and jaw bone. After the surgery, plaintiff underwent radiation treatments and rehabilitation.

Plaintiff subsequently brought this medical malpractice action against Share, Dr. Kowalski and others. Dr. Friedman was not named a party defendant. Plaintiff's complaint, though, alleges that both Drs. Kowalski and Friedman were negligent in failing to diagnose plaintiff's cancer in a timely manner, and that Share is vicariously liable for their negligence under agency principles. Share filed a motion for summary judgment, arguing that it cannot be held liable for the negligence of Dr. Kowalski or Friedman because they were acting as independent contractors in their treatment of plaintiff, not as Share's agents. Plaintiff countered that Share is not entitled to summary judgment because Drs. Kowalski and Friedman were Share's agents. The parties submitted various depositions, affidavits and exhibits in support of their respective positions.

Share is a for-profit corporation. At all relevant times, Share was organized as an "independent practice association-model" HMO under the Illinois Health Maintenance Organization Act (Ill.Rev.Stat.1991, ch. 111 1/2 , par. 1401 et seq.). This means that Share is a financing entity that arranges and pays for health care by contracting with independent medical groups and practitioners. [ ] Share does not employ physicians directly, nor does it own, operate, maintain or supervise the offices where medical care is provided to its members. Rather, Share contracts with independent medical groups and physicians that have the facilities, equipment and professional skills necessary to render medical care. Physicians desiring to join Share's network are required to complete an application procedure and meet with Share's approval.

Share utilizes a method of compensation called "capitation" to pay its medical groups. Share also maintains a "quality assurance program." Share's capitation method of compensation and "quality assurance program" are more fully described later in this opinion.

Share provides a member handbook to each of its members, including plaintiff. The handbook states to its members that Share will provide "all your healthcare needs" and "comprehensive high quality services." The handbook also states that the primary care physician is "your health care manager" and "makes the decisions" about the member's care. The handbook further states that Share is a "good partner in sickness and in health." Unlike the master agreements and benefits contract discussed below, the member handbook which plaintiff received does not contain any provision that identifies Share physicians as independent contractors or nonemployees of Share. Rather, the handbook describes the physicians as "your Share physician," "Share physicians" and "our staff." Furthermore, Share refers to the physicians' offices as "Your Share physician's office" and states: "All of the Share staff and Medical Offices look forward to serving you * * *."

Plaintiff confirmed that she received the member handbook. Plaintiff did not read the handbook in its entirety, but read portions of it as she needed the information. She relied on the information contained in the handbook while Drs. Kowalski and Friedman treated her.

The record also contains a "Health Care Services Master Agreement," entered into by Share and Illinois Masonic. Dr. Kowalski is a signatory of this agreement. The agreement states, "It is understood and agreed that [Illinois Masonic] and [primary care physicians] are independent contractors and not employees or agents of SHARE." A separate agreement between Share and Dr. Friedman contains similar language. Plaintiff did not receive these agreements.

Share's primary care physicians, under their agreements with Share, are required to approve patients' medical requests and make referrals to specialists. These physicians use Share's standard referral forms to indicate their approval of the referral. Dr. Kowalski testified at an evidence deposition that she did not feel constrained by Share in making medical decisions regarding her patients, including whether to order tests or make referrals to specialists.

Another document in the record is Share's benefits contract. The benefits contract contains a subscriber certificate. The subscriber certificate sets forth a member's rights and obligations with respect to Share. Additionally, the subscriber certificate states that Share's physicians are independent contractors and that "SHARE Plan Providers and Enrolling Groups are not agents or employees of SHARE nor is SHARE or any employee of SHARE an agent or employee of SHARE Plan Providers or Enrolling Groups." The certificate elaborates: "The relationship between a SHARE Plan Provider and any Member is that of provider and patient. The SHARE Plan Physician is solely responsible for the medical services provided to any Member. The SHARE Plan Hospital is solely responsible for the Hospital services provided to any Member."

Plaintiff testified that she did not recall receiving the subscriber certificate. In response, Share stated that Share customarily provides members with this information. Share does not claim to know whether Share actually provided plaintiff with this information. Plaintiff acknowledged that she received a "whole stack" of information from Share upon her enrollment.

Plaintiff was not aware of the type of relationship that her physicians had with Share. At the time she received treatment, plaintiff believed that her physicians were employees of Share.

In the circuit court, Share argued that it was entitled to summary judgment because the independent-contractor provision in the benefits contract established, as a matter of law, that Drs. Kowalski and Friedman were not acting as Share's agents in their treatment of plaintiff. The circuit court agreed and entered summary judgment for Share.

The appellate court reversed, holding that a genuine issue of material fact is presented as to whether plaintiff's treating physicians are Share's apparent agents. 296 Ill.App.3d 849, 231 Ill.Dec. 364, 696 N.E.2d 356. The appellate court stated that a number of factors support plaintiff's apparent agency claim, including plaintiff's testimony, Share's member handbook, Share's quality assessment program and Share's capitation method of compensation. The appellate court therefore remanded the cause for trial. The appellate court did not address the theory of implied authority.

ANALYSIS

This appeal comes before us amidst great changes to the relationships among physicians, patients and those entities paying for medical care. Traditionally, physicians treated patients on demand, while insurers merely paid the physicians their fee for the services provided. Today, managed care organizations (MCOs) have stepped into the insurer's shoes, and often attempt to reduce the price and quantity of health care services provided to patients through a system of health care cost containment. MCOs may, for example, use prearranged fee structures for compensating physicians. MCOs may also use utilization-review procedures, which are procedures designed to determine whether the use and volume of particular health care services are appropriate. MCOs have developed in response to rapid increases in health care costs.

HMOs, i.e., health maintenance organizations, are a type of MCO. HMOs are subject to both state and federal laws. [ ] Under Illinois law, an HMO is defined as "any organization formed under the laws of this or another state to provide or arrange for one or more health care plans under a system which causes any part of the risk of health care delivery to be borne by the organization or its providers." Ill.Rev.Stat.1991, ch. 111 1/2, par. 1402(9), now 215 ILCS 125/1–2(9) (West 1998). Because HMOs may differ in their structures and the cost-containment practices that they employ, a court must discern the nature of the organization before it, where relevant to the issues. As earlier noted, Share is organized as an independent practice association (IPA)-model HMO. IPA-model HMOs are financing entities that arrange and pay for health care by contracting with independent medical groups and practitioners. [ ]

This court has never addressed a question of whether an HMO may be held liable for medical malpractice. Share asserts that holding HMOs liable for medical malpractice will cause health care costs to increase and make health care inaccessible to large numbers of people. Share suggests that, with this consideration in mind, this court should impose only narrow, or limited, forms of liability on HMOs. We disagree with Share that the cost-containment role of HMOs entitles them to special consideration. The principle that organizations are accountable for their tortious actions and those of their agents is fundamental to our justice system. There is no exception to this principle for HMOs. Moreover, HMO accountability is essential to counterbalance the HMO goal of cost-containment. To the extent that HMOs are profit-making entities, accountability is also needed to counterbalance the inherent drive to achieve a large and ever-increasing profit margin. Market forces alone "are insufficient to cure the deleterious [e]ffects of managed care on the health care industry." Herdrich v. Pegram, 154 F.3d 362, 374–75 (7th Cir. 1998), cert. granted, 527 U.S. 1068, 120 S.Ct. 10, 144 L.Ed.2d 841 (1999). Courts, therefore, should not be hesitant to apply well-settled legal theories of liability to HMOs where the facts so warrant and where justice so requires.

Indeed, the national trend of courts is to hold HMOs accountable for medical malpractice under a variety of legal theories, including vicarious liability on the basis of apparent authority, vicarious liability on the basis of respondeat superior, direct corporate negligence, breach of contract and breach of warranty. [ ] * * * Share concedes that HMOs may be held liable for medical malpractice under these five theories.

This appeal concerns whether Share may be held vicariously liable under agency law for the negligence of its independent-contractor physicians. We must determine whether Share was properly awarded summary judgment on the ground that Drs. Kowalski and Friedman were not acting as Share's agents in their treatment of plaintiff. Plaintiff argues that Share is not entitled to summary judgment on this record. Plaintiff asserts that genuine issues of material fact exist as to whether Drs. Kowalski and Friedman were acting within Share's apparent authority, implied authority or both.

* * *

As a general rule, no vicarious liability exists for the actions of independent contractors. Vicarious liability may nevertheless be imposed for the actions of independent contractors where an agency relationship is established under either the doctrine of apparent authority [ ] or the doctrine of implied authority [ ].

I. Apparent Authority

Apparent authority, also known as ostensible authority, has been a part of Illinois jurisprudence for more than 140 years. [ ] Under the doctrine, a principal will be bound not only by the authority that it actually gives to another, but also by the authority that it appears to give. [ ]. The doctrine functions like an estoppel. [ ]. Where the principal creates the appearance of authority, a court will not hear the principal's denials of agency to the prejudice of an innocent third party, who has been led to reasonably rely upon the agency and is harmed as a result.[ ]

* * *

We now hold that the apparent authority doctrine may also be used to impose vicarious liability on HMOs. * * * [ ]

To establish apparent authority against an HMO for physician malpractice, the patient must prove (1) that the HMO held itself out as the provider of health care, without informing the patient that the care is given by independent contractors, and (2) that the patient justifiably relied upon the conduct of the HMO by looking to the HMO to provide health care services, rather than to a specific physician. Apparent agency is a question of fact. [ ]

A. Holding Out

The element of "holding out" means that the HMO, or its agent, acted in a manner that would lead a reasonable person to conclude that the physician who was alleged to be negligent was an agent or employee of the HMO. [ ] Where the acts of the agent create the appearance of authority, a plaintiff must also prove that the HMO had knowledge of and acquiesced in those acts. [ ] The holding-out element does not require the HMO to make an express representation that the physician alleged to be negligent is its agent or employee. Rather, this element is met where the HMO holds itself out as the provider of health care without informing the patient that the care is given by independent contractors. [ ] Vicarious liability under the apparent authority doctrine will not attach, however, if the patient knew or should have known that the physician providing treatment is an independent contractor. [ ]

Here, Share contends that the independent-contractor provisions in the two master agreements and the benefits contract conclusively establish, as a matter of law, that Share did not hold out Drs. Kowalski and Friedman to be Share's agents. Although all three of these contracts clearly express that the physicians are independent contractors and not agents of Share, we disagree with Share's contention for the reasons explained below.

First, the two master agreements at issue are private contractual agreements between Share and Illinois Masonic, with Dr. Kowalski as a signatory, and between Share and Dr. Friedman. The record contains no indication that plaintiff knew or should have known of these private contractual agreements between Share and its physicians. Gilbert expressly rejected the notion that such private contractual agreements can control a claim of apparent agency. [ ] * * * We hold that this same rationale applies to private contractual agreements between physicians and an HMO. [ ] Because there is no dispute that the master agreements at bar were unknown to plaintiff, they cannot be used to defeat her apparent agency claim.

Share also relies on the benefits contract. Plaintiff was not a party or a signatory to this contract. The benefits contract contains a subscriber certificate, which states that Share physicians are independent contractors. Share claims that this language alone conclusively overcomes plaintiff's apparent agency claim. We do not agree.

Whether a person has notice of a physician's status as an independent contractor, or is put on notice by the circumstances, is a question of fact. [ ] In this case, plaintiff testified at her evidence deposition that she did not recall receiving the subscriber certificate. Share responded only that it customarily provides members with this information. Share has never claimed to know whether Share actually provided plaintiff with this information. Thus, a question of fact exists as to whether Share gave this information to plaintiff. If this information was not provided to plaintiff, it cannot be used to defeat her apparent agency claim.

* * *

Evidence in the record supports plaintiff's contentions that Share held itself out to its members as the provider of health care, and that plaintiff was not aware that her physicians were independent contractors. Notably, plaintiff stated that, at the time that she received treatment, plaintiff believed that Drs. Kowalski and Friedman were Share employees. Plaintiff was not aware of the type of relationship that her physicians had with Share.

Moreover, Share's member handbook contains evidence that Share held itself out to plaintiff as the provider of her health care. The handbook stated to Share members that Share will provide "all your healthcare needs" and "comprehensive high quality services." The handbook did not contain any provision that identified Share physicians as independent contractors or nonemployees of Share. Instead, the handbook referred to the physicians as "your Share physician," "Share physicians" and "our staff." Share also referred to the physicians' offices as "Your Share physician's office." The record shows that Share provided this handbook to each of its enrolled members, including plaintiff. Representations made in the handbook are thus directly attributable to Share and were intended by Share to be communicated to its members.

* * *

We hold that the above testimony by plaintiff and Share's member handbook support the conclusion that Share held itself out to plaintiff as the provider of her health care, without informing her that the care was actually provided by independent contractors. Therefore, a triable issue of fact exists as to the holding-out element. We need not resolve whether any other evidence in the record also supports plaintiff's claim. Our task here is to review whether Share is entitled to summary judgment on this element. We hold that Share is not.

B. Justifiable Reliance

A plaintiff must also prove the element of "justifiable reliance" to establish apparent authority against an HMO for physician malpractice. This means that the plaintiff acted in reliance upon the conduct of the HMO or its agent, consistent with ordinary care and prudence. [ ]

The element of justifiable reliance is met where the plaintiff relies upon the HMO to provide health care services, and does not rely upon a specific physician. This element is not met if the plaintiff selects his or her own personal physician and merely looks to the HMO as a conduit through which the plaintiff receives medical care. [ ]

Concerning the element of justifiable reliance in the hospital context, Gilbert explained that the critical distinction is whether the plaintiff sought care from the hospital itself or from a personal physician. * * *

This rationale applies even more forcefully in the context of an HMO that restricts its members to the HMO's chosen physicians. Accordingly, unless a person seeks care from a personal physician, that person is seeking care from the HMO itself. A person who seeks care from the HMO itself accepts that care in reliance upon the HMO's holding itself out as the provider of care.

Share maintains that plaintiff cannot establish the justifiable reliance element because she did not select Share. * * *

* * *We reject Share's argument. It is true that, where a person selects the HMO and does not rely upon a specific physician, then that person is relying upon the HMO to provide health care. This principle, derived directly from Gilbert, is set forth above. Equally true, however, is that where a person has no choice but to enroll with a single HMO and does not rely upon a specific physician, then that person is likewise relying upon the HMO to provide health care.

In the present case, the record discloses that plaintiff did not select Share. Plaintiff's employer selected Share for her. Plaintiff had no choice of health plans whatsoever. Once Share became plaintiff's health plan, Share required plaintiff to obtain her primary medical care from one of its primary care physicians. If plaintiff did not do so, Share did not cover plaintiff's medical costs. In accordance with Share's requirement, plaintiff selected Dr. Kowalski from a list of physicians that Share provided to her. Plaintiff had no prior relationship with Dr. Kowalski. As to Dr. Kowalski's selection of Dr. Friedman for plaintiff, Share required Dr. Kowalski to make referrals only to physicians approved by Share. Plaintiff had no prior relationship with Dr. Friedman. We hold that these facts are sufficient to raise the reasonable inference that plaintiff relied upon Share to provide her health care services.

Were we to conclude that plaintiff was not relying upon Share for health care, we would be denying the true nature of the relationship among plaintiff, her HMO and the physicians. Share, like many HMOs, contracted with plaintiff's employer to become plaintiff's sole provider of health care, to the exclusion of all other providers. Share then restricted plaintiff to its chosen physicians. Under these facts, plaintiff's reliance on Share as the provider of her health care is shown not only to be compelling, but literally compelled. Plaintiff's reliance upon Share was inherent in Share's method of operation.

* * *

In conclusion, as set forth above, plaintiff has presented sufficient evidence to support justifiable reliance, as well as a holding out by Share. Share, therefore, is not entitled to summary judgment against plaintiff's claim of apparent authority.

* * *

II. Implied Authority

Implied authority is actual authority, circumstantially proved. [ ] One context in which implied authority arises is where the facts and circumstances show that the defendant exerted sufficient control over the alleged agent so as to negate that person's status as an independent contractor, at least with respect to third parties. [ ] The cardinal consideration for determining the existence of implied authority is whether the alleged agent retains the right to control the manner of doing the work. [ ] Where a person's status as an independent contractor is negated, liability may result under the doctrine of respondeat superior.

Plaintiff contends that the facts and circumstances of this case show that Share exerted sufficient control over Drs. Kowalski and Friedman so as to negate their status as independent contractors. Share responds that the act of providing medical care is peculiarly within a physician's domain because it requires the exercise of independent medical judgment. Share thus maintains that, because it cannot control a physician's exercise of medical judgment, it cannot be subject to vicarious liability under the doctrine of implied authority.

* * *

We now address whether the implied authority doctrine may be used against HMOs to negate a physician's status as an independent contractor. Our appellate court in Raglin suggested that it can. Raglin v. HMO Illinois, Inc., 230 Ill.App.3d 642, 647, 172 Ill.Dec. 90, 595 N.E.2d 153 (1992). Case law from other jurisdictions lends support to this view as well. [ ]

* * *

We do not find the above decisions rendered in the hospital context to be dispositive of whether an HMO may exert such control over its physicians so as to negate their status as independent contractors. We can readily discern that the relationships between physicians and HMOs are often much different than the traditional relationships between physicians and hospitals. * * *

Physicians, of course, should not allow the exercise of their medical judgment to be corrupted or controlled. Physicians have professional ethical, moral and legal obligations to provide appropriate medical care to their patients. These obligations on physicians, however, will not act to relieve an HMO of its own legal responsibilities. Where an HMO effectively controls a physician's exercise of medical judgment, and that judgment is exercised negligently, the HMO cannot be allowed to claim that the physician is solely responsible for the harm that results. In such a circumstance, both the physician and the HMO are liable for the harm that results. We therefore hold that the implied authority doctrine may be used against an HMO to negate a physician's status as an independent contractor. An implied agency exists where the facts and circumstances show that an HMO exerted such sufficient control over a participating physician so as to negate that physician's status as an independent contractor, at least with respect to third parties. [ ] No precise formula exists for deciding when a person's status as an independent contractor is negated. Rather, the determination of whether a person is an agent or an independent contractor rests upon the facts and circumstances of each case. [ ] As noted, the cardinal consideration is whether that person retains the right to control the manner of doing the work. [ ] Facts bearing on the question of whether a person is an agent or an independent contractor include "the question of the hiring, the right to discharge, the manner of direction of the servant, the right to terminate the relationship, and the character of the supervision of the work done." Merlo, 381 Ill. at 319, 45 N.E.2d 665. The presence of contractual provisions subjecting the person to control over the manner of doing the work is a traditional indicia that a person's status as an independent contractor should be negated. [ ] The presence of one or more of the above facts and indicia are not necessarily conclusive of the issue. They merely serve as guides to resolving the primary question of whether the alleged agent is truly an independent contractor or is subject to control.

With these established principles in mind, we turn to the present case. Plaintiff contends that her physicians' status as independent contractors should be negated. Plaintiff asserts that Share actively interfered with her physicians' medical decisionmaking by designing and executing its capitation method of compensation and "quality assurance" programs. Plaintiff also points to Share's referral system as evidence of control.

Plaintiff submits that Share's capitation method of compensating its medical groups is a form of control because it financially punishes physicians for ordering certain medical treatment. The record discloses that Share utilizes a method of compensation called "capitation."[ ]. Under capitation, Share prepays contracting medical groups a fixed amount of money for each member who enrolls with that group. In exchange, the medical groups agree to render health care to their enrolled Share members in accordance with the Share plan. Each medical group contracting with Share has its own capitation account. Deducted from that capitation account are the costs of any services provided by the primary care physician, the costs of medical procedures and tests, and the fees of all consulting physicians. The medical group then retains the surplus left in the capitation account. The costs for hospitalizations and other services are charged against a separate account. Reinsurance is provided for the capitation account and the separate account for certain high cost claims. Share pays Illinois Masonic in accordance with its capitation method of compensation. Dr. Kowalski testified that Illinois Masonic pays her the same salary every month. Plaintiff maintains that a reasonable inference to be drawn from Share's capitation method of compensation is that Share provides financial disincentives to its primary care physicians in order to discourage them from ordering the medical care that they deem appropriate. Plaintiff argues that this is an example of Share's influence and control over the medical judgment of its physicians.

Share counters that its capitation method of compensation cannot be used as evidence of control here because Dr. Kowalski is paid the same salary every month. We disagree with Share that this fact makes Share's capitation system irrelevant to our inquiry. Whether control was actually exercised is not dispositive in this context. Rather, the right to control the alleged agent is the proper query, even where that right is not exercised. [ ]

[The court rejects Share's "quality assurance program" as evidence of control, since it is done primarily to comply with state regulations of the Department of Public Health. The court however allows as evidence of control chart review by Share; control over referral to specialists; and use of primary care physicians as gatekeepers].

We conclude that plaintiff has presented adequate evidence to entitle her to a trial on the issue of implied authority. All the facts and circumstances before us, if proven at trial, raise the reasonable inference that Share exerted such sufficient control over Drs. Kowalski and Friedman so as to negate their status as independent contractors. As discussed above, plaintiff presents relevant evidence of Share's capitation method of compensation, Share's "quality assurance review," Share's referral system and Share's requirement that its primary care physicians act as gatekeepers for Share. These facts support plaintiff's argument that Share subjected its physicians to control over the manner in which they did their work. The facts surrounding treatment also support plaintiff's argument. According to plaintiff's evidence, Dr. Kowalski referred plaintiff to Dr. Friedman. Dr. Friedman evaluated plaintiff and recommended that plaintiff have either an MRI test or a CT scan performed on the base of her skull. Dr. Friedman, however, did not order the test that he recommended for plaintiff. Rather, he reported this information back to Dr. Kowalski in her role as plaintiff's primary care physician. Dr. Kowalski initially sent Dr. Friedman a copy of an old MRI test. Dr. Kowalski later ordered that an updated MRI be taken. In doing so, she directed that the MRI be taken of plaintiff's "brain." Hence, that MRI failed to image the base of plaintiff's skull as recommended by Dr. Friedman. Dr. Kowalski then reviewed the MRI test results herself and informed plaintiff that the results revealed no abnormality. From all the above facts and circumstances, a trier of fact could reasonably infer that Share promulgated such a system of control over its physicians that Share effectively negated the exercise of their independent medical judgment, to plaintiff's detriment.

We note that Dr. Kowalski testified at an evidence deposition that she did not feel constrained by Share in making medical decisions regarding her patients, including whether to order tests or make referrals to specialists. This testimony is not controlling at the summary judgment stage. The trier of fact is entitled to weigh all the conflicting evidence above against Dr. Kowalski's testimony.

In conclusion, plaintiff has presented adequate evidence to support a finding that Share exerted such sufficient control over its participating physicians so as to negate their status as independent contractors. Share, therefore, is not entitled to summary judgment against plaintiff's claim of implied authority.

* * *

CONCLUSION

An HMO may be held vicariously liable for the negligence of its independent-contractor physicians under both the doctrines of apparent authority and implied authority. Plaintiff here is entitled to a trial on both doctrines. The circuit court therefore erred in awarding summary judgment to Share. The appellate court's judgment, which reversed the circuit court's judgment and remanded the cause to the circuit court for further proceedings, is affirmed.

Affirmed.

Notes and Questions

1. Does a subscriber to an IPA-style managed care organization look to it for care rather than solely to the individual physicians? In an IPA, there is no central office, staffed by salaried physicians; the subscriber instead goes to the individual offices of the primary care physicians or the specialists. What justifies extending ostensible agency doctrine to this arrangement?

Managed care advertising often holds out the plan in words such as "total care program", as "an entire health care system". A reliance by the subscriber on the managed care organization for their choice of physicians, and any holding out by the MCO as a provider, is sufficient. See McClellan v. Health Maintenance Organization of Pennsylvania, 413 Pa.Super. 128, 604 A.2d 1053 (1992) (ostensible agency based on advertisements by HMO claiming that it carefully screened in primary care physicians).

In Petrovich, the court allowed both an apparent authority claim and an implied authority claim. Implied authority required a court to find sufficient elements of plan control over a physician to reject the independent contractor defense. In Petrovich, the court found that utilization review, limits on referrals to specialists and hospitals, and other financial constraints were sufficient to create implied authority.

2. IPA-model HMOs that become "the institution", that "hold out" the independent contractor as an employee, and also restrict provider selection are vulnerable to ostensible agency arguments. Where the HMO exercises substantial control over the independent physicians by controlling the patients they must see and by paying on a per capita basis, an agency relationship has been found. See Dunn v. Praiss, 256 N.J.Super. 180, 606 A.2d 862 (N.J.Super.Ct.App.Div.1992); Boyd v. Albert Einstein Medical Center, 377 Pa.Super. 609, 547 A.2d 1229 (Sup. Pa. 1988).

3. The court in Decker v. Saini, 14 Employee Benefits Cas. 1556, 1991 WL 277590 (Mich.Cir.Ct.1991) observed that the application of vicarious liability has a powerful incentive effect on MCOs to select better physicians:

> As a matter of public policy, the Court notes that imposing vicarious liability on HMOs for the malpractice of their member physicians would strongly encourage them to select physicians with the best credentials. Otherwise, HMO's would have no such incentive and might be driven by economics to retain physicians with the least desirable credentials, for the lower prices.

4. Some courts have pushed the boundaries even further, using agency principles to reach consulting physicians chosen by physicians employed by the HMO. In *Schleier v. Kaiser Foundation Health Plan*, 876 F.2d 174 (D.C.Cir.1989), a staff model HMO was held vicariously liable for physician malpractice, not of its employee-physician, but of an independent consulting physician. The court found four grounds for holding the HMO vicariously liable: (1) the consultant physician had been engaged by an HMO-employed physician, (2) the HMO had the right to discharge the consultant, (3) services provided by the consultant were part of the regular business of the HMO, and (4) the HMO had some ability to control the consultant's behavior, since he answered to an HMO doctor, the plaintiff's primary care physician. This judicial willingness to impose respondeat superior liability for the negligence of a consulting, non-employee physician clearly applies to the IPA model HMOs and even PPOs.

5. The development of complex cost and quality controls, which strengthen the supervisory role of the MCO, together with the managed care industry's preference for the capitation method of physician compensation, are likely to lead the courts to hold the IPA model HMO-physician relationship to respondeat superior liability. Even a plan-sponsored network risks exposure to ostensible agency arguments if a court can find that the plan sponsor has created an expectation on the part of patients that the plan will provide high-quality providers of care. If the plan restricts a member's choice of providers, as will be likely in most situations, the network providers look like "agents" of the sponsor. The alternative—disclaimers in a PPO directory or other subscriber material as to quality of care, reminders to patients that they are responsible for choosing their physicians—may provide a legal shield against ostensible agency arguments. Such disclaimers are, however, not very reassuring when marketing to subscribers of a network plan. Capitation has begun to fade as an HMO tool in the face of physician resistance. Use of fee-based service claims that doctors must submit for each procedure is becoming more common. See Leigh Page, Capitation at the Crossroads, 44 AMA News 17 (March 5, 2001).

6. A breach of contract suit can be brought against an MCO on the theory of a "contract" to provide quality health care. In *Williams v. HealthAmerica* 41 Ohio App.3d 245, 535 N.E.2d 717 (Ohio App.1987), a subscriber sued an IPA model HMO, and her primary care physician, for injuries resulting from a delay in referring her to a specialist. The theory was that the physician and HMO failed to deliver quality health benefits as promised, i.e. the right to be referred to a specialist. The court upheld the breach of contract action against the primary care physician but recast the action against the HMO as a tort claim for breach of the duty to handle the plaintiff's claim in good faith.

MCO contracts and literature may also contain provisions to the effect that "quality" health care will be provided or that the organization will promote or enhance subscriber health. The Share literature contained such language. Where such assurances are made in master contracts of HMO-physician agreements, subscribers may be able to bring a contract action under a third party beneficiary theory. In Williams, for example, the court suggested that the subscriber could be a third-party beneficiary of the HMO-physician contract that required the physician to "promote of the rights of enrollees as patients."

A claim for breach of an express contract or an implied contract may also be argued based on representations by an HMO as to quality of care. This would seem to overlap with a malpractice claim to the extent it is based on a contract to provide "adequate and qualified medical care in accordance with the generally accepted standards of the community". Natale v. Meia, 1998 WL 236089 (Sup.Ct. Conn., 1998)(defendant's motion to strike denied) ... But express promises, if proven, can give rise to a separate claim.

Health care providers are not held to guarantee a cure, based on general language. "Mere puffery", as the courts view it, is not the same as a warranty of a good result, and will not create a claim. Pulvers v. Kaiser Foundation Health Plan, 99 Cal.App.3d 560, 160 Cal.Rptr. 392 (1979)(breach of warranty claim rejected on grounds that a warranty of a good result was just "generalized puffing.") However, an assurance of high quality care in marketing materials and brochures might be treated by a court or jury as a promise that standards of quality will be met, leading to warranty liability. In *Boyd* the plaintiff pleaded both ostensible agency and breach of warranty. The concurring opinion argued that summary judgment on the warranty count was inappropriate because there was a factual issue as to "whether the literature in which HMO 'guaranteed' and 'assured' the quality of care to its subscribers, had been distributed to * * * [the plaintiff]."

MCOs also typically market themselves by describing the quality of the providers on the panel. An assertion of quality furnishes courts another reason to impose on the organization the duty to investigate the competency of participating physicians. Such assertions might even be viewed as a warranty that all panel members maintain a certain minimum competence.

7. Common law fraud or state consumer fraud statutes are another possible source of recovery. Representations in contracts and marketing brochures, or omissions of material information from these documents, inducing the patient to subscribe to the MCO or submit to a certain medical treatment, might be actionable. These theories are more demanding, however, often requiring proof of intentional misrepresentation and justifiable reliance.

Common law bad faith claims may be brought against non-ERISA managed car plans. Courts have held that a staff model HMO acts as an insurer when it refers a subscriber to an out-of-network provider, under the contract, and then denies reimbursement for that out-of-network care without reasonable grounds. This kind of non-medical, coverage-related decision is subject to a bad faith analysis. McEvoy v. Group Health Cooperative of Eau Claire, 213 Wis.2d 507, 570 N.W.2d 397 (Wis. 1997) (allowing bad faith action against a non-ERISA HMO for a coverage denial). The managed care organization is liable for any damages from the breach, including damages. Such actions are not intended to be duplicative of malpractice actions. They require a showing "by clear, satisfactory, and convincing evidence that an HMO acted improperly, and that financial considerations were given unreasonable weight in the decision maker's cost-benefit analysis."ID at 405. The court in McEvoy noted that HMO subscribers are "in an inferior position for enforcing their contractual health care rights" (id. at 403.) Such actions are likely to be rare in light of the higher burden of proof required and ERISA preemption,[1] but the question of what "unreasonable weight" means in considering the financial effects of treatment opens the door to more litigation.

1. Pilot Life Insurance Co. v. Dedeaux, 481 U.S. 41, 107 S.Ct. 1549, 95 L.Ed.2d 39 (1987) held that actions such as bad faith sufficiently "relate to" employee benefits plans to fall within ERISA preemption.

B. DIRECT INSTITUTIONAL LIABILITY: CORPORATE NEGLIGENCE

SHANNON v. McNULTY

Superior Court of Pennsylvania, 1998.
718 A.2d 828.

ORIE MELVIN, JUDGE:

Mario L. Shannon and his wife, Sheena Evans Shannon, in their own right and as co-administrators of the Estate of Evan Jon Shannon, appeal from an order entered in the Court of Common Pleas of Allegheny County denying their motion to remove a compulsory nonsuit. This appeal concerns the Shannons' claims of vicarious and corporate liability against HealthAmerica stemming from the premature delivery and subsequent death of their son. We reverse the order refusing to remove the compulsory nonsuit and remand for trial.

This medical malpractice action arises from the pre-natal care provided by appellees, Larry P. McNulty, M.D. and HealthAmerica, to Mrs. Shannon. The Shannons claimed Dr. McNulty was negligent for failing to timely diagnose and treat signs of pre-term labor, and HealthAmerica was vicariously liable for the negligence of its nursing staff in failing to respond to Mrs. Shannon's complaints by timely referring her to an appropriate physician or hospital for diagnosis and treatment of her pre-term labor. The Shannons also alleged HealthAmerica was corporately liable for its negligent supervision of Dr. McNulty's care and its lack of appropriate procedures and protocols when dispensing telephonic medical advice to subscribers.

The case went to trial before a jury, and at the close of the plaintiffs' case HealthAmerica moved for a compulsory nonsuit. The trial court denied the motion. HealthAmerica then proceeded to put on its case by calling two of its triage nurses. At the conclusion of the testimony of the second nurse the court recessed for the day. The following morning the court, sua sponte, reconsidered HealthAmerica's motion for compulsory nonsuit, entertained argument thereon, and granted the nonsuit. The Shannons filed timely post trial motions seeking to have the nonsuit removed. After denial of such motions, this appeal followed.

On appeal the Shannons present two questions for this Court to review:

1. [DID] THE TRIAL COURT [ERR] IN GRANTING A COMPULSORY NONSUIT IN FAVOR OF [APPELLEE], HEALTHAMERICA, AND AGAINST THE [APPELLANTS] [IN THAT APPELLANTS] MADE OUT A PRIMA FACIE CASE AGAINST HEALTHAMERICA FOR BOTH COMMON LAW VICARIOUS LIABILITY REGARDING THE ACTIONS OF HEALTHAMERICA'S TRIAGE NURSES AND EMPLOYEES, AND DIRECT CORPORATE LIABILITY.

2. [DID] THE TRIAL COURT [ERR] IN GRANTING A COMPULSORY NONSUIT AFTER [APPELLEE] HEALTHAMERICA PRESENTED EVIDENCE IN ITS CASE IN CHIEF.

(Appellants' Brief at 2). Initially, we note that the scope of review in an appeal from the denial of a motion to remove a compulsory nonsuit is limited to determining whether the trial court abused its discretion or committed an error of law. [ ] * * *

Generally, in a medical malpractice case the plaintiff must establish: (1) a duty owed by the health care provider to the patient; (2) a breach of that duty; (3) the breach was the proximate cause of, or a substantial factor in, bringing about the harm suffered by the patient; and (4) damages suffered by the patient that were a direct result of that harm. [ ] Moreover, except where it is obvious, the plaintiff must present expert testimony that the health care provider's conduct deviated from an accepted standard of care and such deviation was the proximate cause of the harm suffered.

The theory of corporate liability as it relates to hospitals was first adopted in this Commonwealth in the case of Thompson v. Nason Hospital, 527 Pa. 330, 591 A.2d 703 (Pa.1991). Our supreme court upheld a direct theory of liability against the hospital, stating:

Corporate negligence is a doctrine under which the hospital is liable if it fails to uphold the proper standard of care owed the patient, which is to ensure the patient's safety and well-being while at the hospital. This theory of liability creates a nondelegable duty which the hospital owes directly to a patient. Therefore, an injured party does not have to rely on and establish the negligence of a third party. Id. at 707. (footnote omitted) The court then set forth four general areas of corporate liability:

(1) A duty to use reasonable care in the maintenance of safe and adequate facilities and equipment;

(2) A duty to select and retain only competent physicians;

(3) A duty to oversee all persons who practice medicine within its walls as to patient care;

(4) A duty to formulate, adopt and enforce adequate rules and policies to ensure quality care for patients. Id. The court further stated that "we adopt as a theory of hospital liability the doctrine of corporate negligence or corporate liability under which the hospital is liable if it fails to uphold the proper standard of care owed its patient." Id. at 708.

The evidence introduced by the Shannons may be summarized in relevant part as follows. Mrs. Shannon testified during the trial of this case that she was a subscriber of the HealthAmerica HMO when this child was conceived. It was Mrs. Shannon's first pregnancy. When she advised HealthAmerica she was pregnant in June 1992, they gave her a list of six doctors from which she could select an OB/GYN. She chose Dr. McNulty from the list. [ ] Her HealthAmerica membership card instructed her to contact either her physician or HealthAmerica in the event she had any medical questions or emergent medical conditions. The card contained the HealthAmerica emergency phone number, which was manned by registered nurses. [ ] She testified it was confusing trying to figure out when to call Dr. McNulty and when to call HealthAmerica because she was receiving treatment from both for various medical conditions related to her pregnancy, including asthma and reflux. [ ]

She saw Dr. McNulty monthly but also called the HealthAmerica phone line a number of times for advice and to schedule appointments with their in-house doctors. [ ] She called Dr. McNulty on October 2, 1992 with complaints of abdominal pain. The doctor saw her on October 5, 1992 and examined her for five minutes. He told Mrs. Shannon her abdominal pain was the result of a fibroid uterus, he prescribed rest and took her off of work for one week. He did no testing to confirm his diagnosis and did not advise her of the symptoms of pre-term labor. [ ]

She next called Dr. McNulty's office twice on October 7 and again on October 8 and October 9, 1992, because her abdominal pain was continuing, she had back pain, was constipated and she could not sleep. She asked Dr. McNulty during the October 8th call if she could be in pre-term labor because her symptoms were similar to those described in a reference book she had on labor. [ ] She told Dr. McNulty her pains were irregular and about ten minutes apart, but she had never been in labor so she did not know what it felt like. He told her he had just checked her on October 5th, and she was not in labor.[ ] The October 9th call was at least her fourth call to Dr. McNulty about her abdominal pain, and she testified that Dr. McNulty was becoming impatient with her. [ ]

On October 10th, she called HealthAmerica's emergency phone line and told them about her severe irregular abdominal pain, back pain, that her pain was worse at night, that she thought she may be in pre-term labor, and about her prior calls to Dr. McNulty. The triage nurse advised her to call Dr. McNulty again. [ ] Mrs. Shannon did not immediately call Dr. McNulty because she did not feel there was anything new she could tell him to get him to pay attention to her condition. She called the HealthAmerica triage line again on October 11, 1992, said her symptoms were getting worse and Dr. McNulty was not responding. The triage nurse again advised her to call Dr. McNulty. [ ] Mrs. Shannon called Dr. McNulty and told him about her worsening symptoms, her legs beginning to go numb, and she thought that she was in pre-term labor. He was again short with her and angry and insisted that she was not in pre-term labor.[ ]

On October 12, 1992, she again called the HealthAmerica phone service and told the nurse about her symptoms, severe back pain and back spasms, legs going numb, more regular abdominal pain, and Dr. McNulty was not responding to her complaints. One of HealthAmerica's in-house orthopedic physicians spoke with her on the phone and directed her to go to West Penn Hospital to get her back examined. [ ] She followed the doctor's advice and drove an hour from her house to West Penn, passing three hospitals on the way. At West Penn she was processed as having a back complaint because those were HealthAmerica's instructions, but she was taken to the obstetrics wing as a formality because she was over five (5) months pregnant. She delivered a one and one-half pound baby that night. He survived only two days and then died due to his severe prematurity. [ ]

The Shannons' expert, Stanley M. Warner, M.D., testified he had experience in a setting where patients would call triage nurses. Dr. Warner opined that HealthAmerica, through its triage nurses, deviated from the standard of care following the phone calls to the triage line on October 10, 11 and 12, 1992, by not immediately referring Mrs. Shannon to a physician or hospital for a cervical exam and fetal stress test. As with Dr. McNulty, these precautions would have led to her labor being detected and increased the baby's chance of survival. [ ] Dr. Warner further testified on cross examination that Mrs. Shannon turned to HealthAmerica's triage nurses for medical advice on these three occasions when she communicated her symptoms. She did not receive appropriate advice, and further, if HealthAmerica's triage nurses intended for the referrals back to Dr. McNulty to be their solution, they had a duty to follow up Mrs. Shannon's calls by calling Dr. McNulty to insure Mrs. Shannon was actually receiving the proper care from him.[ ]

CORPORATE LIABILITY

[The court concludes that the third duty of Thompson, the duty to oversee all those who deliver care, is applicable.] * * *

Similarly, in the present case Dr. Warner, on direct examination, offered the following opinion when asked whether or not HealthAmerica deviated from the standard of care:

> I believe they did deviate from the standard of care. I believe on each occasion of the calls on October 10th, 11th, and October 12th, that Mrs. Shannon should have been referred to the hospital, and the hospital notified that this woman was probably in preterm labor and needed to be handled immediately. They did have the alternative of calling for a physician, if they wanted to, for him to agree with it, but basically she needed to be evaluated in a placd [sic] where there was a fetal monitor and somebody to do a pelvic examination to see what was happening with her.

[ ]. When asked whether this deviation increased the risk of harm Dr. Warner stated that "it did increase the risk of harm to the baby, and definitely decreased the chance of [the baby] being born healthy." Id., at 147.

Dr. Warner further testified in response to a series of hypothetical questions as follows:

> Q. I want you to assume that on Saturday, October 10th, that Mrs. Shannon calls Health America and she talks to a triage nurse, and she relates to the triage nurse she is experiencing severe abdominal pain. I want you to assume that she is told, the triage nurse who answered the phone, that she has related these symptoms to Dr. McNulty, and she related Dr. McNulty's response, or lack of response, to her complaints of abdominal pain. I want you to assume that the triage nurse's advice is simply to call the doctor back again. Now, under those facts do you have an opinion, within a reasonable degree medical certainty, whether or not Health America deviated from the standard of care?
>
> A. I do.
>
> Q. What is that opinion?
>
> A. I believe they deviated from the standard of care, the nurse.
>
> Q. We're talking now with respect to October 10th.
>
> A. Yes, sir. The nurse at that time would have a responsibility to know these are signs and symptoms of preterm labor, and to make sure she gets care in a facility where the ability to have fetal monitoring and cervix examination are. She should call up Dr. McNulty and ask him to make arraignments [sic] for that, or she can send the patient directly to the

hospital. She should, in any event, make sure that happens in a very timely fashion. In other words, do it right away, you don't delay in doing this. You want to get her there before it's too late, before the cervix dilates too far, before it's too late to inhibit labor.

* * *

Q. I want you to assume, Dr. Warner, that on October 11, 1992, Mrs. Shannon called Health America again, and again relayed her complaints of either abdominal pain, back pain or side pain. Once again she also relayed her history of what I just told you, and she relayed what Dr. McNulty had done and what he hadn't done up to October 11th, and that the advice from Health America was the same, call Dr. McNulty back again. Now, under that factual scenario do you have an opinion, within a reasonable degree of medical certainty, whether or not Health America deviate from the standard of care on October 11, 1992?

A. I do have an opinion.

Q. And what is that?

A. That they deviated from the standard of care on October 11, 1992, as well. This woman was obviously searching for help. She was worried, and nobody was responding to her. She needed to be brought into the hospital and monitored and examined, and Dr. McNulty did not provide for it. She tlaked [sic] to Health America, who is one of her medical providers, and they at least had to get her into the hospital on an emergency condition, seen right away and monitored and examined right away, and if they called ahead to the emergency room to let them know that, then the emergency room is conditioned to respond, they know they have to respond rapidly to this preterm labor situation before they lose the chance to stop the labor.

Q. Moving down to October 12th, I want you to assume that Sheena Shannon called Health America on October 12, 1992, and relayed the same history. That is, the history now of back pain. I want you to assume that the nurse at Health America asked Sheena whether or not she had experienced any type of trauma over the course of the past year. Although she was also informed of her pregnancy and her gestational status, the nurse under this assumption was told that she had been in two automobile accidents, and the triage nurse then called an internist. The internist under this assumption called Sheena and told Sheena to go to the hospital, West Penn Hospital, for an orthopedic consult. I want you also to assume under this scenario that no provision was made by Health America to this hospital. Now, under that scenario did Health America deviate from the standard of care?

A. Yes, they did deviate from the standard of care. Again she should have been sent to the emergency room right away, and the emergency room notified there was a possibility that she was in preterm labor, regardless of the fact she had prior car accidents. Once again, you can't differentiate back pain caused by preterm labor from other sources of back pain without going through a Physical examination and measurements [sic] that you need to determine whether or not she was in labor or not. So, she had to go in and be seen right away. Her call was at 12:42, as I understand, or about 12:30, I think I saw in one place.

Q. That's right, 12:42.

A. And she was five centimeters at 4:00 a.m., approximately. Since the first part of labor moves rather slowly, especially in a first baby, an hour or two could have made a significant difference. There's a good probability that if they had seen her at 2:00 a.m. she would still be at four centimeters or less, and they could have inhibited labor even on that night if they had gotten her in quickly enough.

Id. at 158–162.

Viewing the evidence in the light most favorable to the Shannons as the non-moving party, our examination of the instant record leads us to the conclusion that the Shannons presented sufficient evidence to establish a prima facie case of corporate liability pursuant to the third duty set forth in Thompson, supra. However, due to the different entities involved, this determination does not end our inquiry. The Welsh case involved a suit against a hospital and thus Thompson was clearly applicable. Instantly, HealthAmerica, noting this Court's decision not to extend corporate liability under the facts in McClellan v. Health Maintenance Organization of Pennsylvania, 413 Pa.Super. 128, 604 A.2d 1053 (Pa.Super.1992), argues that the Thompson duties are inapplicable to a health maintenance organization. We disagree.

In adopting the doctrine of corporate liability the Thompson court recognized "the corporate hospital's role in the total health care of its patients." Thompson, at 708. Likewise, we recognize the central role played by HMOs in the total health care of its subscribers. A great deal of today's healthcare is channeled through HMOs with the subscribers being given little or no say so in the stewardship of their care. Specifically, while these providers do not practice medicine, they do involve themselves daily in decisions affecting their subscriber's medical care. These decisions may, among others, limit the length of hospital stays, restrict the use of specialists, prohibit or limit post hospital care, restrict access to therapy, or prevent rendering of emergency room care. While all of these efforts are for the laudatory purpose of containing health care costs, when decisions are made to limit a subscriber's access to treatment, that decision must pass the test of medical reasonableness. To hold otherwise would be to deny the true effect of the provider's actions, namely, dictating and directing the subscriber's medical care.

Where the HMO is providing health care services rather than merely providing money to pay for services their conduct should be subject to scrutiny. We see no reason why the duties applicable to hospitals should not be equally applied to an HMO when that HMO is performing the same or similar functions as a hospital. When a benefits provider, be it an insurer or a managed care organization, interjects itself into the rendering of medical decisions affecting a subscriber's care it must do so in a medically reasonable manner. Here, HealthAmerica provided a phone service for emergent care staffed by triage nurses. Hence, it was under a duty to oversee that the dispensing of advice by those nurses would be performed in a medically reasonable manner. Accordingly, we now make explicit that which was implicit in McClellan and find that HMOs may, under the right circumstances, be held corporately liable for a breach of any of the Thompson duties which causes harm to its subscribers.

[The court also held that HealthAmerican was vicariously liable for the negligent rendering of services by its triage nurses, under Section 323 of the Restatement (Second) of Torts.]

* * *

JONES v. CHICAGO HMO LTD. OF ILLINOIS

Supreme Court of Illinois, 2000.
191 Ill.2d 278, 246 Ill.Dec. 654, 730 N.E.2d 1119.

JUSTICE BILANDIC delivered the opinion of the court:

This appeal asks whether a health maintenance organization (HMO) may be held liable for institutional negligence. We answer in the affirmative.

The plaintiff, Sheila Jones (Jones), individually and as the mother of the minor, Shawndale Jones, brought this medical malpractice action against the defendants, Chicago HMO Ltd. of Illinois (Chicago HMO), Dr. Robert A. Jordan and another party. The Joneses were members of Chicago HMO, an HMO. Dr. Jordan was a contract physician of Chicago HMO and the primary care physician of Shawndale.

* * *

FACTS

In reviewing an award of summary judgment, we must view the facts in the light most favorable to the nonmoving party. Petrovich v. Share Health Plan of Illinois, Inc., 188 Ill.2d 17, 30–31, 241 Ill.Dec. 627, 719 N.E.2d 756 (1999). The following facts thus emerge.

On January 18, 1991, Jones' three-month-old daughter Shawndale was ill. Jones called Dr. Jordan's office, as she had been instructed to do by Chicago HMO. Jones related Shawndale's symptoms, specifically that she was sick, was constipated, was crying a lot and felt very warm. An assistant advised Jones to give Shawndale some castor oil. When Jones insisted on speaking with Dr. Jordan, the assistant stated that Dr. Jordan was not available but would return her call. Dr. Jordan returned Jones' call late that evening. After Jones described the same symptoms to Dr. Jordan, he also advised Jones to give castor oil to Shawndale.

On January 19, 1991, Jones took Shawndale to a hospital emergency room because her condition had not improved. Chicago HMO authorized Shawndale's admission. Shawndale was diagnosed with bacterial meningitis, secondary to bilateral otitis media, an ear infection. As a result of the meningitis, Shawndale is permanently disabled.

The medical expert for the plaintiff, Dr. Richard Pawl, stated in his affidavit and deposition testimony that Dr. Jordan had deviated from the standard of care. In Dr. Pawl's opinion, upon being advised of a three-month-old infant who is warm, irritable and constipated, the standard of care requires a physician to schedule an immediate appointment to see the infant or, alternatively, to instruct the parent to obtain immediate medical care for the infant through another physician. Dr. Pawl gave no opinion regarding whether Chicago HMO was negligent.

* * *

Chicago HMO is a for-profit corporation. During all pertinent times, Chicago HMO was organized as an independent practice association model HMO under the Illinois Health Maintenance Organization Act (Ill.Rev.Stat. 1991, ch. 111 1/2, par. 1401 et seq.).

In her deposition testimony, Jones described how she first enrolled in Chicago HMO while living in Park Forest. A Chicago HMO representative visited her home. According to Jones, he "was telling me what it was all about, that HMO is better than a regular medical card and everything so I am just listening to him and signing my name and stuff on the papers. * * * I asked him what kind of benefits you get out of it and stuff, and he was telling me that it is better than a regular card."

The "HMO ENROLLMENT UNDERSTANDING" form signed by Jones in 1987 stated: "I understand that all my medical care will be provided through the Health Plan once my application becomes effective." Jones remembered that, at the time she signed this form, the Chicago HMO representative told her "you have got to call your doctor and stuff before you see your doctor; and before you go to the hospital, you have got to call."

Jones testified that when she later moved to Chicago Heights another Chicago HMO representative visited her home. This meeting was not arranged in advance. It occurred because the representative was "in the building knocking from door to door." Jones informed the representative that she was already a member.

When Jones moved to Chicago Heights, she did not select Dr. Jordan as Shawndale's primary care physician. Rather, Chicago HMO assigned Dr. Jordan to her. Jones explained:

> "They gave me * * * Dr. Jordan. They didn't ask me if I wanted a doctor. They gave me him.
>
> * * *
>
> * * * They told me that he was a good doctor * * * for the kids because I didn't know what doctor to take my kids to because I was staying in Chicago Heights so they gave me him so I started taking my kids there to him."

Dr. Mitchell J. Trubitt, Chicago HMO's medical director, testified at his deposition that Dr. Jordan was under contract with Chicago HMO for two sites, Homewood and Chicago Heights. The service agreement for the Homewood site was first entered into on May 5, 1987. The service agreement for the Chicago Heights site was first entered into on February 1, 1990. Dr. Jordan was serving both patient populations in January of 1991 when Shawndale became ill.

Dr. Trubitt stated that, before Chicago HMO and Dr. Jordan executed the Chicago Heights service agreement, another physician serviced that area. Chicago HMO terminated that physician for failing to provide covered immunizations. At the time that Chicago HMO terminated that physician, Dr.

Jordan agreed "to go into the [Chicago Heights] area and serve the patients." Chicago HMO then assigned to Dr. Jordan all of the patients of that physician. Dr. Trubitt explained:

"Q. So then with the elimination of [the other physician], Dr. Jordan then-were the members notified that Dr. Jordan would be their [primary care physician] from that point on?

A. Yes.

Q. They weren't given a choice?

A. At that point in the area there was no choice.

Q. So they weren't given a choice?

A. They were directed to Dr. Jordan."

Dr. Trubitt also explained that Dr. Jordan was Chicago HMO's only physician who was willing to serve the public aid membership in Chicago Heights. Dr. Trubitt characterized this lack of physicians as "a problem" for Chicago HMO.

Dr. Jordan testified at his deposition that, in January of 1991, he was a solo practitioner. He divided his time equally between his offices in Homewood and Chicago Heights. Dr. Jordan was under contract with Chicago HMO for both sites. In addition, Dr. Jordan was under contract with 20 other HMOs, and he maintained his own private practice of non-HMO patients. Dr. Jordan estimated that he was designated the primary care physician of 3,000 Chicago HMO members and 1,500 members of other HMOs. In contrast to Dr. Jordan's estimate, Chicago HMO's own "Provider Capitation Summary Reports" listed Dr. Jordan as being the primary care provider of 4,527 Chicago HMO patients as of December 1, 1990.

Jones' legal counsel and Dr. Trubitt engaged in the following colloquy concerning patient load:

"Q. In entering into an agreement with a provider, is any consideration given to the number of patients to be designated as the primary provider for?

A. Yes, there is consideration given to that element in terms of volume of patients that he is capable of handling.

Q. And who determines the volume of patients he is capable of handling? The Chicago HMO or the provider or-

A. There is some guidelines that HCFA provides.

Q. Who provides?

A. HCFA. The Health [Care Finance Administration], the governmental health and welfare.

Q. Do you happen to know what those limits are with respect to pediatricians?

A. I am going to say I believe they are 3,500 patients to a primary care physician. The number can be expanded depending on the number of physicians in the office and the number of hours of operation.

Q. So you can't tell me whether or not if Dr. Jordan had 6,000 or 6,500 that would be an unusually large number?

A. If he himself had it.

Q. It would be unusually large?

A. It would.

Q. And that would be of some concern to the Chicago HMO, right?

A. Well, yes, if he had those."

In January of 1991, Dr. Jordan employed four part-time physicians, in addition to himself. This included an obstetrician/gynecologist, an internist, a family practitioner and a pediatrician. Dr. Jordan, however, did not explain in what capacities these physicians served. The record contains no further information regarding these physicians.

The record also contains evidence concerning Chicago HMO procedures for obtaining health care. Chicago HMO's "Member Handbook" told members in need of medical care to "Call your Chicago HMO doctor first when you experience an emergency or begin to feel sick." (Emphasis in original.) Also, Chicago HMO gave its contract physicians a "Provider Manual." The manual contains certain provisions with which the providers are expected to comply. The manual contains a section entitled, "The Appointment System/Afterhours Care," which states that all HMO sites are statutorily required to maintain an appointment system for their patients.

Dr. Trubitt testified that Chicago HMO encouraged its providers to maintain an appointment system and also "to retain open spaces on their schedules so that patients who came in as walk-ins could be seen." Retaining space on the schedule for walk-ins was recommended because it offers quicker access to care, keeping patients out of the emergency room with its increased costs, and because, historically, the Medicaid patient population often did not make or keep appointments.

Dr. Jordan related that his office worked on an appointment system and had its own written procedures and forms for handling patient calls and appointments. When a patient called and Dr. Jordan was not in the office, written forms were used by his staff or his answering service to relay the information to him. If Dr. Jordan was in the office, the procedure was as follows:

"Q. * * * [I]f it was a routine appointment for the purpose of having a routine shot or checkup, [the office staff] could make the appointment themselves?

A. Yes.

Q. But if the caller calls and says there is some problem, then they would take the temperature and find out the complaints and refer that call to you; is that correct?

A. That's correct.

Q. And you were the one who would make the determination as to whether or not to schedule an appointment, is that correct?

A. Medical decision, yes.

Q. Medical decision. And I assume there were times when people would call and after you reviewed the information and talked to them that you decided that they didn't need the appointment; is that correct?

A. Of course.

Q. In other words, you would perform some type of triage over the telephone; is that correct?

A. Yes."

Three agreements appear in the record. First, Chicago HMO and the Department of Public Aid entered into a 1990 "AGREEMENT FOR FURNISHING HEALTH SERVICES." This agreement was "for the delivery of medical services to Medicaid recipients on a prepaid capitation basis." Jones and her children, Medicaid recipients, fall within the agreement's definition of beneficiaries.

The preamble to the agreement stated that Chicago HMO "is organized primarily for the purpose of providing health care services." It continued: "[Chicago HMO] warrants that it is able to provide the medical care and services required under this Agreement in accordance with prevailing community standards, and is able to provide these services promptly, efficiently, and economically."

Article V of the agreement described various duties of Chicago HMO, as follows. Chicago HMO "shall provide or arrange to have provided all covered services to all Beneficiaries under this Agreement." Chicago HMO "shall provide all Beneficiaries with medical care consistent with prevailing community standards." In addition, a section entitled "Choice of Physicians" provided in relevant part:

> "[Chicago HMO] shall afford to each Beneficiary a health professional who will supervise and coordinate his care, and, to the extent feasible within appropriate limits established by [Chicago HMO] and approved by the Department, shall afford the Beneficiary a choice of a physician.
>
> There shall be at least one full-time equivalent, board eligible physician to every 1,200 enrollees, including one full-time equivalent, board certified primary care physician for each 2,000 enrollees. * * * There shall be * * * one pediatrician for each 2,000 enrollees under age 17."

Another article V duty stated that, although Chicago HMO may furnish the services required by the agreement by means of subcontractors, Chicago HMO "shall remain responsible for the performance of the subcontractors."

Regarding appointments, this agreement stated that Chicago HMO "shall encourage members to be seen by appointment, except in emergencies." The agreement also stated that "[m]embers with more serious or urgent problems not deemed emergencies shall be triaged and provided same day service, if necessary," and that "emergency treatment shall be available on an immediate basis, seven days a week, 24–hours a day." Finally, the agreement directed that Chicago HMO "shall have an established policy that scheduled patients shall not routinely wait for more than one hour to be seen by a provider and no more than six appointments shall be made for each primary care physician per hour."

The record also contains a second agreement, a 1990 "MEDICAL GROUP SERVICE AGREEMENT" between Chicago HMO and Dr. Jordan, that lists a Chicago Heights office address for Dr. Jordan. This agreement described numerous duties of Dr. Jordan. Pertinent here, Dr. Jordan would provide to

Chicago HMO subscribers specified medical services "of good quality and in accordance with accepted medical and hospital standards of the community." Pursuant to a "PUBLIC AID AMENDMENT TO THE MEDICAL GROUP SERVICE AGREEMENT," Dr. Jordan agreed to "abide by any conditions imposed by [Chicago HMO] as part of [Chicago HMO's] agreement with [the Department]."

The third agreement appearing of record is a second "MEDICAL GROUP SERVICE AGREEMENT" between Chicago HMO and Dr. Jordan. This agreement was entered into in 1987 and lists a Homewood office address for Dr. Jordan.

Both agreements between Chicago HMO and Dr. Jordan provided for a capitation method of compensation. Under capitation, Chicago HMO paid Dr. Jordan a fixed amount of money for each member who selected Dr. Jordan as the member's primary care provider. In exchange, Dr. Jordan agreed to render health care to his enrolled Chicago HMO members in accordance with the Chicago HMO health plan. Dr. Jordan was paid the same monthly capitation fee per member regardless of the services he rendered. For example, for each female patient under two years old, Chicago HMO paid Dr. Jordan $34.19 per month regardless of whether he treated that patient. In addition, Chicago HMO utilized an incentive fund for Dr. Jordan. Certain costs such as inpatient hospital costs were paid from this fund. Chicago HMO would then pay Dr. Jordan 60% of any remaining, unused balance of the fund at the end of each year.

* * *

Analysis

* * *

I. Institutional Negligence

Institutional negligence is also known as direct corporate negligence. Since the landmark decision of Darling v. Charleston Community Memorial Hospital, 33 Ill.2d 326, 211 N.E.2d 253 (1965), Illinois has recognized that hospitals may be held liable for institutional negligence. * * *

* * *

[The court adopts the doctrine of institutional negligence for HMOs, citing to Shannon and Petrovich, supra.]

Having determined that institutional negligence is a valid claim against HMOs, we turn to the parties' arguments in this case. Jones contends that Chicago HMO is not entitled to summary judgment on her claim of institutional negligence. She asserts that genuine issues of material fact exist as to whether Chicago HMO (1) negligently assigned more enrollees to Dr. Jordan than he was capable of serving, and (2) negligently adopted procedures requiring Jones to call first for an appointment before visiting the doctor's office.

Chicago HMO argues that Jones' claim of institutional negligence cannot proceed because she failed to provide sufficient evidence delineating the standard of care required of an HMO in these circumstances. In particular,

Chicago HMO contends that Jones should have presented expert testimony on the standard of care required of an HMO.

Jones responds that she has provided sufficient evidence showing the standard of care required of an HMO in these circumstances. She argues further that her claim does not require expert testimony on this point. In support, Jones relies on Darling, where a claim of institutional negligence was allowed against a hospital without expert testimony because other evidence established the hospital's standard of care. [ ]

[The court discussed the need for expert testimony as to the standard of care in light of Darling and other precedents.

* * *

Darling and its progeny have firmly established that, in an action for institutional negligence against a hospital, the standard of care applicable to a hospital may be proved via a number of evidentiary sources, and expert testimony is not always required. [ ] We likewise conclude that, in an action for institutional negligence against an HMO, the standard of care applicable to an HMO may be proved through a number of evidentiary sources, and expert testimony is not necessarily required. Accordingly, expert testimony concerning the standard of care required of an HMO is not a prerequisite to Jones' claim. Nonetheless, Jones, as the plaintiff here, still bears the burden of establishing the standard of care required of an HMO through other, proper evidentiary sources. We must therefore evaluate the evidence presented on this point to determine whether Jones' claim withstands Chicago HMO's motion for summary judgment. In deciding whether Jones' standard of care evidence is sufficient, we look to whether that evidence can equip a lay juror to determine what constitutes the standard of care required of a "reasonably careful HMO" under the circumstances of this case.

A. *Patient Load*

We first consider Jones' assertion that Chicago HMO negligently assigned more patients to Dr. Jordan than he was capable of serving. Parenthetically, we note that this assertion involves an administrative or managerial action by Chicago HMO, not the professional conduct of its physicians. Therefore, this claim properly falls within the purview of HMO institutional negligence. Jones argues that the standard of care evidence in the record is sufficient to support her claim. She points to Dr. Trubitt's testimony, as well as the contract between Chicago HMO and the Department of Public Aid.

Dr. Trubitt was the medical director for Chicago HMO. He testified that, when Chicago HMO entered into agreements with primary care physicians, it considered the number of patients that the physician is capable of handling. The HMO would look to federal "guidelines" in making this determination. Based on those guidelines, Dr. Trubitt expressed 3,500 as the maximum number of patients that should be assigned to any one primary care physician. He stated that, if Dr. Jordan himself had 6,000 or more patients, then that would be an unusually large number and of concern to Chicago HMO.]

We agree with Jones that Dr. Trubitt's testimony is proper and sufficient evidence of the standard of care on this issue. According to Dr. Trubitt, an HMO should not assign more than 3,500 patients to any single primary care physician. Chicago HMO even concedes in its brief that the maximum patient load to which Dr. Trubitt testified "represent[s] a 'standard of care' whose violation could affect the quality of patient care." This particular standard of care evidence, setting forth a limit of 3,500 patients per primary care physician, is adequate to equip a lay juror to determine what constitutes the standard of care required of a "reasonably careful HMO" under the circumstances of this case. Whether Dr. Trubitt relied on an unidentified federal regulation or some other source in arriving at a maximum patient load of 3,500 is of no consequence. It is enough that Chicago HMO, through its medical director, admitted that it used the 3,500 limit as a guide in assigning patient loads. [ ]

Chicago HMO, however, submits that there is no evidence in the record that Dr. Jordan's patient load exceeded 3,500. We disagree. Chicago HMO's "Provider Capitation Summary Reports" listed Dr. Jordan as being the primary care provider of 4,527 Chicago HMO members as of December 1, 1990. Thus, Chicago HMO's own records show Dr. Jordan's patient load as exceeding the 3,500 limit by more than 1,000 patients. In addition, Dr. Jordan estimated that he himself was designated the primary care physician for an additional 1,500 members of other HMOs. He also maintained his own private practice of non-HMO patients. This evidence supports Jones' theory that Dr. Jordan had more than 6,000 HMO patients.

Chicago HMO, in support of its position, points to Dr. Jordan's testimony that he employed four part-time physicians in his office. We disagree with Chicago HMO concerning the significance of this testimony. Although Dr. Jordan testified that he employed four part-time physicians, he never explained in what capacities these physicians served. In fact, the record contains no further information regarding these physicians. Notably, the agreements between Chicago HMO and Dr. Jordan do not refer to any physicians other than Dr. Jordan himself. The evidence in the record, therefore, supports Jones' theory that Chicago HMO negligently assigned more than 3,500 patients to Dr. Jordan himself. At best, the testimony regarding the four part-time physicians creates a genuine issue of material fact as to how many patients Dr. Jordan actually served himself. Consequently, this limited information in the record about part-time physicians does not entitle Chicago HMO to summary judgment. As earlier noted, it is well established that summary judgment is a drastic remedy and should be awarded only where the right of the moving party is clear and free from doubt.

Chicago HMO also submits that Jones' claim of patient overload must fail because there is no evidence of a causal connection between the number of patients that Dr. Jordan was serving and his failure to schedule an appointment to see Shawndale. We disagree. We can easily infer from this record that Dr. Jordan's failure to see Shawndale resulted from an inability to serve an overloaded patient population. A lay juror can discern that a physician who has thousands more patients than he should will not have time to service them all in an appropriate manner.

We note, moreover, that additional evidence in the record supports Jones' claim. The record indicates that Chicago HMO was actively soliciting new members door-to-door around the same time that it lacked the physicians willing to serve those members. Jones described how she first enrolled in

Chicago HMO while living in Park Forest. A Chicago HMO representative visited her home and persuaded her to become a member, telling her that Chicago HMO "is better than a regular medical card." When Jones later moved to Chicago Heights, another Chicago HMO representative visited her home. Jones explained that this meeting was not arranged in advance. Rather, the representative was "in the building knocking from door to door." Jones also testified that, when she moved to Chicago Heights, Chicago HMO assigned Dr. Jordan to her and did not give her a choice of primary care physicians.

The latter aspect of Jones' testimony was supported by Dr. Trubitt. He explained that, before Chicago HMO and Dr. Jordan executed the Chicago Heights service agreement, another physician serviced that area. When Chicago HMO terminated that other physician, Dr. Jordan agreed "to go into the [Chicago Heights] area and serve the patients." Chicago HMO then assigned to Dr. Jordan all of the patients of that physician. Chicago HMO directed its members to Dr. Jordan; they had no other choice of a physician because "[a]t that point in the area there was no choice." According to Dr. Trubitt, Dr. Jordan was Chicago HMO's only physician who was willing to serve the public aid membership in Chicago Heights. Dr. Trubitt stated that this lack of physicians was "a problem" for Chicago HMO.

The record further reflects that Chicago HMO directed its Chicago Heights members to Dr. Jordan, even though it knew that Dr. Jordan worked at that location only half the time. Chicago HMO entered into two service agreements with Dr. Jordan, the first for a Homewood site in 1987, and the second for the Chicago Heights site in 1990. Dr. Trubitt indicated that Chicago HMO and Dr. Jordan executed the Chicago Heights service agreement at the time that Chicago HMO terminated the other physician. Dr. Jordan confirmed that, in January of 1991, he was dividing his time equally between his two offices. All of the foregoing evidence supports Jones' theory that Chicago HMO acted negligently in assigning more enrollees to Dr. Jordan than he was capable of handling.

Jones also relies on the contract between Chicago HMO and the Department of Public Aid as standard of care evidence. That contract stated that Chicago HMO shall have one full-time equivalent primary care physician for every 2,000 enrollees. We need not address in this appeal whether this contractual provision may serve as standard of care evidence. Our role here is to determine whether Chicago HMO is entitled to summary judgment on the patient overload aspect of the institutional negligence claim. Even if this contractual provision is removed from consideration, Chicago HMO is not entitled to summary judgment. Accordingly, we express no opinion on whether this provision may properly serve as standard of care evidence.

One final matter with respect to patient load remains to be considered. Chicago HMO contends that imposing a duty on HMOs to ascertain how many patients their doctors are serving would be unreasonably burdensome. Chicago HMO asserts that only physicians, and not HMOs, should have the duty to determine if the physician has too many patients.

To determine whether a duty exists in a certain instance, a court considers the following factors: (1) the reasonable foreseeability of injury, (2) the likelihood of injury, (3) the magnitude of the burden of guarding against the injury, and (4) the consequences of placing that burden upon the defendant. [ ] Lastly, the existence of a duty turns in large part on public policy considerations. [ ] Whether a duty exists is a question of law to be determined by the court.[ ]

Here, given the circumstances of this case, we hold that Chicago HMO had a duty to its enrollees to refrain from assigning an excessive number of patients to Dr. Jordan. HMOs contract with primary care physicians in order to provide and arrange for medical care for their enrollees. It is thus reasonably foreseeable that assigning an excessive number of patients to a primary care physician could result in injury, as that care may not be provided. For the same reason, the likelihood of injury is great. Nor would imposing this duty on HMOs be overly burdensome. Here, for example, Chicago HMO needed only to review its "Provider Capitation Summary Reports" to obtain the number of patients that it had assigned to Dr. Jordan. This information is likely to be available to all HMOs, as they must know the number of patients that a physician is serving in order to compute the physician's monthly capitation payments. The HMO may also simply ask the physician how many patients the physician is serving. Finally, the remaining factors favor placing this burden on HMOs as well. Public policy would not be well served by allowing HMOs to assign an excessive number of patients to a primary care physician and then "wash their hands" of the matter. The central consequence of placing this burden on HMOs is HMO accountability for their own actions. This court in Petrovich recognized that HMO accountability is needed to counterbalance the HMO goal of cost containment and, where applicable, the inherent drive of an HMO to achieve profits. [ ]

In conclusion, Chicago HMO is not entitled to summary judgment on Jones' claim of institutional negligence for assigning too many patients to Dr. Jordan.

* * *

Conclusion

An HMO may be held liable for institutional negligence. Chicago HMO is not entitled to summary judgment on Jones' claim charging Chicago HMO with institutional negligence for assigning more enrollees to Dr. Jordan than he was capable of serving. We therefore reverse the award of summary judgment to Chicago HMO on count I of Jones' second amended complaint and remand that claim to the circuit court for further proceedings. As to count III, we affirm the award of summary judgment to Chicago HMO.

* * *

Justice Rathje, also concurring in part and dissenting in part:

I agree with both the majority's affirmance of summary judgment on the breach of contract claim and its determination that plaintiff has waived the breach of warranty claim. I strongly disagree, however, with the majority's holding that Chicago HMO can be liable under a theory of institutional liability.

The majority reasons that, because an HMO is an "amalgam of many individuals" like a hospital, then Chicago HMO can be institutionally liable under the rule set forth in Darling v. Charleston Community Memorial Hospital, 33 Ill.2d 326, 211 N.E.2d 253 (1965). 191 Ill.2d at 293, 246 Ill.Dec. at 664, 730 N.E.2d at 1129. Although both a hospital and an HMO hire many different people for many different reasons, the reasons for holding hospitals liable under this theory do not hold true for Chicago HMO.

Generally, institutional liability attaches when an organization breaches a duty it owes as an organization. Under Darling, hospitals are vulnerable to institutional liability partly because, as organizations, they offer complete medical services, including nurses, doctors, orderlies, and administration. [ ] Hospital facilities include both the place and the staff, and hospitals "assume certain responsibilities for the care of the patient." Darling, 33 Ill.2d at 332, 211 N.E.2d 253. In Darling, the hospital was negligent for two reasons: it failed to properly review the work of an independent doctor, and its nurses failed to administer necessary tests. [ ] The rule set forth in Darling is that a hospital must act as a reasonably careful hospital would and is responsible for reviewing and supervising the medical care given to its patients.[ ]

[The judge notes that in Shannon v. McNulty the HMO hired nurses to work its triage service and advise members on medical decisions, rather than acting only as a vehicle through which member bills were paid.] * * *

* * * Under Chicago HMO's contract with Dr. Jordan, Chicago HMO is responsible for enrolling members, providing the doctor's group with a current list of those members, paying capitation fees, providing a list of hospitals and health care providers, providing other funding, and obtaining the appropriate regulatory licensure for the doctor's group. The doctor's group is solely responsible for providing the health services. Moreover, Chicago HMO's member's handbook specifically explains that the individual doctors are responsible for nurses and all other medical attention. Unlike the HMO in Shannon, which "provid[ed] health care services," Chicago HMO "merely provid[ed] money to pay for services." Thus, institutional liability is inappropriate in this case.

The primary flaw in the majority's analysis is that it attempts to create a rule of general application that fails to take into account not only the differences that exist between a hospital and an HMO but also those that exist among HMOs. To determine whether an HMO should have the same duty to its members that a hospital has to its patients, a court must assess not only whether hospitals are similar to HMOs but also whether the patient's relationship to the hospital is similar to the member's relationship to the HMO. [ ].

Hospitals are "institutions holding themselves out as devoted to the care and saving of human life." Johnson v. St. Bernard Hospital, 79 Ill.App.3d 709, 716, 35 Ill.Dec. 364, 399 N.E.2d 198 (1979). Institutional liability makes sense in the hospital context because a person in need of treatment must be assured that the hospital will abide by a sufficient standard of care. That patient generally does not have the time or opportunity to compare hospital bylaws or look for the hospital with the best administrative policies and the highest standard of care. A person goes to the nearest hospital in an emergency or to a hospital where his doctor has privileges in a nonemergency. In many cases, including most emergent cases, the patient has no time to make an informed choice. In his relationship with a hospital, the patient is at a severe disadvantage, which the law acknowledges by subjecting hospitals to institutional liability.

By contrast, the goal of an HMO is to provide health care in a cost-sensitive manner. B. Furrow, Managed Care Organizations and Patient Injury: Rethinking Liability, 31 Ga. L.Rev. 419, 457 (1997). HMOs offer medical services, but they do not do so in the same way that hospitals do. HMOs offer the funding and the contact with the medical professionals. In Chicago HMO, for instance, the way in which daily business is conducted, the duties of nurses and other staff, and other day-to-day decisions are made by the individual doctor or hospital with whom the HMO has contracted. This type of HMO makes no decision as to what type of care is ultimately given; they only decide whether the HMO will pay for that care.

Moreover, when a person joins an HMO, he knows beforehand what that HMO will cover and, in most cases, chooses which HMO he will join based on his assessment of the costs and benefits. To become a member, that person usually has to contract with the HMO. As a result, the HMO will be held accountable for any failure to comply with its own policies through a contract action.

In this case, the Chicago HMO representative arrived at plaintiff's door and asked her whether she would prefer to receive her public aid medical benefits through the HMO or continue receiving them directly through public aid. He reviewed the policies, and plaintiff made the decision to join, signing a statement that her participation in the HMO was voluntary and that she could disenroll at any time. Plaintiff was given the opportunity to make an informed choice and chose to receive her medical services through an HMO.

Just as hospitals can differ substantially from HMOs, substantial differences may exist among HMOs. Generally, HMOs are organized under one of four major models: (1) staff, in which the providers are all salaried employees of the HMO; (2) medical group, in which the HMO contracts with an organized group of doctors who have combined their practices; (3) independent practice association, in which the HMO contracts with individual physicians who are solo or group practitioners; and (4) network models, in which the HMO contracts with two or more physician group practices who may serve several HMOs at the same time. Both the methods of organization and the methods of reimbursement vary among the models. E. Weiner, Managed Health Care: HMO Corporate Liability, Independent Contractors, and the Ostensible Agency Doctrine, 15 J. Corp. L. 535, 540 (1990). In some cases, an HMO may behave very much like a hospital, and institutional liability might be appropriate in such cases. In most cases, however, an HMO will do everything in its power not to behave like a hospital, precisely to avoid the liability that comes with operating as one. Having a uniform standard of care for all HMOs makes little sense, given the major differences in structure.

Before concluding, I wish to stress that I by no means believe that HMOs should not be held accountable for their actions. Ordinarily, an HMO will be accountable to its members through the contract that is signed by both parties. Unfortunately, in this case, plaintiff was receiving benefits from the HMO through public aid and, therefore, did not contract with the HMO. Consequently, as the majority correctly holds, her particular situation leaves her unable to enforce the policy provisions because she was not a party to the contract. [ ] While I sympathize with plaintiff's unenviable position, the fact remains that plaintiff's theory of liability is not one permissible under our laws.

Notes and Questions

1. Consider the underlying failures of the systems in *Shannon* and *Jones*. In *Shannon*, the treating physician was impatient and inattentive to warning signs, but it was the triage nurses staffing the phone lines who failed to properly direct Shannon to a physician or hospital. How should the system have been designed to avoid such an error? What would you suggest to avoid a repetition of this kind of disaster? In *Jones*, what was the cause of the physician's failure to respond appropriately? Was it his heavy caseload of patients? Or just an erroneous judgment call on that occasion for which it is unfair to blame the MCO? What would you proposed to avoid such a problem in the future?

2. Administration of rules and policies to ensure quality care. Many of the ERISA preemption cases involve claims of negligent design of the managed care plan, including telephone call-in services staffed by nurses, such as those found defective. Other claims of negligent design and administration of the delivery of health care services have been allowed. See McDonald v. Damian, 56 F.Supp.2d 574 (E.D.Pa.1999)(claim for inadequacies in the delivery of medical services). The court in Pappas v. Asbel noted that contractual benefits provided in "such a dilatory fashion that the patient was injured are intertwined with the provision of safe care" This would give right to a negligent administration claim. 555 Pa. 342, 724 A.2d 889, 893 (Pa. 1998). In Pappas, the issue was a delay in transporting the plaintiff to a specialty trauma unit for care. The delay was arguably caused by the utilization review process of the managed care organization, which did not allow transport to the best hospital unit in the area for spinal injuries. Pappas involves a delay induced by a plan determination as to out-of-network care and a benefits question as to which hospitals were available to U.S. Healthcare providers.

2. Selection of providers. Neither *Shannon* nor *Jones* consider the other elements of corporate negligence. The managed care organization, like the hospital, has been held to owe its subscribers a duty to properly select its panel members. In *Harrell v. Total Health Care, Inc.*, 1989 WL 153066 (Mo.App.1989), affirmed 781 S.W.2d 58 (Mo.1989), the court stated that an IPA model HMO owed a duty to its participants to investigate the competence of its panel members and to exclude physicians who posed a "foreseeable risk of harm." This logic also applies to PPOs, which control entry of physicians to the provider panel. While the merits of this claim were not reached, the case suggests that courts are willing to impose upon managed care organizations the duty to determine the competency of the providers on its panel.

The logic of a direct duty imposed on MCOs to properly select providers is even stronger for an MCO than for a hospital. In the hospital setting, the patient usually has selected the physician. He is then admitted to the hospital because his physician has admitting privileges at that hospital. By contrast, in a managed care program the patient has chosen the particular program, but not the physicians who are provided. The patient must use the physicians on the panel. The patient thus explicitly relies on the MCO for its selection of health care providers. The MCO's obligations for the patient's total care are more comprehensive than in the hospital setting. A plan sponsor that establishes provider networks and channels patients to those networks is likely to be liable for negligent selection. If, however, a plan sponsor uses a PPO sponsor as an intermediary to set up PPO networks, the chance of liability is less likely, although a court may still find a duty to properly select and monitor the sponsor.

A duty of proper selection will expose a managed care organization to liability both for failing to properly screen its physicians' competence, and also for failing to evaluate physicians for other problems. If the MCO selects a panel physician or dentist who has evidenced incompetence in her practice, it may risk liability. This is comparable to negligently granting staff privileges to an impaired physician with alcohol or other substance abuse problems, or one with sexual pathologies that might affect patients. See McClellan v. Health Maintenance Organization of Pennsylvania, 413 Pa.Super. 128, 604 A.2d 1053 (1992), where the court allowed a suit against HMO to proceed for negligence in selecting, retaining and evaluating primary care physician, misrepresenting the screening process for selecting its primary care physicians, and breach of contract.

3. The duty to supervise and control staff. Hospitals are required to supervise the medical care given to patients by staff physicians; to detect physician incompetence; and to take steps to correct problems upon learning of information raising concerns of patient risk. A hospital should also properly restrict the clinical privileges of staff physicians who are incompetent to handle certain procedures, or detect concealment by a staff doctor of medical errors.

Managed care organizations are likely to face similar duties to supervise. MCO liability for negligent control of its panel physicians derives from the same common law duty that underlies the negligent selection basis of liability as well as federal and state quality assurance regulations. As courts continue to characterize MCOs as health care providers, suits are likely to increase. Only PPOs with their reduced level of physician control might have an argument that liability should not be imposed for negligent supervision. However, statutes in some states require PPOs to implement quality assurance programs and others contemplate the use of such programs by PPOs. Iowa Code Ann. § 514.21; Ky. Rev. Stat. § 211.461; La. Stat. Ann.—Rev.Stat. § 22:2021; Me. Rev. Stat. Ann. tit. 24 § 2342 & tit. 24–A § 2771. The existence of such systems, with the PPOs having the right to remove a participating physician from the panel based on information generated by the quality assurance mechanism, imposes a duty to supervise. Managed care is likely to be forced to undertake both a duty to select with care and a duty to engage in continuous supervision.

4. Managed care organizations are motivated by goals of both quality and efficiency—the objective of cost sensitive health care. The style of practice in MCOs is different from fee-for-service practice, assuming a more conservative, less intensive level of intervention, specialist use, and hospitalization. Commentators have therefore proposed that courts allow MCO physicians to be judged by a different standard of care than fee-for-service physicians, in recognition of the different approach to care that MCOs have adopted to control costs. Randall Bovbjerg, The Medical Malpractice Standard of Care: HMOs and Customary Practice 1975 Duke L.J. 1375.

Some courts have recognized that managed care plans should give providers leeway to practice a more conservative, cost-effective style. See, e.g., Harrell v. Total Health Care, Inc., 781 S.W.2d 58, 61 (Mo.1989)("People are concerned both about the cost and the unpredictability of medical expenses. A plan such as Total offered would allow a person to fix the cost of physicians' services.").

C. PHYSICIAN INCENTIVE SYSTEMS

Most managed care programs have three relevant features from a liability perspective. First, such programs select a restricted group of health care professionals who provide services to the program's participants. Second, such programs accept a fixed payment per subscriber, in exchange for provision of necessary care. This pressures managed care organizations to search for ways to minimize costs. Third, following from number two, managed care organizations use a variety of strategies to ensure cost effective care. Altering physician incentives is central to managed care, since physicians influence seventy percent of total health spending, while receiving only about twenty percent of each health care dollar. Such plans use utilization review techniques, incentives systems, and gatekeepers to control costs. Managed care organizations create a new set of relationships between payers, subscribers and providers. These new relationships create new liability risks. The subscriber typically pays a fee to the MCO rather than the provider, relinquishing control over treatment and choice of treating physician. The payor in turn shifts some of its financial risk to its approved providers, who must also accept certain controls over their practice.

The argument that physician judgment might be "corrupted" by cost-conserving payment systems in managed care systems has been litigated without much success.

BUSH v. DAKE

State of Michigan, Circuit Court, County of Saginaw, 1989.
File No. 86–25767 NM–2.

PRESENT: HONORABLE ROBERT L. KACZMAREK, CIRCUIT JUDGE.

Defendant Group Health Services of Michigan, Inc. (hereinafter referred to as GHS) has filed a Motion for Partial Summary Disposition pursuant to MCR 2.116(C)(10)), in which defendants Network Family Physicians, P.C., Scott, Gugino, Mulhern, and Brasseur have joined. The motion seeks dismissal of the allegations in Plaintiffs' Complaint a) that GHS's system of financial incentives, risk sharing, and utilization review is contrary to public policy and medical ethics and b) that the use of this system constituted negligence, gross negligence, fraud, a breach of trust, and a tortious breach of the relationship between plaintiff Sharon Bush and her doctors in this particular case. Defendants contend that there is no genuine issue as to any material fact regarding these allegations and that they are therefore entitled to judgment as a matter of law.

This case arises out of the alleged failure of Dr. Dake and Dr. Foltz to timely diagnose and treat plaintiff's uterine cancer. During the period in question, Mrs. Bush was insured by GHS through her husband's employer. As the GHS system requires, she had chosen a primary care physician, Dr. Dake. For any medical problem she might have, it was necessary for Mrs. Bush to first see Dr. Dake and obtain his permission to be examined by a specialist, in order for the specialist's service to be covered by her insurance.

Dr. Dake was one of five physicians comprising Network Family Physicians, P.C. (Network). * * * Network had an agreement with GHS whereby GHS would pay Network a certain amount per month per patient, called a "capitation," for primary care services. In exchange, the physicians would see the patients an unlimited number of times, whenever the patients sought medical care.

GHS set aside a certain amount of money each year for a "referral pool" and a "hospital/ancillary pool" for the Network physicians. The money in these pools would be depleted with each referral to a specialist or hospitalization of a patient during the year. At the end of the year, any money left over in these pools would be divided between GHS and the individual physicians in Network. The result was that the fewer referrals a doctor made and the fewer hospitalizations he ordered for his patients, the more money he made.

The plaintiffs contend that it was this arrangement which led in part to the deficient medical care that Sharon Bush received in this case. Mrs. Bush first consulted Dr. Dake in late August of 1985 with regard to vaginal bleeding and mucous discharge unrelated to menstruation. Dr. Dake prescribed various medications to cure what he considered to be an infection. The condition nevertheless persisted over a period of several months. In January of 1986, the plaintiff asked Dr. Dake for a referral to Dr. Foltz, a specialist in obstetrics and gynecology. Dr. Dake agreed to make the referral, and Mrs. Bush then saw Dr. Foltz on February 18, 1986. Dr. Foltz took a vaginal smear to test for chlamydia, a sexually transmitted disease. When the results of that test came back negative, Dr. Foltz's office advised Mrs. Bush to wait until after her next menstrual period, and then if the bleeding persisted to return to Dr. Foltz for a follow-up visit. When the bleeding did persist and Mrs. Bush attempted to obtain a second referral to Dr. Foltz from Dr. Dake, he refused to make the referral. Eventually, on May 13, 1986, Mrs. Bush presented herself at the emergency room of Saginaw General Hospital, a biopsy was taken, and a diagnosis of cervical cancer was made.

It turned out, in retrospect, that a pap smear, if it had been done, would have revealed the cancer at a earlier stage. In the GHS system, pap smears are to be done by the primary care physician only. However, the primary care physician is not paid anything in addition to the existing capitation for performing pap smears.

The plaintiffs contend that the system in question is wrongful, in that it provides the physicians involved with financial disincentives to properly treat, refer, and hospitalize patients. They contend that this Court should find a) that the system violates public policy and b) that there is a jury question presented as to whether the system itself contributed to the malpractice in this case.

After examining the briefs and statutory and case authority submitted by the parties, the Court agrees with the defendants that it is not for this Court to say whether the HMO system represents sound social policy. It is the Legislature, and not this Court, that determines public policy in this state. * * * In this instance, the Legislature has approved the existence of HMO's, MCLA 333.21001, et seq.; MSA 14.15(21001), et seq., and their use of health care provider incentives, MCLA 333.21023(3); MSA 14.15(21023)(3), risk sharing, MCLA 333.21075; MSA 14.15(21075), and utilization review, MCLA 333.21083(d); MSA 14.15(21083)(d) in an effort to contain health care costs. This Court will not second-guess the wisdom of this legislation.

The Court therefore grants defendants partial summary disposition with regard to the plaintiffs' allegations that GHS's system of financial incentives, risk sharing, and utilization review is contrary to public policy. MCR 2.116(C)(10).

With regard to the second portion of defendants' motion, the Court finds that there is a genuine issue of material fact presented as to whether GHS's system in and of itself proximately contributed to the malpractice in this case. * * * Documentary evidence has been presented which supports the plaintiffs' theory that the manner in which the system operated in this case contributed to the improper treatment and delay in diagnosis of Mrs. Bush's cancerous condition. See *Wickline v. California,* 228 Cal.Rptr. 661, 670 (Cal. App. 2 Dist., 1986). The question should be submitted to the jury for determination at trial.

The Court therefore denies defendants' motion for partial summary disposition with regard to plaintiffs' allegations that the use of the GHS system in this case constituted negligence, gross negligence, fraud, a breach of trust, and a tortious breach of the relationship between Sharon Bush and her doctors.

PEGRAM v. HERDRICH

Supreme Court of the United States, 2000.
530 U.S. 211, 120 S.Ct. 2143, 147 L.Ed.2d 164.

[The treating plan physician examined the plaintiff Herdrich, who had pain in the midline area of her groin. Six days later Dr. Pegram found an inflamed mass in her abdomen, but failed to order an ultrasound at a local hospital, instead making her wait eight additional days for an ultrasound to be performed at a Carle facility more than 50 miles away. Herdrich's appendix ruptured, causing peritonitis. The Seventh Circuit in Herdrich v. Pegram, 170 F.3d 683 (7th Cir.1999) had been impressed by the conflicts of interest in the "intricacies of the defendants' incentive structure." In the words of the Seventh Circuit, "[w]ith a jaundiced eye focused firmly on year-end bonuses, it is not unrealistic to assume that the doctors rendering care under the Plan were swayed to be most frugal when exercising their discretionary authority to the detriment of their membership." On motion for rehearing, Judge Esterbrook J., dissenting, noted that the panel decision looked like a blanket condemnation of managed care generally, in favor of fee-for-service medicine. Even though the panel had tried to distinguish this case by its physician ownership and control, the use of bonuses and salary holdbacks by any managed care plan could be similarly criticized.]

The full opinion can be found in Chapter Nine, discussing ERISA fiduciary duties. The U.S. Supreme Court rejected the reasoning of the Seventh Circuit. With regard to the incentive structure of managed care organizations, Justice Souter, writing for the Court, stated:

> Traditionally, medical care in the United States has been provided on a "fee-for-service" basis. A physician charges so much for a general physical exam, a vaccination, a tonsillectomy, and so on. The physician bills the patient for services provided or, if there is insurance and the doctor is willing, submits the bill for the patient's care to the insurer, for payment subject to the terms of the insurance agreement. [ ] In a fee-for-service system, a physician's financial incentive is to provide more care, not less, so long as payment is forthcoming. The check on this incentive is a physician's obligation to exercise reasonable medical skill and judgment in the patient's interest.

Beginning in the late 1960's, insurers and others developed new models for health-care delivery, including HMOs. [ ] The defining feature of an HMO is receipt of a fixed fee for each patient enrolled under the terms of a contract to provide specified health care if needed. The HMO thus assumes the financial risk of providing the benefits promised: if a participant never gets sick, the HMO keeps the money regardless, and if a participant becomes expensively ill, the HMO is responsible for the treatment agreed upon even if its cost exceeds the participant's premiums.

Like other risk-bearing organizations, HMOs take steps to control costs. At the least, HMOs, like traditional insurers, will in some fashion make coverage determinations, scrutinizing requested services against the contractual provisions to make sure that a request for care falls within the scope of covered circumstances (pregnancy, for example), or that a given treatment falls within the scope of the care promised (surgery, for instance). They customarily issue general guidelines for their physicians about appropriate levels of care. See id., at 568–570. And they commonly require utilization review (in which specific treatment decisions are reviewed by a decisionmaker other than the treating physician) and approval in advance (precertification) for many types of care, keyed to standards of medical necessity or the reasonableness of the proposed treatment. [ ] These cost-controlling measures are commonly complemented by specific financial incentives to physicians, rewarding them for decreasing utilization of health-care services, and penalizing them for what may be found to be excessive treatment [ ]. Hence, in an HMO system, a physician's financial interest lies in providing less care, not more. The check on this influence (like that on the converse, fee-for-service incentive) is the professional obligation to provide covered services with a reasonable degree of skill and judgment in the patient's interest. [ ]

The adequacy of professional obligation to counter financial self-interest has been challenged no matter what the form of medical organization. HMOs became popular because fee-for-service physicians were thought to be providing unnecessary or useless services; today, many doctors and other observers argue that HMOs often ignore the individual needs of a patient in order to improve the HMOs' bottom lines. See, e.g., 154 F.3d, at 375–378 (citing various critics of HMOs). In this case, for instance, one could argue that Pegram's decision to wait before getting an ultrasound for Herdrich, and her insistence that the ultrasound be done at a distant facility owned by Carle, reflected an interest in limiting the HMO's expenses, which blinded her to the need for immediate diagnosis and treatment."

Notes and Questions

1. Bush v. Dake, an unpublished opinion, is one of the early cases raising the issue of the effect of HMO incentives on the medical care received by beneficiaries. While on appeal it was settled. See also, Sweede v. Cigna Healthplan of Delaware, Inc., 1989 WL 12608 (Del.Super.) (claim that doctor withheld necessary care because of financial incentives rejected on facts of case) and Teti v. U.S. Healthcare, Inc., 1989 WL 143274 (E.D.Pa.1989) (RICO claim against HMO for failing to

disclose physician incentives to withhold medical care dismissed). What explains the paucity of such cases, which are greatly outnumbered by articles in the popular and trade press noting their potential? Is it the difficulty of proving what motivates physician decisionmaking? How would you establish that a particular HMO payment structure motivated physicians to forego needed care for their patients? What other countervailing pressures operate on physicians?

2. Financial incentives and patient care. Every medical decision is also a spending decision. Since physicians as agents for patients control a large percentage of the health care dollar, should we trust them to have unfettered freedom to spend the money of others and use others's resources? The record of health care cost inflation suggests that unfettered physician discretion is not desirable. Managed care organizations are institutional structures developed as a response to health care inflation, to better manage the cost of health care by reducing utilization of hospitalization, specialists and testing. See E. Haavi Morreim, Playing Doctor: Corporate Medical Practice and Medical Malpractice, 32 U.Mich. J.L.Ref. 939, 972–73(1999).

The incentives that HMOs create for providers to under-utilize health care for their patients—the possibility that these incentives will "corrupt" the medical judgment of a physician—is raised frequently. The fear with managed care—and its goal of reducing expenditures by its physicians—is that some patients will be undertreated and suffer injury as a result. Bush v. Dake is a early example of these concerns. The U.S. Supreme Court in Pegram, however, acknowledged a national health care policy to use managed care to constrain the rapid health care cost inflation so evidence by the 1970s.

Little evidence exists that HMO incentives have a detrimental effect on patient care. The argument about incentives assumes that physicians' sensitivity to financial incentives is so fine-tuned that they will vary the intensity of care they give to each patient. The alternative possibility is that professional norms, risk of malpractice suits, and the daily pressures of practice will be more powerful forces on physician behavior. This would mean that a physician will treat all patients in light of his sense of best practice as adopted to a particular locality. The evidence has not yet resolved this question of physician response to incentives. Some form of incentive for cost-conservation in health care is desirable, and the ongoing debate is over the extent to which payment incentives can strike the right balance. While incentives may create conflicts of interest, they also give physicians flexibility in their clinical decision-making. The alternative–administrative rules and review mechanisms for denying benefits–is both more inefficient and arguably more constraining of physician decision-making. This debate–incentives versus rules–is an ongoing one. Plaintiffs have nonetheless argued that payment systems can cause a reduction in the quality of care delivered by physicians in managed care organizations, an argument that Pegram finally rejected. Robert H. Miller and Harold S. Luft, Does Managed Care Lead to Better or Worse Quality of Care? 16 Health Affairs 7, 18 (1997); David Orentlicher, Paying Physicians More to Do Less: Financial Incentives to Limit Care, 30 U.Rich.L.Rev. 155 (1996); Uwe E. Reinhardt, The Economist's Model of Physician Behavior, 281 J.A.M.A. 462, 464 (1999); Lawrence C. Baker, Association of Managed Care Market Share and Health Expenditures for Fee–For–Service Medicare Patients, 281 J.A.M.A. 432(1999). See William M. Sage, Physicians As Advocates, 35 Houston L.Rev.1529, 1620 (1999)("... the use of financial incentives in managed care preserves professional autonomy and improves efficiency even if it compromises advocacy at the margin.")

The debate over the use of physician incentives to promote cost sensitive practice will continue. Some managed care companies have decided, in the face of class action litigation and bad publicity, to restrict their use of some incentives. Aetna has announced that it will end the use of financial incentives to physicians that might have the effect of restricting member access to care. Aetna will limit the use of capitated fees, as well as the use of medical guidelines created by actuarial firms and used by some insurers to restrict reimbursement for care. See Milo Geyelin and Barbara Martinez, Aetna Weighs a Managed–Care Overhaul, Wall St. J. A3–10 (January 17, 2001). The REPAIR litigation, discussed below, combined with the possibility that Congress will legislate a patients' bill of rights that expands tort suits against managed care, has undoubtedly spurred these changes in the industry.

D. REPAIR TEAM LITIGATION AND RICO

A series of class action lawsuits was filed in 1999 by a group of lawyers known as the REPAIR Team, short for RICO and ERISA Prosecutors Advocating for Insurance Industry Reform. This group, which had litigated state lawsuits against the tobacco industry, filed class actions lawsuits against several large HMOs–Aetna, Cigna, Foundation, Humana, PacifiCare, Prudential, and United–accusing them of depriving enrollees of adequate treatment and engaging in a fraudulent scheme of misrepresenting coverage and treatment decisions.

MAIO v. AETNA

Third Circuit Court of Appeals, 2000.
221 F.3d 472.

[This case, filed prior to the REPAIR team class action litigation, asserted similar claims against Aetna, Inc., Aetna–U .S. Healthcare, Inc., and Aetna U.S. Healthcare, Inc.'s 24 regional subsidiary health plans (collectively "Aetna" or "appellees") for violations of the Racketeer Influenced and Corrupt Organizations Act ("RICO"), 18 U.S.C. § 1961 et seq., and state law. The case attacked "Aetna's failure to disclose its restrictive and coercive internal policies and practices, which render its advertising, marketing and membership materials false and misleading in violation of RICO." They claimed that "Aetna has engaged in a massive nationwide fraudulent advertising campaign designed to induce people to enroll in its HMO by representing that Aetna affirmatively manages its members' health care so as to, inter alia, raise the quality of care to a 'level of health care never available under the old fee-for-service system,' 'when in fact, Aetna designed undisclosed internal policies to "improve defendants' profitability at the expense of quality of care." The relief sought was compensatory damages and an injunction enjoining appellees from pursuing the "policies, acts and practices" alleged in the complaint, together with punitive damages, treble damages, and attorney's fees under RICO.' "

The class action was brought on behalf of members of a class consisting "of all persons in the United States who are, or were, enrolled in [Aetna's] Health Maintenance Organization (the 'HMO') plans (the 'Plan') at any time during the period from July 19, 1996 to the present (the 'class period')." [FN1] JA–14. The class allegedly consists of millions of both present and former Aetna HMO members who, as a group, "were targeted by [Aetna] and induced into enrolling in Aetna's HMO by virtue of defendants' standardized and uniform misrepresentations and omissions of material facts contained in advertising, marketing and membership* materials." The charges were that (1) Aetna engaged in a fraudulent scheme designed to induce individuals to enroll in its HMO plan by representing "that its primary commitment, in connection with the healthcare services provided to its HMO members, is to maintain and improve the quality of care given to such members and that defendants' policies are designed to accomplish these goals;" (2) Aetna represented that HMO members would receive high quality health care from physicians who are solely responsible for providing all medical care and maintaining the physician-patient relationship, when in reality Aetna's internal policies restrict the physicians' ability to provide the high quality health care that appellants have been promised; (3) despite Aetna's representations that it compensated its physicians under a system that provides them with incentives based upon the quality of care provided, Aetna's provider contracts actually offer the physicians financial incentives to withhold medical services and reduce the quality of care to HMO members. These representations were made through marketing, advertising and membership materials distributed to each and every prospective enrollee including the appellants.]

* * *

The question presented in this appeal therefore is whether the facts as pleaded in the complaint are sufficient to support appellants' assertion that they have suffered a present injury to property, which, according to them, takes the form of a financial loss stemming from their overpayment for their membership in Aetna's HMO plan. To resolve this issue, we must examine the allegations in the complaint and any reasonable inferences that may be drawn from those allegations, and consider their legal significance in view of appellants' injury theory proffered in support of the damage element of their RICO claim.

* * *

For the reasons that follow, we reject appellants' theory that their complaint states valid RICO claims based on the financial losses they purportedly sustained by enrolling in Aetna's "inferior" HMO plan in the absence of allegations to the effect that each appellant suffered negative medical consequences resulting from Aetna's enactment of the policies and practices at issue. Stated another way, in the context of this case, we hold that appellants cannot establish that they suffered a tangible economic harm compensable under RICO unless they allege that health care they received under Aetna's plan actually was compromised or diminished as a result of Aetna's management decisions challenged in the complaint. It seems clear to us that unless appellants claim that Aetna failed to provide sufficient health insurance coverage to the members of their HMO plan in the sense that such individuals were denied medically necessary benefits, received inadequate, inferior or delayed medical treatment, or even worse, suffered personal injuries as a result of Aetna's systemic policies and practices, there is no factual basis for appellants' conclusory allegation that they have been injured in their "property" because the health insurance they actually received was inferior and therefore "worth less" than what they paid for it. Of course, such losses would have to be alleged and proven on an individual basis. Inasmuch as we hold that appellants have not alleged facts sufficient to establish the fact of damage, i.e., appellants' injury to property stemming from their purchase of an "inferior" product, they have no cause of action under RICO.

* * *

Because appellants' property interests in their memberships in Aetna's HMO plan take the form of contractual rights to receive a certain level (quantity and quality) of benefits from Aetna through its participating providers, see Pegram, ___ U.S. at ___, 120 S.Ct. at 2149, it inexorably follows that appellants cannot establish a RICO injury to those property rights (which in turn would cause financial loss in the form of overpayment for inferior health insurance) absent proof that Aetna failed to perform under the parties' contractual arrangement. [ ]

In this factual setting, Aetna's failure to perform (and concomitantly appellants' injury to their property) would be evidenced by appellants' receipt of inadequate, inferior delayed care, personal injuries resulting therefrom, or Aetna's denial of benefits due under the insurance arrangement. Absent allegations of such losses, which appellants specifically indicate are not involved in this case, they cannot establish that they have suffered an injury to their property rights encompassed in their HMO memberships—i.e., their right to receive necessary medical services covered under their plan, and cannot prove a consequential financial loss flowing from their property. [ ]

Apparently recognizing that the property interests at stake are in the nature of contractual rights to health care benefits rather than tangible property rights from which injury is demonstrated by events causing a diminution in value, appellants make a secondary argument that they have pleaded injury in this case by referring to Aetna's failure to implement policies and practices in accordance with its commitment to its members to "raise the quality of health care." [ ] Analogizing to the district court's analysis in Dornberger, see 961 F.Supp. at 522, see reply br. at 8, appellants claim to have suffered economic harm, i.e., lost money, by virtue of Aetna's breach of its specific promise to implement policies and practices which supposedly permitted physicians to provide Aetna's HMO enrollees with quality health care.

Invoking the legal principle that payment for services not rendered can constitute a valid injury to property under RICO, see id. at 523, appellants claim that they suffered that exact loss here-they paid a specific part of their premium dollars for the benefit of Aetna's promises to implement policies designed to foster quality health care and have been injured in their property by Aetna's "failure to perform as promised." Because the "services not rendered" aspect of their injury argument only refers to Aetna's purported promise to implement policies and practices geared towards quality health care, appellants contend that "what the doctors do or don't do is irrelevant." Tr. of Oral Arg. at 14; see also br. at 25–26 ("Plaintiffs do allege . . . that they were denied something Aetna promised it would provide its members as an inducement for, and in consideration of, the members' enrollment. . . . [P]laintiffs and other Class members paid premiums and copayments, not just to receive treatment from physicians, but also to obtain the benefit of Aetna's services in arranging and providing increased quality of care.").

We need not tarry on this argument, as it is premised on an erroneous characterization of Aetna's responsibilities to its enrollees as defined by the parties' contractual arrangement and Aetna's alleged extra-contractual promises to deliver "quality health care." Notwithstanding appellants' creative description of Aetna's obligations to its HMO members, as we have explained they undoubtedly sought from Aetna, and Aetna promised to provide its members, with a different contractual benefit—namely the right to receive covered health care benefits in the form of medically necessary supplies, health care services and treatment through Aetna's participating providers. See Pegram, ___ U.S. at ___, 120 S.Ct. at 2149. Indeed, our review of the relevant contractual provisions and purported extra-contractual promises confirms our understanding of Aetna's obligations to its HMO members as their health insurer. [ ]

Accordingly, regardless of appellants' description of Aetna's obligations to its HMO enrollees, contractual or otherwise, it is obvious that Aetna's primary commitment to its HMO plan members is to provide quality health care services through its participating provider network. Concomitantly, appellants' contractual benefit is their receipt of quality medical services from those sources. We reach this conclusion because the provision and receipt of covered medical care is at the heart of the parties' contractual arrangement and is the driving force behind the purchase of health care insurance. [ ]

It necessarily follows from this observation that appellants' hypothesis that they suffered financial losses as result of Aetna's failure to implement policies designed to increase the quality of health care is untenable. Their argument rests on the faulty proposition that Aetna's implementation of the policies and practices outlined in the complaint amounts to a failure to perform a specific promise to its members, and misconstrues the nature of Aetna's role and its ultimate duty in arranging and providing for its members' health care. [ ] Indeed, while we do not quarrel with appellants' statement that Aetna implemented the managerial policies at issue while performing its role in arranging and providing medical treatment to its members rather than its role as plan administrator, [ ] that observation does not alter the fact that Aetna's contractual duty to its members is to provide medically necessary health care benefits in the form of covered services and supplies, i.e., medication, either directly or through contracts with third party medical providers. [ ] Accordingly, we decline appellants' invitation to define Aetna's duties as narrowly as they suggest.

It is evident to us from the foregoing analysis that given the nature of the property interests at stake, appellants' RICO injury theory predicated on the concept of a "diminution in product value" simply has no application here. Rather, in the context of this RICO suit based on what appellants have deemed to be "inferior" health insurance they received under Aetna's HMO plan, it follows from the nature of their property interests in their HMO memberships that they would be injured only to the extent that they could show that they suffered medical injuries, a denial or delay of medically necessary care, or the receipt of inferior or inadequate care. We emphasize that any personal injuries resulting from Aetna's policies and practices would not constitute a compensable RICO injury, see Genty, 937 F.2d at 918–19, Oscar, 965 F.2d at 786, but instead would serve as the necessary factual predicate for their argument that they suffered an injury to their property interests—their contractual rights to receive insurance coverage and necessary medical services under Aetna's HMO plan—which in turn caused them consequential financial loss in the form of overpayment for the coverage they actually received.

B.

[The court also rejects the claim of RICO injury based on a diminution in property value, since the class members could not show they actually received something "inferior" and "worth less" absent individualized allegations concerning the quantity and quality of health care benefits Aetna provided under its HMO plan.]

* * *

C.

When we analyze appellants' argument as to why they need not plead and prove allegations concerning the level of care they received to establish the fact of damage, i.e., their RICO "injury to property," it becomes evident why their position is fundamentally flawed. Given the total absence of any particularized allegations to the effect that the medical care appellants received pursuant to Aetna's HMO plan was compromised or diminished as a consequence of Aetna's internal policies and practices, the fact of damage, according to appellants' theory of financial injury, obviously is predicated on the concept that the mere possibility that a physician might be influenced by Aetna's policies to provide substandard medical care to Aetna's enrollees as a class demonstrates that the health care insurance they actually received is inferior or "worth less" than the amount appellants expended in premium payments. As the district court described it, appellants' claim of out-of-pocket losses as articulated rests on "a vague allegation that quality of care may suffer in the future. . . ." [ ]

Overall, we are satisfied that if we were to permit appellants to proceed with their RICO claims based on allegations of monetary loss proved solely by reference to what they consider to be the existence of coercive internal policies and practices which inevitably will affect the quality of care they will receive in the future, we would be expanding the concept of RICO injury beyond the boundaries of reason. [ ] * * *

If there were any doubt concerning the result we reach, which there is not, with respect to the message underlying appellants' damages theory, it surely would vanish when considered against the backdrop of the Supreme Court's recent decision in Pegram v. Herdrich, 530 U.S. 211, 120 S.Ct. 2143. Given our analysis, it is evident that in the absence of allegations that the quantity or quality of benefits have been diminished, the only theoretical basis for appellants' claim that they received an "inferior health care product" is their subjective belief that Aetna's policies and practices are so unfavorable to enrollees that their very existence in Aetna's HMO scheme demonstrates that they overpaid for the coverage they received. Indeed, the concept underlying appellants' injury theory is unmistakable—the very structure of Aetna's HMO plan is poor in the sense that its policies and practices inevitably will result in physicians providing inadequate health care to Aetna's HMO enrollees, which in turn means that appellants are paying too much for inferior health care benefits.

Put differently, we believe that the not-so hidden message underlying appellants' RICO claims (and more specifically their injury theory) is as follows: while these policies might be good for Aetna's business (because that they promote increased profits and induce physicians to ration care), they certainly are not beneficial to Aetna's HMO members because they are medically unsound in that they restrict a physician's ability to make independent medical judgments and encourage physicians to withhold otherwise appropriate health care so as to increase Aetna's "bottom line" profits. [ ] Thus, we think it fair to characterize appellants' injury theory as bottomed on the notion that Aetna's policies challenged in the complaint render its HMO structure "bad" in comparison to the other types of health care insurance available in the marketplace.

The force of this position, we believe, has been undermined significantly by the Supreme Court's recent decision in Pegram in which the Court rejected the plaintiff's attempt to challenge the existing structure of an incentive scheme of one particular HMO under the rubric of a breach of fiduciary duty claim under ERISA. * * *

* * *

We read the Court's approach in Pegram as undermining the validity of appellants' RICO injury theory predicated on the notion that their health insurance was rendered "inferior" by Aetna's implementation of its managerial policies outlined in the complaint. In particular, given that the very concept underlying appellants' economic harm is the notion that the structure of Aetna's HMO plan is faulty, we cannot ignore the circumstance that appellants' injury theory in essence asks us to pass judgment on the legal validity of the policies and practices themselves. Accordingly, we find particularly compelling that aspect of Pegram which articulated clearly the myriad of practical problems which undoubtedly arise in a situation in which the federal courts are asked to determine the social utility of one particular HMO structure as compared to another. See id. at ___, 120 S.Ct. at 2150. Indeed, we believe that the Court's observations in evaluating the validity of the plaintiff's ERISA claim in that case apply with equal force where, as here, appellants' theory of economic injury is predicated on the notion that the structure of Aetna's HMO plan, with its "coercive and restrictive" internal policies and practices, renders the health insurance appellants actually received from Aetna less valuable than it otherwise would have been without those management decisions in place.

The critical point here is that if we were to accept appellants' argument that the fact of damage can be demonstrated without specific reference to the level or quality of care actually provided to them under Aetna's HMO plan, we would be making the social and medical judgment that the particular structure of Aetna's HMO plan, by its very nature, places it in the category of a "bad HMO" as opposed to a "good HMO." There is no escaping that analytical step because it is the very nature of Aetna's HMO's structure which, according to appellants' theory, demonstrates that the economic value of their health insurance is reduced, that their insurance is inferior, and that they paid too much in premium dollars for what they actually received. But it seems clear that in view of the Supreme Court's reluctance in Pegram to devise a uniform standard by which federal courts could distinguish one HMO scheme from another in terms of its social utility in the context of an ERISA breach of fiduciary duty claim, we must decline appellants' invitation to pass judgment on the social utility of Aetna's particular HMO structure, albeit in the context of evaluating whether appellants have stated an injury to property under section 1964(c) of RICO. We especially are constrained to reach our result in light of the fact that appellants ask us to make such a determination without reference to the level or quality of care that Aetna's HMO members received while enrolled in its health plan. Cf. id. at ___, 120 S.Ct. at 2157 ("[T]he Federal Judiciary would be acting contrary to the congressional policy of allowing HMO organizations if it were to entertain an ERISA fiduciary claim portending wholesale attacks on existing HMOs solely because of their structure, untethered to claims of concrete harm.").

* * *

In any event, inasmuch as we read Pegram as suggesting that federal courts are ill-equipped to make the kind of social judgment that our acceptance of appellants' injury theory would require us to make, we remain convinced that in order to demonstrate the fact of RICO injury to property in the context of this case, appellants are required to demonstrate that the benefits they received under Aetna's HMO plan were compromised or diminished as a direct consequence of the systemic practices alleged in the complaint. Appellants therefore must allege and prove, for example, that they suffered personal injuries, were denied benefits, or received delayed or inadequate treatment because of the structure of Aetna's HMO plan. In the absence of such allegations, the district court's dismissal was appropriate.

V. Conclusion

Based on the information pleaded in the complaint, we hold that appellants have failed to allege the facts necessary to support their assertion that they paid too much for the health insurance they received from Aetna. Specifically, appellants have not alleged, for example, that they suffered medical injuries, received inadequate or inferior care, or sought but were denied necessary care as a consequence of the structure of Aetna's HMO plan, which includes the "systemic policies and practices" challenged in the complaint. In the circumstances, appellants cannot establish that they suffered a cognizable "injury to business or property" flowing from appellees' conduct, an essential element of a civil action pursuant to section 1964(c) of RICO.

For the foregoing reasons, the district court's judgment of September 29, 1999, will be affirmed.

Notes and Questions

1. What is at the heart of these claims against managed care? That any attempt by an MCO to restrict a physician's decisionmaking is presumptively undesirable? How would you develop standards that allow physicians proper discretion to make treatment decisions while still attempting to control costs? In Chapter One we discussed the uncertainties of much of medical practice and the lack of evidence of effectiveness of much that is done. The RICO statute has been used primarily against organized crime, and RICO claims have not been successful

against managed care plans historically. See Teti v. U.S. Healthcare, Inc., 1989 WL 143274 (E.D.Pa.1989)(RICO claim against HMO for failing to disclose physician incentives to withhold medical care dismissed).

2. For the last several years, the Supreme Court has been reevaluating its interpretation of the McCarran Ferguson Act's deference to state regulation of "the business of insurance." Lower courts had used the Act to void the application of RICO to insurance companies, and had used it to determine the scope of state law of preempted by ERISA. Passed in 1944, the McCarran Ferguson Act was enacted in response to a Supreme Court decision that held, for the first time, that insurance was interstate commerce subject to Congressional legislation. The Act was intended to preclude the contention that federal legislation of general applicability, such as the securities and antitrust laws, were applicable to insurance companies. Instead the McCarran Ferguson Act requires deference to state insurance laws unless federal laws specifically regulate insurance.

In Humana v. Forsyth, 525 U.S. 299, 119 S.Ct. 710, 142 L.Ed.2d 753 (1999), policyholders sued their health plan under RICO for fraudulently failing to pass along to subscribers discounted fee arrangements with providers in the form of reduced co-payment obligations. The health plan argued that application of the federal law would invalidate, supersede, or impair state insurance laws regulating fraudulent acts by insurers and was thus precluded .. The Supreme Court, construing the first clause in the McCarren Ferguson Act, held that it would not. The state law in question, Nevada's insurance fraud statute, permitted private actions against insurers for fraud, in addition to actions by the state insurance commission. The Court held that although the damages recoverable under the federal statute were much greater, the federal and state statute's were complimentary. The Court reasoned that Congress could not have intended federal laws of general applicability to be preempted when they do not impair state insurance regulation. After *Forsyth*, it was clear that the McCarran Ferguson Act does not categorically exempt the insurance industry from liability to consumers under RICO that is applied to all other industries.

2. The REPAIR Team class actions. The REPAIR Team is led by a group of plaintiffs lawyers who were successful in suits against the tobacco companies, and saw managed care as the next vulnerable and destructive institution in our culture. REPAIR's strategy, in the words of one commentator, is to "(r)aise the stakes so high that neither side can afford to lose...." Adam Bryant, Who's Afraid of Dickie Scruggs?, Newsweek, Dec. 6, 1999, at 46.

In their complaints, MCO plaintiffs allege that the managed care organizations have operated the affairs of an enterprise in interstate commerce through a pattern of racketeering activity and have injured the business or property of the plaintiffs as a result, in violation of sections 18 U.S.C. 1964 and 1962(c) of RICO. The racketeering activity is the use of the U.S. mails and wire services to defraud consumers—both by misrepresenting coverage and operations of the health plans, so as to fraudulently induce them to enroll, and by fraudulently misrepresenting the reasons why their claims were denied.

In *Maio*, plaintiffs alleged a violation of RICO based on the alleged misrepresentation that Aetna was primarily concerned with quality of care defendants, when, in fact, Aetna was more interested in profits and cost containment. The district court found this allegation—that "quality of care" might suffer in the future—too vague and hypothetical to confer standing on the plaintiff policyholders. Unlike *Maio*, the REPAIR Team suits allege past injury resulting from a misrepresentation of coverage—not a lack of quality of care in the future or compensation for the denial of particular benefit claims. Their claim depends upon the representations made to class members in their policies and benefit materials, not public advertising.

Plaintiffs allege a pattern of racketeering activity consisting of the MCO's repeated acts of mail and wire fraud over a period of at least four years and the prospect of its continuing. The scheme involves fraudulent misrepresentation of the coverage provided by policies sold by defendants—not the puffery found by the District Court in Maio. The class action plaintiffs contend that defendant's wrongful scheme further involves the fraudulent representations made to subscribers that their claims do not meet the medical necessity conditions in their policies, when defendants have actually only determined that the claims do not meet their undisclosed restrictive criteria.

The class action complaints allege that the enterprise, whose affairs were operated through the pattern of racketeering activity, is an "association-in-fact enterprise" consisting of the national MCO and its subsidiaries, on the one hand, and its network of providers, on the other. They maintain that on-going association of these entities "for a common purpose of engaging in a course of conduct" is sufficient under RICO to allege the existence of an enterprise within the meaning of the statute citing United States v. Turkette, 452 U.S. 576, 583, 101 S.Ct. 2524, 69 L.Ed.2d 246 (1981). National MCOs centralized, national structure and their mechanisms for controlling and directing the affairs of the group support the concept that MCOs and their networks share a common purpose of providing health insurance coverage and medical services to customers and earning profits from providing those services.

In the class cases against MCOs, the injury to policyholders' property that is proximately caused by defendants violations of RICO is the loss of money—the amount of money paid for coverage lost as a result violations MCO's. Plaintiffs believe that the value of the lost coverage can be quantified as the difference between the value of the coverage as represented and the value of coverage actually provided to policyholder, an amount to be established at trial.

Class action plaintiffs contend that premiums are paid for coverage—the transfer of risk to the MCO-insurer—that exists independent of whether the risk materializes. Insureds do not get their premiums back at the end of the year if they never filed a claim. Plaintiff therefor conferred that defendant MCOs are therefore enriched unjustly by the misrepresentation as to "quality" coverage.

Problem: Wanting the "Best"

Cheryl Faber, twenty years old and newly married, joined a managed care organization, Freedom Plus [the Plan], one of several choices offered by her employer, Primerica Bank. Cheryl had examined the literature for the various plan choices during her open enrollment period. She chose the Plan because its literature talked of a "high quality" program, with the "best doctors" in the area, and "no cost-cutting where subscriber health is concerned".

The Plan sets aside a certain amount of money each year for a "referral pool" and a "hospital/ancillary pool" for Plan physicians. The money in these pools is depleted with each referral to a specialist or hospitalization of a patient during the year. At the end of the year, any money left over in these pools is divided between the Plan and the individual physicians.

Cheryl went to her primary care physician in the Plan, Dr. Hanks, for her initial physical examination. Dr. Hanks found small lumps in her breasts, which he noted in the patient record as fibroid tumors. He talked briefly with Cheryl about the lumps, but stated that she shouldn't worry.

A year later Cheryl came back for another checkup. Dr. Hanks had left the Plan. It turned out Dr. Hanks had been the defendant in several malpractice suits filed against him in the five years he had worked for another HMO and he was terminated by that HMO. The Plan could have discovered this by accessing the National Practitioners Data Bank, or by calling up the previous employer.

Cheryl was then examined by another primary care physician, Dr. Wick. Dr. Wick was concerned about the lumps, and she prepared a referral to an oncologist, Dr. Scanem, who had recently joined the panel of specialists affiliated with the Plan. Cheryl went to Dr. Scanem, who ordered a biopsy and confirmed that the lumps were malignant Stage III cancer. Stage III cancers have about a 10% five year survival rate, Stage II a 40% five year survival, and Stage I almost 100% survival with prompt treatment.

Dr. Scanem recommended a treatment regime for Cheryl that included limited radical mastectomy and chemotherapy. He planned to use a new drug for breast cancers that had recently become available through a research protocol in which he was participating. This drug appeared to offer a slightly higher cure rate with young patients such as Cheryl with advanced breast cancer.

The Plan approved Dr. Scanem's recommendations, with the exception of the new drug. The Plan rejected his proposal for use of this drug, stating that it only reimbursed for chemotherapy using the standard drugs used generally by oncologists. The new drug was extremely expensive, and would have increased the cost of Cheryl's chemotherapy by about 200%. Dr. Scanem was angry about the refusal by the Plan to reimburse Cheryl's treatment in full, and told her so. He told her that there was nothing he could do about it, and so he said he would use the standard approach that most oncologists used. Cheryl was a very nervous patient, terrified of her cancer. Dr. Scanem was worried about upsetting her too much, given the other stresses created by the surgery and the side-effects from chemotherapy. She asked him what her chances were, and he said only that she had "a reasonable shot at beating it, with luck and prayer." He did not tell her anything more about the prognosis, nor did she ask.

Cheryl underwent the radical mastectomy and chemotherapy. Optimistic about her chances, Cheryl proceeded to get pregnant. She and her husband also bought a new house, assuming that she would recover and her salary would continue.

Cheryl's cancer proved to be too far advanced to respond to treatment. She died six months after the chemotherapy regime finished. Her fetus could not be saved, in spite of efforts by Plan obstetricians to do so. Her husband lost their new house since he could no longer afford the mortgage payments.

What advice will you give Mr. Faber about the merits of litigation against the Plan?

Chapter 8

REGULATION OF INSURANCE AND MANAGED CARE: THE FEDERAL ROLE

I. INTRODUCTION

Though regulation of health insurance has traditionally been the responsibility of the states, the federal government has taken in recent years an increasingly significant role. The most important federal law affecting health insurance is the Employee Retirement Income Security Act of 1974, ERISA, which has already been alluded to several times in previous chapters. ERISA's primary role in recent years has been deregulatory, as its preemptive provisions have repeatedly blocked state common law actions against health plans as well as state attempts at plan regulation. ERISA also provides its beneficiaries, however, with a positive right to sue to recover denied benefits, while also imposing fiduciary obligations on plan fiduciaries. ERISA regulations promulgated in the last days of the Clinton administration also afford procedural rights to plan beneficiaries.

ERISA is not the only federal statute to affect health plans, moreover. The Americans with Disabilities Act places at least minimal constraints on the ability of employers and insurers to discriminate against the disabled in the provision of health insurance. The Health Insurance Portability and Accountability Act of 1996 (which amended ERISA, as well as other federal statutes), limits the use of preexisting condition clauses while prohibiting intragroup discrimination in coverage and rates. It also offers certain protections in the small group and individual insurance markets. Earlier, the Consolidated Omnibus Budget Reconciliation Act of 1985 provided continuation coverage under certain circumstances. All of these federal initiatives will be considered in this chapter.

II. THE EMPLOYEE RETIREMENT INCOME SECURITY ACT OF 1974 (ERISA)

A. ERISA PREEMPTION OF STATE HEALTH INSURANCE REGULATION

As noted above, ERISA expressly preempts state both regulatory statutes and common law claims that "relate to" employee benefit plans, while at the same time providing for exclusive federal court jurisdiction over cases that could be brought as ERISA claims. The primary ERISA preemption statute (29 U.S.C.A. § 1144), however, explicitly saves from preemption state regulation of insurance, though also prohibiting state regulation of self-insured plans. The task of sorting out ERISA's complex preemption scheme has resulted in a tremendous volume of litigation, including, to date, eighteen Supreme Court decisions.

This subsection discusses ERISA preemption of state regulation, while the next considers preemption of common law claims.

CORPORATE HEALTH INSURANCE, INC. v. TEXAS DEPARTMENT OF INSURANCE

United States Court of Appeals, Fifth Circuit, 2000.
215 F.3d 526.

PATRICK E. HIGGINBOTHAM, CIRCUIT JUDGE:

* * *

This suit is a preemption challenge to Texas's Senate Bill 386. Through that legislation, Texas asserted its police power to protect its citizens in regulating the new field of managed health care in three ways. First, it created a statutory cause of action against managed care entities that fail to meet an ordinary care standard for health care treatment decisions (the "liability" provisions). Second, it established procedures for the independent review of health care determinations to decide whether they were appropriate and medically necessary (the "independent review" provisions). Finally, it protected physicians from HMO-imposed indemnity clauses and from retaliation by HMOs for advocating medically necessary care for their patients.

* * *

Senate Bill 386 became effective on May 22, 1997. Aetna promptly filed suit in the United States District Court, claiming that the Act was preempted by ERISA's general preemption clause, section 514, which preempts "any and all state laws insofar as they . . . relate to any employee benefit plan" and by the Federal Employees Health Benefit Act ("FEHBA"). * * *

The parties filed cross-motions for summary judgment, which the district court granted in part and denied in part. The district court found no FEHBA or ERISA preemption of the liability provisions of Senate Bill 386 but found that ERISA preempted the anti-retaliation, anti-indemnification, and independent review provisions of the legislation. Both Aetna and Texas appeal.

* * *

We have repeatedly struggled with the open-ended character of the preemption provisions of ERISA and FEHBA. We faithfully followed the Supreme Court's broad reading of "relate to" preemption under § 502(a) in its opinions decided during the first twenty years after ERISA's enactment. Since then, in a trilogy of cases, the Court has confronted the reality that if "relate to" is taken to the furthest stretch of its indeterminacy, preemption will never run its course, for "really, universally, relations stop nowhere."[1] Justice Souter, speaking for a unanimous court in Travelers, acknowledged that "our prior attempt to construe the phrase 'relate to' does not give us much help drawing the line here." Rather, the Court determined that it "must go beyond the unhelpful text ... and look instead to the objectives of the ERISA statute as a guide to the scope of the state law that Congress understood would survive."

In Travelers, a New York statute required hospitals to collect surcharges from patients insured by a commercial carrier but not from certain HMOs. The plain purpose of the surcharge was to encourage the HMOs to provide open enrollment coverage. The Second Circuit found that the surcharges "related to" ERISA plans because they imposed economic burdens with an impermissible impact on plan administration and structure. In rejecting the Second Circuit's approach, and in shifting its own approach, the Court observed that such indirect economic influences "d[id] not bind plan administrators to any particular choice," but rather affected the costs of benefits and the "relative costs of competing insurance to provide them." The Court grounded the "relate to" clause in the complex realities of the market for medical services.

[The court proceeded to discuss De Buono and Dillingham, in which the Supreme Court had also narrowed § 514 preemption, ed.]

In each of these three cases, the Court was returning to a traditional analysis of preemption, asking if a state regulation frustrated the federal interest in uniformity. * * * And significantly for our case, this return has included the observation that a broader reading of "relates to" would sweep away common state action with indirect economic effects on the costs of health care plans, such as quality standards which may vary from state to state.

This brings us to the merits of the claim that Senate Bill 386 is preempted. We turn first to its liability provisions. In Section 88.002, the bill provides:

> A health insurance carrier, health maintenance organization, or other managed care entity for a health care plan has the duty to exercise ordinary care when making health care treatment decisions and is liable for damages for harm to an insured or enrollee proximately caused by its failure to exercise such ordinary care.

The statute gives "health care treatment decision" a defined meaning:

> [A] determination made when medical services are actually provided by the health care plan and a decision which affects the quality of the diagnosis, care, or treatment provided to the plan's insureds or enrollees.

The Act also defines the agents for whose health care decisions the entities can be vicariously liable. Further, the Act includes a disclaimer: it

1. De Buono v. NYSA–ILA Med. & Clinical Serv's Fund, 520 U.S. 806, 117 S.Ct. 1747, 138 L.Ed.2d 21 (1997); California Div. of Labor Standards Enforcement v. Dillingham Constr., N.A., Inc., 519 U.S. 316, 117 S.Ct. 832, 136 L.Ed.2d 791 (1997); New York State Conference of Blue Cross & Blue Shield Plans v. Travelers Ins. Co., 514 U.S. 645, 115 S.Ct. 1671, 131 L.Ed.2d 695 (1995).

avoids imposing any obligation on the entity "to provide to an insured or enrollee treatment which is not covered by the health care plan of the entity."

Aetna argues that the liability provisions "relate to" an ERISA plan and affect plan administration. Aetna contends that a claim that medical services were negligently provided will inevitably question the provider's determinations of coverage under an ERISA plan. Texas replies that Senate Bill 356 has avoided the difficult genre of cases complaining of medical care and services which were not provided by excluding a duty to provide treatment not covered by a plan.

We agree with Texas's interpretation of the Act. When the liability provisions are read together, they impose liability for a limited universe of events. The provisions do not encompass claims based on a managed care entity's denial of coverage for a medical service recommended by the treating physician: that dispute is one over coverage, specifically excluded by the Act. Rather, the Act would allow suit for claims that a treating physician was negligent in delivering medical services, and it imposes vicarious liability on managed care entities for that negligence.

This vicarious liability does not "relate to" the managed care provider's role as an ERISA plan administrator or affect the structure of the plans themselves so as to require preemption. Courts have observed that HMOs and MCOs typically perform two independent functions—health care insurer and medical care provider. A managed care entity can provide administrative support for an insurance plan, which may entail determining eligibility or coverage. At the same time, a managed care entity can act as an arranger and provider of medical treatment.

Although state efforts to regulate an entity in its capacity as plan administrator are preempted, managed care providers operate in a traditional sphere of state regulation when they wear their hats as medical care providers. ERISA preempts malpractice suits against doctors making coverage decisions in the administration of a plan, but it does not insulate physicians from accountability to their state licensing agency or association charged to enforce professional standards regarding medical decisions. Such accountability is necessary to ensure that plans operate within the broad compass of sound medicine. We are not persuaded that Congress intended for ERISA to supplant this state regulation of the quality of medical practice. * * *

We also are not persuaded that the liability provisions are preempted as "referring to" ERISA plans. Under this strain of preemption analysis, we examine whether the law acts immediately and exclusively upon ERISA plans or whether the existence of an ERISA plan is essential to the law's operation. A law does not "refer to" ERISA plans if it applies neutrally to ERISA plans and other types of plans. * * * The provisions are indifferent to whether the health care plan operates under ERISA and do not rely on the existence of ERISA plans for their operation.

We see nothing to take the liability provisions from the regulatory reach of states exercising their traditional police powers in regulating the quality of health care. A suit for medical malpractice against a doctor is not preempted by ERISA simply because those services were arranged by an HMO and paid for by an ERISA plan. Likewise, the vicarious liability of the entities for whom the doctor acted as an agent is rooted in general principles of state agency law. Seen in this light, the Act simply codifies Texas's already-existing standards regarding medical care. These standards of care are at the heart of Texas's regulatory power.

We turn to the anti-retaliation and anti-indemnification provisions under sections 88.002(f) and (g) of the Act. The anti-retaliation provision forbids a managed care entity from dropping or refusing to renew a doctor or health care provider for advocating medically necessary treatment. The anti-indemnification provision prohibits a managed care entity from including an indemnification clause in its contracts with doctors and other health care providers that would hold it harmless for its own acts. Aetna contends that these provisions improperly mandate the structure and administration of ERISA plan benefits because ERISA plans are forced to contract with doctors only on those terms.

We are not persuaded that these provisions mandate the structure and administration of plans. * * * The anti-indemnity and anti-retaliation rules govern the managed care entities as health care providers by regulating the terms on which the provider contracts with its agents. The rules do not compel the entities to provide any substantive level of coverage as health care insurers.

* * *

The anti-retaliation and anti-indemnity provisions complement the Act's liability provisions by realigning the interests of managed care entities and their doctors. The liability and indemnity provisions force the managed care entity to share in its doctors' risk of tort liability; the anti-retaliation provision avoids the situation in which the doctor must choose between satisfying his professional responsibilities and facing retaliatory action by the managed care entity. Together, the provisions thus better preserve the physician's independent judgment in the face of the managed care entity's incentives for cost containment. Such a scheme is again the kind of quality of care regulation that has been left to the states.[2]

We come to the statute's provisions for independent review of determinations by managed care entities. * * *

* * *

* * * The Act adds procedures through which patients may appeal "adverse determinations"—

> [A] determination by [an HMO] or utilization review agent that the health care services furnished or proposed to be furnished to an enrollee are not medically necessary or are not appropriate.

The Act further requires that a utilization review agent "comply" with the independent review organization's determination of medical necessity.

It is apparent that "adverse determinations" include determinations by managed care entities as to coverage, not just negligent decisions by a

2. The Supreme Court's most recent discussion of ERISA confirms this analysis. In Pegram v. Herdrich, the Court held that ERISA confers no cause of action against HMOs for providing incentives to their doctors for limiting the costs of testing and treatment. Part of the Court's reasoning was that states are currently allowed to impose malpractice liability on HMOs for such action. 530 U.S. 211, 120 S.Ct. 2143, 147 L.Ed.2d 164 (2000).

physician. The provisions allow a patient who has been denied coverage to appeal to an outside organization. Such an attempt to impose a state administrative regime governing coverage determinations is squarely within the ambit of ERISA's preemptive reach.

Texas and the federal government urge that the preempted independent review provisions are saved under ERISA's saving clause for laws regulating insurance. The Supreme Court has interpreted the clause as designed to preserve Congress's reservation of the business of insurance to the states under the McCarran–Ferguson Act. In determining whether the clause applies, the Supreme Court considers whether the rule regulates insurance as a common sense matter, looking as well to the three McCarran–Ferguson factors as "guideposts:" (1) whether the practice has the effect of transferring or spreading the policyholder's risk; (2) whether it is an integral part of the policy relationship between the insured and the insurer; and (3) whether the practice is limited to entities in the insurance industry. The law need not satisfy each of these tests.

The common sense test measures whether the law is specifically directed toward the insurance industry. A law is so aimed when the state has developed a specific scheme governing insurance, as opposed to a flexible rule used in many legal contexts. Here, the independent review provisions create a regulatory scheme governing health benefit determinations. They do not rely on general legal rights used in other areas of law.

That the provisions apply to managed care entities as well as to traditional insurers does not exclude them from the saving clause. In determining whether a statute regulates the insurance industry, courts have examined whether a statute governs only entities acting as insurers. A statute may regulate insurance if it applies to insurers, health care service contractors, and HMOs. If the law sweeps more broadly, however, covering employers and others not engaged in insurance practices, it cannot be said to be regulating insurance. * * * Our own cases are consistent with this distinction. Here, the preempted provisions apply to HMOs and to utilization review agents for insurers, administrators, and non-ERISA health benefit plans. In making benefit determinations, these entities are functioning as insurers.

The common sense test also considers whether the law plays an integral part in the policy relationship between the insured and the insurer. Laws that create a mandatory contract term between the parties, including procedural requirements, go to the core insured-insurer relationship. Here, the independent review provisions create a procedural right of the insured against the entity. As the independent review provisions are aimed at insuring entities and regulate the insured-insurer relationship, they meet the common sense test of the saving clause.

For the same reasons, the provisions satisfy the second and third prongs of the McCarran–Ferguson test: they are integral to the policy relationship and regulate the insurance industry. While the provisions probably do not meet the first factor of reallocating the risk between the insured and insurer, that failure is not fatal to Texas's saving clause claim.

Our analysis does not end here, however, because even if the provisions would otherwise be saved, they may nonetheless be preempted if they conflict with a substantive provision of ERISA. In Pilot Life v. Dedeaux, the Supreme

Court held that "our understanding of the saving clause must be informed by the legislative intent concerning [ERISA's] civil enforcement provisions." The Court interpreted Congress's intent regarding the exclusivity of ERISA's enforcement scheme very broadly, concluding that the scheme preempts not only directly conflicting remedial schemes, but also supplemental state law remedies. Thus, the saving clause does not operate if the state law at issue creates an alternative remedy for obtaining benefits under an ERISA plan.

Here, the independent review provisions do not create a cause of action for the denial of benefits. They do, however, establish a quasi-administrative procedure for the review of such denial and bind the ERISA plan to the decision of the independent review organization. This scheme creates an alternative mechanism through which plan members may seek benefits due them under the terms of the plan—the identical relief offered under § 1132(a)(1)(B) of ERISA. As such, the independent review provisions conflict with ERISA's exclusive remedy and cannot be saved by the saving clause.

* * *

AFFIRMED IN PART; REVERSED IN PART.

Notes and Questions

1. ERISA only governs employee benefit plans, i.e. benefit plans established and maintained by employers to provide benefits to their employees. It does not reach health insurance purchased by individuals as individuals (including self-employed individuals) or health benefits not provided through employment-related group plans, such as uninsured motorist insurance policies or workers' compensation. Certain church and government-sponsored plans are also not covered. Finally, ERISA does not regulate group insurance offered by insurers to the employees of particular businesses without employer contributions or administrative involvement. See 29 C.F.R. § 2510.3–1(j); Taggart Corp. v. Life & Health Benefits Admin., 617 F.2d 1208 (5th Cir.1980), cert. denied, 450 U.S. 1030, 101 S.Ct. 1739, 68 L.Ed.2d 225 (1981). Nevertheless, ERISA does govern the vast majority of private health insurance provided in America, which is provided through employment-related group plans.

2. Part of the confusion inherent in ERISA preemption decisions is attributable to the fact that there are three distinct forms of ERISA preemption. One of these is express or "ordinary" preemption based on § 514(a) (29 U.S.C. § 1144(a)). Section 514(a) provides that ERISA "supersedes" any state law that "relates to" an employee benefits plan.

Another form of preemption is based on § 502(a) of ERISA (29 U.S.C. § 1132(a)) which provides for federal court jurisdiction over specified types of claims against ERISA plans. The federal courts have, on the basis of § 502(a), permitted ERISA plans to remove into federal court claims that were brought in state courts but could have been brought under § 502(a) in federal court. Removal is permitted under the "complete preemption" exception to the well-pleaded complaint rule. The well-pleaded complaint rule normally permits removal only when federal claims are explicitly raised in the plaintiff's complaint. However, under the "complete preemption" exception to this rule (sometimes called "super-preemption") federal jurisdiction is permitted when Congress has so completely preempted an area of law that any claim within it is brought under federal law, and thus removable to federal court. "Complete preemption" is in reality not a preemption doctrine, but rather a rule of federal jurisdiction.

Third, Section 502(a) also plays another role in ERISA jurisprudence, ousting state claims and remedies that would take the place of § 502 claims. The federal courts have interpreted this section as indicating a Congressional intent to preempt comprehensively the "field" of judicial oversight of employee benefits plans. Thus state tort or contract, or even statutory, claims that could have been brought as claims for benefits or for breach of fiduciary duty under § 502(a) are preempted by § 502(a). Section 502(a) preemption, like § 514(a) explicit preemption, is not comprehensive. In particular, ERISA does not necessarily preempt state court malpractice cases brought against managed care plans that provide as well as pay for health care, as we will see in the next section. Also claims brought by persons who are not proper plaintiffs under § 502(a), or against persons who are not ERISA fiduciaries, may evade ERISA § 502(a) preemption.

Section 502(a) and § 514(a) preemption are not coextensive. Just because a lawsuit invokes a law that might be preempted as relating to an employee benefits claim does not mean that the claim could be brought under § 502(a), and is thus subject to "complete preemption." Not infrequently federal courts remand actions that could not have been brought as § 502(a) claims to state court for resolution of § 514(a) preemption issues. As we see in the principle case, moreover, laws that are saved from preemption by an exception to § 514(a), may still be preempted as inconsistent with § 502(a) field preemption.

3. Early cases interpreting § 514(a) read it very broadly. The Supreme Court's first consideration of § 514(a), Shaw v. Delta Air Lines, 463 U.S. 85, 103 S.Ct. 2890, 77 L.Ed.2d 490 (1983), adopted a very literal and liberal reading of "relates to" as including any provisions having a "connection with or reference to" a benefits plan. The Court rejected narrower readings of ERISA preemption that would have limited its reach to state laws that explicitly attempted to regulate ERISA plans or that dealt with subjects explicitly addressed by ERISA. For over a decade following Shaw, the Court applied the § 514(a) tests developed in *Shaw* expansively in a variety of contexts, almost always finding preemption when it found an ERISA plan to exist. The Court repeatedly expressed allegiance to the opinion that ERISA § 514(a) preemption had a "broad scope" (Metropolitan Life v. Massachusetts, 471 U.S. 724 at 739, 105 S.Ct. 2380, 85 L.Ed.2d 728 (1985)), and "an expansive sweep" (Pilot Life v. Dedeaux, 481 U.S. 41, 47, 107 S.Ct. 1549, 95 L.Ed.2d 39 (1987)). and that it was "conspicuous for its breadth," (FMC v. Holliday, 498 U.S. 52, 58, 111 S.Ct. 403, 112 L.Ed.2d 356 (1990)).

Attending to Supreme Court pronouncements that § 514(a) preemption was to be applied broadly, lower courts in the 1980s and 1990s held to be preempted a wide range of state regulatory programs and common law claims that arguably "related to" the administration of an ERISA plan or imposed costs upon plans. Thus state laws were struck down regulating rates charged by hospitals or pharmacies General Motors Corp. v. Caldwell, 647 F.Supp. 585 (N.D.Ga.1986) (prescription rates); United Health Servs., Inc. v. Upstate Admin. Servs., Inc., 151 Misc.2d 783, 573 N.Y.S.2d 851 (N.Y.Sup.1991) (hospital rates); mandating health insurance coverage for employees (Standard Oil Co. v. Agsalud, 442 F.Supp. 695 (N.D.Cal.1977), affirmed 633 F.2d 760 (9th Cir.1980), affirmed mem. 454 U.S. 801, 102 S.Ct. 79, 70 L.Ed.2d 75 (1981) (striking down the Hawaii Prepaid Health Care Act, subsequently saved by an amendment to ERISA specifically protecting it, 29 U.S.C.A. § 1144(b)(5)); or prohibiting discrimination against persons with AIDS (Westhoven v. Lincoln Foodservice Products, Inc., 616 N.E.2d 778 (Ind.App.1993).

The Supreme Court finally recognized limits to ERISA preemption in New York State Conference of Blue Cross and Blue Shield Plans v. Travelers Ins. Co.,

514 U.S. 645, 115 S.Ct. 1671, 131 L.Ed.2d 695 (1995). *Travelers* held that a New York law that required hospitals to charge different rates to insured, HMO, and self-insured plans was not preempted by § 514(a). Reversing earlier expansive readings of ERISA preemption, the Court expressed allegiance to the principle applied in other areas of the law that Congress is generally presumed not to intend to preempt state law. 514 U.S. at 654. The Court proceeded to note that in cases involving traditional areas of state regulation, such as health care, Congressional intent to preempt state law should not to be presumed unless it was "clear and manifest." Id. at 655. Recognizing that the term "relate to" was not self-limiting, the Court turned for assistance in defining the term to the purpose of ERISA, which it determined to be freeing benefit plans from conflicting state and local regulation. Id. at 656–57. Preemption was intended, the Court held, to affect state laws that operated directly on the structure or administration of ERISA plans, Id. at 657–58, not on laws that only indirectly raised the cost of various benefit options, Id. at 658–64. Accordingly, the court held that the challenged rate setting law was not "related to" an ERISA plan, and thus not preempted.

The Court's post-*Travelers* preemption cases suggest that the Court in fact turned a corner in *Travelers*. It has rejected preemption in the majority of these cases, though it had almost never done so before *Travelers*. Post *Traveler*'s lower court cases have on the whole continued to apply ERISA preemption broadly, generally finding that state programs aimed at regulating insurance and managed care "relate to" ERISA plan, and are therefore preempted. In Prudential Insurance Company of America v. National Park Medical Center, 154 F.3d 812 (8th Cir.1998), for example, the Eighth Circuit concluded that the Arkansas "Patient Protection Act" related to ERISA plans because it explicitly and implicitly made reference to them. The most recent cases, however, evidence a greater reluctance to find preemption, and a greater willingness to recognize the states' rights to regulate managed care, as the principal case illustrates.

4. As *Corporate Health* notes, state law that is otherwise preempted under § 514(a) is saved from preemption if it regulates insurance under § 514(b)(2)(A) (29 U.S.C.A. § 1144(b)(2)(A)). In its early cases interpreting this clause, the Court read it conservatively, applying both a "common sense" test as well as the three part test developed in antitrust cases applying the McCarran Ferguson Act for determining whether a law regulated "the business of insurance," (i.e. 1) whether the regulation affected the transferring and spreading of policy-holder risk, 2) whether it affected the relationship between the insurer and insured, and 3) whether it affected only entities within the insurance industry). Metropolitan Life Insurance Company v. Massachusetts, 471 U.S. 724, 740–44, 105 S.Ct. 2380, 85 L.Ed.2d 728 (1985). The Court applied this test two years later in Pilot Life Insurance Co. v. Dedeaux, 481 U.S. 41, 107 S.Ct. 1549, 95 L.Ed.2d 39 (1987), a case involving a Mississippi common law bad faith breach of contract claim, which held that the state law in that case was not saved from preemption because it was not specifically "directed at" the insurance industry and thus did not meet the McCarran Ferguson criteria. Pilot Life, 481 U.S. at 50–51.

In recent years, however, the Supreme Court has begun to back off the mechanical approach it set forth in *Metropolitan Life* and *Pilot Life* for determining the application of the savings clause. In UNUM Life Insurance Company of America v. Ward, 526 U.S. 358, 119 S.Ct. 1380, 143 L.Ed.2d 462 (1999), the Court specifically held that the three McCarran–Ferguson criteria were merely relevant criteria to a determination of whether the savings clause should be applied, and not conclusive. The Court proceeded to read two of the criteria expansively and withhold judgment on a third in upholding California's notice-prejudice rule against an ERISA challenge. Id. at 1389–90. Perhaps most importantly, Justice Ginsberg, stated in footnote 7:

> In the instant case, the Solicitor General, for the United States as amicus curiae, has endeavored to qualify the argument advanced in Pilot Life [that all state causes of action against ERISA insurers were preempted]. * * * the Solicitor General now maintains that the discussion of § 502(a) in Pilot Life "does not in itself require that a state law that 'regulates insurance,' and so comes within the terms of the savings clause, is nevertheless preempted if it provides a state-law cause of action or remedy." [ ] ("[T]he insurance savings clause, on its face, saves state law conferring causes of action or affecting remedies that regulate insurance, just as it does state mandated-benefits laws."). We need not address the Solicitor General's current argument, for Ward has sued under § 502(a)(1)(B) for benefits due, and seeks only the application of saved state insurance law as a relevant rule of decision in his § 502(a) action.

The Supreme Court in *UNUM* seems to be continuing its trend towards broadening the space left for state regulation of health insurance plans. The decision offers encouragement to states that are eager to move forward with managed care regulation.

5. *Corporate Health* holds that even though a statute (the Texas external appeal statute in this case) is saved from § 514(a) preemption by the savings clause, it may nevertheless be preempted by § 502(a) if it provides a state remedy that takes the place of § 502(a). The Seventh Circuit, however, in Moran v. Rush Prudential HMO, Inc., 230 F.3d 959 (7th Cir.2000), upheld the Illinois external appeals statute, holding that the statute did not displace the civil remedy provided by § 502, but rather modified the insurance contract to include an additional contract term requiring the plan administrator to abide by the decision of the external reviewer and an additional dispute resolution mechanism that needed to be pursued before a § 502 action could be brought. As of this writing, the state of Texas has requested the Supreme Court to resolve the conflict among the circuits.

6. ERISA's § 514(b)(2)(A) savings clause is subject to its own exception, the § 514(b)(2)(B) "deemer" clause. This subsection provides that "neither an employee benefit * * * nor any trust established under such a plan, shall be deemed to be an insurance company or other insurer, * * * or to be engaged in the business of insurance * * * for purposes of any law of any State purporting to regulate insurance companies, [or] insurance contracts, * * *." 29 U.S.C.A. § 1144(b)(2)(B). In FMC Corporation v. Holliday, 498 U.S. 52, 111 S.Ct. 403, 112 L.Ed.2d 356 (1990), the Supreme Court interpreted this clause broadly to except self-funded ERISA plans entirely from state regulation and state law claims.

The deemer clause offers a significant incentive for employers to become self-insured. Self-insurance, however, also has disadvantages—it imposes upon the employer the burden of administering the plan as well as open-ended exposure for claims made to the plan. To avoid these problems, self-insured employers often contract with third-party administrators to administer claims and with stop-loss insurers to limit their claims exposure. The courts overwhelmingly hold that employer plans remain self-insured, even though they are reinsured through stop-loss plans, and prohibit state regulation of stop loss coverage for self-insured plans. See, e.g., Tri-State Machine v. Nationwide Life Ins. Co., 33 F.3d 309 (4th Cir.1994); Lincoln Mutual Casualty v. Lectron Products, Inc. 970 F.2d 206 (6th Cir.1992). Third-party administrators that administer self-insured plans are also protected from state insurance regulation. NGS American, Inc. v. Barnes, 805

F.Supp. 462 (W.D. Texas 1992). Thus an employer who is willing to bear some risk can escape state regulation under the "deemer" clause, even though most of the risk of insuring the plan is borne by a stop-loss insurer and the burden of administering the plan is assumed by a third-party administrator.

7. State statutes requiring external reviews are not the only regulatory statutes to be challenged under ERISA preemption. Perhaps the most litigated regulatory issue has been whether state "any willing provider" legislation is preempted by ERISA. The Eighth Circuit in Prudential Insurance Co. of America v. National Park Medical Center, Inc., 154 F.3d 812 (8th Cir., 1998) and Fifth Circuit in Texas Pharmacy Ass'n v. Prudential Insurance Co., 105 F.3d 1035 (5th Cir.1997) and CIGNA Healthplan of La., Inc. v. Louisiana, 82 F.3d 642 (5th Cir.1996), invalidated the AWP provisions of Arkansas, Texas, and Louisiana respectively, finding that they "related to" ERISA plans, and were not saved from preemption. These holdings were based, in part, on the fact that these statutes were not limited in their reach to traditional insurance plans, since the statutes covered entities such as HMOs, PPOs, and third party administrators.

On the other hand, the Sixth Circuit recently in Kentucky Association of Health Plans, Inc. v. Nichols, 227 F.3d 352 (6th Cir., 2000); and Community Health Partners, Inc. v. Kentucky, 230 F.3d 1357 (6th Cir.2000), applying the more liberal interpretation of the savings clause suggested by Ward, found that the Kentucky AWP statute was saved from preemption. In an earlier case, Stuart Circle Hosp. Corp. v. Aetna Health Management, 995 F.2d 500 (4th Cir.1993), the Fourth Circuit had also upheld a Virginia AWP statute, also finding that the statute properly regulated insurance. The 9th Circuit, in a related case, recently upheld Washington state's alternative provider statute, requiring HMOs and health care service contractors to cover alternative medical treatments, such as acupuncture, massage therapy, naturopathy, and chiropractic services, Washington Physicians Service Ass'n v. Gregoire, 147 F.3d 1039 (9th Cir.1998), finding that the statute did not relate to ERISA plans, and but also that it would be saved from preemption as regulating insurance.

8. Another issue that has arisen occasionally in savings clause litigation is whether health maintenance organizations are in the business of insurance and thus subject to state regulation. Early cases tended to say no, often on very formalistic grounds, see, e.g. O'Reilly v. Ceuleers, 912 F.2d 1383 (11th Cir.1990), as did some of the any willing provider cases, see Texas Pharmacy Ass'n v. Prudential, 105 F.3d 1035 (5th Cir.1997). Recent cases, however, have recognized quite sensibly that:

> In the end, HMOs function the same way as a traditional health insurer: The policyholder pays a fee for a promise of medical services in the event that he should need them. It follows that HMOs * * * are in the business of insurance.

Washington Physicians Service Ass'n v. Gregoire, 147 F.3d 1039, 1046 (9th Cir.1998), See also Kentucky Ass'n of Health Plans v. Nichols, 227 F.3d 352, 364–65, 371 (6th Cir.2000).

9. The topic of ERISA preemption has unleashed a torrent of scholarship. Among the most recent articles discussing ERISA's effect on health insurance regulation are, Karen A. Jordan, Coverage Denials in ERISA Plans' Assessing the Federal Legislative Solution, 65 Mo. L. Rev. 405 (2000); Donald T. Brogan, Protecting Patient Rights Despite ERISA: Will the Supreme Court Allow the States to Regulate Managed Care? 74 Tul. L. Rev. 951 (2000); Jana K. Strain and Eleanor D. Kinney, The Road Paved With Good Intentions: Problems and Poten-

tial for Employer–Sponsored Health Insurance Under ERISA, 31 Loy.U.Chi.L.J. 29 (1999); Edward A. Zelinsky, Travelers, Reasoned Textualism, and the New Jurisprudence of ERISA Preemption, 21 Cardozo L. Rev. 807 (1999); Peter D Jacobson & Scott D. Pomfret, Form, Function, and Managed Care Torts: Achieving Fairness and Equity in ERISA Jurisprudence, 35 Hous. L. Rev. 985 (1998); Scott D. Pomfret, Emerging Theories of Liability for Utilization Review under ERISA Health Plans, 35 Hous. L. Rev. 985 (1998); Karen A. Jordan, The Shifting Preemption Paradigm: Conceptual and Interpretive Issues, 51 Vand. L. Rev. 1149 (1998); Howard Shapiro, Rene E. Thorne, Edward F. Harold, ERISA Preemption: To Infinity and Beyond and Back Again? 58 La. L. Rev. 997 (1998); E. Haavi Morreim, Benefits Decisions in ERISA Plans: Diminishing Deference to Fiduciaries and an Emerging Problem for Provider–Sponsored Organizations, 65 Tenn. L. Rev. 511 (1998); Curtis D. Rooney, The States, Congress, or the Courts: Who Will be First to Reform ERISA Remedies, 7 Annals Health L. 73 (1998); and Karen A. Jordan, Travelers Insurance: New Support for the Argument to Restrain ERISA Preemption, 13 Yale J. Reg. 255 (1996).

B. ERISA PREEMPTION OF STATE TORT LITIGATION

The Employee Retirement Income Security Act of 1974 (ERISA), establishing uniform national standards for employee benefit plans, has broadly preempted state regulation of these plans, as discussed in the previous section. 29 U.S.C.A. § 1144(a) states that ERISA supersedes state laws to the extent that they "relate to any employee benefit plan" covered by ERISA. The interaction of ERISA with state laws that attempt to regulate employee health insurance has caused a great deal of controversy and litigation in malpractice cases. The following cases and notes illustrate judicial struggles to limit ERISA and its "relate to" language.

ESTATE OF FRAPPIER v. WISHNOV

District Court of Appeal of Florida, Fourth District, 1996.
678 So.2d 884.

Speiser, Mark A., Associate Judge.

* * * Appellant, the estate of Robert Frappier Jr., appeals a trial court order dismissing its complaint with prejudice. The estate sued Health Options, Inc., a health maintenance organization (HMO), and two physicians, Drs. Wishnov and Patel, who were assigned by Health Options to attend to the medical needs of Frappier. The estate contended that Frappier died as a result of the medical malpractice of the two doctors.

Health Options, the only party defendant to this appeal, was the subject of counts III through VI of the estate's six count complaint. Count III charged Health Options with direct negligence in selecting the two doctors whom the estate claims were incompetent. Count IV alleged Health Options was vicariously liable for the actions of its agents or apparent agents namely Drs. Wishnov and Patel. Count V was premised upon a corporate liability theory based upon Health Options' breach of a common law and statutory duty to assure the competence of its physicians. Finally, Count VI of the complaint asserted that Health Options breached an implied contractual non-delegable duty to provide appropriate medical care. The trial court dismissed these counts based upon Health Options' contention that the estate's claims "relate to" an ERISA (Employee Retirement Income Security Act) plan and therefore federal question jurisdiction required Frappier's cause of action to be preempted to federal court. [ ]

The estate's motion for rehearing, ultimately denied, alleged that Health Options failed to prove and the trial court failed to determine that an ERISA plan ever existed. The estate now argues that this threshold question must be resolved prior to addressing the issue of whether the dismissed counts are preemptable. We agree and reverse.

Before a state court can conclude that the applicable ERISA federal preemption statute divests it of subject matter jurisdiction, it must be proven that the HMO was an ERISA plan. [ ]

On appeal, the second district concluded that the trial judge failed to make an adequate evidentiary finding as to the propriety of the defendant's assertion that the court lacked subject matter jurisdiction because of federal preemption. Id. at 35. We approve the following quote from the opinion of the second district:

> Thus, the party claiming preemption bears the burden of proof and must establish that Congress has clearly and unmistakably manifested its intent to supersede state law.

* * * On this issue we are compelled to reverse and remand for an evidentiary hearing to determine if Health Options is an ERISA subject to federal preemption.

Nevertheless, presented with the opportunity, we feel compelled to address the merits of the trial court's determination that the estate's claims against Health Options are preempted by the federal ERISA statute. Generally, actions that "relate to" an ERISA are preempted by federal law. Several Florida state decisions have already resolved various ERISA preemption issues. [ ] However, no state case has addressed whether direct negligence or vicarious liability claims against an ERISA are preempted and we therefore seek guidance from federal courts.

The ERISA regulatory scheme was promulgated to entrench as exclusively a federal matter pension plan legislation. Pilot Life Ins. Co. v. Dedeaux, 481 U.S. 41, 107 S.Ct. 1549, 95 L.Ed.2d 39 (1987). The governing provision of ERISA relevant to this discussion is section 514(a) which provides that "this Chapter shall supersede any and all state laws insofar as they may now or hereafter 'relate to' any employee benefit plan." 29 U.S.C.A. § 1144(a).

Properly phrased, the issue becomes whether Frappier's claims against Health Options as delineated in counts III–VI of the complaint are to recover plan benefits due, or to enforce rights, or to clarify rights to benefits under the terms of the plan, as those concepts are detailed in section 502(a)(1)(B) of ERISA, 29 U.S.C.A. § 1132(a)(1)(B). Although Pilot Life suggested an expansive interpretation of the triggering jurisdictional clause of the ERISA federal regulatory scheme, the United States Supreme Court in New York Blue Cross v. Travelers Inc., 514 U.S. 645, 115 S.Ct. 1671, 131 L.Ed.2d 695 (1995), and several more recent lower federal court decisions caution against a literal reading of section 514(a) in determining whether preemption is appropriate. New York Blue Cross directs that in construing the "relate to" phrase of section 514(a), trial courts must analyze the objectives of the ERISA statute to resolve which state laws Congress contemplated would continue to survive the ambit of federal regulation. Id. at ___, 115 S.Ct. at 1677. In other words, statutory or common law claims actionable in state court that are periphery or remotely related to competing laws affecting ERISA should not be preempted to federal court. [ ]

Frappier's claims are grounded on various theories of negligence, breach of an implied contract and vicarious liability (Count IV). * * *

* * *

Thus where, as here, an ERISA is implicated by a complaint for failing to provide, arrange for, or supervise qualified doctors to provide the actual medical treatment for plan participants, federal preemption is inappropriate. [ ] Therefore, even if Health Options is an ERISA subject to federal preemption, we must conclude that the trial court erred in dismissing the vicarious liability count of the instant complaint.

Concerning the direct negligence, corporate liability and implied contract claims, we concur with the lower court's decision that these allegations would be completely preempted because they present issues unequivocally related to the administration of the plan and are within the scope of section 502(a)(1)(B); [ ].

Accordingly, this case is remanded with directions to the trial court to hold an evidentiary hearing to determine whether Health Options is an ERISA plan subject to federal preemption. Upon an appropriate finding, the trial court may dismiss the estate's direct negligence, corporate liability and implied contract claims for a lack of subject matter jurisdiction. However, in no event may the vicarious liability count be dismissed as the same does not "relate to" an employee benefit plan.

PAPPAS v. ASBEL

Supreme Court of Pennsylvania, 2001.
___ Pa. ___, 768 A.2d 1089.

OPINION

MR. JUSTICE CAPPY

[The Pennsylvania Supreme Court, in their earlier decision in *Pappas*, had decided, based on *Travelers,* that medical malpractice claims against U.S. Healthcare were not preempted by ERISA. Their decision was appealed to the U.S. Supreme court, which remanded the case for further consideration in light of their decision in Pegram v. Herdrich.] For all the reasons that follow, we adhere to our original opinion and order.

The facts and procedural history, as set forth in *Pappas I,* bear repeating.

> At 11:00 a.m. on May 21, 1991, Basile Pappas ("Pappas") was admitted to Haverford Community Hospital ("Haverford") through its emergency room complaining of paralysis and numbness in his extremities. At the time of his admission, Pappas was an insured of HMO–PA, a health maintenance organization operated by U.S. Healthcare.
>
> Dr. Stephen Dickter, the emergency room physician, concluded that Pappas was suffering from an epidural abscess which was pressing on

Pappas' spinal column. Dr. Dickter consulted with a neurologist and a neurosurgeon; the physicians concurred that Pappas' condition constituted a neurological emergency. Given the circumstances, Dr. Dickter felt that it was in Pappas' best interests to receive treatment at a university hospital.

Dr. Dickter made arrangements to transfer Pappas to Jefferson University Hospital ("Jefferson") for further treatment. At approximately 12:40 p.m. when the ambulance arrived, Dr. Dickter was alerted to the fact that U.S. Healthcare was denying authorization for treatment at Jefferson. Ten minutes later, Dr. Dickter contacted U.S. Healthcare to obtain authorization for the transfer to Jefferson. At 1:[05]p.m., U.S. Healthcare responded to Dr. Dickter's inquiry and advised him that authorization for treatment at Jefferson was still being denied, but that Pappas could be transferred to either Hahnemann University ("Hahnemann"), Temple University or Medical College of Pennsylvania ("MCP").

Dr. Dickter immediately contacted Hahnemann. That facility advised Haverford at approximately 2:20 p.m. that it would not have information on its ability to receive Pappas for at least another half hour. MCP was then reached and within minutes it agreed to accept Pappas; Pappas was ultimately transported there at 3:30 p.m. Pappas now suffers from permanent quadriplegia resulting from compression of his spine by the abscess.

Pappas and his wife filed suit against Dr. David Asbel, his primary care physician, and Haverford. They claimed that Dr. Asbel had committed medical malpractice and that Haverford was negligent in causing an inordinate delay in transferring him to a facility equipped and immediately available to handle his neurological emergency.

Haverford then filed a third party complaint against U.S. Healthcare, joining it as a party defendant for its refusal to authorize the transfer of Pappas to a hospital selected by the Haverford physicians. Dr. Asbel also filed a cross-claim against U.S. Healthcare seeking contribution and indemnity. * * *

* * *

[The Court restated its earlier conclusion that the U.S. Supreme Court in *Travelers* had recognized "fairly significant bounds on preemption" and had "cautioned that 'nothing in the language of [ERISA] or in the context of its passage indicates that Congress chose to displace general health care regulation, which historically has been a matter of local concern.' *Id.* at 892 (*quoting Travelers,* 514 U.S. at 706, 708–709). Applying Travelers, the Court concluded that the negligence claims were not preempted; in their words, "* * * we held it would have been inappropriate to conclude that Haverford's claims, in which the issue of U.S. Healthcare's allegedly dilatory delivery of contractually-guaranteed medical benefits were intertwined with the question of safe medical care, are preempted by ERISA."]

[The court then recited the facts of *Pegram.*]

The Supreme Court granted certiorari to determine whether treatment decisions made by an HMO, acting through its physicians, are fiduciary acts within the meaning of ERISA. The Court held that they are not. []

In the course of doing so, the Court set forth two guiding principles. First, HMO physicians occupy dual roles. They act like plan administrators when they determine, for example, whether a participant's condition is covered, and as health care providers, when they decide upon the medical treatment a participant will receive. *Id.* at 2153–54.

Second, HMO physicians make three types of decisions. "[P]ure 'eligibility decisions' turn on the plan's coverage of a particular condition or medical procedure for its treatment," *id.* at 2154, such as "whether a plan covers an undisputed case of appendicitis." *Id.* at 2155. " 'Treatment decisions,' by contrast, are choices about how to go about diagnosing and treating a patient's condition: given a patient's constellation of symptoms, what is the appropriate medical response?" *Id.* at 2154. "Mixed eligibility and treatment decisions" are just what their name implies-decisions in which coverage and medical judgment are intertwined. *Id.* at 2154–55. * * *

* * *

While *Travelers* and *Pegram* deal with different aspects of ERISA, for our present purposes, they share common ground. *Travelers* instructs that ERISA does not preempt state law that regulates the provision of adequate medical treatment. *Pegram* instructs that an HMO's mixed eligibility and treatment decision implicates a state law claim for medical malpractice, not an ERISA cause of action for fiduciary breach. Thus, if Haverford's third party claim against U.S. Healthcare arose out of a mixed decision, it is, according to *Pegram,* subject to state medical malpractice law, which is what Haverford asserted. Moreover, under *Travelers,* it is not preempted by ERISA.

* * *

Having looked again at the record, there are facts that are not disputed, in addition to those set forth in *Pappas I,* that are important to our analysis. Dr. Dickter, the physician who first saw Pappas in the emergency room of Haverford on May 21, 1991, at about 11:00 a.m., received permission from Jefferson to admit Pappas to its spinal cord trauma center. Dr. Dickter chose Jefferson because it, unlike other hospitals, had designated space for spinal trauma cases and was able to determine immediately whether it was in a position to receive a new patient. When Dr. Dickter learned at 12:40 p.m. from ambulance personnel that Pappas' transfer to Jefferson was not HMO approved, he telephoned U.S. Healthcare at 12:50 p.m. and asked that it reconsider its decision. Dr. Dickter spoke to Elaine Norman, a U.S. Healthcare representative, and told her that Pappas' condition constituted a neurological emergency that needed immediate attention, and for which he had made arrangements with Jefferson. Ms. Norman advised Dr. Dickter that she was not authorized to take action one way or the other, but that she would consult with someone who was. At 1:05 p.m., Dr. Dickter spoke with Carol DeLark, another U.S. Healthcare representative. She told him that Dr. Liebowitz, one of U.S. Healthcare's physicians who had the authority to decide such matters, reviewed Pappas' case; that the referral to Jefferson, a non-HMO hospital, continued to be denied; and that a referral to the facilities affiliated with Hahnemann, Temple University or MCP was approved. At about 3:30 p.m., through Dr. Dickter's efforts, Pappas was admitted to MCP.

Not surprisingly, U.S. Healthcare argues that its decision about Pappas' referral "constituted a quintessential 'coverage' determination". We, however, disagree. In our view, the undisputed facts in this case, and the inferences drawn from them, establish the sort of mixed eligibility and treatment decision that *Pegram* discussed. Dr. Leibowitz, U.S. Healthcare's physician, reviewed Pappas' case, and rejected another medical doctor's opinion based on his clinical judgment that Pappas needed to be referred to Jefferson for treatment of a medical emergency. Instead of referring Pappas to Jefferson, a non-HMO hospital, as Dr. Dickter recommended, Dr. Leibowitz referred Pappas to one of three other facilities for medical care. He did not, in the Supreme Court's words, only make a "simple yes or no" decision as to whether Pappas' condition was covered; it clearly was. Rather, Dr Leibowitz also determined where and, under the circumstances, when Pappas' epidural abscess would be treated. His was a mixed eligibility and treatment decision, the adverse consequences of which, if any, are properly redressed, as *Pegram* teaches, through state medical malpractice law. This law as *Travelers* teaches, is not preempted by ERISA.

We conclude, therefore, that our reasoning and result in *Pappas I* are consistent with the Supreme Court's decision in *Pegram.* Accordingly, we confirm our original disposition; the order of the Superior Court, reversing the grant of summary judgment to U.S. Healthcare is affirmed. This matter is remanded to the trial court for further proceedings consistent with this opinion.

[Justice Saylor, in dissent, criticizes the majority for oversimplifying Pegram, in terms of conflict preemption and the extent to which ERISA still preempts many health plan decisions. He writes: "First, in my view, *Pegram II* gives cause for the exercise of a degree of caution on the part of state courts and legislators in terms of defining the duties of managed care organizations (or at least those that are deemed to perform administrative functions under ERISA) for purposes of tort jurisprudence. Second, I question whether a full, fair, and final resolution of the conflict preemption inquiry can be effected unless and until some more precise definition is afforded to any duties being ascribed to U.S. Healthcare under state tort law."]

Notes and Questions

1. *Frappier* illustrates the threshold question: is the health plan named as defendant in a tort suit an ERISA-qualified plan? If so, defendant can then remove the case to federal court and argue that the plaintiff's claims are preempted.

Most managed care plans are now ERISA-qualified. If a plan is ERISA-qualified, then state law claims are preempted and the plaintiff is relegated to s. 502(a)(1)(B) of ERISA, 29 U.S.C.A. § 1132(a)(1)(B). § 502(a)(1)(B) states that a civil action may be brought—

> (1) by a participant or beneficiary—
>
> (B) to recover benefits due to him under the terms of his plan, to enforce his rights under the terms of the plan, or to clarify his rights to future benefits under the terms of the plan. . . .

In Massachusetts Mutual Life Insurance Co. v. Russell, 473 U.S. 134, 105 S.Ct. 3085, 87 L.Ed.2d 96 (1985), the Court held that an employee covered under her employer's welfare benefit plan could not recover compensatory and punitive damages for financial losses that allegedly occurred when the benefit plan mishandled the processing of the employee's claim for disability benefits. Section 409(a)'s statement that the fiduciary "shall be subject to such other equitable or remedial relief as the court may deem appropriate" precludes compensatory and punitive damages to compensate beneficiaries for personal injuries. Although a beneficiary can sue a benefit plan, a benefit plan manager, or other fiduciary, she cannot collect any personal compensatory or punitive damages under section 409(a).

See generally Karen A. Jordan, Travelers Insurance: New Support for the Argument to Restrain ERISA Pre-emption, 13 Yale J. on Reg. 255 (1996); Wendy K. Mariner, Liability for Managed Care Decisions: The Employee Retirement Income Security Act (ERISA) and the Uneven Playing Field, 86 Am.J. Pub.Health 863 (1996).

2. The *Pappas* decision interprets Pegram as narrowing the scope of ERISA preemption even further—holding that mixed eligibility and treatment decisions are properly redressed through state medical malpractice law. The U.S. Supreme Court's lengthy discussion of ERISA preemption does suggest, however, that mixed eligibility/treatment decisions are not acts of plan administration and therefore, these potentially "unrelated-to-ERISA" claims can be pursued in state courts.

Do you see problems with this distinction? Does Pappas treat virtually all health plan coverage decisions as "mixed" and therefore not preempted? Can you develop a more helpful set of distinctions for determining when ERISA properly preempts a state malpractice claim?

3. ERISA was interpreted by the federal courts in the first wave of litigation as totally preempting common law tort claims. See, e.g., Ricci v. Gooberman, 840 F.Supp. 316 (D.N.J.1993); Butler v. Wu, 853 F.Supp. 125, 129–30 (D.N.J.1994); Nealy v. U.S. Healthcare HMO, 844 F.Supp. 966, 973 (S.D.N.Y.1994) (plaintiff's attempts to hold an HMO liable under several common law theories held preempted); Altieri v. Cigna Dental Health, Inc., 753 F.Supp. 61, 63–65 (D.Conn.1990) (ERISA preempts plaintiff's negligent supervision claim against an HMO). It appeared from this caselaw that any managed care plan that was ERISA-qualified would receive virtually complete tort immunity.

The federal courts began to split, however, as to the limits of such preemption. Recent decisions have limited the preemption clause of ERISA, holding that many tort theories have little or nothing to do with the administration of pension plan or other benefits. The result has been a litigation explosion against managed care as theories are imported from hospital liability caselaw, fiduciary law, and contract law to use against managed care organizations. Prihoda v. Shpritz, 914 F.Supp. 113 (D.Md.1996) (ERISA does not preempt an action against physicians and an HMO for physicians' failure to diagnose a cancerous tumor, allowing a vicarious liability action to proceed). See also Independence HMO, Inc. v. Smith, 733 F.Supp. 983 (E.D.Pa.1990) (ERISA does not preempt medical malpractice-type claims brought against HMOs under a vicarious liability theory); Elsesser v. Hospital of the Philadelphia College of Osteopathic Medicine, 802 F.Supp. 1286 (E.D.Pa.1992) (same for a claim against an HMO for the HMO's negligence in selecting, retaining, and evaluating plaintiff's primary-care physician); Kearney v. U.S. Healthcare, Inc., 859 F.Supp. 182 (E.D.Pa.1994) (ERISA preempts plaintiff's direct negligence claim, but not its vicarious liability claim). See generally Peter D. Jacobson, Legal Challenges to Managed Care Cost Containment Programs: An Initial Assessment, 18 Health Affairs 69 (1999); Karen A. Jordan, Tort Liability for Managed Care: The Weakening of ERISA's Protective Shield, 25 J. Law, Med. & Ethics 160 (1997).

4. Dukes and the quality–quantity distinction. The watershed decision, opening up a substantial crack in preemption doctrine, was Dukes v. U.S. Healthcare, Inc., 57 F.3d 350 (3d Cir.1995). In *Dukes*, the court found that Congress intended in passing ERISA to insure that promised benefits would be available to plan participants, and that section 502 was "intended to provide each individual participant with a remedy in the event that promises made by the plan were not kept." The court was unwilling, however, to stretch the remedies of 502 to "control the quality of the benefits received by plan participants." The court concluded that ... [q]uality control of benefits, such as the health care benefits provided here, is a field traditionally occupied by state regulation and we interpret the silence of Congress as reflecting an intent that it remain such. The court developed the distinction between benefits to care under a plan and a right to good quality care:

> The plaintiffs are not attempting to define new "rights under the terms of the plan"; instead, they are attempting to assert their already-existing rights under the generally-applicable state law of agency and tort. Inherent in the phrases "rights under the terms of the plan" and "benefits due ... under the terms of [the] plan" is the notion that the plan participants and beneficiaries will receive something to which they would not be otherwise entitled. But patients enjoy the right to be free from medical malpractice regardless of whether or not their medical care is provided through an ERISA plan.

The court distinguished between the quantity of benefits due under a welfare plan and the quality of those benefits. Quality of care could be so poor that it is essentially a denial of benefits. Or the plan could describe a benefit in terms that are quality-based, such as a commitment that all x-rays will be analyzed by radiologists with a certain level of training. But absent either of these extremes, poor medical care—malpractice—is not a benefits issue under ERISA.

5. Chinks in the preemption armor. Theories of liability can be grouped into several categories, depending on the activity engaged in by the managed care organization. This functional organization helps determine what is preempted and what allowed under ERISA

a. Contract claims. The managed care organization as insurer must recruit subscribers to its plan, typically through employment-based plans offered to employees. It must properly enroll these subscribers to ensure they are covered in exchange for their premiums. It must clearly describe any exclusions that operate under its coverage, including exclusions of coverage of certain diseases and "experimental" treatments. Policies also typically impose a requirement of "medical necessity" as a prerequisite to payment for treatment. Policies may impose coverage limitations for certain treatments, such as psychiatric hospitalization. Such coverage restrictions may create a subscriber right to sue under section 502 of ERISA, but the courts have held that malpractice claims for damages for violation of this provision are preempted. See, e.g., Brandon v. Aetna Services, Inc., 46 F.Supp.2d 110 (D.C.Conn.1999)(claim against plan administrator for refusing to pay for in-patient and out-patient care for substance-abuse and anxiety disorder problems; held a benefits issue, preempted under ERISA); Parrino v. FHP, Inc., 146 F.3d 699 (9th Cir.1998)(patient had brain tumor removed and FHP initially refused to authorize payment for proton beam therapy prescribed by physicians as experimental and unnecessary; held that claim is completely preempted); Huss v. Green Spring Health Services, Inc., 1999 WL 225885

(E.D.Pa.1999)(failure of defendant to correctly inform plaintiff of coverage under plan goes to quantity of benefits, and is preempted); Garcia v. Kaiser Foundation Hospitals, 90 Hawai'i 425, 978 P.2d 863 (1999)(plaintiff's claims that plan failed to provide him with reasonable and necessary medical treatment to which he was entitled, preempted; claims included breach of contract, tortious breach of contract, infliction of emotional distress, fraud, unfair and deceptive trade practice, loss of consortium, and punitive damages).

Common law bad faith claims are excluded under ERISA. Pilot Life Insurance Co. v. Dedeaux, 481 U.S. 41, 107 S.Ct. 1549, 95 L.Ed.2d 39 (1987), held that actions such as bad faith sufficiently "relate to" employee benefits plans to fall within ERISA preemption.

b. Operational restrictions on subscriber choices.

Many managed care organizations offer a restricted set of choices for subscribers. Their drug formularies limit the choices of drugs available to plan physicians. Hospital choices are restricted to those which whom the MCO has a contract, as is access to specialists. Use of physician gatekeepers restricts access to hospitals and specialists on the MCO's acceptable list.

The courts have generally held that ERISA preempts claims based on plan strategies to discourage referrals to specialists. Pell v. Shmokler, 1997 WL 83743 (E.D.Pa.1997)(refusal of treating physician to refer plaintiff to pulmonologist is a withholding of benefits, subject to complete preemption); see also Kohn v. Delaware Valley HMO, Inc., 1991 WL 275609 (E.D.Pa.1991).

Pre-certification and other forms of utilization review are designed to filter out demands for "unnecessary" treatments. Such forms of review of physician medical decisions to determine their necessity and cost-effectiveness prior to treatment or hospitalization are either completely preempted under § 502(a)(1)(B) or subject to an ERISA preemption defense under § 514(a). See Jass v. Prudential Health Care Plan Inc., 88 F.3d 1482 (7th Cir.1996)(claim against pre-certification review administrator who denied patient's request of physical therapy to rehabilitate knee after surgery held completely preempted); Kuhl v. Lincoln Nat'l Health Plan of Kansas City, Inc., 999 F.2d 298, 302 (8th Cir.1993)(decision to delay pre-certification of heart surgery preempted); Corcoran v. United HealthCare, Inc., 965 F.2d 1321, 1332 (5th Cir.1992).

Such forms of review may affect the quantity of benefits received directly, but they have attendant effects on quality as well. Thus a failure to provide in-home visits for a subscriber, when the plan allegedly offered such a service, is a benefit issue subject to preemption under § 502. See Kuhl v. Lincoln Nat'l Health Plan of Kansas City, Inc., 999 F.2d 298, 302 (8th Cir.1993)(decision to delay pre-certification of heart surgery preempted); Corcoran v. United HealthCare, Inc., 965 F.2d 1321, 1332 (5th Cir.1992).

Claims that fall within the administrator's core functions–determining eligibility for benefits, disbursing them to the participant, monitoring available funds and recordkeeping—are completely preempted.

Denials based on "medical necessity" determinations are more complicated than the courts have generally acknowledged. They entail two determinations: first, a medical judgment that the patient's condition can be treated by available treatments of varying efficacy and cost; second, an administrative decision of whether to pay for the care, considering the cost-benefit trade-off of the treatment alternatives. The HMO decision can be characterized as a medical determination, although most courts have held that refusals to pay for care that the treating physician recommends are preempted. See Danca v. Private Health Care Sys., Inc., 185 F.3d 1 (1st Cir.1999); Brandon v. Aetna Servs., Inc., 46 F.Supp. 2d 110 (D.Conn.1999); Person v. Physicians Health Plan, Inc., 20 F.Supp.2d 918 (E.D.Va. 1998); Tolton v. American Biodyne, Inc., 48 F.3d 937 (6th Cir.1995); Spain v. Aetna Life Ins. Co., 11 F.3d 129 (9th Cir.1993); Toledo v. Kaiser Permanente Med. Group, 987 F.Supp. 1174 (N.D.Cal.1997); Schmid v. Kaiser Found. Health Plan of the Northwest, 963 F.Supp. 942 (D.Or.1997). Attacks on utilization review necessarily also attack the methods by which benefits are administered or denied.

c. Plan design and delivery of health care services.

MCOs are businesses. They market their care to potential employers and subscribers in a competitive marketplace for health care. They recruit and organize their physicians through their networks. They design a corporate system in which health care is delivered. And they must administer this system in a safe fashion that avoids injury to subscribers caused by the negligence of plan physicians and other providers. Malpractice claims based on vicarious liability, corporate negligence, negligence per se and intentional inflection of mental distress may be allowed under current law as quality of care issues not involving ERISA claims for benefits. Herrera v. Lovelace Health Systems, Inc., 35 F.Supp.2d 1327 (D.C.N.M.1999); Hoose v. Jefferson Home Health Care, Inc., 1998 WL 114492 (E.D.Pa.1998) (claims of negligence in selection of therapists, providing post-operative care, vicarious liability, and negligence in overall supervision of care; the court noted that "this case is noting more than a medical malpractice case", and refused to uphold ERISA preemption).

• Agency doctrine. Under theories of agency, physicians and other professionals may be held liable and that liability imputed to the managed care organization. Such vicarious liability has been held by the majority of courts considering the question not to be preempted by ERISA. Harris v. Deaconess Health Services Corp., et al., 61 F.Supp.2d 889 (E.D.Mo.1999); Herrera v. Lovelace Health Sys., Inc., 35 F.Supp.2d 1327 (D.N.M.1999); Visconti v. U.S. Healthcare, 1998 WL 968473 (E.D.Pa.1998); Petrovich v. Share Health Plan of Illinois, Inc., 188 Ill.2d 17, 241 Ill.Dec. 627, 719 N.E.2d 756 (Ill.1999); Dykema v. King, 959 F.Supp. 736 (D.S.C.1997); Prihoda v. Shpritz, 914 F.Supp. 113 (D.C.Maryland 1996); Pacificare of Oklahoma, Inc. v. Burrage, 59 F.3d 151 (10th Cir.1995); Lupo v. Human Affairs Int'l, Inc., 28 F.3d 269 (2d Cir.1994); Dearmas v. Av–Med, Inc., 865 F.Supp. 816 (S.D.Fla.1994); Gilbert v. Sycamore Municipal Hospital, 156 Ill.2d 511, 190 Ill.Dec. 758, 622 N.E.2d 788 (Ill. 1993).

The plan is irrelevant to the claim, since the claim of agency does not rise and fall with the plan, but is established by reference to reliance and representations, a question of fact not involving the interpretation of an ERISA plan. See Rice v. Panchal, 65 F.3d 637 (7th Cir.1995). If the underlying claim against the treating physician is a failure to treat—a denial of benefits—then it relates to the benefits plan; a vicarious liability claim would also be grounded in this benefits denial claim. The negligence claim then could not be resolved without reference to the benefits determination. In such a situation, one circuit court has held that ERISA completely preempts the agency claim. Jass v. Prudential Health Care Plan, Inc., 88 F.3d 1482 (7th Cir.1996)

The law of vicarious liability varies substantially from state to state, and plans have argued that allowing vicarious liability claims would create a patchwork of regulations affecting ERISA plans, interfering with the administration of benefits and the need for uniformity. However, as the court noted in *Prihoda*, while liability might vary from state to state, "[t]he liability of HMOs ... would not be subject to inconsistent administrative obligations of the type that occur when inconsistent local laws and court decisions cause benefit levels to vary from state to state."

• Treatment recommendations. When a plan or its non-physician employees get involved in treatment orders, they may be liable. In Roessert v. Health Net, 929 F.Supp. 343, 351 (N.D.Cal.1996), the patient sued her HMO, medical group and treating physicians in part for seeking her commitment to a psychiatric facility. The court found that an action for intentional or negligent infliction of mental distress against the HMO and the medical group was not preempted by ERISA. The plan's recommendation to commit could be decided apart from the terms of the plan. If a plan used under-qualified employees to treat a patient and they fail to recognize the seriousness of the condition, the plan is acting as a provider, not in its administrative capacity, and the claim could proceed in state court. Blaine v. Community Health Plan, 179 Misc.2d 331, 687 N.Y.S.2d 854 (S.C. N.Y. 1998)(claim that patient's injuries were caused by the plan's failure to provide her with a physician rather than physician's assistant, failing to provide tests, and failing to adequately supervise the physician's assistant and have written policies governing required supervision.)

If a plan requires that a subscriber first telephone an advisory nurse prior to seeking medical attention, this has been construed as a misdiagnosis and the giving of negligent medical advice rather than as utilization review pre-certification. Crum v. Health Alliance–Midwest, Inc., 47 F.Supp.2d 1013 (D.C.Ill.1999)(advisory nurse told plaintiff with chest pains that he just had gas pains, and he died that evening of acute myocardial infarction); Phommyvong v. Muniz, 1999 WL 155714 (N.D.Tex.1999). But see Jass v. Prudential Health Care Plan, Inc., 88 F.3d 1482 (7th Cir.1996)(nurse's denial of physical therapy held to be a claim for denial of benefits).

• Substandard plan design and administration. Claims of negligent design and administration of the delivery of health care services have been allowed in recent cases. See McDonald v. Damian, 56 F.Supp.2d 574 (E.D.Pa.1999)(claim for inadequacies in the delivery of medical services). In the Pappas case, the court held that a negligence claim against a plan for providing contractual benefits in "such a dilatory fashion that the patient was injured are intertwined with the provision of safe care". The issue was a delay in transporting the plaintiff to a specialty trauma unit for care. The delay was arguably caused by the utilization review process of the managed care organization, which did not allow transport to the best hospital unit in the area for spinal injuries. The case appears to involve both a system-induced delay and also a benefits question as to which hospitals were available to U.S. Healthcare providers and when a proper emergency allowed sending a subscriber outside the hospital network. Under the *Dukes* analysis, it is not clear in such a case where the quality-quantity distinction can be clearly drawn.

• Adoption of policies that discourage physicians from offering needed care. Explicit rules that discourage physicians from giving patients necessary care or hospitalization, such as discharging at-risk patients from hospitals, can be the basis for negligence claims. In Bauman v. U.S. Healthcare, 1 F.Supp.2d 420 (D.C.N.J.1998), plan participants whose newborn infant died on the day following discharge from the hospital sued. They argued that the plan policy that pressured or required that physicians discharge newborn infants and mothers within 24 hours of birth was negligent, and that a policy that discouraged readmission when health problems were identified after the original discharge was negligent. The

Third Circuit held that "when the HMO acts under the ERISA plan as a health care provider, it arranges and provides medical treatment, directly or through contracts with hospitals, doctors, or nurses." 193 F.3d 151. A 24–hour discharge policy fits within a quality of care claim, as does a hospital utilization review policy that discourages readmission.

A challenge to the appropriateness of medical decisions by a plan and its agents, as to quality and level of care and treatment, have been held to fall outside § 502(a) and may be tried in state court. In Moscovitch v. Danbury Hospital, 25 F.Supp.2d 74 (D.C.Conn.1998), the plaintiffs sued the plan and providers for the suicide of their son, on grounds that the plan failed to properly diagnose and assess the decedent's psychiatric condition, failed to monitor, care and treat him and oversee his treatment and failed to prescribe and administer the proper medications. The court held that this was a quality of care issue and the plaintiff can show on remand that the plan crossed the line from making a benefits determination to a treatment decision. See also Cyr v. Kaiser Found. Health Plan of Texas, 12 F.Supp.2d 556 (N.D.Tex.1998)(claims for negligence, fraudulent concealment, and tortious interference with the doctor/patient relationship held not preempted.)

The financial arrangement generally between the managed care organization and a hospital may arguably cause a hospital to commit malpractice, and this does not require courts to review a plan's utilization review or otherwise construe a plan's benefits. Preemption may therefore be avoided. Ouellette v. Christ Hospital, 942 F.Supp. 1160 (S.D.Ohio 1996).

• Substandard plans. A claim that a managed care plan is "substandard", leading to patient injury as a result, would seem to go directly to the administration of a plan and therefore be preempted. However, in Moreno v. Health Partners Health Plan, 4 F.Supp.2d 888 (D.C.Ariz.1998), the District Court held that there is "no relation between an action for medical malpractice and the recovery of benefits or the clarification of rights to future benefits under an ERISA plan". A plan decision to discharge a patient from the hospital to her home rather than a skilled nursing facility is considered a "quality" issue, not suitable for preemption. Miller v. Riddle Memorial Hospital, 1998 WL 272167 (E.D.Pa.1998). Where a plan is responsible for the continuum of care and it proves to be inadequate, even if that means they refuse to cover a benefit at a rehabilitation hospital or other facility, courts have found this to be nothing more a complaint of substandard care, not preempted by ERISA. Snow v. Burden, 1999 WL 387196 (E.D.Pa.1999). If a plan is negligent in failing to provide appropriate screening tests and studies, this can be viewed, not as a benefits denial, but a negligent provision of benefits, not subject to ERISA. Newton v. Tavani, 962 F.Supp. 45 (D.C.N.J.1997).

d. Physician selection and retention.

MCOs must select physicians who have appropriate credentials and training. They must then have procedures in place for reviewing these physicians' conduct and deciding whether or not to retain physicians at the end of their contract periods. Negligence in hiring, employment and supervision of medical personnel involved in treatment is a classic example of corporate negligence, defined in the hospital setting and imported into the managed care environment. As such, it is not subject to preemption, based on the Dukes rationale that such selection relates to the quality of care offered. See, e.g., Giles v. NYLCare Health Plans, Inc., 172 F.3d 332 (5th Cir.1999)(claim for negligence in selecting plan providers remanded); Visconti v. U.S. Healthcare, 1998 WL 968473 (E.D.Pa.1998); Hoyt v. Edge, 1997 WL 356324 (E.D.Pa.1997)(negligent supervision of Plan physicians).

e. Physician payment mechanisms.

One of the primary goals of managed care is conservative, cost-efficient practice. Physician behavior in prescribing, hospitalizing and referring may be altered by designing payment systems that promote cost-sensitive practice through bonuses and penalties. Claims regarding design of and concealment of financial incentives continue to be disallowed under complete preemption doctrine. The claim is that such incentives to undertreat cause a physician to deny benefits to a subscriber, resulting in injury. A plaintiff may claim that a physician negligently diagnosed or failed to treat, and the mere reference to the effect of an incentive system on his or her motivations will not lead to preemption. Lancaster v. Kaiser Foundation Health Plan of Mid–Atlantic States, Inc., 958 F.Supp. 1137, 1145 (E.D.Va.1997)(it may be appropriate for plaintiff to show that an incentive program induced physicians to refrain from ordering tests, to rebut their claim that their decision was based on "sound medical consideration.").

When, however, the claim is that the plan is negligent in the very design of the payment system, the courts have noted that this is an attack on administrative systems designed to curb rising health care costs by rewarding physicians for not ordering tests or treatment. As an attack on the administration of benefits, a denial of benefits as a result triggers section 502(a)(1)(B) and complete preemption. Lancaster v. Kaiser Foundation Health Plan of Mid–Atlantic States, Inc., 958 F.Supp. 1137 (E.D.Va.1997). If the effect of a payment incentive system is recast as having the effect, not of denying benefits, but of discouraging physicians from providing proper care, then it is viewed by some courts as a quality of care issue following the *Dukes* analysis and held not to be preempted. DeLucia v. St. Luke's Hospital, 1999 WL 387211 (E.D.Pa.1999); Ouellette v. Christ Hospital, 942 F.Supp. 1160 (S.D.Ohio 1996). After the Supreme Court decision in *Pegram*, however, where a unanimous court acknowledged the validity of the use by HMOs of various incentives to curb health care costs, it is unlikely that such attacks on the physician incentive systems will prevail.

Courts are steadily eroding ERISA categorical preemption in favor of subscriber rights to sue the organization for injuries. The recasting of malpractice claims as "quality" complaints, rather than benefit denials, has been accepted by several recent federal court decisions. The courts seem inclined to narrow ERISA preemption whenever possible and are likely to continue to do so. The Supreme Court in *Pegram*, acknowledging the role of state malpractice litigation and by using the Dukes "quantity-quality" distinction, has left this door wide open for continued common law litigation that circumvents ERISA preemption.

C. BENEFICIARY REMEDIES PROVIDED BY ERISA

1. Judicial Claims Under ERISA

ERISA takes away, but ERISA also gives. ERISA obligates employee benefit plans to fulfill their commitments to their beneficiaries, and provides a federal cause of action when they fail to do so. But the vision of health insurance that undergirds ERISA is very different from that found in state law.

State insurance regulation has generally been driven by a concern for access rights: e.g., the right of employees to have continued access to insurance coverage when they lose their jobs; the right of insureds to obtain mental health or mammography screening coverage; the right of chiropractors to have their services paid for by insurance; the right of "any willing provider" to participate in a PPO; the right of small businesses to purchase insurance at community rates; the right of beneficiaries to insurer compliance with the insurance contract; and right of beneficiaries to fair procedure. This body of law looks to public utility regulation, and, more recently, civil rights laws, for its models.

The bodies of law that define ERISA, on the other hand, are trust law and classical contract law. ERISA does not compel employers to provide health insurance and prohibits the states from imposing such a requirement. If, however, employers choose voluntarily (or under collective bargaining agreements) to establish health benefit plans, any contributions made by employers (or employees) to such plans are held in trust for all of the participants (employee plan members) and beneficiaries (dependents and others covered under a participant's policy) of the plan and must be paid out according to the contract that defines its terms. If the plan fiduciary or administrator wrongfully withholds benefits, a participant or beneficiary is entitled to sue in federal or state court. If a fiduciary or administrator exercises its properly delegated discretion to withhold benefits that are not expressly granted or denied by the plan, the court must defer to the judgment of the administrator or fiduciary. When the fiduciary or administrator wrongfully withholds benefits, moreover, no matter how egregious its conduct in doing so, the court will merely order the plan to pay the beneficiary the amount due. The statute does not, as interpreted by the Supreme Court, authorize tort relief or punitive damages.

While the limited rights that beneficiaries enjoy under ERISA trouble courts and commentators, they are consistent with ERISA's underlying theory. State insurance law—be it the common law of contra proferentem or statutory mandates enacted by the legislature—focus on the absolute claims of beneficiaries whose life or health is in jeopardy to the assets held by the insurer: your money or my life. They also honor the political claims of providers who demand their turn at the insurance trough. The insurance pot is, apparently, infinitely elastic and must be expanded to fulfil the demands of many claimants, each of whom, considered individually, makes a compelling case.

ERISA, by contrast, sees a zero sum game. The pot is only so big, and when it is empty it is empty. To fudge the rules in favor of one beneficiary may result in the plan not being able to honor the legitimate claims of other beneficiaries. If one claimant who has been treated egregiously by the plan is permitted to recover extracontractual damages from its administrator, these damages will ultimately come out of the pockets of the other beneficiaries, who have themselves done nothing wrong. In a world of scarce resources, not everyone can be taken care of. But the administrator, nevertheless, is also a fiduciary, and there are some limits to its discretion.

DOE v. GROUP HOSPITALIZATION & MEDICAL SERVICES

United States Court of Appeals, Fourth Circuit, 1993.
3 F.3d 80.

NIEMEYER, CIRCUIT JUDGE:

John Doe, a 59–year-old law partner of Firm Doe in Washington, D.C., was diagnosed in late 1991 with multiple myeloma, a rare and typically fatal form of blood cancer. His physician, Dr. Kenneth C. Anderson of the Dana–Farber Cancer Institute, affiliated with Harvard Medical School, prescribed a treatment that involved an initial course of chemotherapy to reduce the percentage of tumor cells. Provided Doe responded to the therapy and achieved a "minimal disease status," Dr. Anderson recommended that Doe then undergo high-dose chemotherapy and radiation therapy combined with an autologous bone marrow transplant. * * * The cost of the entire treatment was estimated at $100,000. Dr. Anderson stated that the prescribed treatment "offers this gentleman his only chance of long-term survival."

John Doe and Firm Doe sought health insurance benefits for the prescribed treatment from Group Hospitalization and Medical Services, Inc., doing business as Blue Cross and Blue Shield of the National Capital Area (Blue Cross). Blue Cross insured and administered Firm Doe's employee welfare benefit plan pursuant to a group insurance contract entered into effective January 1, 1989. Relying on language in the contract that excludes benefits for bone marrow transplants undergone in treating multiple myeloma, as well as for "related" services and supplies, Blue Cross denied benefits. John Doe and Firm Doe promptly filed suit against Blue Cross under § 502 of the Employee Retirement Insurance Security Act (ERISA), 29 U.S.C. § 1132, claiming that Blue Cross denied benefits based solely upon improperly adopted amendments to the group insurance contract and that, in any event, the contract's language as amended did not exclude coverage for the treatment. On cross-motions for summary judgment, the district court entered judgment for Blue Cross, holding that "Blue Cross may properly deny coverage to John Doe and his physicians based on the Group Contract and amendments thereto." This appeal followed

* * *

The group insurance contract to which we must look to resolve the issues in this case was purportedly amended by a letter sent to Firm Doe dated November 30, 1990. The amendment is important because it supplied the language on which Blue Cross relied to deny coverage and gave Blue Cross discretion in deciding eligibility and contract interpretation issues.

* * *

In December 1991 John Doe was evaluated and diagnosed with multiple myeloma, * * *. By letter dated January 30, 1992, John Doe's physician, Dr. Anderson, prescribed a treatment of chemotherapy and radiation that included an autologous bone marrow transplant. On March 30, 1992, Dr. Gregory K. Morris, vice president and medical director of Blue Cross, wrote Dr. Anderson denying the request for coverage of the proposed treatment. Specifically referring to the language of the November 30, 1990, amendment that excludes from coverage treatment of myeloma by means of bone marrow transplant and services and supplies related thereto, Dr. Morris stated that Blue Cross will be "unable to provide benefits for Mr. [Doe]." * * *[4]

4. After denying coverage and rejecting John Doe's appeal, Blue Cross amended the group insurance contract on May 28, 1992, effective August 1, 1992, to confirm its interpretation of the contract and to exclude the treatment for which John Doe had requested precertification. Because ERISA requires that specific reasons for denial of a claim be given, see 29 U.S.C. § 1133, our review in this case is limited to only those reasons which Blue Cross

The November 30 letter was a form letter apparently sent to all administrators of Blue Cross group insurance contracts. It opens by stating that its purpose is to "inform you of updates" to the group contract. It then addresses changes to no less than eight separate aspects of coverage in four single-spaced pages, including one headed "Organ Transplants" that includes the language in question. * * *

John Doe and Firm Doe contend that the amendment was ineffective for two reasons: It was not adopted in accordance with the contract's specified time periods for making amendments, and, even if it was timely, the language of the amendment misled the contract holder, Firm Doe, and its employees about the nature of the changes.

[The court found that the amendment was effective because Blue Cross had provided 30 days notice of the change in accordance with the contract. ed.]

In connection with their second point, John Doe and Firm Doe argue that while the language contained in the section headed "Organ Transplants" purports to "clarify" the types of transplants covered ("In order to clarify which types of transplants are covered, a list of the covered procedures [is] being added to your Contract as follows" (emphasis added)), coverage was in fact narrowed by the amendment because before the amendment transplants were simply not addressed and were therefore presumptively covered so long as they were not excluded under some other provision. They argue, therefore, that Blue Cross failed to disclose the intended effect of the limitation for organ transplants, downplaying the significance of the letter. * * * In short, they maintain that Blue Cross failed to put Firm Doe on notice of an amendment. From our review of the letter and the parties' conduct in response to it, we find this argument unpersuasive.

Health care benefits provided in an employee benefit plan are not vested benefits; the employer may modify or withdraw these benefits at any time, provided the changes are made in compliance with ERISA and the terms of the plan. * * * Firm Doe established its benefit plan through a contract with Blue Cross, and as part of this contract, Firm Doe accepted the provision that "benefits, provisions, terms, or conditions" could be changed by Blue Cross upon timely written notice. We believe that the November 30 letter provided sufficient notice that benefits under the contract were being changed. It states at the outset that the letter is an "update" of the terms of the contract. The body of the letter refers to specific coverages, outlining the changes in the language for each. * * *

Evidence was also presented that Firm Doe in fact relied on the changes made by the November 30 letter in connection with other coverages and it continued to pay premiums under the contract without objection. Moreover, the amendment was circulated well before John Doe evidenced any symptoms of or was diagnosed with cancer. More than 15 months after the amendment was sent, Blue Cross relied on its language in reviewing the coverage, and we believe that it was correct in doing so.

gave for denying coverage. [ ] However, any attempt by Blue Cross to rely on a post-precertification pre-therapy amendment to deny benefits to John Doe, which would be inappropriate to anticipate now, might raise serious questions concerning Blue Cross' duties, both as a fiduciary and under the insurance contract with Firm Doe, and its good faith.

John Doe and Firm Doe contend that even the amended language of their group insurance contract with Blue Cross does not provide a basis for the insurance company's decision to deny John Doe benefits. Before turning to the validly amended contract to review this decision, we must address the appropriate standard of review to apply.

Court actions challenging the denial of benefits under 29 U.S.C. § 1132(a)(1)(B) are subject to the standard of review announced in Firestone Tire and Rubber Co. v. Bruch, 489 U.S. 101, 109 S.Ct. 948, 103 L.Ed.2d 80 (1989). The Court observed there, deriving guidance from principles of trust law, that in reviewing actions of a fiduciary who has been given discretionary powers to determine eligibility for benefits and to construe the language of an ERISA plan deference must be shown, and the fiduciary's actions will be reviewed only for abuse. [ ] If discretionary authority is not provided, denials of claims are to be reviewed de novo. [ ] Thus, where a fiduciary with authorized discretion construes a disputed or doubtful term, we will not disturb the interpretation if it is reasonable, even if we come to a different conclusion independently. [ ] In Firestone, however, the Supreme Court went on to recognize that a conflict of interest could lower the level of deference to be applied to a discretionary decision by a fiduciary:

> Of course, if a benefit plan gives discretion to an administrator or fiduciary who is operating under a conflict of interest, that conflict must be weighed as a "facto[r] in determining whether there is an abuse of discretion."

489 U.S. at 115, 109 S.Ct. at 957

Under the group insurance contract with Firm Doe, the employer, Blue Cross both insures and administers the payment of health care benefits for Firm Doe's employee welfare benefit plan. In its role as plan administrator, Blue Cross clearly exercises discretionary authority or discretionary control with respect to the management of the plan and therefore qualifies as a fiduciary under ERISA. 29 U.S.C. § 1002(21)(A). Only if Blue Cross has also been given discretionary authority with regard to decisions about eligibility for benefits and construction of the plan, however, will those decisions be entitled to deferential review. [ ]

Blue Cross asserts that it has been given discretionary authority to review claims, determine eligibility, and construe contract terms and that our review of its decision to deny Doe benefits is therefore only for abuse of discretion. We agree that the express terms of the group insurance contract give Blue Cross discretion to the extent it claims. The terms were stated in the November 30, 1990, letter of amendment as follows:

> [Blue Cross] shall have the full power and discretionary authority to control and manage the operation and administration of the Contract, subject only to the Participant's rights of review and appeal under the Contract. [Blue Cross] shall have all powers necessary to accomplish these purposes in accordance with the terms of the contract including, but not limited to:
>
> a. Determining all questions relating to Employee and Family Member eligibility and coverage;

b. Determining the benefits and amounts payable therefor to any Participant or provider of health care services;

c. Establishing and administering a claims review and appeal process; and

d. Interpreting, applying, and administering the provisions of the Contract.

John Doe and Firm Doe contend, however, that in denying benefits to John Doe, Blue Cross operated under a conflict of interest, and that therefore no deference to its discretion is warranted. They note that ERISA imposes on fiduciaries a duty of loyalty to act "with respect to a plan solely in the interest of the participants and beneficiaries and for the exclusive purpose of providing benefits ... and defraying reasonable expenses." 29 U.S.C. § 1104(a)(1)(A) [ ] Blue Cross apparently is compensated by a fixed premium, and when it pays a claim it funds the payment from the premiums collected. No evidence has been presented to suggest it has a mechanism to collect from the employer retrospectively for unexpected liabilities. It therefore bears the financial risk for claims made beyond the actuarial norm. John Doe and Firm Doe point out that "each time [Blue Cross] approves a payment of benefits, the money comes out of its own pocket" and argue that Blue Cross' fiduciary role as decisionmaker in approving benefits under the plan therefore "lies in perpetual conflict with its profitmaking role as a business." [ ] They urge that, because of this conflict, when we review Blue Cross' decision to deny Doe benefits, no deference to its judgment is due.* * *

We were first presented with the question of what effect a fiduciary's conflict of interest might have in De Nobel [v. Vitro Corp., 885 F.2d 1180 (4th Cir.1989)]. There, the employee-claimants, who were beneficiaries of an employee retirement plan, contended that decisions of the administrators of the plan were not entitled to deferential review because the administrators operated under a conflict of interest arising from their dual role as plan administrators and employees of the sponsoring company. The beneficiaries argued that decisions by the administrator favorable to the employer would save the plan "substantial sums."[ ] In deciding the case, however, we never reached the effect that a conflict of interest might have on the applicable standard of review because we concluded that no substantial conflict existed when the plan was fully funded and any savings would inure to the direct benefit of the plan, and therefore to the benefit of all beneficiaries and participants. * * *

In this case, Blue Cross insured the plan in exchange for the payment of a fixed premium, presumably based on actuarial data. Undoubtedly, its profit from the insurance contract depends on whether the claims allowed exceed the assumed risks. To the extent that Blue Cross has discretion to avoid paying claims, it thereby promotes the potential for its own profit. That type of conflict flows inherently from the nature of the relationship entered into by the parties and is common where employers contract with insurance companies to provide and administer health care benefits to employees through group insurance contracts.* * *

* * *

Because of the presence of a substantial conflict of interest, we therefore must alter our standard of review. We hold that when a fiduciary exercises discretion in interpreting a disputed term of the contract where one interpretation will further the financial interests of the fiduciary, we will not act as deferentially as would otherwise be appropriate. Rather, we will review the merits of the interpretation to determine whether it is consistent with an exercise of discretion by a fiduciary acting free of the interests that conflict with those of the beneficiaries. In short, the fiduciary decision will be entitled to some deference, but this deference will be lessened to the degree necessary to neutralize any untoward influence resulting from the conflict. [ ] With that lessened degree of deference to Blue Cross' discretionary interpretation of the group insurance contract, we turn to review Blue Cross' decision to deny benefits.

[The court then described the high dose chemotherapy, autologous bone marrow transplantation procedure, ed.]

* * *

Without consideration of a potential bone marrow transplant, treatment of blood cancer by chemotherapy and radiation is accordingly clearly covered by the contract.

* * *

* * * [T]he contract as amended November 30, 1990, provides that an autologous bone marrow transplant for multiple myeloma and "services or supplies for or related to" the transplant are excluded from the plan's coverage.

Blue Cross argues that the language excluding "services or supplies for or related to" the autologous bone marrow transplant reaches to exclude high-dose chemotherapy and radiation treatments because without the autologous bone marrow transplant, the high-dose chemotherapy could not be performed. * * * We believe that such an argument misdirects the analysis required for determining the scope of coverage and fails to accommodate harmoniously all provisions of the contract.

The bone marrow transplant, while necessary to avoid a disastrous side effect, is not the procedure designed to treat the cancer. The first question to be asked, therefore, is whether the cancer treating procedure is covered by the contract, and, as already noted, we have found it is. While Blue Cross is well within its rights to exclude from coverage the ancillary bone marrow transplant procedure, the exclusion should not, in the absence of clear language, be construed to withdraw coverage explicitly granted elsewhere in the contract.

* * *

We additionally note that in determining whether a decision has been made solely for the benefit of the participants, we may take account of the principle that in making a reasonable decision, ambiguity which remains in the scope of the "related to" language must be construed against the drafting party, particularly when, as here, the contract is a form provided by the insurer rather than one negotiated between the parties. [ ]

Because Blue Cross' discretionary interpretation to the contrary is not entitled to the deference we might otherwise accord, * * * we will construe the contract for the benefit of its beneficiaries and enforce the coverage provided by Part 3 of the group insurance contract and not otherwise explicitly excluded.

* * *

AFFIRMED IN PART, REVERSED IN PART, AND REMANDED FOR FURTHER PROCEEDINGS.

Notes and Questions

1. Section 502(a) of ERISA permits a plan participant or beneficiary to sue to "recover benefits due to him under the terms of the plan * * * " in federal or state court. 29 U.S.C.A. § 1132(a)(1). Though on its face this provision permits a suit against a plan for benefits denied, the courts have treated it instead as authorizing a review of the decision of the ERISA plan, i.e. the ERISA administrator is treated as an independent decisionmaker whose decision is subject to judicial review, much like an administrative agency, rather than as a defendant who has allegedly wronged the claimant. See Jay Conison, Suits for Benefits Under ERISA, 54 Univ. Pitt. L. Rev. 1 (1992).

As the principal case notes, Firestone Tire & Rubber Co. v. Bruch, 489 U.S. 101, 109 S.Ct. 948, 103 L.Ed.2d 80 (1989), held that the courts should apply de novo review in reviewing ERISA plan decisions. In doing so the Court rejected the "arbitrary and capricious" standard of review generally applied in earlier lower federal court ERISA review cases. The Court went on to observe, however, that arbitrary and capricious review, rather than de novo review, would apply if "the benefit plan gives the administrator or fiduciary discretionary authority to determine eligibility for benefits or to construe the terms of the plan." 489 U.S. at 115, 109 S.Ct. at 957.

In doing so, the Court created an exception that swallowed the rule, since post-*Firestone* plans are generally drafted to give the plan administrator discretionary authority. Even where de novo review is available, moreover, some appellate courts have cabined it by limiting judicial review to consideration of the evidence considered by the plan administrator, Perry v. Simplicity Engineering, 900 F.2d 963 (6th Cir.1990); or by retaining deferential review for factual determinations of plan administrators and limiting de novo review to plan interpretations. Pierre v. Connecticut General Life Insurance Company, 932 F.2d 1552 (5th Cir.1991), cert. denied, 502 U.S. 973, 112 S.Ct. 453, 116 L.Ed.2d 470 (1991).

Although *Firestone* authorized arbitrary and capricious review where a plan fiduciary is granted decisionmaking discretion, it also observed that if "an administrator or fiduciary * * * is operating under a conflict of interest, that conflict must be weighed as a 'facto[r] in determining whether there is an abuse of discretion.' " 489 U.S. at 114.

The lower courts are sharply divided in their approaches to determining whether an administrator faces a conflict of interest in making the benefit determination, and what effect a conflict should have on the level of review if one is found. See Judith C. Brostron, The Conflict of Interest Standard in ERISA cases: Can it be Avoided in the Denial of High Dose Chemotherapy Treatment for Breast Cancer, 3 DePaul J. Health Care L. 1 (1999); Haavi Morreim, Benefits

Decisions in ERISA Plans: Diminishing Deference to Fiduciaries and an Emerging Problem for Provider Sponsored Organizations, 65 Tenn L Rev. 511 (1998).

At one end of the spectrum, courts hold that if the plaintiff demonstrates that the fiduciary is operating under a substantial conflict of interest, the fiduciary's decision is afforded little deference. See Killian v. Healthsource, 152 F.3d 514 (6th Cir.1998); McGraw v. Prudential Ins. Co. 137 F.3d 1253 (10th Cir.1998). Indeed, some go so far as to hold the decision to be "presumptively void". See Armstrong v. Aetna Life Ins. Co., 128 F.3d 1263 (8th Cir.1997); Brown v. Blue Cross & Blue Shield, 898 F.2d 1556, 1566–67 (11th Cir.1990). Courts applying this test tend to assume that an insurer or self-insured company faces a conflict almost by definition, since approval of any particular claim reduces its profits. See Killian v. Healthsource Provident Administrators, 152 F.3d 514, 521 (6th Cir.1998); Peruzzi v. Summa Med. Plan, 137 F.3d 431, 433 (6th Cir.1998); Edmonds v. Hughes Aircraft Co., 145 F.3d 1324 (4th Cir.1998). Under this "presumptively void" test, a decision rendered by a plan fiduciary operating under a substantial conflict of interest is presumed to be arbitrary and capricious unless the administrator can demonstrate that either (1) the result reached would nevertheless be found to be "right" if subjected to de novo review, or (2) the decision was not made to serve the administrator's conflicting interest.

Courts at the other end of the spectrum insist that conflicts of interest are rarely a problem because of market competition. The denial of any one claim by a benefit plan, they contend, has a negligible effect on the profit margins of a plan, but routine denial of claims will give a plan a bad reputation and make it less competitive. See Mers v. Marriott International Group Accidental Death & Dismemberment Plan, 144 F.3d 1014 (7th Cir.1998); Farley v. Arkansas Blue Cross and Blue Shield, 147 F.3d 774 (8th Cir.1998). Under this interpretation, arbitrary and capricious review, untempered by consideration of conflicting interests, is almost always appropriate.

Courts in the middle take interest conflicts into account only if the plaintiff can show both that a substantial conflict of interest exists and that the conflict in fact caused a breach of the fiduciary's duty and motivated an improper decision See Friedrich v. Intel Corp., 181 F.3d 1105 (9th Cir.1999); Barnhart v. UNUM Life Ins. Co., 179 F.3d 583, 588 (8th Cir.1999); Atwood v. Newmont Gold, Inc. 45 F.3d 1317, 1322 (9th Cir.1995); Elsroth v. Consolidated Edison Co., 10 F.Supp.2d 427 (S.D.N.Y.1998); Sullivan v. LTV Aerospace and Defense Co., 82 F.3d 1251 (2d Cir.1996). For example, the failure of a plan to consult independent reviewers in processing a claim, Woo v. Deluxe Corp., 144 F.3d 1157 (8th Cir.1998); McGraw v. Prudential Ins. Co. of America, 137 F.3d 1253 (10th Cir.1998), or to follow internal plan procedures, Friedrich v. Intel Corp., 181 F.3d 1105 (9th Cir.1999), are evidence of improper decisionmaking. On the other hand, decisions made through the use of independent consultants or by salaried employees who do not face direct incentives to approve or deny claims, or through the application of fair procedures, will generally be accepted. See Hendrix v. Standard Ins. Co., 182 F.3d 925 (9th Cir.1999); Jones v. Kodak Medical Assistance Plan, 169 F.3d 1287 (10th Cir.1999); Hightshue v. AIG Life Ins. Co., 135 F.3d 1144 (7th Cir.1998). Other courts apply a "sliding scale" approach, using an abuse of discretion review standard, but exercising greater scrutiny where a greater conflict is found. See Chambers v. Family Health Plan Corp., 100 F.3d 818, 825 (10th Cir.1996); Sullivan v. LTV Aerospace & Defense Co., 82 F.3d 1251, 1255 (2d Cir.1996); Taft v. Equitable Life Assurance Soc'y, 9 F.3d 1469, 1474 (9th Cir.1993); Van Boxel v. Journal Co. Employees' Pension Trust, 836 F.2d 1048, 1052–53 (7th Cir.1987). Most courts have held that the finding of a conflict of interest does not result in the abandonment of the arbitrary and capricious standard, but rather in giving it "more bite." A few courts, however, apply de novo review when a conflict is found.

What deference, if any, should federal courts afford plan administrators in reviewing ERISA benefit decisions? Should plan drafters be permitted to evade de novo review simply by drafting plan documents to give discretion to plan administrators? Do the interests of plan administrators inevitably conflict with the interests of plan participants and beneficiaries? Does the degree of conflict vary depending on whether the administrator is a self-insured employer, a third-party administrator for a self-insured employer, a risk-bearing insurer, a trust affiliated with a labor union, or a multiple employer trust that administers health benefits for a number of small employers? Should the court in Doe have considered the fact that Blue Cross plans are non-profit? Does the market for insurance in fact correct the conflict-of-interest problem? Should courts be permitted to consider evidence not presented initially to plan administrators when they review plan decisions, or should they be limited to reviewing the plan administrator's decision on the record? Might concern on the part of federal courts about being swamped by insurance claims affect the eagerness of the courts to review these claims? Should it?

2. Whether or not extracontractual damages can ever be available under ERISA is a question that has provoked considerable controversy. At this point the answer seems to be no, though a good argument can be made that this is not the result Congress intended. See George Flint, ERISA: Extracontractual Damages Mandated for Benefit Claims Actions, 36 Ariz. L. Rev. 611 (1994); Note, Available Remedies Under ERISA Section 502(a), 45 Ala. L. Rev. 631 (1994). In Massachusetts Mutual Life Insurance Co. v. Russell, 473 U.S. 134, 105 S.Ct. 3085, 87 L.E.2d 96 (1985), the Supreme Court held that ERISA does not authorize recovery of extracontractual damages by plan participants for breach of fiduciary duty. In Mertens v. Hewitt Associates, 508 U.S. 248, 113 S.Ct. 2063, 124 L.Ed.2d 161 (1993), the Court read provisions of ERISA permitting plan participants and beneficiaries "to obtain other appropriate equitable relief(i) to redress such violations ..." (29 U.S.C.A. § 1132(a)(3)) to not authorize damage actions, as damages are not equitable in nature.

The Supreme Court, however, in its most recent ERISA case to address this issue, held that 29 U.S.C.A. § 1132(a)(3) does authorize individual beneficiaries the right to sue for equitable relief for breaches of fiduciary duty. Varity Corp. v. Howe, 516 U.S. 489, 116 S.Ct. 1065, 134 L.Ed.2d 130 (1996). This case breaks from a long line of cases limiting ERISA relief, and might signal openness on the part of the court to entertaining claims for broader relief for plan participants and beneficiaries.

The effect of these cases is that an ERISA participant or beneficiary denied benefits can only recover the value of the claim itself and cannot recover damages caused by the claim denial. Punitive damages are also unavailable against plan administrators and fiduciaries under even the most egregious circumstances. What effect might the lack of this relief have on ERISA fiduciaries and administrators? To what extent might the fact that ERISA permits courts to award attorneys fees ameliorate this effect? 29 U.S.C.A. § 1132(g).

3. While ERISA preempts state common law, federal courts have, with some hesitancy, developed federal common law in ERISA cases. See Jayne Zanglein, Closing the Gap: Safeguarding Participants' Rights by Expanding the Federal Common Law of ERISA, 72 Wash. U.L Q. 671 (1994); William Carr & Robert Liebross, Wrongs Without Rights: The Need for A Strong Federal Common Law of

ERISA, 4 Stanford L & Pol'y Rev. 221 (1993). Under what circumstances might federal common law or equitable doctrine apply? See Kane v. Aetna Life Insurance, 893 F.2d 1283 (11th Cir.1990), cert. denied, 498 U.S. 890, 111 S.Ct. 232, 112 L.Ed.2d 192 (1990) (court can apply equitable estoppel to interpret but not to change the terms of an ERISA plan); Nash v. Trustees of Boston University, 946 F.2d 960 (1st Cir.1991) (fraud in the inducement can be raised as an affirmative defense in ERISA case); but see Watkins v. Westinghouse Hanford Co., 12 F.3d 1517 (9th Cir.1993) (equitable doctrines may not be relied on to provide remedies not available under ERISA). Should the federal courts adopt state common law of insurance in interpreting ERISA policies, or do different considerations govern in ERISA cases? In particular, could a court apply the contract interpretation principles applied in *HealthChicago* in an ERISA case?

4. ERISA does not by its terms permit providers to sue plans. Courts have generally rejected the argument that providers are "beneficiaries" under ERISA plans. Pritt v. Blue Cross & Blue Shield, Inc., 699 F.Supp. 81 (S.D.W.Va.1988). Providers have been more successful in asserting their rights as assignees of participants and beneficiaries, City of Hope National Medical Center v. Healthplus, Inc., 156 F.3d 223 (1st Cir.1998); Hermann Hosp. v. MEBA Medical & Benefits Plan, 845 F.2d 1286 (5th Cir.1988), though a few courts have held that assignees have no standing to sue as they are not mentioned as protected parties within the statute. Other courts have upheld anti-assignment clauses in plan contracts.

Courts have split on whether providers can recover from insurers when the insurer leads the provider to believe that the insured or the service is covered, and then subsequently refuses payment and claims ERISA protection. Several courts have held that ERISA is intended to control relationships between employers and employees and should not preempt common law or statutory misrepresentation claims brought by providers. Transitional Hospitals Corp. v. Blue Cross & Blue Shield of Texas, 164 F.3d 952 (5th Cir.1999); Hospice of Metro Denver, Inc. v. Group Health Ins. of Okla., Inc., 944 F.2d 752 (10th Cir.1991). Other courts have held that misrepresentation claims are claims for benefits that are preempted by ERISA. Cromwell v. Equicor–Equitable HCA Corp., 944 F.2d 1272 (6th Cir.1991), cert. denied, 505 U.S. 1233, 113 S.Ct. 2, 120 L.Ed.2d 931 (1992). Finally, several courts have allowed a provider to sue an ERISA plan on a contract claim, stating that the claim was not preempted by ERISA because the provider had no standing to sue under ERISA. See, generally, Jeffrey A. Brauch, Health Care Providers Meet ERISA: Are Provider Claims for Misrepresentation of Coverage Preempted: 20 Pepperdine L. Rev. 497 (1993); David P. Kallus, ERISA: Do Health Care Providers Have Standing to Bring a Civil Enforcement Action Under Section 1132(a)? 30 Santa Clara L. Rev. 173 (1990)

5. ERISA also requires health benefit plans to acknowledge and effectuate "qualified medical child support orders." These are state court orders that require a group health plan that covers dependents to extend group medical coverage to the children of a plan participant, even though the participant does not have legal custody of the children. 29 U.S.C.A. § 1169. Under this law, adopted in 1993, a plan participant can be required under court order to pay for family coverage to cover a dependent child not in the parent's custody, even though the parent might have otherwise chosen not to purchase coverage. Who benefits from this law, other than the children it protects?

Problem: ERISA Litigation

John Mendez is in the advanced stages of a condition that results in degeneration of his nervous system. His doctor believes that he would be helped by a new gene therapy. John receives coverage under his employer's self-insured employee benefits plan. The plan has denied coverage for the therapy, claiming that it is experimental. The terms of the plan give the administrator discretion to decide whether or not to cover experimental procedures, but does not define "experimental." John's doctor claims that the procedure is still quite new, but has advanced beyond the experimental stage. What standard will a court apply in reviewing the administrator's decision if John sues under § 502? How does this standard differ from that a court would have applied had John sued an insurer under an individual health insurance policy under standard state insurance contract law?

2. *Administrative Claims and Appeals Procedures Under ERISA*

29 U.S.C.A. § 1133 provides:

In accordance with regulations of the Secretary, every employee benefit plan shall—

(1) provide adequate notice in writing to any participant or beneficiary whose claim for benefits under the plan has been denied, setting forth the specific reasons for such denial, written in a manner calculated to be understood by the participant, and

(2) afford a reasonable opportunity to any participant whose claim for benefits has been denied for a full and fair review by the appropriate named fiduciary of the decision denying the claim.

The Department of Labor promulgated regulations in 1977 permitting an aggrieved ERISA participant to request a review of a decision, review pertinent documents, submit issues and comments in writing, and receive a written decision, including specific reasons for the decision and reference to specific plan provisions on which it is based, usually within 60 days. As indemnification insurance faded into history, and managed care came to the fore, these regulations seemed increasingly archaic. In 1998 then President Clinton directed the Department of Labor to promulgate new ERISA claims procedure regulations to implement recommendations of the President's Advisory Commission on Consumer Protection and Quality in the Health Care Industry, which had issued its final report early that year. Proposed regulations were issued in the fall of 1998, and then sat for two years as the Department mulled over more than 700 letters of comment and heard more than sixty speakers at public hearings. Finally late in November, 2000, again under orders from President Clinton, now in the last few days of his administration, DOL finally issued the final rules.

20 C.F.R. § 2560.503–1 CLAIMS PROCEDURE.

* * *

(b) Every employee benefit plan shall establish and maintain reasonable procedures governing the filing of benefit claims, notification of benefit determinations, and appeal of adverse benefit determinations * * *. The claims procedures for a plan will be deemed to be reasonable only if—

(1) The claims procedures comply with the [procedural requirements of this regulation] * * *;

(2) A description of all claims procedures (including, in the case of a group health plan * * *, any procedures for obtaining prior approval as a prerequisite for obtaining a benefit, such as preauthorization procedures or utilization review procedures) and the applicable time frames is included as part of a summary plan description * * * [a document each plan member must get; describing the plan];

(3) The claims procedures do not contain any provision, and are not administered in a way, that unduly inhibits or hampers the initiation or processing of claims for benefits. For example, a provision or practice that requires payment of a fee or costs as a condition to making a claim or to appealing an adverse benefit determination would be considered to unduly inhibit the initiation and processing of claims for benefits. Also, the denial of a claim for failure to obtain a prior approval under circumstances that would make obtaining such prior approval impossible or where application of the prior approval process could seriously jeopardize the life or health of the claimant (e.g., in the case of a group health plan, the claimant is unconscious and in need of immediate care at the time medical treatment is required) would constitute a practice that unduly inhibits the initiation and processing of a claim;

(4) The claims procedures do not preclude an authorized representative of a claimant from acting on behalf of such claimant in pursuing a benefit claim or appeal of an adverse benefit determination. * * * [I]n the case of a claim involving urgent care, * * *, a health care professional, * * * with knowledge of a claimant's medical condition shall be permitted to act as the authorized representative of the claimant; and

(5) The claims procedures contain administrative processes and safeguards designed to ensure and to verify that benefit claim determinations are made in accordance with governing plan documents and that, where appropriate, the plan provisions have been applied consistently with respect to similarly situated claimants.

(6) In the case of a plan established and maintained pursuant to a collective bargaining agreement * * *—

(i) Such plan will be deemed to comply with the [claims determination and appeal] provisions of * * * this section if the collective bargaining agreement * * * sets forth or incorporates by specific reference—

(A) Provisions concerning the filing of benefit claims and the initial disposition of benefit claims, and

(B) A grievance and arbitration procedure to which adverse benefit determinations are subject.

(ii) Such plan will be deemed to comply with the [appeal] provisions of * * * this section (but will not be deemed to comply with [the claims determination] paragraphs * * *) if the collective bargaining agreement pursuant to which the plan is established or maintained sets forth or incorporates by specific reference a grievance and arbitration procedure to which adverse benefit determinations are subject (but not provisions concerning the filing and initial disposition of benefit claims).

(c) Group health plans. The claims procedures of a group health plan will be deemed to be reasonable only if, in addition to complying with the requirements of paragraph (b) of this section—

(1)(i) The claims procedures provide that, in the case of a failure by a claimant or an authorized representative of a claimant to follow the plan's procedures for filing a pre-service claim, * * * the claimant or representative shall be notified of the failure and the proper procedures to be followed in filing a claim for benefits. This notification shall be provided to the claimant or authorized representative, as appropriate, as soon as possible, but not later than 5 days (24 hours in the case of a failure to file a claim involving urgent care) following the failure. * * *

* * *

(ii) Paragraph (c)(1)(i) of this section shall apply only in the case of a failure that—

(A) Is a communication by a claimant or an authorized representative of a claimant that is received by a person or organizational unit customarily responsible for handling benefit matters; and

(B) Is a communication that names a specific claimant; a specific medical condition or symptom; and a specific treatment, service, or product for which approval is requested.

(2) The claims procedures do not contain any provision, and are not administered in a way, that requires a claimant to file more than two appeals of an adverse benefit determination prior to bringing a civil action under section 502(a) of the Act;

(3) To the extent that a plan offers voluntary levels of appeal (except to the extent that the plan is required to do so by State law), including voluntary arbitration or any other form of dispute resolution, in addition to those permitted by paragraph (c)(2) of this section, the claims procedures provide that:

(i) The plan waives any right to assert that a claimant has failed to exhaust administrative remedies because the claimant did not elect to submit a benefit dispute to any such voluntary level of appeal provided by the plan;

(ii) The plan agrees that any statute of limitations or other defense based on timeliness is tolled during the time that any such voluntary appeal is pending;

(iii) The claims procedures provide that a claimant may elect to submit a benefit dispute to such voluntary level of appeal only after exhaustion of the appeals permitted by paragraph (c)(2) of this section;

(iv) The plan provides to any claimant, upon request, sufficient information relating to the voluntary level of appeal to enable the claimant to make an informed judgment about whether to submit a benefit dispute to the voluntary level of appeal, including a statement that the decision of a claimant as to whether or not to submit a benefit dispute to the voluntary level of appeal will have no effect on the claimant's rights to any other benefits under the plan and information about the applicable rules, the claimant's right to representation, the process for selecting the decisionmaker, and the circumstances, if any, that may affect the impartiality of the decisionmaker, such as any financial or personal interests in the result or any past or present relationship with any party to the review process; and

(v) No fees or costs are imposed on the claimant as part of the voluntary level of appeal.

(4) The claims procedures do not contain any provision for the mandatory arbitration of adverse benefit determinations, except to the extent that the plan or procedures provide that:

(i) The arbitration is conducted as one of the two appeals described in paragraph (c)(2) of this section and in accordance with the requirements applicable to such appeals; and

(ii) The claimant is not precluded from challenging the decision under section 502(a) of the Act or other applicable law.

* * *

(f) Timing of notification of benefit determination.

* * *

(2) Group health plans.

* * *

(i) Urgent care claims. In the case of a claim involving urgent care, the plan administrator shall notify the claimant of the plan's benefit determination (whether adverse or not) as soon as possible, taking into account the medical exigencies, but not later than 72 hours after receipt of the claim by the plan, unless the claimant fails to provide sufficient information to determine whether, or to what extent, benefits are covered or payable under the plan. In the case of such a failure, the plan administrator shall notify the claimant as soon as possible, but not later than 24 hours after receipt of the claim by the plan, of the specific information necessary to complete the claim. * * * The plan administrator shall notify the claimant of the plan's benefit determination as soon as possible, but in no case later than 48 hours after the earlier of—

(A) The plan's receipt of the specified information, or

(B) The end of the period afforded the claimant to provide the specified additional information.

(ii) Concurrent care decisions. If a group health plan has approved an ongoing course of treatment to be provided over a period of time or number of treatments—

(A) Any reduction or termination by the plan of such course of treatment (other than by plan amendment or termination) before the end of such period of time or number of treatments shall constitute an adverse benefit determination. The plan administrator shall notify the claimant, * * * of the adverse benefit determination at a time sufficiently in advance of the reduction or termination to allow the claimant to appeal and obtain a determination on review of that adverse benefit determination before the benefit is reduced or terminated.

(B) Any request by a claimant to extend the course of treatment beyond the period of time or number of treatments that is a claim involving urgent care shall be decided as soon as possible, taking into account the medical exigencies, and the plan administrator shall notify the claimant of the benefit determination, whether adverse or not, within 24 hours after receipt of the claim by the plan, provided that any such claim is made to the plan at least 24 hours prior to the expiration of the prescribed period of time or number of treatments. * * *

(iii) Other claims.

(A) Pre-service claims. In the case of a pre-service claim, the plan administrator shall notify the claimant of the plan's benefit determination (whether adverse or not) within a reasonable period of time appropriate to the medical circumstances, but not later than 15 days after receipt of the claim by the plan. This period may be extended one time by the plan for up to 15 days, provided that the plan administrator both determines that such an extension is necessary due to matters beyond the control of the plan and notifies the claimant, prior to the expiration of the initial 15–day period, of the circumstances requiring the extension of time and the date by which the plan expects to render a decision. * * *

(B) Post-service claims. In the case of a post-service claim, the plan administrator shall notify the claimant, in accordance with paragraph (g) of this section, of the plan's adverse benefit determination within a reasonable period of time, but not later than 30 days after receipt of the claim [subject to one 15 day extension if necessary due to matters beyond the plan's control].* * *

* * *

(g) Manner and content of notification of benefit determination. (1) Except as provided in paragraph (g)(2) of this section, the plan administrator shall provide a claimant with written or electronic notification of any adverse benefit determination. * * * The notification shall set forth, in a manner calculated to be understood by the claimant—

(i) The specific reason or reasons for the adverse determination;

(ii) Reference to the specific plan provisions on which the determination is based;

(iii) A description of any additional material or information necessary for the claimant to perfect the claim and an explanation of why such material or information is necessary;

(iv) A description of the plan's review procedures and the time limits applicable to such procedures, including a statement of the claimant's right to bring a civil action under section 502(a) of the Act following an adverse benefit determination on review;

(v) In the case of an adverse benefit determination by a group health plan or a plan providing disability benefits,

(A) If an internal rule, guideline, protocol, or other similar criterion was relied upon in making the adverse determination, either the specific rule, guideline, protocol, or other similar criterion; or a statement that such a rule, guideline, protocol, or other similar criterion was relied upon in making the adverse determination and that a copy of such rule, guideline, protocol, or other criterion will be provided free of charge to the claimant upon request; or

(B) If the adverse benefit determination is based on a medical necessity or experimental treatment or similar exclusion or limit, either an explanation of the scientific or clinical judgment for the determination, applying the terms of the plan to the claimant's medical circumstances, or a statement that such explanation will be provided free of charge upon request.

(vi) In the case of an adverse benefit determination by a group health plan concerning a claim involving urgent care, a description of the expedited review process applicable to such claims.

* * *

(h) Appeal of adverse benefit determinations.

* * *

(3) Group health plans. The claims procedures of a group health plan will not be deemed to provide a claimant with a reasonable opportunity for a full and fair review of a claim and adverse benefit determination unless * * * the claims procedures—

(i) Provide claimants at least 180 days * * * within which to appeal the determination;

(ii) Provide for a review that does not afford deference to the initial adverse benefit determination and that is conducted by an appropriate named fiduciary of the plan who is neither the individual who made the adverse benefit determination that is the subject of the appeal, nor the subordinate of such individual;

(iii) Provide that, in deciding an appeal of any adverse benefit determination that is based in whole or in part on a medical judgment, including determinations with regard to whether a particular treatment, drug, or other item is experimental, investigational, or not medically necessary or appropriate, the appropriate named fiduciary shall consult with a health care professional who has appropriate training and experience in the field of medicine involved in the medical judgment;

(iv) Provide for the identification of medical or vocational experts whose advice was obtained on behalf of the plan in connection with a claimant's adverse benefit determination, * * *;

(v) Provide that the health care professional engaged for purposes of a consultation * * * shall be an individual who is neither an individual who was consulted in connection with the adverse benefit determination that is the subject of the appeal, nor the subordinate of any such individual; and

(vi) Provide, in the case of a claim involving urgent care, for an expedited review process * * *

* * *

(k) Preemption of State law. (1) Nothing in this section shall be construed to supersede any provision of State law that regulates insurance, except to the extent that such law prevents the application of a requirement of this section.

(2) (i) For purposes of paragraph (k)(1) of this section, a State law regulating insurance shall not be considered to prevent the application of a requirement of this section merely because such State law establishes a review procedure to evaluate and resolve disputes involving adverse benefit determinations under group health plans so long as the review procedure is conducted by a person or entity other than the insurer, the plan, plan fiduciaries, the employer, or any employee or agent of any of the foregoing.

(ii) The State law procedures described in paragraph (k)(2)(i) of this section are not part of the full and fair review required by section 503 of the Act. Claimants therefore need not exhaust such State law procedures prior to bringing suit under section 502(a) of the Act.

(*l*) Failure to establish and follow reasonable claims procedures. In the case of the failure of a plan to establish or follow claims procedures consistent with the requirements of this section, a claimant shall be deemed to have exhausted the administrative remedies available under the plan and shall be entitled to pursue any available remedies under section 502(a) of the Act on the basis that the plan has failed to provide a reasonable claims procedure that would yield a decision on the merits of the claim.

(m) Definitions. The following terms shall have the meaning ascribed to such terms in this paragraph (m) whenever such term is used in this section:

(1)(i) A "claim involving urgent care" is any claim for medical care or treatment with respect to which the application of the time periods for making non-urgent care determinations—

(A) Could seriously jeopardize the life or health of the claimant or the ability of the claimant to regain maximum function, or,

(B) In the opinion of a physician with knowledge of the claimant's medical condition, would subject the claimant to severe pain that cannot be adequately managed without the care or treatment that is the subject of the claim.

(ii) Except as provided in paragraph (m)(1)(iii) of this section, whether a claim is a "claim involving urgent care" within the meaning of paragraph (m)(1)(i)(A) of this section is to be determined by an individual acting on behalf of the plan applying the judgment of a prudent layperson who possesses an average knowledge of health and medicine.

(iii) Any claim that a physician with knowledge of the claimant's medical condition determines is a "claim involving urgent care" within the meaning of paragraph (m)(1)(i) of this section shall be treated as a "claim involving urgent care" for purposes of this section.

* * *

[The rules also provide time frames for appeals, 72 hours for urgent care claims, 30 days for pre-service claims (or 15 days for each stage if two stage appeals are provided), and 60 days for post-service plans. The information that the plan must provide in an adverse appeal decision is similar to that which must be provided under an initial adverse decision.]

Notes and Questions

1. As is discussed in the next chapter, all states have adopted laws prescribing internal review procedures for health plans, and many require external reviews as well. Are these state law provisions enforceable under this regulation? In what respects does this regulation supplement state law?

2. Under what circumstances does the regulation permit arbitration of health care claims? Why does it limit plans to two stage appeals? The 1998 proposed regulations prohibited plan provisions that required claimants to submit claims to arbitration or to file more than one appeal. Can you see why these provisions proved quite controversial?

3. A number of other provisions of the proposed rule proved controversial. Representatives of employers, plans, and plan administrators opposed the provisions of the proposed rule requiring plans to disclose the internal rules, protocols and guidelines on which their decisions were based. Why would they have objected to this requirement? To what extent did they win this battle? Employer and plan representatives did convince the Department not to include a rule it had considered that would have required plans to disclose "after an adverse benefit determination on review, documents and records relating to previous claims involving the same diagnosis and treatment decided by the plan within the five years prior to the adverse benefit determination (up to a maximum of 50 such claims)." 65 Fed. Reg. 70246, 70251. What purpose would such a requirement have served? Why was it abandoned?

4. The Department did not require external reviews, which it considered beyond its authority under the statute set out above.

Problem: Beneficiary Protection Under State Law and ERISA

Review the problems following the Massachusetts managed care regulation statute in the preceding chapter. Which of these problems are addressed by the new ERISA rules, and which are not? How, if at all, do the ERISA rules change the rights that members of insured employment-related managed care plans would be entitled to under the state statute? How does it change the rights to which members of self-insured ERISA plans would be entitled? In particular, how do the rules affect the external review scheme created by the Massachusetts statute? Are the state or federal rules more protective of plan members?

E. PROVIDER FIDUCIARY OBLIGATIONS UNDER ERISA

Subscribers have claimed that managed care's cost-conserving strategies are a breach of ERISA fiduciary obligations. The Supreme Court laid this claim to rest.

PEGRAM v. HERDRICH

Supreme Court of the United States, 2000.
530 U.S. 211, 120 S.Ct. 2143, 147 L.Ed.2d 164.

JUSTICE SOUTER delivered the opinion of the Court.

The question in this case is whether treatment decisions made by a health maintenance organization, acting through its physician employees, are fiduciary acts within the meaning of the Employee Retirement Income Security Act of 1974 (ERISA) [ ]. We hold that they are not.

I

Petitioners, Carle Clinic Association, P. C., Health Alliance Medical Plans, Inc., and Carle Health Insurance Management Co., Inc. (collectively Carle) function as a health maintenance organization (HMO) organized for profit. Its owners are physicians providing prepaid medical services to participants whose employers contract with Carle to provide such coverage. Respondent, Cynthia Herdrich, was covered by Carle through her husband's employer, State Farm Insurance Company.

The events in question began when a Carle physician, petitioner Lori Pegram, examined Herdrich, who was experiencing pain in the midline area of her groin. Six days later, Dr. Pegram discovered a six by eight centimeter inflamed mass in Herdrich's abdomen. Despite the noticeable inflammation, Dr. Pegram did not order an ultrasound diagnostic procedure at a local hospital, but decided that Herdrich would have to wait eight more days for an ultrasound, to be performed at a facility staffed by Carle more than 50 miles away. Before the eight days were over, Herdrich's appendix ruptured, causing peritonitis. [ ]

Herdrich sued Pegram and Carle in state court for medical malpractice, and she later added two counts charging state-law fraud. Carle and Pegram responded that ERISA preempted the new counts, and removed the case to federal court, where they then sought summary judgment on the state-law fraud counts. The District Court granted their motion as to the second fraud count but granted Herdrich leave to amend the one remaining. This she did by alleging that provision of medical services under the terms of the Carle HMO organization, rewarding its physician owners for limiting medical care, entailed an inherent or anticipatory breach of an ERISA fiduciary duty, since these terms created an incentive to make decisions in the physicians' self-interest, rather than the exclusive interests of plan participants.[5]

5. The specific allegations were these:

"11. Defendants are fiduciaries with respect to the Plan and under 29 [U.S.C. §]1109(a) are obligated to discharge their duties with respect to the Plan solely in the interest of the participants and beneficiaries and "a. for the exclusive purpose of:

"i. providing benefits to participants and their beneficiaries; and

"ii. defraying reasonable expenses of administering the Plan;

"b. with the care, skill, prudence, and diligence under the circumstances then prevailing that a prudent man acting in a like capacity and familiar with such matters would use in the conduct of an enterprise of a like character and like aims.

"12. In breach of that duty:

"a. CARLE owner/physicians are the officers and directors of HAMP and CHIMCO and receive a year-end distribution, based in large part upon, supplemental medical expense payments made to CARLE by HAMP and CHIMCO;

"b. Both HAMP and CHIMCO are directed and controlled by CARLE owner/physicians and seek to fund their supplemental medical expense payments to CARLE:

"i. by contracting with CARLE owner/physicians to provide the medical services contemplated in the Plan and then having those contracted owner/physicians:

"(1) minimize the use of diagnostic tests;

"(2) minimize the use of facilities not owned by CARLE; and

"(3) minimize the use of emergency and non-emergency consultation and/or referrals to non-contracted physicians.

"ii. by administering disputed and non-routine health insurance claims and determining:

"(1) which claims are covered under the Plan and to what extent;

"(2) what the applicable standard of care is;

Herdrich sought relief under 29 U.S.C. § 1109(a), which provides that

[a]ny person who is a fiduciary with respect to a plan who breaches any of the responsibilities, obligations, or duties imposed upon fiduciaries by this subchapter shall be personally liable to make good to such plan any losses to the plan resulting from each such breach, and to restore to such plan any profits of such fiduciary which have been made through use of assets of the plan by the fiduciary, and shall be subject to such other equitable or remedial relief as the court may deem appropriate, including removal of such fiduciary.

When Carle moved to dismiss the ERISA count for failure to state a claim upon which relief could be granted, the District Court granted the motion, accepting the Magistrate Judge's determination that Carle was not "involved [in these events] as" an ERISA fiduciary. App. to Pet. for Cert. 63a. The original malpractice counts were then tried to a jury, and Herdrich prevailed on both, receiving $35,000 in compensation for her injury. 154 F.3d, at 367. She then appealed the dismissal of the ERISA claim to the Court of Appeals for the Seventh Circuit, which reversed. The court held that Carle was acting as a fiduciary when its physicians made the challenged decisions and that Herdrich's allegations were sufficient to state a claim:

"Our decision does not stand for the proposition that the existence of incentives automatically gives rise to a breach of fiduciary duty. Rather, we hold that incentives can rise to the level of a breach where, as pleaded here, the fiduciary trust between plan participants and plan fiduciaries no longer exists (i.e., where physicians delay providing necessary treatment to, or withhold administering proper care to, plan beneficiaries for the sole purpose of increasing their bonuses)." Id., at 373.

We granted certiorari [ ] and now reverse the Court of Appeals.

II

Whether Carle is a fiduciary when it acts through its physician owners as pleaded in the ERISA count depends on some background of fact and law about HMO organizations, medical benefit plans, fiduciary obligation, and the meaning of Herdrich's allegations.

A

Traditionally, medical care in the United States has been provided on a "fee-for-service" basis. A physician charges so much for a general physical exam, a vaccination, a tonsillectomy, and so on. The physician bills the patient for services provided or, if there is insurance and the doctor is willing, submits the bill for the patient's care to the insurer, for payment subject to the terms of the insurance agreement. [ ] In a fee-for-service system, a physician's financial incentive is to provide more care, not less, so long as payment is forthcoming. The check on this incentive is a physician's obligation to exercise reasonable medical skill and judgment in the patient's interest.

"(3) whether a course of treatment is experimental;

"(4) whether a course of treatment is reasonable and customary; and

"(5) whether a medical condition is an emergency." App. to Pet. for Cert. 85a–86a.

Beginning in the late 1960's, insurers and others developed new models for health-care delivery, including HMOs. [ ] The defining feature of an HMO is receipt of a fixed fee for each patient enrolled under the terms of a contract to provide specified health care if needed. The HMO thus assumes the financial risk of providing the benefits promised: if a participant never gets sick, the HMO keeps the money regardless, and if a participant becomes expensively ill, the HMO is responsible for the treatment agreed upon even if its cost exceeds the participant's premiums.

Like other risk-bearing organizations, HMOs take steps to control costs. At the least, HMOs, like traditional insurers, will in some fashion make coverage determinations, scrutinizing requested services against the contractual provisions to make sure that a request for care falls within the scope of covered circumstances (pregnancy, for example), or that a given treatment falls within the scope of the care promised (surgery, for instance). They customarily issue general guidelines for their physicians about appropriate levels of care. See id., at 568–570. And they commonly require utilization review (in which specific treatment decisions are reviewed by a decisionmaker other than the treating physician) and approval in advance (precertification) for many types of care, keyed to standards of medical necessity or the reasonableness of the proposed treatment. [ ] These cost-controlling measures are commonly complemented by specific financial incentives to physicians, rewarding them for decreasing utilization of health-care services, and penalizing them for what may be found to be excessive treatment [ ]. Hence, in an HMO system, a physician's financial interest lies in providing less care, not more. The check on this influence (like that on the converse, fee-for-service incentive) is the professional obligation to provide covered services with a reasonable degree of skill and judgment in the patient's interest. [ ]

The adequacy of professional obligation to counter financial self-interest has been challenged no matter what the form of medical organization. HMOs became popular because fee-for-service physicians were thought to be providing unnecessary or useless services; today, many doctors and other observers argue that HMOs often ignore the individual needs of a patient in order to improve the HMOs' bottom lines. See, e.g., 154 F.3d, at 375–378 (citing various critics of HMOs).[6] In this case, for instance, one could argue that Pegram's decision to wait before getting an ultrasound for Herdrich, and her insistence that the ultrasound be done at a distant facility owned by Carle, reflected an interest in limiting the HMO's expenses, which blinded her to the need for immediate diagnosis and treatment.

B

Herdrich focuses on the Carle scheme's provision for a "year-end distribution," n. 3, supra, to the HMO's physician owners. She argues that this particular incentive device of annually paying physician owners the profit resulting from their own decisions rationing care can distinguish Carle's organization from HMOs generally, so that reviewing Carle's decisions under a fiduciary standard as pleaded in Herdrich's complaint would not open the door to like claims about other HMO structures.

6. There are, of course, contrary perspectives, and we endorse neither side of the debate today.

While the Court of Appeals agreed, we think otherwise, under the law as now written.

Although it is true that the relationship between sparing medical treatment and physician reward is not a subtle one under the Carle scheme, no HMO organization could survive without some incentive connecting physician reward with treatment rationing. The essence of an HMO is that salaries and profits are limited by the HMO's fixed membership fees. [ ] This is not to suggest that the Carle provisions are as socially desirable as some other HMO organizational schemes; they may not be. [ ] But whatever the HMO, there must be rationing and inducement to ration.

Since inducement to ration care goes to the very point of any HMO scheme, and rationing necessarily raises some risks while reducing others (ruptured appendixes are more likely; unnecessary appendectomies are less so), any legal principle purporting to draw a line between good and bad HMOs would embody, in effect, a judgment about socially acceptable medical risk. A valid conclusion of this sort would, however, necessarily turn on facts to which courts would probably not have ready access: correlations between malpractice rates and various HMO models, similar correlations involving fee-for-service models, and so on. And, of course, assuming such material could be obtained by courts in litigation like this, any standard defining the unacceptably risky HMO structure (and consequent vulnerability to claims like Herdrich's) would depend on a judgment about the appropriate level of expenditure for health care in light of the associated malpractice risk. But such complicated factfinding and such a debatable social judgment are not wisely required of courts unless for some reason resort cannot be had to the legislative process, with its preferable forum for comprehensive investigations and judgments of social value, such as optimum treatment levels and health care expenditure. [ ]

We think, then, that courts are not in a position to derive a sound legal principle to differentiate an HMO like Carle from other HMOs. For that reason, we proceed on the assumption that the decisions listed in Herdrich's complaint cannot be subject to a claim that they violate fiduciary standards unless all such decisions by all HMOs acting through their owner or employee physicians are to be judged by the same standards and subject to the same claims.

C

We turn now from the structure of HMOs to the requirements of ERISA. A fiduciary within the meaning of ERISA must be someone acting in the capacity of manager, administrator, or financial adviser to a "plan," see 29 U.S.C. §§ 1002(21)(A)(i)-(iii), and Herdich's ERISA count accordingly charged Carle with a breach of fiduciary duty in discharging its obligations under State Farm's medical plan. App. to Pet. for Cert. 85a–86a. ERISA's definition of an employee welfare benefit plan is ultimately circular: "any plan, fund, or program ... to the extent that such plan, fund, or program was established ... for the purpose of providing ... through the purchase of insurance or otherwise ... medical, surgical, or hospital care or benefits." § 1002(1)(A). One is thus left to the common understanding of the word "plan" as referring to a scheme decided upon in advance, see Webster's New International

Dictionary 1879 (2d ed.1957); Jacobson & Pomfret, Form, Function, and Managed Care Torts: Achieving Fairness and Equity in ERISA Jurisprudence, 35 Houston L.Rev. 985, 1050 (1998). Here the scheme comprises a set of rules that define the rights of a beneficiary and provide for their enforcement. Rules governing collection of premiums, definition of benefits, submission of claims, and resolution of disagreements over entitlement to services are the sorts of provisions that constitute a plan. [ ] Thus, when employers contract with an HMO to provide benefits to employees subject to ERISA, the provisions of documents that set up the HMO are not, as such, an ERISA plan, but the agreement between an HMO and an employer who pays the premiums may, as here, provide elements of a plan by setting out rules under which beneficiaries will be entitled to care.

D

As just noted, fiduciary obligations can apply to managing, advising, and administering an ERISA plan, the fiduciary function addressed by Herdrich's ERISA count being the exercise of "discretionary authority or discretionary responsibility in the administration of [an ERISA] plan," 29 U.S.C. § 1002(21)(A)(iii). And as we have already suggested, although Carle is not an ERISA fiduciary merely because it administers or exercises discretionary authority over its own HMO business, it may still be a fiduciary if it administers the plan.

In general terms, fiduciary responsibility under ERISA is simply stated. The statute provides that fiduciaries shall discharge their duties with respect to a plan "solely in the interest of the participants and beneficiaries," § 1104(a)(1), that is, "for the exclusive purpose of (i) providing benefits to participants and their beneficiaries; and (ii) defraying reasonable expenses of administering the plan," § 1104(a)(1)(A).[7] These responsibilities imposed by ERISA have the familiar ring of their source in the common law of trusts. [ ] Thus, the common law (understood as including what were once the distinct rules of equity) charges fiduciaries with a duty of loyalty to guarantee beneficiaries' interests: "The most fundamental duty owed by the trustee to the beneficiaries of the trust is the duty of loyalty.... It is the duty of a trustee to administer the trust solely in the interest of the beneficiaries." 2A A. Scott & W. Fratcher, Trusts § 170, 311 (4th ed.1987) (hereinafter Scott); see also G. Bogert & G. Bogert, Law of Trusts and Trustees § 543 (rev.2d ed. 1980) ("Perhaps the most fundamental duty of a trustee is that he must display throughout the administration of the trust complete loyalty to the interests of the beneficiary and must exclude all selfish interest and all consideration of the interests of third persons"); Central States, supra, at 570–571, 105 S.Ct. 2833; Meinhard v. Salmon, 249 N.Y. 458, 464, 164 N.E.

7. In addition, fiduciaries must discharge their duties

"(B) with the care, skill, prudence, and diligence under the circumstances then prevailing that a prudent man acting in a like capacity and familiar with such matters would use in the conduct of an enterprise of a like character and with like aims;

"(C) by diversifying the investments of the plan so as to minimize the risk of large losses, unless under the circumstances it is clearly prudent not to do so; and

"(D) in accordance with the documents and instruments governing the plan insofar as such documents and instruments are consistent with the provisions of this subchapter and subchapter III of this chapter." 29 U.S.C. § 1104(a)(1).

545, 546 (1928) (Cardozo, J.) ("Many forms of conduct permissible in a workaday world for those acting at arm's length, are forbidden to those bound by fiduciary ties. A trustee is held to something stricter than the morals of the market place. Not honesty alone, but the punctilio of an honor the most sensitive, is then the standard of behavior").

Beyond the threshold statement of responsibility, however, the analogy between ERISA fiduciary and common law trustee becomes problematic. This is so because the trustee at common law characteristically wears only his fiduciary hat when he takes action to affect a beneficiary, whereas the trustee under ERISA may wear different hats.

Speaking of the traditional trustee, Professor Scott's treatise admonishes that the trustee "is not permitted to place himself in a position where it would be for his own benefit to violate his duty to the beneficiaries." 2A Scott, § 170, at 311. Under ERISA, however, a fiduciary may have financial interests adverse to beneficiaries. Employers, for example, can be ERISA fiduciaries and still take actions to the disadvantage of employee beneficiaries, when they act as employers (e.g., firing a beneficiary for reasons unrelated to the ERISA plan), or even as plan sponsors (e.g., modifying the terms of a plan as allowed by ERISA to provide less generous benefits). Nor is there any apparent reason in the ERISA provisions to conclude, as Herdrich argues, that this tension is permissible only for the employer or plan sponsor, to the exclusion of persons who provide services to an ERISA plan.

ERISA does require, however, that the fiduciary with two hats wear only one at a time, and wear the fiduciary hat when making fiduciary decisions. [ ] Thus, the statute does not describe fiduciaries simply as administrators of the plan, or managers or advisers. Instead it defines an administrator, for example, as a fiduciary only "to the extent" that he acts in such a capacity in relation to a plan. 29 U.S.C. § 1002(21)(A). In every case charging breach of ERISA fiduciary duty, then, the threshold question is not whether the actions of some person employed to provide services under a plan adversely affected a plan beneficiary's interest, but whether that person was acting as a fiduciary (that is, was performing a fiduciary function) when taking the action subject to complaint.

E

The allegations of Herdrich's ERISA count that identify the claimed fiduciary breach are difficult to understand. In this count, Herdrich does not point to a particular act by any Carle physician owner as a breach. She does not complain about Pegram's actions, and at oral argument her counsel confirmed that the ERISA count could have been brought, and would have been no different, if Herdrich had never had a sick day in her life. Tr. of Oral Arg. 53–54.

What she does claim is that Carle, acting through its physician owners, breached its duty to act solely in the interest of beneficiaries by making decisions affecting medical treatment while influenced by the terms of the Carle HMO scheme, under which the physician owners ultimately profit from their own choices to minimize the medical services provided. She emphasizes the threat to fiduciary responsibility in the Carle scheme's feature of a year-end distribution to the physicians of profit derived from the spread between subscription income and expenses of care and administration. App. to Pet. for Cert. 86a.

The specific payout detail of the plan was, of course, a feature that the employer as plan sponsor was free to adopt without breach of any fiduciary duty under ERISA, since an employer's decisions about the content of a plan are not themselves fiduciary acts. Lockheed Corp. v. Spink, 517 U.S. 882, 887, 116 S.Ct. 1783, 135 L.Ed.2d 153 (1996) ("Nothing in ERISA requires employers to establish employee benefit plans. Nor does ERISA mandate what kind of benefit employers must provide if they choose to have such a plan").[8] Likewise it is clear that there was no violation of ERISA when the incorporators of the Carle HMO provided for the year-end payout. The HMO is not the ERISA plan, and the incorporation of the HMO preceded its contract with the State Farm plan. See 29 U.S.C. § 1109(b) (no fiduciary liability for acts preceding fiduciary status).

The nub of the claim, then, is that when State Farm contracted with Carle, Carle became a fiduciary under the plan, acting through its physicians. At once, Carle as fiduciary administrator was subject to such influence from the year-end payout provision that its fiduciary capacity was necessarily compromised, and its readiness to act amounted to anticipatory breach of fiduciary obligation.

F

The pleadings must also be parsed very carefully to understand what acts by physician owners acting on Carle's behalf are alleged to be fiduciary in nature. It will help to keep two sorts of arguably administrative acts in mind. Cf. Dukes v. U.S. Healthcare, Inc., 57 F.3d 350, 361 (C.A.3 1995) (discussing dual medical/administrative roles of HMOs). What we will call pure "eligibility decisions" turn on the plan's coverage of a particular condition or medical procedure for its treatment. "Treatment decisions," by contrast, are choices about how to go about diagnosing and treating a patent's condition: given a patient's constellation of symptoms, what is the appropriate medical response?

These decisions are often practically inextricable from one another, as amici on both sides agree. [ ] This is so not merely because, under a scheme like Carle's, treatment and eligibility decisions are made by the same person, the treating physician. It is so because a great many and possibly most coverage questions are not simple yes-or-no questions, like whether appendicitis is a covered condition (when there is no dispute that a patient has appendicitis), or whether acupuncture is a covered procedure for pain relief (when the claim of pain is unchallenged). The more common coverage question is a when-and-how question. Although coverage for many conditions will be clear and various treatment options will be indisputably compensable, physicians still must decide what to do in particular cases. The issue may be,

8. It does not follow that those who administer a particular plan design may not have difficulty in following fiduciary standards if the design is awkward enough. A plan might lawfully provide for a bonus for administrators who denied benefits to every 10th beneficiary, but it would be difficult for an administrator who received the bonus to defend against the claim that he had not been solely attentive to the beneficiaries' interests in carrying out his administrative duties. The important point is that Herdrich is not suing the employer, State Farm, and her claim cannot be analyzed as if she were.

say, whether one treatment option is so superior to another under the circumstances, and needed so promptly, that a decision to proceed with it would meet the medical necessity requirement that conditions the HMO's obligation to provide or pay for that particular procedure at that time in that case. The Government in its brief alludes to a similar example when it discusses an HMO's refusal to pay for emergency care on the ground that the situation giving rise to the need for care was not an emergency, Brief for United States as Amicus Curiae 20–21. In practical terms, these eligibility decisions cannot be untangled from physicians' judgments about reasonable medical treatment, and in the case before us, Dr. Pegram's decision was one of that sort. She decided (wrongly, as it turned out) that Herdrich's condition did not warrant immediate action; the consequence of that medical determination was that Carle would not cover immediate care, whereas it would have done so if Dr. Pegram had made the proper diagnosis and judgment to treat. The eligibility decision and the treatment decision were inextricably mixed, as they are in countless medical administrative decisions every day.

The kinds of decisions mentioned in Herdrich's ERISA count and claimed to be fiduciary in character are just such mixed eligibility and treatment decisions: physicians' conclusions about when to use diagnostic tests; about seeking consultations and making referrals to physicians and facilities other than Carle's; about proper standards of care, the experimental character of a proposed course of treatment, the reasonableness of a certain treatment, and the emergency character of a medical condition.

We do not read the ERISA count, however, as alleging fiduciary breach with reference to a different variety of administrative decisions, those we have called pure eligibility determinations, such as whether a plan covers an undisputed case of appendicitis. Nor do we read it as claiming breach by reference to discrete administrative decisions separate from medical judgments; say, rejecting a claim for no other reason than the HMO's financial condition. The closest Herdrich's ERISA count comes to stating a claim for a pure, unmixed eligibility decision is her general allegation that Carle determines "which claims are covered under the Plan and to what extent," App. to Pet. for Cert. 86a. But this vague statement, difficult to interpret in isolation, is given content by the other elements of the complaint, all of which refer to decisions thoroughly mixed with medical judgment. [ ] Any lingering uncertainty about what Herdrich has in mind is dispelled by her brief, which explains that this allegation, like the others, targets medical necessity determinations. [ ]

III

A

Based on our understanding of the matters just discussed, we think Congress did not intend Carle or any other HMO to be treated as a fiduciary to the extent that it makes mixed eligibility decisions acting through its physicians. We begin with doubt that Congress would ever have thought of a mixed eligibility decision as fiduciary in nature. At common law, fiduciary duties characteristically attach to decisions about managing assets and distributing property to beneficiaries. [ ] Trustees buy, sell, and lease investment property, lend and borrow, and do other things to conserve and nurture assets. They pay out income, choose beneficiaries, and distribute remainders at termination. Thus, the common law trustee's most defining concern historically has been the payment of money in the interest of the beneficiary.

Mixed eligibility decisions by an HMO acting through its physicians have, however, only a limited resemblance to the usual business of traditional trustees. To be sure, the physicians (like regular trustees) draw on resources held for others and make decisions to distribute them in accordance with entitlements expressed in a written instrument (embodying the terms of an ERISA plan). It is also true that the objects of many traditional private and public trusts are ultimately the same as the ERISA plans that contract with HMOs. Private trusts provide medical care to the poor; thousands of independent hospitals are privately held and publicly accountable trusts, and charitable foundations make grants to stimulate the provision of health services. But beyond this point the resemblance rapidly wanes. Traditional trustees administer a medical trust by paying out money to buy medical care, whereas physicians making mixed eligibility decisions consume the money as well. Private trustees do not make treatment judgments, whereas treatment judgments are what physicians reaching mixed decisions do make, by definition. Indeed, the physicians through whom HMOs act make just the sorts of decisions made by licensed medical practitioners millions of times every day, in every possible medical setting: HMOs, fee-for-service proprietorships, public and private hospitals, military field hospitals, and so on. The settings bear no more resemblance to trust departments than a decision to operate turns on the factors controlling the amount of a quarterly income distribution. Thus, it is at least questionable whether Congress would have had mixed eligibility decisions in mind when it provided that decisions administering a plan were fiduciary in nature. Indeed, when Congress took up the subject of fiduciary responsibility under ERISA, it concentrated on fiduciaries' financial decisions, focusing on pension plans, the difficulty many retirees faced in getting the payments they expected, and the financial mismanagement that had too often deprived employees of their benefits. [ ] Its focus was far from the subject of Herdrich's claim.

Our doubt that Congress intended the category of fiduciary administrative functions to encompass the mixed determinations at issue here hardens into conviction when we consider the consequences that would follow from Herdrich's contrary view.

B

First, we need to ask how this fiduciary standard would affect HMOs if it applied as Herdrich claims it should be applied, not directed against any particular mixed decision that injured a patient, but against HMOs that make mixed decisions in the course of providing medical care for profit. Recovery would be warranted simply upon showing that the profit incentive to ration care would generally affect mixed decisions, in derogation of the fiduciary standard to act solely in the interest of the patient without possibility of conflict. Although Herdrich is vague about the mechanics of relief, the one point that seems clear is that she seeks the return of profit from the pockets of the Carle HMO's owners, with the money to be given to the plan for the benefit of the participants. See 29 U.S.C. § 1109(a) (return of all profits is an appropriate ERISA remedy). Since the provision for profit is what makes the

HMO a proprietary organization, her remedy in effect would be nothing less than elimination of the for-profit HMO. Her remedy might entail even more than that, although we are in no position to tell whether and to what extent nonprofit HMO schemes would ultimately survive the recognition of Herdrich's theory.[11] It is enough to recognize that the Judiciary has no warrant to precipitate the upheaval that would follow a refusal to dismiss Herdrich's ERISA claim. The fact is that for over 27 years the Congress of the United States has promoted the formation of HMO practices. The Health Maintenance Organization Act of 1973, 87 Stat. 914, 42 U.S.C. § 300e et seq., allowed the formation of HMOs that assume financial risks for the provision of health care services, and Congress has amended the Act several times, most recently in 1996. See 110 Stat.1976, codified at 42 U.S.C. § 300e (1994 ed., Supp. III). If Congress wishes to restrict its approval of HMO practice to certain preferred forms, it may choose to do so. But the Federal Judiciary would be acting contrary to the congressional policy of allowing HMO organizations if it were to entertain an ERISA fiduciary claim portending wholesale attacks on existing HMOs solely because of their structure, untethered to claims of concrete harm.

C

The Court of Appeals did not purport to entertain quite the broadside attack that Herdrich's ERISA claim thus entails, see 154 F.3d, at 373, and the second possible consequence of applying the fiduciary standard that requires our attention would flow from the difficulty of extending it to particular mixed decisions that on Herdrich's theory are fiduciary in nature.

The fiduciary is, of course, obliged to act exclusively in the interest of the beneficiary, but this translates into no rule readily applicable to HMO decisions or those of any other variety of medical practice. While the incentive of the HMO physician is to give treatment sparingly, imposing a fiduciary obligation upon him would not lead to a simple default rule, say, that whenever it is reasonably possible to disagree about treatment options, the physician should treat aggressively. After all, HMOs came into being because some groups of physicians consistently provided more aggressive treatment than others in similar circumstances, with results not perceived as justified by the marginal expense and risk associated with intervention; excessive surgery is not in the patient's best interest, whether provided by fee-for-service surgeons or HMO surgeons subject to a default rule urging them to operate. Nor would it be possible to translate fiduciary duty into a standard that would allow recovery from an HMO whenever a mixed decision influenced by the HMO's financial incentive resulted in a bad outcome for the patient. It would be so easy to allege, and to find, an economic influence when sparing care did not lead to a well patient, that any such standard in practice would allow a factfinder to convert an HMO into a guarantor of recovery.

11. Herdrich's theory might well portend the end of nonprofit HMOs as well, since those HMOs can set doctors' salaries. A claim against a nonprofit HMO could easily allege that salaries were excessively high because they were funded by limiting care, and some nonprofits actually use incentive schemes similar to that challenged here, see Pulvers v. Kaiser Foundation Health Plan, 99 Cal.App.3d 560, 565, 160 Cal.Rptr. 392, 393–394 (1979) (rejecting claim against nonprofit HMO based on physician incentives). See Brody, Agents Without Principals: The Economic Convergence of the Nonprofit and For-Profit Organizational Forms, 40 N.Y.L.S.L.Rev. 457, 493, and n. 152 (1996) (discussing ways in which nonprofit health providers may reward physician employees).

These difficulties may have led the Court of Appeals to try to confine the fiduciary breach to cases where "the sole purpose" of delaying or withholding treatment was to increase the physician's financial reward, ibid. But this attempt to confine mixed decision claims to their most egregious examples entails erroneous corruption of fiduciary obligation and would simply lead to further difficulties that we think fatal. While a mixed decision made solely to benefit the HMO or its physician would violate a fiduciary duty, the fiduciary standard condemns far more than that, in its requirement of "an eye single" toward beneficiaries' interests [ ]. But whether under the Court of Appeals's rule or a straight standard of undivided loyalty, the defense of any HMO would be that its physician did not act out of financial interest but for good medical reasons, the plausibility of which would require reference to standards of reasonable and customary medical practice in like circumstances. That, of course, is the traditional standard of the common law. [ ]. Thus, for all practical purposes, every claim of fiduciary breach by an HMO physician making a mixed decision would boil down to a malpractice claim, and the fiduciary standard would be nothing but the malpractice standard traditionally applied in actions against physicians.

What would be the value to the plan participant of having this kind of ERISA fiduciary action? It would simply apply the law already available in state courts and federal diversity actions today, and the formulaic addition of an allegation of financial incentive would do nothing but bring the same claim into a federal court under federal-question jurisdiction. It is true that in States that do not allow malpractice actions against HMOs the fiduciary claim would offer a plaintiff a further defendant to be sued for direct liability, and in some cases the HMO might have a deeper pocket than the physician. But we have seen enough to know that ERISA was not enacted out of concern that physicians were too poor to be sued, or in order to federalize malpractice litigation in the name of fiduciary duty for any other reason. It is difficult, in fact, to find any advantage to participants across the board, except that allowing them to bring malpractice actions in the guise of federal fiduciary breach claims against HMOs would make them eligible for awards of attorney's fees if they won. [ ] But, again, we can be fairly sure that Congress did not create fiduciary obligations out of concern that state plaintiffs were not suing often enough, or were paying too much in legal fees.

The mischief of Herdrich's position would, indeed, go further than mere replication of state malpractice actions with HMO defendants. For not only would an HMO be liable as a fiduciary in the first instance for its own breach of fiduciary duty committed through the acts of its physician employee, but the physician employee would also be subject to liability as a fiduciary on the same basic analysis that would charge the HMO. The physician who made the mixed administrative decision would be exercising authority in the way described by ERISA and would therefore be deemed to be a fiduciary. [ ]. Hence the physician, too, would be subject to suit in federal court applying an ERISA standard of reasonable medical skill. This result, in turn, would raise a puzzling issue of preemption. On its face, federal fiduciary law applying a malpractice standard would seem to be a prescription for preemption of state malpractice law, since the new ERISA cause of action would cover the subject of a state-law malpractice claim. See 29 U.S.C. § 1144 (preempting state laws that "relate to [an] employee benefit plan"). To be sure, New York State

Conference of Blue Cross & Blue Shield Plans v. Travelers Ins. Co., 514 U.S. 645, 654–655, 115 S.Ct. 1671, 131 L.Ed.2d 695 (1995), throws some cold water on the preemption theory; there, we held that, in the field of health care, a subject of traditional state regulation, there is no ERISA preemption without clear manifestation of congressional purpose. But in that case the convergence of state and federal law was not so clear as in the situation we are positing; the state-law standard had not been subsumed by the standard to be applied under ERISA. We could struggle with this problem, but first it is well to ask, again, what would be gained by opening the federal courthouse doors for a fiduciary malpractice claim, save for possibly random fortuities such as more favorable scheduling, or the ancillary opportunity to seek attorney's fees. And again, we know that Congress had no such haphazard boons in prospect when it defined the ERISA fiduciary, nor such a risk to the efficiency of federal courts as a new fiduciary-malpractice jurisdiction would pose in welcoming such unheard-of fiduciary litigation.

IV

We hold that mixed eligibility decisions by HMO physicians are not fiduciary decisions under ERISA. Herdrich's ERISA count fails to state an ERISA claim, and the judgment of the Court of Appeals is reversed.

Notes and Questions

1. What exactly does *Pegram* mean for ERISA preemption and for future claims against managed care plans? Speaking for a unanimous Supreme Court, Souter was emphatic: "[t]he eligibility decision and the treatment decision were inextricably mixed, as they are in countless medical administrative decisions every day." He enumerates examples of such mixed decisions: "... physicians' conclusions about when to use diagnostic tests; about seeking consultations and making referrals to physicians and facilities other than Carle's; about proper standards of care, the experimental character of a proposed course of treatment, the reasonableness of a certain treatment, and the emergency character of a medical condition."

Pegram does not directly address the complex preemption issues raised by ERISA caselaw in the federal courts. However, the decision does not suggest expansion of ERISA preemption. To the contrary, the Court objected to extending the reach of federal fiduciary law to medical malpractice on the grounds that it would duplicate state law and and risk preempting state law. Citing to its own caselaw holding that ERISA does not preempt state health law regulation without clear congressional intent to the contrary, the Court concluded that Congress did not consider that ERISA would open federal court doors to fiduciary malpractice claims. The implication is that state courts are a natural forum for such claims.

The Court also suggests that mixed eligibility/treatment decisions are not acts of plan administration, and can therefore be considered as "unrelated-to-ERISA" malpractice claims. So long as medical judgment is involved, a claim may not "relate to" ERISA. State courts would appear to be available for a range of malpractice arguments against managed care plans for a variety of errors, with the risk of ERISA preemption. Many courts have already found ways around ERISA preemption, and the trend is likely to continue.

F. PROVIDER DISCLOSURE REQUIREMENTS

Managed care organizations typically use various financial incentives, such as salary-holdback pools, to affect physician behavior and thereby reduce system costs. This has troubled critics, who fear cost-cutting that might endanger patient care. Critics have therefore advocated disclosure to subscribers of the existence of such incentives that might impact physician decision-making. Federal law requires such disclosure to Medicare beneficiaries under some circumstances.

HEALTH MAINTENANCE ORGANIZATIONS, COMPETITIVE MEDICAL PLANS, AND HEALTH CARE PREPAYMENT PLANS

42 C.F.R. Part 417, S. 417.479.
(Effective April 26, 1996).

(h) Disclosure requirements for organizations with physician incentive plans—

(1) Disclosure to HCFA. Each organization must provide to HCFA information concerning its physician incentive plans as required or requested. The disclosure must contain the following information in detail sufficient to enable HCFA to determine whether the incentive plan complies with the requirements specified in this section:

(i) Whether services not furnished by the physician or physician group are covered by the incentive plan. If only the services furnished by the physician or physician group are covered by the incentive plan, disclosure of other aspects of the plan need not be made.

(ii) The type of incentive arrangement; for example, withhold, bonus, capitation.

(iii) If the incentive plan involves a withhold or bonus, the percent of the withhold or bonus.

(iv) The amount and type of stop-loss protection.

(v) The panel size and , if the patients are pooled according to one of the following permitted methods, the method used * * *;

(vi) In the case of capitated physicians or physician groups, capitation payments paid to primary care physicians for the most recent year broken down by percent for primary care services, referral services to specialists, and hospital and other types of provider * * *

(3) Disclosure to Medicare beneficiaries. An organization must provide the following information to any Medicare beneficiary who requests it:

(i) Whether the prepaid plan uses a physician incentive plan that affects the use of referral services.

(ii) The type of incentive arrangement.

(iii) Whether stop-loss protection is provided.

(iv) If the prepaid plan was required to conduct a survey, a summary of the survey results.

Notes and Questions

1. The Medicare disclosure requirements are a compromise between those who believed that disclosure of incentive plans should be mandatory at the time of

enrollment, and those who maintained that incentive plans are proprietary information exempt from disclosure under the Freedom of Information Act. The Comments to the rules state:

> We agree that disclosure of the incentive plans to patients can aid them in ensuring that they receive needed services. This information in the hands of Medicare beneficiaries and Medicaid recipients will also help physicians to counter pressure from the prepaid plans to reduce services. At the same time, we want to protect the proprietary aspects of the information. * * * We have not asked that more information be provided for the following reasons:
>
> — We do not want to put an undue burden on the prepaid plans.
>
> — We do not require fee-for-service physicians to provide a notice that they have incentives to provide excessive services.
>
> — Certain information in the incentive plans is proprietary information and is exempt from disclosure under the FOIA.

2. Early critics of managed care had called for such disclosures, proposing that

> [A]ll health insurance plans should be required to provide formal disclosure statements to prospective subscribers concerning restrictions on the choice of service and capitation payments and financial incentives for reduced use. These statements should be simple and concise, and supplemented by a more complete description of the arrangement, including fees, out-of-pocket costs, and allowable benefits.

Donald F. Levinson, Toward Full Disclosure of Referral Restrictions and Financial Incentives by Prepaid Health Plans, 317 New Eng. J. Med. 1729 (1987). For a comprehensive legal discussion, see Deven C. McGraw, Financial Incentives to Limit Services: Should Physicians be Required to Disclose These To Patients? 83 Geo. L.J. 1821 (1995).

The critics assumed that patients are not aware of the cost-sensitive nature of incentives operating on physicians in MCOs, such as salary-holdback provisions in some HMO plans. Such plans held back a small percentage of physician salaries in HMOs in a pool, and at the end of the budget year physicians who have too many referrals may "lose" this percentage of their salary, typically 20 percent. Such a pool is intended to create a financial incentive for primary physicians to minimize referrals of members. Under most HMO arrangements, subscribers are not informed of such arrangements, and primary physicians are prohibited from disclosing to subscribers the existence and nature of these incentive arrangements. See, e.g., Alan L. Hillman, et al., How Do Financial Incentives Affect Physicians' Clinical Decisions and the Financial Performance of Health Maintenance Organizations?, 321 New Eng. J. Med. 86 (1989); Alan L. Hillman, Financial Incentives for Physicians in HMOs: Is There a Conflict of Interest?, 317 New Eng. J. Med. 1743 (1987).

The idea is that patients are not aware of the cost-sensitive nature of incentives operating on physicians in MCOs, and should be made aware of them prior to joining, since physicians have a conflict of interest in such MCOs. See e.g., Steven Z. Pantilat, Margaret Chesney and Bernard Lo, Effect of Incentives on the Use of Indicated Services in Managed Care, 170 West. J. Med. 137 (1999); Alan L. Hillman, et al., How Do Financial Incentives Affect Physicians' Clinical Decisions and the Financial Performance of Health Maintenance Organizations?, 321 New Eng. J. Med. 86 (1989); Alan L. Hillman, Financial Incentives for Physicians in HMOs: Is There a Conflict of Interest?, 317 New Eng. J. Med. 1743 (1987).

Disclosure is a remedy that coincides with developments in informed consent, fiduciary law, and Fraud and Abuse legislation. The Stark Amendment, for example, specifically prohibits HMOs with Medicaid contracts from "knowingly making a payment, directly or indirectly, to a physician as an inducement to reduce or limit services provided with respect to Medicare and Medicaid beneficiaries". Omnibus Budget Reconciliation Act of 1986, Pub. L. No. 99–509, § 9313(c), 100 Stat. 2003, as amended by Pub. L. No. 100–203, § 4016, 101 Stat. 1330–64 and H.R. 3299, § 6207. It appears to give the patient options that she or he did not previously have. Such disclosure presents several problems. First, patients may lack a choice of alternative providers, even if disclosure is made. Given the increased prevalence of managed care organizations as employee options, employees face diminishing choices between fee-for-service and managed care physicians. Second, patients already in such MCOs or closed panel plans lack ready flexibility to consult physicians outside the panel who are not themselves subject to financial constraints. Recent writing on the subject includes Stephen R. Latham, Regulation of Managed Care Incentive Payments to Physicians, 22 Am.J.L. & Med. 399 (1996); Henry T. Greely, Direct Financial Incentives in Managed Care: Unanswered Questions, 6 Health Matrix 53 (1996); R.Adams Dudley et al., The Impact of Financial Incentives on Quality of Health Care, 76 The Milbank Quarterly 649 (1998); Marc A. Rodwin, Medicine, Money & Morals: Physicians' Conflicts of Interest 214–217 (1993).

Third, disclosure assumes that cost-sensitive care is less high quality care, when in fact fee-for-service medicine may often result in overtreatment, with its own iatrogenic costs. P. Franks, et al., Sounding Board: Gatekeeping Revisited—Protecting Patients from Overtreatment, 327 New Eng. J. Med. 424, 426 (1992).

The earlier caselaw that discussed the disclosure issue generally rejected such claims. In Teti v. U.S. Healthcare, 1989 WL 143274 (E.D.Pa.1989), affirmed 904 F.2d 696 (3d Cir.1990), the plaintiffs claimed that the HMO's failure to disclose the disincentives for physicians to make specialist or hospital referrals was fraud, breach of contract and RICO violations. The case was dismissed for lack of federal court jurisdiction.

Some courts have been receptive to such claims. In Shea v. Esensten, 107 F.3d 625 (8th Cir.1997), the court considered a claim that the HMO's failure to disclose its practice of giving primary-care physicians financial incentives to minimize referrals to specialists caused employee's death from heart failure. Mr. Shea's physician failed to give him a referral to a cardiologist in spite of warning signs of a cardiac condition. Mr. Shea's widow contended that if her husband had know that his doctor could earn a bonus for treating less, he would have sought out his own cardiologist. The Seventh Circuit agreed that a financial incentive system aimed at influencing a physician's referral patterns is "a material piece of information," Id. at 628, and that a subscriber has a right to know that his physician's judgment could be "colored" by such incentives. The court rested its conclusion on the obligation of an ERISA fiduciary to speak out if it "knows that silence might be harmful." The court held that information about a plan's financial incentives must be disclosed when they might lead a treating physician to deny necessary referrals for conditions covered by the plan. Such a requirement of disclosure, while problematic in some aspects, is consistent with federal policy in HMO regulation and with a trend to use disclosure of information to counteract provider power in health care. For an excellent discussion of these issues, see Tracy E. Miller and William M. Sage, Disclosing Physician Financial Incentives, 281 JAMA 1424 (1999); William M. Sage, Physicians as Advocates, 35 Houston L.Rev. 1529 (1999); Kim Johnston, Patient Advocates or Patient Adversaries?

Using Fiduciary Law to Compel Disclosure of Managed Care Financial Incentives, 35 San Diego L.Rev. 951 (1998); Bethany J. Spielman, Managed Care Regulation and the Physician–Advocate, 47 Drake L.Rev. 713 (1999).

The related disclosure theory is that of informed consent: a physician in an MCO should always discuss with a patient all alternative approaches, even those that are more expensive and therefore are not generally recommended by the cost-sensitive physician. Such an obligation is based upon the line of "informed refusal" cases, such as Truman v. Thomas. Truman imposes on the physician a duty to disclose to a patient the risks of omitting a useful risk-free test, arguably expanding the duty to discuss more expensive diagnostic and treatment procedures that might be useful and helpful to the patient. This could expand the obligations of HMO physicians in situations where some treatments were preferred because of the cost-benefit tradeoff, but exposed patients to slightly higher risks at the same time.

The use of financial incentives in managed care, and the possible effect of these incentives in "corrupting" physician judgment, has led some critics to raise ethical objections to managed care: it creates conflicts of interest of physicians, impairing their judgment; patient trust will suffer as a result. See Council on Ethical and Judicial Affairs, American Medical Association, Ethical Issues in Managed Care, 273 JAMA 330, 330–31 (1995). The Council expressed concern that managed care incentives that make physicians more costs conscious can compromise patient care. "First, physicians have an incentive to cut corners in their patient care, by temporizing too long, eschewing extra diagnostic tests, or refraining from an expensive referral.... Second, even in the absence of actual patient harm, the incentives may erode patient trust as patients wonder whether they are receiving all necessary care or are being denied care because of the physicians' pecuniary concerns.... Financial incentives to limit care exploit the financial motive of physicians" and are less likely to coincide with patients' interests, "because patients generally prefer the risk of too much care to the risk of too little care" *Id.* at 333. Third, patients are less likely to notice the effects of incentives, such as the withholding of a treatment option. See generally Ezekiel Emanuel, Managed Competition and the Patient–Physician Relationship, 329 N.E.J.M. 879 (1993).

"Bedside rationing" is often raised as a threat to medical professionalism and ethical behavior. These critics have contended that neither rationing nor the use of incentives is ethical. While the critics are correct that inappropriate incentives can be damaging, they often fail to acknowledge that physicians have always responded to incentives: fee-for-service may push toward overtreatment, while salaried physicians receive no signals at all about appropriate uses of resources. An ethical model is needed that recognizes the value of physician autonomy and also the need to provide signals as to appropriate use of health care services. Physicians need to think about what they do, and they must also be able to advocate for patients in particular cases. Hall and Berenson propose an approach that recognizes the value of cost-effective medicine in managed care while trying to create an ethical model:

> ... financial incentives should influence physicians to maximize the health of the group of patients under their care; physicians should not enter into incentive arrangements that they would be embarrassed to describe accurately to their patients or that are not in common use in the market; physicians should treat each patient impartially, without regard to source of payment, and in a manner consistent with the physician's own treatment style; if

> physicians depart from this ideal, they must tell their patients honestly; and it is desirable, although not mandatory, to differentiate medical treatment recommendations from insurance coverage decisions by clearly assigning authority over these different roles and by having physicians to advocate for recommended treatment that is not covered.

Mark A. Hall and Robert A. Berenson, The Ethics of Managed Care: A Dose of Realism, 28 Cumb.L.Rev. 287, 288–89 (1999). A properly designed managed care system does not violate professional medical ethics. The purpose of incentive systems are to provide a counterbalance to the inflationary pressures of the American health care system. Such incentives can be provided within a framework that allows sound clinical judgment to be exercised, giving physicians substantial bedside autonomy while also providing incentives for sensitivity to both cost and appropriate care. Hall and Berenson, id. at 304, note that "[t]he strength of various payment methods vary according to at least six dimensions, each with multiple components:" (1) the type of service covered; (2) the practice setting and base reimbursement method; (3) the size of the incentive; (4) the incentive's immediacy; (5) the presence of various counterbalancing monitoring mechanisms; and (6) the relative generosity of the base reimbursement. Such an approach can be found in recent Medicare HMO rules, 61 Fed. Reg. 13430 (to be codified at 42 C.F.R. § 417.479(e)-(f)).

Chapter 9

ACCESS TO HEALTH CARE: THE OBLIGATION TO PROVIDE CARE

A number of factors can impede an individual's access to adequate health care. Ability to pay is a key determinant of access to health care in the U.S. Persons unable to pay, whether out-of-pocket or through insurance or through government programs, must rely largely on voluntary charity or public institutions where available. Medicaid is severely limited in terms of eligibility; between 1975 and 1986 the proportion of poor persons eligible for Medicaid fell from 63% to under 40%, a proportion that persisted for many years. U.S. House of Representatives, Committee on Ways and Means: 1996 Green Book: Overview of Entitlement Programs. Washington, D.C. U.S. Government Printing Office, 1996. Public hospitals have closed in droves. Powerful non-financial obstacles exist as well, including discrimination based on race, gender or medical condition of the patient. See generally, Altman, Stuart H. et al., The Future U.S. Health Care System: Who Will Care For The Poor and Uninsured (1999); Symposium on Nonfinancial Barriers to Health Care, 32 Houston L. Rev. 1187 (1996). See also Sidney D. Watson, Health Care in The Inner City: Asking The Right Question, 71 N.C.L. Rev. 1647 (1993), detailing problems in public hospitals and clinics including waiting time of several weeks to several months for treatment; and Barry Furrow, Forcing Rescue: The Landscape of Health Care Provider Obligations to Treat Patients, 3 Health Matrix 31 (1993), providing statistical information on access to care.

As a general legal principle, private health care providers do not have a duty to provide uncompensated care, and the traditional legal principle of the physician-patient relationship has been that it is a voluntary and personal relationship which the physician may choose to enter or not for a variety of reasons. Legal obligations on the part of providers to furnish care operate as exceptions to this general rule.

Most of the expansion of duties to provide care has been legislative, with state and federal statutes prohibiting discrimination on the basis of certain characteristics of the patient, or mandating treatment for all patients in exchange for the receipt of government funds for the treatment of some patients. Some current legal obligations to provide care have emerged from limited common law doctrines, as you will see in the first set of cases below.

I. PHYSICIANS' DUTY TO TREAT

A. COMMON LAW

RICKS v. BUDGE

Supreme Court of Utah, 1937.
91 Utah 307, 64 P.2d 208.

EPHRAIM HANSON, JUSTICE.

This is an action for malpractice against the defendants who are physicians and surgeons at Logan, Utah, and are copartners doing business under the name and style of the "Budge Clinic." ... [P]laintiff alleges that he was suffering from an infected right hand and was in immediate need of medical and surgical care and treatment, and there was danger of his dying unless he received such treatment; that defendants for the purpose of treating plaintiff sent him to the Budge Memorial Hospital at Logan, Utah; that while at the hospital and while he was in need of medical and surgical treatment, defendants refused to treat or care for plaintiff and abandoned his case ...

* * *

[T]he evidence shows that when plaintiff left the hospital on March 15th, Dr. Budge advised him to continue the same treatment that had been given him at the hospital, and that if the finger showed any signs of getting worse at any time, plaintiff was to return at once to Dr. Budge for further treatment; that on the morning of March 17th, plaintiff telephoned Dr. Budge, and explained the condition of his hand; that he was told by the doctor to come to his office, and in pursuance of the doctor's request, plaintiff reported to the doctor's office at 2 p.m. of that day. Dr. Budge again examined the hand, and told plaintiff the hand was worse; he called in Dr. D.C. Budge, another of the defendants, who examined the hand, scraped it some, and indicated thereon where the hand should be opened. Dr. S.M. Budge said to plaintiff: "You have got to go back to the hospital." ... Within a short time after the arrival of plaintiff, Dr. S.M. Budge arrived at the hospital. Plaintiff testified: "He [meaning Dr. S.M. Budge] came into my room and said, 'You are owing us. I am not going to touch you until that account is taken care of.' " (The account referred to was, according to plaintiff, of some years' standing and did not relate to any charge for services being then rendered.) Plaintiff testified that he did not know what to say to the doctor, but that he finally asked the doctor if he was going to take care of him, and the doctor replied: "No, I am not going to take care of you. I would not take you to the operating table and operate on you and keep you here thirty days, and then there is another $30.00 at the office, until your account is taken care of." Plaintiff replied: "If that is the idea, if you will furnish me a little help, I will try to move."

Plaintiff testified that this help was furnished, and that after being dressed, he left the Budge Memorial Hospital to seek other treatment. At that time it was raining. He walked to the Cache Valley Hospital, a few blocks away, and there met Dr. Randall, who examined the hand. Dr. Randall testified that when the plaintiff arrived at the Cache Valley Hospital, the hand was swollen with considerable fluid oozing from it; that the lower two-thirds of the forearm was red and swollen from the infection which extended up in the arm, and that there was some fluid also oozing from the back of the hand, and that plaintiff required immediate surgical attention; that immediately after the arrival of plaintiff at the hospital he made an incision through the fingers and through the palm of the hand along the tendons that led from the palm, followed those tendons as far as there was any bulging, opened it up thoroughly all the way to the base of the hand, and put drain tubes in. Plaintiff remained under the care of Dr. Randall for approximately a month. About two weeks after the plaintiff entered the Cache Valley Hospital, it became necessary to amputate the middle finger and remove about an inch of the metacarpal bone.

* * *

Defendants contend: (1) That there was no contract of employment between plaintiff and defendants and that defendants in the absence of a valid contract were not obligated to proceed with any treatment; and (2) that if there was such a contract, there was no evidence that the refusal of Dr. S.M. Budge to operate or take care of plaintiff resulted in any damage to plaintiff.

* * *

Under this evidence, it cannot be said that the relation of physician and patient did not exist on March 17th. It had not been terminated after its commencement on March 11th. When the plaintiff left the hospital on March 15th, he understood that he was to report to Dr. S.M. Budge if the occasion required and was so requested by the doctor. Plaintiff's return to the doctor's office was on the advice of the doctor. While at the doctor's office, both Dr. S.M. Budge and Dr. D.C. Budge examined plaintiff's hand and they ordered that he go at once to the hospital for further medical attention. That plaintiff was told by the doctor to come to the doctor's office and was there examined by him and directed to go to the hospital for further treatment would create the relationship of physician and patient. That the relationship existed at the time the plaintiff was sent to the hospital on March 17th cannot be seriously questioned.

We believe the law is well settled that a physician or surgeon, upon undertaking an operation or other case, is under the duty, in the absence of an agreement limiting the service, of continuing his attention, after the first operation or first treatment, so long as the case requires attention. The obligation of continuing attention can be terminated only by the cessation of the necessity which gave rise to the relationship, or by the discharge of the physician by the patient, or by the withdrawal from the case by the physician after giving the patient reasonable notice so as to enable the patient to secure other medical attention. A physician has the right to withdraw from a case, but if the case is such as to still require further medical or surgical attention, he must, before withdrawing from the case, give the patient sufficient notice so the patient can procure other medical attention if he desires. [ ]

* * *

We cannot say as a matter of law that plaintiff suffered no damages by reason of the refusal of Dr. S.M. Budge to further treat him. The evidence shows that from the time plaintiff left the office of the defendants up until the time that he arrived at the Cache Valley Hospital his hand continued to swell; that it was very painful; that when he left the Budge Memorial Hospital he was in such condition that he did not know whether he was going to live or die. That both his mental and physical suffering must have been most acute cannot be questioned. While the law cannot measure with exactness such suffering and cannot determine with absolute certainty what damages, if any, plaintiff may be entitled to, still those are questions which a jury under proper instructions from the court must determine.

* * *

FOLLAND, JUSTICE (concurring in part, dissenting in part).

* * *

... The theory of plaintiff as evidenced in his complaint is that there was no continued relationship from the first employment but that a new relationship was entered into. He visited the clinic on March 17th; the Doctors Budge examined his hand and told him an immediate operation was necessary and for him to go to the hospital. I do not think a new contract was entered into at that time. There was no consideration for any implied promise that Dr. Budge or the Budge Clinic would assume the responsibility of another operation and the costs and expenses incident thereto. As soon as Dr. Budge reached the hospital he opened negotiations with the plaintiff which might have resulted in a contract, but before any contract arrangement was made the plaintiff decided to leave the hospital and seek attention elsewhere. As soon as he could dress himself he walked away. There is conflict in the evidence as to the conversation. Plaintiff testified in effect that Dr. Budge asked for something to be done about an old account. The doctor's testimony in effect was that he asked that some arrangement be made to take care of the doctor's bill and expenses for the ensuing operation and treatment at the hospital. The result, however, was negative. No arrangement was made. The plaintiff made no attempt whatsoever to suggest to the doctor any way by which either the old account might be taken care of or the expenses of the ensuing operation provided for. ... Dr. Budge had a right to refuse to incur the obligation and responsibility incident to one or more operations and the treatment and attention which would be necessary. If it be assumed that the contract relationship of physician and patient existed prior to this conversation, either as resulting from the first employment or that there was an implied contract entered into at the clinic, yet Dr. Budge had the right with proper notice to discontinue the relationship. While plaintiff's condition was acute and needed immediate attention, he received such immediate attention at the Cache Valley Hospital. There was only a delay of an hour or two, and part of that delay is accounted for by reason of the fact that the doctor at the Cache Valley Hospital would not operate until some paper, which plaintiff says he did not read, was signed. Plaintiff said he could not sign it but that it was signed by his brother before the operation was performed. We are justified in believing that by means of this written obligation, provision was made for the expenses and fees about to be incurred. I am satisfied from my reading of the record that no injury or damage resulted from the delay occasioned by plaintiff leaving the Budge Hospital and going to the Cache Valley Hospital. He was not in such desperate condition but that he was able to walk the three or four blocks between the two hospitals. . . .

CHILDS v. WEIS

Court of Civil Appeals of Texas, 1969.
440 S.W.2d 104.

WILLIAMS, J.

On or about November 27, 1966 Daisy Childs, wife of J.C. Childs, a resident of Dallas County, was approximately seven months pregnant. On that date she was visiting in Lone Oak, Texas, and about two o'clock A.M. she presented herself to the Greenville Hospital emergency room. At that time she stated she was bleeding and had labor pains. She was examined by a nurse who identified herself as H. Beckham. According to Mrs. Childs, Nurse Beckham stated that she would call the doctor. She said the nurse returned and stated "that the Dr. said that I would have to go to my doctor in Dallas. I stated to Beckham that I'm not going to make it to Dallas. Beckham replied that yes, I would make it. She stated that I was just starting into labor and that I would make it. The weather was cold that night. About an hour after leaving the Greenville Hospital Authority I had the baby while in a car on the way to medical facilities in Sulphur Springs. The baby lived about 12 hours."

[Dr. Weis] said that he had never examined or treated Daisy Childs and in fact had never seen or spoken to either Daisy Childs or her husband, J.C. Childs, at any time in his life. He further stated that he had never at any time agreed or consented to the examination or treatment of either Daisy Childs or her husband. He said that on a day in November 1966 he recalled a telephone call received by him from a nurse in the emergency room at the Greenville Surgical Hospital; that the nurse told him that there was a negro girl in the emergency room having a "bloody show" and some "labor pains." He said the nurse advised him that this woman had been visiting in Lone Oak, and that her OB doctor lived in Garland, Texas, and that she also resided in Garland. The doctor said, "I told the nurse over the telephone to have the girl call her doctor in Garland and see what he wanted her to do. I knew nothing more about this incident until I was served with the citation and a copy of the petition in this lawsuit."

* * *

Since it is unquestionably the law that the relationship of physician and patient is dependent upon contract, either express or implied, a physician is not to be held liable for arbitrarily refusing to respond to a call of a person even urgently in need of medical or surgical assistance provided that the relation of physician and patient does not exist at the time the call is made or at the time the person presents himself for treatment.

* * *

Applying these principles of law to the factual situation here presented we find an entire absence of evidence of a contract, either express or implied, which would create the relationship of patient and physician as between Dr. Weis and Mrs. Childs. Dr. Weis, under these circumstances, was under no duty whatsoever to examine or treat Mrs. Childs. When advised by telephone that the lady was in the emergency room he did what seems to be a reasonable thing and inquired as to the identity of her doctor who had been treating her. Upon being told that the doctor was in Garland he stated that the patient should call the doctor and find out what should be done. This action on the part of Dr. Weis seems to be not only reasonable but within the bounds of professional ethics.

We cannot agree with appellant that Dr. Weis' statement to the nurse over the telephone amounted to an acceptance of the case and affirmative instructions which she was bound to follow. Rather than give instructions which could be construed to be in the nature of treatment, Dr. Weis told the nurse to have the woman call her physician in Garland and secure instructions from him.

The affidavit of Mrs. Childs would indicate that Nurse Beckham may not have relayed the exact words of Dr. Weis to Mrs. Childs. Instead, it would seem that Nurse Beckham told Mrs. Childs that the doctor said that she would "have to go" to her doctor in Dallas. Assuming this statement was made by Nurse Beckham, and further assuming that it contained the meaning as placed upon it by appellant, yet it is undisputed that such words were uttered by Nurse Beckham, and not by Dr. Weis. * * *

[The court affirmed summary judgment in favor of the defendant.]

HISER v. RANDOLPH

Court of Appeals of Arizona, 1980.
126 Ariz. 608, 617 P.2d 774.

JACOBSON, JUDGE.

* * *

[The trial court entered] summary judgment in favor of the defendant physician, Dr. W. Alan Randolph, and the decedent's spouse has appealed.

* * *

Mohave County General Hospital is the only hospital serving the community of Kingman, Arizona. It maintains an emergency room for the treatment of people in need of immediate medical service. Dr. Randolph and seven other doctors, comprising the medical profession in the Kingman area with admitting privileges at the hospital, established a program with the hospital by which each would take turns in manning the emergency room as the "on call physician" for a 12 hour period.

* * *

From the record it appears that plaintiff's wife, Bonita Hiser, went with her husband to the emergency room at the hospital at approximately 11:45 p.m. on June 12, 1973. She was in a semi-comatose condition and the nurse in charge of the emergency room evaluated her as appearing to be very ill. Mrs. Hiser had an acute diabetic condition described as juvenile onset diabetes of the "brittle" variety. She had been treated in the emergency room at the hospital on the preceding day by Dr. Arnold of Kingman, her regular physician.

The emergency room nurse, after viewing Mrs. Hiser, immediately contacted Dr. Randolph, the "on call physician" at that time. Upon being advised as to who the patient was, Dr. Randolph stated to the nurse, at 11:50 p.m., that he would not attend or treat Mrs. Hiser, and that the nurse should call Dr. Arnold. When the nurse called Dr. Arnold he responded by stating that he would not come to the hospital at that time and that the on call physician should attend Mrs. Hiser. The nurse relayed this information to Dr. Randolph who again refused to attend to or see Mrs. Hiser. The nurse then called Dr. Lingenfelter, Chief of Staff of the hospital. After a subsequent telephone conversation between Dr. Lingenfelter and Dr. Randolph in which Dr. Randolph reiterated that he would not treat Mrs. Hiser, Dr. Lingenfelter came to the hospital and attended Mrs. Hiser, arriving at approximately 12:30 a.m. Dr. Lingenfelter immediately commenced tests and treatment for Mrs. Hiser, whom he regarded as being very ill at the time. Dr. Lingenfelter stayed at the hospital throughout the night until Dr. Arnold arrived in the morning. Mrs. Hiser died at 11:00 a.m. on June 13.

As to the reason for Dr. Randolph's refusal to attend to Mrs. Hiser, a factual dispute exists. Dr. Randolph testified by deposition that the refusal was based upon his inability to adequately treat diabetes. From the evidence presented, however, a trier of fact could conclude that the refusal was based upon a personal animosity between Dr. Randolph and Mrs. Hiser or the fact that Mrs. Hiser's husband was a lawyer. Because the fact that Dr. Randolph refused to treat is undisputed and because of the posture in which this matter reaches us, we assume the refusal was medically unjustified.

* * *

In examining this issue we start with the general rule, with which we agree, that a medical practitioner is free to contract for his services as he sees fit and in the absence of prior contractual obligations, he can refuse to treat a patient, even under emergency situations. [ ]

The question remains whether Dr. Randolph has contracted away this right, while being the doctor "on call" in charge of the emergency room at Mohave General Hospital and being paid the sum of $100 a day to perform those services.

* * *

In our opinion, Dr. Randolph, by assenting to these bylaws [describing the duties of the on-call physician] and rules and regulations, and accepting payment from the hospital to act as the emergency room doctor "on call," personally became bound "to insure that all patients * * * treated in the Emergency Room receive the best possible care," and agreed to insure "in the case of emergency the provisional diagnosis shall be started as soon after admission as possible." Moreover, these services were to be performed for all persons whom the "hospital shall admit ... suffering from all types of disease."

* * *

Reversed and remanded.

Notes and Questions

1. Why did the doctor refuse to treat Mr. Ricks? Ms. Childs? Ms. Hiser? How did the courts approach the claims of the plaintiffs? On what foundation did they place the doctor's duty to treat? Did they examine the reason for the doctor's refusal to treat the patient in these cases? Should the courts distinguish among such cases on the basis of the reason for the physician's refusal?

2. In a footnote in *Hiser,* the court referred to the ethical duty of a doctor to render emergency treatment and noted the distinction between legal obligation and ethical obligation. When should ethical obligations be enforced by law, if ever? Would you support a statute that required physicians to render a certain amount of charity care as a condition of licensure? Would you support such a rule established by a local medical society as a condition of membership?

3. Note that the doctor's duty in *Hiser* is based on his contract with the hospital. Hospital-physician contracting has increased substantially since 1980, as have physician contracts with managed care plans. These latter contracts usually require physicians to treat any subscriber to the plan. How might such a contract apply to discrimination claims? How might such a contractual obligation arise in an abandonment claim? Under *Ricks* or *Childs,* may the doctor be liable to the patient for nontreatment if a current patient's health care plan has refused authorization for the proposed treatment? See discussion of liability in managed care in Chapter 8.

4. Once the court in *Hiser* decided that Dr. Randolph had a duty to treat Ms. Hiser, it went on to discuss whether Dr. Randolph's breach of this duty, and thus the 40–minute delay in treatment, was the proximate cause of Ms. Hiser's death. The court held that the plaintiff must prove that Ms. Hiser "probably died as a result of the 40 minutes delay in treatment." At 778. It stated that "the mere loss of an unspecified increment of the chance for survival is, of itself, insufficient to meet the standard of probability." At 779. Should the law recognize damages for increased stress, anxiety or pain in the absence of proof of any physical injury? See discussion of the problem of causation and damages in Chapter 5.

5. The physician may not have a duty to continue treatment for a variety of reasons, including: 1) termination by mutual consent; 2) explicit dismissal by the patient; 3) services required by the patient that are outside the physician's competence and training; 4) services outside the scope of the original doctor-patient agreement, where the physician has limited the contract to a type of procedure, to an office visit, or to consultation only; 5) failure of the patient to cooperate with the physician. The "lack of cooperation" cases require actions by the patient that suggest an implied unilateral termination of the relationship by the patient. This may occur, for example when the patient refuses to comply with the prescribed course of treatment or fails to return for further treatment. See, e.g., Payton v. Weaver, 131 Cal.App.3d 38, 182 Cal.Rptr. 225 (1982). Of course, all of these defenses are very fact-sensitive.

Problem: Cheryl Hanachek

Cheryl Hanachek, a resident of Boston, discovered she was pregnant during an "action" called by the city's obstetricians in protest against declining insurance payments for physician childbirth services. Ms. Hanachek first called Dr. Cunetto, who had been her obstetrician for the birth of her first child two years earlier. Dr. Cunetto's receptionist informed Ms. Hanachek that Dr. Cunetto was not able to take any new patients because her practice was "full." In fact, Dr. Cunetto had limited her practice due to her patient load.

About two weeks later, Ms. Hanachek called Dr. Simms, who had been recommended by her friends. Dr. Simms' receptionist told Ms. Hanachek that Dr. Simms was not taking any new patients as the fees paid by insurance plans were so low that he was even considering discontinuing his obstetrical practice. Ms. Hanachek reported to the receptionist that she was having infrequent minor cramping, and the receptionist told her that this was "nothing to worry about at this stage." Later that night Ms. Hanachek was admitted to the hospital on an emergency basis. Ms. Hanachek was in shock from blood loss due to a ruptured ectopic pregnancy. As a result of the rupture and other complications, Ms. Hanachek underwent a hysterectomy.

She has brought suit against Dr. Cunetto and Dr. Simms. If you were representing Ms. Hanachek, how would you proceed in arguing and proving your case?

B. THE AMERICANS WITH DISABILITIES ACT

Although the common law does not impose a duty to treat upon a physician in the absence of an established physician-patient relationship, legislatures sometimes, though rarely, have established duties upon the physician.

BRAGDON v. ABBOTT

Supreme Court of the United States, 1998.
524 U.S. 624, 118 S.Ct. 2196, 141 L.Ed.2d 540.

KENNEDY, J., delivered the opinion of the Court, in which STEVENS, SOUTER, GINSBERG, and BREYER, JJ., joined. STEVENS, J., filed a concurring opinion. REHNQUIST, C.J., filed an opinion concurring in the judgment in part and dissenting in part , in which SCALIA and THOMAS, JJ., joined, and in Part II of which O'CONNOR, J., joined. O'CONNOR, J., filed an opinion concurring in the judgment in part and dissenting in part.

We address in this case the application of the Americans with Disabilities Act of 1990 (ADA), 104 Stat. 327, 42 U.S.C. § 12101 *et seq.*, to persons infected with the human immunodeficiency virus (HIV). We granted certiorari to review, first, whether HIV infection is a disability under the ADA when the infection has not yet progressed to the so-called symptomatic phase; and, second, whether the Court of Appeals, in affirming a grant of summary judgment, cited sufficient material in the record to determine, as a matter of law, that respondent's infection with HIV posed no direct threat to the health and safety of her treating dentist.

I

Respondent Sidney Abbott has been infected with HIV since 1986. When the incidents we recite occurred, her infection had not manifested its most serious symptoms. On September 16, 1994, she went to the office of petitioner Randon Bragdon in Bangor, Maine, for a dental appointment. She disclosed her HIV infection on the patient registration form. Petitioner completed a dental examination, discovered a cavity, and informed respondent of his policy against filling cavities of HIV-infected patients. He offered to perform the work at a hospital with no added fee for his services, though respondent would be responsible for the cost of using the hospital's facilities. Respondent declined.

Respondent sued petitioner under § 302 of the ADA, [ ] alleging discrimination on the basis of her disability. Section 302 of the ADA provides:

> "No individual shall be discriminated against on the basis of disability in the full and equal enjoyment of the goods, services, facilities, privileges, advantages, or accommodations of any place of public accommodation by any person who ... operates a place of public accommodation." [ ]

The term "public accommodation" is defined to include the "professional office of a health care provider." [ ]

A later subsection qualifies the mandate not to discriminate. It provides:

> "Nothing in this subchapter shall require an entity to permit an individual to participate in or benefit from the goods, services, facilities, privileges, advantages and accommodations of such entity where such individual poses a direct threat to the health or safety of others." [ ]

... The District Court ruled in favor of the plaintiffs, holding that respondent's HIV infection satisfied the ADA's definition of disability. [ ]

...

The Court of Appeals affirmed. It held respondent's HIV infection was a disability under the ADA, even though her infection had not yet progressed to the symptomatic stage. [ ] The Court of Appeals also agreed that treating the respondent in petitioner's office would not have posed a direct threat to the health and safety of others. [ ] ...

II

We first review the ruling that respondent's HIV infection constituted a disability under the ADA. The statute defines disability as:

> "(A) a physical or mental impairment that substantially limits one or more of the major life activities of such individual; (B) a record of such an impairment; or (C) being regarded as having such impairment."[ ]

* * *

Our consideration of subsection (A) of the definition proceeds in three steps. First, we consider whether respondent's HIV infection was a physical impairment. Second, we identify the life activity upon which respondent relies (reproduction and child bearing) and determine whether it constitutes a major life activity under the ADA. Third, tying the two statutory phrases together, we ask whether the impairment substantially limited the major life activity.

A

[Ed. note: The Court states that the definition of disability in the ADA is drawn from and intended to provide at least as much protection as the definition of handicap in the Rehabilitation Act of 1973.]

1

The first step in the inquiry under subsection (A) requires us to determine whether respondent's condition constituted a physical impairment. The

Department of Health, Education and Welfare (HEW) issued the first regulations interpreting the Rehabilitation Act in 1977. ... The HEW regulations, which appear without change in the current regulations issued by the Department of Health and Human Services, define "physical or mental impairment" to mean:

> "(A) any physiological disorder or condition, cosmetic disfigurement, or anatomical loss affecting one or more of the following body systems: neurological; musculoskeletal; special sense organs; respiratory, including speech organs; cardiovascular; reproductive, digestive, genito-urinary; hemic and lymphatic; skin; and endocrine; or
>
> "(B) any mental or psychological disorder, such as mental retardation, organic brain syndrome, emotional or mental illness, and specific learning disabilities." [ ]

In issuing these regulations, HEW decided against including a list of disorders constituting physical or mental impairments, out of concern that any specific enumeration might not be comprehensive. [ ] ...

* * *

HIV infection is not included in the list of specific disorders constituting physical impairments, in part because HIV was not identified as the cause of AIDS until 1983. [ ] HIV infection does fall well within the general definition set forth by the regulations, however.

* * *

The initial stage of HIV infection is known as acute or primary HIV infection.... The assault on the immune system is immediate. The victim suffers from a sudden and serious decline in the number of white blood cells.... Mononucleosis-like symptoms often emerge between six days and six weeks after infection, at times accompanied by fever, headache, enlargement of the lymph nodes (lymphadenopathy), muscle pain (myalgia), rash, lethargy, gastrointestinal disorders, and neurological disorders. Usually these symptoms abate within 14 to 21 days. HIV antibodies appear in the bloodstream within 3 weeks; circulating HIV can be detected within 10 weeks. [ ]

After the symptoms associated with the initial stage subside, the disease enters what is referred to sometimes as its asymptomatic phase. The term is a misnomer, in some respects, for clinical features persist throughout, including lymphadenopathy, dermatological disorders, oral lesions, and bacterial infections. Although it varies with each individual, in most instances this stage lasts from 7 to 11 years....

* * *

In light of the immediacy with which the virus begins to damage the infected person's white blood cells and the severity of the disease, we hold it is an impairment from the moment of infection.... HIV infection satisfies the statutory and regulatory definition of a physical impairment during every stage of the disease.

2

The statute is not operative, and the definition not satisfied, unless the impairment affects a major life activity. Respondent's claim throughout this case has been that the HIV infection placed a substantial limitation on her ability to reproduce and to bear children. [ ] We ask, then, whether reproduction is a major life activity.

We have little difficulty concluding that it is. As the Court of Appeals held, "[t]he plain meaning of the word 'major' denotes comparative importance" and "suggest[s] that the touchstone for determining an activity's inclusion under the statutory rubric is its significance." [ ] Reproduction falls well within the phrase "major life activity." Reproduction and the sexual dynamics surrounding it are central to the life process itself.

While petitioner concedes the importance of reproduction, he claims that Congress intended the ADA only to cover those aspects of a person's life which have a public, economic, or daily character. [ ] The argument founders on the statutory language. Nothing in the definition suggests that activities without a public, economic, or daily dimension may somehow be regarded as so unimportant or insignificant as to fall outside the meaning of the word "major." . . .

As we have noted, the ADA must be construed to be consistent with regulations issued to implement the Rehabilitation Act. [ ] Rather than enunciating a general principle for determining what is and is not a major life activity the Rehabilitation Act regulations instead provide a representative list, defining term to include "functions such as caring for one's self, performing manual tasks, walking, seeing, hearing, speaking, breathing, learning, and working." [ ] As the use of the term "such as" confirms, the list is illustrative, not exhaustive.

3

The final element of the disability definition in subsection (A) is whether respondent's physical impairment was a substantial limit on the major life activity she asserts. The Rehabilitation Act regulations provide no additional guidance. [ ]

Our evaluation of the medical evidence leads us to conclude that respondent's infection substantially limited her ability to reproduce in two independent ways. First, a woman infected with HIV who tries to conceive a child imposes on the man a significant risk of becoming infected. . . .

Second, an infected woman risks infecting her child during gestation and childbirth . . .

* * *

The Act addresses substantial limitations on major life activities, not utter inabilities. Conception and childbirth are not impossible for an HIV victim but, without doubt, are dangerous to the public health. This meets the definition of a substantial limitation. The decision to reproduce carries economic and legal consequences as well. There are added costs for antiretroviral therapy, supplemental insurance, and long-term health care for the child who must be examined and, tragic to think, treated for the infection. The laws of some States, moreover, forbid persons infected with HIV from having sex with others, regardless of consent. [ ]

In the end, the disability definition does not turn on personal choice. When significant limitations result from the impairment, the definition is met even if the difficulties are not insurmountable.... [ ] We agree with the District Court and the Court of Appeals that no triable issue of fact impedes a ruling on the question of statutory coverage. Respondent's HIV infection is a physical impairment which substantially limits a major life activity, as the ADA defines it. In view of our holding, we need not address the second question presented, *i.e.*, whether HIV infection is a *per se* disability under the ADA.

B

Our holding is confirmed by a consistent course of agency interpretation before and after enactment of the ADA. Every agency to consider the issue under the Rehabilitation Act found statutory coverage for persons with asymptomatic HIV....

* * *

Every court which addressed the issue before the ADA was enacted in July 1990, moreover, concluded that asymptomatic HIV infection satisfied the Rehabilitation Act's definition of a handicap. [ ] We are aware of no instance prior to the enactment of the ADA in which a court or agency ruled that HIV infection was not a handicap under the Rehabilitation Act.

* * *

C

* * *

We also draw guidance from the views of the agencies authorized to administer other sections of the ADA. [ ] ... Most categorical of all is EEOC's conclusion that "an individual who has HIV infection (including asymptomatic HIV infection) is an individual with a disability." [ ] In the EEOC's view, "impairments ... such as HIV infection, are inherently substantially limiting." [ ]

III

[We granted certiorari on the following question:]

> When deciding under title III of the ADA whether a private health care provider must perform invasive procedures on an infectious patient in his office, should courts defer to the health care provider's professional judgment, as long as it is reasonable in light of then-current medical knowledge?

* * *

... The question is phrased in an awkward way, for it conflates two separate inquiries. In asking whether it is appropriate to defer to petitioner's judgment, it assumes that petitioner's assessment of the objective facts was reasonable. The central premise of the question and the assumption on which it is based merit separate consideration.

... Notwithstanding the protection given respondent by the ADA's definition of disability, petitioner could have refused to treat her if her infectious condition "posed a direct threat to the health or safety of others." [ ] The ADA defines a direct threat to be "a significant risk to the health or safety of others that cannot be eliminated by a modification of policies, practices, procedures, or by the provision of auxiliary aids or services." [ ] ...

The ADA's direct threat provision stems from the recognition in School Bd. of Nassau Cty. v. Arline [ ] of the importance of prohibiting discrimination against individuals with disabilities while protecting others from significant health and safety risks, resulting, for instance, from a contagious disease. In *Arline,* the Court reconciled these objectives by construing the Rehabilitation Act not to require the hiring of a person who posed "a significant risk of communicating an infectious disease to others." [ ] ... [A]DA's direct threat provision codifies *Arline*. Because few, if any, activities in life are risk free, *Arline* and the ADA do not ask whether a risk exists, but whether it is significant. [ ]

The existence, or nonexistence, of a significant risk must be determined from the standpoint of the person who refuses the treatment or accommodation, and the risk assessment must be based on medical or other objective evidence. [ ] As a health care professional, petitioner had the duty to assess the risk of infection based on the objective, scientific information available to him and others in his profession. His belief that a significant risk existed, even if maintained in good faith, would not relieve him from liability. To use the words of the question presented, petitioner receives no special deference simply because he is a health care professional. It is true that *Arline* reserved "the question whether courts should also defer to the reasonable medical judgments of private physicians on which an employer has relied." [ ] At most, this statement reserved the possibility that employers could consult with individual physicians as objective third-party experts. It did not suggest that an individual physician's state of mind could excuse discrimination without regard to the objective reasonableness of his actions.

... In assessing the reasonableness of petitioner's actions, the views of public health authorities, such as the U.S. Public Health Service, CDC, and the National Institutes of Health, are of special weight and authority. [ ] The views of these organizations are not conclusive, however. A health care professional who disagrees with the prevailing medical consensus may refute it by citing a credible scientific basis for deviating from the accepted norm. [ ]

[An] illustration of a correct application of the objective standard is the Court of Appeals' refusal to give weight to the petitioner's offer to treat respondent in a hospital. [ ] Petitioner testified that he believed hospitals had safety measures, such as air filtration, ultraviolet lights, and respirators, which would reduce the risk of HIV transmission. [ ] Petitioner made no showing, however, that any area hospital had these safeguards or even that he had hospital privileges. [ ] His expert also admitted the lack of any scientific basis for the conclusion that these measures would lower the risk of transmission. [ ] Petitioner failed to present any objective, medical evidence showing that treating respondent in a hospital would be safer or more efficient in preventing HIV transmission than treatment in a well-equipped dental office.

We are concerned, however, that the Court of Appeals might have placed mistaken reliance upon two other sources. In ruling no triable issue of fact existed on this point, the Court of Appeals relied on the CDC Dentistry Guidelines and the 1991 American Dental Association Policy on HIV. [ ] This evidence is not definitive.... [T]he CDC Guidelines recommended certain universal precautions which, in CDC's view, "should reduce the risk of disease transmission in the dental environment." [ ] The Court of Appeals determined that, "[w]hile the guidelines do not state explicitly that no further risk-reduction measures are desirable or that routine dental care for HIV-positive individuals is safe, those two conclusions seem to be implicit in the guidelines' detailed delineation of procedures for office treatment of HIV-positive patients." [ ] In our view, the Guidelines do not necessarily contain implicit assumptions conclusive of the point to be decided. The Guidelines set out CDC's recommendation that the universal precautions are the best way to combat the risk of HIV transmission. They do not assess the level of risk.

Nor can we be certain, on this record, whether the 1991 American Dental Association Policy on HIV carries the weight the Court of Appeals attributed to it. The Policy does provide some evidence of the medical community's objective assessment of the risks posed by treating people infected with HIV in dental offices. It indicates:

> "Current scientific and epidemiologic evidence indicates that there is little risk of transmission of infectious diseases through dental treatment if recommended infection control procedures are routinely followed. Patients with HIV infection may be safely treated in private dental offices when appropriate infection control procedures are employed. Such infection control procedures provide protection both for patients and dental personnel." [ ]

We note, however, that the Association is a professional organization, which, although a respected source of information on the dental profession, is not a public health authority. It is not clear the extent to which the Policy was based on the Association's assessment of dentists' ethical and professional duties in addition to its scientific assessment of the risk to which the ADA refers. Efforts to clarify dentists' ethical obligations and to encourage dentists to treat patients with HIV infection with compassion may be commendable, but the question under the statute is one of statistical likelihood, not professional responsibility. Without more information on the manner in which the American Dental Association formulated this Policy, we are unable to determine the Policy's value in evaluating whether petitioner's assessment of the risks was reasonable as a matter of law.

* * *

We acknowledge the presence of other evidence in the record before the Court of Appeals which, subject to further arguments and examination, might support affirmance of the trial court's ruling. For instance, the record contains substantial testimony from numerous health experts indicating that it is safe to treat patients infected with HIV in dental offices. [ ] We are unable to determine the import of this evidence, however. The record does not disclose whether the expert testimony submitted by respondent turned on evidence available in September 1994. [ ]

There are reasons to doubt whether petitioner advanced evidence sufficient to raise a triable issue of fact on the significance of the risk. Petitioner relied on two principal points: First, he asserted that the use of high-speed drills and surface cooling with water created a risk of airborne HIV transmission. The study on which petitioner relied was inconclusive, however, determining only that "further work is required to determine whether such a risk exists." [ ] Petitioner's expert witness conceded, moreover, that no evidence suggested the spray could transmit HIV. His opinion on airborne risk was based on the absence of contrary evidence, not on positive data. Scientific evidence and expert testimony must have a traceable, analytical basis in objective fact before it may be considered on summary judgment. [ ]

[P]etitioner argues that, as of September 1994, CDC had identified seven dental workers with possible occupational transmission of HIV. [ ] These dental workers were exposed to HIV in the course of their employment, but CDC could not determine whether HIV infection had resulted. [ ] It is now known that CDC could not ascertain whether the seven dental workers contracted the disease because they did not present themselves for HIV testing at an appropriate time after their initial exposure. [ ] It is not clear on this record, however, whether this information was available to petitioner in September 1994. If not, the seven cases might have provided some, albeit not necessarily sufficient, support for petitioner's position. Standing alone, we doubt it would meet the objective, scientific basis for finding a significant risk to the petitioner.

* * *

We conclude the proper course is to give the Court of Appeals the opportunity to determine whether our analysis of some of the studies cited by the parties would change its conclusion that petitioner presented neither objective evidence nor a triable issue of fact on the question of risk.

JUSTICE STEVENS, with whom JUSTICE BREYER joins, concurring.

... I do not believe petitioner has sustained his burden of adducing evidence sufficient to raise a triable issue of fact on the significance of the risk posed by treating respondent in his office.... I join the opinion even though I would prefer an outright affirmance. [ ]

JUSTICE GINSBURG, concurring.

... No rational legislator, it seems to me apparent, would require nondiscrimination once symptoms become visible but permit discrimination when the disease, though present, is not yet visible. I am therefore satisfied that the statutory and regulatory definitions are well met.... [ ]

I further agree, in view of the "importance [of the issue] to health care workers," that it is wise to remand, erring, if at all, on the side of caution. By taking this course, the Court ensures a fully informed determination whether respondent Abbott's disease posed "a significant risk to the health, or safety of [petitioner Bragdon] that [could not] be eliminated by a modification of policies, practices, or procedures...." [ ]

CHIEF JUSTICE REHNQUIST, with whom JUSTICE SCALIA and JUSTICE THOMAS join, and with whom JUSTICE O'CONNOR joins as to Part II, concurring in the judgment in part and dissenting in part.

* * *

[T]he ADA's definition of a "disability" requires that the major life activity at issue be one "of such individual." [ ] The Court truncates the question, perhaps because there is not a shred of record evidence indicating that, prior to becoming infected with HIV, respondent's major life activities included reproduction [ ] (assuming for the moment that reproduction is a major life activity at all). At most, the record indicates that after learning of her HIV status, respondent, whatever her previous inclination, conclusively decided that she would not have children. [ ] There is absolutely no evidence that, absent the HIV, respondent would have had or was even considering having children. Indeed, when asked during her deposition whether her HIV infection had in any way impaired her ability to carry out any of *her* life functions, respondent answered "No." [ ] It is further telling that in the course of her entire brief to this Court, respondent studiously avoids asserting even once that reproduction is a major life activity *to her*. To the contrary, she argues that the "major life activity" inquiry should not turn on a particularized assessment of the circumstances of this or any other case. [ ]

But even aside from the facts of this particular case, the Court is simply wrong in concluding as a general matter that reproduction is a "major life activity." . . .

* * *

No one can deny that reproductive decisions are important in a person's life. But so are decisions as to who to marry, where to live, and how to earn one's living. Fundamental importance of this sort is not the common thread linking the statute's listed activities. The common thread is rather that the activities are repetitively performed and essential in the day-to-day existence of a normally functioning individual. They are thus quite different from the series of activities leading to the birth of a child.

* * *

But even if I were to assume that reproduction *is* a major life activity of respondent, I do not agree that an asymptomatic HIV infection "substantially limits" that activity. The record before us leaves no doubt that those so infected are still entirely able to engage in sexual intercourse, give birth to a child if they become pregnant, and perform the manual tasks necessary to rear a child to maturity. [ ] While individuals infected with HIV may choose not to engage in these activities, there is no support in language, logic, or our case law for the proposition that such voluntary choices constitute a "limit" on one's own life activities.

* * *

Respondent contends that her ability to reproduce is limited because "the fatal nature of HIV infection means that a parent is unlikely to live long enough to raise and nurture the child to adulthood." [ ] . . . Respondent's argument, taken to its logical extreme, would render every individual with a genetic marker for some debilitating disease "disabled" here and now because of some possible future effects.

* * *

II

I agree with the Court that "the existence, or nonexistence, of a significant risk must be determined from the standpoint of the person who refuses the treatment or accommodation," as of the time that the decision refusing treatment is made. [ ] I disagree with the Court, however, that "in assessing the reasonableness of petitioner's actions, the views of public health authorities ... are of special weight and authority." [ ] Those views are, of course, entitled to a presumption of validity when the actions of those authorities themselves are challenged in court, and even in disputes between private parties where Congress has committed that dispute to adjudication by a public health authority. But in litigation between private parties originating in the federal courts, I am aware of no provision of law or judicial practice that would require or permit courts to give some scientific views more credence than others simply because they have been endorsed by a politically appointed public health authority (such as the Surgeon General). In litigation of this latter sort, which is what we face here, the credentials of the scientists employed by the public health authority, and the soundness of their studies, must stand on their own. The Court cites no authority for its limitation upon the courts' truth-finding function, except the statement in School Bd. of Nassau Cty. v. Arline, [ ] that in making findings regarding the risk of contagion under the Rehabilitation Act, "courts normally should defer to the reasonable medical judgments of public health officials." But there is appended to that dictum the following footnote, which makes it very clear that the Court was urging respect for *medical* judgment, and not necessarily respect for "official" medical judgment over "private" medical judgment: "This case does not present, and we do not address, the question whether courts should also defer to the reasonable medical judgments of private physicians on which an employer has relied." [ ]

Applying these principles here, it is clear to me that petitioner has presented more than enough evidence to avoid summary judgment on the "direct threat" question.... Given the "severity of the risk" involved here, *i.e.*, near certain death, and the fact that no public health authority had outlined a protocol for *eliminating* this risk in the context of routine dental treatment, it seems likely that petitioner can establish that it was objectively reasonable for him to conclude that treating respondent in his office posed a "direct threat" to his safety.

* * *

JUSTICE O'CONNOR, concurring in the judgment in part and dissenting in part.

I agree with The Chief Justice that respondent's claim of disability should be evaluated on an individualized basis and that she has not proven that her asymptomatic HIV status substantially limited one or more of her major life activities. In my view, the act of giving birth to a child, while a very important part of the lives of many women, is not generally the same as the representative major life activities of all persons—"caring for one's self, performing manual tasks, walking, seeing, hearing, speaking, breathing, learning, and working"—listed in regulations relevant to the Americans with Disabilities Act of 1990....

I join in Part II of The Chief Justice's opinion concurring in the judgment in part and dissenting in part, which concludes that the Court of Appeals failed to properly determine whether respondent's condition posed a direct threat. Accordingly, I agree that a remand is necessary on that issue.

Notes and Questions

1. On remand, the Ninth Circuit upheld the District Court's grant of summary judgment in favor of the plaintiff:

> The CDC did not write the 1993 Guidelines in a vacuum, but, rather, updated earlier versions issued in 1986 and 1987, respectively. The 1986 text calls the universal precautions "effective for preventing hepatitis B, acquired immunodeficiency syndrome, and other infectious diseases caused by bloodborne viruses." The 1987 edition explains that use of the universal precautions eliminates the need for additional precautions that the CDC formerly had advocated for handling blood and other bodily fluids known or suspected to be infected with bloodborne pathogens. Neither the parties nor any of the amici have suggested that the 1993 rewrite was intended to retreat from these earlier risk assessments, and we find no support for such a position in the Guidelines' text . . .
>
> The [American Dental] Association formulates scientific and ethical policies by separate procedures, drawing on different member groups and different staff complements. The Association's Council on Scientific Affairs, comprised of 17 dentists (most of whom hold advanced dentistry degrees), together with a staff of over 20 professional experts and consultants, drafted the Policy at issue here. By contrast, ethical policies are drafted by the Council on Ethics, a wholly separate body. Although the Association's House of Delegates must approve policies drafted by either council, we think that the origins of the Policy satisfy any doubts regarding its scientific foundation.
>
> For these reasons, we are confident that we appropriately relied on the Guidelines and the Policy.... Thus, we again conclude, after due reevaluation, that Ms. Abbott served a properly documented motion for summary judgment.
>
> We next reconsider whether Dr. Bragdon offered sufficient proof of direct threat to create a genuine issue of material fact and thus avoid the entry of summary judgment.... The Supreme Court suggested that one such piece of evidence—the seven cases that the CDC considered "possible" HIV patient-to-dental worker transmissions—should be reexamined. Since an objective standard pertains here, the existence of the list of seven "possible" cases does not create a genuine issue of material fact as to direct threat.... Each piece of evidence to which [defendant directs] us is still "too speculative or too tangential (or, in some instances, both) to create a genuine issue of material fact."
>
> ... Upon reflection, we again find that Dr. Bragdon did not submit evidence to the district court demonstrating a genuine issue of material fact on the direct threat issue.

Abbott v. Bragdon, 163 F.3d 87 (1st Cir.1998), cert. denied 526 U.S. 1131, 119 S.Ct. 1805, 143 L.Ed.2d 1009 (1999). What impact does this decision have on the importance of the Supreme Court's decision as to the issue of "direct threat?"

2. How far can the Court's determination that asymptomatic HIV is a disability under the ADA be taken? See e.g., Quick v. Tripp, Scott, Conklin & Smith, P.A., 43 F.Supp.2d 1357 (S.D.Fla.1999) (hepatitis C is a disability); McGraw v. Sears, Roebuck & Co., 21 F.Supp.2d 1017 (D.Minn.1998) (menopause is not a disability); Gutwaks v. American Airlines, Inc., 1999 WL 1611328

(N.D.Tex.1999) (HIV is not a disability because the specific plaintiff had no intention to procreate). In 1999, the Supreme Court decided two more ADA cases concerning the application of the definition of disability. In Sutton v. United Airlines, 527 U.S. 471, 119 S.Ct. 2139, 144 L.Ed.2d 450 (1999) and Murphy v. United Parcel Service, 527 U.S. 516, 119 S.Ct. 2133, 144 L.Ed.2d 484(1999), the Supreme Court held that disabilities that were correctable with devices such as eyeglasses were not disabilities under the Act.

3. Access to dental care has been a particular concern in litigation over refusals to treat persons with HIV. See Scott Burris, Dental Discrimination Against the HIV–Infected: Empirical Data, Law and Public Policy, 13 Yale J. on Reg. 1 (1996), for data on the incidence of refusals to treat, factors that depress lawsuits for discriminatory practices, and an analysis of the impact of legal and other forces on professional behavior. For a discussion of other access issues, see Linda C. Fentiman, AIDS as a Chronic Illness: a Cautionary Tale for the End of the Twentieth Century, 61 Alb. L. Rev. 989, (1998), part of a Symposium on Health Care Policy: What Lessons Have We Learned from the AIDS Pandemic.

4. Although some persons with HIV/AIDS require very specialized treatment, most need the same medical services as other generally healthy individuals and as other chronically or intermittently disabled persons. In 1988, the AMA Council on Ethical and Judicial Affairs announced that "a physician may not ethically refuse to treat a patient whose condition is within the physician's current realm of competence solely because the patient is (HIV) seropositive." Council Report on Ethical Issues, 259 JAMA 1360 (1988). What is the significance of the AMA's use of the word "solely?" Does the AMA's statement address the risk of transmission in medical situations? Does it intend to address unsupported fears of transmission? Does it reach homophobia? Racism? Again, should the reason for refusing the patient make a difference? Many state legislatures have amended their medical practice acts to provide that discrimination against persons with HIV is ground for disciplinary action, and usually this is the only antidiscrimination provision in the medical practice act. See e.g., Wisc. Stat. S 252.14.

5. Chief Justice Rehnquist implies that no risk of transmission is tolerable if the disease is fatal. For a discussion of risk assessment and the ADA, see discussion in Chapter 12.

6. The Americans with Disabilities Act also applies to insurance (see Chapter 9); to governmental health care decisions (see Chapter 10); and to employment (see Chapter 12).

II. HOSPITALS' DUTY TO PROVIDE TREATMENT

A hospital may have a common law duty to provide emergency care. In Wilmington Gen. Hospital v. Manlove, 54 Del. 15, 174 A.2d 135 (1961), the court held that even though a hospital might not have an obligation to have an emergency room, if it did it, must provide emergency care to a person who relies on the presence of an emergency room in coming to the hospital. In New Biloxi Hospital, Inc. v. Frazier, 245 Miss. 185, 146 So.2d 882 (1962), the Mississippi Supreme Court held a hospital liable for the death of a patient who had been taken to the hospital's emergency room by ambulance after suffering a gunshot wound. The patient remained untreated in the emergency room for two hours, despite heavy blood loss and shock, and died twenty-five minutes after transfer to a Veterans Administration hospital. The Mississippi

Supreme Court based their holding on the hospital's breach of the duty to exercise reasonable care once treatment was "undertaken." The Court found that the hospital had undertaken treatment of the patient by virtue of the patient's presence in the emergency room for two hours and his being recorded as an emergency room patient. In Thompson v. Sun City Community Hospital, 141 Ariz. 597, 688 P.2d 605 (1984), the court relied on state hospital regulations and standards of the Joint Commission on Accreditation of Healthcare Organizations to find a duty enforceable through private litigation. Do the varying theories of these cases make a difference in litigating a duty to provide emergency care? The scope of that duty?

The common-law duty of the hospital toward the emergency patient was captured traditionally in the phrase "stabilize and transfer" indicating that once the patient's emergency condition was stabilized, the patient could be transferred. Some few states established broader duties, while in some states there was no statute or case law on the point. Whether the patient was stable at transfer was often a key issue in the legal dispute. For an excellent analysis of the history and scope of this legal doctrine see, Karen Rothenberg, Who Cares? The Evolution of the Legal Duty to Provide Emergency Care, 26 Hous.L.Rev. 21 (1989).

The federal Emergency Medical Treatment and Labor Act. 42 U.S.C.A. § 1395dd (EMTALA) was enacted in response to widespread "patient dumping," a practice in which patients would be transferred from one hospital's emergency room to another's for admission. Several empirical studies of hospital transfers documented this problem. A study in Chicago, for example, reported that transfers from private hospitals to public hospitals increased from 1295 in 1980 to 6769 in 1983, with 24% being unstable at time of transfer. Lack of insurance was the reason given for 87% of the transfers. The cost to the public hospital was $3.35 million, of which $2.81 million would not be reimbursed by insurance, Medicaid or Medicare. Robert L. Schiff *et al.*, Transfers to a Public Hospital, 314 New Eng. J. Med. 552 (1986), one of several studies documenting such transfers. What might explain the substantial increase from 1980 to 1983?

EMTALA applies *only* to hospitals that accept payment from Medicare *and* operate an emergency department. (EMTALA does not require a hospital to offer emergency room services, though some state statutes may). There are two major requirements under the statute. The first requirement is that the hospital give the patient an "appropriate medical screening" upon presentation at the hospital's emergency department and the determination that the patient has an emergency medical condition. The second major requirement is that the hospital stabilize the patient prior to transfer, if transfer is necessary. Violations of these requirements are treated differently when the violations are reported against hospitals or physicians. The statute allows a patient to bring a civil suit for damages for an EMTALA violation against a participating hospital, 42 U.S.C.A. § 1395dd(d)(2)(A); however, no section permits an individual to bring a similar action against a treating physician. Instead, the enforcement sections of EMTALA allow an action against a physician only by the Department of Health and Human Services to bar his participation in Medicare programs and/or to seek administrative sanctions in the form of civil monetary penalties. 42 U.S.C.A.§§ 1395dd(d)(1) & (2)(B). Thus, nothing in the language of the statute permits a private individual to recover personal injury damages from a physician for an EMTALA violation.

BABER v. HOSPITAL CORPORATION OF AMERICA

United States Court of Appeals, Fourth Circuit, 1992.
977 F.2d 872.

WILLIAMS, CIRCUIT JUDGE:

Barry Baber, Administrator of the Estate of Brenda Baber, instituted this suit against Dr. Richard Kline, Dr. Joseph Whelan, Raleigh General Hospital (RGH), Beckley Appalachian Regional Hospital (BARH), and the parent corporations of both hospitals. Mr. Baber alleged that the Defendants violated the Emergency Medical Treatment and Active Labor Act (EMTALA) [ ]. The Defendants moved to dismiss the EMTALA claim under Rule 12(b)(6) of the Federal Rules of Civil Procedure. Because the parties submitted affidavits and depositions, the district court treated the motion as one for summary judgment. See Fed.R.Civ.P. 12(b).

* * *

Mr. Baber's complaint charged the various defendants with violating EMTALA in several ways. Specifically, Mr. Baber contends that Dr. Kline, RGH, and its parent corporation violated EMTALA by:

(a) failing to provide his sister with an "appropriate medical screening examination;"

(b) failing to stabilize his sister's "emergency medical condition;" and

(c) transferring his sister to BARH without first providing stabilizing treatment.

* * *

After reviewing the parties' submissions, the district court granted summary judgment for the Defendants. . . . Finding no error, we affirm.

* * *

. . . Brenda Baber, accompanied by her brother, Barry, sought treatment at RGH's emergency department at 10:40 p.m. on August 5, 1987. When she entered the hospital, Ms. Baber was nauseated, agitated, and thought she might be pregnant. She was also tremulous and did not appear to have orderly thought patterns. She had stopped taking her anti-psychosis medications, . . . and had been drinking heavily. Dr. Kline, the attending physician, described her behavior and condition in the RGH Encounter Record as follows: Patient refuses to remain on stretcher and cannot be restrained verbally despite repeated requests by staff and by me. Brother has not assisted either verbally or physically in keeping patient from pacing throughout the Emergency Room. Restraints would place patient and staff at risk by increasing her agitation.

In response to Ms. Baber's initial complaints, Dr. Kline examined her central nervous system, lungs, cardiovascular system, and abdomen. He also ordered several laboratory tests, including a pregnancy test.

While awaiting the results of her laboratory tests, Ms. Baber began pacing about the emergency department. In an effort to calm Ms. Baber, Dr. Kline gave her [several medications]. The medication did not immediately control her agitation. Mr. Baber described his sister as becoming restless, "worse and more disoriented after she was given the medication," and wandering around the emergency department.

While roaming in the emergency department around midnight, Ms. Baber . . . convulsed and fell, striking her head upon a table and lacerating her scalp. [S]he quickly regained consciousness and emergency department personnel carried her by stretcher to the suturing room, [where] Dr. Kline examined her again. He obtained a blood gas study, which did not reveal any oxygen deprivation or acidosis. Ms. Baber was verbal and could move her head, eyes, and limbs without discomfort. . . . Dr. Kline closed the one-inch laceration with a couple of sutures. Although she became calmer and drowsy after the wound was sutured, Ms. Baber was easily arousable and easily disturbed. Ms. Baber experienced some anxiety, disorientation, restlessness, and some speech problems, which Dr. Kline concluded were caused by her pre-existing psychiatric problems of psychosis with paranoia and alcohol withdrawal.

Dr. Kline discussed Ms. Baber's condition with Dr. Whelan, the psychiatrist who had treated Ms. Baber for two years . . . Dr. Whelan concluded that Ms. Baber's hyperactive and uncontrollable behavior during her evening at RGH was compatible with her behavior during a relapse of her serious psychotic and chronic mental illness. Both Dr. Whelan and Dr. Kline were concerned about the seizure she had while at RGH's emergency department because it was the first one she had experienced . . . They also agreed Ms. Baber needed further treatment . . . and decided to transfer her to the psychiatric unit at BARH because RGH did not have a psychiatric ward, and both doctors believed it would be beneficial for her to be treated in a familiar setting. The decision to transfer Ms. Baber was further supported by the doctors' belief that any tests to diagnose the cause of her initial seizure, such as a computerized tomography scan (CT scan), could be performed at BARH once her psychiatric condition was under control. The transfer to BARH was discussed with Mr. Baber who neither expressly consented nor objected. His only request was that his sister be x-rayed because of the blow to her head when she fell.

* * *

Because Dr. Kline did not conclude Ms. Baber had a serious head injury, he believed that she could be transferred safely to BARH where she would be under the observation of the BARH psychiatric staff personnel. At 1:35 a.m. on August 6, Ms. Baber was admitted directly to the psychiatric department of BARH upon Dr. Whelan's orders. She was not processed through BARH's emergency department. Although Ms. Baber was restrained and regularly checked every fifteen minutes by the nursing staff while at BARH, no physician gave her an extensive neurological examination upon her arrival. Mr. Baber unsuccessfully repeated his request for an x-ray.

At the 3:45 a.m. check, the nurse found Ms. Baber having a grand mal seizure. At Dr. Whelan's direction, the psychiatric unit staff transported her to BARH's emergency department. Upon arrival in the emergency department, her pupils were unresponsive, and hospital personnel began CPR. The emergency department physician ordered a CT scan, which was performed around 6:30 a.m. The CT report revealed a fractured skull and a right subdural hematoma. BARH personnel immediately transferred Ms. Baber back to RGH because that hospital had a neurosurgeon on staff, and BARH did not have the facility or staff to treat serious neurological problems. When RGH received Ms. Baber for treatment around 7 a.m., she was comatose. She died later that day, apparently as a result of an intracerebrovascular rupture.

The district court granted summary judgment for Dr. Kline and Dr. Whelan because it found that EMTALA does not give patients a private cause of action against their doctors. We review this finding de novo because the interpretation of a statute is a question of law. [ ] Because we hold EMTALA does not permit private suits for damages against the attending physicians, we affirm the district court's grant of summary judgment for Dr. Whelan and Dr. Kline.

* * *

Mr. Baber . . . alleges that RGH, acting through its agent, Dr. Kline, violated several provisions of EMTALA. These allegations can be summarized into two general complaints: (1) RGH failed to provide an appropriate medical screening to discover that Ms. Baber had an emergency medical condition as required by *42 U.S.C.A. § 1395dd*(a); and (2) RGH transferred Ms. Baber before her emergency medical condition had been stabilized, and the appropriate paperwork was not completed to transfer a non-stable patient as required by *42 U.S.C.A. §§ 1395dd*(b) & (c). Because we find that RGH did not violate any of these EMTALA provisions, we affirm the district court's grant of summary judgment to RGH.

Mr. Baber first claims that RGH failed to provide his sister with an "appropriate medical screening". He makes two arguments. First, he contends that a medical screening is only "appropriate" if it satisfies a national standard of care. In other words, Mr. Baber urges that we construe EMTALA as a national medical malpractice statute, albeit limited to whether the medical screening was appropriate to identify an emergency medical condition. We conclude instead that EMTALA only requires hospitals to apply their standard screening procedure for identification of an emergency medical condition uniformly to all patients and that Mr. Baber has failed to proffer sufficient evidence showing that RGH did not do so. Second, Mr. Baber contends that EMTALA requires hospitals to provide some medical screening. We agree, but conclude that he has failed to show no screening was provided to his sister.

* * *

While [the Act] requires a hospital's emergency department to provide an "appropriate medical screening examination," it does not define that term other than to state its purpose is to identify an "emergency medical condition."

* * *

[T]he goal of "an appropriate medical screening examination" is to determine whether a patient with acute or severe symptoms has a life threatening or serious medical condition. The plain language of the statute requires a hospital to develop a screening procedure designed to identify such critical conditions that exist in symptomatic patients and to apply that screening procedure uniformly to all patients with similar complaints.

[W]hile EMTALA requires a hospital emergency department to apply its standard screening examination uniformly, it does not guarantee that the emergency personnel will correctly diagnose a patient's condition as a result of this screening.* The statutory language clearly indicates that EMTALA does not impose on hospitals a national standard of care in screening patients. The screening requirement only requires a hospital to provide a screening examination that is "appropriate" and "within the capability of the hospital's emergency department," including "routinely available" ancillary services. 42 U.S.C.A. § 1395dd(a). This section establishes a standard, which will of necessity be individualized for each hospital, since hospital emergency departments have varying capabilities. Had Congress intended to require hospitals to provide a screening examination which comported with generally-accepted medical standards, it could have clearly specified a national standard. Nor do we believe Congress intended to create a negligence standard based on each hospital's capability ... EMTALA is no substitute for state law medical malpractice actions.

* * *

The Sixth Circuit has also held that an appropriate medical screening means "a screening that the hospital would have offered to any paying patient" or at least "not known by the provider to be insufficient or below their own standards."**

* * *

Applying our interpretation of section (a) of EMTALA, we must next determine whether there is any genuine issue of material fact regarding whether RGH gave Ms. Baber a medical screening examination that differed from its standard screening procedure. Because Mr. Baber has offered no evidence of disparate treatment, we find that the district court did not err in granting summary judgment.

* * *

* Some commentators have criticized defining "appropriate" in terms of the hospital's medical screening standard because hospitals could theoretically avoid liability by providing very cursory and substandard screenings to all patients, which might enable the doctor to ignore a medical condition. See, e.g., Karen I. Treiger, Note, Preventing Patient Dumping: Sharpening COBRA's Fangs, 61 N.Y.U.L.Rev. 1186 (1986). Even though we do not believe it is likely that a hospital would endanger all of its patients by establishing such a cursory standard, theoretically it is possible. Our holding, however, does not foreclose the possibility that a future court faced with such a situation may decide that the hospital's standard was so low that it amounted to no "appropriate medical screening." We do not decide that question in this case because Ms. Baber's screening was not so substandard as to amount to no screening at all.

** While a hospital emergency room may develop one general procedure for screening all patients, it may also tailor its screening procedure to the patient's complaints or exhibited symptoms. For example, it may have one screening procedure for a patient with a heart attack and another for women in labor. Under our interpretation of EMTALA, such varying screening procedures would not pose liability under EMTALA as long as all patients complaining of the same problem or exhibiting the same symptoms receive identical screening procedures. We also recognize that the hospital's screening procedure is not limited to personal observation and assessment but may include available ancillary services through departments such as radiology and laboratory.

Mr. Baber does not allege that RGH's emergency department personnel treated Ms. Baber differently from its other patients. Instead, he merely claims Dr. Kline did not do enough accurately to diagnose her condition or treat her injury. [ ] The critical element of an EMTALA cause of action is not the adequacy of the screening examination but whether the screening examination that was performed deviated from the hospital's evaluation procedures that would have been performed on any patient in a similar condition.

* * *

Dr. Kline testified that he performed a medical screening on Ms. Baber in accordance with standard procedures for examining patients with head injuries. He explained that generally, a patient is not scheduled for advanced tests such as a CT scan or x-rays unless the patient's signs and symptoms so warrant. While Ms. Baber did exhibit some of the signs and symptoms of patients who have severe head injuries, in Dr. Kline's medical judgment these signs were the result of her pre-existing psychiatric condition, not the result of her fall. He, therefore, determined that Ms. Baber's head injury was not serious and did not indicate the need at that time for a CT scan or x-rays. In his medical judgment, Ms. Baber's condition would be monitored adequately by the usual nursing checks performed every fifteen minutes by the psychiatric unit staff at BARH. Although Dr. Kline's assessment and judgment may have been erroneous and not within acceptable standards of medical care in West Virginia, he did perform a screening examination that was not so substandard as to amount to no examination. No testimony indicated that his procedure deviated from that which RGH would have provided to any other patient in Ms. Baber's condition.

* * *

The essence of Mr. Baber's argument is that the extent of the examination and treatment his sister received while at RGH was deficient. While Mr. Baber's testimony might be sufficient to survive a summary judgment motion in a medical malpractice case, it is clearly insufficient to survive a motion for summary judgment in an EMTALA case because at no point does Mr. Baber present any evidence that RGH deviated from its standard screening procedure in evaluating Ms. Baber's head injury. Therefore, the district court properly granted RGH summary judgment on the medical screening issue.

Mr. Baber also asserts that RGH inappropriately transferred his sister to BARH. EMTALA's transfer requirements do not apply unless the hospital actually determines that the patient suffers from an emergency medical condition. Accordingly, to recover for violations of EMTALA's transfer provisions, the plaintiff must present evidence that (1) the patient had an emergency medical condition; (2) the hospital actually knew of that condition; (3) the patient was not stabilized before being transferred; and (4) prior to transfer of an unstable patient, the transferring hospital did not obtain the proper consent or follow the appropriate certification and transfer procedures.

* * *

Mr. Baber argues that requiring a plaintiff to prove the hospital had actual knowledge of the patient's emergency medical condition would allow hospitals to circumvent the purpose of EMTALA by simply requiring their personnel to state in all hospital records that the patient did not suffer from an emergency medical condition. Because of this concern, Mr. Baber urges us to adopt a standard that would impose liability upon a hospital if it failed to provide stabilizing treatment prior to a transfer when the hospital knew or should have known that the patient suffered from an emergency medical condition.

The statute itself implicitly rejects this proposed standard. Section 1395dd(b)(1) states the stabilization requirement exists if "any individual ... comes to a hospital and the hospital determines that the individual has an emergency medical condition." Thus, the plain language of the statute dictates a standard requiring actual knowledge of the emergency medical condition by the hospital staff.

Mr. Baber failed to present any evidence that RGH had actual knowledge that Ms. Baber suffered from an emergency medical condition. Dr. Kline stated in his affidavit that Ms. Baber's condition was stable prior to transfer and that he did not believe she was suffering from an emergency medical condition. While Mr. Baber testified that he believed his sister suffered from an emergency medical condition at transfer, he did not present any evidence beyond his own belief that she actually had an emergency medical condition or that anyone at RGH knew that she suffered from an emergency medical condition. In addition, we note that Mr. Baber's testimony is not competent to prove his sister actually had an emergency medical condition since he is not qualified to diagnose a serious internal brain injury.

... [W]e hold that the district court correctly granted RGH summary judgment on Mr. Baber's claim that it transferred Ms. Baber in violation of EMTALA.

* * *

Therefore, the district court's judgment is affirmed.

AFFIRMED

Notes and Questions

1. Under what authority does the federal government require hospitals to provide emergency medical screening and treatment to people who are not covered by Medicare? Is this an appropriate use of that authority? Why did Congress not appropriate Medicare or other funds to reimburse hospitals for EMTALA care? Why did Congress link EMTALA to participation in Medicare rather than Medicaid? How far, if at all, should legal obligations of uncompensated care extend? The cost of the EMTALA obligation has been significant. In December 2000, Congress directed the GAO to study EMTALA. The House Conference Report delineates the following questions:

> (1) the extent to which hospitals, emergency physicians, and physicians covering emergency department call provide uncompensated services in relation to the requirements of EMTALA; (2) the extent to which the regulatory requirements and enforcement of EMTALA have expanded beyond the legislation's original intent; (3) estimates for the total dollar amount of EMTALA-related care uncompensated costs to emergency physicians, physicians covering emergency department call, hospital emergency departments, and other hospital services; (4) the extent to which different portions of the United

States may be experiencing different levels of uncompensated EMTALA-related care; (5) the extent to which EMTALA would be classified as an unfunded mandate if it were enacted today; (6) the extent to which States have programs to provide financial support for such uncompensated care; (7) possible sources of funds, including Medicare hospital bad debt accounts, that are available to hospitals to assist with the cost of such uncompensated care; and (8) the financial strain that illegal immigration populations, the uninsured, and the underinsured place on hospital emergency departments, other hospital services, emergency physicians, and physicians covering emergency department call. H.R. CONF. REP. 106–1004.

Where did the costs now borne by the hospitals fall before the enactment of EMTALA?

See, Lynn Healey Scaduto, The Emergency Medical Treatment and Active Labor Act Gone Astray: A Proposal to Reclaim EMTALA for Its Intended Beneficiaries, 46 UCLA L. Rev. 943 (1999); Michael J. Frank, Tailoring EMTALA to Better Protect the Indigent: The Supreme Court Precludes One Method of Salvaging a Statute Gone Awry, 3 DePaul J. Health Care L. 195 (2000). But see, Lawrence E. Singer, Look What They've Done to My Law, Ma: COBRA's Implosion, 33 Hous. L. Rev. 113 (1996); Erik J. Olson, No Room at the Inn: A Snapshot of an American Emergency Room, 46 Stan. L. Rev. 449 (1994); Maria O'Brien Hylton, The Economics and Politics of Emergency Health Care for the Poor: The Patient Dumping Dilemma, 1992 B.Y.U.L. Rev. 971; Kristine Marie Meece, The Future of Emergency Department Liability after the Ravenswood Hospital Incident: Redefining the Duty the Duty to Treat?, 3 De Paul J. Health Care L. 101 (1999), each examining the impact of EMTALA.

2. The Sixth Circuit, in considering EMTALA, declared the word "appropriate" to be "one of the most wonderful weasel words in the dictionary, and a great aid to the resolution of disputed issues in the drafting of legislation." Cleland v. Bronson Health Care Group, 917 F.2d 266 (6th Cir.1990). Why would Congress choose to leave such a critical term undefined? Leaving this term undefined has generated many court opinions that try to give meaning to the term. *Baber* is typical of the majority of these cases in the standard it uses to decide whether the medical screening provided by the hospital was appropriate. How does this standard differ from that which would be used in a medical malpractice case? In contrast to the standard the courts have applied in relation to the adequacy of medical screening, the standard generally applied to the question of whether the patient was discharged or transferred in an unstable condition is an objective professional standard, as in *Howe* (see below). How should plaintiff structure discovery to meet these two standards? What would be the role for expert testimony, if any? May the plaintiff simply choose to pursue an "unstable transfer or discharge" claim instead of an "inappropriate screening" claim?

3. The Supreme Court, in Roberts v. Galen of Virginia, Inc., 525 U.S. 249, 119 S.Ct. 685, 142 L.Ed.2d 648 (1999), addressed the question of whether improper motive is required under EMTALA for violation of the requirement that the patient be stabilized. In doing so, the Court overturned the decision of the Sixth Circuit. Earlier, the Sixth Circuit in *Cleland* had held that improper motive was required for a violation of the Act in regard to the requirement that the hospital provide an appropriate medical screening. The Supreme Court expressed no opinion on the correctness of the *Cleland* decision. Is it possible to distinguish the two provisions at issue. How are they different? See e.g., Newsome v. Mann, 105 F.Supp.2d 610 (E.D.Ky.2000). The Circuits have almost uniformly held that

EMTALA reaches beyond economically motivated decisions and that proof of motive is not required. Could proof of improper motive be useful to the plaintiff in distinguishing negligent misdiagnosis from an EMTALA claim? How might such proof assist plaintiff in making his or her case? See *Howe*, infra.

4. Another persistent issue in the interpretation of EMTALA is whether the patient is required to have come "to the emergency department" to trigger the obligations of the Act. In Lopez–Soto v. Hawayek, 175 F.3d 170 (1st Cir.1999), the court considered a district court opinion that had held that the Act should be read to require that the patient have come to the hospital's emergency department in order to raise the obligation to provide an appropriate medical screening and that the appropriate medical screening provided must reveal the emergency condition and, thus, trigger the obligation to stabilize the patient. The Court of Appeals reversed and remanded in considering the case of an infant born in the hospital's maternity ward and transferred in distress and without stabilizing treatment.

Federal regulations under EMTALA deal with other questions regarding whether the patient has come to the emergency department. For instance, 49 CFR 489.24(b) states:

> An individual "coming to the emergency department" means ... that the individual is on the hospital property (property includes ambulances owned and operated by the hospital, even if the ambulance is not on hospital grounds). An individual in a nonhospital-owned ambulance off hospital property is not considered to have come to the hospital's emergency department, even if a member of the ambulance staff contacts the hospital by telephone or telemetry communications and informs the hospital that they want to transport the individual to the hospital for examination and treatment. In such situations, the hospital may deny access if it is in "diversionary status," that is, it does not have the staff or facilities to accept any additional emergency patients. If, however, the ambulance staff disregards the hospital's instructions and transports the individual on to hospital property, the individual is considered to have come to the emergency department.

5. Many EMTALA claims are resolved through summary judgment, perhaps reflecting judicial concerns that the Act is too broad. See e.g., Summers v. Baptist Medical Center Arkadelphia, 91 F.3d 1132 (8th Cir.1996). Judge Heaney, who had written the majority opinion in favor of the plaintiff for the Eighth Circuit panel that originally heard the appeal of *Summers* (at 69 F.3d 902 (8th Cir.1995)), dissented from the majority opinion following the court's *en banc* hearing of the case. Judge Heaney writes in his dissent:

> The majority ... accepts as true that Summers complained to the doctor about his chest pains and throbbing chest. Baptist even concedes this point. The Majority assumes, however, that the physician: "through inadvertence or inattention, did not perceive Summers to have cracking or popping noises in his chest, or pain in the front of his chest. This is why no chest x-rays were taken. In the medical judgement of the physician, Summers did not need a chest x-ray. Summers did receive substantial medical treatment. It was not perfect, perhaps negligent, but he was treated no differently from any other patient perceived to have the same condition." ... It was for the jury, not the district court or this court , to determine the relative credibility of the parties and what occurred in the emergency room that day. We should not assume that the doctor did not hear Summers or forgot about his complaints. Nor should we assume that it was the physician's medical judgment that prompted his failure to give Summers a chest x-ray. It is possible that the doctor heard

Summers' complaints and, for no legitimate reason, failed to do anything about them. That alternative would establish the essentials of an EMTALA cause of action.

What is at stake for plaintiffs and defendants when federal courts resolve most EMTALA screening claims on summary judgment rather than submitting the case to the jury?

6. For a guide to the requirements of EMTALA in litigation see, Barry R. Furrow, An Overview and Analysis of the Impact of the Emergency Medical Treatment and Active Labor Act, 16 J. Legal Med. 325 (1995); Wendy W. Berra "Preventing Patient–Dumping: The Supreme Court Turns Away the Sixth Circuit's Interpretation of EMTALA," 36 Hous. L. Rev. 615 (1999); Alicia K. Dowdy et al., The Anatomy of EMTALA: A Litigator's Guide, 27 St. Mary's L. J.463 (1996).

7. Substantial conflicts have occurred between hospitals and managed care plans, which typically require pre-treatment authorization by the plan for services provided by a hospital to an individual subscriber. Hospitals claim that managed care plans take advantage of the hospitals' obligations under EMTALA, counting on the hospital to provide necessary care and allowing the plan more latitude in refusing to authorize or pay for care. Managed care organizations claim that hospitals are facing financial difficulties that require them to overtreat in their emergency departments and to overadmit from the emergency room to generate more revenue, especially from privately insured patients. See e.g., Loren A. Johnson and Robert W. Derlet, Conflicts between Managed Care Organizations and Emergency Departments in California, 164 Western Journal of Medicine 137 (1996); Anna–Katrina S. Christakis (Comment), Emergency Room Gatekeeping: A New Twist on Patient Dumping, 1997 Wis.L.Rev. 295 (1997).

What should an emergency room physician do if the patient's insurance plan denies authorization for tests or treatment? If you were asked to advise a hospital on its emergency department policies manual, what would you advise them to do in this scenario? Does the insurer's refusal to authorize payment provide a defense under EMTALA? Maryland has required payment from managed care organizations participating in the state's medical assistance program to hospitals that have provided emergency care in defined circumstances, including where the care would be required to meet the hospital's obligations under EMTALA. Md. Code Health § 15–103(b)(11).

IN THE MATTER OF BABY "K"

United States Court of Appeals, Fourth Circuit, 1994.
16 F.3d 590.

WILKINS, J.:

The Hospital instituted this action against Ms. H, Mr. K, and Baby"K", seeking a declaratory judgment that it is not required under the Emergency Medical Treatment and Active Labor Act (EMTALA), [ ], to provide treatment other than warmth, nutrition, and hydration to Baby "K", an anencephalic infant. Because we agree with the district court that EMTALA gives rise to a duty on the part of the Hospital to provide respiratory support to Baby "K" when she is presented at the Hospital in respiratory distress and treatment is requested for her, we affirm.

Baby "K" was born at the Hospital in October of 1992 with Anencephaly

. . .

When Baby "K" had difficulty breathing on her own at birth, Hospital physicians placed her on a mechanical ventilator. This respiratory support allowed the doctors to confirm the diagnosis and gave Ms. H, the mother, an opportunity to fully understand the diagnosis and prognosis of Baby "K" 's condition. The physicians explained to Ms. H that most anencephalic infants die within a few days of birth due to breathing difficulties and other complications. Because aggressive treatment would serve no therapeutic or palliative purpose, they recommended that Baby "K" only be provided with supportive care in the form of nutrition, hydration, and warmth. Physicians at the Hospital also discussed with Ms. H the possibility of a "Do Not Resuscitate Order" that would provide for the withholding of lifesaving measures in the future.

The treating physicians and Ms. H failed to reach an agreement as to the appropriate care. Ms. H insisted that Baby "K" be provided with mechanical breathing assistance whenever the infant developed difficulty breathing on her own, while the physicians maintained that such care was inappropriate. As a result of this impasse, the Hospital sought to transfer Baby "K" to another hospital. This attempt failed when all of the hospitals in the area with pediatric intensive care units declined to accept the infant. In November of 1992, when Baby "K" no longer needed the services of an acute-care hospital, she was transferred to a nearby nursing home.

Since being transferred to the nursing home, Baby "K" has been readmitted to the Hospital three times due to breathing difficulties. Each time she has been provided with breathing assistance and, after stabilization, has been discharged to the nursing home. Following Baby "K's" second admission, the Hospital filed this action to resolve the issue of whether it is obligated to provide emergency medical treatment to Baby "K" that it deems medically and ethically inappropriate. Baby "K's" guardian ad litem and her father, Mr. K, joined in the Hospital's request for a declaration that the Hospital is not required to provide respiratory support or other aggressive treatments. Ms. H contested the Hospital's request for declaratory relief. ... [The district court denied the hospital the requested relief and the petitioners appealed to the Court of Appeals.]

* * *

In the application of these provisions to Baby "K", the Hospital concedes that when Baby "K" is presented in respiratory distress a failure to provide "immediate medical attention" would reasonably be expected to cause serious impairment of her bodily functions. [ ] Thus, her breathing difficulty qualifies as an emergency medical condition, and the diagnosis of this emergency medical condition triggers the duty of the hospital to provide Baby "K" with stabilizing treatment or to transfer her in accordance with the provisions of EMTALA. Since transfer is not an option available to the Hospital at this juncture, the Hospital must stabilize Baby "K's" condition.

The Hospital acknowledged in its complaint that aggressive treatment, including mechanical ventilation, is necessary to "assure within a reasonable medical probability, that no material deterioration of Baby "K" 's condition is likely to occur." Thus, stabilization of her condition requires the Hospital to provide respiratory support through the use of a respirator or other means necessary to ensure adequate ventilation. In sum, a straightforward application of the statute obligates the Hospital to provide respiratory support to Baby "K" when she arrives at the emergency department of the Hospital in respiratory distress and treatment is requested on her behalf.

In an effort to avoid the result that follows from the plain language of EMTALA, the Hospital offers four arguments. The Hospital claims: (1) that this court has previously interpreted EMTALA as only requiring uniform treatment of all patients exhibiting the same condition; (2) that in prohibiting disparate emergency medical treatment Congress did not intend to require physicians to provide treatment outside the prevailing standard of medical care; (3) that an interpretation of EMTALA that requires a hospital or physician to provide respiratory support to an anencephalic infant fails to recognize a physician's ability, under Virginia law, to refuse to provide medical treatment that the physician considers medically or ethically inappropriate; and (4) that EMTALA only applies to patients who are transferred from a hospital in an unstable condition. We find these arguments unavailing.

* * *

If, as the Hospital suggests, it were only required to provide uniform treatment, it could provide any level of treatment to Baby "K", including a level of treatment that would allow her condition to materially deteriorate, so long as the care she was provided was consistent with the care provided to other individuals. [ ] The definition of stabilizing treatment advocated by the Hospital directly conflicts with the plain language of EMTALA.

... The terms of EMTALA as written do not allow the Hospital to fulfill its duty to provide stabilizing treatment by simply dispensing uniform treatment. Rather, the Hospital must provide that treatment necessary to prevent the material deterioration of each patient's emergency medical condition. In the case of Baby "K", the treatment necessary to prevent the material deterioration of her condition when she is in respiratory distress includes respiratory support.

* * *

The second argument of the Hospital is that, in redressing the problem of disparate emergency medical treatment, Congress did not intend to require physicians to provide medical treatment outside the prevailing standard of medical care. The Hospital asserts that, because of their extremely limited life expectancy and because any treatment of their condition is futile, the prevailing standard of medical care for infants with anencephaly is to provide only warmth, nutrition, and hydration. Thus, it maintains that a requirement to provide respiratory assistance would exceed the prevailing standard of medical care. However, the plain language of EMTALA requires stabilizing treatment for any individual who comes to a participating hospital, is diagnosed as having an emergency medical condition, and cannot be transferred ... We recognize the dilemma facing physicians who are requested to provide treatment they consider morally and ethically inappropriate, but we cannot ignore the plain language of the statute ...

The Hospital further argues that EMTALA cannot be construed to require it to provide respiratory support to anencephalics when its physicians deem such care inappropriate, because Virginia law permits physicians to refuse to provide such care.

* * *

It is well settled that state action must give way to federal legislation where a valid "act of Congress, fairly interpreted, is in actual conflict with the law of the state," [ ] and EMTALA provides that state and local laws that directly conflict with the requirements of EMTALA are preempted.

* * *

It is beyond the limits of our judicial function to address the moral or ethical propriety of providing emergency stabilizing medical treatment to anencephalic infants. We are bound to interpret federal statutes in accordance with their plain language and any expressed congressional intent. EMTALA does not carve out an exception for anencephalic infants in respiratory distress any more than it carves out an exception for comatose patients, those with lung cancer, or those with muscular dystrophy-all of whom may repeatedly seek emergency stabilizing treatment for respiratory distress and also possess an underlying medical condition that severely affects their quality of life and ultimately may result in their death . . .

SPROUSE, J., dissenting:

. . . I simply do not believe, that Congress, in enacting EMTALA, meant for the judiciary to superintend the sensitive decision-making process between family and physicians at the bedside of a helpless and terminally ill patient under the circumstances of this case. Tragic end-of-life hospital dramas such as this one do not represent phenomena susceptible of uniform legal control. In my view, Congress, even in its weakest moments, would not have attempted to impose federal control in this sensitive, private area.

I also submit that EMTALA's language concerning the type and extent of emergency treatment to be extended to all patients was not intended to cover the continued emergencies that typically attend patients like Baby "K". . . . The hospital argues that anencephaly, not the subsidiary respiratory failure, is the condition that should be reviewed in order to judge the applicability vel non of EMTALA. I agree. I would consider anencephaly as the relevant condition and the respiratory difficulty as one of many subsidiary conditions found in a patient with the disease. EMTALA was not designed to reach such circumstances.

The tragic phenomenon Baby "K" represents exemplifies the need to take a case-by-case approach to determine if an emergency episode is governed by EMTALA. Baby "K" 's condition presents her parents and doctors with decision-making choices that are different even from the difficult choices presented by other terminal diseases . . . Given this unique medical condition, whatever treatment is appropriate for her unspeakably tragic illness should be regarded as a continuum, not as a series of discrete emergency medical conditions to be considered in isolation.

Humanitarian concerns dictate appropriate care. However, if resort must be had to our courts to test the appropriateness of the care, the legal vehicle should be state malpractice law.

Notes and Questions

1. Should Congress amend EMTALA to avoid the result in *Baby K*? Is the interpretation of stabilization in *Baby K* appropriate? Was refusal to treat Baby K discriminatory? Did the court simply apply the requirements of the Act equally to her?

2. If Baby K had never left the hospital, would resuscitation have been required under EMTALA? In Bryan v. Rectors and Visitors of the University of Virginia, 95 F.3d 349 (4th Cir.1996), the Court of Appeals held that the plaintiff did not have an EMTALA claim where the patient had been admitted to the hospital in an emergency condition but where the hospital had entered a "do not resuscitate" (DNR) order some twelve days after admission. The order was entered over the protests of the patient's family. A week after the order was entered, the patient died, according to the plaintiff due to the DNR order. Is this case distinguishable from the Circuit's earlier decision in *Baby K*? See also, Thornton v. Southwest Detroit Hospital, 895 F.2d 1131 (6th Cir.1990). In that case, Elease Thornton suffered a stroke and was admitted to the hospital's intensive care unit through its emergency room. Her doctor wanted her admitted to the Detroit Rehabilitation Institute for post-stroke therapy, but the Institute refused to admit her because her insurance did not cover their services. The doctor then discharged her from the hospital and her condition deteriorated further. Thornton sued the hospital for violation of the Act claiming that the hospital had discharged her before her condition was stabilized. The trial court granted summary judgment in favor of the hospital and the Court of Appeals affirmed. A concurring opinion stated that that release by Thornton's personal physician was "enough evidence" that her condition had stabilized. Was the court's reliance on the attending physician's release appropriate under the Act? Should the duty under EMTALA dissipate over time? Do we need a similar statute that would require continuing treatment?

3. The claims by the hospital and physicians in *Baby K*, that physicians ought to be able to refuse treatment that they consider futile, are considered in the discussion of "medical futility" in Chapter 19.

4. Baby "K" was shuffled back and forth between the nursing home and the hospital six times until she died, shortly after her second birthday, on April 15, 1995. Upon her death her mother, who had fought so hard to keep her alive, said, "She's in heaven. She's in peace. Knowing that she's with God is a comfort." See M. Tousignant, Death of Baby "K" Leaves a Legacy of Legal Precedents, Washington Post, April 7, 1985, p. 8. Baby "K", who was known by her real name, Stephanie, when she died, amassed medical bills of $500,000 during her short life. The hospital bill, which itself ran $250,000, was fully paid by Stephanie's mother's insurance and by Medicaid. Is the cost of her care relevant in determining what care is proper? How would you use that information in making a general policy decision about the treatment that ought to be afforded anencephalic infants? About the treatment that ought to be afforded Stephanie herself?

5. Doctors may disagree over the appropriate emergency treatment. Consider Cherukuri v. Shalala, 175 F.3d 446 (6th Cir.1999):

> Dr. Cherukuri determined by 4:00 A.M. that it would be best to operate on both [accident victims] to stop the internal bleeding.... But he was unable to do so for the next three hours because Dr. Thambi, the anesthesiologist on call, advised strongly against operating and did not come to the hospital. [H]e advised Dr. Cherukuri that the patients should be immediately trans-

ferred.... He advised repeatedly and adamantly that administering anesthesia for the abdominal surgery was too risky because they had no equipment to monitor its effect on the pressure in the brain.

Dr. Cherukuri testified that over the next two hours [he and a nurse] requested Dr. Thambi by phone several times to come to the hospital but he maintained that anesthesia was out of the question and did not come. They tried to locate other anesthesiologists during this period but were unsuccessful.

* * *

While recognizing that Dr. Thambi had made his position very clear that he did not intend to provide anesthesiology because it might kill the brain injured patients, the ALJ concluded that EMTALA required the surgeon to force Dr. Thambi to perform by expressly ordering him to administer anesthesia. The ALJ states ... that the law "necessarily required" Dr. Cherukuri to stop the bleeding for the patients to be considered "stabilized" under the statute and that this required Dr. Cherukuri to force Dr. Thambi against his will to administer anesthesia. Nothing in EMTALA demands such a confrontation, and for good reasons.

In this case, the action had been brought by the federal government against Dr. Cherukuri, and a fine of $100,000 was overturned by the court. (As discussed earlier, EMTALA does not permit private actions against physicians but does provide for government enforcement of the Act against both physicians and hospitals.) Would a private plaintiff suing the hospital in this case have been successful? How would the plaintiff structure his claim?

HOWE v. HULL

United States District Court, Northern District of Ohio, 1994.
874 F.Supp. 779.

POTTER, SENIOR JUDGE.

Plaintiff brought suit in the current action alleging that on April 17, 1992, defendants refused to provide Charon medical treatment because he was infected with HIV. Plaintiff claims that defendants' actions violate the Americans with Disabilities Act (ADA), the Federal Rehabilitation Act of 1973 (FRA) [and] the Emergency Transfer and Active Labor Act (EMTALA). The defendants vehemently dispute these claims and allegations and have moved for summary judgment on all of plaintiff's claims.

* * *

On April 17, 1992, Charon and plaintiff Howe were traveling through Ohio, on their way to vacation in Wisconsin. Charon was HIV positive. That morning Charon took a floxin tablet for the first time. Floxin is a prescription antibiotic drug. Within two hours of taking the drug, Charon began experiencing fever, headache, nausea, joint pain, and redness of the skin.

Due to Charon's condition, Charon and plaintiff ... sought medical care at the emergency room of Fremont Memorial Hospital. Charon was examined by the emergency room physician on duty, Dr. Mark Reardon.

Dr. Reardon testified that Charon suffered from a severe drug reaction, and that it was his diagnosis that this reaction was probably Toxic Epidermal

Necrolysis (TEN). This diagnosis was also recorded in Charon's medical records. Dr. Reardon also testified regarding Charon's condition that "possibly it was an early stage of toxic epidermal necrolysis, although I had never seen one . . . ."

* * *

Dr. Reardon determined that Charon "definitely needed to be admitted" to Memorial Hospital. Since Charon was from out of town, procedure required that Charon be admitted to the on-call physician, Dr. Hull. Dr. Reardon spoke with Dr. Hull on the telephone and informed Dr. Hull that he wanted to admit Charon, who was HIV-positive and suffering from a non-AIDS related severe drug reaction.

. . . Dr. Hull inquired neither into Charon's physical condition nor vital signs, nor did he ask Dr. Reardon about the possibility of TEN. During this conversation, it is undisputed that Dr. Hull told Dr. Reardon that "if you get an AIDS patient in the hospital, you will never get him out," and directed that plaintiff be sent to the "AIDS program" at MCO. When Dr. Hull arrived at the hospital after Dr. Reardon's shift but prior to Charon's transfer, he did not attempt to examine or meet with Charon.

It is undisputed that Charon was never admitted to Memorial Hospital . . . .

Charon was transferred to the Medical College of Ohio some time after 8:45 P.M. on April 17. After his conversation with Dr. Hull and prior to the transfer, Dr. Reardon told Charon and plaintiff that "I'm sure you've dealt with this before . . ." Howe asked, "What's that, discrimination?" Dr. Reardon replied, "You have to understand, this is a small community, and the admitting doctor does not feel comfortable admitting [Charon]."

Plaintiff and defendants dispute whether Charon's physical condition was stable at the time of transfer and whether Charon's physical condition deteriorated during the transfer.

Charon was admitted and treated at the Medical College of Ohio (MCO). Despite the TEN diagnosis, Charon was not diagnosed by MCO personnel as having TEN and, in fact, was never examined by a dermatologist. After several days, Charon recovered from the allergic drug reaction and was released from MCO.

* * *

It is important to note that, even if Memorial Hospital did transfer Charon solely because of his HIV status, there will be no liability under the EMTALA if he was stabilized prior to the transfer. If Charon's condition was not stable, however, defendant could be liable if it provided Charon with substandard care due to his HIV status. [ ] The initial inquiry then, focuses on whether the defendants stabilized Charon before the transfer.

[A medical expert] testified that he did not agree that there was no material deterioration of Charon's condition during the transfer, and that there was a "50/50 chance" that a material deterioration in Charon's condition would occur at the time of transfer. [He] further testified that Charon's vital signs were dangerous, that he would have been uncomfortable transferring Charon, and that Charon was in near shock condition. From this testimony, a reasonable jury could find that defendant had not stabilized Charon prior to transfer.

* * *

Much of this case turns on what in fact Dr. Reardon's initial diagnosis of Charon's condition was. Dr. Reardon testified that the diagnosis was TEN, and this is supported by the entry Dr. Reardon made in the medical records.... Plaintiff's expert, however, testified that TEN was not the "likely or even probable" diagnosis. Dr. Reardon also never told Dr. Lynn, the admitting physician at MCO, about the TEN diagnosis. Given [these factors], a jury could reasonably conclude that the TEN diagnosis was a fabrication or ad hoc justification for Charon's transfer.... Dr. Hull's statement about AIDS patients could cause a reasonable jury to believe that the sole reason for transfer was Charon's HIV status. Plaintiff also presented evidence that Charon was not given the appropriate medical treatment by defendant. Further, if the jury found that Charon's actual diagnosis was simply a non-AIDS-related severe allergic drug reaction, that jury could reasonably conclude that Memorial Hospital transferred Charon, while he was unstable, without providing him with necessary medical care that was within their capability to provide.

* * *

[The Court denies defendants' motion for summary judgment.]

* * *

Defendant Memorial Hospital and defendant Hull also move for summary judgment on plaintiff's ADA claim as well as plaintiff's FRA [Rehabilitation Act] claim, on the basis that the evidence does not establish that Charon was denied treatment solely on the basis of his HIV status, and that plaintiff was not "otherwise qualified" for treatment due to the TEN diagnosis.

* * *

[D]iscrimination can take the form of the denial of the opportunity to receive medical treatment, segregation unnecessary for the provision of effective medical treatment, unnecessary screening or eligibility requirements for treatment, or provision of unequal medical benefits based upon the disability [ ]. A defendant can avoid liability by establishing that it was unable to provide the medical care that a patient required. [ ]

Similarly, to establish a prima facie case under the FRA the plaintiff must show

> a) the plaintiff has a disability; b) plaintiff was otherwise qualified to participate in the program; c) defendants discriminated against plaintiff solely on the basis of the disability; and d) the program received federal funding. 29 U.S.C. § 794(a).

As this Court has already stated, a reasonable jury could conclude that the TEN diagnosis was a pretext and that Charon was denied treatment solely because of his disability. Further, there is no evidence to support the conclusion that Memorial Hospital was unable to treat a severe allergic drug reaction. In fact, the evidence indicates that Dr. Reardon initially planned to admit Charon for treatment. Therefore, Charon was "otherwise qualified" for treatment within the meaning of the FRA. Defendants' arguments in this regard are not persuasive.

The Court notes that defendant Memorial hospital argues that the "solely on the basis of ..." standard that appears in the FRA should be imported into the ADA as well. This argument is without merit.

The FRA states that "no otherwise qualified individual with a disability ... shall, solely by reason of his or her disability ... be subjected to discrimination...." [ ]. The equivalent portion of the ADA reads "No individual shall be discriminated against on the basis of disability...."[ ]. It is abundantly clear that the exclusion of the "solely by reason of ... disability" language was a purposeful act by Congress and not a drafting error or oversight.... [ ]

The inquiry under the ADA, then, is whether the defendant, despite the articulated reasons for the transfer, improperly considered Charon's HIV status.... [T]he Court finds plaintiff has presented sufficient evidence to preclude a grant of summary judgment on these claims.

Notes and Questions

1. In the trial after the court's denial of defendants' summary judgment motions in *Howe*, the jury returned a verdict in favor of the plaintiff on the Rehabilitation Act claim, awarding plaintiff's estate $62,000 in compensatory damages and punitive damages of $150,000 against Dr. Hull and $300,000 against the hospital. The jury found in favor of the defendants on the plaintiff's EMTALA claim and on his state claim of emotional distress. The ADA claim was tried to the bench, and the judge found that defendants' actions violated the Act and awarded injunctive relief.

2. The trial court noted in its findings that Dr. Reardon had recorded Dr. Hull's statements about AIDS patients in the official emergency room record and also recorded that Charon's allergic reaction was not related to AIDS or HIV infection in any way. Was it appropriate for Dr. Reardon to document this? Would it have been ethical for him to have omitted this from the patient's record?

3. Would the hospital in *Baby K* have been obligated to provide resuscitation under the ADA or Rehabilitation Act? In its findings, the District Court in *Howe* stated:

> Clearly, where the disability and the medical condition for which treatment is sought are unrelated, the health care provider may not properly consider the disability in referring the patient elsewhere. The more complicated question, however, concerns a medical condition that is complicated by the disability. Given the disposition of this case, the Court need not reach, and specifically declines to address, whether a health care provider may properly consider an individual's disability when that disability complicates the medical condition for which the individual is seeking treatment.

In Baby "K", the Court of Appeals did not reach the question of the application of the disability acts. The District Court, however, held that the Rehabilitation Act and the ADA required a hospital to provide resuscitation and ventilator support. 832 F.Supp. 1022 (E.D.Va.1993).

4. Haavi Mooreim offers the following as indicators of "discriminatory" decisions to withhold treatment: where the medical judgment is based on "inaccurate facts" resulting from presumptions or prejudices against person's with the

patient's medical condition; where the reasoning underlying the treatment decision is "irrational" as for example where a surgeon would decide not to perform surgery only because of the high risk of mortality even though the surgery would provide the patient's only hope of survival; or where the decision is based on "inappropriate values" such as a conclusion that certain persons are by race or gender inherently inferior. E. Haavi Morreim, Futilitarianism, Exoticare, and Coerced Altruism: The ADA Meets Its Limits, 25 Seton Hall L. Rev. 883 (1995). How would this framework apply to *Howe*? To *Baby K*? See also, Mary A. Crosley, Of Diagnoses and Discrimination: Discriminatory Nontreatment of Infants with HIV Infection, 93 Colum. L. Rev. 1581 (1993) and Medical Futility and Disability Discrimination, 81 Iowa L. Rev. 179 (1995); David Orentlicher, Destructuring Disability: Rationing of Health Care and Unfair Discrimination Against the Sick, 31 Harv. C.R.–C.L. Rev. 49 (1996).

5. In Johnson v. Thompson, 971 F.2d 1487 (10th Cir.1992), parents of infants born with spina bifida claimed that their children were selected for nontreatment in an experiment, without their knowledgeable consent and in a discriminatory fashion based on the infants' physical handicap *and* on the families' socio-economic status. The parents lost their § 504 claim. How might the result have differed under the ADA?

6. Other federal statutes create a duty to furnish care upon hospitals. For example, the federal Hill–Burton Act, enacted in 1946, provided federal financing for the construction and expansion of private health care facilities through the early 1960's. (42 U.S.C.A. § 291) Facilities receiving funding under the Act were required to assure that they would make the federally financed facility "available to all persons residing in the territorial area of the applicant" (the "community service obligation") and would provide in the financed facility a reasonable volume of services to people unable to pay therefore. This latter free care requirement was interpreted to extend for twenty years after the federal financing, and so most Hill–Burton financed facilities are no longer required to provide free care under the statute. The community service obligation continues indefinitely. For commentary on the Hill–Burton litigation, see Kenneth Wing, The Community Service Obligation of Hill–Burton Health Facilities, 23 B.C.L.Rev. 577 (1982); James Blumstein, Court Action, Agency Reaction: The Hill–Burton Act as a Case Study, 69 Iowa L.Rev. 1227 (1984); and Sylvia A. Law, A Right to Health Care That Cannot be Taken Away: The Lessons of Twenty–Five Years of Health Care Advocacy, 61 Tenn. L.Rev 771 (1994). See the discussion of tax exempt status in Chapter 13.

Note: Title VI and Racial Discrimination In Health Care

> Class theory maintains that the primary factor affecting differences in health care status between racial groups is socioeconomic.... The class theory, however, oversimplifies the issue and completely ignores the independent role of race in American society. Race influences not only life-style, personal behavior, psycho-social behavior, physical environment, and biology, but also socioeconomic status. Thus race has a double influence.
>
> Racism in America establishes separate and independent barriers to health care institutions and to medical care. Those who advocate for the class theory ignore the fact that removing economic barriers does not remove racial barriers.

Vernellia R. Randall, Racist Health Care: Reforming an Unjust Health Care System to Meet the Needs of African–Americans, 3 Health Matrix 127 (1993). See also, David R. Williams and Chiquita Collins, US Socioeconomic and Racial Differences in Health: Patterns and Explanations, 21 Annual Review of Sociology 349 (1995). The literature on race inequality in health care is substantial and empirically based. In addition to Professor Randall's article, see Sidney Dean Watson, Minority Access and Health Reform: A Civil Right to Health Care, 22 J. of Law, Med. & Ethics 127 (1994); Council on Ethical and Judicial Affairs, Black–White Disparities in Health Care, 263 JAMA 2344 (1990); and Barbara A. Noah, Racial Disparities in the Delivery of Health Care, 35 San Diego L.Rev. 135 (1998); Evidence of Race–Based Discrimination Triggers New Legal and Ethical Scrutiny, BNA Health Law Reporter, Dec. 16, 1999. Under legislation enacted in 2000, the National Institutes of Health will be establishing a National Center on Minority Health and Health Disparities. AMA, HHS Announce Pact to Eliminate Racial, Ethnic Disparities in Health Care, BNA Health Law Reporter, Dec. 7, 2000.

If poverty and race intersect with diminished health, in terms of increased risk of heart disease, diabetes, low birth weight and other illnesses and injuries, how should equality in health care be defined? Are institutional decisions such as the decision to move from urban to suburban locations; to require pre-admission deposits or admission only by a physician with staff privileges; to require that the nursing-home resident or family have resources adequate to support a year or two years of care upon admission in order to be eligible for a Medicaid bed in the facility when it is needed; to place childbirth services at a suburban rather than urban hospital within an integrated delivery system; to acquire physician practices only in high income areas; or to limit the home-care agency's services to a particular geographic area discriminatory on the basis of race? Does discrimination depend on the intent or motive of the decision maker? If a hospital transferred all patients (after stabilizing treatment) who could not provide proof of ability to pay, is that hospital acting in a racially discriminatory manner if 89% of those transferred were African–American or Hispanic? See Robert L. Shiff, et al., Transfers to a Public Hospital: A Prospective Study of 467 Patients. 314 NEJM 552 (1986), reporting data concerning pre-EMTALA hospital transfers.

Title VI of the Civil Rights Act of 1964 (42 U.S.C.A. § 2000d et seq.) prohibits discrimination on the basis of race, color or national origin by any program receiving federal financial assistance and provides for both federal enforcement and private actions. Private activity under Title VI has recently increased but with limited success thus far. The most successful of these is a challenge to Tennessee's Medicaid plan in Linton v. Tennessee Commissioner of Health and Environment, 65 F.3d 508 (6th Cir.1995). In this litigation, the district court judge found that the state Medicaid plan allowing nursing homes to limit the number of "beds" certified for Medicaid reimbursement within the facility violated Title VI. The Sixth Circuit affirmed the district court's acceptance of the remedial plan submitted by the state over the objections of nursing home providers. See also, Latimore v. County of Contra Costa, 77 F.3d 489 (9th Cir.1996) (table), opinion at 1996 WL 68196, in which the Court of Appeals affirmed dissolution of a preliminary injunction against use of county financing in reconstruction of a hospital in one area of the county while residents in poorer sections of the county received inadequate health care. The district court dissolved the injunction after the county had expanded hospital, clinic and transportation services to residents in areas represented by the plaintiffs. But see, Madison–Hughes v. Shalala, 80 F.3d 1121 (6th Cir.1996) challenging HHS' failure to collect racial data concerning the delivery of covered health services that would allow examination of minority access to federally funded health care. The Court of Appeals held that the court had no jurisdiction since the collection of data was not mandated by Title VI.

Scholars reviewing the implementation of Title VI by the government or in private litigation generally have concluded that its effectiveness has been limited by ineffective federal enforcement and by other barriers to private litigation. A leading expert and litigator in Title VI cases proposes new civil rights legislation for health care. See Sidney Dean Watson, *supra*. For a description of current federal enforcement activity under Title VI, see Donna E. Shalala, Federal Efforts to Remove Nonfinancial Barriers to Health Care, 32 Houston L. Rev. 1195 (1996).

Problem: Emmaus House I

You are a volunteer attorney for a nonprofit organization that provides services to the homeless through a community center called Emmaus House. You and several other attorneys come to Emmaus House to offer legal services a couple of hours each week as part of a program organized by the local bar association. While you are there, the director of the center comes rushing into the cubicle where you are conducting interviews and tells you there is an emergency.

Mr. Jack Larkin, a homeless man who comes frequently to the center, is complaining of chest pains and shortness of breath. He has had these episodes before and, in fact, went to the public hospital very early this morning because of them. The doctor at the public hospital examined Mr. Larkin and concluded that he was not having a heart attack but rather was suffering from influenza. You and the director get Mr. Larkin into your car and take him to the nearest hospital which happens to be Eastbrook Memorial, a private hospital. Mr. Larkin is guided to a cubicle where the emergency room physician examines him. The doctor then tells you that they are going to transfer Mr. Larkin to the public hospital, twenty minutes away. What do you do?

Assume that Mr. Larkin is admitted to the public hospital but dies within the week. If you brought suit against Eastbrook, what would you have to prove? How would you structure discovery? Do you have a claim against the doctor?

Problem: Emmaus House II

Elaine Osborne lives in Springfield. There is no public hospital. The state contracts with private hospitals for care of the indigent although it is approximately a year in arrears in reimbursing these hospitals for indigent care they have already provided. Ms. Osborne works in a minimum-wage job that provides no health insurance. As a woman with no dependent children, she would not qualify for Medicaid even if she meets the income standards for eligibility.

Ms. Osborne discovered a lump in her breast, and a mammogram provided at a free public health fair has revealed suspicious tissue in the breast. The doctor who reviewed the results recommended a biopsy which must be performed by a surgeon. Ms. Osborne went to the emergency department of each of the local hospitals but was told that she was not in need of emergency care. The hospitals each required a cash deposit prior to admitting Ms. Osborne for the biopsy because she has no insurance, does not qualify for Medicaid, and may not qualify for state assistance due to her income. Does Ms. Osborne have a claim against the hospitals or the doctors?

Six months later, Ms. Osborne goes to Westhaven Hospital complaining of pain and shortness of breath. She was admitted to Westhaven because it was suspected that she had had a heart attack or was suffering from arterial blockage. The physicians eventually concluded, however, that her pain and shortness of breath was due to the spread of the breast cancer. Ms. Osborne was discharged from the hospital with a prescription for pain medication. Where should Ms.

Osborne go for treatment of these symptoms of the breast cancer? Does she have a claim against Westhaven?

Index

References are to Pages

References are to Pages

References are to Pages

References are to Pages

†